Aquinas, Bonaventure, and the Scholastic Culture of Medieval Paris

In this volume, Randall B. Smith provides a revisionist account of the scholastic culture that flourished in Paris during the High Middle Ages. Exploring the educational culture that informed the intellectual and mental habits of Thomas Aquinas and Bonaventure, he offers an in-depth study of the prologues and preaching skills of these two masters. Smith reveals the intricate interrelationships between the three duties of the master: *lectio* (reading), *disputatio* (debate), and *praedicatio* (preaching). He also analyzes each of Aquinas and Bonaventure's prologues from their student days to their final works, revealing both their artistry and their instructional character. Written in an engaging style, this book serves as an invaluable resource that will enable scholars and students to read thirteenth-century sermons, prologues, and biblical commentaries with greater understanding and ease.

Randall B. Smith is a full professor of theology at the University of St. Thomas in Houston, Texas. He is the author of *How to Read a Sermon by Thomas Aquinas* 2016.

Aquinas, Bonaventure, and the Scholastic Culture of Medieval Paris

Preaching, Prologues, and Biblical Commentary

Randall B. Smith
University of St. Thomas, Houston

Shaftesbury Road, Cambridge CB2 8EA, United Kingdom

One Liberty Plaza, 20th Floor, New York, NY 10006, USA

477 Williamstown Road, Port Melbourne, VIC 3207, Australia

314–321, 3rd Floor, Plot 3, Splendor Forum, Jasola District Centre, New Delhi – 110025, India

103 Penang Road, #05–06/07, Visioncrest Commercial, Singapore 238467

Cambridge University Press is part of Cambridge University Press & Assessment, a department of the University of Cambridge.

We share the University's mission to contribute to society through the pursuit of education, learning and research at the highest international levels of excellence.

www.cambridge.org
Information on this title: www.cambridge.org/9781108789356

DOI: 10.1017/9781108893084

© Cambridge University Press & Assessment 2021

This publication is in copyright. Subject to statutory exception and to the provisions of relevant collective licensing agreements, no reproduction of any part may take place without the written permission of Cambridge University Press & Assessment.

First published 2021
First paperback edition 2024

A catalogue record for this publication is available from the British Library

Library of Congress Cataloging-in-Publication data
NAMES: Smith, Randall B., 1959– author.
TITLE: Aquinas, Bonaventure, and the scholastic culture of medieval Paris : preaching, prologues, and biblical commentary / Randall B. Smith, University of St. Thomas, Houston.
DESCRIPTION: Cambridge, United Kingdom New York, NY, USA : Cambridge University Press, 2020. | Includes bibliographical references and index.
IDENTIFIERS: LCCN 2020013839 (print) | LCCN 2020013840 (ebook) | ISBN 9781108841153 (hardback) | ISBN 9781108789356 (paperback) | ISBN 9781108893084 (epub)
SUBJECTS: LCSH: Scholasticism–France–Paris. | Philosophy, Medieval–France–Paris. | Thomas, Aquinas, Saint, 1225–1274. | Bonaventure, Saint, Cardinal, approximately 1217–1274.
CLASSIFICATION: LCC B734 .S65 2020 (print) | LCC B734 (ebook) | DDC 189/.40944361–dc23
LC record available at https://lccn.loc.gov/2020013839
LC ebook record available at https://lccn.loc.gov/2020013840

ISBN 978-1-108-84115-3 Hardback
ISBN 978-1-108-78935-6 Paperback

Cambridge University Press & Assessment has no responsibility for the persistence or accuracy of URLs for external or third-party internet websites referred to in this publication and does not guarantee that any content on such websites is, or will remain, accurate or appropriate.

To my beloved Tamara:
Poet, muse, wife

Contents

Acknowledgments   *page* ix

Introduction   1

PART ONE · PRELIMINARIES

1 · Preaching and *Principia* at the University of Paris   25
2 · The Basic Elements of the Thirteenth-Century "Modern Sermon"   45
3 · *Principia* and the *Sermo Modernus*   67

PART TWO · THOMAS AQUINAS: THE LOGICIAN WHO LEARNED TO PREACH

4 · *Rigans Montes*: Thomas's Inception *Principium*   79
5 · *Hic Est Liber*: Thomas's *Resumptio*   99
6 · Thomas's Student Prologues   128
7 · After Inception: Early and Late Prologues   151
8 · I Have Seen the Lord: Thomas's Protreptic Prologue to His *Commentary on the Gospel of John*   173
9 · Aquinas, *Sermo Modernus*–Style Preaching, and Biblical Commentary   198

PART THREE · BONAVENTURE: THE SCHOLASTIC WITH THE SOUL OF A POET

10 · Bonaventure's Inception *Principium*: *Omnium Artifex*   233
11 · Bonaventure's *Resumptio*: An Early Attempt to Think through the Hierarchy of the Sciences   251
12 · Searching the Depths of the Lombard: The Prologue to Bonaventure's *Sentences* Commentary   289
13 · Exalting Our Understanding: The Prologue to Bonaventure's *Commentary on the Gospel of John*   306
14 · The Spirit of the Lord Is Upon Me: The Prologue to Bonaventure's *Commentary on the Gospel of Luke*   319

15 • Bonaventure, *Sermo Modernus*–Style Preaching, and
Biblical Commentary   328

16 • A Master's Praise of Scripture: The Prologue to Bonaventure's
Breviloquium   344

17 • The Union of Paris and Assisi: The Prologues to Bonaventure's
Later Collations   363

18 • The *Reduction of the Arts to Theology* Redux: The Prologue to the
Collations on the Six Days of Creation   383

19 • Summary and Concluding Remarks   412

Appendix 1: Outlines of the Divisiones Textus *of the Books of the Bible from the
Inception* Resumptio *Addresses of Four Thirteenth-
Century Masters*   427

Works Cited   435
Index   443

Appendix 2: Bonaventure's Principium *Address at Paris: An Outline
Translation is available at www.cambridge.org/9781108841153.*

Acknowledgments

THERE ARE two kinds of people in the world: those who read "Acknowledgments" and those who don't. If you're reading this, you are among the first group. That's not good or bad, it's just different – different from most people in the world, one would imagine. But whether readers are inclined to read "Acknowledgments" or not, it is incumbent upon writers to write them because no one produces a book without the help of others. And in the case of this book, it required quite a lot of help from many – so many, in fact, that I won't be able to fit them all into this page. So, for example, if I tried to mention all the baristas who nurse-maided me with coffee over the months and years of the book's production, I wouldn't have had room for anything else. Yet, they all have my gratitude.

Let me begin, though, with the one person about whom I can safely say, No one is more responsible for this book finally seeing print than Susan Needham, the woman I consider to be the best editor in the country. I have often viewed editors as an annoyance, as people who usually miss your humor and mess with your prose. But once I had something edited by Susan Needham, I knew that henceforth I would want her to read and edit everything I ever wrote. That's not possible, but it would be something profoundly to be wished. I would be a better writer. I once thought of writing an acknowledgment that began, "Writing this book was like a journey through purgatory, and Susan Needham was the Virgil to my wayward Dante – except Dante was cleverer, more talented, and took instruction better." Yet, for all that, Susan Needham is not likely to get stuck like Virgil at the final exit out of Purgatory. She has my undying gratitude. Her daughter Anne ably did the index to the volume, so my gratitude to the Needham family extends to multiple generations.

Thanks are also due to my excellent copy-editor, Theresa Kornak and to my editor, Beatrice Rehl at Cambridge University Press, who did yeoman's work shepherding the book past many obstacles. I am grateful to Alasdair MacIntyre, Edward Houser, Mary Catherine Sommers, Christopher Blum, Henk Schoot, and Kevin White for having made useful comments on various parts of the manuscript. And I must express my thanks to our friends Catherine Peters, Elias and Victoria Sundaram, Phil Bess and his late wife Barbara, and John and Alicia Nagy for their emotional support at various stages of the book's production.

In addition to these, I must also thank the staff of the de Nicola Center for Ethics and Culture at the University of Notre Dame, and its past and present directors, David Solomon and Carter Snead, for their support. I am also grateful to the Scanlan Foundation for making possible course releases that allowed me to complete work on this book. But special thanks must go to John O'Callaghan, director of the Jacques Maritain Center, which remains one of the best research centers in the nation and where much of the work on this book was done, along with his wife Mary, for their continuing friendship and unflagging support.

Finally, there is no question for anyone who knows me that none of this would have been possible – scarcely a word would have been written – without the constant love, support, and inspiration of my wife, the incomparable Tamara Nicholl-Smith.

Introduction

THE YOUNG candidate – some thought too young – sat behind a large podium at the front of the room. To his left, seated in a long line of chairs, were the junior masters of the university; to his right sat the chancellor and all the senior masters. The previous evening had been spent responding to bachelors and masters in a complex series of "disputed questions." But now the presiding master stood and placed on his head a biretta and said aloud: "I place on you the magisterial biretta in the name of the Father, and of the Son, and of the Holy Spirit. Amen." The young candidate had become a master, and after birettas had been distributed to the other masters to place on their own heads, the gathered company sat down to hear the new master deliver his inaugural lecture: the *principium*. It was spring, 1256, and the new master was the Dominican friar, Thomas d'Aquino, the son of a minor nobleman from Italy, who had grown up in a small castle not too far from the site of the great Benedictine abbey at Monte Cassino, where the newly incepted master had studied as a youth.[1]

Two years earlier, in 1254, Giovanni di Fidanza from Bagnoregio in Umbria, a friar of the Franciscan order who had taken the religious name Bonaventure and was several years Thomas's senior, was incepted in a similar ceremony.[2] Whereas Brother Thomas had been only a few years in residence at Paris, having spent his early years studying at the Benedictine abbey of Monte Cassino, after which he had studied grammar, logic, and the *libri naturales* of Aristotle with the Dominicans at Naples, young Giovanni, by contrast, had been resident at the University of Paris for many years by the time of his inception, having begun his studies in the Arts there as a layman nearly twenty years earlier in 1235 at

---

[1] For the chronology of Thomas's life and work, see Jean-Pierre Torrell, O.P., *Saint Thomas Aquinas: The Person and His Work*, trans. Robert Royal (Washington, DC: Catholic University of America Press, 1996). Still good, however, is James Weisheipl, O.P., *Friar Thomas d'Aquino: His Life, Thought, and Works* (Washington, DC: Catholic University of America Press, 1974, 1983).

[2] The best research on the chronology of Bonaventure's life and the date of his inception as master can be found in Jay Hammond, "Dating Bonaventure's Inception as Regent Master," *Franciscan Studies*, vol. 67 (2009): 179–226.

the age of 14. He had attained the rank of Master of Arts by the time he was 22, at which point he entered the Franciscan novitiate and began his studies as an *auditor theologiae*.

There he studied for some years under the great Franciscan master Alexander of Hales who, as legend has it, said of young Giovanni that "it seemed as though Adam never sinned in him." After entering the Franciscan order in 1244 at age 23, Bonaventure advanced quickly in his studies. He was licensed as a *lector biblicus* by John of Parma, Minister General of the order, in 1248 and began lecturing cursorily on the Bible, but only to his fellow friars at the Cordeliers, the Franciscan House of Studies. In 1248, he was officially granted the status of *baccalarius biblicus*, a "bachelor of the Bible," at the University of Paris. In 1250, he advanced to the status of *baccalarius sententiarius* "bachelor of the *Sentences*." By 1253, he was ready to be incepted as a master.

By this time, however, serious disputes had broken out between the secular masters and the friars at the University. In February of 1252, the secular masters had published a letter, *Quoniam in promotione*, in which they demanded that no religious order could have more than one chair at the University. The Dominicans already had two, so this demand presented a decisive challenge to them. The Franciscans had only one chair at the University, and it was occupied by William of Middleton, so the Franciscans simply kept Bonaventure lecturing in the private chair at the Franciscan House. During March of 1253, riots broke out in Paris, and a student was killed. The University decreed that all lectures should cease until the town made proper reparations. Despite the decree, the two Dominican masters and the Franciscan William of Middleton continued lecturing. In retaliation, the University expelled all three masters and began the formal process of excommunication.

Unlike the Dominicans, who continued their fight against the secular masters and the University until 1256 (when Thomas was incepted, but only after the intervention of Pope Alexander IV), the Franciscans under John of Parma appear to have made peace with University officials two years earlier by consenting to all the University's demands: the Franciscans would henceforth abide by all University statutes; they would not seek more than one chair; and they would remove William of Middleton from his chair. William was removed from the public chair in theology recognized by the University and took up a position teaching in the private chair at the Franciscan House, while Bonaventure left the private chair and made ready to take the public chair at the University. First, however, he had to be incepted.[3]

Every regent master in theology at the University of Paris in the thirteenth century had to receive his position in an official inception ceremony, usually held in the great hall (the *aula*) of the Bishop of Paris, during which the candidate would deliver a brief sermon that came to be known as the *principium in aula*. Sometime later, usually on the first day before classes were scheduled to begin, the new Master was also required to deliver a *resumptio* (a "resumption" address), which constituted his first act as a fully incepted Master.[4]

---

[3] Hammond, "Dating Bonaventure's Inception," 225, holds that the "almost three year silence regarding any secular opposition to the Franciscans [between 1254 and 1257] strongly suggests that Bonaventure was received into the *consortium magistrorum* at the time of his inception [in 1254]. While this must be explained more clearly, it undermines the dominate narrative that he remained unrecognized by the University until 1256 or 1257."

[4] For an invaluable introduction to the inception ceremony and to the entire genre of the medieval *principium* address, see Nancy Spatz, *Principia*: *A Study and Edition of Inception Speeches Delivered*

There were clear rules in the University's documents about what the subject matter of each of these two addresses should be: the *principium in aula* was to contain "a commendation of Scripture and a comparison of Scripture to other fields of study," and the *resumptio* was to set forth a "division and description of the books of the Bible."[5] This inception ceremony was seen as the culmination of a long course of study and the commencement of a long and fruitful scholarly career for which the master had spent many years preparing.

The Three Types of *Principia*

The *principium in aula* was not the only *principium* these aspiring medieval masters were asked to compose. They had been prepared for their inception by writing many *principia* – what we often call "prologues" – to their biblical commentaries and to each book of their commentary on the *Sentences* of Peter Lombard.

Since we will be discussing *principia* of various types, it will be good to get clear on the different items in the medieval university that fell under this one heading.[6] At the University of Paris in the thirteenth century, "*principium*" could refer to one of three things: (1) the inaugural lecture of a course, (2) a written prologue to a commentary, or (3) the address a candidate would give during his inception as regent master.[7] Let's begin with the first of these.

When a bachelor or master began a course in the thirteenth century, he would give an inaugural lecture in which he would extol the importance of the text on which he would be lecturing and exhort the students to prepare themselves for the discipline of study. This introductory lecture was also called an *introitus*, an *ingressus* or an *accessus*, terms that indicate the character of the address. This lecture was supposed to provide an "entrance" (*ingressus*) or "introduction" (*introitus*) by which the students could "enter into" the text to

---

Before the Faculty of Theology at the University of Paris, ca. 1180–1286 (Cornell University Dissertation, 1992), esp. 39–50. Spatz uses the term *principium* for the first address delivered in the bishop's hall, and "resumption *principium*" for the second. I have chosen to simplify the terminology and call the first, the master's *principium* and the second, his *resumptio,* although I have sometimes used the phrases "*resumptio* address" or "resumption address." All contemporary descriptions of the inception ceremony for the masters at Paris are based ultimately on the early fourteenth century document that can be found in the *Chartularium Universitatis Parisiensis*, 2:693–694. See also the description of the inception ceremony in Weisheipl, *Friar Thomas*, 96–110.

[5] See Spatz, *Principia*, 62. We do not have both the *principium in aula* and the *resumptio* addresses for each master, so it is not possible to make a final judgment. For a description of the extant thirteenth-century *principa in aula*, see Spatz, 130–145; for the *resumptio* addresses, see Spatz, 145–155.

[6] We have an analogous problem in English books with the terms "preface," "prologue," and "introduction," the meaning and usage of which are flexible and interchangeable.

[7] See Mariken Teeuwen, *The Vocabulary of Intellectual Life in the Middle Ages*, Études sur le vocabulaire intellectual du Moyen Âge 10 (Turnhout: Brepols, 2003), esp. 315: "The term *principium* is generally used, in the context of the medieval university, for the inaugural lecture of a course. In the context of a student's career an inaugural lecture of this kind marked the transitions from one phase to another, and was, usually, a solemn and public occasion. Bachelors of Theology, who were first allowed to teach on the Bible and then on Peter of Lombard's *Sententiae*, held *principia* or inaugural lectures on each of these occasions, in which they eulogized the texts and gave short analyses or introductions."

be studied. It gave them "access" (*accessus*) by "drawing them nearer" to the subject. All these terms suggest what I will later describe in more detail as the "protreptic" function of these *principia*.[8]

Nothing approaching a complete inventory of these biblical *principia* has yet been made.[9] Although, as Athanasius Sulavik reports, "A surprising number of *principia* [of this first sort] have survived – more than one hundred fifty . . . only a small proportion, perhaps only five to ten percent, can be securely linked to an author and date. The majority of these are anonymous, difficult to date, and scattered throughout sermon collections and works of biblical exegesis."[10] The challenge in identifying such *principia* is that "they were often taken for sermons on account of their structure, style, and length."[11] This is because when masters delivered these inaugural *principia* lectures, they employed the same *sermo modernus* style they used in preaching.

It is important not to confuse these introductory lectures with the *principium in aula* address a master would give at his inception. There are more *principia in aula* addresses remaining to be discovered for the masters we know incepted at Paris, but even if we had them all, there would not be "more than one hundred fifty."[12] In one collection of "*principia*," for example, seven *principia* are ascribed to the Dominican John of Naples, who was master of theology at Paris between 1315 and 1317.[13] John did not incept seven times during those two years; these seven *principia* are the introductory lectures he delivered at the beginning of successive terms.

This brings us to the second type of *principium*. What seems likely is that, if a master's lectures on a book of the Bible were recorded, corrected, and sent to the stationers for copying, the *principium* he had delivered verbally at the beginning of the term was published as the *principium* (what we call the "prologue") of the text.[14] Just as schoolmen

---

[8] For an excellent introduction to the genre of the classical philosophical protreptic, see Mark D. Jordan, "Ancient Philosophic Protreptic and the Problem of Persuasive Genres," *Rhetorica: A Journal of the History of Rhetoric*, vol. 4, no. 4 (Autumn 1986): 309–333.

[9] See Gilbert Dahan, "Genres, Forms and Various Methods in Christian Exegesis of the Middle Ages," in *Hebrew Bible/Old Testament: The History of Its Interpretation I/2*, ed. M. Sæbø (Göttingen: Vandenhoek & Ruprecht, 2000), 215.

[10] Athanasius Sulavik, "*Principia* and *Introitus* in Thirteenth Century Christian Biblical Exegesis with Related Texts," in *La Bibbia del XIII secolo, storia del testo, storia dell'esegesi*, eds. Giuseppe Cremascoli and Francesco Santi (Florence: SISMEL, 2004), 269–270. So, for example, *principia* are listed in various places and under various titles in Friedrich Stegmüller's *Repertorium biblicum medii aevi*, 11 vols. (Madrid, 1950–), now online at http://repbib.uni-trier.de/cgi-bin/rebihome.tcl; as for example, *Alius prologus in principio* [11456], *Principium vet. et nov. test.* [11455], *Principium biblicum* [10026, 12], and *Principium in sacra Scriptura* [8650].

[11] Sulavik, 272–273.

[12] According to Sulavik, 270–271: "Sixteen thirteenth-century *principia* [in the sense of "inaugural addresses"] attributed to the following, have been published: Thomas Chobham, Robert Grosseteste, Odo of Châtereaux, John of La Rochelle, Albert the Great, Thomas Aquinas, Nicholas Pressoir, Odo of Chateauroux, Matthew of Aquasparta, Peter John Olivi, and Stephen of Besançon."

[13] See Sulavik, 273.

[14] For the best overview of the nature and function of these prologues to medieval biblical commentaries, especially as an *accessus* guiding the reader's interpretive perspective and interests, see A. J. Minnis, *Medieval Theory of Authorship: Scholastic Literary Attitudes in the Later Middle Ages* (London: Scolar Press, 1984; 2nd ed. Philadelphia: Pennsylvania State University Press, 1988, 2009).

of the thirteenth century would call both the original oral dispute and the later written document a "disputed question," so also he would call both the preparatory exhortatory address delivered orally on the first day of the term and the later written version a "*principium.*"

Along with (1) the inaugural lecture of a course, and (2) a written prologue to a commentary, the word *principium* was also used to refer to (3) the address a candidate would give during his inception ceremony. The third type of *principium* was what we have been calling the *principium in aula*. In an attempt to clarify matters, Athanasius Sulavik sets up a distinction between a *principium*, a term he associates solely with an inception address, and an *introitus*, the term he uses for the prologue to an individual book of the Bible. While the distinction is useful, it seems not to have been one commonly observed in the thirteenth century, when the word *principium* could apply to either.

So, for example, the manuscript in which Joshua Benson discovered St. Bonaventure's inaugural *principium in aula* address contained a collection of both inaugural addresses and commentary prologues (or what Prof. Sulavik would call an *introitus*).[15] Scholars have long known of collections of medieval sermons; Bonaventure made a collection of his sermons, one for each Sunday of the liturgical year, many of which may not have been preached before an actual congregation.[16] Such collections were likely meant to serve as samples from which other preachers could learn. We now know that collections of *principia* were also sometimes kept, both inception addresses and first lectures of the term, likely for similar reasons: as examples from which prospective masters could learn.[17]

In much of the modern literature on inception *principia*, the master's two addresses – what I have called earlier the *principium in aula* and the *resumptio* – are sometimes both called a *principium*.[18] There may be medieval precedent for this confusing usage, since the *resumptio* address was usually delivered the day before classes commenced and thus may have been thought of as the new master's first introductory lecture. In his *resumptio*, the master was required to provide a *divisio textus* of all the books of the Bible, and as we will see, an elaborate *divisio textus* was a common feature in thirteenth century introductory lectures and prologues.

---

[15] See Joshua C. Benson, "Bonaventure's Inaugural Sermon at Paris," *Collectanea Franciscana* 82 (2012): 517–562.

[16] See *The Sunday Sermons of St. Bonaventure*, tr. Timothy Johnson, Works of Bonaventure, vol. 12 (St. Bonaventure, NY: Franciscan Institute Publications, 2008).

[17] Recent research by Michèle Mulcahey on the manuscript Firenze, Conv. Soppr. G.4.936, indicates that *principia* and *introitus* were gathered together for the purpose of lecturing on the Bible at the Dominican *studium* in Florence during the last quarter of the thirteenth century. As Mulcahey notes, a copy of Thomas Aquinas' *principium* survives in a collection of sixteen introductory sermons on the entire Bible. These were preserved by Thomas' student, Remigio de'Girolami, who refers to them as "*Prologi super Bibliam.*" Twenty introductions to individual books of the Bible and several prologues to the books of Peter Lombard's *Sentences* follow these introductory sermons. See M. Mulcahey, *First the Bow Is Bent in Study: Dominican Education Before 1350* (Toronto: P.I.M.S., 1998), 391–394 and Sulavik, 273, nn. 13–18.

[18] So, for example, if one were to look up the text published under the title "Principium Biblicum Alberti Magni," edited by Albert Fries, in *Studia Albertina: Festschrift für Bernhard Geyer*, ed. H. Ostlender (Münster Westf.: Aschendorff, 1952), 128-147, a quick glance at the text reveals that it contains a long *divisio textus* of all the books of the Bible, suggesting that this is actually Albert's *resumptio*.

In her dissertation on thirteenth-century inception *principia*, Nancy Spatz attempted to clarify matters for her readers by calling the first address (*in aula*) a "*principium*" and the second on the first day of class a "resumption *principium*."[19] These terms were helpful in the context of her work, because she dealt exclusively with inaugural addresses. They would be less useful for our purposes, however, since we will be dealing with inaugural addresses and written prologues both. In this text, therefore, when I am referring to the first of the two inceptiòn addresses, I will call it a "*principium* address" or a *principium in aula* address." The second of the two inaugural lectures I will call a "*resumptio*" or "*resumptio* address."

Principia and the Thirteenth-Century "Modern Sermon"

One especially crucial element connecting all three types of *principia* is that they all employ the contemporary *sermo modernus* style of preaching. This style of preaching had become popular – indeed it was nearly ubiquitous in Western Europe – from the mid-thirteenth century to the late fourteenth.[20]

I will have more to say about the *sermo modernus* style and its origins in Chapter 2, but very briefly, the three basic characteristics of this style of preaching were

1. The *thema*

    Sermo modernus sermons were structured around an opening biblical verse, the *thema*, which served as a mnemonic device that provided the structure for the topics covered in the sermon.

2. The *divisio*

    After a short introductory prologue (or *prothema*), the preacher would divide the opening biblical *thema* verse, typically into three or four sections. Thomas's sermon *Ecce rex tuus*, for example, took as its *thema* verse the passage from Matthew 21.5: *Ecce rex tuus venit tibi mansuetus*. For the purpose of his sermon, Thomas divided the verse into four parts that provided the topics for each of the four parts of his sermon: *Ecce / rex tuus / venit tibi / mansuetus*.

3. The *dilatatio*

    After the medieval preacher had made his basic division of the *thema*, he then had to develop or "dilate" each. *Dilatatio* is sometimes translated "amplify," but I prefer to stay closer to the Latin original. There were many creative ways of dilating upon a word or a group of words recommended by the preaching manuals of the day.[21]

---

[19] For a good explanation of the sometimes confusing nomenclature used in inception ceremonies (*aula, vesperies, collatio, principium*), see Nancy Spatz, "Imagery in University Inception Sermons," in *Medieval Sermons and Society: Cloister, City, University*, ed. J. Hamesse, Kienzle, et al. (Louvain-La-Neuve: Fédération Internationale des Instituts d'Études Médiévales, 1998), esp. 331–333.

[20] Michèle Mulcahey, for example (*First the Bow*, 403, n. 10), notes that John of Wales, a Franciscan master at Paris around 1270, wrote in his *De arte praedicandi* that the older style of homily "did not sit particularly well with modern listeners, who liked to see the clear articulation of a sermon developed from a scriptural *thema*," as was Thomas's practice. Indeed, by 1290, the Italian Dominican Fra Giacomo da Fusignano, prior of Santa Maria sopra Minerva in Rome would write that the older style was suitable only for preaching to the ignorant.

[21] For more on all three, see Randall B. Smith, *Reading the Sermons of Thomas Aquinas: A Beginner's Guide* (Steubenville, OH: Emmaus Road, 2016). Henceforth, merely "*Reading the Sermons.*"

This style of preaching, which involved developing content from the divided words of an opening biblical verse, will seem odd, perhaps even a bit off-putting, to many of us today. But it was clearly not considered odd or off-putting to listeners in Thomas's time. Manuscript evidence and contemporary accounts show that the *sermo modernus* style of preaching that Thomas and his contemporaries employed was not something that was *forced* on the medieval congregations of the time; rather it became very popular, very fast, because there was a demand for it. All *principium* addresses at Paris in the thirteenth century were crafted in this style, as were all the prologues of biblical commentaries. They were all structured around the divisions of an opening *thema* verse and dilated according to the contemporary rules of preaching.

Thomas's two inception addresses can be found under several different titles and are sometimes confusingly called Thomas's two *principium* addresses, but they can be identified by their "incipits": the first words of the biblical verse on which each is based. The first of these, Thomas's *principium in aula* was based on the passage from Psalm 103:13 beginning *Rigans montes de superioribus*; the second, Thomas's *resumptio*, is known by its beginning phrase taken from Baruch 4:1: *Hic est liber mandatorum*.[22]

---

[22] Both addresses are sometimes found under the general heading: *Commendatio Sacrae Scripturae*, although this can vary. In the "Brief Catalogue of Authentic Works" at the back of Weisheipl, *Friar Thomas*, for example, #35 on p. 373 reads: "*Commendatio Sacrae Scrijpturae*: Two *principia* (Paris, April or May 1256)." And then: "These two *sermones* were discovered by Uccelli in Florence, Bibl. Cent. MS Conv. Soppr. G. 4. 36 (Santa Maria Novella), and immediately recognized as *principia*, i.e., inaugural lectures. The first *Commendatio S. Scripturae* is based on the text 'Rigans montes de suprioribus,' etc. (Ps. 103:13), and was presented by Thomas on the second day of his inception as master in theology in the spring of 1256 (Tocco, *Hystoria*, c. 16). The second *sermo* compliments the first and is more traditional as a *commendatio*. It is a division of all the books of Scripture, based on the text of Baruch 4:1, 'Hic est liber mandatorum,' etc. Mandonnet, assuming that Thomas was a *cursor biblicus* at Paris for two years before reading the *Sentences*, claimed that the second *sermo* was Thomas's *principium* when he began cursory reading of the Bible in 1252. However, we have argued that Thomas was never *cursor biblicus* at Paris, and that the *sermo secundus* was delivered by Thomas on the first *dies legibilis* following inception, i.e., at his *resumptio*, 'in which lecture he brought to completion his incomplete inaugural lecture given *in aula*.'" For an invaluable discussion of the two addresses and their place in the context of the entire inception ceremony, see Weisheipl, 96–110, esp. 103–104 for Weisheipl's argument that *Hic est liber* was also part of the master's inception ceremony and thus *not* from an earlier period when Thomas was a *cursor biblicus*.

In the "Brief Catalogue of the Works of Saint Thomas Aquinas" by Giles Emery in Torrell, *St. Thomas*, 338, *Rigans montes* and *Hic est liber* are described, in agreement with Weisheipl's judgment, as "two *Principia*, i.e., inaugural lectures . . . held on the occasion of the *inceptio* of the new *magister in actu regens* in Paris between 3 March and 17 June 1256."

In the "Corpus Thomisticum," that invaluable on-line resource containing the complete works of Aquinas in Latin (corpusthomisticum.org), one will find the first *principium* address under the title "Principium Rigans montes" in the "Opuscula theologica," while the second *principium* address, "Hic est liber," is found further down, in the "Opera probabilia authenticitate" section under "Sermones" with the heading "Principium biblicum."

Finally, one will find English translations of both *principia* addresses on Thérèse Bonin's invaluable website "Thomas Aquinas in English: A Bibliography"(www.home.duq.edu/~bonin/thomasbibliography.html) under the general heading "Commentaries on Scripture," by clicking on the link "*Commendatio Sacrae Scripturae* (2), Thomas' inaugural lectures," which will take one to an online version of Ralph McInerny's English translations of both *principia* which appeared first in: *Thomas Aquinas: Selected Writings* (Harmondsworth: Penguin, 1998), 5–17. On the linked website,

The situation is somewhat different with Bonaventure's inception *principium* and *resumptio* addresses, but no less confusing. Whereas *Rigans montes* and *Hic est liber mandatorum* have appeared in lists of Thomas's authentic works since his death, it was until recently assumed that Bonaventure's two inception addresses were lost. In the 1974 celebration commemorating the seventh centenary of Bonaventure's death, Bonaventure scholar Ignatius Brady bemoaned the fact that two important texts of Bonaventure's had not yet been discovered: his *principium biblicum* and what he (Brady) called his "*principium magisteriale* or *aulicum*, which he described as a "*recommendatio s. scripturae* or *recommendatio sacrae doctrinae* given in brief form by the doctorandus in the aula/hall of the bishop and repeated at length soon after his promotion."[23] Brady went on to lament that, although we possess these lectures for other great medieval theologians such as John of La Rochelle and Thomas Aquinas, Bonaventure's remained missing.

Since Brady gave that address, scholars have clarified that the *recommendatio s. scripturae* or *recommendatio sacrae doctrinae* given in brief form by the doctorandus in the aula/hall of the bishop was not repeated. Rather, the new master delivered a second address at his *resumptio* which contained another "commendation" of Sacred Scripture, this second one containing a *divisio textus* of all the books of the Bible, which is what Brady may have been referring to by the term "*principium biblicum*." Most importantly, since Brady's address, Bonaventure scholar Joshua Benson was able to identify a manuscript containing Bonaventure's inaugural *principium* and *resumptio* addresses. Most startling was the fact that this manuscript showed that the text we have traditionally come to now as the *De reductione artium ad theologiam* had been, in its original version with a different opening paragraph, Bonaventure's *resumptio*.[24]

Inception and the Three Duties of the Master

Study of these prologues and *principia* addresses provides important insights into how medieval theologians were trained and what habits of mind they developed. The methodology and habits of mind involved in engaging in "disputed questions" was naturally also quite important, but this element of the pedagogy and practice of the medieval university has long been known and studied. Understanding the culture of preaching, prologues, and *principia* at Paris will provide us with a complementary set of perspectives on the habits of mind they brought to their work.

At the end of the twelfth century, Peter Cantor (d. 1197) had identified the three duties of the medieval master as *lectio* ("reading," i.e., "lecturing" or commenting on texts, especially

---

however, one will find, somewhat oddly, the second of the two *principia* ("Hic est liber") listed first, and the first of them ("Rigans Montes") below it.

[23] See Ignatius Brady, "The *Opera Omnia* of Saint Bonaventure Revisited," in *Proceedings of the Seventh Centenary Celebration of the Death of Saint Bonaventure*, ed. Pascal Foley (St. Bonaventure, NY: The Franciscan Institute, 1975), 47–59; quoted from Joshua C. Benson, "Identifying the Literary Genre of the *De reductione artium ad theologiam*: Bonaventure's Inaugural Lecture at Paris," *Franciscan Studies*, vol. 67 (2009): 149–150.

[24] See Joshua Benson, "Bonaventure's *De reductione artium ad theologiam* and Its Early Reception as an Inaugural Sermon," *American Catholic Philosophical Quarterly*, vol. 85, no. 1 (2011): 7–24.

the Bible), *disputatio* (disputation), and *praedicatio* (preaching).²⁵ This threefold distinction became classic in the thirteenth century. The inception ceremony at Paris served as the capstone of the prospective master's education by requiring the candidate to demonstrate all three basic duties of the master: *disputatio*, *praedicatio*, and *lectio*. The candidate had to engage in a complex series of disputed questions (*disputatio*) on the first and second days, after which he would deliver his *principium in aula*, a sermon in praise of Scripture (*praedicatio*). Finally, in his *resumptio*, the newly incepted master was required to give the same kind of introductory lecture he would subsequently give at the beginning of each course in which the students had to undertake an in-depth reading and study of a biblical text. The goal of this *lectio*, this first lecture of a course, was to prepare the students to read with interest and understanding. This normally meant laying out at the beginning of the course a *divisio textus* of the book about to be commented upon. In the master's *resumptio*, he demonstrated his ability to do this (and showed his acquaintance with all the Scriptures) by laying out a *divisio textus* of all the books of the Bible.²⁶

To get a sense of what the inception ceremony was preparing the young master for, one might first glance at any of the works normally associated with medieval thinkers crafted in the style of the medieval *disputatio*. To get a sense of the other two duties of the master, however, we need to look at a medieval biblical commentary, a product of *lectio*, paying special attention to the prologue, which would have been written in the style common in medieval preaching.

These written prefaces (also called *principia*, as we have seen) served both protreptic and preparatory purposes: they prepared the students by revealing the "skeleton" of the work and also exhorted them to take up the study seriously. The master provided his students, who were faced with a mass of intimidating and confusing verbiage, with a useful *ingressus* into the material, especially a suitable *divisio textus* of the work. But even this was not enough. He also had to inspire them, by explaining what wisdom was to be attained by their study of the book on which he intended to lecture.

What Should a Good Prologue Do?

In one sense, a prologue, from the Greek *pro* (before) and *logoi* (words), is simply some words found before the body of a text. But if the preface was written by the author himself, why not simply begin the book and put whatever is in the prologue in chapter 1? Why call it a "prologue"? What purpose does a prologue serve?

One obvious answer is that a prologue should introduce the book to the reader. What I am calling a "Prologue" is sometimes called an "Introduction." But substituting words in this way does not get us any closer to answering the question; it merely shifts the debate, so

---

[25] Peter Cantor, *Verbum Abbreviatum* 1: *In tribus igitur consistit exercitum sacrae scripturae: circa lectionem, disputationem et praedicationem* ... (In these three consists the exercise of Sacred Scripture: lecture, disputation, and preaching). See *Verbum Abbreviatum Petri Cantoris Parisiensis. Verbum adbreviatum. Textus conflatus*, ed. M. Boutry, Corpus Christianorum, Continuatio Mediaeualis, 196 (Turnhout: Brepols, 2004).

[26] Note in Peter Cantor's original comment that all three duties were related to the "exercise" (*exercitum*) of sacred Scripture.

that now we have to ask: "What would a good 'introduction' be?" Or, taking a cue from the name of the medieval *principium*: How best to *begin*? How does one set a good foundation for reading and reading well?

In *Three Rival Versions of Moral Enquiry*, Alasdair MacIntyre compares the major presuppositions of what he calls "the encyclopedic stance" of modern thought – that truth "not only is what it is, independent of standpoint, but can be discovered or confirmed by any adequately intelligent person, no matter what his point of view" – with that of an earlier, classical view of the philosophic craft which held that a prior commitment was required on the part of the student who aspired to study and study well.[27] The kind of transformation required, argues MacIntyre, was of the sort "which is involved in making oneself into an apprentice to a craft," the craft in this case being philosophical enquiry.[28] It was essential, therefore, that the enquirer learn first "how to make him or herself into a particular kind of person" before he or she could move forward "towards a knowledge of the truth about his or her good and about *the* good."[29]

The customary modern way of writing a prologue reflects the modern "encyclopedic" stance toward education, which presupposes that anyone with sufficient background information, no matter what his or her point of view, prior ideological commitments, or manner of life, can read and learn what a text intends to teach. It is for this reason that many modern prologues tend to read like encyclopedia articles. We get a biography and background of the author; information about the historical, literary, intellectual, and cultural context within which the author worked and wrote; details about the manuscript tradition of the text, if they are relevant; comparisons with or comments about other works by the same author; and perhaps comments about the work's reception and interpretation through the ages. These are the categories commonly found in most encyclopedia articles. Such details are useful if one is doing a research paper on the author or the work. Such prologues rarely appear to have taken as their primary goal exciting the reader about the work.

A notable exception would be C. S. Lewis's introduction to Sr. Penelope Lawson's translation of Athanasius's *On the Incarnation*. Since one cannot find this translation of *On the Incarnation* without Lewis's introduction, even on-line, it seems clear that Lewis's introduction remains a principal draw to this particular translation.[30] One can even find Lewis's introduction published separately from the translation. Some of this popularity can be explained by Lewis's large following, but not all of it. Why, then, has this little introduction retained its popularity?

Lewis was by training a scholar of medieval and renaissance literature and thus was deeply imbued with the spirit of those two historical periods. Two of his many books could be considered "introductions" and both very successful: *The Discarded Image: An Introduction to Medieval and Renaissance Literature* and the revealingly titled *A Preface to*

---

[27] Alasdair MacIntyre, *Three Rival Versions of Moral Enquiry: Encyclopedia, Genealogy, and Tradition* (Notre Dame: University of Notre Dame Press, 1990), 60.

[28] MacIntyre, *Three Rival Versions*, 61.

[29] Ibid.

[30] This introduction appears many places on the web, and the volume has been re-printed by St. Vladimir's Seminary Press, but the original copy in the United States was Athanasius, *On the Incarnation*, trans. by a religious of C.S.M.V. (New York: Macmillan, 1946). It was published with Lewis's introduction two years earlier in England by Centenary Press.

Paradise Lost. Lewis understood that readers need information, but also, and just as importantly, they need to be drawn imaginatively into the spirit and mind of the writer. His were not merely repackaged encyclopedia articles; his genius was to realize that readers had first to be persuaded that there was something valuable and important to be gained from entering upon the task of reading a book. Readers had to be convinced of the beauty of a text — that it contained something worthy to be loved and learned from — if they were going to be able to read well.[31]

Thirteenth-century prologues sought to communicate relevant background information, but this was not their only or even their primary aim. We will misjudge them if we imagine that Thomas or Bonaventure were attempting to do what a modern "encyclopedic" prologue does but doing it badly. Their prologues were designed to bring about the kind of transformation Prof. MacIntyre describes as the necessary preparation for reading.[32] Medieval prologues were meant as an exhortation to enter into a practice and a specific tradition of philosophical and theological enquiry. And in this way Thomas and Bonaventure's prologues served the purposes of the classic philosophical protreptic.

Classical Protreptic and Its Purposes

For those not acquainted with the term, a philosophic "protreptic" was, as the Greek term suggests, an "exhortation" which had "as its explicit aim," writes Mark D. Jordan in one of the best articles on the genre, "the winning of a student for philosophy."[33] One of the most famous of these was Cicero's *Hortensius*, now lost, which Augustine credits with having won him over for philosophy before he was eventually converted to Christianity. Cicero's *Hortensius* is sometimes said to have been adapted from an earlier work by Aristotle, the *Protrepticus*, which was reportedly one of the most famous and influential books of philosophy in the ancient world. It too, like the *Hortensius*, is now lost.

Sections of larger works could also serve a protreptic function. "This is famously true," argues Prof. Jordan, "of the first two chapters of Aristotle's *Metaphysics*, which borrow textually from his *Protreptikos*." There are also well-known examples of philosophical protreptic in Cicero's *Tusculan Disputations* and Lucretius's *De rerum natura*.[34] There are

---

[31] Mortimer Adler declared in the first edition of *How to Read a Book* (New York: Simon and Schuster, 1940), 15, that his book was "not about reading in every sense but only about that kind of reading which its readers do not do well enough, or at all, except when they are in love."

[32] Cf. MacIntyre, *Three Rival Versions*, 133: "The concept of having to be a certain sort of person, morally or theologically, in order to read a book aright — with the implication that perhaps if one is not that sort of person, then the book should be withheld from one — is alien to the assumption of liberal modernity that every rational adult should be free to and is able to read every book."

[33] Mark D. Jordan, "Ancient Philosophic Protreptic and the Problem of Persuasive Genres," *Rhetorica: A Journal of the History of Rhetoric*, 4, no. 4 (Autumn 1986): 309.

[34] See, for example, *Tusculan Disputations* 5.2.5–5.4.11, a section that begins (in the English translation of C. D. Yonge) with this encomium: "O Philosophy, thou guide of life! thou discoverer of virtue and expeller of vices! what had not only I myself, but the whole life of man, been without you? To you it is that we owe the origin of cities; you it was who called together the dispersed race of men into social life; you united them together... You have been the inventress of laws; you have been our instructress in morals and discipline; to you we fly for refuge; from you we implore assistance; and as I formerly submitted to you in a great degree, so now I surrender up myself entirely to you.

protreptic moments scattered throughout the Platonic dialogues, but the protreptic character stands out nowhere more prominently than in the *Gorgias* and the *Republic*, in both of which the give-and-take between the interlocutors seems specially crafted to convince the reader that, to make progress in wisdom, he or she must become a willing, disciplined enquirer searching for truth, not merely seeking money, power, or status. The protreptic was an invitation to a way of life, and the lives of the classical philosophers, such as those preserved by Diogenes Laertius and others, were said in antiquity to have served as invitations to the way of life of the philosophic school they represented.[35]

Nor was the practice of composing protreptic discourses confined to philosophy. There were protreptics to music (Chamealon), medicine (Galen), rhetoric (Themistius), and later, even a protreptic to martyrdom by Origen. Basil the Great's famous "Address to Young Men on Greek Literature" was often listed in ancient manuscripts under the heading *logos protreptikos*. Practitioners of nearly every discipline considered it important that they compose exhortations to engage in the study of the discipline and to adopt its goals and standards of excellence.

As Prof. Jordan's survey of ancient protreptic shows, the character of individual protreptics varied greatly depending upon the views of the philosophical school.[36] Yet we might discern a pair of common goals among all such protreptic works. The first is suggested by a comment attributed to Philo of Larissa, a second century BC member of the Platonic Academy, who is said to have compared the goals of the philosopher and the physician.[37] According to Philo, the physician's first task was to offer therapy for illness and his second was to refute the advice of false counselors; so too with the philosopher, his first

---

For one day spent well, and agreeably to your precepts, is preferable to an eternity of error. Whose assistance, then, can be of more service to me than yours, when you have bestowed on us tranquillity of life, and removed the fear of death?" So also Lucretius's *De rerum natura*, see 2.7–32 contains (in the English translation of W. E. Leonard) this exhortation to the Epicurean philosophy of life in which the greatest wisdom was to know how to minimize pain.

> *O wretched minds of men! O blinded hearts!*
> *In how great perils, in what darks of life*
> *Are spent the human years, however brief!*
> *O not to see that nature for herself*
> *Barks after nothing, save that pain keep off,*
> *Disjoined from the body, and that mind enjoy*
> *Delightsome feeling, far from care and fear!*
> *Therefore we see that our corporeal life*
> *Needs little, altogether, and only such*
> *As takes the pain away, and can besides*
> *Strew underneath some number of delights.*

[35] Cf. Jordan, "Protreptic," 314, esp. n. 40, and Bernard Frischer, *The Sculpted Word: Epicureanism and Philosophical Recruitment in Ancient Greece* (Berkeley: University of California Press, 1982).

[36] Jordan, "Protreptic," 328–329, argues that protreptic would be difficult if not impossible to define as a "genre in the ordinary poetic sense, that is, as dictating a certain combination of form, diction, and subject-matter." The problem is that "[e]ach school's notions about the human good issue[d] in views about how the good [could] be taught, and these views issue[d] in judgments about appropriate modes of composition." Thus we find that "[d]ifferent protreptics ... exhibit different motives in relation to the differently conceived philosophic ends."

[37] Stobeaus, *Anthol.*, 2.7.2.

Introduction 13

task was to show the good of philosophy and his second was to refute accusations, attacks, and malicious assaults against it. As the physician must both treat the causes of illness and aid what produces health, so the philosopher must remove what begets false opinion and shore up healthy thought.[38]

These two are not mutually exclusive, however. Treating the causes of illness helps produce health. But along with keeping the patient away from bad things, optimal health depends upon the physician instilling in the patient a knowledge of and a desire for good things, things conducive to his or her flourishing rather than destructive of it. As Alasdair MacIntyre has noted, to become a successful apprentice to a craft tradition, one must learn to distinguish "between what in particular situations it really is good to do and what only seems good to do to this particular apprentice but is not in fact so."[39] One crucial role of the protreptic, therefore, writes Prof. Jordan, was to compare the claims to knowledge of the other schools or disciplines with those of the true philosopher in such a way as to show that "every other form of knowledge is found lacking."[40]

To engage in the study of the discipline and to adopt its goals and standards of excellence was also by necessity an invitation to the way of life. The sort of decision envisioned here is captured nicely by Prof. MacIntyre's use of the analogy with apprenticing to a craft. When one chooses to become an apprentice, one is not merely choosing to engage in a particular form of *technē*, one is choosing as well and as importantly to enter into an entire way of life and to orient one's goals according to the standards of excellence handed down by one's teachers.

As Jordan points out, students – that is, potential future apprentices – had to "be won" at several different levels: "for the love of wisdom generally, for the choice of a particular school, for full commitment to the rigors of an advanced discipline."[41] Protreptics, thus, were designed to force the listener to make a choice. "Protreptics are just those works," argues Prof. Jordan,

> that aim to bring about the firm choice of a lived way to wisdom – however different the form of those works and their notions of wisdom might be… Each author confronts a hearer whose choice is the target of many other persuasions. The unity of the philosophic protreptic [as a genre] – and its great rhetorical interest – would seem to lie in this 'exigence,' in the hearer's moment of choice before ways-of-life.[42]

In the following chapters, I will argue that *principia*, of all three types, were meant to serve just such protreptic purposes: to inspire in the master's audience a love of the highest wisdom, but also to convince his listeners that the most profound and secure source of that wisdom could be found in sacred Scripture. To gain access to this wisdom, however, students would have to enter upon a new way of life and commit themselves to an advanced discipline of study.[43] This exhortation to a certain discipline of study was not "biblical" in

---

[38] Cf. Jordan, "Protreptic," 316–317.
[39] MacIntyre, *After Virtue*, 61.
[40] Jordan, "Protreptic," 321.
[41] Ibid., 309.
[42] Ibid., 310.
[43] There is obviously a certain irony here. The present book about these two great Parisian masters is itself a species of scholarship in the "encyclopaedist" tradition. I have tried to make a convincing

the manner of study that characterized the monastic schools, and yet it remained distinctly "biblical" in its own way. It sought to convince its audience to place the Bible as the highest authority, beyond that of even the most preeminent classical philosophers. The new opportunities for learning that arose in the thirteenth century presented new challenges, and the masters we will be studying knew they had to address them.

The master's task was to convince his students that the Scriptures were not merely a book of folk tales for simple people, but a source of wisdom more profound than that even of the greatest philosophers of antiquity. Students would have to see beneath the surface simplicity of the text and plumb its depths with *humility*, a key Christian virtue unknown to Aristotle. They would have to become *docile* – that is, "teachable" – if they were to attain the real treasures hidden within the words of the text, just as the Apostles were able to see the divinity of Christ, the Word made flesh, because they were humble men, while the scribes and learned men of Christ's day could not because they approached Him with pride and arrogance, not searching deeply in humility for the divine Truth, but assuming they knew more than they actually did.

The *Divisio Textus*

The Benedictine monk Galdericus, the first regent master of theology at the College of Cluny, who incepted at the University of Paris during the years 1258-1259, told the assembled members of the university community in his *resumptio* address:

> In the *principium* of a science or a book, the intention of doctors is accustomed to touch on two things. They are accustomed first to commend the science in order to have benevolent listeners (*auditores benevolos*). Also, they are accustomed to treat the causes and offer a general division in order to render them docile and attentive (*dociles et attentos*). Yesterday we showed, from the word proposed [i.e., the *thema* verse], that Sacred Scripture is commendable and surpasses all others. Now the causes will be treated and the division of the books..."[44]

Here Galdericus identifies two key elements of a *principium*, whether "of a science" – and by this we have to imagine he means the *principium* of a course – or "of a book," by which it is clear he means a "prologue." The first key element involved "commending the science" in order to produce benevolent listeners – what I have been describing as the "protretpic"

case for the approach these medieval masters chose, and I have done so with the hope that readers will read them more readily, more eagerly, and with greater appreciation. But I have not written an Introduction that would have been, from the classical or medieval point-of-view, sufficiently exhortatory or protreptic. This is simply to admit that very few of us, if any, can escape entirely the presuppositions, categories, and expectations of our age. Nor should we necessarily attempt to do so. I hope it is clear from the content of this book that I have tremendous respect for modern scholarship of the "encyclopaedic" sort. I take it I do no disservice to the benefits provided by my own age to suggest that other ages had their own benefits and that we might learn valuable lessons from them as much as they might have benefited from our specialized skills.

[44] Quoted from Spatz, 136; see also n. 13.

dimension of the *principium*.⁴⁵ But there was something more needed, and it involved "treating the causes and offering a general division of the books." By the "causes" of Scripture, Galdericus was referring to the four Aristotelian causes: the author or "efficient cause"; the subject or "material" cause; the manner of proceeding the author employs, which would be the "formal cause"; and the purpose or "final cause" of the work. And then, after all this, a good *principium* lecture of a course or a good prologue should provide a good *divisio textus*. Why this?

In Mortimer Adler's popular guide *How to Read a Book*, he recommends looking over the book's table of contents as an important first step for reading. He also recommends noting all the section headings and throughout each chapter, a skill he calls "seeing the skeleton" of the book. He describes this preparatory step as "setting forth the major parts of the book, and showing how they are organized into a whole, by being ordered to one another and to the unity of the whole."⁴⁶ When done properly, a good *divisio textus* is meant to achieve precisely this goal: seeing the parts in relation to the whole.

Having students grasp the material in this way helps them to recollect what they have read. The memory arts, which were an important part of the pedagogy of the Middle Ages,⁴⁷ long emphasized that when one is faced with a vast amount of information it should be "gathered together" under six or seven headings. If the six or seven items stored in one's short-term memory could be associated with the information one hoped to recall, bringing to mind the shorter list would provide "access points" to the larger store of information in one's long-term memory. The smaller list was stored in one's "memory" (*memoria*); the process by which the longer list was called to mind was known in the Middle Ages (hearkening back to Aristotle) as "recollection" (*reminiscentia*).⁴⁸ It was part of the medieval master's skill set that he had to be able to organize a large amount of information effectively under a few headings and then make memorable associations to help his audience recollect the rest.

And yet memory and recollection are merely the first steps. A good *divisio textus* helps provide a hermeneutical lens through which the text can be viewed more clearly. Show students Fra Angelico's *Annunciation*, ask what he or she saw and an obvious answer is likely to be: "It's a picture of an angel." That much is obvious. But the significance of that angel must be understood in the context of the whole scene: it is an annunciation to *Mary*. So too with thoughtful books: one can appreciate the beauty of a single passage, but often one's fuller appreciation of the significance of that one passage comes only with understanding how it fits into the whole.

It is revealing, for example, that most of the medieval masters whose *divisio textus* of the books of the Bible we will be reviewing thought it was important that the New Testament

---

⁴⁵ Although it is worth noting that rendering listeners "benevolent" was also the goal of the *exordium* of a speech in classical rhetoric.

⁴⁶ Adler, 163.

⁴⁷ On the popularity and widespread use of the arts of memory in the Middle Ages, see Mary Carruthers, *The Book of Memory: A Study of Memory in Medieval Culture* (Cambridge: Cambridge University Press, 1990).

⁴⁸ See, for example, Thomas Aquinas's commentary on Aristotle's *Memory and Recollection* in: Thomas Aquinas, *Commentaries on Aristotle's "On Sense and What Is Sensed" and "On Memory and Recollection,"* trans. Kevin White and Ed Macierowski (Washington, DC: Catholic University of America Press, 2005).

books correspond with the Old: the books of the Mosaic Law with the Gospels, for example, the historical books with the Acts of the Apostles, and the prophetic books with the Epistles. In their eyes (as revealed by the way they "divided" the text), the Old Testament and the New are not just a random collection of books that happened to make it into the canon. Rather each book is an essential part of a coherent whole, each with its own role to play in God's plan of salvation. The way the medieval masters "divided" the books in order to "unite" them provides us important information about how they viewed the Bible as a whole.

Suzanne Reynolds argues in her book *Medieval Reading: Grammar, Rhetoric, and the Classical Text* that, "The twelfth century saw an increase in the production of classical texts, an expansion of education, and a series of crucial debates about language, signification, and interpretation. All of these are part of a gradual shift in reading itself, broadly from the ruminative *lectio* of monastic meditation to the more public, structured reading processes of the classroom."[49] The *divisio textus* designed to give the reader a clear vision of the parts in relation to the whole and the protreptic exhortation directed to the students to undertake the discipline of reading with love and respect – these two would have been especially helpful to medieval students coming from what was still a mostly oral culture into what was increasingly a literary, book-centered educational environment at the University of Paris.[50]

A Culture of Preaching and Prologues

There are two approaches to intellectual history. The first sets out to provide a synthetic treatment of a host of writers over an extended period of time. The second consists in selecting a few representative or especially fertile thinkers to probe their work more deeply and at greater length. For the purposes of this book, I have chosen the second approach. I will provide an in-depth study of the work of two of the most preeminent medieval masters of the thirteenth century: Thomas Aquinas and Bonaventure.

The work of these two men is especially useful, not only because they remain among the best known thinkers of the period, but also because they incepted as masters at roughly the same time. Approaching the two masters in this way would be akin in modern academic culture to comparing the development of two prominent philosophers who graduated from the same institution in the same year, both of whom worked with the same dissertation director, but who went on to have very different careers and distinctively different work.

I will argue, based on an analysis of the work of these two masters, both of whom, although they became preeminent, had a very standard training at Paris, that there was a great deal of continuity among the three skills of the medieval master: *lectio*, *disputatio*, and

---

[49] Suzanne Reynolds, *Medieval Reading: Grammar, Rhetoric and the Classical Text* (Cambridge: Cambridge University Press, 1996), 1. It is also worth noting that in that famous passage in *Verbum Abbreviatum* 1 in which Peter Cantor lays out the three duties of the master – *lectio, disputatio,* and *praedicatio* – he specifies that "studious reading (*lectio*) is as it were the foundation and substratum of the rest" (*quasi fundamentum et substratorium sequentium*).

[50] For an extensive study of the two cultures, oral and literary, as they developed in the eleventh and twelfth centuries, see Brian Stock, *The Implications of Literacy* (Princeton, NJ: Princeton University Press, 1983).

praedicatio – more, perhaps, than has been previously recognized. The three elements we find in the master's inception addresses – a series of disputed questions, a protreptic exhortation to the study of Scripture, and a *divisio textus* of the entire Bible – are expressions of all three duties. But the relationship between the three runs even deeper.

Although medieval preachers were warned that "preaching" was not the place for "disputation" – a warning that suggests this may have been a common temptation – both practices manifested a similar mindset, one characterized by division of a topic into its constituent parts. Each of those parts was then developed in its own right but always with an eye to how the parts fit together into a coherent whole. This approach also characterized medieval biblical commentaries, which were usually scribal transcriptions of the *lectiones* that masters delivered at the University. As I will show, the composition of these biblical commentaries was highly influenced by the contemporary methods employed in *sermo modernus*–style preaching, both in terms of their style and their purpose. That is to say, they were written in a style reminiscent of medieval *sermo modernus*–style preaching, and they were written with an eye to *training prospective preachers* with material especially useful for *sermo modernus*-style preaching. It is for this reason that I have described the academic culture of the University of Paris in the thirteenth century as "a culture of preaching, prologues, and biblical commentary."

It is worth noting in advance that I spend relatively little time on the arts of *disputatio* in the current volume, not because they are unimportant, but simply because there are plenty of good treatments of that topic available. There has been so much emphasis on *disputatio*, in fact, that some people associate the word "scholastic" almost solely with texts written in the style of the "disputed question." An unsuspecting student looking up "scholastic method" on the web would before long likely find a comment similar to this one on encyclopedia.com: "From its earliest, obscure beginnings there were two essential features of scholastic method: exposition (*lectio*) and disputation (*disputatio*). Disputation was undoubtedly the more original and characteristic feature..." Notice that *praedicatio* is missing entirely from this description.

One of the chief goals of the present work is to show that leaving out *praedicatio* in this way is to miss one of the primary intellectual and cultural driving forces of the thirteenth century. With this study, I hope to broaden our current understanding of the term "scholastic." So while I have no desire to de-emphasize the undisputed importance of the "disputed question" among medieval theologians of the thirteenth century, I intent to show that the language of the "disputed question" was not the only language of the schools and that the language and patterns of *sermo modernus*–style preaching were also a characteristic element of the theological training at Paris.

I suggest that the medieval method of *divisio* and *dilatatio* united by a central *thema* was both an expression of a cultural mindset and a means of transmitting it. Bachelors were trained to craft these *principia* regularly, and this way of approaching a text or a topic continued to characterize their work, throughout their careers. This way of thinking about the practice of reading – structured, organized, and with an eye toward memory and recollection – would bear fruit in Thomas's and Bonaventure's later works, although in very different ways.

In my analysis, I examine primarily the prologues of these authors and examine everything else in relation to them. My contention is that this in-depth study of a good number of these prologues of various types gives us access to the mindset of medieval scholars, especially how they approached the task of reading. It provides us too with a glimpse of the literary culture that characterized the medieval universities: one that was increasingly "bookish," but still in large part oral.

Getting a good sense of the habits of mind that informed these prologues, however, requires reading a good number of them. So too, seeing the relationship between the style of these prologues and the other work of these scholastic masters is not something that will become evident from reading only one prologue, any more than becoming acquainted with a master's preaching style can be achieved by reading only one sermon. So I have chosen to focus on only two authors and examine a larger spectrum of their prologues, from their earliest novice work to the prologues they wrote as mature scholars shortly before their deaths.

The Structure of the Book

The book is divided into three major parts.

Part I Preliminaries
Part II Thomas Aquinas, the Logician Who Learned to Preach
Part III Bonaventure, the Scholastic with the Soul of a Poet

A few words are in order about each.

Part I Preliminaries

In Part I, I sketch out some of the necessary historical and cultural context that will help us flesh out what I describe throughout the book as the culture of preaching, prologues, and biblical commentary at the University of Paris in the thirteenth century.

Chapter 1, "Preaching and Principia at Paris," traces the historical development of what has been called the "homiletic revolution of the thirteenth century" from its roots in the late twelfth century to its expression in the pedagogy at the University of Paris in the thirteenth.

Because most modern readers would find the preaching style employed in the thirteenth century – the so-called "modern sermon" or *sermo modernus* style of preaching – odd, difficult to understand, perhaps even off-putting, I review some of the basic elements of this unique style of preaching in Chapter 2.

The culmination of a young bachelor's training in preaching was his inception address. The thirteenth-century development of the distinctive literary forms used in those addresses – the *principium in aula* and the *resumptio* – is the subject of Chapter 3.

The remainder of the book is divided into two major parts. In the first, I examine the prologues of Thomas Aquinas, and in the second, I make a similar examination of the prologues of Bonaventure of Bagnoregio.

Part II Aquinas, the Logician Who Learned to Preach

I begin the part on each master by examining the *principium in aula* address the man gave at his inception and then, in a subsequent chapter, his *resumptio*. The reason for starting with each man's *principium* and *resumptio* is that it allows us to compare their proficiency at roughly equal points in their respective careers and to view their development, both prior to their inception and after it, in relation to that key moment.

A word is in order, however, about why I have chosen to consider Aquinas's inception addresses before Bonaventure's, given that Bonaventure likely incepted two years *before* Aquinas. My reasons are pedagogical rather than chronological.

An anonymous reviewer of this volume noted the remark of R.-A. Gauthier concerning Aquinas's debt to Bonaventure in *Quodlibet* 7.7 on the question of manual labor. Aquinas held this quodlibet in Lent of 1256, very close to the time of his inception as master, and he basically rewrote Bonaventure's treatment of the question, channeling and simplifying Bonaventure's dense exposition. To go from Bonaventure's treatment to that of Thomas, says Gauthier, is to pass "from the luxuriance of a virgin forest to a French garden."[51] "Would not this be the proper order to consider these two great masters?" wondered my reviewer.

It is hard to deny a reviewer who is at once so learned and so clever. And yet the quotation the reviewer cites could just as well be used to argue for the order I have proposed. It is precisely *because* Bonaventure's work is so much more "luxuriant," so much more complex, so much more "overgrown" than Aquinas's, that I chose to treat Aquinas first. A basic pedagogical principle, traceable back to Aristotle, holds that one should start with what is simpler and move to what is more complex. My goal is to get readers accustomed to the *sermo modernus* style in its simpler form in the work of Aquinas before moving on to the much more "luxuriant" expression of that style in Bonaventure's prologues.

There is also no indication in current scholarship of any influence of Bonaventure's inception on Aquinas's, even if we could say for sure that Aquinas was present at Bonaventure's inception. So although there might have been *some* value in placing Bonaventure's inception addresses first to indicate to readers that they could *search* for an influence, interested readers can make that search without my switching the order, especially because I have included an English translation of Bonaventure's *principium* in the accompanying website.

For these reasons, I begin with Aquinas. And in Chapter 4, I begin the section on Aquinas with an examination of Thomas' *principium in aula* inception address (*Rigans montes*).

Chapter 5 follows with an examination of Thomas's *resumptio* address (*Hic est liber*), in the course of which I give special attention to the *divisio textus* of the books of the Bible that were a common feature of these addresses.

In Chapter 6, I examine several prologues Thomas wrote as a *lector biblicus* and then analyze the general prologue he wrote for his *Commentary on the Sentences of Peter Lombard*.

In Chapter 7, I examine in the first part of the chapter two prologues Thomas wrote as a young master at Paris: the prologue to his treatise *Contra Impugnantes* (1256) and the prologue to his commentary on Boethius's *De Trinitate* (1257–1258). In the second part of the chapter, I examine two prologues from Thomas's later career: the general prologue to

---

[51] *Sancti Thomae de Aquino Opera Omnia*, 25.1, *Quaestiones quodlibetales* (Paris: Edita Leonis XIII, 1984), 81. Translated from the French original.

his series of commentaries on the epistles of St. Paul (begun perhaps 1265 or 1268; finished 1271–1272) and the prologue to his commentary on the Psalms (1272–1273).

In Chapter 8, I examine what I take to be Thomas's most highly developed and theologically sophisticated prologue: the prologue to his *Commentary on the Gospel of John* (1272–1273).

In Chapter 9, "Aquinas, *Sermo Modernus*–Style Preaching, and Biblical Commentary," I discuss some of the scholastic "habits of mind" we see revealed in these prologues and the light they shed on Thomas's other work. I also examine the relationship between thirteenth-century biblical commentary and thirteenth century *sermo modernus*–style preaching. Many of the methods of commentary were adopted from contemporary methods of preaching, and it is clear that the goal of such commentaries was to prepare young friars to be able to preach in the *sermo modernus* style.

Part III Bonaventure, the Scholastic with the Soul of a Poet

In Chapter 10, we turn to our analysis of the work of St. Bonaventure and, as was my practice with St. Thomas, we begin with an analysis of Bonaventure's *principium in aula* address (*Omnium artifex*), only recently identified by Prof. Joshua Benson.

In Chapter 11, I examine the text Prof. Benson has identified as Bonaventure's *resumptio* address – the text that, with minor alterations, has been known to scholars for years as the *De reductione artium ad theologiam* ("On the Reduction of the Arts to Theology").

In Chapter 12, I examine the general prologue to Bonaventure's *Commentary on the Sentences of Peter Lombard*. In this chapter as in the others in this part, we are interested in the development of Bonaventure's skill in the use of the *sermo modernus* style, but we will also be comparing Bonaventure's skill at these early points in his university career with Thomas's at roughly the same points.

In Chapters 13 and 14, I undertake an examination of Bonaventure's early prologues, the products of his student years. As Bonaventure's prologues are much longer and more complicated than Thomas's, it will be necessary to discuss each in its own chapter. In Chapter 13, I discuss the prologue to his *Commentary on the Gospel of John*, and in Chapter 14, the prologue to his *Commentary on the Gospel of Luke*.

In Chapter 15, "Bonaventure, *Sermo Modernus*–Style Preaching, and Biblical Commentary," I show the extent to which Bonaventure's early biblical commentaries were done using the methods of *sermo modernus*–style preaching with an eye to training young friars to preach in the *sermo modernus* style.

In Chapter 16, I turn to another of Bonaventure's early prologues, although one that was *not* a product of his student years: the prologue to the *Breviloquium*, his short summary of the main elements of Christian doctrine.

In Chapters 17 and 18, I turn to several of Bonaventure's later works. In Chapter 17, we examine the prologue to his *Collations on the Ten Commandments* and the *Collations on the Seven Gifts of the Holy Spirit*. And in Chapter 18, we look at his infamously difficult *Collations on the Six Days of Creation*. With all three *Collations*, the goal is to show what light can be shed on the complex style of these works by seeing them as employing a creative development of the *sermo modernus*-style of preaching.

Finally, in Chapter 19, I offer some brief conclusions regarding (1) the changes needed in our understanding of the historical and cultural setting at Paris, especially regarding the connotations we attach to the term "scholastic"; (2) the significance of the inception addresses as revelatory of the fundamental skills of the master and how they were related; and (3) the characters of the authors, their similarities and differences, and how their common education at Paris bore fruit in very different ways.

One final note: I wrote this book aware that different readers will likely use it in different ways. Some will be interested only in Thomas, others only in Bonaventure. Some may be interested only in the historical and cultural "preliminaries" part, others only in the chapters on the relationship between preaching and biblical commentary in the thirteenth century. Still others may pick up the book simply to read about a particular prologue.

So although the chapters are meant to form a coherent whole, I have also done my best to organize the book so that it can be more easily accessed as a reference tool. So, for example, one reason I have divided the major parts into "Preliminaries," "Aquinas," and "Bonaventure" rather than interweaving my analysis of the two masters together is so that readers interested in one master or the other can go right to that part.

I have, in addition, done my best to make each chapter stand on its own, so that a reader studying just one chapter would be able to find nearly everything he or she needs in that chapter without having to refer to earlier chapters. Although I have tried to keep unnecessary repetition to a minimum, crafting each chapter to be able stand on its own in this way made some repetition unavoidable. The goal has been to produce a book whose parts are as useful as possible for a wide range of scholars with varied interests in the subjects covered.

PART ONE

Preliminaries

1

Preaching and *Principia* at the University of Paris

THE INCEPTION *principium* addresses we will examine and all the prologues, oral or written, even those for highly academic material such as the *Commentary on the Sentences of Peter Lombard*, shared one common characteristic: they were all crafted in the style used in sermons during the thirteenth century, the so-called *sermo modernus*, or "modern sermon" style.[1]

---

[1] It is necessary to distinguish, however, between University sermons (*sermones*) and what are sometimes called in English "sermon-conferences" (*collationes*). Literally, *collatio* simply means "a gathering." By the thirteenth century, it could refer to one of two types of address: one liturgical, one not. Masters of the Sacred Page at the University of Paris were required to preach a University sermon when they were assigned the task. And when they were given that task, they not only had to preach a *sermo* during the day; they were also required to preach a *collatio* at vespers the same evening utilizing the same *thema* verse they had used that morning. This was one sort of *collatio*. It required a formal *sermo modernus*-style structure. There was, however, it seems, another form of *collatio* that was more of a "conference address" than a "sermon," strictly speaking. So, for example, the Leonine edition of Thomas's sermons does *not* include Thomas's well-known *collationes* on the Ten Commandments, the Creed, the Our Father, or the Hail Mary. These four are also listed separately in Fr. Gilles Emery's "Brief Catalogue of the Works of Saint Thomas Aquinas" at the back of Fr. Jean-Pierre Torrell's biography of Thomas Aquinas. There are, I would argue, good reasons for this custom of distinguishing Thomas's sermons from these *collationes* on the Ten Commandments, the Creed, the Our Father, and the Hail Mary, just as there are similarly good reasons for not including Bonaventure's *collationes* on the Seven Gifts of the Holy Spirit and on the Six Days of Creation in with his long list of sermons. They are not the same sort of address. Although Thomas and Bonaventure often used the methods of sermon development in these religious addresses, they did not conform to the form of the thirteenth-century sermon. Hence, if it is asked why Thomas did not use the *sermo modernus*–style of preaching in his "sermons" on the Ten Commandments, the answer is that these were not "sermons." They were no more "sermons" than Bonaventure's *Collationes in hexameron* were "sermons." They were religious addresses, not sermons delivered in the context of the Mass or a related liturgical service such as preaching at vespers. See Randall B. Smith, *Reading the Sermons of Thomas Aquinas: A Beginner's Guide* (Steubenville, OH: Emmaus Press, 2016), xxvii–xxix.

Prologues, *principia*, and sermons had not always been done this way. The *sermo modernus* style was a product of the early thirteenth century. Previously, sermons were less stylized and usually involved a verse-by-verse, running commentary on the biblical text.[2] Even in the middle of the thirteenth century, when Thomas and Bonaventure were students at Paris, it was not uncommon for a *cursor biblicus* or even a master to copy out one of St. Jerome's prologues and then draw the reader's attention to a few important points in it.[3]

The *sermo modernus* style that masters such as Thomas and Bonaventure used in crafting their sermons and prefaces arose in the early thirteenth century, a product of what has been called the "homiletic revolution of the thirteenth century."[4]

Prior to Alan of Lille's 1199 work *De arte praedicatoria* ("On the Preacher's Art"), only three works could qualify as serious theories of preaching: St. Augustine's fourth-century work *De doctrina christiana*, Pope St. Gregory the Great's sixth-century *Cura pastoralis*, and Guibert de Nogent's eleventh-century *Liber quo ordine sermo fieri debeat* ("A Book About the Way a Sermon Ought to Be Written").[5] Within the next twenty years after the publication of Alan of Lille's *De arte praedicatoria*, however, a whole new rhetoric of preaching had spread across Europe and hundreds of theoretical manuals had been written for aspiring preachers to learn from.[6] By the middle of the thirteenth century, this new style had been fully developed, complete with its own technical vocabulary and stable pattern of organization.[7]

How did these developments come about so rapidly? "The plain truth," says James J. Murphy, author of *Rhetoric in the Middle Ages*, "is that we do not yet know the complete answer."[8] We are not, however, without knowledge of concurrent events that can help us understand the context within which this sudden explosion of interest in preaching arose. These concurrent events are worth examining here, since the preaching and teaching careers of both Thomas and Bonaventure should be seen against the cultural and historical backdrop of this "homiletic revolution," which by their time was well underway.

---

[2] See *The Sermon*, ed. Beverly Kienzle (Turnhout: Brepols 2000), esp. Thomas N. Hall, "The early medieval sermon"; Beverly Mayne Kienzle, "The twelfth-century monastic sermon"; and Mark A. Zier, "Sermons of the twelfth century schoolmasters and canons."

[3] As we will see, both Thomas and Bonaventure observed this traditional practice in their early careers.

[4] See James J. Murphy, *Rhetoric in the Middle Ages: A History of Rhetorical Theory from Saint Augustine to the Renaissance* (Berkeley: University of California Press, 1974), 309 ff.

[5] Murphy, *Rhetoric*, 309. For a nice overview of these works and their influence on preaching, see Murphy, 269–308.

[6] For an invaluable introduction to the various preaching aids that became available, see David d'Avray, *The Preaching of the Friars: Sermons Diffused from Paris before 1300* (Oxford: Oxford University Press, 1985), esp. 14–28, 163–203.

[7] Murphy, *Rhetoric*, 309–310. For an excellent survey of the development of the style, see Nicole Nicole Bériou, *L'avènement des maîtres de la Parole: La Prédication à Paris au XIIIe siècle*, vol. 1 (Paris: Institut d'Études Augustiniennes, 1998), 133–214; Richard and Mary Rouse, *Preachers, Florilegia and Sermons: Studies on the Manipulus florum of Thomas of Ireland* (Toronto: Pontifical Institute of Mediaeval Studies, 1979), 65–87; and Murphy, *Rhetoric*, 311–355.

[8] Murphy, 310.

Preaching and the Fourth Lateran Council

One key event that contributed to the thirteenth century's "homiletic revolution" was the Fourth Lateran Council of 1215, canon 10 of which lamented:

> It often happens that bishops, on account of their manifold duties or bodily infirmities, or because of hostile invasions or other reasons, to say nothing of lack of learning, which must be absolutely condemned in them and is not to be tolerated in the future, are themselves unable to minister the word of God to the people, especially in large and widespread dioceses.[9]

Declaring that "the food of the word of God is above all necessary, because as the body is nourished by material food, so is the soul nourished by spiritual food, since 'not by bread alone does man live but in every word that proceeds from the mouth of God'" (Matthew 4:4), the council decreed that bishops should henceforth provide men "suitable for carrying out fruitfully the office of sacred preaching" (*idoneos ad sanctae praedicationis officium salubriter exequendum*), commissioning them to visit the people diligently in place of the bishop to instruct them, both by word and example.[10] These designated preachers were to be "supplied appropriately with necessities" lest they be compelled to abandon their work for lack of them.[11] Lest anyone imagine these were mere suggestions or pious wishes, the council declared that, "If anyone neglect to comply with this, he shall be subject to severe punishment."[12]

It may seem odd to modern Catholics to imagine a time when preaching was not a regular occurrence at Mass. But such was often the case in the early Middle Ages. As Richard and Mary Rouse have pointed out,

> In the twelfth century much of the preaching was monastic, preached by monks to a monastic congregation. The homily, thoughtful, usually brief, and simple in organization, was the customary vehicle of monastic preaching. Sermons to the laity were not totally lacking, of course; in particular, preaching to the lay faithful was associated with the Crusades, and with wandering evangelists such as Robert d'Arbrissel. But the ordinary parish priest was not expected, and often not competent to prepare and deliver regular sermons. The task of routine preaching to the lay faithful was the responsibility of the bishops, who were required to preach once each Sunday. When this requirement was fulfilled, and it often was not, the result might be no more than one sermon per diocese per week...[13]

---

[9] See *Conciliorum Oecumenicorum Decreta*, curantibus J. Alberigo, et al., 3rd ed. (Bologna: Istituto per le scienze religiose, 1973). Available at: www.internetsv.info/Archive/CLateranense4.pdf and www.documentacatholicaomnia.eu/01_10_1215-1215-_Concilium_Lateranum_IIII.html

[10] Ibid.

[11] Ibid. "Quibus ipsi cum indiguerint congrue necessaria ministrent ne pro necessariorum defectu compellantur desistere ab incoepto."

[12] On the tenth canon and the Lateran Council, see Rouse, *Preachers*, 56–60.

[13] Rouse, *Preachers*, 43. Compare this scarcity with the surfeit of sermons in the thirteenth century, about which Jean Leclercq points out, "Le sermon est sans doute le genre littéraire le plus abondamment représenté dans la production du XIIIe siècle." J. Leclercq, *"Le magistère du prédicateur*

It is notable also that Peter Cantor (also known as "Peter the Chanter"), who in the *Verbum abbreviatum* famously defined the three duties of the master as *lectio* (reading), *disputatio* (debate), and *praedicatio* (preaching), later in the same work spent an entire section inveighing against "the evil silence (*taciturnitatem*) especially of the *prelati*." One manifestation of this "evil silence," according to Peter, was their failure to preach: "Evilly they pass over in silence when preaching is to be done" (*Tacetur etiam male ad praedicandum*).[14]

Note that the Council's intention was to encourage not only more preaching to the laity, but also more *learned* preaching. The concern was not only that many of the faithful were not hearing the Word of God preached to them, but also that when they did hear preaching, it was too often from preachers incompetently prepared, lacking either the rhetorical training or the theological resources, or both, to preach the faith of the Church accurately and reliably, or from wandering evangelists who, though they possessed rhetorical power, often preached a message at odds with the theology of the Church. The Council's goal, therefore, was to encourage a new generation of preachers with the time and resources to gain the rhetorical skill and theological training to preach to a new population of educated laypeople.

Yet, since Peter Cantor died in 1197, and the *Verbum abbreviatum* was written before 1187, we can say that the concern over the lack, not only of good preaching, but of any preaching at all, preceded the Fourth Lateran Council by several decades at least.[15] As David d'Avray has suggested:

> In a sense the decree on preaching of the Fourth Lateran Council is one chapter in a history which goes back to Caesarius of Arles in the sixth century. He presided over the Council of Vaison in 529, at which it was laid down that priests – "not only in cities but also in all parishes" – had the right to preach to the people. The implication is that preaching by the bishop alone was not enough. The same solution and much the same wording were adopted at the reform synod of Arles in 813. The other local reform synods of that year do not appear to go so far as Arles in extending the bishops' right and duty to preach to ordinary priests, but Charlemagne and his advisers clearly believed that preaching was a responsibility of priests as well as bishops. In declaring that the bishops needed help with preaching the Fourth Lateran Council was thus restating an idea that had been around for a very long time.[16]

Better preaching was one of the prime goals of Charlemagne's educational program and thus of what we today call the "Carolingian Renaissance." In his famous *Admonitio generalis*

---

au XIIIe siècle," *Archives d'histoire doctrinale et littéraire du Moyen Age* 15 (1946): 105—147, esp. 143–144. For a different perspective, see D. W. Robertson, "Frequency of Preaching in Thirteenth-Century England," *Speculum* 24, no. 3 (July, 1949): 376–388.

[14] Peter Cantor, *Verbum abbreviatum*, 62.

[15] For a good treatment of Peter Cantor and his historical milieu, see J. W. Baldwin, *Masters, Princes and Merchants: The Social Views of Peter the Chanter and His Circle*, 2 vols. (Princeton, NJ: Princeton University Press, 1970). Richard and Mary Rouse suggest that, at this point in time, "the Church considered preaching largely as a missionary function, aimed at the conversion of non-believers"; for those who were Christians by birth and heritage, "the faith was transmitted principally through the sacraments." See Rouse, *Preachers*, 43–44.

[16] d'Avray, *Preaching*, 30.

Preaching and Principia at the University of Paris

of 789, for example, Charlemagne associated the duty to preach with the first and most important commandment of the law:

> Before all else, that the catholic faith is to be diligently taught and preached to all the people by the bishops and priests, because this is the first commandment of the Lord God almighty in the law: "Hear, O Israel, that the Lord your God is one God. And that He is to be loved with all your heart and with all your mind and with all your soul and with all your strength."[17]

Yet, as noble as these earlier efforts at reform may have been, none appears to have been as successful as those in the thirteenth century. What explains the difference? Hume's famous warning about not mistaking causality with contiguity and coincidence is worth remembering. Whether the Fourth Lateran Council of 1215 caused the "homiletic revolution" of the thirteenth century, was one of its first major effects, or simply helped to amplify a movement that was already afoot is not a question we can resolve here. What we can say with David d'Avray, however, is that the "decree marks, even if it did not cause, the beginning of a new age in the history of preaching."[18]

The Demand for Preaching among More Educated Laymen

If the dictates of the Council alone are insufficient to explain the "homiletic revolution" of the thirteenth century, what other influences can we find among contemporaneous events that might have led to their successful implementation? Another key factor was likely the increasing presence of a more literate and educated populace in the growing number of medieval towns in western Europe. "Cities," writes d'Avray, "provided an environment in which the relatively new classes of merchants and lay lawyers could flourish; for the latter literacy was indispensable and for the former a decided advantage."[19] The emergence and success of the University of Bologna, founded nearly at the same time as the University of Paris, specializing in the schooling of a literate class of academically trained lawyers rather than in the academic preparation of a literate class of preachers, as at Paris, suggests that the demand for people with such skills had increased dramatically since the twelfth century.

During the thirteenth century, confraternities, of which the first is often said to have been founded at Paris in 1208, also sprung up, sometimes by the dozen, in every city and town across Europe, to respond to the needs and desires of this new literate class of laymen.[20] Regarding one such group, the *humiliati*, which was especially popular and

---

[17] See *Charlemagne: Translated Sources* (Lambrigg, Kendal, Cumbria: P. D. King, 1987), 214, section 61.

[18] d'Avray, *Preaching*, 16. The full quotation is: "Still, most scholars would agree that the decree marks, even if it did not cause, the beginning of a new age in the history of preaching, and that it calls attention to the gravity of the problem – too few popular sermons – which the friars in the event went far towards solving." I consider the importance of the friars in a later section.

[19] d'Avray, *Preaching*, 30.

[20] G. G. Meersseman, *Ordo fraternitatis: confraternite e pietà dei laici nel Medioevo* (Rome: Herder, 1977).

influential in Italy, Jacques de Vitry (d. 1240) comments in his *Historia occidentalis*, "The laity as well as the clerics do not omit to say all the canonical hours by day and by night; and nearly all of them are literate (*litterati*)." Notably, the author goes on some ten lines later to point out that "the brothers, both the clerics and the literate laymen," had authority given them by the pope himself to preach "not only in their own congregation, but in the streets and cities and in secular churches," as long as they had the permission of the local bishop.[21] "By the end of the thirteenth century," writes d'Avray, "the cultural gap between clergy and laity had been narrowed... Far from all of their lay public were simple and ignorant people."[22]

I am not suggesting that everyone or even the majority of people in medieval society were literate. Clearly there were still large numbers who did not have the ability to read. Yet we should be careful of labeling them as "unliterary." Many cultures have existed throughout history, and exist still today, in which the common people are literary, though not literate. In such societies, their knowledge of great texts – whether the stories of Homer's *Iliad*, the Scottish Tam Lyn, or the Hebrew Psalms – comes from listening to them repeatedly spoken or sung. In this form they were passed down from generation to generation orally by memory.

We should not imagine, therefore, that the common folk in medieval towns and villages were entirely ignorant of the Scriptures, even if they could not read them. Many would have heard Bible verses spoken and sung constantly. It is likely that medieval preachers came to understand in such circumstances that a form of preaching and lecturing that would allow their points to be more easily recalled was crucial. The arts of memory and recollection in this setting would have been invaluable to students, masters, and preachers.[23]

The social milieu in which Thomas and Bonaventure studied and taught was a culture in transition between orality and literacy. Books were becoming more common, and yet only the richest owned more than a few. Monks and friars who attended a university were required to read not only the Scriptures but also a host of other large, complicated books. It was not uncommon for students at Paris to have committed to memory not only all the Psalms but large portions of the rest of the Bible as well. Teaching was still done mostly orally, often with only the master possessing a written copy of the book he was commenting upon during his *lectio*. Many points had to be committed to memory.

So although there were still large portions of the population unable to read, the population as a whole, especially in the towns and cities, was becoming increasingly literate, or at least *literary*, and thus more eager for learned sermons. For similar reasons, people were less

---

[21] *The Historia Occidentalis of Jacques de Vitry*, ed. J. F. Hinnebusch, O.P. (Fribourg: The University Press, 1972), c. 28, 144–145: "Omnes horas canonicas diebus et noctibus laici sicut et clerici non pretermittunt. Fere omnes litterati sunt... Fratres autem eorum tam clerici quam laici literati a summon pontifice, qui regulam eorum et canonica instituta confirmauit, auctoritatem habent predicandi, non solum in sua congregatione sed in plateis et ciuitatibus, in ecclesiis secularibus, requisite tamen consensus eorum qui present locis illis prelatorum."

[22] d'Avray, *Preaching*, 43.

[23] On the importance of the arts of memory and recollection in the Middle Ages, see Mary Carruthers, *The Book of Memory: A Study of Memory in Medieval Culture*, 2nd ed. (Cambridge: Cambridge University Press, 2008) and her anthology with Jan M. Ziolkowski, *The Medieval Craft of Memory: An Anthology of Texts and Pictures* (Philadelphia: University of Pennsylvania Press, 2003).

forgiving of illiterate, thoughtless ones. The problem facing the Church was not only how to provide preachers but also how to train preachers who could measure up to the rhetorical and intellectual expectations of the newly educated class of laypeople who knew more about secular matters but not always about matters pertaining to their Christian faith.

With such an audience, the simple moral lessons or pious exhortations that might have been adequate in an earlier age would have ceased to be so any longer, and the allure of rhetorically sophisticated but doctrinally unorthodox preaching became all the harder to resist. "One is not certain," write Richard and Mary Rouse, "whether it was in reaction against these unorthodox preachers that the Church began to emphasize and encourage sermons by the orthodox; or whether, in effect, the Church began in earnest to emphasize the sermon as a vehicle for instruction simply because there was an audience receptive to preaching."[24] For our purposes, we needn't make this an either – or proposition. The Fourth Lateran Council intended to encourage not only more preaching to the laity, but also more *learned* preaching – preaching that would communicate more reliably the authentic faith of the Church.

Training large numbers of such preachers who could sort through various "opinions" in order to discern the authentic truths of the faith and then preach these truths convincingly to a more literate, intellectually discriminating audience was a tall order. But this challenge was taken up by two distinctive, novel institutions founded early in the thirteenth century that, had history been different, might not have had much to do with one another, but whose fortunes in the thirteenth century became intimately intertwined. I am speaking of course of the universities and the friars.

The Friars and Preaching

A key factor missing in attempts at the reform of preaching in the Church in previous centuries was the existence and widespread influence of a large number of highly educated members of religious orders specially trained for preaching and not bound by the vow of stability taken in Benedictine-type orders. By contrast, in the thirteenth century, the new orders of friars were able to travel widely across Europe preaching and teaching, but also carrying with them the model of a new style of preaching.

The year 1215, the date of the Fourth Lateran Council, was also the year that Dominic de Guzman, with six "brothers," established a new religious order in a house in Toulouse. Guzman attended the council with his diocesan bishop, Foulques of Toulouse, and little more than a year later, in January 1217, he obtained from the new pope, Honorius III, a mandate, *Gratiarum omnium*, that gave general approval to the work of preaching already begun at Toulouse.

From the very beginning, Dominic and his brothers were devoted to the dual works of preaching and teaching. Early on, Dominic and his brothers were called both the *ordo praedicatorum* (order of preachers) and the *ordo doctorum* (order of teachers). Early Dominicans and those who were sympathetic to them would frequently assert that "an

---

[24] Rouse, *Preachers*, 44.

order of preachers is necessarily an order of doctors."[25] Dominic could have required a simple education of his friars, but he did not. The preaching of the "Order of Preachers" was to be based on sound biblical theological training – training necessitated not only by the need to preach and provide moral instruction to a more educated laity, but also by the appearance in the late twelfth century of heresies that had inundated certain areas – among them the Albigensians in southern France and the Joachimites in Italy – which threatened to swell beyond those boundaries if concerted action was not forthcoming.

The late twelfth century also witnessed the rise of wandering preachers who, although not attached to a heretical sect, preached doctrines not to be trusted. Their increased popularity suggested a new hunger among the laity for evangelical preaching. The tragedy from the institutional Church's point of view was that this hunger was not always being nourished with the solid food of the Gospel message.

In 1209, six years before the founding of the Dominican order in Toulouse, Francis of Assisi had gained from Pope Innocent III unofficial approval for an early rule for *his* new order. Early on, Francis and his "lesser brothers" had not lavished special emphasis on preaching *verbally*. Francis's special skill was to preach by deed and example. The "Earlier Rule" (the *regula non bullata*) of 1221 directed only that "no brother preach contrary to the rite and practice of the Church or without the permission of his minister."[26] It further insisted, however, that "all the brothers preach by their deeds."[27] When the officially approved "Later Rule" of St. Francis came out in 1223 (the *regula bullata*), it notably contained an entire chapter on preaching (chapter 9), in which Francis directed:

> The brothers may not preach in the diocese of any bishop where he [the bishop] has opposed their doing so. And let none of the brothers dare to preach in any way to the people unless he has been examined and approved by the general minister of this fraternity, and the office of preacher has been conferred upon him. Moreover, I admonish and exhort those brothers that when they preach their language be well-considered and chaste for the benefit and edification of the people, announcing to them vices and virtues, punishment and glory, with brevity, because our Lord when on earth kept his word brief.[28]

---

[25] For a somewhat dated, but still basically sound description of the early order, its relation to the Fourth Lateran Council, and especially of the equation *ordo praedicatorum* equals *ordo doctorum*, see Pierre Mandonnet, *St. Dominic and His Work*, vol. 1, trans. Sister Mary Benedicta Larkin, O.P. (New York: Herder, 1945), 25, 47, 115–134. Available at: http://laity.stdombenicia.org/stdominicandhisworks.pdf

[26] "Early Rule" (*Regula non bullata*), no. 17. See *Francis of Assisi: Early Documents*, vol. 1, eds. Regis J. Armstrong, et al. (New York: New City Press, 1999) [hereafter FAED], 75.

[27] Ibid. Indeed, it seems as though Francis envisioned that his "lesser brothers" would work in and among the townspeople using the skills and in the occupations for which they had been trained before entering the order. After finishing their work, they were not to accept money, but they were allowed to accept food and a place to sleep. This, it seems, was to be their primary way of preaching. Cf. "Earlier Rule," chapter 7: "Let the brothers who know how to work do so and exercise that trade they have learned, provided it is not contrary to the good of their souls and can be performed honestly... and *Let everyone remain* in that trade and office *in which he has been called*. And for their work they can receive whatever is necessary excepting money... And it is lawful for them to have the tools and instruments suitable for their trades." I am indebted to my colleague Edward Houser for this insight.

[28] FAED, vol. 1, 104–105.

As Michael Blastic notes, admonishing the brothers that their words be "well-considered and chaste" (*examinata et casta*) suggests that the preacher's words were to be "sincere and have integrity," but also "pure in doctrine, that is, in concord with Catholic teaching, without doctrinal error or lack of clarity."[29] These words from 1223 clearly echo the concerns of the Fourth Lateran Council to have preaching that was both well prepared and doctrinally sound, but also that was done only with permission of the local bishop, a clear allusion to the problem of the wandering evangelists leading the people astray with unorthodox preaching. Yet the caveat that the preaching should be kept brief suggests Francis had still not yet entirely embraced with complete fervor the ministry of verbal preaching in the way that, decades later, Franciscans such as St. Bonaventure did, who as Minister General preached sermons that were both long and involved.

Yet, we also find an account in the early Assisi Compilation of stories about St. Francis, assembled roughly between 1244 and 1260, suggesting that, after he had composed the Canticle of Brother Sun, Francis sent for Brother Pacifico, saying that he wanted

> to give him a few good and spiritual brothers to go through the world preaching and praising God. He said that he wanted one of them who knew how to preach, first to preach to the people. After the sermon, they were to sing the Praises of the Lord [the Canticle of Brother Sun] as minstrels of the Lord. After the praises, he wanted the preacher to tell the people: "We are minstrels of the Lord, and this is what we want as payment: that you live in true penance." He used to say: "What are the servants of God if not his minstrels, who must move people's hearts and lift them up to spiritual joy?" And he said this especially to the Lesser Brother, who had been given to the people for their salvation.[30]

Michael Blastic suggests that the admonition here about finding someone who "knew how to preach" implies someone who had learned the more formal style of the *sermo modernus*, which he wanted the brothers to combine with the singing of the Canticle of the Sun so as to move the faithful in both mind and heart.[31] Whatever Francis's original intentions, it was not long before the Franciscans were, like the Dominicans, devoting themselves fully to the ministry of preaching verbally in the new style to the laity.[32]

One way scholars have gauged the increase in interest in preaching in the thirteenth century has been by the large number of treatises on preaching produced after the turn of the century. We find that by 1230 both the Dominicans and the Franciscans had produced

---

[29] Michael Blastic, "Preaching in the Early Franciscan Movement," in *Franciscans and Preaching: Every Miracle from the Beginning of the World Came about Through Words*, ed. Timothy Johnson (Leiden, The Netherlands: Brill, 2012), 32.

[30] The Assisi Compilation, 83. FAED, vol. 2, 186.

[31] Blastic, "Preaching," 38.

[32] Francis's early reticence about verbal preaching, especially in long and complicated sermons, compared to what would eventually arise once the "lesser brothers" such as John of La Rochelle and Bonaventure entered the order, likely helps explain Richard and Mary Rouse's comment (*Preachers*, 59), "The Franciscans likewise, in a manner unforeseen by St. Francis, were quickly and inevitably drawn into a preaching ministry." On the early developments in this ministry among the Franciscans, see the article by Michael Blastic cited earlier (n. 28) and the introduction by Timothy J. Johnson to *The Sunday Sermons of St. Bonaventure*, trans. Timothy J. Johnson, Works of St. Bonaventure, 12 (St. Bonaventure, NY: Franciscan Institute, 2008), esp. 22–31.

several of their own treatises on preaching.³³ Among those by the Dominicans, there was Stephen of Bourbon's *Tractatus de diversis materiis praedicabilibus*, Humbert of Romans' *De eruditione praedicatorum*, and Thomas of Waley's *Ars praedicandi*. Among those by the Franciscans, the *Ars concionandi* has sometimes been attributed to Bonaventure, although it was likely not written by him. Yet, given its manuscript history in Franciscan sources and its later association with Bonaventure, it likely derives from some Franciscan source, if not Bonaventure himself.³⁴ And if, as Timothy J. Johnson suggests in his introduction to *The Sunday Sermons of St. Bonaventure*, Bonaventure wrote and gathered a collection of sermons to serve as a teaching guide for his Franciscan brothers, then this too would be another example of the contemporary interest in homiletics and the *sermo modernus* style of preaching among the Franciscans.³⁵

In 1227, a mere twelve years after the Fourth Lateran Council, the Council of Trier ordered that priests should instruct their parishioners on the articles of faith, the Ten Commandments, and the virtues and vices. "Ignorant and inexperienced priests" were not to presume to preach to their parishioners lest they become "teachers of error" (*magistros erroris*). They were, however, actively to encourage attendance when learned men came to preach, and most especially friars, both Dominican and Franciscan, who were to be "warmly received and treated with charity" (*benigne recipiatis et caritative pertractetis*) so the people might "hear the word of God from them."³⁶

Unlike the Benedictines and their various offshoots, the Dominicans and Franciscans had constitutions that allowed and even supported traveling, peripatetic preachers. Early on, however, they needed the help of institutions to help educate their members. Such institutions needed to be sound in theological doctrine and sophisticated enough intellectually to help them refute the many errors being propounded in various parts of Europe, but they also had to be sufficiently literary to help train the preachers needed to address an increasingly literate society in a new style that took training to master. Several scholars have argued that the thirteenth-century preaching revival of the friars was as successful as it was in large part because the friars were uniquely able to educate their members to make effective use of the new preaching aids available.³⁷ It was not enough merely that such preaching aids were available; there had to be a population trained to use them as well.

---

³³ Fr. Thomas Charland has compiled a list in *Artes Praedicandi: contribution à l' histoire de la rhétorique au moyen âge*, Publications de l'Institut d'Etudes Medievales d'Ottawa 7 (Paris/Ottawa: J. Vrin/Institute of Medieval Studies, 1936), 17–106.

³⁴ On the complicated manuscript history, see Smith, *Reading the Sermons*, 44–45, n. 30.

³⁵ See *The Sunday Sermons of St. Bonaventure*, trans. Timothy J. Johnson, 31: While the text of the *Sunday Sermons* provided others even outside the Order with a homiletic model for the entire liturgical year or specific Sundays as the manuscript tradition attests, the *Sunday Sermons* are best appreciated when considered as Bonaventure's institutional message to those who affirmed and embraced the second generation Minorite construction of the evangelical life *that emphasized preaching*" [emphasis added].

³⁶ Council of Trier, Statute 7 (*De decanis*); Mansi 23:31–32. Quoted from Rouse, *Preachers*, 59, n. 57.

³⁷ See, e.g., d'Avray, *Preaching*, 21–22: "The thirteenth century marks a turning-point in the history of medieval preaching, not just because of the proliferation of preaching aids but because there were for the first time organizations – the mendicant orders – whose members were properly trained to make use of these tools." And in the same work, 203: "the preaching revival of the friars was more successful than the Carolingian one because they succeeded in closing the gap between preaching aids and their users. In this context the role of Paris is prominent. On the one hand, a large number

The monastic schools still existed, but they were increasingly superseded by new educational institutions springing up across Europe. Among them were the cathedral schools such as the famous one in Chartres, the schools of canons regular such as the Royal Abbey School of the Canons Regular of St. Victor in Paris, and the *studia generalia* associated with the priories of the new religious orders. The most influential of the new educational institutions, however, was the medieval university; and when it came to preaching, the most influential by far was the University of Paris.

Preaching and the University of Paris

In the thirteenth century, Paris outstripped all other cities as a center for sermon production and the publication of preaching manuals.[38] Efforts at preaching reform in Paris went back at least to the time of Maurice de Sully, bishop of Paris from 1160 until his death in 1196, who, in contrast to the common practice of the time, urged his priests to preach every day.[39] Moreover, a good number of the masters of theology at Paris in the late twelfth century showed greater interest than their predecessors such as Abelard and Peter Lombard in preaching and the training of preachers. Masters such as Stephen Langton, Peter Cantor, Peter of Poitiers, Prepositinus, and Alan of Lille not only were celebrated preachers themselves but also produced elaborate reference works directed at teaching others the skill. All except Stephen Langton made and circulated collections of biblical *distinctiones* for use in preaching.

A word of clarification is in order here about these collections of *distinctiones*. These reference works should not be confused with the "distinctions" one finds in scholastic *summae*. A collection of biblical *distinctiones* was a reference work, usually alphabetized (Peter Cantor's *Summa Abel* takes its name, for example from the first entry: "Abel"), which provided for a given scriptural term "several figural meanings, and for each meaning provided a passage of scripture illustrating the use of the term in the given sense."[40] Richard and Mary Rouse provide the following example from the *Summa Abel* of Peter Cantor. Under the heading *avis* (bird), one finds these entries:

> *Tending unto the heights*, namely the just. Whence fish and birds are of the same matter. But fish, that is evil men, remain in the waters of this age; birds, that is good men, tend unto the heights.

---

of purpose-built preaching aids were available... On the other hand, the influential and fairly numerous minority of friars who were selected to study at Paris were particularly well equipped to handle these preaching aids confidently and effectively." See also the comment in Rouse, *Preachers*, 43: "The Church, in the thirteenth century, changed its view on the nature and importance of preaching, and increasingly recognized the sermon as a major instrument of the Church's ministry. As a natural concomitant, there was a marked increase in preaching, especially by preachers who were school-trained and, thus, more apt to use and to devise tools."

[38] d'Avray, *Preaching*, 22: "In the thirteenth century Paris far outstrips any other place as a centre of sermon production. It did not have a monopoly – important sermon collections were written elsewhere – but it is more important than other centres by an order of magnitude." Cf. Rouse, *Preachers*, 48: "The most plentiful evidence of increased interest in preaching comes from the Paris schools in the late twelfth to early thirteenth centuries."

[39] See Rouse, *Preachers*, 61.

[40] I have taken this useful "omnibus definition" from Rouse, *Preachers*, 68.

Remaining on high, namely an angel. Whence: "In the secret of your private chamber, detract not the king, because the birds of heaven will announce it." (Eccl 10:20)

Falling down from on high, namely the proud. Whence: "If you ascend into heaven as an eagle, from thence I will bring you down." (Obadiah 4)

Rapacity, namely the devil. Whence in the parable of the seed it is said that the birds of the sky ate it. (Luke 8:5)

Consumption, that is the tumult of evil thoughts. Whence Abraham drove birds away from the flesh of the sacrificed [animals]. (Gen 15:11)

Prelates. Whence the bird nested in the mustard bush (Matt 13.31-32), that is, the prelate in the catholic faith.[41]

Thus if a preacher found the word *avis* or "bird" in his *thema* verse, he could develop a sermon about the height of angels, the rapacity of devils, or the perennial problems of prelates.

Thirteenth-century preachers made abundant use of this sort of imagery. For the practice to become widespread, reference materials were required that would allow preachers who might not have had the memory or intellectual training of a Thomas or a Bonaventure to engage in it. There is evidence that even these two creative geniuses made use of collections of *distinctiones*. According to Robert J. Karris, Bonaventure inserted thirty-six such *distinctiones* into his *Commentary on the Gospel of Luke*, sixteen of which he seems to have crafted himself, but twenty of which he borrowed from the Dominican Hugh of St. Cher.[42]

One does not find serious scholars with extensive clerical duties such as Peter Cantor, Peter of Poitiers, Prepositinus, and Alan of Lille spending the time to produce such elaborate reference works unless there is a demand for them.[43] What is especially noteworthy for our purposes is the fact that all of the writers who produced these various preaching aids did so in and around Paris. One might have imagined that major reference works of this sort would have been produced – one at Paris, one at Oxford, one further south, perhaps at Bologna or in Naples. Instead, at this early stage at least, we find Paris as the center of the movement. "It is plain, in fact," write Richard and Mary Rouse, "that the schools at Paris were not merely one center, but the primary center of a concentrated interest in and effort toward enhancing the role of the sermon in the ministry of the church."[44] So too we find David d'Avray affirming of Paris that this "most important center for the dissemination of ideas to a mass lay public happened also to be the intellectual capital of Europe in general and of the Franciscan and Dominican orders in particular."[45]

---

[41] See Richard and Mary Rouse, "Biblical 'Distinctiones' in the Thirteenth Century," *Archives d'histoire doctrinale et littéraire du moyen age* 41 (1974): 27–37.

[42] Robert J. Karris, "St. Bonaventure's Use of *Distinctiones*: His Independence of and Dependence on Hugh of St. Cher," *Franciscan Studies*, vol. 60 (2002): 1.

[43] The best short introduction to these biblical *distinctiones* is the article by Richard and Mary Rouse cited earlier. In addition, see Philip Moore, *The Works of Peter of Poitiers: Master in Theology and Chancellor of Paris (1193–1205)* (Notre Dame: University of Notre Dame Press, 1936), 78–96, and Beryl Smalley, *The Study of the Bible in the Middle Ages* (Oxford: Blackwell, 1952), 246–249.

[44] Rouse, *Preachers*, 50.

[45] d'Avray, *Preaching*, 4, 6.

That Paris would be an important center for learning is no surprise. In the thirteenth century, Paris was the largest city in Europe by a wide margin, and as historian Marc Bloch has pointed out, thanks to the fertile soil of the Ile-de-France, it was one of the wealthiest.[46] It made sense, therefore, that someone with the ambition of Abelard would gravitate there in the twelfth century. Indeed, his presence there, though notoriously troubled, helped to make the city an important center for the study of logic. But he was not alone. The Royal Abbey School of St. Victor produced several major scholars, among them one of Bonaventure's favorite authorities, the man known as *alter Augustinus*, Hugh of St. Victor. Once the Dominicans and Franciscans opened and staffed important priories in the city and began teaching at the University of Paris, the die was cast.

We still might wonder, however, how and why *preaching* became a central concern not only in the archdiocese of Paris, but also at the University of Paris. Did the University soak up the concern for preaching from the city as if by osmosis – simply because it was "something in the air"? Perhaps. But there were other, more tangible factors at work as well.

Historian Ian P. Wei has suggested that the three most significant documents in the establishment of the University of Paris were the charter King Philip Augustus granted it in 1200; the statutes Robert of Courson established for the University in 1215; and the papal bull *Parens scientiarum*, which Pope Gregory IX sent its faculty in the spring of 1231.[47] Although the faculty and students of the University had *in principle* been granted their corporate independence by the king in 1200 and by the pope in 1215, the bishop of Paris and the chancellor continually refused to recognize this independence, culminating in the bishop ordering that the whole University be excommunicated because they had made a constitution without his consent. This, however, was precisely what the 1215 statutes had permitted them to do, so the University repeatedly called for papal intervention. And in a 1219 bull, the pope decreed that the University could not be excommunicated without papal permission.

Tensions continued to build, however, culminating in a series of student riots in 1229. When local authorities were sent to quell the riots, several students were killed. As a result, the entire University community, faculty and students both, left the city. In response, Pope Gregory IX sent letters of reproach to William of Auvergne, the bishop of Paris, and Philip, his chancellor, for handling the situation badly. He exhorted the French king, Louis IX, to invite the students and masters back to Paris and to assure them of a safe return to the city. This he did, also reaffirming the privileges granted the University by Philip Augustus in 1200.

It took two years to sort everything out, and the University didn't resume classes until the fall of 1231. In the previous April and May of that same year, Pope Gregory IX had issued a series of papal bulls with a view to restoring order and helping re-found the University. The most important of these for our purposes was the first, *Parens scientiarum* ("Parent of the sciences"), in which Gregory began laying out his vision for what the University should become.[48] The bull begins: "Paris, parent of the sciences ... city of letters, and precious,

---

[46] See Marc Bloch, *The Ile-de-France: The Country around Paris* (Ithaca, NY: Cornell University Press, 1971), esp. 16–30, 74–99.

[47] The document can be found in the *Chartularium universitatis parisiensis*, ed. Denifle, vol. 1, n. 79.

[48] My discussion throughout this section is highly indebted to Ian P. Wei's book *The Intellectual Culture in Medieval Paris: Theologians and the University, c. 1100–1330* (Cambridge: Cambridge University Press, 2012), esp. 92–105. I have found no other book as clear or as valuable a guide to the history and culture of the founding years of the University of Paris as this superb volume.

shines forth." In the lines that follow, the pope praises the University as "wisdom's special workshop" (*officina sapientie speciali*) in which the masters and students mine and refine silver and gold, from which "those prudent in mystical eloquence" (*prudentes eloquii mistici*) produce precious ornaments to adorn the bride of Christ, and take iron out of the earth to manufacture "the breastplate of faith, the sword of the spirit, and other Christian arms" needed to fight the evil powers.

As Ian Wei has shown, Gregory borrowed the associations he makes in his letter from the *Moralia in Job*, the work of his papal namesake, Pope Gregory the Great. The metallurgy images can be traced to Job 28:1-2:

Silver hath beginnings of its veins, and gold hath a place wherein it is melted.
Iron is taken out of the earth, and stone melted with heat is turned into copper.

The imagery in the Book of Job suggests both the mining of the ore and its purification by fire. But Gregory took the image one step further to propose the *uses* to which the mined and refined metals should be put. Gold and silver should adorn the bride of Christ "in mystical eloquence," and iron "solidified in firmness" (*fortitudine solidatur*) should produce the armaments that protect her. "As a stone freed by heat in art is purified," says Gregory, "so stony hearts blown on by the fervor of the Holy Spirit catch fire and are made to proclaim the praises of Christ with resonant preaching." (*Et lapis calore solutus in es veritur, quia corda lapide Sancti Spiritus afflata fervore dum ardent, incendunt et fiunt predicatione sonora preconantia laudes Christi.*) The second half of that sentence might also be translated: "by preaching, they [stony hearts] are made resonant, proclaiming the praises of Christ." Both translations fit the original Latin.

Read in the first way, the passage suggests that it is the preaching that becomes "resonant." Read in the second way, it is the transformed students who do.[49] Either way, the underlying message seems clear: the mission of the University was to find the precious metals in these young men, purify them, and put them to use for the Church – praising, preaching, and defending the faith.[50]

University statutes specified that, even as a young *baccalarius biblicus*, a student was required to preach every year at least two collations or a sermon and a collation "in his own person, to prove himself in eloquence and the art of preaching."[51] Masters and students were required to attend all University sermons, and preaching competence was required for a student to advance through the stages of his career as a bachelor and eventually to receive the license. The final test of one's competence was the *principium in aula* and *resumptio* addresses the bachelor was required to deliver during his inception as a master.

---

[49] These two translations are suggested by Wei; see *Intellectual Culture*, 102–104. The first translation takes "sonora" as an ablative singular with "praedicatione." In the second version, "sonora" is taken as a neuter plural referring back to "corda."

[50] Ian Wei says simply: "the fundamental purpose of the university was to transform men into preachers, tying them into the pastoral mission of the church." Wei, *Intellectual Culture*, 3. Cf. also 107: "[T]he Parisian masters of theology in the late twelfth and early thirteenth centuries repeatedly asserted their deep commitment to preaching, as a technique by which they would teach their students, as a key aspect of the pastoral work that they would teach their students to perform, and as the means by which they and their students would bring about reform of both clergy and laity."

[51] *Chartularium*, vol. 2, no. 1189, 699, item 27. Quoted from Wei, 235.

Whether due to the demands of the Fourth Lateran Council, the increased demands from an increasingly literate laity for more intellectually serious preaching, the influence of the educated members of the new mendicant orders, or papal exhortations to take up the mission of training preachers, preaching clearly became a key part of the intellectual, moral, and spiritual life of the University of Paris during the thirteenth century.[52] Thus, as Ian Wei writes, "preaching was soon established as an enduring feature of university life."[53]

This is not to deny the importance of logic and disputation, arts for which Paris had already become renowned. But perhaps we should take as our guide Peter Cantor who, in the *Verbum abbreviatum*, after listing the three main duties of the master – *lectio*, *disputatio*, and *praedicatio* – immediately adds: "But since the office of preaching is common to teachers and pastors, the privilege by merit goes to the science of preaching." (*Cum igitur officium predicandi doctoribus et pastoribus sit commune, merito predicationis scientiam optinet privilegium.*)[54]

Peter proceeded in the same text to compare the relationship between the three duties to the parts of a building:

Reading is, as it were, the foundation and basement for what follows, for through it the rest is achieved. Disputation is the wall in the building of study for nothing is fully understood or faithfully preached, if it is not first chewed by the tooth of disputation. Preaching, which is supported by the former, is the roof, sheltering the faithful from the heat and wind of temptation. We should preach after, not before, the reading of Holy Scripture and the investigation of doubtful matters by disputation.[55]

On this view, disputation is not an end unto itself, but a means to the end of better, more well-informed, more judicious preaching, as the building of foundation and walls of a building support the roof.

Not everyone would have shared this view, of course. There were undoubtedly those who would have viewed disputation and preaching as two very distinct, largely unrelated skills: not only schoolmen, whose intellectual vanity might have tempted them to consider disputation a more intellectually serious skill and an end unto itself, but also monks, who could have been forgiven for assuming that preaching had little or nothing to do with disputation. It takes a special mindset and a very distinctive notion of the relationship between faith and reason to believe, on the one hand, that the fruits of disputation can nourish good preaching and, on the other, that the "pastoral" concern for the lives and faith of plain persons outside the academy can force a salutary discipline on one's philosophical disputations. Although medieval preaching manuals were careful to note that "preaching should not seem to be a disputation,"[56] this warning did not shake the conviction among the Franciscan and Dominican masters that preaching should be nourished by the fruits of disputation.

---

[52] Good discussions of the question can be found in David d'Avray, *The Preaching of the Friars*; Nicole Bériou, *L'avènement des maîtres de la Parole*; and Ian Wei, *The Intellectual Culture in Medieval Paris*.
[53] Wei, *Intellectual Culture*, 107.
[54] Peter Cantor, *Verbum abbreviatum* 1.
[55] Ibid., 6.
[56] The anonymous author of the thirteenth century *Ars concionandi* (3.40) warns preachers "ne praedicatio videatur esse disputatio."

Along with the general questions of the relationship between faith and reason, preaching and disputation – questions that might arise in any culture or milieu – undoubtedly the more specific concerns animating the intellectual life of thirteenth-century Paris also played a role. One such concern resulted from the pointed criticism that monks such as Bernard of Clairvaux and William of St. Thierry had made in the twelfth century of the new purveyors of the dialectical art, such as Abelard and Gilbert of Poitiers. The monks held that to know religious truth, it was necessary to reject the world and live virtuously. They regarded the schoolmen as presumptuous in their application of reason to faith and accused them of pursuing knowledge for the wrong reasons: in search of novelty rather than to serve God, or out of desire for fame and profit. So too they believed the schoolmen failed to take responsibility for how their audience received their teaching, especially when the audience lacked the necessary moral and spiritual formation. Perhaps in response to these criticisms, many of the early statutes of the University of Paris were designed to inculcate in the students both the intellectual skills and the moral virtues thought necessary for good learning. "Rules about conduct and behaviour were therefore interspersed with rules about, for example, curriculum," says historian Ian Wei, "precisely because life and learning were understood to be linked."[57]

It seems likely, therefore, that a key purpose of Pope Gregory IX's 1231 bull *Parens scientiarum* was to respond to the monastic criticisms of this new institution, the university. Gregory, while giving due weight to the legitimate concerns of the monks, set out to show how the university, properly understood and judiciously organized, could preserve the traditional monastic ideals while serving the contemporary needs of the Church in a new and important way. If the *academic* efforts of the schoolmen could be disciplined and harnessed for the good of the Church – say, toward the goal of better preaching to the laity, a need in the Church that the monastic orders had done little to address – this might go a long way to blunting the criticism the schoolmen had been receiving. This was a vision of a university education in which scholars were to be transformed by preaching and, by preaching to others, would help transform the Church.[58]

Consider, in this context, Thomas's announced goal for writing the *Summa theologiae* and Bonaventure's for writing the *Breviloquium*: their common goal was to provide a sound foundation in theology to inform the preaching and teaching of the younger friars. Thomas intended the "disputed question" format of the *Summa* to serve the ends of preaching and teaching.[59] So too with Bonaventure's *Breviloquium*: although it was not written in the form

---

[57] Wei, *Intellectual* Culture, 99.
[58] Cf. Wei, *Intellectual Culture*, 107.
[59] On the pedagogical goals of the *Summa*, see, e.g., Jean-Pierre Torrell, O.P., *Saint Thomas Aquinas: The Person and His Work*, trans. Robert Royal (Washington, DC: Catholic University of America Press, 1996), esp. 144–145, who suggests that Thomas set for himself at Rome "the task of forming the friars in moral theology and in the pastoral work of confession, which went along with the mission of preaching that had been entrusted to the order." Leonard Boyle had famously argued in his 1982 pamphlet *The Setting of the* Summa theologiae *of St. Thomas* (Toronto: Pontifical Institute of Mediaeval Studies, 1982) that Thomas wrote the *Summa* when from experience he found Lombard's *Sentences* and the early Dominican manuals unsuitable teaching texts for his students at Santa Sabina in Rome. Fr. Boyle emphasized that with the *Summa*, St. Thomas set out to fill a gap in the teaching of "dogmatic theology" that existed in the earlier Dominican manuals. My emphasis on preaching should not be taken as contradicting Boyle's thesis. Rather, my contention

of a disputed question, Bonaventure's short text employed the deductive mode of reasoning, also common in the schools, to assist "beginning theologians" (*novi theologi*) to understand the Scriptures more adequately and to preach more capably.[60] This commonality between these two great lights of the thirteenth century suggests that the goals of the education at the University of Paris, especially among the friars, were similar, and a key part of that education was the pedagogy of preaching.

Preaching and Prologues

Yet, as important as the art of preaching was to the thirteenth century and to the University of Paris's understanding of its calling within the Church to transform men into preachers, we have no record of any classes in preaching. Students and masters were required by University regulations both to hear and to give sermons,[61] so young aspiring preachers would certainly have had plenty of exposure to the preaching of others. But this alone seems insufficient to explain how they came to master the complexities of the *sermo modernus* style. Modern scholars have suggested that the training students acquired at the University would have helped them to use the increasing number of preaching aids more capably.[62] This alone, however, does not explain how or when the friars actually learned to use them. One can listen to hundreds of sermons without getting any closer to preaching like St. Bonaventure. One cannot merely watch; one must *do*. Students had to have occasions to sit down with the books in front of them and *write something down* – something concrete with a distinct end in mind.

It is likely that most, if not all, young friars got their first training and first experiences preaching in the enclosed privacy of their religious house. Humbert of Romans, in his "Instructions on the Offices of the Order" (*Instructiones de officiis ordinis*), relates that it was the duty of the master of students to give young friars their first training in preaching.[63]

---

is that solid dogmatic theology was foundational for a solid moral theology, and both were foundational for good preaching.

[60] *Breviloquium*, prol. 6.5. See also Dominic Monti's Introduction to the *Breviloquium*, The Works of St. Bonaventure (Franciscan Institute, 2005), xivxxii, esp. xxi, where he suggests that Aquinas's "reasons for composing his celebrated *Summa theologiae* [were] remarkably similar to Bonaventure's own." It was not "simply an academic contribution to theology"; rather, [o]ver the years of teaching, Bonaventure had become convinced that there was a critical need in the education of young friars, and in [the *Breviloquium*] he attempted to supply it." With regard to the "deductive" method of the *Breviloquium*, he writes that, although the technique of dialectic "has become 'almost synonymous with what has come to be known as the Scholastic method,' [it] was not the only one that medieval theologians employed to probe the meaning of the Christian faith" (xxiii). The other was the deductive, which Bonaventure adopted in the *Breviloquium*.

[61] Wei, *Intellectual Culture*, 230.

[62] David d'Avray, for example, has argued (*Preaching*, 203) that "the preaching revival of the friars was more successful than the Carolingian one because they succeeded in closing the gap between preaching aids and their users. In this context the role of Paris was prominent."

[63] I am indebted for the information in the following two paragraphs to Michèle Mulchahey's superb book *First the Bow is Bent in Study: Dominican Education Before 1350* (Toronto: Pontifical Institute of Mediaeval Studies, 1998), esp. 188–193, since I was not able to locate a copy of Humbert's *Opera de vita regulari*, vol. 2, containing the *Instructiones*, in any US library.

He was to introduce them to the right reference materials for preparing a sermon and counsel them on their presentation: not repeating points needlessly, not speaking too long so as to tax the listener's patience. Humbert of Romans even suggested that the master of students might sit near enough to the young preacher to be able to give him a nudge if he went on too long.[64]

The prior, sometimes with the help of a board of advisers, made the decision whether a brother was ready to go on a preaching assignment outside the convent; their judgment was based on what they had seen him do at home. Moreover, within the convent, the brother was to be notified well in advance if visitors were to be present when he was scheduled to preach; otherwise the visitors were restricted from attending. Rules prohibited priors from sending a brother out to preach in public who had not first been "exercised among his brothers" in giving sermons.[65] It was only after he had shown himself capable that the young friar was permitted to preach publicly before the whole University community.

During their years as a bachelor, friars were required by University statute only to deliver one sermon and one *collatio* each year. Such an infrequent assignment was hardly sufficient practice for the life of preaching for which they were being groomed, especially given the importance both University and ecclesiastical authorities had placed on the training of preachers. It is more likely, therefore, that these annual preaching assignments were less a practice-in-preaching than an *examination of progress* made through practice done elsewhere.

It would be instructive if we had some written records of these early preaching attempts. But as far as I know, we do not, unless some of the really poor sermons scholars have uncovered represent some of these early attempts. I am not aware of anyone who has attempted to make such a judgment.

What we do possess, however, are the written prologues these future masters wrote when they were just starting out as bachelors, all of which were composed in the *sermo modernus* style. When a young friar became a *lector biblicus*, he would be assigned to give cursory lectures on some book of the Bible, and he would have begun that course by writing a *principium*, which he would have delivered on the first day of the term to introduce his students to the book he was to lecture on. If the *reportatio* of the course was later published, the *principium* would show up as the *prologus* of the commentary. These written orations would have been among the young friar's first public uses of the *sermo modernus* style. Thomas Aquinas, for example, produced some fairly rudimentary prologues to his cursory commentaries on Jeremiah and Lamentations early on. His later prologue to his cursory commentary on Isaiah is stronger and shows a much better grasp of the style.[66]

The requirement to write and deliver these *principia* addresses in the *sermo modernus* style at the beginning of each term would have provided the occasion for the young friar to produce a written text that could be critiqued in an academic fashion in a way that a sermon, especially one delivered in the convent, could not. A preached sermon was not an academic product; a written prologue was. An early draft of a written prologue was something a master or religious superior could go over with the young *lector biblicus*; he

---

[64] See Humbert of Romans, *Instructiones de officiis ordinis*, c. 12.2; cf. Mulchahey, 192.

[65] See, e.g., the *Acta provinciae Romanae* (Salerno, 1279), 51; quoted from Mulchahey, *First the Bow*, 190.

[66] See my discussion of these prologues in Chapter 6.

could help him edit it, making suggestions for improvement and pointing out resources that might be used to improve the text. Such assistance would have been especially important if the oral *principium* was to be published as a "prologue" to the written commentary. It is likely that this process was not much different from the sort of critique the young bachelors were given before preaching in front of the community or the public.

Several years later, when the young friar was finally elevated to the position of "bachelor of the Sentences" (*baccalarius sententiarum*), he would be relieved of his obligations to preach regularly before the entire University community, but he was still required to write prologues for each book of his *Sentences* commentary, all of which were to be composed in the *sermo modernus* style.

Students could read collections of model sermons, and they were required to attend all University sermons, so they heard preaching constantly. But their most consistent practice writing in the *sermo modernus* style – choosing an appropriate *thema* verse, dividing it, and then dilating its parts – was writing prologues. It was a constant practice during their years at the University, even when preaching was not.

Why We Are Examining the Prologues as Evidence of a Culture of Preaching

Since a young friar's prologues were evidence of his level of mastery in the art of preaching in the *sermo modernus* style, this book on the preaching culture at Paris is also a book on prologues. Why not merely concentrate on sermon collections? In an earlier work, I did just that and concentrated on all the extant sermons of Thomas Aquinas.[67] The limitation inherent to this approach is that a person's sermons were collected only *after* he had become a master. And even when we have several surviving sermons of a master, they are often scattered examples, hard to date. Even for someone as prominent as Aquinas, only nineteen extant sermons remain, several only in fragments. This circumstance makes it difficult to gain a sense of how the friar developed his skills during his early career and impossible to watch his early development *before* he became a master. The only way we have to investigate how a particular master honed his skill in preaching in the *sermo modernus* style from his early years as a "biblical bachelor" to his more advanced years as a "bachelor of the *Sentences*," regent master, and beyond, therefore, is to read and compare his written prologues.[68]

I will focus our attention here on the prologues of two masters whose other works are widely known: Thomas Aquinas and Bonaventure, one Dominican and one Franciscan,

---

[67] Randall B. Smith, *Reading the Sermons of Aquinas: A Beginner's Guide* (Emmaus Press, 2016).

[68] Restricting my study to the prologues also removes from consideration the much-disputed question of how often friars trained at Paris such as Thomas and Bonaventure would have preached in the vernacular rather than in Latin. Would Thomas have preached in German when he was with Albert in Germany? Would he have used the local dialect in Orvieto, Rome, and Naples? If so, how was the translation made from his training in Latin to these other languages or dialects? These are interesting questions to which we currently have no answers, so for our present purposes, I am bypassing them.

who both finished their studies at Paris at roughly the same time. There was a difference-in-sameness about these two that made them especially suitable for comparison. They were both friars, but from different orders. They both studied at the University of Paris at roughly the same time, which helps to negate differences that might be attributed to changed institutional circumstances at the University. And since the works of both are widely known, each having attained a similar prominence among his devotees, it was not necessary to spend a great deal of time discussing their other works, since for those wishing to know more about either thinker, there are plenty of excellent secondary sources already available. These serendipitous parallels have allowed me to focus my attention on the art of preaching displayed in their prologues. Two friars, both from Italy, but trained in different religious orders, both having been trained in the same university and at roughly the same time: Did the rigorous and highly structured education they received force a dull sameness? Our examination of Thomas and Bonaventure will show us clearly that it did not.

To summarize:

1. Thomas and Bonaventure received their scholarly training and began their careers during this period of tremendous ferment, creativity, and increased interest in popular preaching, whose early stage was marked by the Fourth Lateran Council in 1215, but whose roots go back earlier into the late twelfth century.
2. The friars and the University of Paris were key efficient causes in this reform movement. They pushed reforms based on better preaching, which in turn was tied to extensive intellectual and theological formation.
3. In the interests of stemming the tide of bad preaching and diminishing the allure of popular wandering unorthodox preachers, Church authorities, in part through the pronouncements of councils and synods, helped to encourage and promote this reform movement with a new generation of well-trained, doctrinally sound preachers and teachers.
4. This new generation of well-trained preachers was expected to preach and appeal to a newly educated populace that seems to have been not only open to popular preaching and piety but eager for it.
5. These efforts to train a new generation of preachers bore fruit in the early thirteenth century with the development of a new style of preaching: the so-called *sermo modernus* style. This new preaching style and the institutional resources to support it were well developed by the time Thomas and Bonaventure incepted as masters of theology at Paris. Aspiring preachers at the time developed their skills in this complex new style of preaching by writing prologues that employed the style.

Since the prologues we will be examining in the following chapters all employ the *sermo modernus* style, it will be worth summarizing its basic characteristics – a task to which we turn in the next chapter.

2

The Basic Elements of the Thirteenth-Century "Modern Sermon"

TO UNDERSTAND the *sermo modernus* style of preaching, it is necessary to understand how it differed from what preceded it. In the early fourteenth century, Thomas Waleys, an Oxford Dominican, looking back on the "homiletic revolution" of the thirteenth century, wrote a widely circulated tract entitled "On the manner of composing sermons" (*De modo componendi sermones*). The difference between the "modern" sermons of the thirteenth century and the "ancient" sermons of the Church Fathers, said Waleys, was that, whereas the "ancient" sermon consisted of a verse-by-verse commentary on the entire Gospel reading for the day, the "modern" sermon was built around a *thema* or single Bible verse.[1] Indeed, as Michèle Mulcahey notes, "The theme [that is, the *thema*] of a *sermo modernus* was often likened by the authors of preaching manuals to the root of a tree which was the sermon, or similarly it was the trunk from which sprung the various branches."[2]

"Although a brief *thema* is used when preaching to clerics," says Waleys, "nevertheless, in some parts, for example in Italy, commonly, when preaching not to clerics but to the people, a brief *thema* is not used; rather the whole Gospel which is read in the Mass is taken for the *thema*, and the whole is expounded upon, and many beautiful and devout things are said." Waleys considered the older style still the best for preaching to the laity: "In my judgment, this manner of preaching to the people is not only easier for the preacher, but also more useful for the listener among all the modes of preaching. And such was the ancient manner of preaching of the saints, as is clear in their homilies." Waleys decried

---

[1] Thomas Waleys (Thomas of Wales), *De modo componendi sermons*, in *Artes Praedicandi: contribution à l'histoire de la rhétorique au moyen âge*, ed. T. Charland, Publications de l'Institut d'Etudes Medievales d'Ottawa 7 (Paris/Ottowa: J. Vrin / Institute of Medieval Studies, 1936), 344.

[2] See Michèle Mulcahey, *First the Bow Is Bent in Study: Dominican Education Before 1350* (Toronto: Pontifical Institute of Mediaeval Studies, 1999), 404–405, quoting a passage from the manuscript in Anger, Bibliothèque municipale, MS 1582, fol. 132: "Unde, quia thema est quasi radix totius sermonis et per ipsum fundamentum totius aedificii fabrica consurgit." For more on the *thema*, see Charland, *Artes praedicandi*, 111–124.

those who preach to the uneducated in the manner appropriate to clerics. "When they fill their sermons with such theological subtleties," says Waleys, they make it all but impossible that "multiple errors" and "unfitting phantasies" (*phantasiae ineptae*) will not arise in the minds of their listeners. Waleys thought it "better simply not to preach to the people at all than to preach to them in this way."[3]

Waleys appears to have been swimming against the tide, however, for as Michèle Mulcahey points out, the Franciscan master John of Wales wrote in his 1270 treatise "On the Art of Preaching" (*De arte praedicandi*) that the older "*sermo antiquus*" homily of the sort Waleys favored "did not sit particularly well with modern listeners, who liked to see the clear articulation of a sermon developed from a scriptural theme" (i.e., *thema*). So too in 1290 the Italian Dominican Fra Giacomo da Fusignano, prior of Santa Maria sopra Minerva in Rome, wrote that the older style was suitable only for preaching to the ignorant. To other, more intelligent and literate listeners, this sort of exposition was, he thought, unnecessary. The sermon "more common to modern preachers" (*modernis praedicatoribus communior*), writes Fra Giacomo, was one in which a *thema* was divided into various parts.[4]

After stating his opening *thema* – a Bible verse normally chosen from among the lectionary readings for the day – the medieval preacher would make a *divisio* of the verse into several parts, each of which was associated with a separate section of the sermon. When Thomas crafted a sermon for advent in the year 1271, for example, he chose as his *thema* the first six words from Matthew 21:5, one of the verses of the Gospel reading for the day: *Ecce rex tuus venit tibi mansuetus*. The whole verse reads (in English translation): "Behold your king comes to you, meek, sitting upon a donkey." Thomas did not wish to use the last phrase of the verse (*sedens super asinam*, "sitting upon a donkey"), so he simply left it out. After stating his *thema*, Thomas then "divided" it into four parts or "members":

1. *Ecce* ("Behold"), in which he discusses the coming (advent) of Christ;
2. *rex tuus* ("your king"), in which he discusses the conditions of His coming;
3. *venit tibi* ("he comes to you"), in which he discusses the benefit of His coming; and
4. *mansuetus* ("meek"), in which he discusses the way of His coming[5]

Bonaventure, in like manner, in the *principium* given at his inception took as his opening *thema* a verse from Wisdom 7:1, *Omnium artifex docuit me sapientia* ("The creator of all things has taught me wisdom"), which he divided into these four parts:

1. *Artifex* ("the maker");
2. *omnium* ("of all things");
3. *sapientia* ("wisdom"); and
4. *docuit me* ("he has taught me")

Bonaventure divided each of these four into four more subdivisions. Although the preacher often had limited freedom in choosing his opening *thema* verse, he had much more freedom

---

[3] See Waleys, *De modo componendi*, in *Charland*, 344–345.
[4] See Michèle Mulcahey, *First the Bow*, 403, n. 10: "Est autem hoc satis populo rudi utilis. Ceteris literatis et intelligentibus auditoribus populariis exposicio non est necessaria."
[5] I discuss this sermon in greater detail in *Reading the Sermons of Thomas Aquinas*, 4–11. See also the analytic outline on 240–243.

in choosing how to divide it. The medieval preaching manuals provided extensive guidance on how this could be done and done well.⁶

After the preacher had divided the opening *thema* into three or four parts, he then had to develop or "dilate" (the Latin term was *dilatatio*) each member of his original *divisio*. The preaching manuals also gave guidance on how this could be done. In his sermon *Ecce rex tuus*, Thomas dilated the first *divisio* according to different uses of the word *ecce* ("behold"). When we say "behold," we could be (1) asserting something certain; (2) indicating a determination of time; (3) showing something previously hidden; or (4) comforting a person, as in "Behold, I bring you tidings of great joy." Each of these Thomas associates with the advent of Christ: (1) it is certain; (2) it happened at a determinate point in time; (3) he was made visible; and (4) his coming comforts us. Moving on to the second member of his opening *divisio*, the words *rex tuus* ("your king"), Thomas dilates these according to the four characteristics of a king: a king suggests unity; a king has fullness of power; a king has fullness of jurisdiction; and a king brings equity of justice.⁷ Christ, says Thomas, possesses each of these to a supreme degree. The process of dilation is repeated with *venit tibi* and *mansuetus*, each word or group of words suggesting a topic or topics to the writer. When the sermon was preached, the *thema* verse also served as a mnemonic device to help the listeners identify their place within the progress of the whole and then recall the contents of the sermon after it was finished. To recall the contents of the sermon, one merely had to bring to mind the opening *thema* verse, and each word would suggest the topics the preacher had associated with it.⁸

In sum, the three basic elements of the *sermo modernus*–style sermon were (1) the *thema*, (2) the *divisio* of the *thema*, and (3) the *dilatatio* of each of the parts created by this opening *divisio*. Members created by the opening *divisio* could be subdivided and then subdivided again if the preacher wished.⁹ In the sermon *Ecce Rex Tuus*, for example, Thomas subdivides "your king" (*rex tuus*), one of the four parts of his opening *divisio*, into two parts: one dealing with the characteristic of a "king" (as we saw earlier) and another dealing with the significance of calling him "your" king. Further subdivisions of such subdivisions were not uncommon.

Medieval preachers also sometimes added a relatively brief introductory section after the statement of the *thema* verse, the *prothema*, which had its own *divisio* and *dilatatio* and

---

⁶ For more on the various methods of *divisio*, see *Reading the Sermons of Thomas Aquinas*, 49–112.

⁷ For more on some of the most common methods of *dilatatio*, see *Reading the Sermons of Thomas Aquinas*, 113–180.

⁸ On the difference between "memory" and "recollection" and on their importance for appreciating the *sermo modernus* style, see *Reading the Sermons of Thomas Aquinas*, 11–19. For a fuller treatment of the arts of memory in the Middle Ages, see Mary Carruthers, *The Book of Memory: A Study of Memory in Medieval Culture* (New York: Cambridge University Press, 1990). See also D'Avray, *Preaching of the Friars*, 193–194, who in response to the objection that university preaching would have been quite different from popular preaching, mentions in passing, "A schematic framework of rhythmic divisions and subdivisions would be easy to fix in the mind. Guibert de Tournai, discussing the *original principium* of division (in his huge work called *Erudimentum doctrine*), states that its purpose is to avoid confusion and help the memory (*ut cesset confusion et adiuvetur memoria*). This could have been true for popular as well as for learning preaching."

⁹ For a nice example, see Thomas Aquinas's sermon *Homo quidam erat dives* (Sermon 15 in the Leonine edition), or my outline of it in *Reading the Sermons of Thomas Aquinas*, 285–292.

finished with a brief prayer. A *prothema* was not always included in every sermon, nor does it seem ever to have been included in a prologue.[10]

The *Thema* Verse: Finding Words to Fit the Occasion

The division and development of an opening *thema* verse was the hallmark of the *sermo modernus* style. What modern readers of medieval sermons must understand, however, is that medieval preachers did not preach on their biblical *thema* verse in the sense of doing exegesis. Rather the *thema* verse was used as a mnemonic device, a memory aid, to give structure to the sermon. Each word or group of words from the *thema* verse suggested a different section of the sermon. However a medieval master ultimately decided upon his *thema*, "the most important thing a preacher had to bear in mind when selecting it," as Michèle Mulcahey points out, "was that it should contain latent within it the whole of the sermon he imagined, to be drawn out through a complex yet organic development."[11]

The *Forma praedicandi*, an early fourteenth-century preaching manual written by Englishman Robert of Basevorn, provides this example. Let us say that the sermon was to commemorate the feast day of one of the doctors of the Church. The preacher might choose as his *thema* the verse from Proverbs 14:35 ("The intelligent minister is acceptable to the king") and divide it as follows: "intelligent" might be associated with his *mental perfection*; "minister" might be taken to refer to his *spiritual humility*; and "acceptable to the king" might be associated with his *brotherly kindness*. What one must *not* do, however, is to select words for the *divisio* that are too similar to the words in the *thema*. So, for example, it would *not* be correct to divide the *thema* above so that "intelligent" is associated with the saint's *intellectual perfection*, "minister" associated with *ministerial humility*, or "acceptable to the kind" associated with *fraternal acceptance*. To repeat the words in this way would show a lack of artfulness and also drain the words of the *divisio* of their force and communicative power.[12]

How was the *thema* chosen? According to Mulcahey: "This verse was sometimes taken from the liturgical readings for the day, it seems, but they were also taken from anywhere else in the Scriptures if the occasion warranted it, regardless of whether the passage was from the liturgical readings for the day or not."[13] Her general observation is borne out by a review of Aquinas's sermons. In roughly half of Thomas Aquinas's nineteen extant sermons, he seems to have taken the *thema* from within the lectionary reading for the day.[14] One finds the same tendency in the Sunday Sermons of St. Bonaventure.[15] Both of these great masters, as far as we can tell, usually took their *thema* from the day's readings

---

[10] Both Thomas and Bonaventure sometimes included a prothema and sometimes did not.
[11] Mulcahey, *First the Bow*, 404.
[12] Robert of Basevorn's *Forma praedicandi* can be found in the Latin original in Charland, *Artes Praedicandi*, 233–323, and in English translation in Robert of Basevorn, *The Form of Preaching*, tr. Leopold Krul, O.S.B., in *Three Medieval Rhetorical Arts*, ed. James J. Murphy (Berkeley: University of California Press, 1971), 109–215.
[13] Mulcahey, *First the Bow*, 404.
[14] See Smith, *Reading the Sermons*, Appendix 2.
[15] Cf. *The Sunday Sermons of St. Bonaventure*, trans. Timothy J. Johnson, The Works of St. Bonaventure 12 (St. Bonaventure, NY: Franciscan Institute Publications, 2008).

when they were preaching at Sunday masses. On special feast days, they sometimes allowed themselves to select a verse from elsewhere in the Scriptures. It is noteworthy, however, that when a medieval master set out to write a prologue for a biblical commentary, he rarely chose a *thema* verse from the biblical book upon which he was commenting.

After choosing an appropriate *thema*, the medieval preacher's next task was to make a suitable "division" (*divisio*) of the verse and a "dilation" (*dilatatio*) of each of the parts. The preaching manuals of the thirteenth and early fourteenth centuries identified several possible ways of carrying out the *divisio* and *dilatatio*. The lists varied somewhat, but the methods were basically the same.[16] We begin logically with the first of the two: crafting the *divisio*.

Divisio: An Ordered Structure of Parts to the Whole

According to Robert of Basevorn's *Forma Praedicandi*, essential to a good *divisio* was that the preacher make clear how the parts were ordered to the whole. It was also essential that the division should be exhaustive and complete.[17] Consider again the threefold *divisio* we examined above of the verse from Proverbs 14:35:

the intelligent // minister // is acceptable to the king

---

[16] The following analysis is based on the rules in Robert of Basevorn, *Forma praedicandi*, esp. chapter 33 and the *Ars concionandi*, section 1, the Latin of which can be found among the works of dubious authenticity in Bonaventure, *Opera Omnia* (Ad Claras Aquas Quaracchi ex typographia Collegii s. Bonaventurae, 1882–1901), 9–21. English translations are from Harry Charles Hazel, "A Translation, with Commentary, of the Bonaventuran '*Ars Concionandi*'" (PhD diss., Washington State University, 1972). I am not proposing that either of these works had a direct influence on Thomas or Bonaventure; I put them forward merely as representing the status of the craft during that period. Interested readers might also fruitfully compare the "Thomistic" tract on preaching translated by Harry Caplan and published as "A Late Medieval Tractate on Preaching" in *Studies in Rhetoric and Public Speaking in Honor of James Albert Winans* (New York: Century, 1925), 61–90, with the two "Franciscan" tracts I will be drawing upon below. Both the Caplan "Thomistic" tract and Robert of Basevorn's text are from the early fourteenth century, while the *Ars concionandi* is likely earlier, sometime in the late thirteenth century. All three contain basically the same rules and advice.

[17] The reader might fruitfully compare the medieval method of *divisio* employed in the *sermo modernus* style with the method of *divisio* commonly used in the exegesis of texts. A useful article on the topic is John F. Boyle's "The Theological Character of the Scholastic 'Division of the Text' with Particular Reference to the Commentaries of Saint Thomas Aquinas," in *With Reverence for the Word: Medieval Scriptural Exegesis in Judaism, Christianity, and Islam*, ed. J. D. McAuliffe et al. (Oxford: Oxford University Press, 2003), 276–283. As Boyle points out, a scholastic "division of the text" always involved the articulation of a "theme that provides a conceptual unity to the text" and always "begins with the whole and then continues through progressive subdivisions, every verse stand[ing] in an articulated relation not only with the whole but ultimately with every other part, division, and verse of the text" (276). "For the scholastic division of the text to work," he adds, "the unity must be an intrinsic conceptual unity; there must be a unifying idea in the light of which the whole can be seen and, still more important, each part can be understood" (277). In other words, the parts must fit together correctly and the whole they come together to form must be *complete*: an apt description of what a good *divisio* of the *thema* in a sermon was supposed to do.

According to Robert, having made this *division*, the preacher could then associate the first word, "intelligent," with "the splendor of truth by which God is celebrated in the power of one's vision." With the next, "minister," he might associate "the course of purity by which one lives with affection." Finally we are left with the words "is acceptable to the king." What does one do with them? According to Robert, the preacher might speak of "hope for the sweetness of charity" and the purity of life by which one hopes to become "acceptable to the king."

Notice that, in this *divisio*, the powers of vision and feeling – that is, reason and will – are the two basic parts of a whole – namely, the soul. The preacher might have used the same *thema* to point out that it is *faith* that disposes us to the knowledge of truth; *hope* that adds certitude to the life of purity; and *charity* that is the reward of the king that brings us to our ultimate end with him in heaven. What is crucial in either case is that the preacher make his *divisio* in such a way that the parts "fit" into a structured "whole" and that the list of parts is complete. If the preacher had mentioned only faith and hope, the congregation would ask, "Where is charity?" Similarly, one could make a *divisio* according to the three sides of a triangle or according to the four corners of the earth – north, south, east, and west – but what one *should not* do is mention only two sides of a triangle or only three directions: north, south, and east.

After deciding upon an appropriate *divisio*, the preacher was to "declare" it. The rules for "declaring" these parts were not entirely dissimilar from the rules governing "parallelism" in English grammar today, according to which it is appropriate in English to say "He likes running, hiking, and swimming," but *not* "He likes running, hiking, and *to swim*." Nor is it acceptable to say "He likes to run, to hike, and swimming." The individual words or phrases in the list must be "parallel" in their construction.

So too, in the "declaration of parts," a medieval preacher had to formulate each of the parts according to an acceptable pattern of parallel verbal constructions. A common way of achieving this parallelism was to set up a similar pattern based on one of the parts of speech. Adjectives, verbs, adverbs, nouns, participles, and prepositions worked well for this purpose, advised Robert, but pronouns, conjunctions, and interjections did not. Three illustrative examples based on Robert's threefold division (the intelligent // minister // is acceptable to the king) will have to suffice.

One way of "declaring the parts" of the *divisio*, for example, would be by using adjectives, as for example if the preacher were to declare: "In these words [the *thema* verse] we are taught, first, *honorable excellence* ["intelligent"]; second, *compensative patience* ["minister"]; and third, *ineffable friendship*" ["acceptable to the king"]. Using a descriptive pair of adjectives was recommended and seems to have been common: not just *excellence*, but *honorable excellence*; not just *patience*, but *compensative patience*, and so on.

Another way of crafting the "declaration of parts" was to use verbs, as for example: "The first ["intelligent"] *perfects oneself* as oneself; the second ["minister"] *draws the love* of others; and the third *makes one happy* with God" ["acceptable to the king," i.e., God]. Another type of verbal series is: "The first commands the beginning by which there is a start; the middle by which there is progress; and the third, the end by which there is an exit."

A third method of declaring the parts involved using prepositions. Robert provides a simple example based on the famous verse from *Ecclesiasticus*, "Vanity of vanities, all is vanity." One could formulate the declaration of parts of this *thema* verse in this way: "All things were subject to vanity, namely those which were made *for* man; in those which were made *by man*; and in those which were made *in* man."

St. Bonaventure was especially adept at crafting these parallel constructions. In Sermon 29 for the second Sunday after Pentecost, for example, for which the *thema* verse was taken from Luke 14:16, "A certain man made a great supper and invited many," Bonaventure says that "Our Lord ... commends three things in the proposed verse, which render any supper complete and perfect: first the excellence of the singular dignity; second, the affluence of abundant bounty; third, the benevolence of welcoming cordiality."[18] The three characteristics of the supper are not merely its "dignity," its "bounty," and its "cordiality," nor merely its "excellence," its "affluence," or its "benevolence." One will almost always find in Bonaventure's works a triad such as "the excellence of the singular dignity," "the affluence of abundant bounty," and "the benevolence of welcoming cordiality."

In subsequent subdivisions, the declaration of the parts can get even more complex. In this sermon, Bonaventure sets up a threefold subdivision of the third part, "the benevolence of welcoming cordiality." Here is the way Bonaventure formulates the three parts of that subdivision:

> Our Lord, by reason of his cordiality and benevolence, did not wish to be alone at the supper, but instead *called many* from various nations. For first, he urgently calls without ceasing by instructing through teachings and examples (*instanter sine desitione instruendo per documenta et exampla*); second, freely without recompense by attracting through benefits and promises (*gratis sine recompensatione alliciendo per beneficia et promissa*); and third, generally without exception by threatening through eternal punishments" (*generaliter sine acceptione comminando per aeterna supplicia*).[19]

Although the most common method of formulating the "declaration of parts" involved phrases using words all of one type, whether verb, adverb, adjective, or participle – or, as with Bonaventure, a complex collection of these in a certain order – there were other methods. Using the same threefold *divisio* – the intelligent // minister // is acceptable to the king – the preacher could formulate the "declaration of parts" in various other ways. One way would be to use descriptive nouns: "minister" might be taken to refer to a person's *spiritual humility*; "intelligent" might be referred to his *mental perfection*; and "acceptable to the king" might be taken to refer to his *brotherly kindness*. Or one might use nouns with a modifying adjective, in which case "minister" might refer to an *innocence of life*; "intelligent" might refer to the greater *knowledge following from this innocence*; and "acceptable to the king" might be taken as referring to the *gratifying satisfaction* that follows from both. The preacher might also formulate the *divisio* to answer questions such as who, what, when, and why. He could say what kind of man a priest ought to be (namely, *intelligent*), what he should do for others (*minister*), and whom he should please by this life and acts (he should be "acceptable to the king," that is, to Christ).

Another common method employed the properties or attributes of nouns. Robert of Basevorn's example of this method was designed for a sermon on the Trinity, for which the preacher might employ the following declaration of parts: "In the first [word or phrase from the *thema*], there is a likeness to the *wisdom* of the Son; by the second, we understand the *clemency* of the Holy Ghost; and by the third, the *power* of the Father. The relevant nouns

---

[18] Bonaventure, *Sunday Sermons*, no. 29, section 1.
[19] Bonaventure, *Sunday Sermons*, no. 29, section 10.

in this example are "wisdom," "clemency," and "power." Notice that by linking these three with the Son, the Holy Spirit, and the Father, the preacher has made a nice, complete series, which is what he is supposed to do.

The preacher was supposed to be attentive to the specific attributes and properties of the nouns he was using. If the preacher was using the opening *thema* "The intelligent minister is acceptable to the king," for example, he should note that the word in the verse is "intelligent," not "learned"; that it is a "minister," not "*magister*" (teacher); and that it says "*acceptable* to the king," not "rejected." If there were different words in the *thema* verse, this would necessitate a different declaration of parts.

Consider a *divisio* based on this verse from Ezra 32:7: "I will cover the sun with a cloud." One could set up a threefold *divisio* based on a metaphorical appropriation of the properties of the nouns in this way: "First, the sun shines alone with the gravity of law and judges; but later it comes under the cloud by the kindness of the Incarnation; and finally at the judgment it is covered with the equity of the sentence, because it does not respect the person [that is the status] of the man." If the *thema* verse had used the image of the moon rather than the sun, or if the sun had not been said to be "covered with a cloud," but was shining hot in the middle of the day, or if the sun were not covered by a cloud but instead eclipsed by the moon, then the declaration of parts would have had to be different, and the new declaration could not have been associated with the law, the Incarnation, and status of mankind in the same way.

These examples show that the medieval preacher had plenty of options, even when he was dealing with a single biblical verse. I have taken the time to go over some of these options because, as we will see, Thomas and Bonaventure often used these same methods when they wrote their prologues.

Dilatatio: Methods of "Unfolding" a Sermon

After the preacher had "divided" his opening *thema* and "declared the parts," it remained for him to develop each section. Medieval preaching manuals contained rules and advice on how this was to be done. The common term for this "developing" of content from the words of the *thema* verse was *dilatatio*. *Dilatatio* literally means "an expanding" (as in the English "dilation"), but it may help to think of it as an "unpacking" or "unfolding" of the semiotic possibilities inherent in the words of the *thema* verse.

Both the *Ars concionandi* and the *Forma praedicandi* list these eight methods of "dilating" a word or phrase from the opening *thema*.

1. By proposing a discussion based on a noun as it occurs in definitions or classifications (*proponendo orationem pro nomine, sicut fit in diffinitionibus seu quibuscumque notificationibus*)
2. By subdivisions of the original *divisio* (*per divisionem*)
3. By reasoning or argumentation (*ratiocinando vel argumentando*)
4. By "chaining" together concordant authorities (*per auctoritates concordantes*)
5. By setting up a series running from the positive through the comparative and arriving finally at the superlative in the manner of "good, better, best" (*ut ponendo superlativum curratur ad positivum et comparativum*)

The Basic Elements of the Thirteenth-Century "Modern Sermon" 53

6. By devising metaphors through the properties of a thing (*excogitando metaphoras per proprietetem rei*)
7. By expounding the *thema* in diverse ways accordingly to the literal, allegorical, tropological, and/or anagogical senses (*exponere thema diversimode: historice, allegorice, moraliter, anagogice*)
8. By a consideration of causes and their effects (*per causas et effectus*)

Since some of these phrases may be rather cryptic, allow me to illustrate with examples of each.

Method 1: Proposing a Discussion Based on a Noun as It Occurs in Definitions or Classifications

Let us say that the *thema* for the sermon is to be taken from Wisdom 10:10, which says that Wisdom "led the just man in the right paths, and showed him the reign of God, and gave him the knowledge of holy things." And let us say that the preacher divides this passage by saying that Wisdom does three things for the just man: first, "she *led the just man in the right paths*"; second, she "*showed him the reign of God*"; and third, she "*gave him the knowledge of holy things*."

Our question now is how the preacher can "develop" or "dilate" each of these three. For our present purposes, let us focus on only the first of these three, in which Wisdom is said to have "led the just man in the right paths." According to the nearly identical instructions in both the *Ars concionandi* and Basevorn's *Forma praedicandi* (to which henceforth I will refer simply as "our manuals"), one could "dilate" this phrase, first, by defining the "just man" as "he who gives everyone his proper due." Then the preacher might further develop this thought by expounding upon how "giving everyone his proper due" applies, first, to God, second, to one's neighbor, and finally, to oneself.

Alternatively, the preacher might define "justice" and then develop the idea by expounding upon those things that are *contrary to* justice, such as vices of various sorts or surrender to the passions. Or he might discuss the virtues *related to* justice, such as prudence, temperance, and fortitude, suggesting that *prudence* is "the ability to discern good things from evil"; *fortitude* "the sustaining of difficulties because of love"; and *temperance* "the firm command of sensual desires." The preacher would then introduce this discussion or conclude it using words such as these: "Therefore, prudence consists in *discerning*, fortitude in *enduring*, temperance in *checking illicit passions*, and justice in *giving to each one his proper due*."[20] Using this method, the preacher would have succeeded in taking one word from his *thema* verse – in this case "just" – and turning it into a discussion about not only justice, but about all of the cardinal virtues. And given that the original context proposes that "Wisdom" is "leading the just man," the preacher might also declaim on the relationship between Wisdom and the virtues, or on how God's "Wisdom" is the Holy Spirit, and then develop the relationship between the virtues and the Gifts of the Holy Spirit. The possibilities are nearly endless – so much so that the *Ars concionandi* bids the aspiring preacher to notice "how an expansion can be made in the oration by using a noun, not only

[20] *Ars concionandi* 3.33.

by indicating what is contained in the [word] itself, but also by indicating other things which can be drawn from it."[21]

Yet, medieval preachers were also warned that there were limits – that they "should not attempt to take up definitions or descriptions of everything indiscriminately."[22] A judgment about how faithfully a particular preacher has observed those limits will depend to a large degree upon each reader's taste and tolerance for such things. Readers who merely want to "get to the point and be done with it" will likely find these "dilations" on various related topics annoying. Others who enjoy word games, word associations, and the connections between ideas will find the method rather ingenious and more delightful.

Method 2: Creating Subdivisions

After the original division of the opening biblical *thema*, a preacher would sometimes make further subdivisions within one or more of the "members" of his opening *divisio*. Both Thomas and Bonaventure loved this method. If you look at one of the early sections of Thomas's *Veniet desideratus* (Sermon 1), you will find a complex series of divisions and subdivisions – so complex, in fact, that the translator, Fr. Hoogland, saw fit to insert a complex numbering system into his English translation to help the reader keep the sections straight.[23]

The *thema* for the entire sermon is taken from Haggai 2:8: "He who is desired by all the nations together will come, and he will fill this house with glory" ("veniet desideratus cunctis gentibus et implebo domum istam gloria").[24] Thomas divides the *thema* into three parts. Regarding the first, "he will come," he proposes that it is God's Son himself who comes down from the heavens. In the second, "who is desired by all the nations together," he shows that Christ mercifully fulfills the desires of all the patriarchs. And in the third, "and he will fill this house with glory," he shows how Christ freely bestows his pleasing benefit. So far, this is nothing more than a simple threefold division of the *thema*.

But when we come to Thomas's *dilatatio* of the first part, "he will come" (*veniet*), here is what he says: "I interpret 'he will come' insofar as it is absolutely necessary for us." That is to say, when someone says "he *will* come," one means that it *will* happen and thus there is a certain "necessity" involved. He continues (with Fr. Hoogland's numbering inserted):

> Well, the coming of the Savior was necessary for three reasons: first, because the world was imperfect in many ways; second, because man was cast down from his rightful honor in a foul way; and third, because God was offended by man in a wondrous way. Therefore, he came (1.1) in order to grant to the whole world the highest grade of dignity; (1.2) in order to

---

[21] Ibid.
[22] Ibid.
[23] Cf. *Thomas Aquinas: The Academic Sermons*, trans. Mark-Robin Hoogland, C.P. The Fathers of the Church: Mediaeval Continuation, vol. 11 (Washington, DC: Catholic University of American Press, 2010), 23–33. All English translations of Thomas's sermons will be taken from this volume.
[24] Fr. Hoogland cites the source of this verse as Hag 2:7. I found it in a modern Vulgate edition, however, in Hag 2:8; *Biblia Sacra Vulgata*, 5th ed. (Stuttgart: Deutsche Bibelgesellschaft, 1983) – all citations are from this edition.

The Basic Elements of the Thirteenth-Century "Modern Sermon" 55

lead man back to his proper human state; and (1.3) in order to take away the offense of man against God.

But with this, Thomas is only warming up. For he continues, dilating upon the notion of "dignity" in section 1.1:

> Now the grade of dignity in the world fell short in three respects: (1.1.1) one grade of *union* is more wonderful than the others; (1.1.2) one way of generation is more sublime than the others; and (1.1.3) one way of perfection is more excellent than the others. Yet, when Christ came into this world, he accomplished a new *union* [cf. 1.1.1], he took on a new *generation* [cf. 1.1.2] and he brought along a new *perfection* [cf. 1.1.3].

What we find in the section that follows (which is a subsection of why Christ's coming was "necessary") is how Christ has "granted the whole world the highest grade of dignity" in three ways: a new sort of *union*, a new sort of *generation*, and a new sort of *perfection*. These specific categories allow Thomas to include some serious Christology in his sermon. Allow me to quote in full the relevant passages that follow, along with my own subdivision system (parenthetical capital letters) added on top of Fr. Hoogland's numbering system (numbers with periods). In each case, Thomas proposes several species of, first, *union*; second, *generation*; and third, *perfection*, only the last of which will apply to Christ. Here are the next three paragraphs of his text in outline form that follow directly after Thomas says, "Yet, when Christ came into this world, he accomplished a new *union*; he took on a new *generation*; and he brought along a new *perfection*."[25]

> (1.1.1) In the world, one grade of *union* was lacking, the one more wonderful than the others. For in our world there are four kinds of union:
>
> (A) The first is the union of something corruptible with something corruptible, as in natural things.
> (B) The second is the union of something corruptible with something incorruptible, as in human beings.
> (C) The third is the union of something incorruptible with something incorruptible, as in spiritual things: a union of *essentia* and *potentia*.
> (D) The fourth, however, was lacking: the union of something temporal with something eternal. Well, this union was made when "the Word became flesh and dwelt among us," as it says in Jn 1.14; "when he emptied himself (and took on the form of a slave; made in the likeness of human beings he was, through his way of life, found a man)."
>
> (1.1.2) Also, the one way of *generation* was lacking that is more wonderful than the others. For there are four kinds of generation in the broad sense of the word:
>
> (A) The first is from the Father without a mother, the generation that occurs eternally.
> (B) The second is without a father and without a mother, in the beginning, as with the first parents.
> (C) The third is from a father and a mother, the generation that occurs all around us.

---

[25] I have shortened this passage in places for length while attempting to preserve the sense and complexity of the whole.

(D) The fourth did not exist before, namely, the generation from a mother without a father in time. Well, this generation was made when the Virgin conceived, when, as we read in Isaiah 10, "the stone is hewn from the mountain without hands.". . . The stone hewn from the mountain [without hands] is Christ, born from the Virgin without a human action.

(1.1.3) Also lacking was the one grade of *perfection* that is more excellent than the others, although anything that is connected with *its end is **perfect***. Hence, a creature is most perfect when united with its Creator. Well, a creature is conjoined with its Creator with a triple connection:

(A) The first is a union in respect of strength, by reason of a dependency in all things.
(B) The second is in respect of the [human] species: through the grace in just people, since according to Dionysius love [*amor*] is a unifying force.
(C) The third union concerns the thing itself, by essence. This did not exist before, but it came into being when the human nature was taken on by the Son of God in unity of supposit or person. In taking on the human nature in a certain way the whole world was taken on, because, according to Gregory, "in a way every creature is a human being."

Recall that all of these divisions and subdivisions were in service of showing how Christ has granted the whole world the highest grade of dignity (1.1).

After he has finished his "dilation" of this section, Thomas must still take up, in section 1.2, how Christ leads man back to his proper human state and, in 1.3, how he takes away the offense of man against God. Each of these subsections will have further subsections, just as we saw with section 1.1. And *all of this*, please recall, is simply in service of Thomas's "unfolding" of the first phrase in his *divisio*: "he will come."

As we will see, both Thomas and Bonaventure made abundant use of the method of division and subdivision in their sermons and prologues. From the testimony of their contemporaries, we have every reason to believe that they were capable of mentally keeping track of each and every one of them.

As I mentioned earlier, we might fruitfully compare the medieval method of division and subdivision employed in the *sermo modernus* style of preaching with the divisions and subdivisions commonly used at that time in the exegesis of biblical texts. The method is similarly reminiscent of the divisions and subdivisions one finds in scholastic *summae* and disputed questions. David d'Avray classifies all of these as expressions of what he calls "the subdividing mentality" of the scholastics, of which sermons and disputed questions were two species of the same genus, and biblical commentaries a third.[26] We will have several occasions in the text that follows to note that, in the prologues to several of Thomas's and Bonaventure's biblical commentaries, the *sermo modernus* style can be found together with a complex *divisio textus*, and at times, even with several disputed questions.

---

[26] See David d'Avray, *The Preaching of the Friars: Sermons Diffused from Paris before 1300* (Oxford: Oxford University Press, 1985), 176–179, esp. 176: "One feature which thirteenth-century mendicant sermons do share with the academic genres to which I would restrict the word 'scholastic' is the passion for dividing and sub-dividing."

Method 3: Argumentation

As we noted in the previous chapter, the famous medieval scholar Étienne Gilson once wrote that "the place for disputes is the School, the place for the sermon is the church."[27] In this, he was simply echoing a warning made by thirteenth-century preaching manuals that a sermon should not sound like a disputation: that is, it should not proceed by setting forth premises from which a conclusion is then deduced (*non praemittantur propositiones, et postea inferatur conclusio*).[28] Clearly, such advice would have become necessary only after preachers had gained the education in logic offered at universities such as those at Paris, Oxford, and others. Yet, to say that a sermon should not proceed in the manner of a disputation was not the same as saying that a sermon should not make use of arguments, since "argumentation" was universally recognized as a method of *dilatatio*.

According to the *Ars concionandi*, the type of argument especially fitting for a sermon involved reasoning by opposing two contraries, one of which is approved, the other being made the object of reproach, "thereby demonstrating a type of cause." The *Ars concionandi* proposes this example. To argue that continence should be fostered, the preacher should speak about riotous living and show that it destroys the body, the soul, possessions, and reputation, whereas continence does the reverse. *Therefore*, one ought to "practice continence."

So too in Thomas's Sermon 11 (*Emitte Spiritum*), he proposes a set of contraries: "Everything man knows he knows either because he finds out or because he learns it." "So how is man led to the knowledge of God?" he asks. It cannot be that he *learns it* by his own powers. Therefore, he must *find out* these things having been told by God's own divine revelation to him." Similarly, elsewhere in the same sermon, he posits the general principle that stipulates that "all things that are moved to a certain end must have something that moves them to that end." Now, the things moved to a natural end are moved by something in nature. But things moved to a supernatural end cannot be moved by something in nature, says Thomas, so they must have a "supernatural mover."

Another method of argument proceeds by asking rhetorical questions. In Sermon 11, Thomas asks several: "But how has God created all things?" "But what is the first movement of the will?" and "What then is the reason for the mission of the Holy Spirit?" He also gives voice to objections he suspects may exist in the mind of his listener, such as "You will say: 'You must not summon such people nor lead them to religious life," or "You will say: 'It is good for boys to preach, so that they let go of the secular world and come to Christ in religious life, but it is not good to attract or allure them with temporal benefits," or again: "You will say: 'It is allowed to attract boys to religious life but not to let them take vows." Why not? "You will say: 'Because many who had taken vows returned [into the world]. I then will say what the Apostle says: 'Will the unbelief of those make the faith empty?'" (Rom 3:3).

Scholastically trained preachers such as Thomas and Bonaventure resisted the temptation to turn the sermon into another version of a disputed question, but they also understood that simple arguments were not foreign to a good sermon, especially with

---

[27] Étienne Gilson, "Michel Menot et la Technique du Sermon Médiéval," in *Les Idées et Les Lettres* (Paris: Vrin, 1932), 134.

[28] *Ars concionandi* 3.40.

university audiences accustomed to hearing arguments. Yet, although arguments were not at all *foreign* to preaching in the thirteenth century, they were usually not the single most essential element. Nor were the arguments used in sermons usually of the same type as those in "disputed questions." Arguments in sermons were simpler, involving fewer steps, where more of the argumentative force depended on the juxtaposition of contraries or the listing of costs suffered or benefits gained. Such was the case, similarly, as we will see, when these preachers wrote prologues, even if the prologue was for a very technical, dialectical text, such as Peter Lombard's *Sentences*.

Method 4: Concordance of Texts or the "Chaining" of Authorities

Medieval preachers occasionally used arguments in their sermons, but they loved to quote Bible verses even more than make arguments. A medieval sermon of the *sermo modernus* style would be noteworthy to any modern audience precisely because of its dual nature. On the one hand, it would sound extremely "scholastic" because of its definitions, distinctions, and arguments. But it would also sound extraordinarily "biblical," given that one does not go more than a sentence or two without finding another biblical verse. Michèle Mulcahey notes that, "The use of [biblical] *auctoritates* by some preachers became so extensive that a whole sermon was sometimes virtually no more than an uninterrupted sequence of quotations." "The problem facing the preacher," she suggests, "was how to connect all his *auctoritates* in a logical and pleasing fashion. The usual method was to build up 'chains' of authorities by concording them all either *verbaliter*, verbally, with a key word of the member under discussion, or *realiter*, that is, by means of analogous ideas, or both."[29] This practice, sometimes described as the "chaining" of authorities was, as Mulcahey notes, "a device universally employed by the preachers of the thirteenth and fourteenth centuries."[30]

Like other medieval preachers, both Thomas and Bonaventure relished this method of "expanding" a sermon. And given the prodigious memory and wide knowledge of the Scriptures enjoyed by both men, they were extraordinarily adept at finding several Bible verses to support nearly every passing remark.

Consider, for example, this passage from Thomas's Sermon 1 (*Veniet desideratus*), a sermon for the First Sunday in Advent. In this passage, Thomas repeats the famous argument from St. Anselm's *Cur deus homo*, but he does so in the rhetorical setting of a *sermo modernus* style sermon.

> Thus a certain case, so to speak, was set in motion from the beginning of the world for the coming of the Lord. For truth required that man would die, because it is written in Numbers 15:30: "A soul that sins through pride will be cut off from his people." But mercy required that man would be set free. The Psalmist says (Ps 77:8–9): "Will God reject in eternity (so that he would not remember) that he was more favorable until now, or will he until the end (abandon his grace)?" Justice, however, required in the end that he be condemned, because Genesis 2:17 reads: "On whatever day you will eat from it, you will

---

[29] Michèle Mulcahey, *First the Bow*, 410.
[30] Ibid., 409.

die." And Deuteronomy 17:12 says: "A person who will be so proud as to disobey an order of the wise one will die by decree of the judge." But peace requires that a settlement be arranged and the disposition be changed. The Psalmist says (Ps 85:6): "Will you be angry with us in eternity or do you extend your wrath from generation to generation?" And therefore Isaiah asked (Isa 16:1): "Send out the lamb, Lord, to the rulers of the earth." And Moses says (Exod 4:13): "I beseech you, Lord, send the one whom you will send." But since God is "good and merciful" (2 Macc 1:24), he could "not deny himself" (2 Tim 2:13), but he answers through Jeremiah (Jer 31:20): "My inner parts are stirred up because of him; I will show him great mercy." And Hosea 11.8: "My heart is turned within me; my penance has turned likewise." Thus the Lord has sent someone to settle [the debt]: not a human being, not an angel, but God's Son, who satisfied through mercy so that it did not fall short of justice in anything. And so it happened that there was in the same man justice to the full and infinite mercy, and so "just and mercy have kissed" (Ps 85:11).

That, if the reader was not yet clear on the concept, is "chaining." What we have here is essentially the core argument of Anselm's *Cur Deus homo* summarized in one paragraph, enunciated almost entirely by the chaining together of biblical verses.[31] This is the way to give a fairly sophisticated theological argument in preaching, not in the terms and tropes of Greek philosophy, but speaking almost entirely in the language of Sacred Scripture.

Method 5: Setting Up a Series: Good, Better, Best

The short, one-sentence description in Latin of this method is harder to understand than the method itself. The rather complicated way the *Ars concionandi* describes the method is to say that the *dilatatio* is carried out "through those words which have the same meaning and which agree in root, although they carry incidental differences. Therefore, if a superlative has been proposed, one can proceed to the positive and comparative."[32] This is a complicated way of saying that the preacher should set up a series along the lines of "good-better-best."

The example the *Ars concionandi* gives is as follows. Suppose the division of the *thema* verse has left the preacher with this bit of the verse from Psalm 44:4, "Bind your sword around your thighs, strongest one." This verse can be dilated by suggesting that the people bound by the sword *strongly* are those who are married; those bound even *more strongly* are the continent; and those bound *most strongly* are the virgins. Or consider the passage from the Song of Songs 5:1 which reads, "I have drunk, dearest one." One might dilate this verse by suggesting that those are *dear* who live in charity, although of an imperfect type; those are *dearer* who can endure adversity for the sake of Christ but with some annoyance; and those are *dearest* who laugh in the midst of their humiliations.[33]

What can also be done, however, is to dilate by cataloguing the three ways in which something is a "better" sort of happiness or a "more excellent" sort of virtue. In Thomas's

---

[31] Cf. Anselm, *Cur Deus homo*, esp. I.11–15, 24–25; II.6–11.

[32] *Ars concionandi* 3.42: "per ea eiusdam sunt cognitiones, quae scilicet conveniunt in radice, licet diversitatem habeant. Posito igitur superlative, discurraatur ad positivum et comparativum."

[33] Ibid.

Sermon 1 (*Veniet desideratus*), Thomas praises Christ in three respects, claiming that his "grade of union is more wonderful than the others," his "way of generation is more sublime than others," and his "way of perfection is more excellent than others." He then discusses each of these in turn. Similarly in Sermon 13 (*Homo quidam*), a sermon on the story of "a certain man" (that is, Christ) who "made a great dinner," Thomas stipulates that the dinner is called "great" for three reasons: (1) the greatness of the provision, (2) the greatness of the delight in taste, and (3) the great virtue that results.

Method 6: The Use of Metaphors

Dilating using the metaphorical meanings of terms is one of the most common techniques to be found in the sermons of both Thomas and Bonaventure. There are about as many different ways of doing this as there are different ways of giving various metaphorical meanings to terms. Allow me to offer a few examples from Thomas's sermons.

In Sermon 4 (*Osanna filio Dauid*), for example, Thomas suggests that our salvation consists "in the stability of eternity." As a ship whose safety is threatened in a dire storm is not considered "safe" or "saved" until it has arrived at its destination in a stable harbor, "in the same way," says Thomas, "a human being is not saved during his life on earth [*in via*], but only in our heavenly homeland [*in patria*]."

So too in Sermon 6 (*Caelum et terra transibunt*), we find a fairly straightforward *dilatatio* by metaphor based on Luke 21:33, which reads: "Heaven and earth will pass." Dilating upon the word "heaven," Thomas says that this word describes the situation of the just man in four ways: (1) because heaven is of great brightness; (2) because it has a splendid appearance; (3) because it is in motion; and (4) because it is high in location. Each of these characteristics can be applied metaphorically to the just man, says Thomas, because: (1) the just man should "shine brightly," in that he ought to be full of the light of heavenly wisdom; (2) he ought to be "like a circle by a wide mercy or like an orbit by a broad devotion and perfect love"; (3) he should be "set in motion" always by a spiritual carefulness"; and (4) the just man ought to be "high" by excelling others in holiness.

Here are two final examples, the first relatively straightforward and the second relatively more complex, both from Sermon 11 (*Emitte Spiritum*), a sermon on Pentecost, for which the opening biblical *thema* is the famous verse Psalm 104:30, "Send forth your Spirit, and they will be created, and you will renew the face of the earth." Dilating upon the first half of the verse ("Send forth your Spirit, and they will be created"), Thomas suggests that the word "spirit" seems to imply four things: first, "a fineness of substance," since "we usually call substances without a body 'spirits'"; second, a "perfection of life," since "as long as animated creatures have a spirit, they live"; third, an "incitement of motion," as when we say of a person that he has an impulsive spirit; and fourth, a "hidden origin," as when someone is disturbed but does not know what is disturbing him, and will often attribute it to a spirit. Thomas then applies each property – fineness of substance, perfection of life, incitement of motion, and hiddenness of origin – metaphorically to the Holy Spirit.

We find a somewhat more complex example in the second half of the same sermon, where Thomas is dilating on the last part of the opening *thema*: "and you will renew the face of the earth." "Who receives this renewal?" asks Thomas. "The face of the earth" is the obvious answer. "The face of the earth," says Thomas, refers in one sense to the whole world, but in another sense it refers to the human mind, because "just as we see with our face in a corporeal way, so we see with the mind in a spiritual way." So, metaphorically speaking, and for the purposes of this sermon, the "face" of the earth is the human mind. What is involved, then, in "renewing the face of the earth" in this sense? Well, says Thomas (making full use of the associations one derives from the image of a face), a face is "renewed" when it is (1) clean, (2) uncovered, (3) directed toward God, and (4) firm (as in the phrase "set your face firmly and truly on God"). Each of these metaphorical ways in which a "face" can be "renewed" is then taken to be a way in which God renews our mind.

Consider the first of these, for example: *cleaning* one's face. Thomas quotes the verse in Matthew 6:17 that says, "When you fast . . . anoint your head and wash your face," which he interprets as meaning "wash your face *with the tears of a moved heart*," so that you will be able to receive the renewal of the Holy Spirit. So the metaphorical "chain," if you will, has gone like this: "face of the earth" was metaphorically taken to mean the human mind; renewing the human mind was metaphorically related *back to* the physical human face; the physical human face is "washed by tears"; and so the conclusion is that the Holy Spirit can "renew the face of the earth" when men weep with a humble and contrite heart and open their minds to the Truth.

Some readers may find this chain of associations between the human face and the phrase "renew the face of the earth" to be a bit of a stretch. Yet, most readers, even in a modern audience, will understand the meaning of the phrase "a bit of a stretch" in that last sentence, even though there is no actual physical stretching going on. We use metaphors in speech all the time, often without even noticing that we are doing so. When medieval preachers noticed the *metaphorical potency* of words and used that expressive power of language in their preaching, was it really so different from what poets often do with words? In these sermons, preachers such as Thomas were certainly stretching the expressive power of the words; but then, so do great poets. The trick in making these associations in a sermon is that the association should be *close enough* to be suggestive, but also *odd enough* to be interesting, evocative, and thus memorable.

Bonaventure had a special love for complex metaphors. For the prologue to the first book of his *Sentences* commentary (which we will discuss in greater detail in Chapter 12), he chose as his *thema* the verse from Job 28:11, "The depths of rivers he hath searched, and hidden things he hath brought forth to light" (*profunda quoque fluviorum scrutatus est et abscondita produxit in lucem*).[34] In his dilation of this verse, Bonaventure associates the material cause of the Lombard's *Sentences* with the word *fluviorum* ("of rivers") and the four properties of a material river, which he identifies as (a) perpetuity (*perennitatem*), since rivers are always flowing; (b) spaciousness (*spatiositatem*), which distinguishes a river from a brook or a stream; (c) circulation (*circulationem*), for as it says in Ecclesiastes 1.7: "All the rivers run into the sea, yet the sea doth not overflow: unto the place from whence the rivers come, they return, to flow again"; and finally (d) cleansing (*emundationem*), for the waters cleanse the earth through which the river runs so that it is not polluted.

---

[34] See *Opera Omnia S. Bonaventurae* (Ad Claras Aquas (Quaracchi): Collegii s. Bonaventurae, 1882–1901), vol. 1, 1–6.

From these four properties of a material river, Bonaventure metaphorically discerns the four properties of what he calls a "spiritual river." The spiritual river is *perpetual* in that it involves an emanation of persons, and this emanation is without beginning or end. So too the first book of the *Sentences* deals with the emanation of persons in the Trinity. The second property of a material river is its *spaciousness*, and this Bonaventure associates with the subject matter of the second book of the *Sentences*: creation. The third property of a material river is its *circulation*, and just as in a circle, the beginning is joined to the end, so in the Incarnation, the subject of the third book of the *Sentences*, the highest is joined to the lowest, God to man. The fourth property of a material river is *cleansing*. So too the fourth book of the Lombard's *Sentences* deals with the sacraments, which cleanse us "from the pollution of sin."

Method 7: A Fourfold Exposition According to the Historical, Allegorical, Moral, and/or Anagogical Senses of Scripture

It is sometimes claimed, mistakenly, that the allegorical, moral, and anagogical senses of Scripture – also called the spiritual senses – were largely abandoned in the thirteenth century, having given way to a greater focus on literal sense of the Scriptures.[35] Although it is true that a new interest in and emphasis on the literal sense of the Scriptures arose in the late twelfth and the early thirteenth century, we still find all four senses of Scripture in the preaching of the high Middle Ages as means of "dilating" a term or phrase in the opening *thema*.

A nice example of a *dilatatio* based on the spiritual senses can be found near the end of Thomas's Sermon 2 (*Lauda et laetare*), a sermon for Advent, where Thomas is dilating upon the last part of the *thema* from Zechariah 2:10 ("'Sing praise and be glad, daughter of Zion, for behold, I come and I will dwell in your midst,' says the Lord"). Dilating upon the phrase "I will dwell," Thomas suggests that Christ "dwells with us" in three ways. First, he dwells "with all people, in a general way, through the substance of the flesh, as we read in John 1:14: 'The Word became flesh and dwelt among us.'" Second, he dwells with the saints "in a special way, through infused grace, as we read in 2 Cor 5:16: 'I will dwell among them and I will be their God.'" Finally, Christ dwells with the just in heaven "in a familiar way" (*familiariter*) by being present before their eyes, as the Psalmist says (5:12): "Forever they will exult and you will dwell among them." The first of these three sorts of "dwelling" refers to Christ; the second is moral, dealing with how grace makes possible our obedience to the moral law; and the third is anagogical, dealing with the activities of the saints in heaven.

Bonaventure makes a fascinating use of the three spiritual senses in Collation 7 of his *Collations on the Seven Gifts of the Holy Spirit* in a discussion of the gift of counsel. This

---

[35] There are others, of course, who assume that benighted medieval scholars used *nothing but* an allegorical approach to the Scriptures until the Protestant scholars of the sixteenth century or those of the nineteenth century (depending upon your viewpoint) finally restored biblical scholarship to its authentic dedication to the *literal* sense. It was Beryl Smalley's lonely task to disabuse many twentieth-century biblical scholars of this mistaken notion. See, for example, her classic *The Study of the Bible in the Middle Ages* (Oxford: Blackwell, 1941; Notre Dame, IN: University of Notre Dame Press, 2007).

collation is the last one in a series of three collations – 5, 6, and 7 – all based on this passage from Proverbs 31:10–13:

> Who shall find a valiant woman (*mulierem fortem*)? Far and from the uttermost coasts is the price of her. The heart of her husband trusts in her, and he shall have no need of spoils. She will render him good, and not evil, all the days of her life. She hath sought wool and flax, and hath wrought by the counsel of her hands (*consilio manuum suarum*).[36]

With this as his *thema* verse, Bonaventure is able to discourse upon the gifts of both fortitude ("Who shall find a valiant woman?") and counsel ("the counsel of her hands").

In Collation 7, after distinguishing three types of "counsel" – according to the judgment of right reason, according to the command of good will, and according to the practice of virtue – in section 9 Bonaventure turns directly to the verse: "She hath sought wool and flax, and hath wrought by the counsel of her hands." "Coarse clothing is made from wool," explains. "Finer clothing is made from flax. Warm clothing is made of wool. Lighter clothing is made from flax. Further, outer garments are made of wool. Undergarments are made of flax." These three properties will provide the basis for an understanding of the verse that is allegorical, anagogical, and tropological. Allegorically, says Bonaventure, "wool" and "linen" signify the Old and New Testaments – the Old Testament being more coarse or rough, like wool, and the New Testament being finer, like flax. In terms of anagogy, says Bonaventure, "wool from which warm clothing is made signifies the revelation of prayer because prayer is like heat. On the other hand, flax from which softer clothing is made signifies delights." Tropologically, according to the moral sense, wool, from which outer garments are made, signifies external things, while flax, from which undergarments are made, signifies the inner experiences of just people.

Notice in all these examples how Bonaventure and Thomas employ the three spiritual senses as *one method among others* of "dilating" or "unfolding" a biblical verse. The spiritual senses have not been abandoned or forgotten – as we'll see, Bonaventure will use the three spiritual senses to structure the entire second half of his *resumptio* address, a text we now call the *De reductione artium ad theologiam* – but they no longer serve as the foundations of preaching. The rules of *divisio* and *dilatatio* serve that purpose instead.

Method 8: The Consideration of Causes and Their Effects

The final method of *dilatatio* is the consideration of causes and their effects. Given Thomas and Bonaventure's training in dialectic, this method of "dilating" a point comes naturally, and they use it frequently; indeed, they will often "chain" together a whole series of cause-and-effect relationships.

In Thomas's Sermon 11 (*Emitte Spiritum*), for example, in a section in which he is "dilating" the opening *thema* from Psalm 104:30, which contains the words "Send forth your Spirit," Thomas suggests that the word "Spirit" implies four things: first, the fineness of

---

[36] English: Zachary Hayes, tr., *Collations on the Seven Gifts of the Holy Spirit*, The Works of St. Bonaventure, 14 (St. Bonaventure, NY: The Franciscan Institute, 2010). Latin: *Collationes de septem donis Spiritus Sancit* in *Opera Omnia Sanctae Bonaventurae* (Quarrachi), vol. 5.

substance; second, the perfection of life; third, the incitement of a movement; and fourth, a hidden origin. When he comes to the fourth of these considerations – the one in which he suggests that the word "spirit" implies or suggests a "hidden origin" – Thomas "dilates" the point by saying, "Faith teaches and reason argues that all visible and changeable things have a hidden cause. What is that cause? That cause is God." "But how has God created all things?" asks Thomas. Not out of necessity, he insists, but out of His own free will. But why, then, did He create the world? "For sure, it is love [*amor*]," answers Thomas, and adds: "We celebrate now the feast of the Holy Spirit, and the Spirit is the principle of being in all things. Thus the Spirit has a hidden origin, the property of which is love [*amor*]."

Similarly, when he considers the third characteristic that he suggests is implied by the word "spirit" – namely, "the incitement of a movement" – Thomas says:

> For we see in the world different movements, natural and voluntary ones, in people and in angels. Where do these different movements come from? They must come from one first mover, evidently from God. The Psalmist says: "you will change them, and they will be changed" [Ps 102:27]. And God moves by his will. But what is the first movement of the will? For certain it is love [*amor*].

Readers of the *prima pars* of Thomas' *Summa of Theology* will recognize the cause–effect relationship sketched ever so briefly here as one of the "five ways" of demonstrating the existence of a Creator: reasoning from effect to cause, from the things that are moved to a first, unmoved mover. Readers of the *prima pars* might also notice how different the argument sounds in a sermon. In the context of his sermon, Thomas has the rhetorical freedom to add this final, important point about the "first mover": He moves because of His love and is the "first mover" because He *is* love.

So too in Bonaventure's Sermon 1 (*Veniet desideratus*), whose *thema* verse is from Haggai 2:8: "The one desired by all the nations will come," dilating upon the word *veniet* ("he will come"), Bonaventure notes, "If someone asks the principal reason and cause for God coming in the flesh, the best reason is the most excellent liberality of God by which, according to which, and because of which the Word became incarnate."[37] The *cause* of the Incarnation is God's liberality, which Bonaventure distinguishes as consisting of three types: first, that of a "most gracious mediator displaying the remedies of peace and harmony"; second, that of a "most truthful doctor offering proofs of piety and justice"; and third, that "of a most humble king, demonstrating examples of humility and subjection, that is, of poverty and indigence." Our response to God's liberality should be made accordingly: we should love him as a mediator, revere Him as a doctor, and imitate him as a precursor. Distinguishing in this way allows Bonaventure in the following sections to develop each of these points in turn and thus "expand" his content.

Building the Elements of the Sermon

Notice how, in all the examples, these methods of *dilatatio* are frequently used in conjunction with one another. A cause-and-effect discussion is often built upon an

---

[37] Bonaventure, *Sunday Sermons*, no. 1, section 3.

"interpretation of names" or a guiding metaphor, and each of these will provide opportunities for a concordance of texts and the "chaining" of biblical authorities.

In this regard, consider this wonderful passage from Thomas's Sermon 18 (*Germinet terra*) celebrating the Feast of the Birth of the Virgin Mary, where Thomas, dilating upon the opening biblical *thema* from Genesis 1:11, "Let the earth put forth the green plant that brings forth seed and the fruit-bearing tree that yields fruit" – a passage that, let us be honest, is not one that most of us would have immediately associated with a sermon on the Virgin Mary – claims that Mary was a "green plant." He explains:

> She is a green plant because of her virginity. It says in Jer 12.4: "Every plant of the land will wither," but the Blessed Virgin was a green plant through her virginity. Hence it says in Luke 1.26–27: "The angel Gabriel was sent to the Virgin Mary." See that in the greenness we observe (1) moisture, (2) beauty, and (3) usefulness or necessity. First, I say that in the greenness we see moisture as a cause, since moisture is the cause of greenness. Thus we read in Sirach [Ecclesiasticus] 40.16: "Greenness on all waterfronts." And you should know that, just as every plant withers because of fire or the sun, so the concupiscence of the flesh makes the greenness of virginity wither. It says in Job 31.12: "It is a devouring fire aimed at consumption." But by what is the greenness of virginity nurtured? Surely by heavenly love [*amor*].

Here, we begin first with a metaphor: Mary is like a green plant because of her virginity. We move next to a consideration of the implications of the "greenness" of a plant: it indicates moisture, beauty, and usefulness. Then we are presented with a cause-and-effect relationship: moisture is a cause of greenness. Next, we get another metaphor: concupiscence of the flesh (lust) is like a fire or like the heat of the sun. Then we get another cause-and-effect relationship: What does fire or heat from the sun do to green plants? It withers them. This consideration leads us back into another metaphor: just as heat withers a green plant, so concupiscence destroys virginity. And we finish (this little section at least) with another cause-and-effect relationship: by what is the greenness of virginity nurtured? It is nurtured by heavenly love, which is metaphorically like water from heaven that causes the greenness of the plant.

Note that each stage of development along the way, each cause-and-effect relationship, provides another lively opportunity for the "chaining" of biblical passages. In this little section, Thomas's metaphorical consideration of "greenness" and "moisture" lead him to the passage from Ecclesiasticus 40:15–16 that reads: "Never a branch will the posterity of the wicked put forth; dead roots they are that rattle on the wind-swept rock. Yet how green yonder rushes grow by the river's bank!" One sentence later, his consideration of heat and the sun leads him to make another concordance-type search – whether he made this search in an actual printed concordance or merely by searching his memory is immaterial at the moment – and this search turns up the passage in Job 31:12, "that fire, once lighted, will rage till all is consumed, never a crop shall escape it." The result is biblical authority associated with a metaphor based on the results of a cause-and-effect analysis that is itself based on another metaphor and an interpretation of a name. Here, as elsewhere, the methods of *dilatatio* overlap and intersect with one another as the author develops the content of the sermon.

I suggest that none of this is just for play – although it is playful. These methods of *dilatatio* are the means by which a medieval preacher can, if he is capable, craft an intellectually sophisticated sermon with a serious theological point in such a way that it will be both compelling and memorable to his audience. In Thomas's Sermon 18 (*Germinet terra*), the serious theological point has to do with the interesting (and somewhat ironic) relationship between the virginity of Mary and her ultimate fecundity: the green plant will bring forth seed, the "seed" is Christ, and the "fruit-bearing tree" is the cross of Christ, the fruits of which are many. Yet, by his use of the imagery, Thomas has also made clear that Mary's "yes" to God was *made possible by* the grace of God, by the divine love that waters her "greenness" as rain nourishes a green plant.

Having chosen as his biblical *thema* a verse from the book of Genesis dealing with creation, Thomas also confirms in the minds of his listeners the idea that the divine Word who created us in the beginning is the same Word who creates us anew by means of his Incarnation, death on the Cross, and Resurrection from the dead. Preaching in this way does not involve "dumbing down" or "watering down" one's theology. It does, however, involve spurring interest by making beautiful and memorable rhetorical associations.

Granted, a preacher could just *make* these theological points straightforwardly about the fruits of Mary's virginity, her cooperation in Christ's salvific sacrifice on the Cross, and the prevenient grace and divine love that makes possible her cooperation with the God's salvific act in the dry categories of the theological textbook without any of Thomas's metaphorical associations. Or he could choose, as Thomas has done here, to discuss Mary's virginity and the divine love that makes its "fruit" possible in relation to the greenness of plants and the fecundity of creation itself. The question is, which of the two is more likely to remain memorable for most audiences?

For any reader who doubts that medieval preachers could keep up this sort of division and development of a Bible verse, sermon after sermon, for an entire year or more, there is no better example than Bonaventure's *Sunday Sermons*. In that volume, the reader will find fifty sermons total for the entire liturgical year, each of which fits the basic *sermon modernus* pattern we have outlined earlier. The unavoidable conclusion is that this was simply the way medieval preachers of the thirteenth century preached. They developed the art and the style of the "modern sermon" until it became second nature to them. As we will see, one of the ways they learned the style and applied it was through the writing of prologues, both for their courses and for commentaries on the books of the Bible and for their commentaries on the *Sentences* of Peter Lombard.[38]

---

[38] Whether this complexity could possibly have characterized popular preaching as well as university preaching is a question I will not address here. However, see d'Avray, *Preaching*, 193: "So far as sermon form or technique is concerned, [the thesis that university preaching and popular preaching are fundamentally different] is not the conclusion of recent writers." So too Richard and Mary Rouse, *Preachers, Florilegia and Sermons: Studies on the Manipulus florum of Thomas of Ireland* (Toronto: Pontifical Institute of Mediaeval Studies, 1979), 84: "the type of sermon evolved at the University of Paris through the course of the thirteenth century was an admirable instrument for routine preaching to laymen." Whether further scholarship brings this conclusion into question is largely immaterial to our current concerns, since the prologues we will be examining were crafted with a university audience in mind.

3

Principia and the *Sermo Modernus*

IN THE modern world, we don't assume that sermons and book prologues should be done in the same style, or that book prologues and introductory lectures should share the same style, let alone that either of these should be written as sermons. Yet the *sermo modernus* style we have just described was used in all three types of *principia* distinguished in Chapter 2: introductory lectures, book prologues, and inception addresses. What order of development resulted in all three making use of the same style is unknown to us. Whether masters first developed a new method of introducing students to a book that would help them keep its sections in memory and then later found it useful for sermons, or whether a style of preaching was incorporated into the methodology of the classroom, we do not know. What we do know is that by the time Thomas and Bonaventure incepted as masters at Paris in 1256 and 1254 respectively,[1] the *sermo modernus* style was accepted as the default mode for delivering *principia* of any type, written or oral, and no one seems to have questioned the practice.

There is no need for our present purposes to attempt to trace the origins and development of the *sermo modernus* style from its origins in the late twelfth century to its embryonic stages in the early thirteenth century up to its more highly developed stages in the mid to late thirteenth century.[2] The earliest records we have of masters who incepted at Paris reveal

---

[1] The date of Bonaventure's inception is disputed. For a nice review of the arguments, see Jay M. Hammond, "Dating Bonaventure's Inception as Regent Master," *Franciscan Studies* 67 (2009): 179–226.

[2] To get a sense of the development, see the descriptions in the following essays, all of which can be found in the invaluable volume edited by Beverly Kienzle, *The Sermon*, Typologie des sources du Moyen Age occidental, Fasc. 81–83 (Turnhout: Brepols, 2000). Compare (a) Thomas N. Hall, "The Early Medieval Sermon," 203–269; (b) Mark Zier, "Sermons of the Twelfth Century Schoolmasters and Canons," 325–362, and (c) Nicole Bériou, "Les Sermons Latin après 1200," 363–447. For a good sense of the changes in the late twelfth century, see in particular, Zier, "Twelfth Century Schoolmasters," 340–344. For a good comparison of original sermon material, I would also suggest a comparison of Gregory the Great's *Homilia XXIX in Evangelia* (Kienzle, 248–265), delivered in AD 593 – also available in English translation in *Gregory the Great: Forty Gospel Homilies*, trans.

that their inception *principia* addresses were always delivered as sermons and always crafted in the *sermo modernus* style. This is not to say there was no development over the course of the thirteenth century. Quite the contrary, there was. It is merely that the art of the *principia* address developed in tandem with the developments in the *sermo modernus* style. As the *sermo modernus* style became more formalized and refined, so did prologues and *principia* addresses.³

How much development had there been? In a superb, unpublished dissertation, Nancy Spatz lists the eleven medieval masters of theology at Paris whose inception addresses had been discovered by the time she finished her work.⁴ They are (with the date of each master's inception):

Stephen Langton (1180)
Odo of Châteauroux (1230)
John of La Rochelle (1238)
Albert the Great (1245)
Guy of Aumone (1256)
Thomas Aquinas (1257)
Galdaricus (1258)
Nicholas of Pressoir (1273)
Henry of Ghent (1275)
Matthew of Aquasparta (1276)
Stephen of Besançon (1286)

Some thirteen years after Spatz's dissertation, Catholic University of America scholar Joshua Benson discovered Bonaventure's inaugural *principium*, bringing the total to twelve.⁵

David Hurst (Collegeville, MN: Cistercian Publications, 1990), 226–235 – with Peter Comestor's *Sermo LV primus de adventu domini* (Kienzle, 353–362), delivered in the late twelfth century, with any of Thomas or Bonaventure's "academic," sermons; for which, see either *Thomas Aquinas: The Academic Sermons*, trans. Mark-Robin Hoogland (Washington, DC: Catholic University of America Press, 2010) or *The Sunday Sermons of St. Bonaventure*, tr. Timothy J. Johnson, Works of St. Bonaventure 12 (St. Bonaventure, NY: Franciscan Institute Publications, 2008). For another good comparison, see J. P. Bonnes, "Un des plus grands prédicateurs du XIIe siècle: Geoffrey du Louroux, dit Geoffrey Babion," *Revue bénédictine* 56 (1945–1946): 174–215, who juxtaposes two sermons based on the same *thema* verse – Psalm 81:1, *Deus stetit in synagoga deorum, in medio autem deos diidicat* – the first composed by Geoffrey Babion (d. 1158) and the second by Peter Comestor (d. ca. 1179).

³ For more on the developments in the *sermo modernus* style in the thirteenth century, see Richard and Mary Rouse, *Preachers, Florilegia and Sermons: Studies on the Manipulus florum of Thomas of Ireland* (Toronto: Pontifical Institute of Mediaeval Studies, 1979), 65–90. See also David d'Avray, *The Preaching of the Friars: Sermons Diffused from Paris before 1300* (Oxford: Oxford University Press, 1985), esp. 163–203. For an interesting textual analysis, one might compare the series of sermons for the academic year 1230–1231 at Paris, published in M.-M. Davy, *Les sermons universitaires parisiens de 1230-32: contribution à l'histoire de la prédication médiévale*, Études de philosophie médiévale, 15 (Paris, J. Vrin, 1931) with a similar collection of 216 sermons preached during the academic year 1272–1273 in *Bib. Nationale* MS lat 16461.

⁴ Nancy Spatz, *Principia: A Study and Edition of Inception Speeches Delivered Before the Faculty of Theology at the University of Paris, ca. 1180–1286* (PhD diss., Cornell University 1992), 77–78.

⁵ See esp. Joshua Benson, "Bonaventure's Inaugural Sermon at Paris," *Collectanea Franciscana* 82 (2012): 517–562.

Principia *and the* Sermo Modernus

These are not all the masters who incepted at Paris, merely the ones for whom *principium* addresses have been discovered and identified. They provide us with a valuable resource nonetheless.

To get a sense of the development over the course of the thirteenth century, it will be instructive to compare the earliest *principium* address we possess, that of Stephen Langton who incepted in 1180, with the one by Odo of Châteauroux from 1230, and both of these with another inception address (probably a *resumptio*[6]) delivered in 1245 by Thomas's teacher, Albert the Great.[7] Our concern is primarily to note the remarkable developments in the *sermo modernus* style from Langton to Odo to Albert, a space of only sixty-five years or roughly two generations.

Stephen Langton (1180): Rudimentary Beginnings

Stephen Langton begins his *principium* not with a biblical verse per se, but with a summary of verses from Exodus 12:34 and 39 and Exodus 16:4.[8]

> We read that the sons of Israel when they set forth from Egypt bore dough (*farinam conspersam*) tied in their cloaks on their shoulders (cf. Ex 12:34), from which they made hearth cakes (*panes sucinericios*; cf. Ex 12:39). Then in the desert they received manna from heaven (*manna celeste*; cf. Ex 16:4). Nevertheless when they arrived in the land of promise, they ate of the fruit of that region.[9]

So also for us, adds Stephen, before we come into the land of promise and eat of the fruit of that land, we must be fed by a twofold spiritual food: first, by the wheat born out of Egypt, and second, by the manna from heaven. This twofold distinction will provide the structure for much of the sermon that follows. The topics of the first half he associates with "the wheat born out of Egypt" while those in the second half he associates with "the manna from

---

[6] This address might be Albert's *principium*, but Nancy Spatz argues that it is Albert's *resumptio* precisely because it contains a *divisio textus* of the books of the Bible. See Spatz, *Principia*, 65–66. Whether it is a *principium* address or not is irrelevant to our present comparison, however, since masters employed the *sermo modernus* style in both their *principium* and *resumptio* addresses.

[7] See in particular M.-M Davy, *Les sermons universitaires parisiens de 1230-32* for the sermons themselves, and Bériou, "Les sermons latins," in Kienzle, *The Sermon*, 394–402 for an analysis that puts these developments in perspective.

[8] For the text of Stephen's *principium*, see Phyllis B. Roberts, *Studies in the Sermons of Stephen Langton* (Toronto: Pontifical Institute of Mediaeval Studies, 1968), 224–237. It also appears in Roberts's *Selected Sermons of Stephen Langton* (Toronto: Pontifical Institute of Mediaeval Studies, 1980), 17–34.

[9] Stephen has not quoted directly from any of the texts to which he is referring. Exodus 12:34 reads: "The people therefore took dough before it was leavened; and tying it in their cloaks, put it on their shoulders" (*populus conspersam farinam antequam fermentaretur: et ligans in palliis, posuit super humeros suos*). Ex 12:39 adds: "And they baked the meal, which a little before they had brought out of Egypt in dough: and they made hearth cakes unleavened" (*Coxeruntque farinam, quam dudum de AEgypto conspersam tulerant : et fecerunt subcinericios panes azymos*). Several chapters later, then, in Ex 16:4, we find: "And the Lord said to Moses: Behold I will rain bread from heaven for you" (*Dixit autem Dominus ad Moysen: Ecce ego pluam vobis panes de caelo*). Stephen takes just a phrase from each. Indeed, he may not be quoting at all, merely summarizing from memory.

heaven." In both instances, however, the topics Stephen discusses are only distantly related to the biblical images he uses to suggest them.

His discussion of the "wheat born out of Egypt," for example, begins: "As temporal things are worthless to us, 'let the wheat be born away from Egypt,' that is, let the deceits of the world be shattered." In what follows, he transitions somewhat awkwardly from a discussion of the wheat (in context, it is unleavened dough) to a discussion of the plagues of Egypt. "So that we may know from which grains we ought to collect this wheat," says Stephen, "let us recall to memory the plagues of Egypt so that the calamities of the mortal life may be revealed by the character of the assault" posed by each plague. The notion here is that recalling the ten plagues will help us "gather the right wheat," just as after the ten plagues the Israelites gathered the grain God commanded for their journey into the wilderness.

This is not the place to review each of the ten "plagues" and how each discloses for Stephen another "calamity of the mortal life," but to illustrate his method, consider his treatment of the "eighth plague," the plague of the locusts that consume all the vegetation in the land (cf. Ex 10:12). "The consuming locusts are like the stroking caresses of adulation," claims Stephen. "For the touch of the adulator is well compared to locusts: just as locusts grow torpid in a time of cold, but in heat leap about swiftly, so the adulator in a time of adversity is closed in upon himself in silence, but in a time of prosperity impudently exercises himself." "Shattering adversity does not diminish the good," says Stephen, but "stroking adulation dies away" in times of adversity. Hence this is the sort of "plague" we must avoid when we are "gathering together grains" to roll into our unleavened dough for our journey into the wilderness. The association of locusts with "stroking caresses" image may seem odd, but it is memorable, which is the point.

Having finished with the "ten plagues" (the ten possible calamities of human life) with which he associated the "wheat born away from Egypt," he next turns to his consideration of the manna from heaven. This manna, the "bread from heaven," is the Sacred Scripture given for man's spiritual nourishment by God. The image of the manna gathered in the wilderness gives Stephen several pages in which to discuss topics such as how and in what ways the manna was to be gathered, how it was spread over the whole earth like hoar-frost, how it provided more for those who needed more and less for those who needed less, and how after the sun got hot, it melted. Each image suggests another characteristic of the Sacred Scriptures. The fact that the manna provided more for those who needed more and less for those who needed less, for example, corresponds to the fact that the Scriptures provide both spiritual meanings for the learned and simpler meanings for the unlearned.

In the last section of the *principium*, Stephen departs from the twofold structure he set out at the beginning of "wheat born out of Egypt" and "manna from heaven in the wilderness" in order to discuss the five qualities he believes are needed to teach and to study: cleanness of life, simplicity of heart, attention of mind, humility, and mildness.

Although this is an engaging *principium* address that touches upon many of the same themes that will appear in the *principia* of later masters, it does not yet exhibit all the characteristic elements of the *sermo modernus* style. Later masters will quote an opening biblical verse and then divide it into parts, dilating on each one separately, whereas Stephen merely paraphrases and then selects two images suggested by this paraphrase around which to structure his sermon. His practice of associating his theological points with biblical imagery is similar but not identical to the *sermo modernus* style, and the sermon lacks the full range of methods of *divisio* and *dilatatio* that later, thirteenth-century preachers will employ. In short, the methods of the *sermo modernus* style are not as formal or as well developed as they would become in later decades.

Odo of Châtearoux (1230): Still Lacking a Clear Structure

Stephen's *principium* was delivered in 1180, Odo of Châtearoux's in 1230.[10] The changes that occurred in that half century are substantial. Odo begins his *principium* with a verse from Ezekiel 10.2: *Ingredere in medio rotarum quae sunt subtus cherubim, et imple manum tuam prunis ignis quae sunt inter cherubim, et effunde super civitatem* ("Go in between the wheels that are under the cherubim and fill your hand with the coals of fire that are between the cherubim, and pour them out upon the city"). Whereas Stephen Langton had used his opening biblical citation simply as a source for imagery and not as a structuring device, Odo starts out in the manner that will later become standard, making a *divisio* of his opening *thema* into two parts. "In these words," says Odo, "spiritually understood, there are prescribed for us two forms: namely the forms of achieving to the height of the position of authority in theology or as a master; and the forms of teaching after reaching it." The first of these – namely, how one ought to undertake becoming a master – is signified by the words: "Go in between the wheels that are under the cherubim and fill your hand with the coals of fire that are between the cherubim," while the second of these – the form of teaching and reading that a person ought to follow once he has become a master – is signified by the second part of the opening verse: "and pour them out upon the city."

How does one become a master? One must "Go in between the wheels." But before you can "go in" (*ingredere*), you have to subject yourself to the burden and be cleansed of the impureness of the world, a cleansing signified by the man "clothed in linen" who is mentioned earlier in Ezekiel 10:2, a verse that begins: "And he [the Lord] spoke to the man that was clothed with linen and said: 'Go in between the wheels that are under the cherubim and fill your hand with the coals of fire that are between the cherubim, and pour them out upon the city.'" Note here how Odo's *principium* presupposes on the part of the listener an advanced knowledge and memory of the Scriptures sufficient to remember the words in Ezekiel 10:2 immediately preceding those he has chosen for his *thema* verse. The listeners must remember that the Lord says these words about going "in between the wheels" to a man "clothed with linen." Those who fail to make this connection quickly and naturally would have trouble understanding why Odo transitions into a long string of references to Scriptural passages containing the word "linen."[11]

---

[10] The text of Odo's *principium* is unedited, but a transcription of an early, badly damaged manuscript (Paris, B.N. lat. 15948) appears in Spatz, *Principia*, 221–231.

[11] I had this confusion at first. Note that by "advanced knowledge of the Scriptures," I do not mean that all of Odo's listeners would have *read* the biblical text exhaustively. See my comment in Chapter 2 about cultures which are "literary" but not highly "literate" or "bookish." Odo's audience would have consisted of university scholars and students, many of whom would have known biblical passages from chanting them or hearing them read during meals.

Following an extended discussion of the purifications needed to become a master in theology – suggested for the most part by associations with linen or by things suggested by other scriptural texts that contain the word "linen" – Odo concludes:

> Truly therefore, the one who takes upon his shoulder the burden of the master in the theological faculty ought to be clothed in linen as another Samuel, 'girded with a linen Ephod' [1 Samuel 2:18]. And then it will be able to be said to him: "Go in between the wheels that are under the cherubim" [Ezekiel 10:2]; otherwise, he will not be worthy to go in.

Using the word "linen" in this way to link or "chain" biblical authorities together because they all use that word is a characteristic of the more developed *sermo modernus* style. Stephen Langton used the images of "wheat" and "manna" from Exodus, but he did not "chain" together biblical authorities around a single word in the way Odo does here with "linen," something undoubtedly made easier by lists of biblical *distinctiones* such as Peter Cantor's *Summa Abel*.[12]

In Odo's *principium*, the words in Ezekiel 10:2 allow him to move rapidly from associations related to "going between" the wheels of the chariot to associations with "linen" and quickly back again. Returning to the image of the chariot wheels allows Odo to pose the rhetorical question: "What are these wheels if not the fourfold exposition of the Scriptures?" which involves him in a series of associations with the wheels of four chariots and the horses that pull those chariots. So, for example, the third chariot represents the anagogical understanding of the Scriptures, which "elevates human cognition to the contemplation of eternal things." This is the fiery chariot, says Odo, "by which Elijah was taken up into heaven" [2 Kgs 2:11]. The wheels of the chariot are faith, the gifts of knowledge, understanding, and wisdom; the horses drawing the chariot are prayer (*oratio*), meditation (*meditatio*), and affection (*affectioi*); and the ecstasy of the driver is divine inspiration.

After this extended discussion of the four senses suggested by the four chariots and their wheels, which the man in clean linen is meant to "go into," we get a further discussion of what Odo thinks it means to "go in" (*ingredere*) between the wheels rather than merely circle about them, which brings us finally, in line 223 out of 259 lines total, to the meaning associated with the wheels being "under the cherubim (*subter cherubym*) – namely, that our knowledge of heavenly things is not complete – and to an extended discussion of the meaning of the "coals of fire," which he says are "the words of the Lord and the testimonies of the Scriptures," and in what way these (that is, the words of the Scriptures) are meant to make us "on fire."

Having finished all this, Odo makes a brief peroration starting at line 251, in which he announces:

> But if the things we have said above are true, as indeed they are true, then what sort of audacious foolishness have I that I would dare to take unto myself so grave an office? But I have faith in him who is worthy to open the book and break open its seals through whom,

---

[12] See my discussion of these lists of *distinctiones* in Chapter 1; also Richard and Mary Rouse, "Biblical 'Distinctiones' in the Thirteenth Century," *Archives d'histoire doctrinale et littéraire du moyen age* 41 (1974): 27–37.

if any will enter in, he will find pasture, by whose face the fire is spread and the coals are set on fire. In his holy name and undivided Trinity, Father, Son, and Holy Spirit, I am set free for this office.

And with that, he is done – at least for the time being.

The attentive reader may have noticed that Odo never got to the second part of his opening *divisio*: the words "and pour them out upon the city." Recall that "the way in which one ought to undertake becoming a master" was associated with the words "Go in between the wheels that are under the cherubim and fill your hand with the coals of fire that are between the cherubim." Odo managed to dilate upon the words "in between," "the wheels," "under the cherubim," and "the coals of fire" and was able to add a section on another word, "linen," that appeared earlier in the same verse. But Odo never got to the second subject he proposed in his opening *divisio*: "the form of teaching and reading a person ought to follow once he has become a master," which he associated with words "and pour them out upon the city." Did he just run out of time? This is possible, but not likely.

What is more likely is that we have Odo's *principium in aula* address but are still lacking his *resumptio* address containing the continuation of his dilation of the biblical verse from Ezekiel 10:2, which, according to Odo's original plan, was to be associated with the forms of teaching (*forma docendi*) and reading (*legendi*) that ought to be followed. These final two topics appear well-suited to introducing a discussion of either (a) the parts of Scripture (as we find in Thomas's *principium*) or (b) a description of the hierarchy of the other disciplines showing how they lead to and culminate in the Scriptures (as Bonaventure did in his *resumptio*).[13] Given that Odo's *principium in aula* dealt with the personal moral and spiritual preparation needed to read and interpret the Scriptures, and given that it included a discussion of the various senses of Scripture, he had certainly prepared the way for a commendation of the Scriptures and its various parts in his *resumptio*. But since we don't have (or at least haven't yet identified among the many manuscripts waiting to be catalogued) Odo's *resumptio* address, we just don't know.

What we can say with some certainty about Odo's *principium* is that, while it exhibits more characteristics of the *sermo modernus* than were evident in Stephen Langton's *principium*, it still does not have all the elements of the style that we will find in later years. Although in Odo's *principium* we have a clear statement of the biblical *thema* at the outset rather than a mere paraphrase (as in Langton's), and though Odo structures his address according to this *divisio*, what Odo does *not* do as extensively as later masters is to further subdivide the opening biblical verse into distinct subsections around which he might then build up the content of his sermon.

So, for example, if Odo's *principium* had been given in later years, we might have expected him, after dividing his opening biblical verse from Ezekiel 10:2 into two basic parts, to further sub-divide the first part into four sub-divisions, such as: "Go in" (*ingredere*) / "in the middle of the wheels" (*in medio rotarum*) / "which are under the cherubim" (*quae sunt subtus cherubim*) / "and fill your hand with the coals of fire that are between the cherubim" (*et imple manum tuam prunis ignis quae sunt inter cherubim*). This series of subdivisions would have allowed Odo to take up roughly the same topics he does in his current *principium*

---

[13] See my discussion in Chapter 11.

address: (1) what it means to "go in" between the wheels rather than merely circulate around them; (2) the four chariots as the four senses of Scripture; (3) the wheels "under the cherubim" which signify that our knowledge of heavenly things is not complete; and (4) a discussion of the "coals of fire," which are "the words of the Lord and the testimonies of the Scriptures," and the ways in which they can make us "on fire."

Odo's *principium* differs from the more developed style of later masters in that he does not make the divisions and structure of his text clear with his first *divisio* of the *thema*. Michèle Mulcahey has pointed out, "The preacher of a *sermo modernus* habitually declared in advance precisely how he intended to divide his text, as well as what its members were going to be. This announcement of the skeleton of the sermon at the outset ... is very much the signature of the thirteenth- or fourteenth-century preacher."[14] Neither Stephen Lanagton's nor Odo's opening *thema* verse provides the sort of rigorous order and structure that will become customary among later preachers.

Albert the Great (1245): The Style Fully Realized

The fifty years between Stephen Langton's *principium* and Odo of Châtearoux's saw the emergence of a more formal structure with more clearly defined divisions. So too, if we compare Odo's *principium* with Albert's *resumptio* address in 1245 a mere fifteen years later, we find an even more pronounced development.[15]

Albert began, as had become customary by this time, by stating his *thema*, which was from Ecclesiasticus (Sirach) 24.33: "Moses commanded a law in the precepts of justice, and an inheritance to the house of Jacob, and the promises to Israel" (*Legem mandavit nobis Moyses in praeceptis iustitiarum et hereditatem domui Iacob et Israel promissiones*). Then Albert did something we have seen no earlier master do: he gives something like a *prothema*, an introductory section to the sermon. Properly speaking, a *prothema* would have another biblical *thema* verse (or, more accurately, a *prothema* verse) whose divisions would help structure the preacher's introductory comments in the *prothema*. Instead, Albert began with a series of introductory comments about the basic terms in his opening biblical *thema* from Ecclesiasticus, such as "law" and "justice." "Law," he says, are precepts of justice, and "justice" is that by which "sins are avoided and God is served by means of the virtues." He then associates these two functions of justice – avoiding sin and serving God – with the verse in Psalm 36(37):27, where it says "Decline from evil and do good" (*declina a malo, et fac bonum*).[16] If Albert's structure were more formal, this Psalm verse could have served as his *prothema* verse. At the time of Moses, says Albert, those who observed the law were given blessings; those who did not were showered with maledictions; the repentant were restored

---

[14] Mulcahey, *First the Bow is Bent*, 405.

[15] The Latin text can be found as "Principium Biblicum Alberti Magni," edited by Albert Fries, CSSR, in *Studia Albertina: Festschrift für Bernhard Geyer zum 70. Geburtstage*, ed. Heinrich Ostlender, Beiträge zur Geschichte der Philosophie und theologie des Mittelalters, Suppl. 4 (Münster Weste: Aschendorffsche Verlag, 1952), 128–147. Fries discusses the text in "Eine Vorlesung Alberts des Grossen über den biblischen Kanon," *Divus Thomas* 28 (1950): 194–213.

[16] Compare this Psalm verse with Thomas's famous statement in ST I–II, q. 94, a. 2 about the law being directed to "doing good and avoiding evil."

to the inheritance of their fathers. A biblical gloss on the text suggests to Albert that "all this should be understood finally as referring to Christ, who is as it were the end and completion of the law and who truly fulfills the 'promises to Israel.'"[17]

After this brief series of introductory comments,[18] Albert finally announces the division of his opening biblical *thema* from Ecclesiasticus: "Briefly, therefore, in these words, three things are contained, namely the author of the law *in ministerio* where it says 'Moses'; the mode of the law where it says 'commanded for us,' and the contents of the law where it says 'in the precepts of justice.'" This is the standard way of beginning a sermon in the developed *sermo modernus* style. The structure is made plain by announcement of the *divisio* of the opening biblical *thema* into its various parts, each of which is then developed (dilated) in turn.[19]

First, as to the author of the law "as to its minister" (*in ministerio*), this was Moses, says Albert (as his *thema* verse indicates), but the ultimate author of the law "in authority" (*in auctoritate*) is God alone, who gives the law not for his own utility, but for all.

Second, the mode (*modus*) of the law – or what we might describe as the "manner by which" the law operates – is associated with the words "he commanded," for one commands an inferior and those who are absent. The Scriptures contain both "commands for inferiors," as in the books in which we find precepts of justice, and "promises for future generations" to come.

The contents of the law, finally, are associated with the words: "in the precepts of justice and, an inheritance to the house of Jacob, and the promises to Israel." Why such a long phrase for the third *divisio*? Because there are three things in the law, according to Albert: precepts of justice that lead to merit (*praecepta iustitiarum ad meritum*), a promised inheritance as a reward (*hereditas promissa ad praemium*), and the promises concerning redemption by Christ in the signification of the law (*promissiones de Christo redimente in legis significationibus*). The first of these – namely, the precepts of justice – are contained in the Pentateuch, the Wisdom books, the Psalms, and the Prophets. The second element related to the law, "a promised inheritance as a reward," is communicated through the historical books of the Old Testament. And the third element, "the promises concerning redemption by Christ in the signification of the law" – these are contained in the New Testament.[20]

---

[17] One might compare these remarks with Thomas's discussion of the Old Law and its fulfillment in the New Law in ST I–II, qq. 98–105.

[18] Let me repeat: I am not claiming that these prefatory comments amount to a true *prothema*. The results are tantalizing similar in certain respects – the preacher makes an immediate detour, after which he returns to re-state his opening *thema* verse – but Albert's comments do not have the finished style of an actual *prothema*. Richard and Mary Rouse are critical of M.-M. Davy's edition of the collection of sermons given at Paris in 1230–1231 on precisely these grounds: for attributing *prothemata* to sermons that don't (in their view) have them. For their critique, see Rouse, *Preachers*, esp. 72–73. I wish to leave the argument over what constitutes a true *prothema* to others.

[19] See my discussion in *Reading the Sermons of Aquinas*, chapter 3, "*Divisio*: Approaches to Dividing the Opening *Thema*," 49–113. Better yet, glance at any of the sermons in Thomas Aquinas, *The Academic Sermons* or *The Sunday Sermons of St. Bonaventure*.

[20] I have translated the Latin *promissiones de Christo redimente in legis significationibus* very literally as "the promises concerning redemption by Christ in the signification of the law." The sense of the phrase, I take it, refers to the promises concerning the redeeming of Christ which were promised, that is "signified," in the law, the prophets, the historical books, and the Psalms.

With this, Albert was off and running on his (very long and elaborate) *divisio textus* of the books of the Bible.

Unlike some *resumptio* addresses, the transition between the first section of the address and the second *divisio textus* section is seamless; there is no odd break between the two. Albert was able to use his opening biblical *thema* to introduce the divisions with which he began his analysis of the biblical books. Even Thomas did not accomplish such a seamless transition. As we will see, Thomas finishes the dilation of his opening biblical *thema* from Baruch 4:1, "This is the book of the commandments of God, and the law that is forever. All that keep it shall come to life . . .," with a discussion of the three sorts of "life" to which the Scriptures lead us: the life of grace, the life of justice in works, and the life of glory. Thomas signals the transition to his *divisio textus* simply by saying: "Sacred Scripture leads us to this life in two ways, by commanding and by helping." This twofold division sets up a distinction between "law" and "grace," which corresponds to the division between the books of the Old Testament and those of the New. Note that the twofold division in the Scriptures is suggested here, however, only by one word, "life," and not by a division within the opening biblical *thema*, as in Albert's *principium*.

Albert's sermon proceeds in a more structured fashion than those of the earlier masters, and he associates the parts of the sermon much more clearly with the individual words and phrases from the opening biblical *thema*. Thomas's *principium* address twelve years later will be even more formally structured. Yet, as we have seen, this new style did not spring up overnight. It had long been in the works, with preachers refining the practice over the previous decades. By the time Thomas incepted as a master at Paris, the basic forms were in place.

PART TWO

Thomas Aquinas
The Logician Who Learned to Preach

4

Rigans Montes
Thomas's Inception **Principium**

As I mentioned in the Introduction, I have chosen to treat Thomas and Bonaventure's inception addresses first before considering their earlier and later works. There are several reasons for beginning with each master's inception addresses and not with earlier or later works. First, each man's inception addresses were delivered to a similar audience and were written according to the same University regulations. It is revealing to see how the two men approached the same assignment in different ways. Second, the master's *principium* marks a definite beginning to each man's career. However good or ill their earlier student efforts might have been, when they were incepted, the educational development of the two masters should have been equal. Both had been through the required two years as a *cursor biblicus* and four as *baccalarius sententiarum*, and both were judged worthy by their superiors for taking on the duties of a master. Shortly after each man was incepted, however, their careers veered off in very different directions: Bonaventure became the master general of the Franciscan order but remained in Paris; Thomas remained teaching as a master of theology but left Paris for other assignments after only three years. The inception addresses of the two masters constitute the last point at which their educational development remained similar enough that the effort to compare their efforts is meaningful.

I have also chosen to examine Thomas's *principium in aula* and *resumptio* addresses before considering Bonaventure's even though Bonaventure likely incepted two years earlier than Thomas for reasons that I discussed in the Introduction to this volume. Thomas's inception addresses were shorter, simpler, and adhered to the University of Paris regulations more closely.

First, according to University regulations, although the *principium* address was one of the high points in the inception ceremony of a new master, it was supposed to be delivered "briefly" (*breve*) and "quickly terminated" (*celeriter terminato*).[1] Brother Thomas's *principium*

---

[1] Cf. James Weisheipl, *Friar Thomas d'Aquino: His Life, Thought, and Works* (Washington, DC: The Catholic University of America Press, 1983), 99. Fr. Weisheipl is quoting from the earliest account we have of the inception ceremony "secundum usum Parisienem," which is contained in a Bologna

was fairly brief, requiring maybe ten minutes to read; Brother Bonaventure's was much longer, requiring forty minutes or more.²

Second, the University statutes called for a "commendation and partition of sacred Scripture" (*Scripture sacre commendationem et particionem*).³ Thomas did what most masters seem to have done in their *resumptio* addresses, namely provide a *divisio textus* of the books of the Bible.⁴ But if Joshua Benson is right in identifying an early version of the *De reductione artium ad theologiam* as Bonaventure's *resumptio*, then Bonaventure seems to have gone his own way. Rather than providing a *divisio* of the books of the Bible, he chose instead to discuss how all the disciplines work together to help foster the understanding needed for the interpretation of sacred Scripture.⁵ Both approaches fit the bill as "commendations" of the sacred Scriptures, but Thomas's choice was more in accord with the stipulation that the master provide a *particionem* of the sacred Scriptures.

The Circumstances and Origins of Thomas's *Principium*

The *thema* verse on which Thomas based his *principium* was taken from Psalm 103 (104):13: *Rigans montes de superioribus suis; de fructu operum tuorum satiabitur terra* ("From your lofty abode, you water the mountains; the earth is sated with the fruit of your works").⁶ Although the manuscripts of Thomas's inception *principium* address and *resumptio* were not discovered until the late nineteenth century,⁷ scholars have known since Thomas's death which *thema* verse he used because the story about it was legendary.

As we have noted already, Thomas and his Dominican confreres faced a great deal of opposition at Paris from the secular masters in the spring of 1256 when Thomas was

---

manuscript published in *Chartularium Universitatis Parisiensis*, ed. H. Denifle, O.P., and E. Chatelian, vol. 2 (Paris: 1891), no. 1188, 691–695. See esp. 693–694. This passage can be found in the last line of 693.

² For the Latin text of Bonaventure's *principium*, see Joshua Benson, "Bonaventure's Inaugural Sermon at Paris," *Collectanea Franciscana* 82 (2012), 517–562. The actual text of Bonaventure's *principium* is fifteen pages in length, from p. 537 to 552. Thomas's *principium* in the same font would run about four pages.

³ *Chartularium*, vol. 2, no. 1188, 694. Note that this is the requirement for *biblici*, not *baccalarii*.

⁴ For an argument and overview of the manuscript evidence suggesting that the *principium* and *resumptio* were separate events within the inception ceremony, see Nancy Spatz, *Principia: A Study and Edition of Inception Speeches Delivered Before the Faculty of Theology at the University of Paris, ca. 1180–1286* (PhD diss., Cornell University, 1992), esp. 55–65.

⁵ See Joshua Benson, "Bonaventure's Inaugural Sermon at Paris," *Collectanea Franciscana* 82 (2012): 517–562.

⁶ This translation is my own. Other English translations appear in quotations from other authors in the following pages. Some of them translate the first clause with some version of "You water the hills from your upper rooms." I chose to translate the verse this way because "rooms" is not in Thomas's Latin, and because "hills" seems too weak for *montes* and for the associations Thomas wishes to make with that word. "Lofty abode" may seem a bit lofty linguistically, but it preserves the sense of God's "rooms" without inserting the word. And it is a more colloquial expression than "From your places above."

⁷ The manuscript of two *principia* were discovered together in the late nineteenth century by Pietro Antonio Uccelli in the convent library at Santa Maria Novella in Florence (Florentine MS G. 4. 36) and were first published in 1912.

appointed regent master. The secular masters had forbidden their students to take courses with the Dominicans and Franciscans and had even attempted to have them excommunicated. It was only through the forceful intervention of Pope Alexander IV that the excommunication against the Dominicans was lifted and the order given that Thomas and Bonaventure both be admitted straightaway to the faculty. Thomas was chosen to take the chair designated for the Dominicans even though, at age thirty or thirty-one, he did not meet the University's requirement that masters were not to incept before age thirty-five.[8]

"Thomas was terribly upset," Fr. Weisheipl tells us in his biography of St. Thomas, basing his judgment on several contemporaneous sources. At first the young friar "tried to excuse himself on the grounds of insufficient age and learning," but his efforts were for naught. "Since obedience left him no escape," writes Fr. Weisheipl, "he had recourse as usual to prayer."[9] What happened next is attested to by an equally large number of contemporary sources.[10] "With tears," writes Thomas's medieval biographer Bernardo Gui, Thomas begged "for inspiration as to the theme he should choose for his inaugural lecture." Afterward he fell asleep and had a very clear dream, in which, according to Bernardo Gui:

> He seemed to see an old man, white haired and clothed in the Dominican habit, who came and said to him: "Brother Thomas, why are you praying and weeping?" "Because," answered Thomas, "they are making me take the degree of master, and I do not think I am fully competent. Moreover, I cannot think what theme to take for my inaugural lecture." To this the old man replied: "do not fear: God will help you to bear the burden of being a master. And as for the lecture, take this text, "Thou waterest the hills from thy upper rooms: the earth shall be filled with the fruit of thy works" [*Rigans montes de suprioribus suis; de fructu operum tuorum satiabitur terra*]. Then he vanished, and Thomas awoke and thanked God for having so quickly come to his aid.[11]

Among those attesting to the authenticity of the story – at least as far as its originating with Thomas himself – was Peter of Montesangiovanni, a monk at the Cistercian monastery of Fossanova, where Thomas fell ill and died on his way to the Council of Lyons. Peter

---

[8] The whole affair is described succinctly by Torrell, 50–51 and by Weisheipl at more length, 79–83. The discrepancy in Thomas' age, whether he was thirty-one or thirty-two, is due to disagreements over when he was born: 1225 or 1226. In his 1993 biography of St. Thomas, *Initiation à saint Thomas d'Aquin: Sa personne et son oeuvre* (Paris: Cerf, 1993), published in English translation as *Saint Thomas Aquinas, vol. 1. The Person and His Work* (Washington, DC: The Catholic University of America Press, 1996, 2005), Fr. Torrell suggested the date as 1224/1225. In his more recent, updated version of the biography, Father Torrell opts for a later date (1226). See *Initiation à saint Thomas d'Aquin: Sa personne et son* oeuvre (Paris: Cerf, 2015). Everyone agrees, however, Thomas was not yet thirty-five, the age required for inception as master, when he incepted. For a valuable resource on University life in general, see Mariken Teeuwen, *The Vocabulary of Intellectual Life in the Middle Ages* (Turnhout: Brepols, 2003).

[9] Weisheipl, *Friar Thomas*, 96.

[10] Cf. K. Foster, *The Life of Saint Thomas Aquinas*, 69. "The story has been transmitted by three different sources," Fr. Torrell tells us in his biography of St. Thomas, "all of which lead back to Thomas himself." See Torrell, *Saint Thomas*, 51.

[11] Quoted from Weisheipl, 96. Weisheipl's translation of the Psalm verse is different from mine, which I warned readers about earlier.

testified under oath during Thomas's canonization hearing that he heard Thomas tell this story to the then-prior of Fossanova at the request of his *socius*, Reginald, several days before his death. Jean-Pierre Torrell writes in his biography of Aquinas:

> According to the testimony of Peter of Montesangiovanni, a monk of Fossanova, at [Thomas's] canonization process, Thomas himself told this story to the prior of Fossanova in the presence and at the request of Reginald, several days before his death. Peter of Caputio, another witness at the process in Naples, reported that he had learned this fact when he was in the priory of Saint-Jacques, during the reading that was done to the friars at times of bleeding. He adds that all the friars in Paris were convinced that the *frater antiquus* who appeared had been none other than Saint Dominic himself. Except for this last detail, where the hagiographical process seems to be at work, the different stories agree, and historians have every reason to believe that we have here a personal confidence that goes back to Thomas himself.[12]

Modern readers may remain skeptical about whether the source of the verse was St. Dominic – St. Thomas never identified the man – but it is noteworthy what Thomas did *not* receive in the dream. He did not receive the subject matter or the points he should make. What came to Thomas in the dream was simply the mnemonic text – the *thema* verse – that will serve as a structuring device for the *principium*. Thus, if we were curious to know whether Thomas began his preparation for his sermons with the points he wanted to make and then searched the Bible for just the right mnemonic device, or whether he found the mnemonic device first and then allowed the words of the text to suggest the topics he would treat, the story of the dream and the fact that Thomas nearly always preached on some part of the lectionary reading assigned for the day suggests that he usually began with the *thema* verse.

This is interesting for many reasons, not the least of which is that the process is very *unlike* that of the ancient Greek orators, who crafted their orations *first* and only *later* associated the points with their mnemonic structuring device, such as the rooms in their house or the particular sights on a walk around the city. It would likely never have occurred to an ancient orator to imagine that he could *create* a speech just by taking his usual mnemonic walk around the house or the town. The topics of a prospective oration – a speech in the Senate, let us say, or a speech on behalf of a plaintiff in court – would have been entirely unrelated to the architectural elements and would have become associated with them only later when the orator was memorizing his speech.[13]

Thomas and his contemporaries, by contrast, began with the mnemonic device as a way of discovering and developing a topic. In the ancient world, the process of "finding" the points (or topics) for a speech was called *inventio;* choosing how to develop or arrange those points into a coherent and persuasive whole was called *dispositio* (arrangement); and each

---

[12] Torrell, *Saint Thomas*, 51.
[13] The primary classical sources for the art of memory include the *Rhetorica ad Herennium* (Bk III), Cicero's *De oratore* (Bk II, 350–360), and Quintilian's *Institutio Oratoria* (Bk XI). The classic description of how memory can be trained by associating the points one wishes to make with visual images of places can be found in Cicero's *De oratore*, Bk II, 351–354.

was distinct from the process of memorization, which came later.¹⁴ By the time Thomas was crafting his *principium*, the two processes had been united in a unique and important way, undoubtedly because the words of the biblical text were thought to possess a special fecundity that other sorts of mnemonic devices lacked. As I have argued in more detail elsewhere:

> Medieval preachers knew these five canons, as they had all studied their Quintillian, Cicero, and the *Rhetorica ad Herennium*. What the *sermo modernus* style offered them was a new method of *inventio* – that is, of discerning one's topic and one's approach to the topic. This was an *inventio* guided by the structure of, and indeed by the nature of the word in, the opening biblical *thema* verse. The words of the verse suggested the topics to be covered, and the order of those words would determine the *dispositio* – or as the medievals called it, the *divisio* – of the parts of the speech. The *sermo modernus* style became popular precisely because it provided not only a method of *inventio*, of finding a topic – and in this case, one keyed very purposefully to the scriptural reading for the day – but also a method of constructing and ordering the material of the sermon. The whole process, then, was designed to foster *memoria*, for the opening biblical verse functioned, as we have shown repeatedly, as an elaborate mnemonic device to help the listeners associate the topics covered with the words in the verse. The art of memory, then, was not only something that the preacher did for himself (indeed, medieval preachers rarely memorized their sermons). Rather, the arts of *memoria* were something the preacher used to help the congregation remember. This was, I would argue, a genuinely new development in the rhetorical arts, and at the center of this new sort of rhetoric stood the Christian Scriptures.¹⁵

Thomas experienced in a very dramatic way the truth of the promise Christ made when he told his disciples not to be anxious about what they should say when they were brought before the authorities, "for the Holy Spirit will teach you in that very hour what you ought to say" (Luke 12:12; cf. Mark 13:11; Matthew 10:19). People sometimes imagine that this process would be a divine dictation: that God would whisper in a person's ear the words he or she should say, like Cyrano whispering to young Christian what he should to say to Roxanne standing at her window. Thomas's experience was different. The first step was to remember the words God had *already given* in the Scriptures and to call to mind *just the right set of words* for the occasion. Once Thomas had the right key words, he could proceed from there, and the Spirit would teach him what to say, as if God's promise had been: "Do not be anxious what you are to say, Brother Thomas, for I will give you the right biblical verse as a *thema*, and from those words, you will be able to derive a clear set of points that will impress that unruly and unforgiving audience at Paris."¹⁶

---

¹⁴ The five canons of rhetoric, expressed in their most developed form in Quintillian's *Institutio Oratoria*, are *inventio* (invention), *dispositio* (arrangement), *elocutio* (style), *memoria* (memory), and *actio* (delivery).

¹⁵ R. Smith, *Reading the Sermons of Aquinas: A Beginner's Guide* (Steubenville, OH: Emmaus, 2016), 168–169.

¹⁶ It is more likely, however, that God would simply say: "Trust me."

In its original context, the passage from Psalm 103 Thomas uses to structure his praise of sacred Scripture is part of an encomium of praise to God as creator of the heavens and the earth, reminiscent of the creation account in Genesis 1.

> ⁵He set the earth on its foundations,
>   so that it should never be moved.
> ⁶ You covered it with the deep as with a garment;
>   the waters stood above the mountains.
> ⁷ At your rebuke they fled;
>   at the sound of your thunder they took to flight.
> ⁸ The mountains rose, the valleys sank down
>   to the place that you appointed for them.
> ⁹ You set a boundary that they may not pass,
>   so that they might not again cover the earth.
> ¹⁰ You make springs gush forth in the valleys;
>   they flow between the hills;
> ¹¹ they give drink to every beast of the field;
>   the wild donkeys quench their thirst.
> ¹² Beside them the birds of the heavens dwell;
>   they sing among the branches.
>   (Psalm 103:5–12)[17]

Nothing on a surface reading of this text would recommend its use in a sermon in praise of sacred Scripture. A more obvious passage would have been Isaiah 55:10–11:

> ¹⁰ For as the rain and the snow come down from heaven
>   and do not return there but water the earth,
> making it bring forth and sprout,
>   giving seed to the sower and bread to the eater,
> ¹¹ so shall my word be that goes out from my mouth;
>   it shall not return to me empty,
> but it shall accomplish that which I purpose,
>   and shall succeed in the thing for which I sent it.

Thomas uses a similar image of rain coming forth from the clouds and watering the ground to make it fertile in his *principium*, but he never refers to this passage from Isaiah among the many biblical references in his inception address. The passage revealed to Thomas in the dream had absolute priority.

Teaching Through Intermediaries

Thomas approached the task of translating the Psalm verse given to him in the dream into a full-fledged inception address by prefacing his comments with a passage from

---

[17] Unless otherwise noted, Scripture passages have been quoted from the English Standard Version.

Pseudo-Dionysius's *Celestial Hierarchy* 5: "It is the most sacred law of the divinity that things in the middle should be led to his most divine light by first things" (*per prima media adducantur ad sui divinissimam lucem*). Reversing the order, Thomas then states the principle this way: "The King and Lord of the heavens set down this law from all eternity that the gifts of his Providence should come to the lower through intermediaries."[18] There are, then, from the outset, two directions in view here: one that comes down from heaven through intermediaries and another that leads above from below. Either way, whether the gifts are coming to the lower through intermediaries or the lower are being led to the higher through intermediaries, the process is directed by "the most sacred law of" God's divine providence.

By choosing this text from Pseudo-Dionysius, Thomas reminds his listeners that God often comes to us indirectly, through *intermediaries*, and not always by direct divine inspiration. What are creation, the sacraments, the Church, and the Bible itself but *intermediaries* that mediate divine wisdom to us so we may be led, step by step, back to God? They are intermediaries, as was also the flesh of the Son of God incarnate. We come to know the incarnate God first *through the senses*. Thomas moves directly from Dionysius's statement on intermediaries to a passage from Augustine's *De trinitate* to bear witness to the idea that there is in nature a hierarchy of moving principles, all of them meant to come under the guidance and direction of the divine wisdom: "Just as the coarser and weaker are ruled in a certain order by more subtle, powerful ones, so all bodies (are ruled) by the rational spirit of life."[19]

Mining the metaphorical potential of his *thema* verse, Thomas draws an analogy between the physical and spiritual realms: just as the mountains are watered from above and send forth streams to water the valley below, so God sends forth his grace to masters so that they may teach His wisdom to their students.

> It is plain to the senses that from the highest clouds rain flows forth by which the mountains and rivers are refreshed and send themselves forth so that the satiated earth can bear fruit. Similarly, from the heights of divine wisdom the minds of the learned, represented by the mountains, are watered, by whose ministry the light of divine wisdom reached to the minds of those who listen.[20]

An Implicitly Incarnational Approach to Teaching and Learning

Setting his *principium* in this context allowed Thomas, in a sermon stipulated by regulation to be in praise of sacred Scripture, to address not only the dignity of the

---

[18] Thomas Aquinas, *Rigans Montes*, proemium. English: Ralph McInerny, tr., *Thomas Aquinas: Selected Writings* (New York: Penguin, 1998), 13–17. Latin: "Corpus Thomisticum," www.corpusthomisticum.org/otd.html

[19] Augustine, *De trinitate*, III:4.9: "quemadmodum igitur crassiora et infirmiora per corpora subtiliora et potentiora quodam ordine reguntur, ita omnia corpora per spiritum vitae rationale." The titulus for this chapter reads: "God Uses All Creatures as He Will, and Makes Visible Things for the Manifestation of Himself."

[20] *Rigans montes*, proemium.

Scriptures, but also the dignity with which the teachers and students of sacred doctrine were supposed to be imbued. Just as the rains come forth from above and water the mountains, and the streams flow downward into the rivers so the earth can be irrigated and made to bear fruit, so too divine wisdom comes down first to the "learned" – the Latin has *mentes doctorum*, "minds of the doctors," or "teachers" in the proper sense of *doctores*, which comes from the Latin *doceo*, "to teach" – and from them it flows down to the students. The rain that waters these mountains is the sacred teaching of the Scriptures. The teachers who have been refreshed by these sacred waters are then in turn to pour forth this wisdom on their students, as the mountains pour forth water onto the plains, irrigating them so they might bear much spiritual fruit.

Students do not learn directly from God, nor are they always able to learn from the Scriptures on their own without being taught to read and interpret the word-signs correctly. If students of the Scriptures are to be enabled to read and interpret these word-signs correctly, they must first come to a greater understanding of the things in the world, so that from our knowledge of these things, our minds may ascend by stages to a progressively fuller knowledge of the Creator. Indeed, the nature of the *principium* itself suggests the practice. From our knowledge about physical things – in this case mountains, flowing water, plains, and fruit-bearing plants – we come to know (under Thomas's tutelage as teacher) some important lessons about how we come to know about God.

There is, thus, an implicit incarnational mentality underlying Thomas's *principium*. The classic statement of the relationship between "signs" and "things" is found in Augustine's *De doctrina christiana*, who suggests that we know signs (and words for Augustine are a type of sign) by knowing the things these signs represent.[21] And yet we also learn from words. From the inspired words of sacred Scripture, we learn about the Word made flesh who teaches us in and through His Incarnation that the created realities of this world are "signs" that point us to the uncreated Word through whom "all things were made" and without whom "nothing was made that has been made" (John 1:3).[22] This "incarnational" approach allows Thomas later in his *principium* to propose Christ's dignity and humility as a model for both masters and students.

Using this same image of the mountains being watered from above, Thomas can remind the masters in his audience where the source of all true wisdom lies: in God as He has revealed Himself to us in His Word (Christ), and as we come to know Him in his word (the sacred Scriptures). Wisdom, he reminds them, is from above, not first and foremost from masters. Masters are called, like St. Paul, to "pass on what they themselves received" (1 Corinthians 15:3), not to imagine that they should set forth their own doctrines or pretend to possess their own wisdom. What this role as an *intermediary*, not an ultimate source, of

---

[21] See Augustine *De doctrina christiana*, esp. Bk 1.
[22] Note that Thomas's approach, utilizing Pseudo-Dionysius's *Celestial Hierarchy* to set up a discussion of intermediaries, allows him to discuss the dispositions that ought to characterize teachers and students. Bonaventure, by contrast, restricts himself to the praise of sacred Scripture. Bonaventure's discussion of the kind of education necessary to prepare students properly to read the Scriptures is reserved for his *resumptio*. It is also worth noting, however, that Bonaventure, by reputation less of an "Aristotelian" than Thomas, makes use of several passages from Aristotle right at the beginning of his *principium*, whereas Thomas never quotes Aristotle even once. Thomas's more thorough praise of Scripture will come in his *resumptio* address. Masters seem to have taken it as their charge not only to praise Scripture but also to address the dispositions with which they should be read.

Rigans Montes: *Thomas's Inception* Principium 87

divine wisdom requires of them is that they live the noblest form of life, freeing themselves from all their "base" desires for status and prestige, as did Christ, the teacher who was one with God and yet emptied himself of His divinity to take on our humanity.

A Sacramental Metaphysics of Teaching

In his commentary on this text, Simon Tugwell suggests that Thomas has in mind a related philosophical theme.²³ Tugwell notes that Thomas wrote the short work *On Being and Essence* during the years before he incepted as a master, probably while he was working on his commentary on the first book of Peter Lomabard's *Sentences*. This work, says Tugwell, helped solidify Thomas's deep, lifelong conviction "that there can never be any separation between God and his creatures."

> The idea that God somehow "withdraws" in order to give his creatures space to be could never begin to make sense to Thomas; if God withdrew then being is the last thing any creature could achieve. The freedom and inner consistency of creatures is not something that has to be defended against divine interference; it is precisely the gift that is made by the divine presence. The fact that things exist and act in their own right is the most telling indication that God is existing and acting in them.²⁴

For Thomas, the question of human teaching is merely "one aspect of the more general and extremely important question of whether secondary causes of any kind exercise any authentic causality."²⁵

Do teachers really teach? Or does only God teach? Christ warns in Matthew 23:10 that none was to call himself "teacher" (*magister* in the Latin Vulgate). So what did Thomas think he would be doing as an incepted *magister* or "teacher"?

Father Tugwell tells us that some of Thomas's contemporaries had concluded from an argument in St. Augustine's *De magistro* that no human being, strictly speaking, should be called a "teacher."²⁶ William of Auxerre interpreted him this way.²⁷ Thomas, as we have seen, does not take this approach. In the following year, in his *Disputed Question on Truth* (*De veritate*), q. 11, a. 1, he would argue more fully against Avicenna's notion that, in learning, "intelligible forms flow into our mind from the agent intelligence" (*formae intelligibiles effluent in mentem nostram ab intelligentia agente*), the teacher being present

---

²³ Simon Tugwell, O.P., "Aquinas: Introduction," in *Albert and Thomas: Selected Writings*, Classics of Western Spirituality (New York: Paulist Press, 1988), 214.

²⁴ Tugwell, *Albert and Thomas*, 215.

²⁵ Ibid., 268–269.

²⁶ Ibid., 268.

²⁷ See *Summa Aurea* IV, ed. J. Ribaillier (Paris: Éditions du Centre national de la recherche scientifique, 1980–1986), 88, 97, 116. In these passages, however, William is discussing the powers imputed to the baptized, not teachers *per se*. William's approach to the question of human teachers in these passages is similar to one Bonaventure and other Franciscans will champion decades later: the exterior human teacher does nothing without Christ, who is the interior teacher, illuminating the mind.

merely as an instrument that prepares the material for the reception of these forms (*omnia inferiora agentia naturalia non sunt nisi sicut praeparantia materiaum ad formae susceptionem*), and against the early Platonic conception, as can be found in the *Meno*, that teaching is helping the student to remember what was already present.[28]

Thomas rejects both positions because each rules out the possibility that natural or "secondary" causes ("secondary" to God's "primary" causality) can act as true causes in the world. Thomas rejects the Avicennian position because it rules out any possibility of a chain of causes, since on this view, the first cause, as the "giver of forms," is the only real cause. He rejects the Platonic conception too because a cause that only removes an impediment also is not a cause in the truest sense. For Thomas, any approach to the nature of teaching that diminishes the status of secondary causality in the world, that "attributes to first causes alone all effects coming about in inferior things," not only "derogates from the order of universe, which is woven together by the order and connection of causes" (*derogatur ordini universi, qui ordine et connexione causarum contexitur*); worse, it insults God, who "out of the eminence of his goodness makes things not only to be but also to be causes" (*ex eminentia bonitatis suae rebus aliis confert non solum quod sint, sed et quod causae sint.*)

Saying a teacher does not really teach is, for Thomas, like saying that a physician does not really treat disease or that medicine does not really cure disease.[29] When we deny that the physician treats disease or that medicine cures disease in the belief that only God truly cures, this for Thomas is to deny natural causality and God's power as Creator to make things exist such that they can act as true causes in the world. Thomas would insist that both the medicine and God cured the man, each in its own domain, just as the medicine and the physician cured the man, each in its own way. To assert God's divine causality is not to deny the natural causes we see around us in the world. Quite the contrary. For Thomas, "[t]he fact that things exist and act in their own right is the most telling indication that God is existing and acting in them."[30]

On Thomas's account, things would not exist and would have no causality if it were not for God. To deny things their proper causality is to deny God's power and goodness to impart true causality to them. It is to treat God as if He were jealous of the doctor or the medicine, which would be absurd, since both owe their existence and causality entirely to God. The healing power of the physician and the healing power of the medicine: each plays its own role in God's creative and redemptive plan, a plan revealed most fully in the Incarnation. What God reveals through Christ in the Incarnation is the truth of creation – the truth that all of creation is created through God's Word and is thus an expression, an embodiment, and an instrument of God's creative and redemptive love. This is a sacramental notion of creation in which things in the world, including human persons, are meant to see themselves as instruments of God's grace because, in fact, that is what they were created to be.

---

[28] Throughout this section, I am quoting the English translation of *De veritate* 11.1 in Robert W. Mulligan, James V. McGlynn, and Robert W. Schmidt, trans., *Truth*, 3 vols., Library of Living Catholic Thought (Chicago: Regnery, 1952–54; reprint, Indianapolis: Hackett, 1994).
[29] Thomas himself employs this analogy in his *responsio* in *De veritate* 11.1.
[30] Tugwell, 215.

A Real Relationship Between Teacher and Students: The Duties of Teaching and Learning

On this view, physicians, teachers, and all others should not understand themselves as parallel entities having no causal connection with each other, for so to understand themselves would be to subscribe to a modern "parallelist" form of body–soul dualism, such as that of Leibniz. According to Leibniz, the body and soul do not influence one another, they merely act *as if* they were interacting, because they both operate according to a preestablished harmony set in place by God.[31] If this were true, however, then the physician acts and I am cured, not because the physician acted with knowledge and skill, but only because God chose to cure me while, quite separately, the physician was acting. And if this were true, the physician would not have been a true cause; his would have been merely a parallel action. Thomas insists, however, that there is a true causal interaction. And because there is a true causal interaction, there is also a personal, not just an extrinsic, connection between teacher and student.

And yet neither should the physician or the teacher see him- or herself as the *sole* cause of the healing or the teaching. Physicians and teachers are creatures with capacities given to them by God who are called upon to deal intelligently with other creatures created by God, all of which operate according to their intrinsic created natures. A physician cannot merely cure by an act of will, nor can a teacher simply place ideas into the student's head as if he were placing a bird in a cage. The teacher and student should both see themselves as cooperators with God, not as replacements for God or those replaced by God. And just as a physician must operate in accord with the created laws of physics and human biology in order to heal the patient, so too a teacher must act in accord with the created nature of the human mind in order to teach.

How do human beings learn? How do they arrive at the truth? One's answers to these questions determines what he or she thinks goes on in teaching and learning. Thomas holds that "certain seeds of the sciences preexist in us" (*praeexistunt in nobis quaedam scientiarum semina*). These are "the first concepts of understanding, which by the light of the agent intellect are immediately known through the species abstracted from sensible things." These "first concepts of understanding" include the notions of being and the one, which the intellect grasps immediately.[32] According to Thomas, "When, therefore, the mind is led from these general notions to actual knowledge of the particular things, which it knew previously in general and, as it were, potentially, then one is said to acquire knowledge."[33]

This can be done by the student alone – we learn many things by ourselves – but it can be aided by a teacher who shows the student the proper path such discursive reasoning should

---

[31] For a brief introduction, consult Mark Kulstad and Laurence Carlin, "Leibniz's Philosophy of Mind," *The Stanford Encyclopedia of Philosophy* (Winter 2013 edition), https://plato.stanford.edu/archives/win2013/entries/leibniz-mind/

[32] *De veritate*, q. 11, a. 1 resp.: "primae conceptiones intellectus, quae statim lumine intellectus agentis cognoscuntur per species a sensibilibus abstractas, sive sint complexa, sicut dignitates, sive incomplexa, sicut ratio entis, et unius, et huiusmodi, quae statim intellectus apprehendit."

[33] Ibid.: "quando ergo ex istis universalibus cognitionibus mens educitur ut actu cognoscat particularia, quae prius in universali et quasi in potentia cognoscebantur, tunc aliquis dicitur scientiam acquirere."

take. One man is said to teach another, says Thomas, when he shows the student the course of reasoning (*decursum rationis*) that he himself followed. The student, attending to what has been proposed, comes to knowledge of what he previously did not know.[34] Although knowledge preexists in us potentially, in "seeds" as it were, what is in us potentially must be "brought to actuality from this state of potency through a proximate external agent, and not through the first agent alone."[35] This is not to deny the role of the first cause. Merely to affirm that the agency of the first cause does not preclude the role of another, proximate agent that helps the intellect to learn. "Therefore, says Thomas, "just as the doctor is said to heal the patient through the activity of nature, so a man is said to cause knowledge in another through the activity of the learner's own natural reason, and this is teaching."[36]

The human mind too is a true cause. Human thinking, real discursive reasoning, not mere illumination without ratiocination, is a reality. Thomas is clear in *De veritate* that the natural light of reason is from God, and *in this sense*, we owe all to God. But we also owe to God the realization that we are made capable of thinking on our own. On Thomas's account, this is what a good teacher helps a student learn to do. Students can and often do learn to think on their own. But the teacher can be an example and guide. Yet, the student can also check the teacher by working through the arguments for him- or herself. As Thomas argues in *Quodlibet* 3, q. 4, a. 2, students are not excused for making an error when they submissively follow the false opinions of their teachers.

The teacher cannot (and should not try to) replace the student's own mind, any more than God simply replaces any learner's mind. The student and teacher must be in a cooperative relationship: the student cooperating with the teacher as guide, and the teacher cooperating with God's Truth, the divine light, as it has been revealed in and through (a) creation, (b) the Word made flesh, and/or (c) God's Scriptural word. These three are, for Thomas, not mutually exclusive, but rather mutually inclusive and reinforcing. Thomas's view is both contemplative and active. Our task is to attend to the order of the created, natural realm closely and carefully and then act as best we can in harmony with the order instilled in it and us by the Creator.

What, then, should a student expect from a teacher? What duties follow for a teacher upon such a view? The first is that a teacher should make good arguments. The second is that a teacher ought to live a holy life. Both are essential.

Consider again the analogy of the teacher and the physician. The physician cannot simply stand aside and let God cure, even though "miraculous" cures sometimes do occur that exceed the physician's abilities. To effect a cure, the physician must understand the principles of human biology and anatomy and know how to apply them wisely to the particular concerns of healing. And yet the physician must also recognize that he or she is not the ultimate lord of nature to command as he or she wills; that there are domains

---

[34] Ibid.: "unus alium dicitur docere quod istum decursum rationis, quem in se facit ratione naturali, alteri exponit per signa et sic ratio naturalis discipuli, per huiusmodi sibi proposita, sicut per quaedam instrumenta, pervenit in cognitionem ignotorum."

[35] Ibid.: "formae enim naturales praeexistunt quidem in materia, non in actu, ut alii dicebant, sed in potentia solum, de qua in actum reducuntur per agens extrinsecum proximum, non solum per agens primum."

[36] Ibid.: "sicut igitur medicus dicitur causare sanitatem in infirmo natura operante, ita etiam homo dicitur causare scientiam in alio operatione rationis naturalis illius: et hoc est docere."

beyond his or her control; and that he or she, understanding and acting in accord with the given natures of things as God has created them, can foster cures. These two – reliable knowledge of the craft and the wisdom to use it rightly – are both essential to make a physician "good."

What physicians need, therefore, to be able to do the good they called upon to do is, first, constant training in the application of principles to particulars and second, constant prayer that they might be guided in learning and in the proper use of their craft. Prayer without pursuing knowledge can be disastrous and is an insult to the universe and to God as Creator. Learning without prayer can be disastrous in a different way; it can lead to overweening pride in one's ability to control nature rather than to learn from it – a pride that can lead to a refusal to work with and for others rather than merely operate on them as another species of "thing" subject to one's putative control.

So too with teachers. Teacher must learn to make good arguments – learn to see the relationship between principles and conclusions – in order to guide their students. Personal holiness is not enough. Getting metaphysical principles wrong can lead even very holy people to make serious mistakes, such as when a pious person refuses to take their sick child to the doctor in the mistaken belief that it would demean God's power not to let God cure their child. God is not in causal competition with human doctors and natural medicines. They are in providential cooperation as Creator and creature, primary and secondary causes.

Good teachers must also understand, however, that they do not teach *their own* truth, but God's. The teacher has no business trying to make disciples for himself, for it is not *his* truth he shares. Teachers, like the mountain, reflect light from above. On their own, without the reflected light of the sun, they bring darkness and shadows.[37]

Masters, insists Thomas, must excel in both intellect and holiness; not merely in intellect alone (consider the unfortunate example of Abelard) or holiness alone. Thomas stresses that students must be able to *look up to* their teachers, making in this way a fruitful use of the "mountain" imagery supplied by the biblical *thema* verse he received in the dream.

Students too are called upon to cooperate and become like the master in their dedication to both holiness and learning. Students must learn to "look up" and receive the life-giving rains from above: both by praying for wisdom and guidance, and through study. They must learn to use correctly the reason God has given them. In their teachers, students should see an embodiment of their own vocation to become *like the mountains*, able to defend the faith as the mountains protect the land from invaders, eager to transfer the wisdom they have been given as a gift from above, and never to portray themselves arrogantly as the source of the truth they teach.

In his essay on Thomas's *principium*, Fr. Tugwell insists on two fundamental points. The first is that "in line with the Dionysian principle with which he begins his lecture, Thomas always insists that God's providence disposes things in such a way that creatures do have a real effect on one another."[38] The second is this: "Thomas, conscious of the high role of the

---

[37] I have changed Thomas's image slightly while retaining his Pseudo-Dionysian idea of mediation. Thomas pictures the mountains as a medium that transfers rain. I have proposed an image in which the mountains reflect light. In both instances, the mountains can provide only what they have gotten from above.

[38] Tugwell, 268–269.

teacher as an instrument of divine providence, says … it is only by God's gift that anyone could be adequate for the task, so he needs to ask God to make him adequate."[39]

Following Fr. Tugwell's lead, we have introduced material here from Thomas's longer and more developed reflections on teaching and causality in *De veritate*. Since this disputed question was completed shortly after Thomas's inception, it is easy to imagine that these considerations were not far from his mind when he composed his *principium*.[40]

The Font of Wisdom: Paris or God?

Even if Thomas received his opening *thema* verse in a dream, he still had to choose how he would "dilate" the verse. His association of the mountains with the masters whose flowing waters make fruitful the plains might have been crafted to correct another use of this image of "flowing waters" that had become notorious two years earlier.

After expelling and excommunicating the friars, University officials publicly circulated a letter defending their decision that began:

> The right hand of the Most High planted at Paris the paradise of delights (*paradisum voluptatis*), the venerable gymnasium of letters, whence the fount of wisdom rises (*sapientie fons ascendit*) which, distributed in four faculties of theology, jurisprudence, medicine, and rational, natural, and moral philosophy, like the four rivers of Paradise flowing through the four climes of the world, waters and irrigates the whole earth. From which, how multifarious the spiritual and temporal advantages Christendom experiences is clearer than light to all.[41]

The biblical reference underlying the image here is from Genesis 2.10, where it is written: "And a river went out of the place of pleasure (*de loco voluptatis*) to water paradise, which from thence is divided into four heads." These four rivers were later interpreted as watering and irrigating "the whole earth," although this is not specified in the text of Genesis itself.

The metaphor the writer has in mind is fairly clear, if in some ways unfortunate. Not only was it not entirely prudent to boast that Paris was the original source (the font) of wisdom for "the whole world" – what did they suppose the Pope or the masters at Oxford or Bologna would say to *that*? – comparing Paris of the day to Paradise was something of a stretch.[42] Conditions there had been so notoriously antagonistic and unwelcoming to the University students and masters that they had been forced to pack up and leave the city for several years. The failure of the friars to join them in their exile was one of the chief reasons for the secular masters' displeasure with them. It may be that the author of the letter meant

---

[39] Ibid., 269.
[40] On the dating, see the "Brief Catalogue" in Torrell, 334.
[41] This letter can be found in the *Chartularium universitatis Parisiensis*, I, 252–258; and in English translation in: *University Records and Life in the Middle Ages*, ed. and trans. Lynn Thorndike (New York: Norton, 1975; repr. of New York: Columbia University Press, 1944), 56–64, esp. 57.
[42] It may, however, have become a commonplace. Even in the 1270s, we find an unnamed friar concluding his sermon by inviting the congregation to pray for the University of Paris so that God would protect in peace "this fountain from which streams flow through the whole church of God." See Bériou, "La predication au béiuinage de Paris," 137.

to suggest by using this image of the Garden of Eden that it was the friars who ruined the educational "paradise" that Paris had been by their disobedience to the rules of the Garden (refusing to join in their strike) and by demanding things too high for them (desiring to have more regent masters than the seculars wished to grant them).[43]

Another difficulty with the letter's use of the image of Paris as the paradise in Genesis 2 is this: Did they *really* mean to compare Paris to the place of the fall of all mankind? They likely did themselves no great service – and caused knowing laughs among some of their readers – when they quoted the text of the Vulgate literally, describing Paris as a "paradise of delights" (*paradisum voluptatis*), literally, "a paradise of voluptuousness." This was not an entirely judicious choice of words, one would have thought, given the bawdy reputation of the students in Paris.

Thomas was undoubtedly wiser in his *principium* address, therefore, to use an image that made clear that the font of divine wisdom was in heaven above, not planted in Paris. Masters, on this view, were merely *intermediaries*, who were to pass on to others what had been entrusted to them. Masters had to be nourished at the font of wisdom *first* – the font in heaven, the font that existed mystically in the inspired word of the Sacred Scriptures – and only *afterward* would they be able to pass on what they themselves had received, taking care along the way not to contaminate the pure, life-giving water from above by adding their own impurities. Which would take precedence: the canons of scholarship established at the University of Paris, or the canonical Scriptures of the Catholic Church handed down from the patriarchs, prophets, and apostles? Thomas took the occasion of his *principium* address to make his views on the matter abundantly clear.[44]

The *Divisio* and *Dilatatio*

After quoting the *thema* of the sermon, a medieval preacher would next make a *divisio* of the *thema* in order to establish the basic structure of his sermon and then develop or "dilate" each of the parts. Common ways of dividing the *thema* would have included a twofold *divisio* (e.g., You water the mountains from the places above them / the earth is

---

[43] See my discussion of the dispute in the Introduction.
[44] The thirteenth-century Franciscan brother Salimbene of Adam (or "of Parma") indicates in his chronicle of the order that the Franciscan master general John of Parma had taken a somewhat different approach two years before Thomas's inception when he preached a sermon to the whole University community, at the conclusion of which he proclaimed to the assembled masters: "You are our lords and masters; we, your servants, sons, and disciples. And if we have any learning, we wish to acknowledge that it has come from you. I place myself and the Brothers who are under my rule under your discipline and correction." Brother Salimbene reports that, when the collected masters "heard these things, they were all satisfied and 'their spirit was appeased with which they swelled against' the brothers" [Judges 8:3]. This series of conciliatory comments, along with the Franciscan agreement to abide by the secular masters' demands, may help explain why Bonaventure was allowed to incept some two years earlier than Thomas. See *The Chronicle of Salimbene of Adam*, trans. Joseph L. Baird, Giuseppe Baglavi, and John Robert Kane (Binghamton, NY: Medieval & Renaissance Texts & Studies, 1986), 299–300. In his *principium*, Thomas did not directly address any part of this controversy, but it may not have been far from his mind.

sated with the fruit of your works), a threefold *divisio* (e.g., You water the mountains / from the places above them / the earth is sated with the fruit of your works), or a fourfold *divisio* (e.g., You water the mountains / from the places above them / the earth is sated / with the fruit of your works). Each was commonly used in the *sermo modernus* style, but on this occasion, Thomas chose a fourfold *divisio*.

Thomas begins his *principium* by identifying the four subjects he wishes to correlate with his *thema* verse: the *height* of the spiritual doctrine to be taught, the *dignity* that should exist in those who teach this spiritual doctrine, the *condition* or qualities required of the listeners, and the *manner of communicating* this spiritual doctrine.

Thomas's usual practice in his later Sunday sermons would be to take up topics in the order they appeared in the *thema* verse. From those examples, we might have expected Thomas to coordinate his opening fourfold division – height, dignity, condition, and order – with the four parts of the opening biblical verse in this manner: (1) *watering the mountains* (the "height" of the doctrine suggested by the word "mountains"); (2) *from the places above them* (the "dignity" of the teachers suggested by the words "places above"); (3) *the earth is sated* (the "condition" of the students suggested by the lowliness of the earth); and (4) *with the fruit of your works* (the order or manner of communicating suggested by either "fruit or "works"). Although this approach would have worked perfectly well, this is not what Thomas does.[45]

Rather, Thomas allows himself the freedom to range back and forth among the images as needed, so that the first topic, the *height* of the spiritual doctrine, is suggested not by the word "mountains" (*montes*), which is first in the sentence, but by the words "from the places above" (*de superioribus suis*), which appear later. The second topic, the dignity of those who teach, is suggested by the first word in the verse, "mountains" (*montes*). The reason for the transposition likely had to do with Thomas's desire to draw a picture in which, although the masters have (or are supposed to have) a certain height, they must realize that they would remain "desiccated" and "dry" if they did not receive watering from above themselves. They are, on this view, not the *source* of the water that flows down from them, merely the conduit through which that water is meant to flow.

After the *height* of the spiritual doctrine to be taught (associated with the word *superioribus*) and the *dignity* that should exist in those who teach this spiritual doctrine (associated with the word *montes*), the third topic is the *condition* or qualities required of the listeners, which Thomas associates with the word *terra* ("earth"). Finally, at the end of his *principium*, Thomas touches upon various issues related to the *manner of communicating* the spiritual doctrine, which he associates, interestingly, not with a single word, but with the order of the words in the whole Psalm verse. This was an uncharacteristic approach to dilating the content of a sermon which can be found nowhere else in Thomas's extant sermons.

Thomas treats three points within each *divisio*, so the overall structure can be outlined as shown in Box 4.1.

---

[45] I do not mean to suggest that Thomas *never* reversed the strict ordering of the parts of his opening *thema* verse, only that it was rare. On this, see especially the analytical outlines of each of Thomas's sermons at the back of Smith, *Reading the Sermons*.

> **Box 4.1** Structure of Thomas's *Divisio*
>
> A. Height of Spiritual Doctrine ("from the places above"):
>   1. Its origins (from above)
>   2. Subtlety of its matter (beyond human comprehension)
>   3. Sublimity of the end (life eternal in heaven)
> B. Dignity Required of Teachers ("mountains")
>   1. To keep their minds set on things above (so that they may *preach*)
>   2. To be illuminated by the sun's rays first (so that they can *teach*)
>   3. To defend the faith from errors as the mountains protect from enemies (in *disputation*).
> C. Condition Required of Listeners ("the earth is sated with fruit")
>   1. Lowliness of humility
>   2. Stable and firm in rectitude
>   3. Fruitful in listening
> D. Manner of Communicating (relationship between "places above" and "mountains")
>   1. The order of communicating
>   a. Masters should not teach everything they know.
>   b. The minds of the doctors cannot possess all of divine wisdom, nor can the minds of students hold even what the masters know.
>   2. God possesses this wisdom by nature, humans only by participation.
>   3. God communicates this wisdom by his own power, masters only as ministers.

We will consider each of these four *divisiones* in the text that follows in turn, beginning with Thomas's discussion of the "height" of the doctrine to be taught.

Height

"Height" is associated not with the masters but with the doctrine they are called upon to teach and is suggested by the words *de superioribus* ("from the places above"). The "height" of this teaching derives from three things. The first is its origin, for it is "from above" (*sursum*). The second is the "subtlety of its matter" (*ex subtilitate materiae*), because it concerns matters "so high" that they are beyond the comprehension of human beings.

We might also imagine Thomas wants his audience to think of the "subtlety" of the clouds or of the ethereal spheres on which the stars and planets were fixed. There are some things, says Thomas, that all know, such as the existence of God; other things, however, are higher (*altiora*) and require the wisdom of the wise. Still others are so high (*altissima*) that they entirely transcend the grasp of human reason, but these have been made known by the Holy Spirit through the text of Sacred Scripture.

The "height" of the spiritual teaching is also due, thirdly, to "the sublimity of the end" (*ex finis sublimitate*). If we were to ask the masters what their ultimate goal should be: Prestige? Superior distinction among their colleagues? A devoted following of disciples? – Thomas would reply that their ultimate goal should be no less than the salvation of souls. Such is Thomas's exalted sense of the vocation of the teacher. Note in all this how Thomas is progressively drawing the eye of the mind upward, from the plains to the mountains, from the mountains to the sky, from the sky above the mountains to the spheres above the sky, and finally to the outermost sphere, the empyrean or uppermost heaven.

Dignity

"Dignity" is what the masters are supposed to possess. We should not fail to appreciate the ingenious transition between the last Scripture passage on the "height" of the spiritual doctrine and the next section on the "dignity" of the masters, which he associates with the word "mountains" (*montes*). He ends the first section on the "height" of spiritual doctrine with this passage from Colossians 3:1–2: "Therefore, if you have risen with Christ, seek the things that are above, where Christ is seated at the right hand of God. Mind the things that are above, not the things of earth." He begins his next section on the responsibility of the masters, then, with this: "Thus the holy teachers by despising earthly things cleave to heavenly things alone," just as the mountains rise above the earth and are "neighbors" (*vicini*) of the heavens.[46] Because the masters are called upon to help their students get to heaven, they too must have their own sights set on heavenly things. The "dignity" of the masters must be in accord with the "height" of the spiritual doctrine they are called upon to deliver. They must raise their eyes and their minds to the things above, for if they have their minds focused on earthly things – power, prestige, position, or status – they will not gain the waters from above they need to nourish their students below. So they must, like the mountains, remain "above."

The second way the masters should be like mountains is that, just as the mountains are the first to be illuminated by the rays of the sun, so too masters should be the first to be illumined by the light of divine wisdom.

Finally, masters should be like the mountains so that, just as mountains protect a kingdom from its enemies, so too the masters should defend the faith against errors.

Thomas then associates the three kinds of *dignity* he has just identified (all suggested by the word "mountains") with the three duties of the master: *praedicare, legere,* and *disputare*.[47] Masters should have their hearts and minds "fixed in highness of life," just as the mountains are fixed in the heavens, so they may fittingly *preach*. They should seek to be "illumined" (*illuminati*) by the rays of divine light, so they might fittingly "teach by reading" (*doceant legendo*) – an obvious reference to the way in which medieval masters would often teach by reading and commenting upon a text. Finally, masters should seek to be "armed" (*muniti*) with divine wisdom so they might "refute errors in disputation" (*ut errores confutent disputando*), protecting the faith from errors just as the mountains protect the kingdom from its enemies.

Condition Required of Students

Even in this remarkably short address, Thomas was not willing to skip over the responsibilities and obligations of the students, which he associates with the next words in his *thema* verse: "the earth is sated" (*satiabitur terra*).[48]

---

[46] "Dignity" is discussed in *Rigans montes*, 2.
[47] As I noted in Chapter 1, this threefold list can be traced back to a comment by Peter Cantor (d. 1197) in the first chapter of the *Verbum Abbreviatum*.
[48] *Rigans montes*, 3.

As the earth is low, says Thomas, so too should the students be "low" as the earth in humility. As the earth is stable and firm, so the students should be stable and firm with rectitude, not tossed to and fro and carried about by every wind of change. Finally, as the earth bears fruit when watered, they should be fruitful. "Therefore *humility* is required of the students with respect to the learning that comes from listening, *rectitude* with respect to the judgment of what is heard," and "*fruitfulness* in discovery," by which from a few things heard, the good listener may bear much fruit.[49]

In the final section of the *principium*, Thomas does not turn, as the canons of the *sermo modernus* style would have led us to expect, to the remaining words in the opening *thema* verse: "from the fruit of your works" (*de fructu operum tuorum*). Rather he turns instead back to the first two parts of the verse he has already "dilated": "Watering the mountains" (*rigans montes*) and "from the places above them" (*de superioribus suis*).[50] This is the only place I have found in Thomas's extant sermons where he goes back to the beginning of the *thema* verse rather than moving on. This may have been due to the fact that this *principium* was a product of Thomas's early preaching career when he had not yet mastered the required elements of the style.

Manner of Communicating

Having dealt with the *height* of the spiritual doctrine, the *dignity* that ought to characterize the masters, and the *condition* that ought to characterize the students, Thomas now turns to the *manner* in which this spiritual doctrine ought to be communicated, which he associates with the relationship between "the mountains" and "the places above them."

First, says Thomas, masters should not try to preach to "the simple" everything they know. This would be akin to flooding the plain with water rather than irrigating it. The students, as novices, cannot take in all that the master knows, and should they try, they would not then be able to grow into well-integrated thinkers themselves. This comment complements his advice to both students and masters to embrace humility. As masters should embrace and exemplify their humility before the vastness of divine wisdom, so students should embrace an analogous humility before both the vastness of divine wisdom and the more advanced wisdom of their masters. They cannot learn if they will not submit themselves to a higher wisdom.

Whereas God has wisdom "naturally" (*per naturam*) – for the "upper places" are said to be "his" (*de superioribus suis*) – masters merely "participate" (*participant*) in that divine wisdom. They share something that does not have its source in them. This is why teachers are said to be, like the mountains in the Psalm verse, "watered from on high." And whereas God communicates wisdom by His own power (*Deus propria virtute sapientiam communicat*) – He by Himself is said to water the mountains – masters, says Thomas, do not communicate wisdom "except as ministers" (*non communicant nisi per ministerium*). The water that nourishes the plains and causes them to bear much fruit should be understood to have its

---

[49] Ibid.
[50] Ibid., 4.

source from *above* the mountains, and not from the teachers themselves. "Although no one by himself, of himself, is sufficient for such a ministry," says Thomas, "he can hope to have this sufficiency from God."

> "Not that we are sufficient of ourselves to think anything as from ourselves, but our sufficiency is from God" (2 Cor 3:5). Thus "if any of you is wanting in wisdom, let him ask it of God, who gives abundantly to all men ... and it will be given to him" (James 1:5). Let us pray Christ will grant it to us. Amen.[51]

Getting the Most from the Gift and Communicating a Lot in a Short Time

With this "Amen," Thomas finishes with an address delivered "briefly" (*breve*) and "quickly terminated" (*celeriter terminato*) as per University regulation[52] – a little over ten minutes, by my reckoning, if read out loud – and yet remarkably full. In that short space, Thomas managed to praise the Scriptures for their *height* ("places above"); exhort the masters to a greater *dignity* ("mountains"); exhort the students to the appropriate *humility* ("earth"); and give advice on the proper manner of communicating the divine teaching, for the "places above" do not rain down all their water upon the mountains, and the mountains should not flood the plains beneath them nor pretend they have sucked the heavens dry of all the moisture they have to give. Above all, he continually directed the attention of his listeners *above*, toward the divine source of true wisdom, and not merely toward himself or toward Paris and its various disputes. All in all, we'd have to say it was an inspiring and full ten-minute address, more easily recollected if one can remember its opening *thema*: "Watering the mountains" (masters) / "from his places above" (divine wisdom) / "the earth" (the students) / "is sated with the fruit of your works" (the students are to bear fruit by receiving the divine wisdom that comes from heaven through the mediation of their masters). Such was the mnemonic power of the *sermo modernus* style of preaching.

Thomas made a lot out of the gift he was given in his dream. But he also had resources that he had received from his human teachers: those who had taught him grammar, rhetoric, and logic and how to read and interpret the Scriptures; from those who had introduced him to the thought of Pseudo-Dionysius and the relationship between primary and secondary causality. He also had the God-given gift of his own creative intellect and a profound desire for the truth. All of these, under God's divine providence, allowed him to nurture the gift of that dream to fruition. His *principium* provided a good, solid example of "height" connected to "humility" for his fellow friars, students, and masters to emulate.

Having finished his *principium in aula*, it remained now for Thomas to deliver his *resumptio* address with its characteristic *divisio textus* of the books of the Bible. It is to the examination of that address that we turn in the next chapter.

---

[51] *Rigans montes*, 5.
[52] Cf. *Chart. Univ. Paris.* II, 693 (final lines): *statim magister novellus cum benedictione incipit suum breve principium de commendatione de Scripture sacre. Quo celeriter terminato ....*

5

Hic Est Liber

Thomas's Resumptio

MODERN SCHOLARSHIP suggests that the *principium in aula* was one part of a series of required steps in a master's inception. There were disputed questions at or around the hour of vespers the day before the *principium* and others on the day of the official inception before the assembled masters, four in all. Although the possibility exists that what I have been calling *resumptio* addresses were the inception addresses given when a young *baccalarius* incepted as a *biblicus*, for the present, we will continue to accept the thesis that, in the thirteenth century, the *principium in aula* and the *resumptio* were two parts of a multistage ceremony.[1] We have special reason to believe that Thomas's second "commendation of Sacred Scripture" entitled *Hic est liber* came from his inception as a master, since he never incepted as a *biblicus* at Paris. As both Fr. Weiheipl and Fr. Torrell indicate, it is likely that Thomas delivered *Hic est liber* – an address that contained a continuation of his praise of Sacred Scripture and a *divisio textus* or *partitio* of all the books of the Bible – on the first day of classes after his inception.[2]

This *divisio* of all the books of the Bible was sometimes integrated into one of the parts of the sermon, sometimes not. It was sometimes simply appended to the end of the sermon. If it was integrated into one of the divisions of the sermon, the result was a distinctly medieval creation: a *divisio* within a *divisio*. The listing of the divisions of the books of the Bible would have been related to one of the divisions of the opening *thema* verse.[3]

Thomas's mentor Albert the Great, for example, when he incepted in 1245, took as the *thema* verse for his *resumptio* address a passage from Ecclesiasticus 24:33: "Moses commanded a law in the precepts of justice, and an inheritance to the house of Jacob, and the

---

[1] For a review of the arguments and relevant texts, see Nancy Spatz, *Principia: A Study and Edition of Inception Speeches Delivered Before the Faculty of Theology at the University of Paris, ca. 1180–1286* (PhD diss., Cornell University, 1992), 55–65.

[2] See my discussion of the ceremony in the Introduction for the references.

[3] Indeed the reader should be careful not to mistake the *divisio* of the opening *thema* verse with the *divisio textus* of the all the books of the Bible. This long *divisio textus* of all the biblical books was generally added after the master had finished dilating the last of the divisions of the *thema*.

promises to Israel" (*Legem mandavit Moses in praeceptis iustitiarum et hereditatem domui Iacob et Israel promissiones*).[4] "Three things are contained in these words," declared Albert. The minister of the law (Moses); the manner in which the law was given (he commanded it to us); and the contents of the law, which are signified in the three remaining parts of the *thema* verse.

At this point in his *principium*, Albert transitions seamlessly into his *divisio textus*. The Scriptures (which Albert describes here simply as "the law" based on the first word in his *thema* verse "*legem*") contain, first, the precepts of justice for merit (*praecepta iustitiarum ad meritum*). These can be found in the Pentateuch and in the five books which are attributed to Solomon, and the Psalms and Prophets. Second, we find the inheritance promised as a prize (*hereditas promissa ad praemium*) for those observing the law. These are revealed in all the historical books of the Old Testament. Finally, the end or goal of the law and the truth of the promises about Christ's redemption contained in the things signified by the law (*promissiones de Christo redimente in legis significationibus*), these are contained in the whole New Testament. This is only the beginning of Albert's very long and complex *divisio* of each book of both the Old and New Testament. The opening *thema* verse is used to set up a basic structure, but once Albert gets into the details of each book, the complexity outstrips what he can associate with these few words in a single biblical verse.

The Art of Resuming

Being able to carry on a coherent series of reflection over the course of several days – indeed, over the course of a whole academic term – was an essential skill for any Master. The multiple stages of the inception ceremony allowed the Master to exhibit publicly his ability to carry out just such a coherent series of reflections over the course of several days.

Consider, for example, the four disputed questions which were assigned over the multiple days of the inception. Two questions were disputed in the afternoon of the first day at vespers, although the candidate proposed his magisterial determination only on the second of the two questions. At the ceremony *in aula* on the second day, the third and fourth questions were disputed, but the newly incepted master proposed a determination only of the third. The incepting master did not intervene in the disputation of either the first question (on the first day) or the fourth question (on the second day in the bishop's *aula*). Instead he provided a lengthier discussion and determination of the first and fourth questions (the *determinatio valde prolixa*) on the first eligible day following his inception when he was also to give his *resumptio* address.

Day 1: Questions 1 and 2 are disputed; the Master determines only Question 2.

---

[4] See "Principium Biblicum Alberti Magni," ed. Albert Fries, CSSR, based on Cod. Vat. Lat. 4245, ff. 22va–24ra, in *Studia Albertina: Festschrift für Bernhard Geyer*, ed. H. Ostlender (Münster: Aschendorf, 1952), 128–147. Cf. also A. Fries, "Eine Vorlesung Alberts des Grossen über den biblischen Kanon," *Divus Thomas* 28 (Feb. 1950), 195–213, and "Der Schriftkanon bei Albert der. Grossen, *Divus Thomas* 29 (Feb. 1951), 3, 4.

Day 2: Questions 3 and 4 are disputed; the Master determines only Question 3. He also delivers his *principium in aula* address in praise of sacred Scripture.

Day 3: (first eligible day after the *principium*): The Master gives an extended determination of Questions 1 and 4 and delivers his *resumptio* address, also in praise of sacred Scripture, but also containing a *divisio textus* of all the books of the Bible.[5]

The process was clearly complicated, but it appears to have been designed with an eye to forcing the Master to "resume" and continue coherently a train of thought or argumentation left off previously. What Masters were being asked to demonstrate was whether they could carry through with a topic of discussion, a train of thought, or a chain of logical inferences from one class to the next. This requirement suggests a pedagogical culture which took seriously the ability to lecture, not just once, but day after day, in a clearly articulated and coherent fashion, to students needing just this sort of structure to help guide them over the course of a whole term.

So too, the practice of resuming a sermon or collation after a break was not only a common practice for masters at Paris, it was a stipulated requirement of their office. According to University regulations, when masters were assigned to preach a University sermon, they were required to preach a *collatio* at vespers later the same evening using the same *thema* verse they used for the morning's sermon.[6] When Thomas preached the sermon *Ecce rex tuus*, for example (Sermon 5 in the Leonine and in Fr. Hoogland's English translation), he chose as his *thema* verse the first six words from Matthew 21:5: *Ecce rex tuus venit tibi mansuetus* ("Behold your king comes for you, meek"). He then made a fourfold division of this *thema*, saying:

> Now on this Sunday the Church celebrates the first coming of Christ, and we can see four things in the verse mentioned above: first, the manifestation of the coming of Christ, where it says: "Behold"; second, who the one is that is coming, where it says: "your king"; third, the benefit of his coming: "comes for you"; and fourth, the way of his coming, where it says: "meek."[7]

In his morning sermon, Thomas completed the *dilatatio* of the first two words, *Ecce* and *rex*. Later that evening at vespers, Thomas began his *collatio* by reviewing briefly the topics he had covered in the morning's sermon associated with the words *Ecce* and *rex*, and then picked up right where he left off, with *tuus*, *venit*, *tibi*, and *mansuetus*.

---

[5] This outline is based on the description in James Weisheipl, *Friar Thomas d'Aquino: His Life, Thought, and Works* (Washington, DC: Catholic University of America Press, 1974, 1983), 98–101.

[6] *Chartularium Universitatis Parisiensis*, ed. H. Denifle, O.P., and E. Chatelian, vol. 2 (Paris: 1891), no. 1188, 692. See item (4): "Item, nota, quod theologi habent aliquod festum, quo ipsi non legunt, licet in illo festo legatur in aliis facultatibus, nichilominus in illa die fit sermo de mane, et collatio in vesperis in Cordigeris, vel in Jacobitis." And item (17): "Item, nota, quod quando unus prelatus vel unus magister in theologia facit sermonem de mane in Universitate in aliquot festo in aliqua domo Mendicantium vel alibi: tunc ille qui facit collationem post prandium, debet accipere illud thema in collatione, quod assumptum fuit per prelatum vel per magistrum, qui fecit sermonem eadem die."

[7] For the complete sermon in English translation, see *Thomas Aquinas: The Academic Sermons*, trans. Mark-Robin Hoogland, C.P., The Fathers of the Church: Mediaeval Continuation, 11 (Washington, DC: Catholic University of American Press, 2010), 62–78. For an analytical outline of this and all the sermons and their accompanying *collationes*, see R. Smith, *Reading the Sermons of Aquinas: A Beginner's Guide* (Steubenville, OH: Emmaus, 2016), Appendix 1, esp. 240–243.

Another fascinating example of how a single *thema* verse could serve as a bridge between the sermon and the *collatio* can be found in Sermon 18, *Germinet terra*, which was delivered on the Feast of the Birth of the Blessed Virgin Mary (8 September). The *thema* verse was taken from Genesis 1:11: *Germinet terra herbam virentem et proferentem semen, lignumque pomiferum faciens fructum* ("Let the earth sprout forth the green plant that brings forth seed, and the fruit tree that bears fruit"). Since the vespers service fell on the eve of the celebration of the Cross of Christ, Thomas used the first half of the *thema* verse in the morning to deliver a sermon in praise of Mary, based on the words "Let the earth sprout forth the green plant that brings forth seed" – the "green plant" being Mary. He then used the second half of the *thema* ("and the fruit tree that bears fruit") in the evening address to impress on his audience the importance of the Cross – the "tree" that bear much fruit.

The *sermo modernus* style allowed preachers to make just this sort of "break" and "resumption" in an orderly fashion in his *thema* without much difficulty at any one of the divisions he set up at the outset of his sermon. The skills the new master was required to exhibit in the medieval inception ceremony suggest that medieval universities valued continuity and coherence in instruction and were willing to make sure they had teachers who could provide them.

A Second *Principium* and Commendation of Sacred Scripture

If Fr. Weisheipl is correct, Thomas's "second *principium* address," which often goes by the title *Hic est liber*, was delivered shortly after the first one. To clearly distinguish this "second *principium*" from the first, I have called it Thomas's *resumptio* address. Devoted Latinists annoyed by my use of the locutions "a *principium* address" and "*resumptio* address" would rightly complain that no one at the time would have said: "Let's go to Thomas Aquinas's *principium* address." They would have said, simply: "Let's go to Thomas Aquinas's *principium*." The word "address" doesn't appear in the Latin, and it's redundant. This is certainly true, but I have adopted the locution in order to distinguish between (a) the *principium* given at the beginning of a semester, (b) the *principium in aula* given during the inception, and (c) the "second *principium*" (as some people call it) delivered at the *resumptio*.

Consider, by comparison, the multiple uses we make in contemporary English of the word "lecture." Students ask: "Are you going to Prof. Smith's lecture today?" If the questioner means "lecture" in a generalized way, it would be possible for the person answering to say: "Yes, I'm going. Do you think he will give a lecture today or lead a discussion? In academic circles, it is not uncommon to call any academic presentation a "lecture," even if the speaker does not read a prepared lecture. I once heard a student ask another: "Do you have notes from Monday's lecture?" To this his fellow classmate replied: "Yes, but she didn't lecture; she just went over the reading." The student had "lecture notes" on something the student himself admitted wasn't a "lecture."

Analogously, we might imagine that a student in Thomas's day might have said to a colleague: "Are you going to Friar Thomas's *principium* today?" To which his fellow student might have replied: "I thought there weren't any lectures today. Oh wait, that's right; Brother Thomas is incepting today! He is giving his master's *principium*. I have to go." (Attendance was required of all students and masters.) So too, we might imagine one student asking another: "Did you hear Friar Thomas's *principium* this morning?" To which his fellow student, if he had just arrived back in town, might have replied: "I thought

Brother Thomas incepted last week?" At which point the first student might reply: "Yes, he did, but this is his *resumptio*."

I hope the reader will not consider this Wittgensteinian flourish merely frivolous. I am seeking to be clear about terminology that, precisely because it is not technical, might be confusing. Common usage of terms of the sort we employ and encounter every day is more likely to confuse those of us who do not speak the language. When we live within a linguistic environment, the distinctions between various uses of a term are more obvious to us. To those who are not accustomed to them, they would be less so.

The *resumptio* address was likely also called a *principium* because, other than the *divisio textus* of the books of the Bible in its concluding section, the first part had the same structure and purpose as the first *principium* address. The second, like the first, was another "commendation of Sacred Scripture" delivered in the *sermo modernus* style. It began with a *thema* verse, which the Master divided and dilated in the manner that had become customary for all University sermons. After the master had finished dilating the points in this little sermon, he would then lay out the parts of the stipulated *divisio textus* of the books of the Bible. So, in effect, the master really did provide a "second *principium*." It is simply that we must not mistake this "second" *principium*, the *resumptio*, with the *principium in aula*, delivered several days earlier.

Hic Est Liber: A Law That Gives Life

Since Thomas does not report having received a second dream with another *thema* verse for his *resumptio*, he presumably had to choose his own. For this occasion, he chose the passage from Baruch 4.1: "This is the book of the commandments of God, and the law, that is forever: all they that keep it, shall come to life: but they that have forsaken it, to death" (*Hic est liber mandatorum Dei, et lex quae est in aeternum: omnes qui tenent eam pervenient ad vitam: qui autem dereliquerunt eam, in mortem*).[8] This was the same verse that in 1238, a little more than twenty years earlier, the Franciscan John of La Rochelle had chosen when he incepted. It was also the verse chosen by secular master Henry of Ghent when he incepted in 1275 or 1276, nearly twenty years after Thomas.

Using Old Testament passages that praised the law seems to have been common among thirteenth-century masters. As we have seen, Thomas's teacher Albert the Great used a passage from Ecclesiasticus (24:33). The Franciscan Matthew Aquasparta, who incepted in 1277/78, used the passage from Psalm 93 (94):12: "Blessed is the man whom you shall instruct, O Lord: and shall teach him out of your law." Indeed, of the seven surviving *resumptio* addresses delivered at the University of Paris in the thirteenth century, five began by praising the sacred Scriptures as a book of *law*.

On this occasion, Thomas chose to make a threefold *divisio* of his *thema*: (1) "This is the book of the commandments of God"; (2) "and the law that is forever"; and (3) "all they that

---

[8] Throughout, I quote the Latin from the best modern critical edition of *Hic est liber*, which is still found in vol. 1 of *Opuscula Theologica*, ed. R. A. Verardo (Turin: Marietti, 1954). Unless otherwise noted, all English translations are mine. A good English translation can be found in Ralph McInerny, trans., 'The Inaugural Sermons,' in *Thomas Aquinas: Selected Writings* (Harmondsworth: Penguin, 1998), 5–17.

keep it, shall come to life." Thomas makes this threefold *divisio* with an eye to associating each of these with the three effects that St. Augustine claimed characterize a skilled speaker: he or she should speak in order to teach the ignorant (*doceat ignaros*), delight the bored (*delectet tediosus*), and change the lazy (*flectat tardos*).[9] According to Thomas, the Scriptures accomplish each of these, although he alters Augustine's terms slightly from *doceat*, *delectet*, and *flectat* to *instruit*, *allicit*, and *flectit*.[10] Scripture "teaches the ignorant," says Thomas, with the "eternal truth with which it instructs (*ab aeterna veritate qua instruit*); it "delights the bored" by "the utility with which it entices" (*ab utilitate qua allicit*); and it "changes the lazy" by "the authority with which it moves" (*ab auctoritate qua flectit*). Each of these Thomas associates with a separate part of his *thema* verse.

Scripture's "authority" Thomas associates with the first part of the verse: "This is the book of the commandments of God." "The eternal truth with which it instructs" he associates with the words "and the law that is forever." And "the usefulness with which it entices" he associates with the words "All that keep it shall come to life."

The authority of the Scriptures is shown in three things, says Thomas: its origin, the efficacy with which it is imposed, and the efficacy that comes from the uniformity of its sayings. The first of these – its origin – Thomas associates with the words "of God" because the Scriptures are from God; the second – the efficacy with which it is imposed – is suggested by the words "the commandments" because commands bring about a change in behavior; and the third – the efficacy that comes from the uniformity of its sayings – is suggested by the words "This is the book." These words suggest that the Scriptures should be considered a single book.

Thomas next moves on to the phrase "and the law that is forever," which he associates with the second of the three reasons to commend sacred Scripture: because of the "eternal

---

[9] Thomas's reference here is to Augustine, *De doctrina christiana* 4.12.27: "A certain eloquent man has said…that an eloquent man ought to speak so as to teach, to delight, and to persuade." (*Dixit ergo quidam eloquens, et verum dixit, ita dicere debere eloquentem ut doceat, ut delectet, ut flectat.*) The unnamed "certain eloquent man" (*quidam eloquens*) to whom St. Augustine is referring is Cicero, who in *De oratore* 1, 21, 69 says: "The eloquent orator, then … is a man who speaks in the forum and in civil cases in such a manner as to prove, to delight, and to persuade" (*erit igitur … is qui in foro causisque civilibus ita dicet, ut probet, ut delectet, ut flectat*). It is St. Augustine who changed the first of the three key terms from *probet* ("to prove") to *doceat* ("to teach"). Yet it is worth noting that in Thomas's *resumptio*, the way in which the Sacred Scriptures "teach" is with truth that is "immutable and eternal" ("*Veritas Scripturae huius doctrinae est immutabilis et aeterna*"), with the result that Thomas is not very far from Cicero's original "to prove" (*probet*) after all. Stephen of Besançon, who incepted as master of theology at Paris in 1286, would later use this same threefold *divisio* in his own *resumptio* address. It was obviously a well-known text.

[10] Cicero's original *probet*, *delectet*, and *flectat* (to prove, delight, and persuade) had become in Augustine's *De doctrina christiana*, *doceat*, *delectet*, and *flectat* (to teach, to delight, and to persuade) and subsequently Thomas's: *instruit*, *allicit*, and *flectit* (to instruct, to entice, and to persuade). Although the terms are not identical, the sense is basically the same. The irony of Thomas's use of this passage from *On Christian Doctrine* to praise the eloquence of sacred Scripture is that Augustine himself admits in his *Confessions* (e.g., 3.5.9) and in the early books of *On Christian Doctrine* (e.g., 2.6.6) that, when he first encountered the Christian Scriptures, he found them wanting in literary skill precisely because they didn't "delight" him and didn't measure up to the eloquence of Cicero. By the time Augustine wrote the fourth book of *On Christian Doctrine* some years later, however, he had changed his view and admitted that the Scriptures contained more beauty than he previously could appreciate (see esp. 4.5–7).

truth with which it instructs." The "law is forever" – that is, it is "immutable and eternal" – because of three things, says Thomas: first, because of the *power* of the lawgiver, which is God; second, because of the *immutability* of the lawgiver (who is "forever"); and third, because of the *truth* of the law.

Coming finally to the third division of the opening verse, "all who keep it shall come to life," Thomas dilates the verse by affirming that the life which the Scriptures promise and to which they lead is of three sorts: first, the life of grace; second, the life of justice, consisting in works; and third, the life of glory.

Hence, to summarize, the Scriptures are to be commended for three things:

1. The authority with which it moves: "This is the book of the commandments of God" – a phrase that suggests:
   A. Its origin: "of God"
   B. Its efficacy: "commandments"
   C. Its uniformity: "This is the book"
2. The eternal truth with which it instructs: "and the law that is forever" – a phrase that suggests:
   A. The power of the lawgiver (which is God)
   B. The immutability of the lawgiver (who is eternal and "forever")
   C. The truth of the law
3. The usefulness with which it entices: "all who keep it shall come to life" – it is "useful" because the *life* the Scriptures promise and to which they lead is of three types:
   A. The life of grace
   B. The life of justice
   C. The life of glory

Therefore, the Scriptures fulfill the requirements of a great oration, because they teach (with eternal truth), they move (with the authority of God), and they delight (with the promise of new life). And using the *sermo modernus* style, Thomas was able to fit all of this content into an extraordinarily efficient five minutes.

Baruch 4:1 in Other Early *Principia* Addresses

How much creativity could different authors show when they used the same biblical *thema* as their structuring device? Did using the same structuring device result in the same topics, and roughly the same content in a sermon or *principia*? Since two other masters used this same verse from Baruch 4:1 as a *thema* for their inception addresses – the Franciscan John of La Rochelle, who incepted roughly twenty years prior to Thomas, and the secular master Henry of Ghent who incepted roughly twenty years after – we have an answer to that question.[11]

---

[11] For the text of John of La Rochelle's *resumptio*, see "Deux leçons d'ouverture de Cours Biblique données par Jean de La Rochelle," ed. Delorme, O.F.M., *La France Franciscaine* 16 (1933): 345–360. The text of interest for our purposes is the second of the two. For the text of Henry's *resumptio*, see Henry of Ghent (Henrico de Gandavo), *Lectura Ordinaria Super Sacram Scripturam*, ed. Raymond Macken, in *Opera Omnia*, vol. 36 (Leuven: Leuven University Press, 1980), 5–27. The first lecture would presumably have been Henry's *principium in aula*. The second was likely Henry's *resumptio* and contains Henry's *divisio textus* of the Bible. All English translations are mine. See Spatz, *Principia*, 63–65 and 72–73 for why these texts should be accepted as each master's *resumptio*.

What is especially interesting about each of these addresses is that both John and Henry divide the original structuring biblical verse (the *thema*) in four parts in order to associate each with one of the four Aristotelian "causes": formal, final, material, and efficient – something Thomas, though a devoted Aristotelian in his own right, does *not* do, choosing instead, as we have seen, to associate the parts of his opening *thema* with the three "Ciceronian" characteristics of a great oration. John and Henry do not, however, divide the *thema* verse at the same points, nor do they associate the same words with the same Aristotelian cause.

John associates the words "This is the book of the commandments" with the material cause of the Bible, whereas Henry associates these words with the efficient cause. John associates the words "and the law that is forever" with the formal cause; Henry claims they describe the material cause. Both Masters associate the words "all those who keep it shall come to life" with the final cause. But whereas John goes back to the first phrase in the *thema* and associates the efficient cause with the words "of God" (in the phrase "This is the book of the commandments *of God*"), Henry grabs the first half of the next verse from Baruch 4:2 – *Convertere igitur, Iacob et apprehende eam, et ambula per viam ad splendorem eius* ("Turn back, O Jacob, and apprehend it [the law], and walk in the way by its splendor") – and associates these with the formal cause.

John of La Rochelle		Henry of Ghent	
"This is the book of the commandments"	Material Cause	"This is the book of the commandments"	Efficient Cause
"and the law that is forever"	Formal Cause	"and the law that is forever"	Material Cause
"all they that keep it shall come to life: but they that have forsaken it, to death"	Final Cause	"all they that keep it shall come to life"	Final Cause
"of God"	Efficient Cause	"Turn back, O Jacob, and apprehend it, and walk in the way by its splendor" (Baruch 4:2)	Formal Cause

John of La Rochelle

Let's examine some of the details. John begins his *resumptio*, as we have seen, by associating the words "This is the book of the commandments" (*Hic est liber mandatorum*) with the material cause (the *materia*) of the Pentateuch, the books with which he begins his *divisio textus* of the Scriptures. The "commandments," he says, "are the *materia* of the Law." It will be fourteen more pages in the critical edition before John will get to the second division of his *thema*. In those fourteen pages, he sets out his entire *divisio textus* of all the books of the Bible.

Recall, as I mentioned earlier, that Albert the Great associated his *divisio textus* with the last part of his *thema* verse. Most masters appended the complete *divisio textus* to the end of their *resumptio*. This is what Thomas Aquinas did. John of La Rochelle is the only master I am aware of who associated his complete *divisio textus* with the first part of his *thema*.

After fourteen pages spent laying out his outline of all the books of the Bible, John finally returns to his opening *thema* (at the bottom of page 359 in the Delorme edition) and associates the next words, "and the law that is forever" (*et lex quae est in aeternum*), with the formal cause of the Scriptures, saying that the knowledge (*scientia*) one derives from Scripture is distinguished from all others in its manner of acting, because the Scriptures are written "both within and without" (as it says in Ezekiel 2:10). The external, literal sense of the Scriptures is suggested here by the words "law" and "commandment," while the internal, spiritual sense that remains forever is suggested by the phrase "the law that is forever."

The words "This is the book" can also be taken as describing the *formal cause*, says John. These words distinguish the Law from the Gospel because, whereas the Law is particular, intended for a particular people and a particular time (suggested by the specifying pronoun "this"), the Gospel is universal.[12]

John associates the final cause of the Scriptures with the next phrase, "all they that keep it shall come to life: but they that have forsaken it, to death," since the purpose of the Scriptures is to direct its readers to eternal life and help them avoid death. This life is promised, however, only to doers of the law, not to those who merely read or listen. He quotes as an authority Aristotle, who in *Ethics* 2.4 writes about those who want to be philosophers, but do not act justly, merely taking refuge in theory – these, says Aristotle, "behave like patients who listen attentively to their doctors, but do none of the things they are ordered to do."

At this point, John has a problem, because he has used up all the parts of his original *thema* on the material, formal, and final causes respectively, with the result that he has no more words left from his opening *thema* verse with which to associate the points he wants to make about the efficient cause of the Scriptures. So he goes back to the first part of the *thema* verse and associates the efficient cause of the Scriptures with the words "This is the book ... *of God*." Who, then, is the *efficient* or "moving cause" of the Scriptures? First and foremost, God. And with this, John brings his *resumptio* to a close.

John seems much less adept at dividing and dilating his opening *thema* as later masters would be. His word associations are also more complicated and less orderly than the associations of these later masters. Furthermore, he starts dilating his first *divisio* at the beginning of the *principium*, only to break off with a long digression that contains his *divisio textus* of the Scriptures. And then, only a few short sentences from the end, he returns to finish dilating the remaining parts of the *thema*. The result is that the opening *thema* verse does not really give a proper structure to the whole. It seems as though the use of the *thema* as a structuring device was still fairly new to him, or perhaps it was simply that the *sermo modernus* style was not yet as fully developed as it would become later.

---

[12] If the reader wonders whether the little word "this" (*hic*) has taken on more significance that than seems reasonable, it is important to remember that these medieval preachers are not doing exegesis. The verbal association is meant to bring the point back to mind during the process of recollection. If the association is odd, it may for that reason be even more memorable, thus serving its purpose. On this, see my discussion in *Reading the Sermons*, 11–15.

Henry of Ghent

Henry of Ghent, by contrast, was proficient at employing the methods of *divisio* and *dilatatio*, and he employs verbal associations that are orderly and clear.[13]

According to Henry, the first characteristic of the Scriptures is "the sublimity of their authority," which is from God who inspired them and is their efficient cause. This authority is suggested by the words "This is the book of the commandments."

The second characteristic of the Scriptures is "the profundity of their truth" – "truth" being, as it were, the *materia* out of which the Scriptures are formed. "The profundity of the truth" of the Scriptures is suggested, then, by the words "And the law that is forever."

The third characteristic of the Scriptures is "the fruitfulness of their use," by which "all who keep it shall come to life," words referring, says Henry, to the final cause of the Scriptures.

The fourth characteristic that sets the sacred Scriptures apart from all others, finally, is "the variety of its mode," which pertains to the *form* or formal cause, and this is communicated by the words from Baruch 4.2: "Turn back, therefore, O Jacob, and apprehend it, and walk in the path toward its splendor" (*Convertere igitur, Iacob et apprehende eam, et ambula per viam ad splendorem eius*).

On this view, the "matter" of the Scriptures is "the truth." But this truth is expressed in a variety of forms – or more precisely, communicated "in a variety of modes." This variety of modes, says Henry, consists in this: that "frequently while the letter signifies one thing, the meaning intended is another." On this point, Henry is echoing a key point made forty years earlier by John: that the sacred Scriptures transcend all the sciences (*scientias*) by its manner of speaking, because in one and the same sentence, it both narrates and reveals. The Scriptures narrate with respect to the literal sense which is signified, says Henry, by the words "apprehend it" in the verse from Baruch 4:2, and it reveals by means of the mystical sense, which is signified by the words "and walk in the path toward its splendor." The sense here is that we "apprehend" the truth of the literal sense more easily and straightforwardly, and then we walk in the path toward the splendor of that truth by means of the mystical senses. Indeed, says Henry, the splendor of the mystical senses "shines forth from the literal sense as from a cloud." John of La Rochelle had made a similar point about the unique mystical senses of the Scriptures using a different image declaring that the Scriptures are written "both within and without" (Ezekiel 2:10).

This comparison between John and Henry's use of Baruch 4:1 shows that different masters could deploy and develop the same biblical *thema* differently. Different masters, even those separated by twenty or forty years, could make similar, sometimes identical points, but not associate these points with the same words in the opening *thema* verse. John of La Rochelle and Henry both made use of the four Aristotelian causes in their *resumptio* addresses, for example, but they associated the formal, final, efficient, and material causes with different parts of the *thema* verse. Thomas, though a devoted student of Aristotle himself, did not structure his *resumptio* around the four Aristotelian causes, as we have seen. Rather, although he used the same *thema* verse from Baruch, he structured his *resumptio*

---

[13] Henry's *resumptio*. can be found in *Lectura ordinaria super sacram scripturam*, ed. Raymond Macken. See n. 11 for the full reference.

around the three "Ciceronian" characteristics of a successful oration: "to teach," "to delight," and "to change."

Not only did masters make different uses of the same *thema*; they also incorporated the required *divisio textus* in various ways. John started his *resumptio* with his *divisio textus* immediately after the opening statement of his *thema* verse. Thomas added his *divisio textus* to the end of his *resumptio*, after he had finished dilating the last part of his *thema*. Albert the Great, like Thomas, put his *divisio textus* at the end of his *resumptio* address, but he incorporated it nicely into the dilation of the last part of his *thema*. The Franciscan Matthew of Aquasparta, who incepted 1277–1278, was able to incorporate his *divisio textus* into the dilation of the last part of his *thema*, just as the Dominican Albert had years before.

Wherever the *divisio textus* was incorporated, it is clear that it was an important part of the *resumptio* address of any new master.[14] Reading through these lists of the various books of the Bible can be a laborious task, and for this reason, many readers skip over them in frustration, the way some readers skip over the famous "catalogue of ships" in Homer's *Iliad* or the genealogies of Jesus in the Gospels of Matthew and Luke. They are long lists filled with dozens of names, the importance of which is not always clear. Although I understand the frustration, I propose that these *divisiones textus* of the books of the Bible are actually invaluable for what they reveal about how these medieval masters conceived of the Scriptures.

The Theological Character of the Scholastic *Divisio Textus*

The lists and divisions of the biblical books included in the *resumptio* addresses of these medieval masters were not only a useful textual guide for students; they were also an important theological statement about the unity and diversity of salvation history.

In an article on what he describes as "that splendid scholastic device: the division of the text," John Boyle describes the method this way: "In a division of the text, a commentator states some theme that serves as an interpretive key for this commentary... With the theme stated, the commentator begins to divide the text, dividing each division in turn into smaller and smaller parts down to the verse or even smaller."[15]

---

[14] Unless it was replaced by a *divisio* of all the arts in relation to theology, as seems to have been the case with Bonaventure, the Cistercian Guy of Aumone, who incepted in 1256, and the first Cluniac master, Galdericus, who incepted in 1259. For more on Guy of Aumone, see Spatz, 103–107. For Galdericus, see Spatz, 111–117, and by the same author, "A Newly Identified Text: The Inception Speech of Galdericus, First Cluniac Regent Master of Theology at the University of Paris," *Archives d'histoire doctrinale et littéraire du moyen âge* 61 (1994), 133–147. We will have more to say about this practice in the chapter on Bonaventure's *resumptio*.

[15] See John Boyle, "The Theological Character of the Scholastic 'Division of Text' with Particular Reference to the Commentaries of Saint Thomas Aquinas," in *With Reverence for the Word: Medieval Exegesis in Judaism, Christianity, and Islam*, ed. J. McAuliffe, B. Walfish, and J. Goering (Oxford: Oxford University Press, 2003), 276–283. For the quoted line, see by the same author, "Authorial Intention and the *Divisio Textus*," in *Reading John with St. Thomas Aquinas*, ed. M. Levering and M. Dauphinais (Washington, DC: Catholic University of America Press, 2005), 3–8; quoted line on 7.

Described this way, the method of doing a *divisio textus* sounds very similar to the process by which a preacher crafted a thirteenth century *sermo modernus* style sermon. One begins by stating a theme (a *thema*), which one divides and subdivides in order to fit together in a sensible and orderly fashion the parts of the whole. The finished literary product is different, of course – a sermon as opposed to a *divisio textus* in a biblical commentary – but both reveal the sort of mindset St. Thomas expressed famously in the first chapter of his *Summa contra Gentiles* where he affirms that "it belongs to the wise man to order" (*quod sapientis est ordinare*) and "they are to be called wise who order things rightly" (*sapientes dicantur qui res directe ordinant*).[16] Crafting a suitable *divisio textus* was a way for a master to order the material in such a way as to enable his students to see the parts in relation to one another and to the whole. In a good *divisio textus*, no book stands in isolation, rather each stands in a rich and organic set of relations to the rest.[17]

But this was not merely a textual matter for these medieval masters, as if the master thought of themselves as doing no more than providing a convenient outline to help the students study.[18] The division of the text was, as Prof. Boyle has suggested, "precisely a means to arrive at ways of seeing the fundamental unity of revealed truth."[19] In the modern world, given our contemporary presuppositions about "texts," students are unlikely to view the words of a text, let alone the divisions of a text, as somehow revelatory of reality itself. For many students, what they read is "just" a text – no more than words on a page whose relation to anything in the "real world" remains doubtful or uncertain. For medieval thinkers, words were *signs* revelatory of *things*. Clarifying the meaning of the words on a page was not the *same as* understanding the realities signified by those words, but it was an important first step. Calling things by the right name was essential. Indeed, a good definition was meant to capture the essence of the thing. Seeing the similarities and differences between one thing and another was also a crucial part of "defining" and understanding them.

Consider, for example, the difference in our modern context of contrasting the "Old Testament" with the "New Testament" as opposed to talking about "the New Testament" in contrast to "the Hebrew Scriptures." When the early Christian fathers read the Psalms and the prophets, they read them looking for ways in which the text might *prefigure* Christ. A Jewish rabbi from the same time period would not have read them this way. For the rabbi, they would not have been part of the *Old* Covenant, as they were for the Church fathers; they were simply expressions of *the* Covenant. So too, students gets one interpretive lens on the Hebrew Scriptures if they think of the Torah (the Law) as the foundation of the whole book and then divide the remaining books between the Nevi'im (the Prophets) and the Kethuvim (the Writings); whereas they get a very different perspective if they read the Pentateuch as simply the first five books of a long series of books that include the "historical books," the "wisdom literature," and the "prophets."

---

[16] *Summa Contra Gentiles*, Bk 1, chapter 1.
[17] Cf. Boyle, "Authorial Intention," 7–8. In the original, Prof. Boyle is speaking about the division of a single book of Scripture. His point remains valid, in my view, when the scope is widened to include a *divisio* of the whole of the Scriptures.
[18] Modern professors sometimes supply such outlines to their students. One finds them also in the scholarly introductions to classic texts.
[19] Boyle, "Theological Character," 277.

So too, in the thirteenth century, it was one thing to envision the distinction between the Old Testament and the New in terms of the distinction between "signs" (Old Testament) and "things" (New Testament), as some Masters did, as opposed to distinguishing between them in terms of "law" (Old Testament) and "grace" (New Testament). Similarly, one's expectations might be very different reading the books of Kings and Chronicles under the heading "historical books" as opposed to reading them as moral "*exempla*" – examples (both good and bad) of the moral strictures contained in the law. In the first case, the student likely reads the books with an eye to their historical accuracy and veracity. In the second, the accuracy of the details of the historical event would be less important than understanding how the events exemplify the moral lesson intended.

So although the master's *divisio textus* certainly had a pedagogical value – it likely helped students remember all the books of the Bible in their proper order and prepared them to begin their studies on each individual book – the exercise of crafting these *divisiones* was also part of an effort to identify the unity of divine purpose behind and among the various books of the Bible, one rich enough that it could suitably be expressed only in a variety of forms, genres, and texts. So too, the effort to understand the unity of divine purpose behind and among the various books of the Bible was in turn part and parcel of their effort to understand the unity of divine purpose within God's salvific plan itself, from the creation recounted in Genesis to the end of history promised in the Book of Revelation.[20]

The Master's *Divisio*: A Unique Vision

Although crafting a *divisio textus* of all the books of the Bible was a required part of the inception ceremony for decades, no two were ever quite the same. There were sometimes similarities, but it appears to have been a requirement that each master should come up with his own distinctive version.

To give the reader a sense of the similarities and difference, I have provided in the appendices to this volume an outline of the *divisio textus* from the *resumptio* addresses of four masters who incepted at Paris over a roughly forty-year period between 1238 and 1278. To the two masters whose *resumptio* addresses we examined above, the Franciscan Master John of La Rochelle and the secular Master Henry of Ghent, we add another Franciscan, Matthew of Aquasparta, a personal pupil of Bonaventure's who incepted in 1277 or 1278.[21] This sampling is far from exhaustive, but it should provide us with sufficient context to appreciate Thomas's *divisio textus*, which we will consider separately in the text that follows. Thomas's inception in 1256 fell roughly halfway between the earliest inception, John of La Rochelle's in 1238, and the latest, Matthew of Aquasparta's in 1277/1278.

Since the reader can find full outlines in the appendices, I will focus attention here on five key points of comparison.

---

[20] Cf. Boyle, "Theological Character," 277: "For the scholastics, the division of the text is precisely a means to arrive at ways of seeing the fundamental unity of revealed truth."
[21] For John of La Rochelle's and Henry of Ghent's *principium in aula* and *resumptio*, see the references in n. 10. For Matthew of Aquasparta's text, see *Quaestiones Disputatae Selectae* (Florence: Quaracchi, 1903), 16–22.

First, the most basic division is the one between the Old and New Testaments, but masters establish the distinction between them in a variety of ways.

Unsurprisingly, the most basic division is between the Old Testament and the New. The Latin term they use is *testamentum*. Thomas uses this term in places, but in the *prima secundae* of his *Summa Theologiae*, he prefers "Old Law" and "New Law."

One popular way of distinguishing the Old Testament from the New in the thirteenth century was in terms of the distinction in Augustine's *De doctrina christiana* between "signs," which was associated with the Old Testament, and "things," associated with the New.[22] This statement by Henry is typical: "Since, therefore, according to Augustine, in the first book of *On Christian Doctrine*, 'every doctrine is either of signs or of things,' and Sacred Scripture is a doctrine, it contains both things and signs: signs in the Old Testament, things in the New."[23] John mentions "signs" (Old Testament) and "things" (New Testament) at the beginning of his *resumptio*; Matthew mentions it in the last section right before he begins his *divisio textus*.[24]

It is worth noting that Augustine himself never used the distinction between "signs" and "things" in the *De doctrina* to distinguish the Old Testament from the New.[25] The medieval application of this distinction between *signs* and *things* to the distinction between the Old Testament and the New was made possible by a creative synthesis of Augustine's discussion in *De doctrina* with his famous affirmation in the *Quaestiones in Heptateuchum* that "what lies hidden in the Old Testament is made manifest in the New."[26] Support would also have been found in *De spiritu et littera*, where Augustine says that God's grace "hid itself under a veil in the Old Testament, but it has been revealed in the Gospel of Christ according to the most perfectly ordered dispensation of the ages."[27] Reliance on this passage would explain the comment in Henry's *resumptio* that "the Old Testament was principally about signs predicting future grace revealed in the New Testament."[28] Henry provides no reference, nor did the editor supply a citation; but the reference to grace, predicted and revealed, makes it likely Henry was echoing that similar passage in Augustine's *De spiritu*.

---

[22] Cf. Augustine, *De doctrina christiana*, esp. II.1–3. Peter Lombard made the pair even more prevalent in the thirteenth century by arranging the *Sentences* around this distinction.

[23] Henry of Ghent, *Lectura ordinaria*, 12: "Cum igitur, secundum Augustinum, 1° De doctrina christiana, *omnis doctrina uel rerum est, uel signorum*, et sacra scriptura sit doctrina quaedam, aut igitur est rerum vel signorum. Signorum est in veteri testament, rerum vero in novo."

[24] See p. 14 in Matthew's *Quaestiones Disputatae Selectae*; his *divisio textus* begins on p. 16.

[25] John, Henry, and Matthew all refer to passages in the *De doctrina christiana*, but none of the passages they cite refer to the division between the Old and New Testaments. See, for example, Matthew's references to *De doctrina christiana* on 14. He, like John and Henry, bases the division between the Old Testament and the New on Augustine's comment in *De doctrina* II.6.7–8 about interpreting things hidden in the Scriptures by reference to things stated more clearly elsewhere. Yet, in the original context, this is a general comment, not one specifically about the relationship between the New Testament and the Old.

[26] See Augustine, *Quaestiones in heptateuchum* 2.72: "et in Vetere Novum lateat, et in Novo Vetus pateat."

[27] Augustine, *De spiritu et littera*, 27:15: "Haec gratia in Testamento vetere velata latitabat, quae in Christi Evangelio revelata est dispensatione temporum ordinatissima…"

[28] Henry of Ghent, *Lectura Ordinaria*, 12: "Vetus enim testamentum principaliter erat de signis prognosticis futuram gratiam novi testament indicantibus."

Hic est Liber: *Thomas's Resumptio*

The distinction between *sign* and *thing* is, however, merely one of a series of distinctions thirteenth-century masters used to distinguish the Old Testament from the New. Others included the distinction between judgment (OT) and mercy (NT); severity (OT) and piety (NT); labor (OT) and rest (NT); onerous burdens (OT) and light ones (NT); lessening evil deeds (OT) and helping men to do good (NT); temporal goods (OT) and eternal goods (NT); and finally, Thomas's distinction between the law (OT) and grace (NT).[29]

Second, all three masters have "law" as a key component of their *divisio* and make clear efforts to correlate the Old Testament with the New.

All three masters contrast the Old and the New Testaments as two types of "law."[30] This distinction allowed them to associate books and sections of the Old Testament with those in the New in imaginative and creative ways. All three Masters sub-divide the books of the Old Testament into the laws, set forth in the five books of the Pentateuch; the *exempla* ("moral examples") found in the historical books; the admonitions and exhortations to wisdom found in the sapiential (wisdom) books; and finally the prophecies in the books of the prophets. These divisions are then taken to correspond in various ways to analogous divisions in the New Testament. Matthew of Aquasparta is clearest in this regard. He suggests that "the Lord's precepts" in the four Gospels corresponding to the five books of the Mosaic Law; the historical *exempla* in the historical books correspond to the Acts of the Apostles; the Pauline and canonical epistles corresponding to the sapiential books of the Old Testament; and the Book of Revelation corresponds to the Old Testament prophetic books, because it (the Book of Revelation) deals with the future state of the Church.

John of La Rochelle, although he begins with the same distinction between the law and the historical *exempla* in the Old Testament, does not distinguish the New Testament books in these terms. He begins instead by characterizing the law as a kind of "teaching" (*doctrina*). The Old Testament is filled with various *doctrina*: teaching by means of law (the Pentateuch); teaching by means of historical *exempla* (the historical books); teaching by words of admonition (the sapiential books); and the teaching of truths to be believed about Christ (the prophetic books). When he turns his attention to the New Testament, he makes a twofold *divisio* between the evangelical teaching in the four Gospels and the apostolic teaching in the remaining books and epistles. However, in the final stages of his *divisio* of the books of the Old Testament, John also associates the four Major Prophets with the four Gospels: Daniel with Matthew, Jeremiah with Mark, Ezekiel with Luke, and Isaiah with John.

Both Matthew and Henry employ another means of associating the Old Testament and the New. Both masters associate Isaiah with the Incarnation, Jeremiah with Christ's passion and death, Ezekiel with His death and resurrection, and Daniel with the judgment at the end of time. Individual verses in each book suggest these associations. So, for example, the passage in Isaiah 7:14, "the Virgin shall conceive and bear a son," was widely taken to apply to the Incarnation and birth of Christ.[31] The passage in Daniel 7:13–14 about

---

[29] For a good example, see the list of distinctions in Henry of Ghent, *Lectura Ordinaria*, 13–16.

[30] So too, when Thomas later wrote the *Summa Theologiae*, he distinguished the Old Testament from the New by distinguishing the "Old Law" from the "New Law." See ST I–II, qq. 98–108.

[31] With the notable exception, as Beryl Smalley has pointed out, of Andrew of St. Victor. See Smalley, *The Study of the Bible in the Middle Ages* (Notre Dame, IN: University of Notre Dame

the apocalyptic "Son of Man" who comes on the clouds of heaven at the end of time and to whom the Ancient One will give "all dominion, glory, and power" had long been associated with the final apocalypse in the Book of Revelation.

Each Master crafted his own, unique *divisio textus* of the books of the Bible, but all of them were seeking to work out the implications of Augustine's claim that the Old Testament contained latently "in figures" what was manifested "in reality" in the New. While affirming plainly the distinction between the Old Testament and the New, they also sought to identify a unity of the divine plan behind the distinction.[32]

Third, much more effort is expended on partitioning the Old Testament than the New

Although a chief concern among all three masters was to show how the Old Testament is a prefiguration culminating in the New, oddly enough, all three masters – and this will be true of Aquinas as well – spend much more space dividing and subdividing the books of the Old Testament than they do the New. The Old Testament is admittedly much larger than the New, with a greater number and variety of books, but this alone does not explain the difference. These masters supply exhaustive categories and subcategories to account for each book of the Old Testament, but when they came to the New Testament, they listed each of the four Gospels and then lumped all the remaining books into broad categories such as "Pauline epistles" and "canonical epistles" without listing the individual books.

Consider, in this regard, the very detailed *divisio textus* of all the Pauline epistles Thomas provides in the prologue to his *Commentary on the Epistles of St. Paul*, based on the *thema* verse from Acts 9:15, "This man is for me a vessel of election to bear my name before the Gentiles, kings, and the children of Israel" (*vas electionis est mihi iste, ut portet nomen meum coram gentibus, et regibus, et filiis Israel*), which I discuss in detail in Chapter 7. None of this material appeared in his *resumptio* address, where he mentions none of the epistles by name but says of them collectively only that they deal with "the power of grace."

It was not uncommon for masters to expend nearly all their efforts partitioning and categorizing all the various books of the Old Testament and to devote comparatively less time dealing with the individual books of the New.

Fourth, even when the three masters use the same divisions, they often create their own subdivisions and descriptions.

Although written over a roughly forty-year spread, several of the basic categories these masters used remain remarkably constant: the categories of law, *exempla*, and prophets figure in all three treatments of the Old Testament, although John of La Rochelle and

---

Press, 1989), esp. 232–234. Andrew was roundly criticized for holding this view, however, by his religious confrere Richard of St. Victor in *De Emmanuele*.

[32] Cf. Henri de Lubac, *Catholicism: Christ and the Common Destiny of Man* (San Francisco: Ignatius, 1947, 1950, 1988), 176–177, who describes "the same fundamental principle" shared by the early Church fathers: "From the beginning 'the harmonious agreement of the Law and the Prophets with the Testament delivered by the Lord' was the 'rule of the Church'. In the conjunction of the two Testaments was woven a single vesture for the Word, together they formed one body..." For a long list of references to fathers of the early Church from both East and West who gave expression to "this 'consonantia' of the two Testaments – which is more than their mere 'concord'," see de Lubac, 176, n. 41.

Henry of Ghent place *exempla* as a subcategory under "law," whereas Matthew of Aquasparta gives it its own separate category.

Another complication involves the question of what to do with the Wisdom literature and the Psalms. John and Henry, perhaps taking their cue from Christ's words in Luke 24:44, "Everything must be fulfilled that is written about me in the Law of Moses, the Prophets and the Psalms," made a threefold *divisio* between law, prophets, and Psalms foundational. Matthew took a different approach and included the Psalms as a species of prophecy. And whereas Matthew separates the Wisdom books into their own separate category, John and Henry included them under *exempla*, categorizing them as "paternal" admonitions delivered in words, rather than examples in deeds such as we find in the historical books.

This is not the only place where Matthew of Aquasparta's *divisio* departs from the pattern laid down by his Franciscan predecessor John of La Rochelle. Indeed, there are greater similarities between the *divisio* of the Franciscan master John of La Rochelle and the secular master Henry of Ghent, who incepted forty years later, than there are between the two Franciscans John and Matthew of Aquasparta. Given that Matthew's teacher was Bonaventure, and Bonaventure's was John, we might have expected Matthew to be the one repeating John's categories, not Henry. Henry of Ghent had studied with the Dominican Albert the Great, and yet Henry is the one we find echoing the Franciscan master of forty years earlier. This may suggest there was not a distinctly "Franciscan" or "Dominican" way of crafting a *divisio* and that perhaps the lines of influence did not always fall into traditional patterns of ecclesiastical inheritance. More study would be needed to verify this conclusion, however.

The most numerous and complicated series of divisions and subdivisions are always to be found among the *exempla*. Clearly the effort to categorize all the books of the Old Testament from Joshua, Judges, Kings, and Chronicles up to Job, Tobit, Judith, and Esther was no small task: there are many books of varying genres and the relationships among them is not obvious – unlike the five books of the Pentateuch, which have a much clearer unity. And yet, even the five books of the Pentateuch were also subjected to divisions and subdivisions. John and Henry both made divisions among the books of the Pentateuch in order to account for various elements of the natural and Mosaic laws.

It had become a commonplace by the thirteenth century to distinguish the four "major prophets" – Isaiah, Jeremiah, Ezekiel, and Daniel – from the others, the twelve so-called "minor prophets." This distinction was made centuries earlier, likely for purely utilitarian reasons, "major" and "minor" being designations of the size, not the importance, of the book. Matthew of Aquasparta testifies to the fact that, even in his day, the books of the twelve Minor Prophets were bound together in one volume, as were the four books of the Major Prophets. But by the thirteenth century, it had also become a commonplace to associate the books of the four "major prophets" with the four Evangelists – Matthew, Mark, Luke, and John – and to associate the books of the twelve Minor Prophets with the twelve apostles. In this way, a *theological* significance was attributed to what had originally been simply a decision about binding and book-making. But these associations between the four Major Prophets and the four Gospels and between the twelve prophets and the twelve apostles, although not immediately apparent to us, were a commonplace to these medieval masters. Which bring us to our fifth and final point.

Fifth, it is likely that these many of these *divisiones* were crafted with an eye toward (a) memory, and (b) their usefulness as aids to preaching.

With regard to all these odd categories and complicated attempts to relate the books of the Old Testament with the books of the New, we might wonder: Why all the fuss? Why expend so much time and energy creating these divisions and associations? This was not just the strange obsession of a single scholar; it was a mandatory exhibition of skill required of every incoming master at the University of Paris. We would have a better appreciation of these divisions and distinctions if we understood them, first, as examples of the "memory culture" that characterized the High Middle Ages, and second, as expressions of the increased concern to foster better preaching that arose in the thirteenth century in the wake of the Fourth Lateran Council.

Let me begin with the first of these: the *divisio* as an aid to memory. As Mary Carruthers has ably demonstrated in her book *The Book of Memory: A Study of Memory in Medieval Culture*, the culture in which Thomas and Bonaventure worked was a "memory culture" devoted to the arts of memory.[33] These arts were invaluable not only because of the relative lack of actual books, but also because, even though more written books were becoming available, there was a related need to keep different types of information relevant to the study of these books stored in one's memory.

I argued in an earlier chapter (and have argued in more detail in my book on the sermons of Aquinas) that the *divisiones* in *sermo modernus* style sermon were memory aids – mnemonic devices intended to help the listener recall the major points of the sermon by bringing to mind the opening biblical *thema* verse. This was especially helpful for providing continuity during the break between the morning's sermon and the evening's continuation at vespers. By University regulation, masters assigned to preach at the first were also required to preach at the second and use the same *thema* verse.[34]

Above I compared the process of crafting a "modern sermon" with Prof. John Boyle's description of *divisio textus* as a process wherein "a commentator states some theme" which serves to unite his commentary, and then "[w]ith the theme stated, the commentator begins to divide the text, dividing each division in turn into smaller and smaller parts...".[35] The goal of both the *divisio* by which the "modern sermon" was constructed and the *divisio textus* by which a text was divided was to divide a large mass of material into smaller, more easily grasped memory "cells" or "units" and then associate each of these with the parts of something easily memorized or something already known by heart, such as a single Bible verse.

The classic example of memory and recollection in oratory was a Roman orator memorizing a speech by associating the various parts with the buildings, piazzas, and temples he passes each day on his walk around the city. The walk isn't something he has to commit to memory; to be useful for this purpose, it must be something he knows so well already that he can bring it to mind automatically. He must be able to do that walk in his mind, so that, as he comes mentally to each new sight along his route, he can recollect the point he

---

[33] Mary Carruthers, *The Book of Memory: A Study of Memory in Medieval Culture* (Cambridge: Cambridge University Press, 1990; now in a second edition, 2008).
[34] See *Reading the Sermons of Aquinas*, esp. 4–18.
[35] Boyle, "Authorial Intention," 7.

associated with it. It was likely that orators who used this method walked the same route over and over, practicing the speech as they went. Seeing the progression of sights along the walk had presumably become second nature to them. It was the strength of the associations with each of these sights along the way that allowed the orator to recall a long speech in the proper order from beginning to end. Making memorable associations was the trick.

The difference between the *divisio* which established the structure of the *sermo modernus* sermon and the *divisio textus* of the sort a master would make when he was commenting on a book is that, in the first case, each of the elements of the sermon had to be associated with a single Bible verse. Associating all of the books of the Bible individually with the words of one *thema* verse would have been impossible. Indeed, medieval preachers were generally prudent in this regard, realizing that one should not try to collect more than four or five items under any one heading.

Consider, in this connection, Matthew of Aquasparta's *divisio* of the books of the Old Testament. Note that he has divided the various books into an orderly series of five books in five categories.

Law: Genesis, Exodus, Leviticus, Numbers, Deuteronomy
Exempla **(general)**: Joshua, Judges, Kings, Chronicles, Ezra-Nehemiah
Exempla **(notable persons)**: Job, Tobit, Judith, Esther, the Maccabees
Wisdom: Proverbs, Ecclesiastes, Ecclesiasticus, Wisdom, Song of Songs
Prophets: Psalms (a special case), Isaiah, Jeremiah, Ezekiel, Daniel

What remains is simply to remember that there are twelve "minor prophets" corresponding to the twelve apostles. However complex these scholastic *divisiones textus* became, it is noteworthy that Parisian masters did not as a rule list out individually all twelve Minor Prophets or all of the Pauline and canonical epistles. These lists would have been too long. A good list for memorizing usually contained no more than four or five items.

Although the practice of making these *divisiones* has much to do with the memory culture with which the medieval university was imbued, the particular categories and associations we find in them were likely crafted with an eye to fostering good preaching. Consider, for example,

John of La Rochelle and Henry of Ghent's subcategories under *exempla*. Both subdivide Kings, Chronicles, Ezra, and Nehemiah according to the books dealing with the active life (Kings and Nehemiah) and those concerning the contemplative life (Chronicles and Ezra). Nehemiah is associated with the active life because he undertook to repair the city of Jerusalem; Ezra is associated with the contemplative life because he repaired the Temple and restored observance of the Mosaic Law. This imaginative contrast between the "active" and the "contemplative" life as exemplified in the lives of Nehemiah and Ezra is precisely the sort of imagery that makes for lively preaching. In contemporary practice, we are more likely to hear about Martha, who represents the "active life," taking care of the household chores, while her sister, Mary, who represents the "contemplative life," sits listening at the feet of Jesus.

So too, it is much easier to conceive of what one might say about the various complex historical details in the books of Joshua, Judged, Kings, and Chronicles if one thinks about them as source books for "*exempla*": illustrative moral stories and examples which can be incorporated into one's preaching. Modern preachers, by contrast, have a hard time knowing *what* to say about these complicated historical accounts, so many preachers simply avoid preaching on them altogether.

The classic way of dealing with the problem that medieval preachers inherited from the early Church was to relate the books of the Old Testament with the books of the New in accord with St. Augustine's dictum that what lies hidden in the Old Testament is made manifest in the New. Even in our own day, when the council fathers at the Second Vatican Council came to the conclusion that the lectionary needed to be reformed to include more readings from the Old Testament, the way they chose to incorporate these texts was to select an Old Testament reading that corresponded to the reading from the Gospel. This is why, although the Gospel readings are organized so as to guide the congregation systematically through Matthew (Year A), Mark (Year B), and Luke (Year C), the readings from the Old Testament are taken from all over, depending upon what passage appears that day in the Gospel. Although jumping from one Old Testament book to another from week to week is not a particularly good way to read through the Old Testament or even to understand individual books such as Exodus, Leviticus, or any of the prophets, it is a more suitable way to organize the lectionary for the purposes of preaching. Something similar was at work, I suggest, in the organization of these *divisiones* of the biblical books in the thirteenth century.

Thomas Aquinas's Divisio Textus

We turn now to Thomas Aquinas's *divisio textus*, a complete outline of which can be found in the Appendix to this volume. The goal of our prior examination of the *divisiones* crafted by other thirteenth-century masters was to provide a better context within which we might then be able to take note of how Thomas's work resembles theirs in certain ways but differs in others.

In agreement with his fellow masters, Thomas sees the Old Testament primarily in "legal" terms, as various kinds of law or various ways of applying the law. So, for example, he divides the Old Testament according to the various types of precepts it contains, the basic division being between those precepts that *bind* and those that merely *warn*. The binding precepts, says Thomas, are to be understood as analogous to "the commands of a king who can punish transgressors"; those that merely warn are analogous to "the precepts of a father who must teach." Thomas further subdivides this first category into two, suggesting that the precepts of a king are of two kinds: one that establishes the laws and another that induces to observance of the law, which is customarily done through his heralds and ambassadors. The result is a division of the Old Testament into three basic parts: books containing royal commandments; books containing heraldic inducements to obey the commandments; and books containing fatherly warnings to act justly. This threefold distinction replaces the more common division among other masters between law, *exempla*, and prophets.

Thomas's threefold division into *commandments*, *inducements*, and *admonitions* is in its own way, however, an echo of John of La Rochelle's division of *precepts*, such as we find in the Pentateuch; *exempla*, such as we find in the historical books; and *admonitions*, such as we find in the Wisdom books. Thomas tucks the prophets under the heading "heralds who induce observance of the law," while John had put them into their own separate category.

Although some of the terms are the same, Thomas crafts his own unique set of categories and subdivisions. So, for example, the division of some historical books in one category ("heralds who induce the observance of the law"), some in another (under "precepts of a father who teaches – by deed"), is unique to Thomas.

John of La Rochelle had suggested that the four Major Prophets speak about the head, namely Christ, while the twelve Minor Prophets speak about the body, the Church. Thomas affirms, by contrast, that the Major Prophets were those who "were sent to the whole people and called for observance of the whole law," while the Minor Prophets were sent to particular tribes of Israel, each for different reasons. Thomas is, in fact, the only master who mentions any of the Minor Prophets by name, listing Hosea and Jonah as two who imparted edicts of the law "for special reasons to special tribes." Thomas does say elsewhere (echoing John of La Rochelle) that the Major Prophets speak about Christ, with Isaiah foretelling the Incarnation, Jeremiah the Passion, and Ezekiel the Resurrection, but he differs from John by making no mention of the Minor Prophets speaking about "the body," the Church.

Unlike John, Henry, and Matthew, Thomas does not use the term *exempla*. Rather he uniquely associate certain books with each of the four cardinal virtues: justice with Chronicles, temperance with Judith, fortitude with Maccabees and Tobit, and prudence with Ezra-Nehemiah and Esther. Further on, he associates three of the "sapiential" books – Proverbs, Ecclesiastes, and the Song of Songs – with the three categories of virtue listed by Plotinus. The political virtues, which involve the use of this world, he associates with Proverbs. The purgative virtues, which involve contempt for worldly goods, he associates with Ecclesiastes. Finally, the virtues of the purged soul wholly cleansed from worldly cares and given over to contemplation alone, he associates with the Song of Songs.

Although Thomas is renowned as one of the prime expositors of the natural law, it is interesting to note that, in his *resumptio*, he does not follow John of La Rochelle's lead in associating the natural law with the book of Genesis. This may have something to do with the fact that, in John's *divisio*, the natural law involves primarily conserving the individual and the species before the Fall and resisting concupiscence and blood lust after the Fall. In the *Summa Theologiae*, by contrast, Thomas employs a threefold distinction that he inherited from Cicero's *De officiis* (IV.1) in order to differentiate between (a) the inclination to preserve one's life, (b) the inclination to procreate and raise the young, and (c) the inclination to live in society and know the truth about God.[36] The last of these, which is the most important for Aquinas, is missing from John's schema. Thomas would also not have agreed with John's claim that the origin of the judicial precepts were to be found in the Noahide law against eating meat mingled with blood (cf. Genesis 9.4). On Thomas's account, the judicial precepts were divine positive law precepts given by God through Moses in the Mosaic Law.

Whatever accounts for its absence, the natural law does not show up explicitly anywhere in Thomas's *divisio textus*. One might wish to claim that it is present implicitly, but if so, it is in connection with the virtues, which are mentioned explicitly.

---

[36] Cf. ST I–II, q. 94, a. 2.

Whereas John of La Rochelle says that New Testament is divided into two parts: the *evangelical*, dealing with Christ, and the *apostolic* – the second of which is divided into *origins* (Acts of the Apostles), *doctrine* (Epistles), and *consummation* of the Church (Apocalypse) – Thomas divides the New Testament into *the origin of grace* (the Gospels), *the power of grace* (the Pauline Epistles), and *the execution of the power of grace* in the progress of the Church, in whose development there are three stages: the beginning of the Church, treated in the Acts of the Apostles; the progress of the Church, treated in the canonical epistles; and the end of the Church, which we find in the Apocalypse.

Whereas other masters described the New Testament as the locus of laws, teachings, and moral *exempla*, no one else but Thomas mentions the centrality of grace. Significantly, when Thomas many years later finally crafted a *divisio textus* of the Pauline epistles (and outline of which I have inserted into his *divisio*) he did so precisely in terms of the various modes and categories of grace, as he had suggested years before at his inception.

Thomas's *divisio* has fewer explicit associations between the Old and the New than those of John, Henry, and Matthew, rather he puts more emphasis on the grace of Christ as a unique gift enabling us (a) to live in accord with the precepts and admonitions of the Old Law, and (b) to develop the virtues exemplified in the Old Testament books.

Note as well that when Thomas writes his *Summa theologiae*, he will propose the same *divisio* to distinguish between the Old Law and the New Law as he did years before in his *resumptio*. In the prologue to ST I-II, q. 90, Thomas lays out the *divisio textus* of the final part of the *prima secundae*, saying:

> We have now to consider the extrinsic principles of acts. Now the extrinsic principle inclining to evil is the devil, of whose temptations we have spoken in the first part. But the extrinsic principle moving to good is God, Who both instructs us by means of His Law, and assists us by His Grace: wherefore in the first place we must speak of law; in the second place, of grace.

This was the basic *divisio* Thomas employed years before in his *resumptio*: the Old Testament commanding or warning by law or precept, the New Testament or "New Law" helping with gifts of grace. Thomas was among the first to use the term "the New Law," but Henry of Ghent picked it up some years later and incorporated it into his *resumptio*.

Thomas's *divisio* was both elegant and simple. It does some things better than others, but it could not do everything. A *divisio* of this sort was not meant to be "the last word." If this had been the goal, University officials would not have asked for a new one from each incepting master. These *divisiones* of the books of the Bible were meant, rather, as a "first word": a beginning task for the newly incepted master to demonstrate his ability to lay out a beginning lecture and a beginning outline for his incoming students. In years to come, Thomas would be expected to lecture on whatever books of the Bible the needs of the students dictated. In those circumstances, his first task would be to give a *principium*, a prologue lecture in the *sermo modernus* style, as part of which he would lay out for his students a *divisio textus* to aid his students in their reading and to give them a road map of the lectures to come. In his *resumptio* and its accompanying *divisio textus*, Thomas demonstrated not only the skills necessary for inception as a master theologian, but also the skills of laying out an admirably clear outline for his students, the hallmark of the great and marvelously lucid teacher he would become.

Why Do a *Divisio Textus*?

There clearly seems to have been a presumption at Paris during this period that a fully certified master should be capable of laying out this sort of fully worked out *divisio textus*. Why was this particular intellectual skill valued? I know of no explicit comments from University officials as to *why* it was required; we only know *that* it was. And yet several contemporary masters spoke of its value. Henry of Ghent defended the practice in his *principium*, claiming that it was important "because we often take more easily divided into parts what we are not capable of swallowing whole," therefore "in order that we might temper the difficulty of sacred Scripture for ourselves as much as possible, we approach it by first dividing it into parts."[37] On this account, crafting a suitable *divisio textus* was an aid to memory and understanding, and it was a pedagogical tool to help oneself and one's students assimilate a large mass of material.

So too the Dominican master Stephen of Besançon stated near the beginning of his *resumptio* delivered at Paris in 1286:

> In the *principium* of a science or of a book, the intention of doctors is accustomed to touch on two things. They are accustomed to commend learning in order to have benevolent listeners (*auditores benivolos*). Also, they are accustomed to treat the causes and offer a general division in order to render them docile and attentive (*dociles et attentos*). Yesterday we showed, from the word proposed [i.e., the biblical *thema* verse], that Sacred Scripture is commendable and surpasses all others. Now the causes will be treated and the division of the books..."[38]

Those who know the classical rhetorical tradition will recognize within that last paragraph an echo of the famous "three purposes" of the introduction or *exordium* of any speech (which, it is worth noting, the *Rhetorica ad Herennium* calls the "*principium*" of a speech). In the first book of the *Rhetorica*, the author (who, during the Middle Ages, was thought to be Cicero) declares: "The *principium* immediately prepares the soul of the hearer to attend to our speech. Its purpose is to enable us to have hearers who are attentive (*adtentos*), receptive (*dociles*), and well-disposed (*benivolos*)."[39] So too in Cicero's *De inventione* 1.15.20, we read: "An exordium is an address bringing the mind of the hearer into a suitable state to receive the rest of the speech; and that will be effected if it has rendered him well disposed towards

---

[37] Henry of Ghent, *Lectura ordinaria super sacram scripturam*, 12: "Sed quia plerumque per partes divisum facilius capiemus quod integrum deglutire non valemus, ut igitur difficultatem sacrae scripturae quantum possumus nobis temperemus, primo eam dividendo per partes aggrediamur." Translation quoted from Spatz, 152.

[38] "In principio scientie vel libri circa duo versari solet doctorum intencio. Solent primo scienciam commendare ut habeant auditores benevolos. Solent eciam causas tangere et generalem divisionem premitterre ut reddant eos dociles et attentos. Heri ex verbo proposito sacram scripturam commendabilem ostendimus, et omnes alias precellentem. Modo cause tangende sunt et librorum divisio;..." Translation quoted from Spatz, 153. For Latin, see Spatz, 61–62, n. 33, her transcription of Hereford Cathedral Library, ms. P.iii.3, f. 113r.

[39] [Cicero], *Rhetorica ad Herennium*, trans. Harry Caplan, Loeb Classical Library (Cambridge, MA: Harvard University Press, 1954), 1.4.6: "Principium est cum statim auditoris animum nobis idoneum reddimus ad audiendum. Id ita sumitur ut adtentos, ut dociles, ut benivolos auditores habere possimus."

the speaker (*benivolum*), attentive (*attentum*), and willing to receive information (*docilem*)."⁴⁰ And again in Quintillian's *Institutio oratoria* 4.1.5:

> The sole purpose of the exordium is to prepare our audience in such a way that they will be disposed to lend a ready ear to the rest of our speech. The majority of authors agree that this is best effected in three ways, by making the audience well-disposed (*benivolum*), attentive (*attentum*) and ready to receive instruction (*docilem*). I need hardly say that these aims have to be kept in view throughout the whole speech, but they are especially necessary at the commencement, when we gain admission to the mind of the judge in order to penetrate still further.⁴¹

Note in each of these passages the different English translations of the Latin *docile*. We get "receptive," in the first case; "willing to receive information," in the second; and "ready to receive instruction," in the third. Although in the modern world the word "docile" carries connotations of being tractable and easily managed, the Latin word *docilis* is related to the Latin verb *docere*, "to teach," and means "easily taught."

The three purposes of an exordium or *principium* – to make listeners attentive (*attentos*), receptive (*dociles*), and well-disposed (*benivolos*) – were well known in the Middle Ages, both because the classical rhetorical texts quoted above were widely distributed and because of the praise given the art of rhetoric in Book 4 of Augustine's *De doctrina christiana*:

> Now, the art of rhetoric being available for the enforcing either of truth or falsehood, who will dare to say that truth in the person of its defenders is to take its stand unarmed against falsehood? That those who are trying to persuade men of what is false are to know how to introduce their subject, so as to put the hearer into a friendly (*benevolum*), or attentive (*intentum*), or teachable frame of mind (*docilem*), while the defenders of the truth shall be ignorant of that art? That the former are to tell their falsehoods briefly, clearly, and plausibly, while the latter shall tell the truth in such a way that it is tedious to listen to, hard to understand, and, in fine, not easy to believe it? That the former are to oppose them to melt, to enliven, and to rouse them, while the latter shall in defense of the truth be sluggish, and frigid, and somnolent? Who is such a fool as to think this wisdom? Since, then, the faculty of eloquence is available for both sides, and is of very great service in the enforcing either of wrong or right, why do not good men study to engage it on the side of truth, when bad men use it to obtain the triumph of wicked and worthless causes, and to further injustice and error?⁴²

---

⁴⁰ C. D. Yonge, trans, *The Orations of Marcus Tullius Cicero*, vol. 4 (London: George Bell & Sons, 1888): "Exordium est oratio animum auditoris idonee comparans ad reliquam dictionem quod eveniet, si eum benivolum attentum docilem confecerit."

⁴¹ Quintillian, *Institutio oratoria*, trans. H. E. Butler, Loeb Classical Library (Cambridge, MA: Harvard University Press, 1922), 4.1.5: "Causa principii nulla alia est quam ut auditorem quo sit nobis in ceteris partibus accommodatior praeparemus. Id fieri tribus maxime rebus inter auctores plurimos constat, si benivolum attentum docilem fecerimus, non quia ista non per totam actionem sint custodienda, sed quia initiis praecipue necessaria, per quae in animum iudicis ut procedere ultra possimus admittimur."

⁴² Augustine, *De doctrina christiana*, trans. James Shaw, Nicene and Post-Nicene Fathers, First Series, vol. 2, ed. Philip Schaff. (Buffalo, NY: Christian Literature Publishing, 1887), 4.2.3. See also the

This passage inspired generations of medieval preachers to embrace the arts of rhetoric, as we can see in the passage quoted above from Stephen of Besançon's *principium* address.

But let's take a closer look at that passage. Note how Stephen says that, in the *principium* of a science or of a book, doctors: (a) "commend learning in order to have benevolent listeners," and (b) "treat the causes and offer a general division in order to render the docile and attentive." *Treating the causes* in this context meant the four Aristotelian causes: the efficient (author), material (subject matter), formal (manner of proceeding), and final (purpose) causes of the text. On Stephen's understanding, therefore, in commending the Sacred Scriptures, as he had done in his *principium in aula*, he had accomplished only *one* of the three goals of a *principium*: making listeners "benevolent." It was to be by means of the *resumptio*, with its account of the four causes and its *divisio textus*, that students would be rendered "docile" (teachable) and "attentive."

Although modern readers generally don't think of a completed *divisio textus* as an effective means of rhetoric or of rendering students "teachable" and "attentive," the masters of theology at Paris in the thirteenth century appear to have believed that a *principium* address delivered at the beginning of the term, along with its appropriate *divisio textus* of the book to be commented upon, would, like the parts of the medieval sermon, help to focus the student's attention in appropriate ways. The *principium* was meant as an exhortation to get the students interested in the subject matter and to render them good-willed toward the study they were about to undertake. The *divisio textus* was meant to help focus their attention on the main points to be covered and provide a suitable road map of the complex terrain ahead. Just as acquainting oneself with a good road map in advance of a journey, noting the major obstacles and twists and turns in the road, can help us not lose our way, so too having a good *divisio textus* can help students not lose track of where they are in the context of the whole of the text as they move from section to section.

Modern theories of education recommend that teachers break vast amounts of material down into more readily digestible sections and then communicate clearly to students as they move from one section to the next. Anyone who has taught an "Introduction to the Bible" course knows how difficult it is to give students an adequate picture of the whole of the Bible, given the vast collection of books and different literary genres. It is usually necessary to skip over and even ignore many books. What masters like John of La Rochelle, Henry of Ghent, Matthew of Aquasparta, and Thomas Aquinas attempted to do instead was to provide their students with an adequate road map of the whole terrain before setting out on the journey into any one region.

Latin in Augustine, *De doctrina christiana*, Oxford Early Christian Texts (Oxford: Oxford University Press, 1995), 196: "Nam cum per artem rhetoricam et vera suadeantur et falsa, quis audeat dicere, adversus mendacium in defensoribus suis inermem debere consistere veritatem, ut videlicet illi qui res falsas persuadere conantur, noverint auditorem vel bene volum vel intentum vel docilem proemio facere; isti autem non noverint? Illi falsa breviter, aperte, verisimiliter et isti vera sic narrent ut audire taedeat, intellegere non pateat, credere postremo non libeat? Illi fallacibus argumentis veritatem oppugnent, asserant falsitatem, isti nec vera defendere nec falsa valeant refutare? Illi animos audientium in errorem moventes impellentesque dicendo terreant, contristent, exhilarent, exhortentur ardenter; isti pro veritate lenti frigidique dormitent? Quis ita desipiat ut hoc sapiat? Cum ergo sit in medio posita facultas eloquii, quae ad persuadenda seu prava seu recta valet plurimum, cur non bonorum studio comparatur, ut militet veritati, si eam mali ad obtinendas perversas vanasque causas in usus iniquitatis et erroris usurpant?

Thus the two ultimate goals of the *principium* address were, as Stephen of Besançon suggests, first, to commend the importance of the Scriptures, and second, to help make the audience members more "attentive" by providing an instructive division of the material. As we have seen, these are the basic goals of any *exordium* or prologue: first, to render the audience interested and open by commending the subject matter; and second, to divide the topic so as to make the audience more attentive to your points and to make those points easier to recall later.

In the mid-thirteenth century, all these elements of the rhetorical arts were focused on the sacred Scriptures. So, for example, the audience was to be made "benevolent" not toward the speaker per se, but toward the Scriptures. *They* are what must be commended. So too the audience was to be made "docile" and "attentive" not toward the message of the master per se, but toward the Scriptures, for the Scriptures are what really do the teaching. The medieval prologue, rather than prompting good will toward the speaker, turns the attention of the audience toward the Scriptures as the source of wisdom and eloquence.

A final clue to the value and importance of the *divisio textus* can be found in the prologue to Thomas's *Summa contra gentiles*, quoted earlier, where he addresses the "office of the wise man" (*officium sapientis*). They are called "wise," says Thomas, "who order things rightly" (*qui res directe ordinant*). So too, "it belongs to the wise man to consider the highest causes" (*sapientis est causas altissimas considerare*). Therefore, concludes Thomas, although there is a certain limited wisdom among those who possess knowledge about particular things, "the name of the absolutely wise man" (*nomen autem simpliciter sapientis*) must be "reserved for him whose consideration is directed to the end of the universe" (*finem universi*), which is also "the origin of the universe" (*universitatis principium*). It made sense, therefore, on this understanding of "wisdom," to insist that the master who wished to show himself truly "wise" should be able to show that he could discern the "order" between and among the books of the Bible, since, for Christian theologians of the thirteenth century, the "origins" and "end" of the universe were thought to be revealed most definitively by God Himself in those books.

Categorizing the Books of the Bible: Then and Now

Finally, it might be instructive to consider for a moment how approaching the books Bible guided by the perspective of these medieval *divisiones* would have differed from the ways we approach these books in the modern world. In the modern world, a Bible is usually a single book with a Table of Contents. Medieval students would have encountered the Scriptures very differently. They generally would not have been able to use a single, bound Bible for study purposes. They might have seen or handled a large, bound volume in liturgical settings, but it is unlikely that any individual student, especially a member of a mendicant order, could have possessed a single, bound volume containing all the books of the Bible.

The books of what we now call "the Bible" ("the book") and what they called "the sacred Scriptures" ("the sacred writings") would usually have been available to students outside of liturgical contexts only in smaller collections of books: law, prophets, historical books. Given that their students most often experienced the Scriptures only in scattered parts, these medieval masters may have felt the need to express to their students some principle of unity to help clarify why they should consider this scattered collection of books one unified whole.

Currently, the books in modern Christian Bibles are usually organized according to genres, starting with the five books of the Law, followed by the historical books, the Psalms and Wisdom literature, and finally by the four Major Prophets and the twelve Minor Prophets. What is missing in this presentation is any sense of how each individual book relates to all the others within a unified and ordered pedagogy, or how the order of the books correspond to the order of salvation history. So too, in modern "study Bibles," one often finds a useful scholarly introduction at the beginning of each book – an "encyclopedic" prologue of the modern sort, which I described in the Introduction. Such prologues often contain valuable information about *that one book*, but not only do they embody the modern "encyclopedic" presuppositions about reading, they also provide the reader little sense of the connections and relationships between the book being introduced and the other books in the canon.

Medieval masters, by contrast, sought to communicate to their students not merely a textual unity, but also a sense of the unity of salvation history – a sense that these books were part of a single divine will meant to transform their readers in important ways in order to bring them to their ultimate union with God in heaven, both by instructing them in truths they needed to understand and in the virtues they needed to develop in order that they might fully realize their true nature in the love of God and neighbor.

Consider the difference to the student between approaching the Old Testament as a series of books in an ancient library, or as a series of artifacts of an ancient religious society – Isaiah as an expression of 8th century BC Jewish history and culture, Jeremiah as an expression of sixth-century national and religious concerns, and so on – as opposed to approaching the books of Isaiah, Ezekiel, and Jeremiah as an application of Torah to the life of the People of God and/or as a foretaste and prefiguration of the New Covenant in Christ. It is one thing to read the Scriptures as the remnants of scholarly work catalogued in a library of ancient manuscripts, quite another to read them as inspired texts by which the Triune God has communicated Himself to humankind in order to invite them into a deeper communion of selfless love with Him and with each other. I do not wish to be mistaken on this point, however. A mature biblical faith should be open to the possibility that the books of the Bible are *both* expressions of the time, place, and culture in which they were written *and* an inspired revelation of God. My present aim was simply to note the differences in the way the reader approaches the text if he or she privileges one interpretive lens over the other.

The *divisiones textus* of these medieval masters witnessed to a belief that every book of the Bible had its own proper place within the whole – a "whole" that was profoundly important for human flourishing. It is also worth noting that these *divisiones textus* of the books of the Bible were included in a *resumptio* address which by University statute had as its purpose a commendation in praise of the sacred Scriptures as the highest source of wisdom. As we have seen, medieval masters were less interested in producing *the definitive* arrangement of the biblical books as they were in helping the students to understand that each individual book played its part in the larger project of the whole, the purpose of which was to lead mankind back to God by teaching us in manifold ways the Way of God's Own Wisdom.

When preached and presented in this way, the Scriptures were not understood to be just another book or set of books to be read the way one might read a shelf of books containing

Aristotle, Cicero, or Homer. The Scriptures were not just another "text"; they were the "word of God," and as such they both charted a trajectory for human flourishing and enabled the journey. The Scriptures on this view were not *separate from* the work of the Spirit; they were an especially important *expression of* the Spirit. There was not "reading the Scriptures" on the one hand, and the interior work of the Spirit, on the other. Rather, the reading had to be animated by the interior work and illumination of the Spirit, or the text would be empty and the understanding false. For these medieval masters, the Scriptures had their proper place within the framework of salvation history and God's salvific plan for mankind. They were meant not merely to *inform*, but to *change* the reader.

Even when we do not agree with this or that judgment or with a characterization of this or that biblical text, we should laud these medieval masters for making the attempt to present a unified pedagogy to their students, one designed to foster their students' future vocations as teachers and preachers of the word within the communities of faith to which they had pledged their lives and one meant to be an integral means to their full flourishing as complete and whole human persons.

We tend to think of medieval theologians as an especially intellectual lot. It would be foolish, given the intellectual sophistication of their work, to deny that they were. Yet these intellectual efforts were always self-consciously directed to a definite end or *telos*: one that was not merely "scholarly" or "intellectual," but also distinctly *theological* and *personal*. The *principium* and *resumptio* addresses were meant to serve a protreptic purpose. They were meant as exhortations to study, to embrace the means to wisdom being proposed by the master and the school.[43]

We return again to Alasdair MacIntyre's *Three Rival Versions of Moral Inquiry* and the contrast he describes between what he terms "the encyclopaedic stance" of modern thought and an earlier, "classical" view. Whereas the "encyclopaedist" presumes "that truth not only is what it is, independent of standpoint, but can be discovered or confirmed by any adequately intelligent person, no matter what his point of view," earlier thinkers presumed that "a prior commitment was required" on the part of the student who aspired to study and study well.[44]

Deep philosophical presuppositions lie behind the encyclopedia-like prologues one finds in the modern "study Bible," among which are (a) that one needn't share the faith of the author to understand the book fully and (b) that what one needs in order to read well is simply a sufficient amount of background information of the right sort. As valuable as these modern prologues can be, they do not usually presume that the reader needs to be spiritually prepared to read or that they need to be educated about the sort of transformation reading the book is meant to achieve. Judgments of this sort, about what is necessary for good

---

[43] For more on the history and character of philosophical protreptics, see my discussion in the Introduction to the present volume, esp. Mark D. Jordan, "Ancient Philosophic Protreptic and the Problem of Persuasive Genres," *Rhetorica: A Journal of the History of Rhetoric*, vol. 4, no. 4 (Autumn 1986), 309–333.

[44] Alasdair MacIntyre, *Three Rival Versions of Moral Enquiry: Encyclopedia, Genealogy, and Tradition* (Notre Dame, IN: University of Notre Dame Press, 1990), 60. For more, see my discussion in the Introduction to this volume. This chapter and the previous one have as one of their aims illustrating the theses about the protreptic nature of medieval prologues expressed in the Introduction.

reading and what is not, distinguish the presuppositions behind the production of modern prologues from medieval *principia* such as Thomas's.

Learning to Write a *Principium*

Incepting Masters like John, Henry, and Thomas did not learn to produce sophisticated *principia* overnight or in a weekend seminar. They had to be trained, and the quality of their skill had to be tested regularly to ensure they were developing satisfactorily. There were undoubtedly training programs to help aspiring preachers develop their skills in preaching. We know a good deal about the preaching manuals they were given and the preaching aids available to them, but we have as yet no clear picture of how preachers developed their skills during their years at the University. What we do know is that they were required to write a prologue, also called a "*principium*," to each of the works they produced, both as a *baccalarius biblicus* and as a *baccalarius sententiarum*. Although we do not have the early student sermons of either Aquinas or Bonaventure, we do have their early efforts at writing prologues. And it is to Aquinas's early prologues as a "biblical bachelor" that we turn in the next chapter.

6

Thomas's Student Prologues

REVIEWING WHAT our researchers have shown thus far, recent scholarship suggests that the late twelfth and early thirteenth centuries saw an increased interest in and demand for better preaching to the laity. This concern for better preaching, which may have been percolating within the Church for some decades, was expressed in an official directive of the Church at the Fourth Lateran Council in 1215. The call for better preaching was taken up by many but animated in a special way during the founding of the new mendicant orders, the Dominicans and Franciscans. The directives of the Lateran Council and various popes, in addition to the efforts of local bishops, scholars, and the efforts of the newly founded mendicant orders, led to the formation of a theology curriculum at the University of Paris designed to help train a new generation of preachers who could preach clearly, powerfully, and with doctrinal integrity to an increasingly educated laity where heretofore there had often been either no preaching or the preaching of heretical doctrines.

There seems to have arisen within the cradle of this new educational reform movement, especially at the University of Paris, a new style of preaching, the *sermo modernus* or "modern sermon," which was characterized by being structured around a single biblical verse or *thema*. The preacher would "divide" this *thema* verse into various parts around which he would build his sermon by associating words from each member of his opening *divisio* with the topics he wanted to cover. In this way, he would "expand" or "dilate" the members of each division into the message of his sermon. The biblical *thema* verse served as both a mnemonic device to help the listeners keep the topics of the sermon stored in an orderly fashion in memory and as what we could call today a "writing prompt" that helped drive the process of *inventio*, discovery of a topic, and *dispositio*, arrangement of the address to be given. The result was a sermon whose structure was organized as an aid to the memory, but not primarily the memory of the speaker, since there is no evidence that medieval preachers memorized their sermons in the way classical orators such as Cicero memorized theirs; rather it aided the memory of the listeners, especially students who had to recall the points in the morning's sermon when the same "theme" was taken up later that same day at vespers. In these circumstances, the preacher could review the basic points of the morning's sermon by calling to mind the parts of the *thema* he had dilated that morning, after which he could pick up right where he had left off with the next word in the sentence.

An important use of the *sermo modernus* style outside a strictly liturgical setting at Mass or vespers was in the *principium in aula* and *resumptio* addresses given by medieval masters during their inception ceremonies. Modern scholars often find these *principium* addresses in collections of sermon material, so it seems likely that the *principium in aula* and *resumptio* were considered at the time to be a species of sermon. If the *principium* and *resumptio* addresses of an incepting master were understood to be a kind of sermon, albeit one delivered outside a liturgical context, then it makes sense that masters who delivered them adopted the style of preaching most common at the time.

The term *principium*, as we have seen, could apply to any of three different, but related, types of writings. The prologue to a whole document or section of a document was called a *principium*. But the first introductory lectures in a course also bore the name *principium*, as did the master's inception addresses. In all of these, we find bachelors and masters consistently and repeatedly employing the *sermo modernus* style of composition. Writing prologues and preaching sermons in the *sermo modernus* style seems to have been as much a part of the pedagogical culture at Paris as was participation in disputed questions.

In this and subsequent chapters, I hope to show that a common set of mental habits served as the foundation for the arts of *lectio*, *praedicatio*, and *disputatio*. Although medieval preachers were warned that "preaching" was not the place for "disputation," both arts seem to have manifested a similar approach. A topic, problem, question, or text was divided into what were taken to be its constituent parts, each of which could be analyzed or developed in its own right, but always with an eye to how the parts fit together into a coherent whole.

The *sermo modernus* style of composition – *divisio* and *dilitatio* of an organizing *thema* verse – was both an expression of a cultural ethos and a means of transmitting it. Bachelors were required to write prologues regularly in their student years using the *sermo modernus* style. They were required to preach using the same style. When they incepted as masters, they delivered their opening addresses in this style. And when they began each new course of lectures on a book of the Bible, they crafted a prologue to be published with the printed commentary in this style. This was a culture of preaching and prologues. Producing these works repeatedly throughout their years at Paris required and instilled certain mental habits – habits that stayed with these masters throughout their careers, continuing to shape much of their subsequent work.

In this chapter, we will examine several of Thomas's early prologues to the "cursory" lectures he gave on the Old Testament books of Jeremiah, Lamentations, and Isaiah. These, I will argue, are early rudimentary efforts, composed when Thomas was still a student and learning the skills of the *sermo modernus* style.

After examining Thomas's early efforts as a *cursor biblicus*, we will turn next to his general prologue to his *Sentences* commentary. Some readers may not be aware that bachelors of the *Sentences* had to write a *sermo modernus*–style prologue for each book of their commentary, but they did. The prologue to Book One also served as a general prologue to Lombard's *Sentences* as a whole.

We begin, however, with Thomas's earliest efforts: the prologues to his cursory commentaries on the books of Jeremiah, Lamentations, and Isaiah. Fr. Torrell has suggested that Thomas likely lectured on these books while studying with Albert in Cologne before his departure for Paris in 1252.[1] If Thomas did write these prologues in Cologne, then the requirement that scholars craft a *sermo modernus*-style prologue was observed both in Paris and Cologne. It is also possible, however, that since the Order always had in mind that Thomas would return to Paris, he may have been asked to write prologues in the "Parisian" style knowing he would have to do so when he returned to Paris.

Jeremiah

In these early commentaries, Thomas followed the custom, common at the time, of prefacing his commentary on the biblical text with (a) his own prologue; (b) a copy of St. Jerome's prologue found in the Vulgate; and (c) a short exposition, mostly by way of a *divisio textus*, of Jerome's prologue.[2] For the prologue to this commentary, Thomas chose as his *thema* verse a passage from 2 Maccabees 15:14 that mentions Jeremiah by name: "This is a lover of the brothers, and of the people of Israel: this is he who prays much for the people and for all the holy city, Jeremiah the prophet of God" (*Hic est fratrum amator, et populi Israel; hic est qui multum orat pro populo et universa sancta civitate, Jeremias propheta Dei*).[3] The prologue that follows begins in the customary way, with a statement of the fundamental *divisio* according to which Thomas will organize the rest.

> With regard to the author [Jeremiah], the present authority [the *thema* verse] designates three things: namely, the office, disposition, and act. In his office, he is shown to have prophetic dignity, whence it says: "Jeremiah the prophet of God." In disposition, to have fraternal charity: whence it says: "this is the lover of the brothers." In act, to have pious compassion, whence it says: "this is he who prays much for the people and for all the holy city."

So what is Jeremiah's *office*? Thomas replies that Jeremiah is called a *prophet of God* "to differentiate him from others who are not prophets of God." He follows this with a long description of the three different kinds of prophets – prophets of heaven, prophets of the devil, and prophets of God – followed by another long description of the three things that characterize the prophets of God: they are inspired by God, sent by God, and testify to God.

Jeremiah's "affect" or *disposition* is one of fraternal charity, says Thomas, and this is shown in the *thema* where it says that he is "the lover of the brothers." But instead of listing the three or four ways Jeremiah was a "lover of the brothers," as might have been expected, Thomas characterizes Jeremiah by way of contrast, explaining that the disposition of prophets varies in a threefold way. Some are lovers of profit who despoil people of their riches. Some are lovers of human favor who deceive people with their blandishments. But

---

[1] Jean-Pierre Torrell, *Saint Thomas Aquinas*, vol. 1: *The Person and His Work*, rev. ed. (Washington, DC: The Catholic University of America Press, 2005), 337.

[2] The exception is Thomas's commentary on Lamentations. The reason is that Jerome never wrote a prologue to Lamentations.

[3] Latin text: *Sancti Thomae de Aquino in Jeremiam prophetam expositio*, Textum Parmae 1863, editum ac automato translatum a Roberto Busa SJ, available at www.corpusthomisticum.org/cph.html. Unless otherwise noted, all English translations are mine.

the third kind are lovers of the people who instruct with true doctrines, and such was Jeremiah.

We have covered Jeremiah's *office* and *disposition*. What, then, was Jeremiah's *act*? According to the *thema* verse from Maccabees, Jeremiah's distinctive act was prayer: "this is he who prayed much." His prayer is "much" or "great" says Thomas, in three ways: first, in the height of his contemplation; second, from the magnitude of his compassion; and third, from the great assiduousness he showed in his prayer, since it began before the Babylonian Captivity and continued on after it had begun. Three things are necessary for a prophet, says Thomas: prophetic dignity (*prophetalis dignitas*), fraternal charity (*fraternalis caritas*), and compassionate piety (*compassionis pietas*).

With this, Thomas has finished "dilating" the three parts of his opening *divisio*. But he was not yet finished. After explaining that "the prophet is situated as it were in the middle between God and the people," conjoined to God by the gift of prophecy and to the people by a bond of charity, he returns to his opening threefold *divisio*. "From these three," he says – office, disposition, and act – "another three are immediately apparent": the manner (*modus*), the utility (*utilitas*), and the subject matter (*materia*) of the prophet's book.

From the office, says Thomas, we know the manner: "he proceeds through similitudes and figures, which is more properly the mode of prophets." From the prophet's disposition of fraternal charity, we come to understand the utility of the book: for as is said in Ecclesiasticus 6:16, "A faithful friend is the medicine of life and immortality," so the goal of the prophetic book is to live well and to arrive at the glory of immortality. Finally, the subject matter is clear from the act. The prophet's distinctive *act*, we will recall, was prayer, and so the subject matter of the book concerns "the captivity of the people, which excited prayer of compassion."

After finishing this relatively brief prologue of his own, Thomas copied out St. Jerome's prologue to Jeremiah, found in most versions of the Vulgate, after which he offered his own exposition of Jerome's prologue. This exposition did not follow the format of the *sermo modernus* style with yet another *thema* verse. Instead, as was common practice, Thomas produced a step-by-step *divisio textus* of Jerome's text. In his prologue to this *divisio*, Thomas affirms that Jerome does three things: first, he renders the readers attentive (*reddit attentos*); second he makes them docile (*dociles facit*); and third, he makes them good-willed (*benevolos*).

These three – to render attentive, docile, and attentive – were, as I pointed out in Chapter 5 in a discussion of the *resumptio* of Stephen of Besançon, who used the same three terms, understood classically to be the three goals an orator should seek to accomplish in the *exordium* of his speech. Stephen altered the Latin term *exordium*, however, which he would have found in his source, Quintillian's *Institutio oratoria* 4.1.5, to a Latin term more relevant to his own purposes: *principium*. By this slight change in the wording, Stephen adopted the three classic goals of the *exordium* of a speech and applied them to the *principium* or "prologue" of a science or a book, and by extension, to his own "prologue" to the Scriptures.

Thomas makes a similar move here by applying the three goals of an *exordium* to Jerome's prologue (which would also have been called a *principium*). Note, however, that with Thomas, we have a further extension of the original concept. Here, Jerome is making the readers attentive, docile, and good-willed not to himself as the person about to give a speech, and not to his *principium* address. Jerome's achievement, rather, is to prepare the readers of the book of the prophet Jeremiah by making them attentive *to the Scriptures*, docile *to the Scriptures*, and good-willed to receiving the instruction *of the Scriptures*.

In good scholastic, *sermo modernus* style, Thomas further subdivides each division. Jerome makes the reader "attentive" in two ways: first by pointing out the profundity of the Scriptures, and second, by noting the authority of the one writing. Regarding the first, for example, the profundity of the Scriptures, Jerome does two things: he commends the profundity of the mystery, and he shows the cause, which is the unity of the Holy Spirit who inspired the text. There is no need to elaborate all the details here, since our concern is primarily with Thomas's prologues, but Thomas successfully divides and subdivides Jerome's text down to its most basic units.

Here we see in action an early example of the practice of *divisio textus* that will be required of the incepting master at his *resumptio*. This was the way a medieval master of theology commented upon the Scriptures and many other books. And it was the way he often approached the structure of his own works, as we will see in Chapter 9, where we will review how Thomas provided an analytical outline to his *Summa theologiae* in instructive *divisio textus* prologues scattered throughout his text.

Lamentations

Thomas began his prologue to Lamentations with a *thema* verse from Ezekiel 2:9: "Behold, a hand was sent to me, wherein was a book rolled up: and he spread it before me, and it was written within and without: and there were written in it lamentations, and canticles, and woe" (*Ecce manu missa est ad me, in qua erat liber in volutus. Et expandit illum coram me; qui erat scriptus intus et foris: et scriptae errant in eo lamentationes et carmen, et vae*).[4] The word "lamentations" in this verse obviously suggested itself here for use in a prologue to the Book of Lamentations, but there is no indication in Ezekiel itself that this verse refers to Lamentations.

Thomas makes a fourfold division of the verse, representing the author, the manner, the utility, and the subject matter of the work. He associates the *author* with the phrase "behold, a hand was sent to me"; the *manner* in which the book is written with the phrase "wherein was a book rolled up"; the *utility* of the work with the phrase "it was written within and without"; and finally the *subject matter* of the work with the phrase "and there were written in it lamentations, and canticles, and woe." With each of these four, Thomas also associates a description. In the author, we see goodness; in the manner, we see the difficulty of the work; in the utility, we find a multiplicity; and in the subject matter, diversity.[5]

Let's examine each of these. The *author* of the work is suggested by the phrase "behold a hand was sent to me." Why a hand? This hand, says Thomas, is the wisdom of God by

---

[4] Latin text: *Sancti Thomae de Aquino in Threnos Jeremiae expositio*, Textum Parmae 1863, editum ac automato translatum a Roberto Busa SJ, available at www.corpusthomisticum.org/cth.html. All English translations are mine. This commentary is sometimes listed as of "dubious authenticity," but both Weisheipl and Torrell list it as authentic. See James A. Weisheipl, *Friar Thomas d'Aquino: His Life, Thought, and Works*, 2nd ed. (Washington, DC: The Catholic University of America Press, 1983), 45, 369–370 and Torrell, *St. Thomas*, 27, 337–338.

[5] Perhaps because this is an early work, Thomas does not announce his *divisio* clearly at the beginning of the prologue. We have to search for the parts of the opening *thema* verse as we read. Thomas's later practice, especially in his sermons, would be to state the *divisio* clearly at the beginning so neither his readers nor his listeners would be unclear about the associations he wished to make.

which all things are made. This wisdom opens the intellect to seeing, speeds the tongue to speak, and directs the hand to write. This wisdom spoke through the prophets in diverse ways, dividing the gifts of wisdom among them so that all that was handed over to man exteriorly through a minister might be perfected interiorly through authority. This wisdom is so high that we can take nothing from it unless it is sent to us. And so the goodness of the author is designated by the phrase "behold a hand was sent to me." This wisdom is sent to us in a threefold way, says Thomas: in the creation of things, in internal inspiration, and most preeminently in the Incarnation when "before the corporeal eyes, invisible wisdom appeared."

The *manner* in which the book is written is suggested by the phrase "wherein was a book rolled up." The phrase also suggests the difficulty of the work. For this book is "rolled up," says Thomas, due to the ornateness of its words, the profundity of its mysteries, and the variety of its similitudes. These three are also signified, says Thomas, by the three covers in which the vessels of the sanctuary are folded to ready them for travel, as recounted in Numbers 4:6–13. There, the sons of Aaron are commanded to wrap the ornaments of the tabernacle in various, colored cloths when the camp was set to move forward. The Ark of the Covenant was to be wrapped in the multicolored veil that covered the door; the censers, the cups and bowls, the candlesticks, and various other items were to be wrapped and covered with a violet cloth; and the altar itself was to be wrapped in a purple cloth.[6] Thomas associates each of these with a way the book is "rolled up." The many colors of the veil from the door represent the diversity of similitudes in the Book of Lamentations. The cloth of violet color signifies the celestial mysteries, with which the Book of Lamentations is impregnated. And the purple cloak signifies the ornateness of the words.

Thomas dilated the first *divisio* on the author of the book, which he associated with the phrase "behold a hand was sent to me," by the method described in Chapter 2 as "devising metaphors through the properties of a thing" (*excogitando metaphoras per proprietetem rei*).[7] He dilates the second *divisio*, which deals with the manner in which the work was written (its *form*), with an elaborate allegory on the image of a "book rolled up." The spiritual senses have not by this time been lost or discarded; they have become one of several means of dilating a text. It is not uncommon to find in Bonaventure's prologues and collations an elaborate allegory such as this one inserted into the middle of a long string of arguments and distinctions. Medieval preachers such as Thomas and Bonaventure had a host of methods of developing topics at their disposal, and they made abundant use of all of them.

How, then, can all the textual complexity of a book like Jeremiah's be understood – the book which is a "hand sent to me," a book "rolled up" with similitudes, mysteries, and ornate words? Answer: It requires the aid of the Holy Spirit, who "spreads it before me." As Thomas points out, an important principle of exposition holds that "the Sacred Scriptures ought to be exposited by the same Spirit by which they were written."[8] The author of the

---

[6] The description itself is actually a bit more complicated. Those interested in the details should consult Numbers 4:1–14.

[7] This is #6 of the methods of *dilatatio* listed in Chapter 2.

[8] Thomas attributes the phrase to Augustine (*sicut Augustinus dicit*). I have not been able to find it in any of the extant works of Augustine. In *The Catechism of the Catholic Church*, we also find the statement that "Sacred Scripture must be read and interpreted in the light of the same Spirit by

book, as Thomas stated earlier, was *Wisdom* – the same Wisdom by Whom the world was created, the prophets inspired, and Who later became incarnate as a man. It is with the aid of this Wisdom that the Scriptures must be interpreted and understood. And so the opening *thema* says, "and he spread it before me," because God opens the words of the Scriptures, reveals the hidden mysteries, and explicates the similitudes. Note in all this there has been no mention of Jeremiah or any other human author.[9]

The complexity and difficulty of Lamentations due to the ornateness of its words, the profundity of its mysteries, and the variety of its similitudes also suggests its *utility*, which is suggested by the phrase "it was written within and without." Lamentations, says Thomas, contains written wisdom both in "the husk of the literal sense" (*in cortice litteralis sensus*) and in "the hidden places of the sentential understanding" (*in abditis sententialis intelligentiae*). By this latter term, it is clear Thomas has in mind the spiritual or figurative senses. He cites the passage from John 10:9: "I am the door. By me, if any man enter in, he shall be saved: and he shall go in, and go out, and shall find pastures," creating thereby a verbal connection between the book "written within and without" and the door by which the sheep "go in and go out," which is Christ. What is the utility of the book? Its multiple senses lead to us to the Wisdom that created the world and us – that is, to Christ, the Word and Wisdom of God made flesh; Christ, who both reveals the meaning of Scripture and is revealed by the Scriptures; Christ who is the author, subject matter, and goal of the written text.

We come finally to the subject matter (the *materia*) of the text which, according to Thomas, is suggested by the last phrase in the opening *thema* verse: "and there were written in it lamentations, and canticles, and woe." These three – lamentations, canticles, and woe – express the diversity of elements in the book. Why lamentations? Because, says Thomas, the author is lamenting the death of Josiah. Why a song? Because the author sings a song deploring the trampling of the people; as in Ezekiel 32:18, it says: "Son of man, sing a

---

whom it was written." The Catechism footnotes a passage in *Dei verbum* 12, which in turn footnotes the following passage in St. Jerome's Commentary on Galatians 5:19–21: "Whoever understands Scripture in a manner other than that demanded by the meaning of the Holy Spirit in which it was written, even though he doesn't separate himself from the Church, can nevertheless be called a heretic." This is similar, but St. Thomas's formulation is much closer to the Latin original in *Dei Verbum*, 12: *Sed, cum Sacra Scriptura eodem Spiritu quo scripta est etiam legenda et interpretanda sit.* Thomas asserts the principle often. See, e.g., Thomas's *Quodlibet* 12, q. 17, proem.: "Dicendum, quod ab eodem spiritu Scripturae sunt expositae et editae"; ST II-II, q. 176, art. 2, obj. 4: "quia Scripturae eodem spiritu exponuntur quo sunt editae"; *Lectures on 1 Corinthians*, chapter 14, lecture 1, no. 813 (on 1 Cor 14:1–4): "Et sic dicitur propheta omnis qui discernit doctorum Scripturas, quia eodem spiritu interpretatae sunt quo editae sunt." A clue to Thomas's reference to Augustine might be found in Thomas's *Commentary on Romans*, chapter 1, lecture 5, no. 80, where he says: "However as Augustine also says, the meaning of Sacred Scripture is gathered from the actions of the saints. For it is the same Spirit who inspired the Sacred Scriptures (*idem enim Spiritus quo Sacrae Scripturae sunt editae*): men moved by the Holy Spirit spoke from God (2 Pet 1:21) and who moves holy men to act: all who are led by the Spirit are sons of God (Rom 8:14)." Here, however, it is the actions of the saints that help us interpret the meaning of Scripture because the Spirit inspired both the Scriptures and the saints. The sense here is similar but not identical.

[9] Although Thomas always affirms that the ultimate author of the Scriptures is the Holy Spirit, he usually also identifies a human author.

mournful song for the multitude."[10] Why is there woe? Because of the devastation of the whole city of Jerusalem.

Alternatively, says Thomas, these three – lamentations, canticles, and woe – can be referred to the three senses by which the book can be expounded. "Woe" refers to the typical, tropological, or moral sense, by which the author deplores the servitude of sin. "Song" refers to the mystical sense, by which he deplores the widowhood of the Church. And "lamentations" refers to the historical sense, by which he deplores the captivity of Judea.

At the end of his prologue, Thomas makes several further comments unrelated to his opening *thema* verse – they appear to be something like a coda – about an alternative title of the book, *Threni*, Greek for "lamentations," a title one sometimes finds in Latin as well,[11] which he then somewhat confusingly relates to the Latin *Terni* or "threes" because the book is set up in a pattern of threes: the first two chapters have three lines under each Hebrew letter, and the third chapter has three clauses under each Hebrew letter. The pattern of threes breaks down after that, however, so Thomas's association of *Threni* with *Terni* and groups of three simply doesn't work.

This is the work of a beginner, after all. Yet there has been remarkable progress since Thomas wrote his prologue to the Book of Jeremiah. The prologue flows more easily; he involves himself in fewer confusing digressions; his images are more effective; and his associations are cleaner and clearer. All in all, it is superior to his prologue to Jeremiah. Neither, however, achieves the quality and caliber of his prologue to Isaiah.

Isaiah

For the prologue to his *Commentary on Isaiah*, Thomas chose as his *thema* this passage from Habakkuk 2:2-3: "Write the vision, and make it plain upon tablets: that he that reads it may run through it. For as yet the vision is far off, and it shall appear at the end" (*Scribe visum, et explana eum super tabulas, ut percurrat qui legerit eum: quia adhuc visus procul, et apparebit in finem*).[12] "From these words," says Thomas, "three things can be understood concerning the book of the prophet Isaiah, which we have in our hands; namely the author, the manner, and the subject matter." As in his other early prologues, one must search through the body of the prologue to find the parts of the opening *thema* verse Thomas associates with each of these three: author, manner, and subject matter. The *author* of the work is expressed by the words, "Write the vision." The *manner* of the work is expressed by the words, "and make it plain upon tablets, that he that reads it may run

---

[10] "The multitude" in Ezekiel 32:18 is actually the multitude of Egypt, not the multitude ruined by the Babylonian Captivity. Thomas's point, however, is simply that, as this verse from Ezekiel suggests, what one does to deplore the trampling of the multitude is to sing a mournful song.

[11] Indeed, this commentary is most often denominated "*In Threnos Jeremiae Expositio*" or simply "*Super Threnos*."

[12] Latin text: *Sancti Thomae de Aquino expositio super Isaiam ad litteram*, Textum Leonino 1969 praebito adaequatum ac translatum a Roberto Busa SJ, available at www.corpusthomisticum.org/cisoo.html. Unless otherwise noted, all English translations are mine.

through it." And the *subject matter*, finally, is expressed by the final part of the verse: "For as yet the vision is far off, and it shall appear at the end."

"Write the Vision"

We begin with the *author* of the book and the phrase, "Write the vision." As was his common practice, Thomas further subdivides this phrase into three subdivisions, which correspond to the author, the minister of the author, and the office of the minister. The author is shown in the command that comes directly before the *thema* verse, where it says, "And the Lord answered me, and said: Write the vision." Since the author of the Sacred Scriptures is the Holy Spirit, the text says, "*The Lord* answered me and said . . ." Yet, although it is the Lord who commands, he commands *someone else* to "write." This is the "minister of the author," the prophet Isaiah, "the organ of the Holy Spirit."

What was it his "*office*" or "duty" (*officium*) as God's prophet to write? "Write the vision," says the opening *thema* verse. What Christians call a "prophet" was at one time called a "seer." As the Lord says in Numbers 12:6: "Hear my words: if there be among you a prophet of the Lord, I will appear to him in a vision, or I will speak to him in a dream."

"And Make It Plain Upon Tablets"

The *manner* in which the book is written is expressed in the next part of the *thema* verse: "make it plain upon tablets: that he that reads it may run over it." The *manner* of the book is that it is plain and open, not composed of the complex similitudes one finds in the Book of Lamentations. Thomas further subdivides this *divisio* into three: "make it plain," "upon tablets," "so that he that reads it may run over it." The first expresses how the vision is "made plain"; the second, the reason it is made plain; and the third, the consequent utility.

Regarding the first, the prophet *makes plain* his vision in a threefold manner: first, he makes use of similitudes; second, he employs definitive statements (*sententiae*); and third, he uses beautiful words. This prophet excels others in all three, claims Thomas. First, he uses beautiful and *courtly* similitudes (*curiales similitudines*), that is, similitudes drawn from courts of Uzziah, Jotham, Ahaz, and Hezekiah, the kings of Judah to whom Isaiah prophesied (cf. Isaiah 1:1). Such similitudes are invaluable, says Thomas, because reason derives what it knows from sensible things, and therefore "it captures more perspicaciously the things whose likenesses it sees with the senses." For this reason, the Scriptures use sensible figures. This prophet also excels in the expression of definitive statements (*sententiae*), so much so, claims Thomas, that his book seems to be not merely prophecy, but more like a gospel.[13]

---

[13] Thomas likely had in mind passages such as "The Virgin shall conceive and bear a son" (Is 7:14); "The voice of one crying in the desert: Prepare ye the way of the Lord, make straight in the wilderness the paths of our God" (Is 40:3); "Surely he hath borne our infirmities and carried our sorrows" (Is 53:4); "he has delivered his soul unto death, and was reputed with the wicked: and he has borne the sins of many, and prayed for the transgressors" (Is 53:12); "Behold, I have given you to be the light of the Gentiles, that you may be my salvation even to the farthest part of the earth" (Is

And Isaiah excels, finally, in the beauty of his words, suggesting he must have been a nobleman of urbane eloquence.[14]

According to the opening *thema* verse, the prophet "made it plain" *upon tablets*. There are three types of "tablet," says Thomas: the tablets of the law, the stony tablets of the heart, and the tablets of a soft and fleshy heart. The first, the tablets of the law, are those that Moses brought down from Mt. Sinai. The second and third tablets are identified in 2 Corinthians 3:3 where Paul says: "you are the epistle of Christ, ministered by us, and written not with ink, but with the Spirit of the living God; not on *tablets of stone*, but on *the fleshly tablets of the heart*" [emphasis mine].

The first tablet, namely of the written law, was "written by the finger of God" (Exodus 31:18). And yet since the Scriptures are in places obscure and full of mysteries, it was necessary for prophets such as Isaiah to trace over the words of this first tablet plainly with the finger of man to help clarify their teaching.

The second tablet is the tablet of stony hearts. It was necessary to write over them with refutations, says Thomas, as it says in Matthew 15.7-8: "Well has Isaiah prophesied of you, saying: This people honors me with their lips: but their heart is far from me."

The third tablet is the tablet of fleshy hearts. On this, one can write plainly, not merely to clarify obscurity or to refute error, but to instruct those with the heart to learn.

We can infer from what Thomas says that we are meant to see a correspondence between the *manner in which* Isaiah writes – "making it plain" with clear similitudes, forceful *sententiae*, and eloquent words – and the *reasons for* writing this way. Crafting clear similitudes with sensible figures is the way Isaiah "writes over" the obscure words of the Scriptures. Fashioning forceful *sententiae* is the way Isaiah "writes over" the tablets of a stony heart with refutations. And by employing the eloquent and beautiful language of the court, Isaiah helps inspire and instruct those with fleshy hearts who are open to his teaching.

"So That He That Reads It May Run Through It"

This brings us to the third subdivision under the *manner* of the work: namely its utility. The utility of the prophet's "making it plain upon the tablets" is shown in the phrase that follows: "so that he that reads it may run through it" (*ut percurrat qui legerit eum*). To "run through" it (*percurrat*), says Thomas, means to arrive quickly at the end by running. And in this case, the "end" is threefold: there is the end of the law, the end of the precept, and the end of life. The end of the law, as we read in Romans 10:4 "is Christ, unto justice to everyone that believes." "The end of the precept is charity," as it says in 1 Timothy 1:5. And the end of life is death, although those who persevere even to the end will be saved. So the

---

49:6); "The spirit of the Lord is upon me, because the Lord hath anointed me: he hath sent me to preach to the meek, to heal the contrite of heart, and to preach a release to the captives, and deliverance to them that are shut up" (Is 61:1). In fact, there are more than sixty-one passages from Isaiah quoted or referenced in the New Testament.

[14] Thomas is merely repeating a judgment Jerome expressed in his prologue. But modern biblical scholars also surmise that the person responsible for the Book of Isaiah was educated and attached to the royal court.

thema verse reads "he that reads it" – namely, the book of Isaiah – "may run through it," as if to say, "he who reads, without the obstacle of doubt," runs quickly, arriving at his threefold end: first, he arrives at belief in Christ (the end of the law); by believing, he loves (the end of the precept), and in love, he perseveres and achieves his salvation (the end of life).

"For as Yet the Vision Is Far Off"

With this, we come finally to the *subject matter* of the book and the next part of the opening *thema*: "For as yet the vision is far off." According to Thomas, the subject matter of the Book of Isaiah is "principally" (*principaliter*) the appearance of the Son of God, which is why it is read in Church during Advent.[15] But there is a threefold appearance of the Son of God: the first by which He appeared in the flesh as man; the second by which he appears through faith; and the third by which he will appear in glory. According to Thomas, these appearances (or advents) describe the *subject matter* of the book.

"For as yet, the vision is far off," says Thomas, because when the Book of Isaiah was written, Christ's Incarnation was still "far off," and not merely chronologically. Something is "far off," says Thomas, when it excels in majesty and is beyond our understanding; thus it is written in Job 36:25–26: "everyone beholds afar off; behold, God is great, exceeding our knowledge." So too Christ was "far off" because hidden, as in Ephesians 3:8-9 Paul says that the grace was given him to preach "the unsearchable riches of Christ, and to enlighten all men, that they may see what is the dispensation of the mystery which hath been *hidden from eternity* in God" (emphasis mine). In a third way, Christ's Incarnation was "far off" because it was long awaited and anticipated by the Old Testament fathers; as we are told in Hebrews 11:13: "All these died according to faith, not having received the promises, but beholding them *afar off*."

But what was "far off" at the time of Isaiah was "made close" by the coming of Christ. What was "far off" in the sense of far above our knowledge was "made close" because in Christ, "the Word was made flesh" (John 1:14). What was "far off" in the sense of "hidden from all eternity" was made public when "the only begotten Son who is in the bosom of the Father declared him" (John 1:14). And what was long awaited and anticipated was finally possessed, as Christ says in Matthew 25:34: "Come, ye blessed of my Father, possess you the kingdom prepared for you from the foundation of the world."

"And It Shall Appear at the End"

Thus far, Thomas has dilated each part of his opening *thema* verse from Habakkuk 2:2-3 except the last: "and it shall appear at the end." What is this "end"? According to Thomas, it is threefold. Christ's coming brought, first, the end of the rule of the law; as we read in Galatians 4:4–5: "But when the fullness of the time was come, God sent his Son, made of a woman, made under the law, that he might redeem them who were under the law." It brings also the end of idolatry; as we read in Isaiah 19:1: "Behold the Lord will ascend upon a

---

[15] This fact was noted by nearly all of the incepting masters in the *resumptio* addresses we examined earlier.

swift cloud, and will enter into Egypt, and the idols of Egypt shall be moved at his presence." And Christ's coming at the end of time will bring the end of all misery, as it says in Revelation 21:4: "And God shall wipe away all tears from their eyes: and death shall be no more, nor mourning, nor crying, nor sorrow shall be any more, for the former things are passed away."

An outline of this prologue would look something like this the one shown in Box 6.1.

Box 6.1 Outline of Thomas's Prologue to His *Commentary on Isaiah*

Thema: Habakkuk 2:2–3: "Write the vision, and make it plain upon tables: that he that reads it may run over it. For as yet the vision is far off, and it shall appear at the end."

I. "Write the vision": the author of the work
   A. "And the Lord answered me and said . . .: Author: the Lord
   B. "Write . . .": Isaiah is the minister of the Lord
   C. "the vision": the office of the minister: he is commanded to write the vision
II. "and make it plain upon tables that he that reads it may run over it": the manner in which the work was written
   A. "make it plain": how it was written (the manner in which)
      1. Similitudes
      2. *Sententiae*
      3. Beautiful words
   B. "upon tables": the reason it was written this way
      1. Table of the law: clarifying obscure passages in Scripture
      2. Stony table of the heart: *sententiae* for refuting these
      3. Fleshy table of the heart: beauty and eloquence for instructing these
   C. "that he that reads it may run over it": the utility (running is to arrive quickly at the end): three ends
      1. End (goal) of the law is Christ
      2. End (goal) of the precept is charity
      3. End of life is death, but ultimate goal is salvation for those who believe in Christ
III. "For as yet the vision is far off, and it shall appear at the end": the subject matter of the work: the appearance of the Son of God
   A. "appear": threefold appearance:
      1. He appeared in the flesh as man
      2. He appears through faith
      3. He will appear in glory at the end of time
   B. What was "far off" is "made close" by Christ
      1. Excels our understanding: the Word is made flesh
      2. Hidden: made public in Christ
      3. Long awaited: possessed with Christ
   C. "and it shall appear at the end": Christ's coming brought an end to:
      1. The rule of law
      2. Idolatry
      3. Misery and death

Note that what Thomas has learned to do more effectively than in his earlier efforts is to set up a simple threefold structure with a series of simple threefold subdivisions. This was a schema favored by Bonaventure, who loved dividing and subdividing in threes. The results are not always flashy, but it makes a nice, clear structure with a predictable "rhythm."

We have no way of knowing which cursory commentary was written first.[16] But in my judgment, the prologue to his Isaiah commentary is the most well balanced and shows the greatest skill. He doesn't do too much with the words of his *thema*, the images are creative but not too much of a stretch, and he fits everything neatly into the limits of his opening *thema* verse.

Let me emphasize again that these were all early works of a student who was not yet even a bachelor of the *Sentences*. Yet, writing these mini-sermon–like prologues was part of his training; it was the required way of introducing one's *lectiones* on a book of the Bible. The lecturer delivered a *principium* to the course verbally that eventually became the prologue in the written version of the commentary. What distinguished the lectures of a master from those of a bachelor who gave "cursory" lectures was that the bachelor was not permitted to "determine" any theological issues that arose in the text. The lectures of the bachelor were introductory, meant to "run over" the main points of the text in cursory fashion for beginning students.

Whether it was a bachelor or a master, however, there was always another pressing concern: fostering good preaching. I will have more to say on this topic in Chapter 9.

Thomas's Prologue to His *Sentences* Commentary

It should be clear by now that such prologues were an accepted part of the genre of the biblical commentary in the thirteenth century, so if a bachelor was producing such a commentary, it was simply expected that he would write a prologue. But bachelors of the *Sentences* were also required to write a prologue in the same *sermo modernus* style for each book of their commentary on Peter Lombard's *Sentences*. Whether the *sermo modernus* style of preaching influenced the manner in which masters of theology delivered their prologues, or whether the scholastic method of doing prologues influenced the style of preaching remains unclear. What is clear is that we have a certain *modus operandi* that had become a standard practice by Thomas's time – so much so that it had become something of a distinctive and identifiable literary form of its own.

Bonaventure introduced his commentary on the *Sentences* with a prologue based on Job 28:11: "The depths of rivers he hath searched, and hidden things he hath brought forth to light" (*profunda quoque fluviorum scrutatus est et abscondita produxit in lucem*). Albert had introduced his with a prologue based on Ecclesiasticus (Sirach) 24:5-6: "I came out of the

---

[16] The Leonine editors of the 1974 edition of the *Super Isaiam* argued that the commentary was written during Thomas's first year of teaching in Paris, 1252–1253. Fr. Weisheipl subsequently argued that it was written during Thomas's years as a *baccalarius biblicus* with Albert in Cologne. The precise resolution of this argument has no bearing here other than to say both agree that at least the first part of the *Super Isaiam* was an early work written sometime before Thomas's inception as a master. For more on this, see *Expositio Super Isaiam ad Litteram*, Leonine, vol. 28 (1974), 19–20 and Weisheipl's review in *The Thomist* 43 (1979): 331–337.

mouth of the most High, the firstborn before all creatures: I made that in the heavens there should rise light that never fails, and as a cloud I covered all the earth" (*Ego ex ore Altissimi prodivi, primogenita ante omnem creaturam. Ego feci in caelis ut oriretur lumen indeficiens, et sicut nebula texi omnem terram*). Writing prologues this way, based on an opening biblical *thema*, was simply the custom of the time.

I begin our discussion of Thomas's prologue to his *Sentences* commentary with a textual caveat. The reader who searches out these prologues in a Latin edition may not always have an easy time discerning the structure provided by the opening biblical *thema*, first, because editors haven't noticed the role it plays, so they divide the text in other ways, and second, because Thomas's use of the biblical *thema* in his *Sentences* commentary is not always as crisp and clear as it is in his sermons. The *sermo modernus* style is unmistakable, however, once the reader notices it. To get a sampling of the method, it will suffice for our purposes to examine the prologue to Book One, which is also the prologue to the entire commentary.

Thomas begins this prologue with the following long verse from Ecclesiasticus (Sirach) 24:40–42:

> I, wisdom, have poured out rivers. I, like a brook out of a river of a mighty water; I, like a channel of a river, and like an aqueduct, came out of paradise. I said: I will water my garden of plants, and I will water abundantly the fruits of my meadow.[17]

Thomas makes a fourfold *divisio* of this *thema* that he associates with each of the four books of Lombard's *Sentences*.

Book One: "I, wisdom, have poured out rivers." (*Ego sapientiam effudi flumina.*)
Book Two: "I flow forth like the streams of an immense water." (*Ego quasi trames aquae immensae de fluvio.*)
Book Three: "I, like a channel of a river, and like an aqueduct, came out of paradise." (*Ego quasi fluvii dioryx, et sicut aquaeductus exivi de paradiso.*)
Book Four: "I said, I will water my garden of plants, and I will water abundantly the fruits of my meadow." (*Dixi: Rigabo hortum meum plantationum, et inebriabo prati mei fructum.*)[18]

After "declaring the parts" of his *divisio*, Thomas digresses to provide a brief *introductio*. This was not uncommon in sermons. These "introductions" were sometimes long enough that they merited their own *thema*, *divisio*, and *dilatatio*. Scholars often call this secondary *thema* verse and its attendant material a "*prothema*." In this short, introductory section, Thomas argues that for us to know anything about God, it must be derived from God's own wisdom, since only God himself knows himself fully and perfectly and that it is Christ, "the wisdom of God who was also made by God into wisdom for us," who most fully reveals God to us. As the Gospel of Matthew declares: "No one knows the Father except the Son

---

[17] Happily, an English translation with facing Latin of this prologue is available at that invaluable web site "Thomas in English: A Bibliography," which links to Hugh McDonald's translation of the prologue and question 1, articles 1–5 of Book One at www.vaxxine.com/hyoomik/aquinas/sent1.html. There are, however, as of this writing, a number of errors remaining in this translation, as it is still a work in progress, so the reader should refer frequently to the original Latin text.

[18] We will have occasion in the text that follows to note a source of confusion in Thomas's Latin text. He seems to have read *parti* where most editions have *prati*.

and he to whom the Son wishes to reveal him" (Mt 11:27); and the Gospel of John: "No one has ever seen God, except the Only Begotten who is in the bosom of the Father" (Jn 1:18).

This conclusion brings Thomas back to the first part of his opening *thema* verse; he applies this Gospel teaching from Matthew and John to his Old Testament text from Sirach and suggests that the one speaking these words in Sirach is the Son. The Son is the one who says: "I, wisdom, have poured out rivers.'" "These rivers," says Thomas, "I understand as the flowing of the eternal procession whereby the Son from the Father, and the Holy Spirit from both, proceed in an ineffable manner." In this way, Thomas can associate the words of the first part of the *thema* verse from Sirach with the subject of the first book of Lombard's *Sentences*: namely, the Trinity.[19]

The subject matter of the second book of the *Sentences*, says Thomas, is "the production of creatures as it pertains to God's wisdom, for He has not only speculative wisdom concerning created things, but also operative wisdom, as an artisan of the products of His art." John's Gospel tells us it is through "the Word made flesh" who was "in the beginning with God" that all creation was brought into being: thus "all things were made through him" (see John 1:1–5). Once again, it is the Son who is speaking the words of Sirach: "This therefore is rightly said in the person of the Son," says Thomas: "I flow forth like the steams of an immense water." In these words are signified the "order" (*ordus*) and "manner" (*modus*) of creation, for just as streams are derived from a river, so too the temporal procession of creatures is derived from the eternal procession of the persons in the Godhead.

The image Thomas uses here may be a little confusing at first, since in English, "streams" flow *into* rivers, not out of them. In Latin, however, "*trames*" means a "branch" of a river or even a "stream bed." A "branch" of a river generally flows *into* a river. So Thomas is likely referring to a river overflowing during a heavy rain and filling dry stream beds with water, perhaps even cutting new channels in the earth. Note that the streams flow forth from an "immense" water, an image suggesting an overflowing abundance. There will be further evidence to suggest this is the image Thomas has in mind in a moment.

However we interpret these "streams" (*trames*), the referent is clear: the words "I, wisdom, have poured out rivers" refers to the procession of the Persons in the Trinity. From "the rivers" we get another flowing forth, but this time into much smaller rivulets or streams, which is the "order" of creation flowing forth from the Trinity.

The "manner" of creation is suggested by the same phrase – "I flow forth like the streams of an immense water" – in two ways: first, because the One who creates, although He makes all things full, cannot himself be measured, which is signified by the word "immense"; and second, because "as a stream proceeds outside of the riverbed, so the creature proceeds from

---

[19] One of the difficulties involved in noticing the role of the opening biblical *thema* as a structuring device in this prologue is that Thomas does not here conform to the practice, which will become standard for him later on, of re-stating the entire opening biblical *thema* and then immediately articulating the division of the various parts, relating each to the subject matter of each of the four books of the *Sentences*: namely, the Trinity (Book One), Creation (Book Two), the Incarnation (Book Three), and the Sacraments (Book Four). Instead, in each case, Thomas dives right into his description of the contents of the book, returning only later to make his reference to the key words in the opening biblical *thema*.

God outside the unity of God's essence, in which as in a riverbed the flow of the persons is contained."

Note how Thomas showed care here in his use of the image of "flowing forth" found in his opening *thema* verse so as to avoid implying any hint of Plotinian "emanationism," the view of creation that holds that lesser beings "flow from" or "pour forth out of" higher principles in stages from the ultimate principle: the "One."[20] The danger is to imagine that, as creation flows forth from the Son, so too *in a similar way*, the Son flows forth from the Father. Were this true, then the Son would be, as the Arians claimed, the first created thing. So we must carefully distinguish the "procession" of the persons in the Trinity from the "procession" of creation from the Son. This Thomas does by specifying that "as a stream proceeds outside of the riverbed, so the creature proceeds from God outside the unity of God's essence, in which as in a riverbed the flow of the persons is contained." The procession of persons in the Trinity is one thing: they are three Persons sharing one Substance. Creation is quite another. Created things do not share in the unity of God's essence; the Son and the Spirit do. What God creates is separate from Himself; it does not share His essence. The Son and Spirit, although separate from the Father, "proceed" forth from Him in such a way that all three share the same divine essence.

As we have seen, Thomas associates the first sentence in his *thema* verse – "I, wisdom, have poured out rivers" – with the first book of the *Sentences*, whose subject is the Trinity, and the second sentence in the same *thema* verse – "I, flow forth like the streams of an immense water" – with the second book, whose subject is creation. The third book of the *Sentences* deals with the Incarnation. How, we might wonder, is Thomas going to associate the doctrine of the Incarnation with the third part of the *thema* verse, the phrase "I, like a channel of a river, and like an aqueduct, came out of paradise"?

The third thing that pertains to God's Word and Wisdom, says Thomas, is "the restoration of his works" (*operum restauratio*), "for a thing should be repaired by the same thing whereby it was made; hence the things that were made by wisdom would best be repaired by wisdom." This reparation was brought about by the Son, says Thomas, who, in becoming man, not only restored mankind, but also restored all creation, which was made for man's sake. Yet, what does this standard theological teaching about the Incarnation have to do with the phrase, "I, like the channel of a river, and like an aqueduct, came out of paradise"? Note first, that the word "paradise" here refers not to the Garden of Eden, but to the glory of the Father; as Christ says in John 16:28: "I came forth from the Father and have come into the world." So Christ's "coming out of paradise" refers to His coming forth from the Father into the world in His Incarnation. Note, second, that there are two kinds of "coming forth" implied in the *thema* verse: (1) "like a channel of a river" and (2) "like an aqueduct." The first of these, the "channel" (*dioryx*) Thomas associates with the *manner* of Christ's coming forth, and the second, the "aqueduct" (*aquaeductus*) with its *fruit*.

---

[20] For a good short description of the classical philosophical sources that produced "emanationist" thinking in the early Church, see J. N. D. Kelly, *Early Christian Doctrines*, rev. ed. (New York: Harper Collins, 1978), 20–29. For a good short introduction to Plotinus in particular, who is generally taken to be the primary source of emanationist thinking, see A. H. Armstrong, *Plotinus: A Volume of Selections in a New English Translation* (New York: Collier, 1963), esp. the Introduction.

The *manner* of Christ's coming forth from the Father is suggested by the image of the "channel of a river" (*fluvii dioryx*), because as the water flowing through a channel is extremely swift (*rapidissimus*), so also the Son comes forth from the Father's glory "as if by a certain strong impetus of love for our reparation" (*quasi impetu quodam amoris nostrae reparationis*).[21] The *fruit* of Christ's coming is suggested by the image of an aqueduct: just as an aqueduct brings water from one source to many places, making them fertile, so from Christ "flowed forth the kinds of diverse graces to plant the Church." The order of the *thema* verse also reminds us of the order of the topics in the third book of the *Sentences*, which treats first of the mysteries of our restoration (which, as we have seen, Thomas associates with the words "channel of a river") and second, of the graces that come to us from Christ (which Thomas associated with the image of an aqueduct watering a field).

The Incarnation and the graces that come to us from Christ, which are covered in the third book of the *Sentences*, prepare the way for the fourth book, which deals with the sacraments of Christ. If we have been following along with Thomas's opening *thema* verse, we will know that he needs to associate this topic with the last sentence from Sirach 24.40–42: "I said: I will water my garden of plants, and I will water abundantly the fruits of my meadow." Here is how he does it. We first must remember, as we have each time, that the person speaking is God's Word and Wisdom.

What belongs to wisdom, and especially to God's Wisdom, says Thomas, is "the perfection, by which things are preserved unto their end" (*perfectio, qua res conservantur in suo fine*). Wisdom 8:1 tells us that Wisdom "reaches from end to end strongly and arranges all things sweetly." This verse especially pertains to the Son, says Thomas, because, first, He leads us to our end, the Father's glory, but also because He "arranges sweetly" the means necessary to help prepare us to achieve that end. These are "the medicines of the sacraments" (*sacramentorum medicamenta*), by which "the wound of sin is removed from us" (*quibus a nobis peccati vulnus abstergitur*). As we might expect, Thomas associates each of these with words from his *thema* verse. The preparation that comes through the "medicine

---

[21] There is a potential confusion in the Latin text at this point that will not affect the ultimate point Thomas wishes to make, but that may confuse readers who refer to the Latin text. The version of the Latin Vulgate I have given above reads: *ego quasi fluvii dioryx*. This is an accurate rendering of the Greek, *diōrux* (διωρυξ), which is the Greek word for "channel," "canal," or perhaps "trench." This is its meaning in Latin as well, the Greek word having been taken over into Latin without change. In some versions of the Vulgate, however, one finds, instead of *dioryx*, the word *doryx* or *dorix*. *Dorix* is what the reader will find, for example, at the website where the English translation by Hugh McDonald I have been using appears. What Mr. McDonald has in his Latin version of the text, then, is this: *ego quasi fluvius Dorix*, which at the very beginning of the prologue he translates as "I, like a channel of a river," but which later he translates differently as: "I, like the river Dorix." When it comes to Thomas's comments on this verse, McDonald makes a very sensible decision to translate what he finds in his Latin text and renders *Dorix enim fluvius rapidissimus est* as "For the Dorix river is the swiftest." The problem is that one will look in vain to find any evidence of a Dorix River, either in Europe or in ancient mythology, to which Thomas might be referring. That doesn't mean Mr. McDonald isn't right; it merely means we have a bit of an unresolved confusion. I have chosen in my text to stick with the Latin/Greek *dioryx* and translate it as "channel." The implication, then, is that the water in trenches and irrigation channels dug from a river flows very quickly out into the fields, where it irrigates the crops and brings forth much fruit. I believe that this is the image Thomas wants to associate with the coming of Christ in the Incarnation.

of the sacraments" he associates with the words "I will water my garden of plants." The "garden" is the Church, says Thomas, and this garden is watered by Christ and by the rivers of the sacraments, which flowed from his side on the cross. Thus the ministers of the Church, who dispense the sacraments, are called "irrigators" (*rigatores*) by St. Paul in 1 Corinthians 3.6, where he says: "I have planted; Apollos has irrigated" (*ego plantavi, Apollo rigaviti*). The end for which we are being prepared, finally – we are being "led forth into glory" (*inductio in gloriam*) – is suggested by the last words in the *thema*: "I will water abundantly the fruits of my meadow." There is, however, as we will see, some confusion surrounding a key word in that phrase.

Were the reader to refer to any standard version of the Latin Vulgate, he or she would find just what I've written earlier: in Latin, *inebriabo prati mei fructum*; in English, "I will water abundantly the fruits of my meadow." The problem is that Thomas's Latin has, in place of *prati* (from *pratus*, "meadow"), *parti* (from *partus*, or "birth"). Where this discrepancy comes from is hard to say. Whether *parti* rather than *prati* was in Thomas's manuscript copy of Ecclesiasticus (Sirach) or whether he simply read it this way is difficult to know without more information, and information of the sort most readers would find tedious.[22] What we can say is that, because of the way he reads this verse, Thomas associates Christ's "leading us into glory" (*inductio in gloriam*) with the phrase: "and I will water the fruit of my giving birth" (*parti mei fructum*). Those given birth by Christ (*partus ipsius Christi*) "are the faithful of the Church, whom he bore like a mother by his labor." So too "the fruit of this birth" are "the saints who are in glory" (*fructus autem istius partus sunt sancti qui sunt in gloria*).

The confusion between *partus* ("birth") and *pratus* ("meadow") would be more serious were Thomas providing a commentary on the text of Ecclesiasticus, because he would have misread the text. Here, however, although the error makes for some confusion (but only for

---

[22] By way of illustration: In the Latin text one finds at "corpusthomisticum.org" (taken from the Busa edition, which was in turn taken from the 1856 Parma edition, which coincidentally is the same Latin original one will find in Hugh McDonald's facing Latin–English text), the *thema* from Ecclesiasticus 24.40 at the top of the prologue has *prati* or "meadow," but further on down the page, we find *parti*. In Fr. Mandonnet's more recent edition of Thomas's *Scriptum* on the *Sentences* (*Scriptum super Sententiis*, P. Mandonnet ed., vol. 1, p. 1, Paris: Lethielleux, 1929), we find at the top of the first page: "*Ribabo hortum plantationum, et inebriabo* **partus** *mei fructum*" [emphasis mine], but there is also an asterisk in the text directing the reader to a note below that reads simply: "*Fluvii Diorix; . . .prati mei fructum*," with no further explanation. Whether Fr. Mandonnet found a manuscript with this version of the biblical text at the top of the page or simply changed the opening biblical verse to bring it into agreement with what Thomas says below in his prologue is impossible to say, because he gives us no indication one way or the other.

Without the original manuscripts, it is difficult to say what may have happened to cause this discrepancy between the first statement of the biblical verse and subsequent restatements. My colleagues Mary Catherine Sommer and Ed Houser have suggested another likely scenario, however. They note that the original manuscript would likely not have contained the entire word *prati*, but only an abbreviation that would have looked something like this: *p̄r̄ti*. Thus we may not have a scribal error, but a case where one word could have been taken in either of two ways: either as *prati* or as *parti*. The person who transcribed the manuscript for the modern critical edition may have read "*p̄r̄ti*" at the top and written *prati*, which is what every copy of the Vulgate would have told him was the proper way to read it, in a place where Thomas had read *parti*. It will be difficult to say anything more definite until we get the Leonine edition of the *Sentences* commentary with all of the accompanying manuscript apparatus.

scholars who check up on such things), Thomas has neither misinterpreted the text of Sacred Scripture (since he's not commenting on it) nor misrepresented the text of the Lombard. The image of "giving birth" works so nicely here that I was left wishing the original did say "the fruit of my giving birth" rather than "the fruit of my meadow." But it doesn't. Yet, despite all this, Thomas still managed to communicate to his audience the subject matter of the fourth book of the *Sentences*, the first part of which deals with the sacraments, and the second part of which deals with the glory of the resurrection.

So let's review how Thomas has employed the four parts of his *thema* verse to identify and distinguish four ways the Wisdom of God "flows forth." The first "flowing forth" of the Wisdom of God was when the Son proceeded from the Father (the subject of Book One of the *Sentences*). This "procession" of the Son did not, however, involve the creation of a separate substance or a separation of the Son from the unity of the divine essence. The second "flowing forth" of God's wisdom was when the world was created through God's Word and Wisdom (the subject of Book Two). This "flowing forth" was into a separate "channel," suggesting that created things have essences separate from God's divine essence. The third "flowing forth" of God's wisdom was when the Word of God became incarnate – when the Word became flesh, uniting Himself to His own creation. Flowing forth from His side, finally, we have the rivers of the sacraments that irrigate the meadow and make it fruitful, that is, that prepare the faithful for glory with God (the subject of Book Four).

"And so," concludes Thomas, "from the aforementioned words, the intention of the books of the *Sentences* is clear." We, because of our knowledge of the *sermo modernus* style, know that when Thomas says "from the aforementioned words" (*ex praedictis verbis*), he is referring to his opening biblical *thema* from Sirach 24:40–42 which he has "dilated" in such a way as to reveal the order and contents of the four books of Peter Lombard's *Sentences*.

"I, wisdom, have poured out rivers": Book One deals with the Trinity and the "flowing forth" of the Son and the Spirit from the Father.

"I flow forth like the streams of an immense water": Book Two deals with Creation, the "flowing forth" of created things from the Son, who as an "immense water" is infinitely superior to that which He produces.

"I, like a channel of a river, and like an aqueduct, came out of paradise": Book Three deals with the restoration of God's works by Christ, who "came out of paradise" by coming forth from the Father with the force and impetus of a "channel of a river," and "like an aqueduct" in that, just as aqueducts bring water to make fertile the earth, and many aqueducts are produced from one river, so from Christ flowed forth the diverse graces to plant the Church.

The fruit of that planting, finally, we find in Book Four – "I will water my garden of plants, and I will water abundantly the fruits of my birth" – the first part of which deals with the sacraments by which Christ "waters his garden of plants," and the second part that deals with "the fruits of his birth," namely the life of the saints in glory.

However odd we may find these verbal associations or indeed the whole process, a certain undeniable cleverness is exhibited here. If I may be permitted a comparison to a modern analogue, the impetus to figure out all the inventive associations Thomas employed here is not dissimilar to the impetus that many years ago caused young people to spend hours trying to figure out all the images in Don McLean's hit song "American Pie." Who was "the jester"? (Bob Dylan.) What was "the day the music died"? (The day Buddy Holly died in a plane crash.) What was "the marching band" that "refused to yield"? (The Beatles.) At our age, none of us had read an actual allegory, and none of us was particularly "intellectual," but we talked endlessly about these interesting verbal associations. People who find the medieval practice bizarre would do well to rediscover their childhood fascination with word games. As we have seen, medieval people loved these verbal associations. They showed cleverness, provided a clear structure, and helped the audience remember what was said.

Prologues, Preaching, and Practices

It seems clear enough that writing these *sermo modernus*-style prologues was considered an integral part of the training to become a master of theology at Paris. It prepared him for his duties of lecturing (*lectio*) and preaching (*praedicatio*). Writing prologues was, I suggest, a "practice" in the sense in which Alasdair MacIntyre has defined that term in *After Virtue*: "any coherent and complex form of socially established cooperative human activity through which goods internal to that form of activity are realised in the course of trying to achieve those standards of excellence which are appropriate to, and partially definitive of that form of activity, with the result that human powers to achieve excellence, and human conceptions to the ends and goods involved, are systematically extended."[23]

By the thirteenth century, writing prologues in the *sermo modernus* style had become a "complex form of socially established cooperative human activity." When the Lombard wrote his *Sentences*, this was an individual act of creative genius, albeit one that built on the creative genius of his predecessors. When in later years generations of students were required to write commentaries on his *Sentences*, it became a "practice." It wasn't merely something students individually chose to do; it was a "socially established" activity "through which goods internal to that form of activity" – namely, theological knowledge and wisdom – were "realized in the course of trying to achieve those standards of excellence ... appropriate to, and partially definitive of that form of activity." Students had to write *good* commentaries on the *Sentences* if they were to qualify to become masters. And yet one's designation as a "master" was not an end unto itself; it was, rather, recognition that one had achieved a standard of excellence and was ready to "systematically extend" and help realize the goals of excellence and the common goods of the community – both of the Church and of the University.

Such was the case also with writing prologues: it was a "socially established" activity. Writing prologues was something that the communities, both academic and religious, within which bachelors lived and studied expected them to learn to do. The standards of excellence were set by the community, not by the bachelor or even by his religious superior. There was a history and tradition of this practice: bachelors looked to collections of sermons, preaching manuals, inception *principia*, and the prologues of earlier commentaries to learn how to write prologues and write them well. "Writing them well" and with "excellence" meant crafting them in such a way as to realize goods of the community. Good prologues exhorted the students to enter upon the discipline of study precisely in

---

[23] Alasdair MacIntyre, *After Virtue: A Study in Moral Theory*, 3rd ed. (Notre Dame, IN: University of Notre Dame Press, 1981, 1984, 2007), 187.

such a way and with such dispositions – with humility and docility – that would enable them to achieve the highest wisdom.

And note, *all* of these various written products of one's student years had to be written in the prevailing sermon style. The pedagogy of writing good prologues was an exercise in the practice of writing good sermons. Not every preacher in every parish had to learn to write prologues; but those whose vocation included university teaching had to know how to exhort their students, to draw them away from the temptations to pride and introversion that beset the academic life and to direct them into the higher path of Christian contemplation and study.

The protreptic dimension of this practice invited students into a way of life, one based on a particular understanding of human flourishing and the wisdom that would lead to it. Because of the educational level these students had achieved and the academic vocation many would undertake in later years, this protreptic also involved a particular understanding of the role that learning and study should play (and the dangers such learning and study might present) in one's journey to wisdom and human flourishing. There were also, therefore, definite views expressed on the dispositions with which students had to approach their studies. Students were required to engage in certain practices – prayer was among them, but so were disputation, reading texts analytically, preaching, and writing prologues – that were meant to develop in them certain habits, dispositions, and virtues of the mind and the will.

It is important to remember that Thomas did not spend his early years at the University of Paris and thus did not begin his years as a *cursor biblicus* after years of training in the *sermo modernus* style, as did Bonaventure. Thomas's primary courses of study during his five years at the *studium generale* at Naples had been logic and Aristotle's natural philosophy. The *studium* at Naples had been founded by Emperor Frederick II "where teaching was to be carried out," notes Weisheipl, "not for the sake of knowledge alone, but for the advantage of the state; it was, in fact, a nursery for imperial offices rather than for ecclesiastical preferment."[24] Naples had a large law school, but a theology faculty of only one professor. So, although Thomas was fortunate to study the *libri naturales* of Aristotle at Naples and receive a solid education in logic, his training in higher-level theological studies was probably lacking. At Naples, Thomas became acquainted with the Dominicans, but he had not yet entered the Order, so it was unlikely that he would have had much training in preaching during that time, especially in the new *sermo modernus* style, since it was not especially favored among the older religious orders in rural Italy.

And yet, according to his earliest biographers, Thomas was known to be an excellent preacher not only to educated audiences, but also to ordinary laymen, even the uneducated. William of Tocco, who in his old age spoke as a witness at Thomas's canonization enquiry in 1319, testified that he himself had heard Brother Thomas preach and that, on these occasions, "many people came to hear him preach."[25] Another early biographer, Bernardo Gui, says of him:

---

[24] Weisheipl, *Friar Thomas*, 13.
[25] See the testimony of William of Tocco in "From the First Canonisation Enquiry," section LVIII, in: Kenelm Foster, O.P., trans., ed., *The Life of St. Thomas Aquinas: Biographical Documents* (London: Longmans, Green, 1959), 97.

To the ordinary faithful he spoke the word of God with singular grace and power, without indulging in far-fetched reasoning or the vanities of worldly wisdom or in the sort of language that serves rather to tickle the curiosity of a congregation than do it any real good. Subtleties he kept for the Schools; to the people he gave solid moral instruction suited to their capacity; he knew that a teacher must always suit his style to his audience.

The people, says Gui,

> heard him with great respect as a real man of God. He was a teacher who taught others to do what he himself was already doing, or rather God in him, according to that saying of the Apostle, 'I dare speak of nothing except of what Christ has done in me' (Rom 15.18). Hence his words had a warmth in them that kindled the love of God and sorrow for sin in men's hearts.[26]

A study of Thomas's early prologues suggests that, although he did not start out at Paris and Cologne as a master of the *sermo modernus* style, he was a quick study. He began haltingly, not entirely sure of himself in his early prologues on Jeremiah and Lamentations, but within several years, he was writing longer, more sophisticated prologues. He never wrote prologues or sermons as long and as complex as either Albert or Bonaventure; Thomas's strength was his ability to combine a penetrating intellect with admirable simplicity. Knowing that "a teacher must always suit his style to his audience," Thomas was able to preach "to the ordinary faithful . . . the word of God with singular grace and power."

Developing the Practice and Employing the Habits of Mind

Practices, if they are to remain healthy, must have a history of their refinement. Practices are always situated within a tradition, but they are also the means by which that

---

[26] Cf. Bernardo Gui, *The Life of St. Thomas Aquinas*, c. 29; quoted from Foster, *Biographical Documents*, 47–48. Both William of Tocco and Bernardo Gui indicate that Thomas preached to the faithful in his native Italian, and when in Naples, in South Italian (cf. Foster, *Biographical Documents*, 74, n. 68). Sadly, none of these sermons have survived. We have only a few of the sermons that Thomas preached in Latin. This is why Fr. Hoogland gave his recent translation of Thomas's sermons the subtitle *The Academic Sermons*, for these sermons were likely all intended for a more educated, *academic* audience that understood Latin. If we want to know what style Thomas adopted when speaking to less educated audiences, we would do well to look at his *collationes* on the Ten Commandments, the Ave Maria, the Pater Noster, and the Creed, all of which have an admirable simplicity so often missing from other great medieval preaching. St. Bernard's renowned sermons on the *Song of Songs*, for example, are unquestionably masterpieces, but as one who has tried to teach them to students, I can report that they can be tough going. Bernard himself warns that they are not "milk for babes," but "meat for adults." By comparison, Thomas's discussions of the Ten Commandments in the *Collationes de decem praecepta* are a model of clarity and simplicity. Those acquainted with Thomas primarily through the *Summa theologiae* or his Aristotelian commentaries or any of the disputed questions – texts that will undoubtedly give a picture of St. Thomas as decidedly *cerebral*, which is certainly not untrue, but perhaps also not the whole truth about him – would do well to read Thomas's more simple presentations and note that he was able, as Benardo Gui says of him, to give to each group to which he was speaking "instruction suited to their capacity." Indeed, it was perhaps because Thomas spent as much time as he did *outside* university circles, preaching to laymen and teaching novices, that he was able to produce a work with the clarity and precision of his *Summa theologiae*.

tradition is both passed on and developed within a new historical context. In two previous chapters, we examined how the practice of crafting *principia in aula* and *resumptio* addresses was refined over the decades between John of La Rochelle and Henry of Ghent. In this chapter, we examined Thomas Aquinas's early prologues when he was still a bachelor and witnessed the development of his proficiency.

We turn in the first section of the next chapter to an examination of two of Thomas's prologues from the years shortly after his inception as master: the prologue to his treatise *Contra impugnantes* (1256) and the prologue to his commentary on Boethius's *De trinitate* (1257–58). We then examine two prologues he wrote later in his career: the general prologue to his commentaries on the Epistles of Paul (c. 1272) and the prologue to his commentary on the Psalms (1273). Each prologue holds an intrinsic interest, but our overarching goal is to consider how the practice of crafting prologues during Thomas's student years at Paris affected his work as a master in the years after inception. Did masters continue to observe the form of the prologue or, once it was no longer required, did they abandon it? Did the habits of mind formed by writing these prologues during his student years influence his later work, and if so, how? These are the questions we take into our analyses in the next several chapters of Thomas's later work. We will be asking the same questions when, in the second half of this volume, we examine the development of Thomas's contemporary, the Franciscan Bonaventure of Bagnoregio.

7

After Inception
Early and Late Prologues

We have seen that writing prologues was a key part of a young developing master's education. Thomas wrote prologues to his cursory biblical commentaries and to his *Sentences* commentary. He was also required to deliver two prologues – two *principia* – during his inception as a master, one at his *principium in aula* and the other at his *resumptio*, both of which were to be in praise of the sacred Scriptures. All were crafted in the *sermo modernus* style, which was the style of preaching that had become customary – indeed standard – by the late thirteenth century. Other than in his sermons, did this style of composition continue to influence Thomas after his inception as a master? The answer is yes.

To illustrate, we will examine in the first section of this chapter two prologues from Thomas's early work as a master: the prologue to his treatise *Contra impugnantes* (1256) and the prologue to his commentary on Boethius's *De trinitate* (1257–1258). In the second section, we will examine two prologues from Thomas's later career: the general prologue to his series of commentaries on the epistles of St. Paul (begun perhaps 1265 or 1268; finished 1271–1272) and the prologue to his commentary on the Psalms (1272–1273).[1] In Chapter 8 we will examine Thomas's most highly developed and theologically sophisticated prologue: the prologue to his *Commentary on the Gospel of John* (1272–1273).

I TWO EARLY PROLOGUES
Contra Impugnantes

We have recounted in Chapter 1 some of the troubles the Dominicans and Franciscans had with the secular masters at Paris. These difficulties continued even after Bonaventure and Thomas incepted as masters. The leader of the secular masters,

---

[1] The dating of the commentary on the Psalms is somewhat unclear. Some consider it early; others, such as Frs. Weisheipl and Torrell, think it may have been Thomas's final work. I am considering it as a late work.

William of Saint-Amour, published a major attack against the mendicants in March or April of 1256 entitled *Tractatus de periculis nouissimorum temporum*.[2] Fr. Torrell summarizes its contents thus:

> That work, which survives in several versions, presents itself as a warning to the bishops and other pastors of the Church about the perils of the last days before the Antichrist. It seeks to make them aware of the danger that the false preachers described by Saint Paul will pose to the Church. The essence of William's proposed remedy consists in sending all the religious back to their monasteries (from which they should never have departed) to perform manual labor.[3]

As Torrell rightly notes: "This simplistic proposition shows the depth of the misunderstanding: William never comprehended that the mendicant religious were not monks, nor to what extent the order of preachers was defined by study and preaching."[4] William's treatise was condemned by Pope Alexander IV in October of 1256, but its influence was widespread and lasting.

Thomas was incepted in the spring of 1256, before that papal condemnation, while the dispute was still raging. I recounted in Chapter 4 the difficulties Thomas had being accepted as a master, and it was only as a result of to the direct intervention of Pope Alexander IV that his inception occurred. In the spring of 1256, the year of his inception, in what was likely his first published work as a master, Thomas wrote *Contra impugnantes dei cultum et religionem* in defense of the mendicants at Paris.[5] Thomas was now a master, and his student days were behind him. Yet he continued the practice of prefacing his work with a *sermo modernus*-style prologue. Clearly such prologues were not merely "student exercises." Students were assigned to write prologues, because once they were incepted as masters, they would be expected to write and deliver such prologues regularly.

At the outset of the *Contra impugnantes*, Thomas set forth as his *thema* this verse from Psalm 82(83):3–4: "Lo, your enemies have made a noise: and those who hate you have lifted up the head. They have taken malicious counsel against your people, and have consulted against your Saints. They have said: 'Come, and let us destroy them, so that they be not a nation; and let the name of Israel be remembered no more.'"[6] Using long *thema* passages

---

[2] For the Latin text with English translation, see G. Geltner, trans., William of Saint-Amour, *De periculis novissimorum temporum*, Dallas Medieval Texts and Translations 8 (Paris: Peeters, 2008).

[3] Jean-Pierre Torrell, *Saint Thomas Aquinas*, vol. 1: *The Person and His Work*, rev. ed. (Washington, DC: The Catholic University of America Press, 2005), 79.

[4] Torrell, *St. Thomas*, 79–80.

[5] Fr. Weisheipl has suggested that Thomas disputed the question of the role of manual labor in the religious life during his inception ceremony. The record of this disputation exists, he believes, and has been appended to *Quodlibet* 7 as question 7 [17–18], a text that is often known by the title *De opere manuali religiosorum*. This suggests that Thomas was deeply engaged in the dispute from the very beginning of his tenure as master at Paris. See James A. Weisheipl, *Friar Thomas d'Aquino: His Life, Thought, and Works*, 2nd ed. (Washington, DC: The Catholic University of America Press, 1983), 104–109.

[6] English trans.: John Procter, trans. *An Apology for the Religious Orders* (London: Sands, 1902; reprint, Westminster, MD: Newman, 1950). Both the English and Latin text have been quoted from dhspriory.org/thomas/

ContraImpugnantes.htm. NB: The sections of this text are not numbered so there will be no subsequent citations.

such as this one seems to have been Thomas's practice only early in his career; later he gained the skill to associate everything he wanted to say with a single sentence or two.[7]

After stating his *thema*, Thomas offers a brief *introductio*, something he had done in the general prologue to his *Commentary on the Sentences*. In a sermon, this would have been called a *prothema* if it had its own separate *thema* verse and separate development. The passage Thomas inserts from Augustine's *De doctrina christiana* – "Almighty God, the Lover of mankind, makes use of us ... both for the sake of His own goodness, and for our advantage" – serves as something of a *sed contra* to William of Saint-Amour's claim that the mendicants were the instruments of the Antichrist. Since Thomas does not divide or dilate this passage, it serves more as an "introduction" rather than a proper *prothema*. Thomas uses Augustine's authority to argue that God has appointed ministers to help Him achieve our salvation, but the work of these ministers is often opposed by Satan and his emissaries.

After this brief *introductio*, Thomas repeats his opening biblical *thema* from Psalm 82 and proceeds to his statement of the division of the parts. He makes a threefold *divisio* in places we might not have expected because he does not always divide the Psalm at the natural break between sentences. So we get: (1) "Lo, your enemies have made a noise: and those who hate you have lifted up the head." (2) "They have taken malicious counsel against your people," and (3) "have consulted against your Saints." A twofold subset of (3) is expressed in the final two clauses: (3a) "They have said: 'Come, and let us destroy them, so that they be not a nation"; and (3b) "let the name of Israel be remembered no more.'"

We begin with the first: "Lo, your enemies have made a noise." In these words, says Thomas, the Psalmist describes the hatred borne by the ministers of Satan to God. "They who formerly spoke secretly against You do not fear now to oppose You publicly." Noting that the verse says "your enemies have made *a noise*," Thomas says that it is called a "noise" rather than a "voice," because the clamor of Satan's ministers is an "unreasoning tumult." Thomas will rarely allow himself to be this caustic in future years, even in disputes. But this is early, and his fellow friars and the reputation of their beloved order was being attacked.

Next, says Thomas, the Psalmist points out how the Antichrist and his ministers wage war against the whole human race when he says: "They have taken malicious counsel against your people." Thomas had another version that read: "They have devised crafty things, that they may deceive them."[8] "This reading agrees with the words of Isaiah (3.12)," says Thomas, "'O my people, those who call you blessed, the same deceive you.' They deceive, as the Gloss adds, 'with flattering words.'" Using alternative readings of a verse and words from the Gloss to dilate is evidence of a novice, and Thomas rarely does it later on.

Third, the Psalmist shows how the ministers of Satan persecute the servants of God, in the words: "They have consulted against your saints." These "ministers of Satan" nourish two designs against the saints, says Thomas: first, they wish to sweep them from the face of the earth, which the Psalmist refers to in the words: "Come, and let us destroy them, so that they be not a nation"; and second, if they cannot destroy the saints, these ministers of Satan seek at least to ruin their good name among men so their words produce no fruit,

---

[7] See, for example, the analytical outlines of each of Thomas's extant sermons in the Appendix to R. Smith, *Reading the Sermons of Thomas Aquinas: A Beginner's Guide* (Steubenville, OH: Emmaus, 2016). No *thema* is longer than two sentences; most are only one.

[8] super populum tuum malignaverunt consilium, vel astute cogitaverunt, secundum aliam litteram, ad eos decipiendum

something Thomas associates with the words: "Let the name of Israel be remembered no more."

How do these ministers of Satan persecute the servants of God and seek to ruin their good name? Thomas lists seven ways.

1. "They [the ministers of Satan] seek to deprive them [the saints] of the means of study and of becoming learned, in order that they may be unable either to confute the adversaries of the truth, or to draw spiritual consolation from the Scriptures."
2. "They seek to prevent the religious from consorting with learned men, in order that, thus, their life may fall into disrepute."
3. "They seek to hinder religious from preaching, and from hearing Confessions, by which means they might effect much good to souls."
4. They seek to oblige the members of the religious orders "to labor with their hands, that so they may become weary of, and be disgusted with, their state of life; and that they, may be impeded in the discharge of their spiritual functions."
5. They "malign the religious, and blaspheme against their perfection," that is, the poverty of the mendicants.
6. They try to deprive religious of alms, and of all other means of subsistence.
7. They endeavor to "tarnish the reputation of the Saints; and that, not only by word, but by letters, sent to all parts of the world."

Regarding these "letters sent to all parts of the world," Thomas quotes Jeremiah 23:13: "From the prophets of Jerusalem, corruption is gone forth into all the land." In an earlier chapter on Thomas's *principium*, I mentioned that the secular masters at the University of Paris had circulated a letter widely after they had expelled and excommunicated the friars in which they boasted, somewhat intemperately, that the University of Paris was a "paradise of delights," whence "the fount of wisdom rises which, distributed in four faculties of theology, jurisprudence, medicine, and rational, natural, and moral philosophy, like the four rivers of Paradise flowing through the four climes of the world, waters and irrigates the whole earth."[9] Thomas likely still had this letter in mind, for he would have begun this treatise in defense of the mendicants just a few months after his inception. Thomas's rejoinder to the claim that the secular masters at Paris were "watering and irrigating the whole earth" was his charge that, on the contrary, with their letters they "spread forth corruption into all the land."

Thomas found no way of associating each of the seven items on this list with words in his opening biblical *thema*, which might have made the list more complicated than it is. Only the first part of the prologue fully conforms to the *sermo modernus* style. But the characteristic notes of the style are still apparent.

It is worth noting in passing that, among Thomas's nineteen extant sermons, there is only one in which Thomas digresses at length from the structure offered by the *sermo modernus* style. It occurs in Sermon 9, *Exiit que seminat*, a sermon in which he also defends the mendicant life. In his dilation of the word *exiit* ("went out"), Thomas digresses from his usual order and spends an extraordinary amount of space at the end of his morning sermon

---

[9] This letter can be found in the *Chartularium universitatis Parisiensis*, I, 252-58; and in English translation in: *University Records and Life in the Middle Ages*, ed. and trans. Lynn Thorndike (New York: Norton, 1975; repr. of New York: Columbia University Press, 1944), 56–64. See esp. 57.

and at the beginning of his evening *collatio* defending the practice of calling young men to the religious life of the friars. Clearly Thomas was passionate about the topic and, as a consequence, had a hard time keeping his angry comments within the boundaries set by the limits of his opening *thema* verse.

Commentary on Boethius's *De Trinitate*

Thomas's commentary on Boethius's *De trinitate* is another early text, composed during his first period at Paris, probably in the years 1257–1258, sometime between the middle of his work on the *De veritate* and the beginning of the *Summa contra Gentiles*. According to Fr. Torrell, Aquinas is the only thirteenth-century author we know to have commented on Boethius's text.[10]

Some have suggested that Thomas meant for this commentary to be the grand theological synthesis he eventually produced in the *Summa contra gentiles* and the *Summa theologiae*. Whether this was his intention or not, it is clear Thomas abandoned the work after a short span, having commented only as far as the first lines of chapter 2 of the *De trinitate*, up through the threefold distinction Boethius makes between natural science, mathematics, and theology.

For the prologue to this commentary, Thomas took as his opening *thema* the passage in Wisdom 6:24: "From the beginning of her nativity, I will investigate and bring the knowledge of her to light." (*Ab initio nativitatis investigabo et ponam in lucem scientiam illius.*)[11] What follows immediately after the statement of the *thema*, however, is another long *introductio* in which Thomas points out that, whereas philosophers move from knowledge about created things to knowledge of the Creator, among theologians the order is the reverse: the study of the Creator comes before that of creatures. This is the order followed by Boethius whose starting point (*principium*) was in that highest origin of things (*in ipsa summa rerum origine*), the Trinity.

This *introductio* goes on for so long that the reader must search a good way down in the prologue to find where Thomas returns to the opening biblical *thema* and says: "Whence it is that the above-quoted words [that is, from Wisdom 6.24] are applicable to him [namely, Boethius]: 'From the beginning of her birth, I will investigate and bring the knowledge of her to light.'"[12] "In these words," says Thomas, "three things can be noted with regard to the present work": namely, its matter, manner, and purpose. Thomas associates each of these with one of the three parts of his opening biblical *thema*: From the beginning of her birth/ I will investigate / and bring the knowledge of her to light.

The "matter" (*materia*) of Boethius's treatise, says Thomas, is the Trinity of Persons in the one, divine Essence – "that Trinity which has its source in the primal nativity in which

---

[10] Torrell, *St. Thomas*, 345.
[11] Latin text: Boethius, *Theological Tractates. The Consolation of Philosophy*, Loeb Classical Library, 74 (Cambridge, MA: Harvard University Press, 1973). English: Erik C. Kenyon, trans. 2004. Facing English and Latin text can be found at www.logicmuseum.com/authors/aquinas/superboethiumq1.htm. References are given to paragraph numbers in this translation.
[12] In the online version of the text at logicmuseum.com, this sentence appears at para. 2, which appears three long paragraphs after the original statement of the *thema*.

divine wisdom is eternally generated by the Father." Notice the word "nativity" in that last sentence; Thomas chose it intentionally in order to associate the "matter" of the treatise with the first words of the opening biblical *thema*: *Ab initio nativitatis* ("from the beginning of her nativity"). "This nativity is the beginning of every other nativity," says Thomas, such as those we see around us in the created realm, but which are only "imperfect," because, in contrast with the processions in the Trinity, "the one generated [in the created realm] received only a *part* of the substance of the generator, or only a similitude" (*genitum aut partem substantiae generantis accipit aut substantiae similitudinem*), and not, as in the Trinity, the whole substance, such as the Father bestows upon the Son.[13]

Next we find the manner (or *modus*) in which Boethius treats the Trinity in this word: "I shall investigate" (*investigabo*). There are two possible ways of writing a treatise on the Trinity, says Thomas: one is "by means of authorities" (*per auctoritates*), the other "by means of reasoned arguments" (*per rationes*). Whereas Augustine used both methods, says Thomas, Ambrose and Hilary of Poitiers used mostly authorities. Since Boethius chose the second of these – reasoned arguments rather than authorities – the manner of his work is indicated by the words: "I shall investigate." Thus in Sirach 39:1 we read: "'Wisdom,' namely, knowledge of the Trinity; 'of all the ancients,' that is, which the ancients affirmed solely on the grounds of authority; 'the wise man will seek out,' that is, he will investigate by reason."[14] So too, notes Thomas, Boethius's first words in his own prologue affirm that his was "an investigation carried on for a very long time (*"Investigatam diutissime"*).

Finally, the purpose (*finis*) of the work, says Thomas, is that "the hidden things of faith may be made manifest so far as possible in this life" (*occulta fidei manifestentur, quantum in via possibile*). Thomas associates this purpose with the final words in the opening biblical *thema*: "and I will bring the knowledge of her to light."

We can recall the subject matter, manner of proceeding, and purpose of Boethius's *De trinitate* simply by bringing to mind one phrase and noticing its three parts: "From the beginning of her birth/ I will investigate / and bring the knowledge of her to light." The subject matter is the eternal "birth" of the Son and Holy Spirit from the Father. The manner of treating this subject is by means of reasoned investigation. And the goal is to bring to light the knowledge of the invisible things of faith, especially those concerning the divine Trinity. This is pure *sermo modernus* style.

Between the Early and Later Prologues

Thomas composed this prologue for his *Commentary on Boethius's* De trinitate, probably in 1257–1258. Several years earlier, he had composed another prologue in the same style for his *Commentary on Boethius's* De hebdomadibus, likely written during Thomas's first regency at Paris (1252–1256). We will examine in the next section Thomas's general prologue to the course of lectures he gave on the epistles of St. Paul and then the prologue he composed to his *Commentary on the Psalms*. The lectures on the epistles of Paul may have been begun during Thomas's second regency at Paris (1268–1272), but they were likely

---

[13] Kenyon, para. 3.
[14] Ibid., para. 5.

composed later, during his regency at Naples (1272–1273), the period when he wrote the prologue to his *Commentary on the Psalms*.

A word is in order, however, about what falls between the "early" prologues we examined earlier and the "later" ones we will examine in the text that follows. During this intermediate period, Thomas continued to write prologues, but he did not continue composing them in the *sermo modernus* style. Thomas wrote prologues for many, but not all, of his commentaries on the works of Aristotle between 1269 and 1272, but none of them was written in the *sermo modernus* style. So too, even when Thomas composed a biblical commentary during this period – his *Commentary on Job* was likely written during his four years as a Conventual Lector at Orvieto (1261–1265) – this too lacked a *sermo modernus* style prologue.

Yet, when Thomas returned to Paris for his second regency in 1268 and began his lectures on the *Gospel of St. Matthew*, he once again used the *sermo modernus* style for his prologue – perhaps because it was required or at least "expected" at Paris. But he continued to use it later when he lectured on the Bible at Naples.

One conclusion we might draw is that the *sermo modernus*–style prologue was a distinctively "academic" literary form, one whose use was required whenever one was working in a university setting.[15] Early in his career, when Thomas was teaching at institutions that required prologues of this sort, he wrote them. Later, in the years before his second regency, when it was not required, his prologue style became much less formal or else he abandoned the *sermo modernus* style altogether. When he returned in the last years of his life to teach at the universities at Paris and then Naples, he once again wrote prologues in the required style. His years of preaching not only kept him in constant practice, but they also undoubtedly helped him master the style, given that his later prologues are some of his best.

II TWO LATER PROLOGUES

Commentary on the Epistles of St. Paul

Thomas wrote a relatively brief prologue to each of the Pauline epistles, but he also composed a general prologue to the entire series, which was published at the beginning of his *Commentary on Romans*. It is still not entirely clear when Thomas began and/or completed these commentaries.[16] Current scholarship suggests these commentaries date from a relatively late period in Thomas's career – perhaps as late as the last two years of his life.[17] Whenever they were written, it is certain, writes Torrell, "that Thomas thought of his commentary as a whole."

---

[15] We cannot conclude that this literary form was only used for prologues to lectures on books of the Bible since, as we have seen, Thomas used it in his early prologues to other works.
[16] One can find the complicated details and arguments in Torrell, *St. Thomas*, 250–255. There is also a good overview of the debate in Anthony Giambrone, O.P., "The Prologues to Aquinas' Commentaries on the Letters of St. Paul," in *Towards a Biblical Thomism: Thomas Aquinas and the Renewal of Biblical Theology*, ed. P. Roszak and J. Vijgen (Navarre, Spain: Eunsa, 2018), esp. 23–25.
[17] It may have been begun, however, as early as 1265, so I am treating it before Thomas's prologue to his commentary on the Gospel of John, which can be more certainly dated to 1270–1272. For our purposes, we are considering both simply as two witnesses to Thomas's later practice.

> The proof of this is given in the Prologue that he placed at the head of this whole. He proposes there a general plan of the Pauline epistles, according to which each one corresponds to a precise design. Certainly, he could have placed this [the prologue] here [at the beginning] at the time of a second version, but in fact he refers to this plan at the start of each epistle, which shows quite well that he was conscious of the unity of his intention, even for the parts simply reported on [for which we have only an uncorrected *reportatio*].[18]

Assuming Torrell is right that Thomas wrote the general prologue *before* he wrote the remaining commentaries on Paul's letters, it would have been written later in his career.

Yet, though late, we should note several important similarities between this later prologue and the *resumptio* address Thomas gave years earlier at his inception. Both contain a "commendation" of the text and its author, which is followed by a thematic *divisio textus*. In his master's *resumptio*, Thomas crafted a thematic *divisio* of all the books of the Bible. For this general prologue, he crafted a similar thematic *divisio* of all the epistles of Paul.[19] And in both instances, the basic structure of Thomas's comments were generated and organized by means of the division and dilation of an opening *thema* verse from the Bible.[20]

In this case, Thomas chose as his opening *thema* a verse from Acts 9:15: "this man is a vessel of election of mine, to bear my name before the Gentiles, and to kings, and to the sons of Israel" (*vas electionis est mihi iste, ut portet nomen meum coram gentibus, et regibus, et filiis Israël*).[21] Although there is no statement of the opening *divisio*, a quick survey of the whole prologue shows that Thomas has in mind a fourfold division: this man is: a vessel / of election / of mine to bear my name / before the Gentiles, and to kings, and to the sons of Israel" This "vessel" to the Gentiles is, of course, St. Paul. Now there are four things we can say about this or any vessel: how it is made (*constitutionem*), what it holds (*repletionem*), what it is used for (*usum*), and the fruit (*fructum*) of its use.

The Constitution of the Vessel

First, what are the properties of this "vessel"? "What sort of vessel this was," says Thomas, "is described in Sirach (50.10): 'as a solid vessel of gold adorned with every

---

[18] Torrell, *St. Thomas*, 255.

[19] Including the Epistle to the Hebrews which, in the thirteenth century, was thought to have been authored by Paul, an opinion modern scholars do not share.

[20] I have included an outline of the *divisio* of the books of the Bible Thomas proposed in his *resumptio* in the Appendix to this volume. Into it, I have inserted an outline of his *divisio* of the Pauline epistle. This was possible because (a) Thomas did not specify in his *resumptio* how the Pauline epistles were to be divided, so the new *divisio* did not take the place of an older one, and (b) Thomas retained a basic consistency in his overall conception, so the later *divisio* fit neatly into the earlier.

[21] English: Fabian Larcher, O.P., trans., *Commentary on the Letter of Saint Paul to the Romans*, ed. John Mortensen and Enrique Alarcón, with parallel Latin and the Greek text of the epistle (Lander, WY: The Aquinas Institute, 2012). E-text: aquinas.cc. See also for the Latin text.

sort of precious stone'" (*quasi vas auri solidum, ornatum omni lapide pretioso*).²² Having started with the word *vas* or "vessel" from Acts 9:15, Thomas has now bent the *sermo modernus* rules somewhat and added a subsidiary verse to lend structure the subsection that follows. St. Paul is a "vessel" which is "golden (*auri*), "solid" (*solidum*), and "adorned with every sort of precious stone" (*ornatum omni lapide pretioso*). It would not be wrong to think Thomas probably had in mind a richly adorned Eucharistic chalice.

Paul was a "golden" vessel, says Thomas, because of the shining brilliance of his wisdom (*propter fulgorem sapientiae*). He was "solid" in the virtue of charity (*virtute charitatis*). And he was "adorned with every sort of precious stone," that is, he was "adorned" with all the virtues (*omnibus virtutibus*).²³

In the next paragraph, Thomas praises these three distinguishing marks – St. Paul's wisdom, charity, and virtues – using a complex metaphor whose interpretation is made more difficult by a textual confusion. The original Latin text has: "*Quale autem fuerit istud vas patet ex hoc quod alia propinavit* . . ." Fabian Larcher, the English translator, translates this as: "The nature of this vessel is thus indicated by the sort of things it poured out." This interpretation is slightly odd, however, since *propinavit*, from the Latin verb *propino, -are, -avi, -atum*, means to "drink to someone's health" or to "pledge," although it can also mean simply "to give to drink." So too, the next paragraph contains a description of the things *contained in* the cup. One would have thought that the discussion of the contents of the cup would have preceded the discussion of what was poured out. Larcher's translation makes more sense, however, if we consider the entire context.

Thomas may be saying that "what sort of thing this vessel was is made clear" from *the sort of things it was used to pledge to* in the sense in which someone raises a glass and "drinks" or "pledges" or "toasts" to a person's health or marriage or graduation from college. That is possible. It could also suggest, however, that what the vessel was – its character – is made clear from what people were given to drink from it. The latter would be closer to Larcher's translation.

If we ask *either* to what sort of thing this vessel was raised up as a pledge *or* what were people given to drink from this vessel, Thomas answers: First, "Paul taught the mysteries of the most lofty divinity, which requires wisdom." Second, he "extolled love in the loftiest terms." Third, he "taught men about the different virtues."²⁴ Using the verb *propinavit* might suggest that wisdom, charity, and the virtues are the blessings one gives when one lifts up the cup in front of others during the "blessings" before the feast, as one lifts up the

---

²² The Latin text indicates that the passage is taken from Ecclesiasticus (now generally called Sirach) 50:10; the English indicates it is quoted from Sirach 50:9. In the Latin Vulgate, it can be found in Sirach 50:10. But in the Septuagint and most English translations it is found in Sirach 50:9.

²³ Strictly speaking, Thomas has violated several of the basic rules of the *sermo modernus* style here. The three descriptive clauses are supposed to be parallel, and it is not considered good style to repeat the word "virtue." Once he had written *propter fulgorem sapientiae* (because of shining wisdom), he should have made the next clause something like *propter firmitatem charitatis* (because of the firmness of his love), and the final one something like, "he was adorned with precious stones *propter multitudinem virtutum* (because of the multitude of his virtues).

²⁴ Here, as earlier, these clauses should, strictly speaking, be parallel, and Thomas should not repeat words.

Scriptures (and, more particularly, the Pauline epistles) to read before coming to the Eucharistic feast. What blessings are offered when one "raises" this vessel at mass – namely, St. Paul, or, by extension, his writings? Wisdom is given about the mysteries of the most lofty divinity; love is extolled; and the virtues are taught.

In this first section we are still dealing with Thomas's discussion of the make-up or "constitution" of the vessel (which, as we know, is St. Paul); we don't get to the question of the "contents" of the vessel until the next paragraph. But as we will see, there is a connection between what was "poured out" of the vessel (using Fr. Larcher's translation) – what was given people to drink – and what was contained in it.

The Contents of the Vessel: A Vessel of Election to Bear Christ's Name

So what are the "contents" of the vessel? Different vessels hold different liquids, says Thomas; so too, "God fills men with diverse graces as though with diverse liquids." So with what sort of "liquid" – that is to say, with what sort of graces *of election* – filled the vessel, St. Paul?

The opening biblical *thema* provides the answer: Paul was a "vessel of election" to "bear my name" (*ut portet nomen meum*), and this in three ways:

> For he possessed this name in the knowledge of his intellect (*in cognitione intellectus*), according to that verse in 1 Cor 2.2: "For I decided to know nothing among you except Christ."
>
> He also possessed the name in the love of his affections (*in dilectione affectus*), according to that verse in Rom 8.35: "Who will separate us from the love of Christ?" and in 1 Cor 16.21: "If any one does not love our Lord Jesus Christ, let him be accursed."
>
> And finally, he possessed it [i.e., "Christ's name] in the constant practice of his life (*in tota vitae suae conversatione*); hence it is said in Gal 2.20: "It is no longer I who live, but Christ who lives in me."

In this passage, we hear an echo of the three characteristics of the cup and of the blessings given with the cup mentioned earlier: wisdom, love, and virtue. The pattern is repeated three times as variations on a theme.

Constitution	Blessings (when raised as a pledge or poured out)	Contents
Paul was "golden" in the shining brilliance of wisdom	Paul taught the mysteries of highest divinity	Paul possessed the name of Christ in his intellect
"solid" in great love	He extolled love in the loftiest terms	He possessed the name of Christ in the love of his affections
"adorned with precious stones": the virtues	He taught the virtues	He possessed the name in the constant practice of his life [in accord with the virtues]

The drink offered to people by the vessel (St. Paul) were teachings (a) about the mysteries of the divinity, (b) about love, and (c) about the virtues. Paul was able to offer this drink because he possessed (as a vessel of election) "the name of Christ" (a) in his intellect, (b) in the love of his affections, and (c) in the constant practice of his life in accordance with the virtues. Paul was able only to offer what he himself had been given. He was *made* a vessel *by election*, and thus filled with the graces of election, precisely *so that* he could "bear Christ's name" to the nations.

We should also not miss the Eucharistic significance of this pattern. As the cup at mass contains the Blood of Christ "poured out for us," so also this cup – namely, St. Paul – "bears Christ" to the people. Just as the Eucharistic cup has the character it does because of the importance of what it contains – it is "golden, solid, and adorned with every sort of precious stone" – so also the "vessel," St. Paul, has the character *he* has because of the graces of Christ he has been given. His wisdom is the wisdom of Christ; his love is the love of Christ; and the virtues that characterize his life come from his life being lived for Christ. In commending St. Paul, Thomas is actually commending the grace of Christ, which is the subject of Paul's epistles.

The Use of the Vessel: To Bear Christ's Name

Which brings us to the question: "What is the vessel *used for*?" We already have the preliminary answer: it carries the divine name. But why does the divine name need to be carried? Why doesn't everyone already possess Christ's "name"? Thomas has an ingenious answer. It was necessary for the name to be "carried," says Thomas, "because it was far away from men" (*quia longe erat ab hominibus*) because of sin. Thomas cites two wonderful Old Testament verses to illuminate and emphasize the point; the first from Isaiah 30:27: "Behold the name of the Lord comes from afar," and the second from Psalm 119:155: "Salvation is far from us on account of sin."

If the Lord is "far off," how then is the Lord to be brought near to us? "Just as the angels bestow God's light upon us as being far from God," says Thomas, "so the apostles brought us the gospel teaching from Christ." And similarly "just as in the Old Testament, after the law of Moses, the prophets were read, who handed on the teaching of the law ... so also, in the New Testament, after the Gospels, the teachings of the apostles are read, who handed on to the faithful the things which they heard from the Lord." On this view, St. Paul is something like an angel, a messenger of God, bringing God's light to our darkened intellects. And he is like a prophet who, although he comes after the decisive revelation of God to His people (on Sinai in one case, in Galilee and Jerusalem in the other), hands on what he himself has received and faithfully imparts God's teaching (His *doctrina*) to the people of God.

How does Paul "carry Christ's name"? He does so, first in his body, says Thomas, by imitating Christ's life and sufferings. He does so, second, in his speech, because he spoke a message of hope. Just as the dove returned to the ark bearing an olive branch in its mouth (Genesis 8:11), which signified God's mercy and peace, so also Paul can be signified by a dove because he brings an "olive branch" – that is, a message of mercy and peace – to the "ark" that signifies the Church.

The third way St. Paul "carries the name" of Christ, finally, is by writing his epistles, through which, to those not yet born, he might hand on the "sense of Scripture" (*sensum Scripturae*). This last point is connected thematically with the one that precedes it, since on this view, it is Paul who in his epistles hands on the "teaching" (*doctrina*) of the New Testament – so much so that Thomas says of his epistles that "almost the whole teaching of theology" is contained in them (*fere tota theologiae continetur doctrina*). On this account, it was Paul who set the model for doing theology, as for Thomas it was also Paul who modeled the practice of using arguments in theological discourse (see ST I, q. 1, a. 8) and Paul who showed Christians how to read the Old Testament in light of the New.

Paul's excellence in bearing God's name – his excellence as a vessel – is shown by his being called a "chosen vessel" (*vas electionis*). He is also called "a chosen vessel *of mine*" (*vas electionis est mihi*) because in his dedication, he sought nothing of his own, but only what was Christ's.

The Fruit of the Vessel: To Bear Christ's Name to the Nations

What, then, was the "fruit" of this vessel? According to Thomas, the "fruit" of this vessel

> is expressed by the words *before the Gentiles*, whose teacher he was ... and *to kings*, to whom he preached the faith of Christ: for example to Agrippa, as in Acts 16.38, and even to Nero and his princes. Hence it is said in Phil 1.12–13: "What has happened to me has really served to advance the gospel, so that it has become known throughout the whole praetorian guard that my imprisonment is for Christ" (Phil 1.12). And again, in Isaiah 49.7: "Kings shall see and princes shall arise" (Is 49.7). And *to the sons of Israel*, against whom he argued about Christ: "But Saul increased all the more in strength, and confounded the Jews who lived in Damascus by proving that Jesus was the Christ" (Acts 9.22).

And with this, Thomas has completed his fourfold consideration of the "vessel" – its constitution, contents, use, and fruit – *and* he has made use of all the words in his opening biblical *thema*. What is left for him to do? He has commended Paul, praising him as a vessel of Christ's grace. But he has yet to say anything about Paul's *letters*. The letters, therefore, are the subject of the remainder of the prologue.

He discusses the letters using the classic fourfold Aristotelian *causes* of the work: the efficient, material, formal, and final causes. Thomas associates each of the four causes with the original four divisions of his opening *thema* verse. Having dilated the four parts of his opening *thema* in one way to commend Paul, he now dilates them differently to describe the letters. As we will see in Section III, this ability to dilate the same *thema* verse in two, sometimes three ways was the kind of advanced skill Bonaventure possessed and developed to a fine art. It was a skill Thomas developed only later in his career.

The Four Causes of the Work

"From the words of our text, therefore," says Thomas – and by this he means the opening biblical *thema* – "we can gather the four causes of the work, i.e., of Paul's letters." The first, the author of the work, or its efficient cause, is associated as we have seen above, with the word *vessel*. Second, the subject matter (*materia*) of the work is communicated by the words *my name*, "of which the vessel is full," says Thomas, "because this entire teaching is about the teaching (*doctrina*) of Christ." Third, the manner (*modum*) of the work, which would be its form, is letters – letters that "*bear* Christ's name." Finally, the final cause of the work is "in the utility mentioned above" (*in utilitate praedicta*): namely, to bear Christ's name *among the Gentiles* (alternatively, "to the nations"), *and to kings, and to the sons of Israel*.

The *Divisio Textus*

Having finished his "commendation" of Paul in the first part of his prologue and the description of the four causes in the second, Thomas moves in the final section, in a manner akin to what we saw above with his *resumptio* address, to a *divisio textus* of all the Pauline epistles.

Notice how Thomas transitions nicely into his *divisio textus* using the last words of his *thema*. The purpose of the letters was to bear Christ's name "among the Gentiles, and to kings, and to the sons of Israel." These three – Gentiles, kings, and the sons of Israel – set up the beginning elements of his *divisio textus*. Paul wrote fourteen letters, says Thomas, "nine of which instructed the church of the Gentiles; four, the prelates and princes of the Church, i.e. *kings*, and one to the people of *Israel*, namely the letter to the Hebrews."

Who is the author? Paul. What is the form? Letters. What is the *fruit* of the vessel? These letters to the Gentiles, the kings, and the sons of Israel. What is the subject matter (*materia*) of the letters? Thomas tells us in the next sentence: the "entire teaching is about Christ's grace." Christ's grace is what unifies them. How, then, can we *distinguish* them?[25]

Christ's grace "can be considered in three ways," says Thomas. It can be considered, first, as it is in the Head, namely Christ, and this is covered in the letter to the Hebrews.

Christ's grace can be considered, second, as it is in the chief members of the Mystical Body of Christ, and this is covered in the letters to the prelates of the Church, both spiritual and temporal. He instructs the spiritual prelates of the Church about establishing, preserving, and governing ecclesial unity in the first letter to Timothy; about resistance against persecutors of the Church in the second letter to Timothy; and about defense against heretics in the letter to Titus. Paul instructs temporal lords, finally, in the letter to Philemon.[26]

---

[25] I have provided an outline of Thomas's *divisio* in Appendix 1. See the insertion in the *divisio textus* of the books of the Bible from Thomas's *resumptio*.

[26] With regard to the last, the reader should recall that the letter to Philemon deals with an important Christian at Colossae named Philemon whose servant Onesimus secretly fled to Rome, where he was baptized by Paul. Paul sent the servant back to Colossae with this letter begging him to forgive his servant and embrace him as a brother. In his introductory comments to his commentary on Philemon, Thomas echoes this same point about the "spiritual" prelates and "temporal" prelates, saying: "For as it was shown above how spiritual prelates should relate to their subjects, so here [in the letter to Philemon] he shows how temporal masters should relate to their temporal servants, and how the faithful servant to his master."

Christ's grace can be considered, third, "as it is in the Mystical Body itself, namely the Church," and Paul deals with this topic in the letters to the Gentiles (i.e., the Romans, Corinthians, Galatians, Ephesians, Philippians, and Thessalonians). This is a long list. How do we distinguish these?

The letters to the Gentiles can be distinguished from one another, says Thomas, according to the three ways the grace of Christ can be considered. First, as that grace is *in itself*. This is the subject matter of the letter to the Romans.

Second, Christ's grace can be considered as it exists in the sacraments of the Church, which is the subject matter of the two letters to the Corinthians. The first deals with the nature of the sacraments, and the second with the dignity of the minister of the sacraments. In the letter to the Galatians, "superfluous sacraments" (*superflua sacramenta*) are rejected against those who wanted to join the old sacraments to the new.

Third, Christ's grace can be considered in view of the unity it produces in the Church. The establishment of ecclesial unity is treated in the letter to the Ephesians; the consolidation and progress of this unity is treated in the letter to the Philippians. The defense of this ecclesial unity against certain errors is covered in the letter to the Colossians; against existing persecutions is covered in the first letter to the Thessalonians; and against persecutions to come in the second letter to the Thessalonians.

The Purpose of the *Divisio*

Modern scholars would likely consider this set of thematic divisions too clever by half since, as everyone knows, Paul wrote these letters in an ad hoc way, when occasion demanded, not with an intentional order in mind, treating systematically the various topics related to Christ's grace.

Yet, criticizing Thomas in this way for crafting a thematic *divisio textus* which St. Paul would not have had in mind is to make an unfortunate "category mistake." As seems clear from our examination of the various *resumptio* addresses at the University of Paris during the thirteenth century, medieval theologians and their audiences do not seem to have viewed these thematic divisions of the biblical text as somehow ironclad and invariable, since each master had to come up with his own as the test of his skill as a potential teacher.

Recall again the important role the memory arts played in medieval pedagogy and how invaluable medieval people thought it was for someone to possess a good memory. The virtue of Thomas's thematic *divisio textus* is that provides a mnemonic structure by means of which all the Pauline epistles can be remembered, and remembered in such a way as to underscore that they all communicate important lessons about the grace of Christ. Even modern biblical scholars might see the value in this as a pedagogical device.

The irony is that, if we criticize Thomas for being guilty of textual anachronism – attributing to St. Paul's epistles a unified intent and thematic structure which was not present when they were written – we would be guilty of our own textual anachronism for failing to understand the character of the literary form and the pedagogical intention behind a *divisio textus*. Our contemporary criticism of Thomas would be valid only if Thomas actually thought that with his *divisio textus*, he was actually capturing St. Paul's intention in writing each of his epistles. But this, I would suggest, is to misunderstand the nature and intention of the *divisio textus*.

Thomas and his contemporaries did not presume that they could *know* St. Paul's intentions in writing. This is more of a modern conceit, heightened by modern biographical and psychological schools of interpretation. For good or for ill, one rarely finds medieval exegetes guessing at or theorizing about a *human* author's intentions the way modern literary critics are wont to do. Rather Thomas and his fellow masters proposed these thematic textual *divisiones* primarily as pedagogical tools.

Prologues such as this one with its accompanying *divisio textus* were written to serve both pedagogical and protreptic purposes. They were philosophical exhortations to the students and other prospective readers to appreciate the importance of the text they were about to study. In this way, the prologue serves the basic purposes of any *principium* or exordium: to render the audience good-willed (*benevolum*), attentive (*attentum*), and teachable (*docile*).[27] First, the master had to render his audience interested and open by commending the text and/or its author; second, he divided the text to make the audience more attentive to his points. These first two served, then, to prepare the student's minds, in terms of attention, interest, and focus, to make them more teachable.

In this prologue, that toward which the audience was to be made benevolent was not the author *of the prologue* – Thomas himself; the goal was to make them benevolent toward St. Paul. Paul is the one being commended, although the *way* Thomas commended Paul showed it was really a commendation of *Christ*, because all of Paul's gifts were due to the grace of Christ. This served as a nice foretaste of the subject matter of the epistles, in fact, because all of them deal with *the grace of Christ*. That toward which the audience was to be made "attentive" and "docile" were the letters of Paul because ultimately *they* are what do the teaching.

Commentary on the Psalms

It is not known with any precision when Thomas commented on the Psalms. The great Dominican editor of Thomas's sermons, Louis Bataillon, at one point suggested that they should not be considered mature works of Aquinas. He argued that it was unlikely that Thomas would have waited to the end of his career to comment on so important a text. This view was received favorably by his Dominican confrère Simon Tugwell, who believed that the commentary belonged to the very beginning of Thomas's career.[28] The majority of scholars, however – a list including Frs. Glorieux, Eschmann, Weisheipl, and Torrell – have all dated it to Thomas's final years teaching at Naples (1272–1273). After the French publication of his biography of Aquinas, Fr. Torrell was sent two additional pieces of evidence that favor a later dating. This appears to have convinced even Fr. Bataillon, who wrote: "The commentary on the

---

[27] As mentioned in Chapter 5, these were the three goals of the *exordium* or "beginning" of any speech according to the classical rhetorical tradition going back to Cicero: to render one's listeners good willed, attentive, and docile. See, for example, Augustine, *De doctrina christiana* IV.2.3 and Cicero, *De oratore* 2.82.

[28] See Tugwell, *Albert and Thomas: Selected Writings*, Classics of Western Spirituality (Mahwah, NJ: Paulist Press, 1988), 246 and n. 474.

Psalms is almost certainly the last instruction of Thomas."[29] For our present purposes, we will consider it a mature work.

In *The Medieval Theory of Authorship*, author A. J. Minnis discusses Thomas's prologue to the Psalms at some length and with great sophistication.[30] He notes that the thirteenth century saw a greater appreciation for certain key elements of the literal sense – in particular the role of the human author and the author's distinctive literary forms and style – with the development and use of what he terms the "Aristotelian prologue," so called because this style of formulating a prologue was based on the four Aristotelian causes: the efficient cause or author of the work, the material cause or subject matter of the work, the formal cause or form of the work, and the final cause or purpose of the work. Minnis shows that, during the thirteenth century, this simple, four-part prologue gradually came to replace a series of more complicated prologues that had been popular in the twelfth century.[31] Yet, while it is true that Thomas's prologue to his Psalm commentary is structured around the four Aristotelian causes, those four causes are associated with the parts of the biblical verse that introduces the prologue and then dilated in the *sermo modernus* style.

In the prologue to his Psalms commentary, Thomas uses as his opening *thema* this passage from Ecclesiasticus 47:9: "In his every work, he gave confession to the holy one and the most high, with a word of glory" (*In omni opere suo dedit confessionem sancto et excelso in verbo gloriae*).[32] One reason for quoting this verse from Ecclesiasticus in a prologue to the Psalms is that the passage in its original context refers to David, whom Thomas takes to be the author of the Psalms.[33] Yet Thomas shows himself willing in other places to use a biblical *thema* having nothing to do with a particular author to describe that author. Perhaps the most obvious example is in Thomas's Sermon 16 (*Inveni David*), where Thomas uses the passage from Psalm 88:21, "I have found David my servant; with my holy oil I have anointed him; my hand will assist him and my arm will make him firm," to refer to the fourth-century saint, Nicholas of Myra. Here, in the prologue to his Psalm commentary, the correspondence between the *thema* verse and the reputed author, King David, was fortuitous. Yet, as was always the case with the opening *thema* verse, its primary purpose was to provide a mnemonic structuring device around which the rest of the prologue could be developed. As we have seen, Thomas does not always make a fourfold *divisio*, nor does he always associate the parts of the *divisio* with the four Aristotelian causes. But as A. J. Minnis has shown, this format was becoming more popular in the thirteenth century, and Thomas employed it here.[34]

---

[29] See Torrell, *St. Thomas*, 258, esp. n. 36. The Bataillon quotation was taken from this note; the original can be found at L. Bataillon, "La diffusione manoscritta e stampata dei commenti biblici de San Tommaso d'Aquino," *Angelicum* 71 (1994): 579–590, esp. 589.

[30] Alastair J. Minnis, *Medieval Theory of Authorship: Scholastic Literary Attitudes in the Later Middle Ages* (Philadelphia, PA: University of Pennsylvania Press, 1984; 2nd ed. 1988), esp. 86–90.

[31] See Minnis, *Medieval Theory*, esp. 75f.

[32] "Sancti Thomae de Aquino in psalmos Davidis exposition proemium, Reportatio Reginaldi de Piperno," Textum Parmae 1863 editum et automato translatum a Roberto Busa SJ, online at www.corpusthomisticum.org/cps00.html. All English translations are mine.

[33] Most medieval exegetes insisted on this, even though St. Jerome did not agree. Cf. Jerome, *Epistola* 140, *Ad Cyprianum Presbyterum*.

[34] See Minnis, *Medieval Authority*, esp. chapter 1 on the development of the "Type C," "Aristotelian" prologue. In the third section, we will see that Bonaventure incorporates all four Aristotelian causes into his prologues much more often than Thomas does.

The Four Causes of the Work

The phrase "In his every work" suggests the *materia* (the subject matter) of the Psalms: "The matter of the work is clear," says Thomas, "because it concerns every work of the Lord." The work of God is fourfold: it involves creation, governance, reparation, and glorification, and all four are covered in the Psalms. Many psalms praise the works of *creation*; others deal with God's *governance*; still others speak of God's work of *reparation* because they "speak of Christ and all the effects of grace." Although this may sound odd to modern readers of the Psalms, according to Thomas, "all the things which pertain to the faith of the Incarnation are so clearly treated in this book that it seems almost a gospel, and not prophecy."[35] Finally, the Psalms treat of God's work of *glorification* because "through it, he invites us to glory. Indeed, the Psalter is the most frequently used book in the Church, says Thomas, "because it contains the whole of the Scriptures." As I have pointed out, an important goal of these prologues was to provide the students with a protreptic exhortation to consider the book seriously and study it eagerly. An Old Testament book that is, according to Thomas, "almost a Gospel," "contains the whole of the Scriptures," and is the most frequently used book in the Church might just pique a young student's interest.

The mode or the *form* of the Psalms is suggested by the next phrase in the epigraph: "he gave confession." Several different literary modes are used in Scripture: the narrative mode, which is found in the historical books; the admonitory, the exhortatory, and the imperative modes, which are found in the law, the prophets, and the wisdom books; the disputative mode, which is found in the book of Job; and finally, the beseeching or laudatory mode, which is the mode found in the Psalms. According to Thomas, "whatever is said in the other books in the aforementioned modes, is found [in the Psalms] in the mode of praise and prayer." The "beseeching" mode of the Psalms is suggested by the phrase "he gave confession."

Next, the final cause or *purpose* of the Psalms is prayer, which is the elevation of the mind to God – something which Thomas associates with the phrase "to the holy one and the most high." But the soul is elevated to God for four reasons: first, for admiring the loftiness of His power, which is the elevation of faith; second, for tending toward the excellence of eternal beatitude, which is the elevation of hope (and both faith and hope are suggested by the phrase "to the most high"); third, the soul is elevated, for clinging to divine goodness and sanctity, which is the elevation of charity; and fourth for imitating divine justice in work, which is the elevation of justice. These last two are suggested by the phrase "to the holy one." The purpose of the Psalms, therefore, says Thomas, "is that the soul may be conjoined with God, as *to the holy one and the most high*."

Finally, the author or *efficient cause* of the Psalms is signified by the last part of the epigraph: (In his every work / he gave confession / to the holy one and most high) *in a word of glory*. Why are the Psalms a "word of glory"? Because, says Thomas, whereas the other sciences are written by means of human reason, the sacred Scriptures are written by means of the inspiration of the Holy Spirit. They are, therefore, the "word of the Lord" – that is, "the word of glory." The Book of Psalms is called the "word of glory," therefore, for four reasons. First, its teaching emanates from the glorious work of God. Second, this book

---

[35] As the reader may recall, Thomas made a similar comment about the Book of Isaiah in the prologue to that commentary. Verses from both Old Testament books show up repeatedly and in crucial places in the gospels.

contains the glory of God, which it announces. Third is the manner in which the book is expressed; for "glory," says Thomas "is the same as clarity," and whereas other prophets utilized images, figures, or dreams, "this one taught unveiled concerning the truth." Therefore the revelation of this prophet was glorious, because laid open (*aperta*)." Fourth, the Psalms are called the "word of glory" because through them "God invites us to glory."

After the Exhortation: Background Information

After he has finished dilating the four parts of his opening *divisio*, Thomas provides the reader with some background information of the sort we are accustomed to getting in modern prologues: information about the translation of the Psalms; how they are to be interpreted; and the order of the Psalms within the collection. We might consider this long "coda" to his *sermo modernus*–style prologue Thomas's own version of the Jerome-style prologue. As the reader may recall, Thomas's early practice as a *baccalarius biblicus* was to write a *sermo modernus*–style prologue, after which he would copy out one of Jerome's prologues and then provide a *divisio textus* exposition of it. Thomas's practice here in his Psalm commentary is a development of that earlier practice. Now that Thomas was a master and not a bachelor, he felt confident enough to provide his own Jerome-style prologue. As we will see in a moment, the potential confusions surrounding the text and interpretation of the Psalms would seem to have dictated this extra step.

Aquinas informed his students, rightly, that there were three Latin translations of the Psalms. The first was made in the early centuries of the Church and is now commonly called the *Vetus Latina* or the *Psalterium Vetus*; it was a translation from the Greek Septuagint and provided the basis for Jerome's first revision of the Psalter. The second translation was the one done by Jerome himself from the Greek Septuagint. This version was "sung in France" in Thomas's day and served as the basis for most Gregorian chant. It is still to this day commonly called the *Versio Gallicana* or the *Psalterium Gallicanum*. The third translation was done by Jerome, who translated from the Hebrew into Latin, a version now commonly called the *Versio iuxta Hebraicum*. Although important as a scholarly tool, this version never appears to have been used in the liturgy in any church. And so Thomas comments that "it is not sung in any Church," but then adds: "although many own a copy."

How to Interpret the Psalms

Following these details about the three versions of the Psalms, we find under the heading "mode of exposition" fascinating reflections on how to interpret the Psalms. Thomas is aware, and warns his reader, that Theodore of Mopsuestia, an exegete of the Antiochene School, was condemned (posthumously) at the Second Council of Constantinople in 553 for claiming that passages such as the verse in Psalm 21, "They divide my garments among them," should not to be taken literally as referring to Christ. According to Theodore, the passage referred literally to David and was only subsequently applied to Christ. Although by this point in his career, Thomas was no longer copying out

Jerome's prologues in addition to his own, his response to this problem shows how much he depended still upon Jerome. Thomas writes:

> Blessed Jerome therefore expounding on Ezekiel passed on to us a rule that we will observe in the Psalms; namely, that events are to be expounded as prefiguring something about Christ or the Church" (*scilicet quod sic sunt exponendae de rebus gestis, ut figurantibus aliquid de Christo vel Ecclesia*). Prophecies however sometimes are said of things which were of the time then, but are not principally said of those things, but insofar as they are a figure of future things; and therefore the Holy Spirit ordained that when such things were said, we should infer things that exceed the condition of the event, so that our attention might be raised to that which is prefigured.

Thomas cites several examples, but for our purposes, we'll focus on just one: his statement that "we read some things about the Kingdom of David and Solomon which were not to be fulfilled in the reign of those men, but were fulfilled in the reign of Christ of whom those are a figure."[36] Consider for a moment the following passage from 2 Samuel 7 that contains God's promise to David to establish an eternal covenant with one of his descendants:

> *The LORD spoke to Nathan and said:*
> *"Go, tell my servant David . . .*
> *'When your time comes and you rest with your ancestors,*
> *I will raise up your heir after you, sprung from your loins,*
> *and I will make his kingdom firm.*
> *It is he who shall build a house for my name.*
> *And I will make his royal throne firm forever.*
> *I will be a father to him,*
> *and he shall be a son to me.'"*
>
> (2 Sm 7:4–5a, 12–14a)

David's son was Solomon, and Solomon did build the first temple in Jerusalem after his father's death. So this passage clearly seems to refer to Solomon. But does it?

Note the promises. Along with "It is he who shall build a house for my name," we also find these three in particular:

> *I will make his kingdom firm.*
> *I will make his royal throne firm forever.*
> *I will be a father to him, and he shall be a son to me.*

The problem with applying these promises to Solomon is that, although his kingdom was firm during his life, it split into the northern and southern kingdoms after his death. So too, after the kingdom was divided, the northern kingdom of Israel eventually fell to the Assyrians in 722 BC and the southern kingdom of Judah fell to the Babylonians in 598 BC. Thus neither the kingdom nor the royal throne seems to have been "made firm"

---

[36] My exposition at this point goes beyond Thomas's few, simple comments. It is meant to make clear what might be left unclear by Thomas's comments.

forever. Indeed, it ended shortly after Solomon's death. As for the promise that "I will be a father to him, and he shall be a son to me," Solomon was renowned in the Scriptures both for his sins and for his idolatry. The Scriptures tell us he had taken hundreds of foreign wives and even more concubines, on the model of an Eastern potentate, and had ordered hundreds of shrines to be built to their gods in Jerusalem. There are things in the textual "promise to David" that seem to "exceed the condition of the event" – "the event" being Solomon's kingdom and its aftermath.

What early Christians such as St. Jerome concluded, therefore, was that the promises in 2 Samuel 7 were truly fulfilled only with the coming of Christ, when with the Incarnation, death, resurrection, and ascension to the right hand of the Father, (a) He established the "kingdom of God"; (b) He "made his royal throne firm forever" in heaven; and (c) as the Son of God, He fully realized the promise that God would be "father to him, and he shall be son to me." Thus although the prophet writing 2 Samuel 7 may have had Solomon in mind or may have had no idea in whom his words would be fulfilled, exegetes such as St. Thomas and St. Jerome believed that this prophet, whoever he was, was working as the instrument of the Holy Spirit who knew the true identity of the man in whom his words would find their fulfillment.

So although these promises may have been fulfilled in part, figuratively, in Solomon, who built a temple for the Lord, early Christians such as St. Jerome believed these words referred most fully and most properly to Jesus Christ, the co-eternal Son of God; the one who after the temple of His body was destroyed, raised it up in three days (John 2.19); the one in whom the Kingdom of God was established; and the one whose throne with the Father in heaven is made firm forever.

Instead of claiming, as Theodore of Mopsuestia seems to have done, that the Psalm text literally refers to Solomon and only allegorically refers to Christ, Thomas, following Jerome, says that the text literally and most properly, refers to Christ because its promises are fulfilled only in Him.[37] Not that they make absolutely no reference to Solomon, but they refer to him only inchoately, imperfectly, and as a prefiguration of Christ. These words, says Thomas, should be explained "as being about the kingdom of Solomon, insofar as it is a symbol of the Kingdom of Christ in which all the things said there will be fulfilled."

In a similar vein, Thomas writes that the first fifty psalms "treat figuratively" (*figuraliter tractatur*) "of David's tribulations, the attacks upon him, and his liberation," in the sense that these psalms were meant to pre-*figure* – to provide people with the categories to lead

---

[37] I am not attributing to Thomas a doctrine of the *sensus plenior*, a view popularized in the twentieth century especially by Fr. Raymond Brown, on which see *The 'Sensus Plenior' of Sacred Scripture* (Baltimore, MD: St. Mary's University Press, 1955); and his articles: "The History and Development of the Theory of a *Sensus Plenior*," *Catholic Biblical Quarterly* 15 (1953): 141–162; "The Problems of the *Sensus Plenior*," *Ephemerides Theologicae Lovanienses* 43 (1967): 460–469. The controversy over the *sensus plenior* was whether it should be considered a part of the literal sense or one of the figurative senses. Thomas does not speak of a *sensus plenior* here. He clearly holds that statements such as the one in Psalm 21(22), "They divided my garments among them," is said literally (*dicitur ad litteram*) of Christ, not David. This is less troublesome for him than for modern exegetes because for Thomas, the ultimate author of the text is the Holy Spirit, and for this reason, whether the human author knew the person to whom his words would properly refer at some future date was not as much a burning question for him as it became for exegetes in the twentieth century.

their minds to – Christ's infinite kingdom, the tribulations of His sacrificial death, and His liberation from the bonds of death in the resurrection of the body.

The *Divisio Textus*

In the final section of his prologue, Thomas discusses the significance of having 150 psalms and mentions several ways of dividing them.[38] The number 150 is fitting, says Thomas, because this number is composed of 70 and 80; 7 represents the course of time because it is the number of days in the week, and 8 represents the state of the future life because Christ rose on "the first day of the week," or the eighth day. This signifies that in the Psalms "there is a treatment of those things that pertain to the course of the present life and to future glory." Or perhaps by 7 the Old Testament is signified, since the fathers of the Old Testament observed the Sabbath on the seventh day, and by 8 is signified the New Testament, since Christians celebrate the resurrection of the Lord on the eight day. This signifies that in the Psalms "are contained the mysteries of the Old and New Testament" (*continentur mysteria veteris et novi testamenti*).

Thomas mentions, but he does not seem to bless, the notion that the Psalter can be divided into five books, each of which is concluded with the phrase: "Amen, amen." On this view, the first division would fall at the end of Psalm 40; the second, at the end of Psalm 71; the third, at the end of Psalm 88; and the fourth, at the end of Psalm 106. But as Thomas notes, "amen, amen" does not always refer to the end of the book, because in other books where the phrase appears, it does not always appear at the end of the book.

Thomas notes rightly that the Psalms are not ordered chronologically, since some things that happened earlier historically show up in later psalms. The division Thomas seems to favor distinguishes the Psalms into three groups of fifty: the first group having to do with penitence, the second with justice, and the third with the praise of eternal glory.[39]

What follows these considerations is Thomas's attempt at a *divisio textus* of the first fifty psalms which, as he has said, treat "figuratively" (or perhaps we should say "prefiguratively") of David's tribulations, attacks upon him, and his liberation. According to Thomas, David prayed against a twofold attack: the first were attacks against the entire people of God (Psalms 41–50), which signify persecutions against Christ and the Church; the second were attacks against David's own person, both by those who persecuted him in the temporal order and those who lived unjustly (Psalms 31–40). While David reigned, he suffered a twofold tribulation: from the entire people (Psalms 21–30) and from two persons especially: Absalom and Saul. "By this," says Thomas, "is signified the persecution which the saints suffer either from those of their own household" (signified by Absalom) "or from outsiders" (signified by Saul); so too Christ suffered from Judas (of his own household), and from the Jews (outsiders). Psalms 1–10 deal with the suffering from those of one's own household, while Psalms 11–20 treat of the sufferings from outsiders.

---

[38] Most modern Bibles have 151 Psalms, although some have several more, for reasons we won't go into here, but in Thomas's day, Psalters contained 150 in total.

[39] Thomas's designation of the first fifty Psalms as having to do with penance should be distinguished from the four "penitential Psalms" designated by Cassiodorus (Psalms 6, 32, 38, 51, 102, 130, and 143 in modern Bibles, or Psalms 6, 31, 37, 50, 101, 129, and 142 in the Septuagint and Latin Vulgate).

Why Read the Psalms?

The first task of a good prologue was to give the student *a reason to read*, just as the master at his inception had to commend the value of Sacred Scripture before providing a suitable *divisio textus* of all its books. The student needs a reason to care, a reason to think a text will be important, before he will be willing to attend patiently to the intricate details of a complex *divisio textus*.

Why read the Psalms? For Thomas, it was not because they were said to be the words of a famous Old Testament king, nor because they reveal how he reacted to various events in his eventful life. In Thomas's prologue, David's name shows up in the first line but rarely does so thereafter. When Thomas identifies the author of the work, he associated the author with the phrase "with the words of glory," which signifies that the author is the Holy Spirit. And the events that seem to be referred to in the words of the Psalms are only "figuratively" about David's tribulations in his limited earthly kingdom, whereas they are lastingly significant because they "prefigure" realities concerning Christ, His Church, and his everlasting heavenly kingdom. The events of David's tribulation are over, and neither we nor Thomas's readers can take part in them. The realties prefigured by David's tribulations having to do with Christ and His Church are realities that exist now and everlastingly, and in these, we can participate fully if we so choose.

Summarizing his account of the four Aristotelian causes, Thomas says:

> Therefore the material (*materia*) of this work is clear: it is about every work of the Lord. The style (*modus*) of the work: it is deprecative and laudative. The end purpose (*finis*): that we are raised to be joined to the most High and Holy One. The author [efficient cause] is the Holy Spirit that reveals this.

For Thomas, the question "Why read the Psalms?" could be answered this way: because the Psalms are prayers or praises that treat every work of the Lord, and by reading the Psalms, we are raised to glory, "to be joined to the most High and Holy One." A book of prayers about every work of God, inspired by God, which unites us to God, might be one worth reading, one would think. It is not likely anyone would be much interested in the details about the different translations or the order and numbering of the Psalms unless one had first become interested in the book itself.

In these latter two prologues – to the Psalms and to the Pauline epistles – Thomas exhibits a greater proficiency in using the *sermo modernus* style. These later prologues are longer and more sophisticated than his earlier prologues to Boethius's *De trinitate* and the *Contra impugnantes*, even if he still has not mastered all the rules consistently. The differences between his prologue to the Pauline epistles and his earlier halting attempts at writing prologues for his cursory commentaries on Jeremiah and Lamentations is the difference between an unsure, inexperienced novice and a master. Thomas was a quick study and learned to write clear, beautiful sermons and prologues. In the next chapter, we will examine what I take to be Thomas's most highly developed and most effective protreptic prologue: his exhortation to his students to embrace the wisdom of the Gospel of St. John.

By the time he had matured in his career as a preacher and a master, Thomas had gained significant skill in using the art of the *sermo modernus* style. But it is worth noting that Thomas did not begin his studies at Paris and Cologne with this skill, and he did not develop it overnight. These were hard-earned skills that he developed over years of preaching and writing prologues.

8

I Have Seen the Lord

Thomas's Protreptic Prologue to His Commentary on the Gospel of John

ONE OF Thomas's most elegant and most philosophically profound prologues was one of his last: the prologue to his *Commentary on the Gospel of John*, crafted during his second regency at Paris (1268–1272).[1] The entire prologue was structured around a single sentence from Isaiah 6:1: "I saw the Lord seated on a throne high and lofty, and the whole earth was full of his majesty, and the things that were under him completely filled the temple" (*Vidi dominum sedentem super solium excelsum et elevatum, et plena erat omnis terra maiestate eius, et ea quae sub ipso erant, replebant templum*).[2]

---

[1] References are to the online version of Thomas Aquinas, *Commentary on the Gospel of John*, trans. J. Weisheipl, O.P. (Albany, NY: Magi Books, 1980) at http://dhspriory.org/thomas/SSJohn.htm. Latin texts were taken from this website as well. References will be to the section numbers in that translation: e.g., "John Prologue, 3," would refer to the Prologue, section 3, in the Weisheipl translation.

[2] Fr. Weisheipl notes in one of the several invaluable essays at the back of the Magi Press volume – essays not reprinted on the dhspriory website noted earlier – that the text of Is 6:1 that appears here with all three of its parts – *Vidi Dominus sedentem super solium excelsum et elevatum, et plena erat domus a maiestate eius, et ea quae sub ipso erant erant replebant templum* – cannot be found this way in any of the ordinary editions of the Latin Vulgate that have come down to us, nor in the Clementine version, the Greek Septuagint, or the Hebrew Masoretic text of Isaiah. It does, however, show up this way in Thomas's running gloss on the book of Isaiah (cf. the *Expositio super Isaiam ad litteram*, in *Opera omnia*, ed. Leon. 28 [Rome 1974], 6:1, lines 96–103). Thomas's teacher Albert the Great quotes it as well in the prologue to his *Commentary on the Second Book of the Sentences* (cf. ed. Bourgnet 27:1–3). Thus the "historical and textual problem," as Weisheipl points out, "is to locate the vulgate tradition to which the Bible of Thomas and Albert belonged," which, as he also points out, "has not yet been done" (see Weisheipl, *Commentary*, 447–449).

The Latin text of Isaiah 6:1 the reader will find in modern critical editions of the Latin text reads as follows: *Vidi Dominum sedentem super solium excelsum et elevatum, et ea quae sub eo erant implebant templum*. In other words, it is identical to the version Thomas uses with regard to its first and third parts, but the second part in Thomas's version is missing. One can scarcely blame Thomas for the imperfections in the texts available to him in his time and circumstances. This might be more of a concern if Thomas had been commenting on the verse, and if he were deriving from it a meaning

"These are the words of a contemplative," says Thomas (referring to Isaiah), and yet, "if we regard them as spoken by John the Evangelist, they apply quite well to showing the nature of this Gospel." Recall that for Thomas and his contemporaries, a key to reading and interpreting the Scriptures involved recognizing its Christocentric character. Thomas believed he could use a text spoken by Isaiah to elucidate John's Gospel because of their intrinsic connectedness through Christ.

When Isaiah says, "I saw the Lord," he spoke truly, but he may not have realized that the *person* he was seeing was Jesus Christ. This verse occurs during the commissioning of the prophet, whose mouth is purified when a burning coal is applied to his lips so he can speak "fittingly" of the Lord. The Book of Isaiah may be understood to speak fittingly of the Lord, since passages from Isaiah show up repeatedly in the Gospels and are directly prophetic of events that happen to Christ. Of special importance are those passages from the songs of the "suffering servant" in Isaiah, chapters 42–53. On Thomas's account, just as Isaiah's mind was elevated up above what reason alone could grasp so that he was privileged to see the coming of the Christ, so too John's mind was elevated above what reason alone could grasp so that he was privileged to see the full truth of Christ's divinity. Thus John was especially *contemplative* precisely because he grasped in an especially full way Christ's *divinity*.

In accord with the canons of the *sermo modernus* style, Thomas describes the threefold nature of John's contemplation in relation to the three dominant images in his *thema* verse: high, full, and perfect: "I saw the Lord seated on a throne *high* and *lofty*" (*excelsum et elevatum*); "the whole house was *full* (*plena*) of his majesty"; and "the things under him *completely filled* (*replebant*) the temple." The image of the temple being *completely filled* allows Thomas to describe this as "perfect" (*perfectere*) or "complete." These three phrases will also suggest the matter, the order, and the end of the Gospel.[3]

John's Contemplation Was "High"

John's contemplation was "high," says Thomas, because it rose to knowledge of God, the highest object of contemplation, and this in four ways, each of which is suggested by the phrase: "I saw the Lord seated on a throne high and lofty." One can come to a knowledge of God, says Thomas, by *authority* (which is suggested by the phrase "I saw *the Lord*"); by reasoning from *eternity* (which is suggested by the phrase *seated*, that is, "presiding without any change"); by reasoning from *dignity* or *nobility* (which is suggested by the throne's being *high*); and by reasoning from *incomprehensibility* (which is suggested by the throne's being *lofty*).

---

not contained within the actual text itself. But this is not the case. The text is simply a mnemonic structuring device.

[3] Strictly speaking, according to the canons of the *sermo modernus* style, Thomas was not supposed to use the same word in his dilation that appears in his *thema*. Rather, he should have said something like John's contemplation was "high" in the preeminent authority of his knowledge, "full" in the magnificent breadth of its extension, and "perfect" in the divine joy of its end. Compare Thomas's practice here, for example, with any of Bonaventure's prologues in the next section. Thomas's complex use of the words in the *thema* likely made this option less desirable. The result is greater clarity.

The attentive reader may notice that the word "high" is doing double service here: Thomas uses it to suggest the basic distinction between "high," "full," and "perfect" on the one hand, while also using it to suggest "dignity" as opposed to "authority," "eternity," and "incomprehensibility" on the other. That's fine, as long as the chain of associations is clear. The goal ultimately is to use the word to recall a list of various associations. And since a word can have multiple associations, it can send the reader off into various directions mnemonically to recall various trains of thought.

Knowing God from His Authority

Some have arrived at the knowledge of God from his *authority*, says Thomas, but by "authority" here he does *not* mean the sort of authority to which he is referring in the *Summa theologiae* when, in the first question of the *prima pars*, he lists as an objection that "authority is the weakest kind of proof."[4] In the *Summa*, Thomas will turn that argument on its head, saying that "although the argument from authority based on human reason is the weakest," yet "the argument from authority based on divine revelation is the strongest."[5] Here, however, the notion of "authority" is very different; it is, as Thomas describes it, the "authority in governing" (*gubernandi auctoritas*) by which God directs all created things back to Himself as their source and ultimate end.

> For we see the things in nature acting for an end, and attaining to ends which are both useful and certain. And since they lack intelligence, they are unable to direct themselves, but must be directed and moved by one directing them, and who possesses an intellect. Thus it is that the movement of the things of nature toward a certain end indicates the existence of something higher by which the things of nature are directed to an end and governed. And so, since the whole course of nature advances to an end in an orderly way and is directed, we have to posit something higher which directs and governs them as Lord; and this is God.[6]

Those who know Thomas's *Summa theologiae* will recognize this argument as the famous "fifth way" of arriving at knowledge of God's existence – i.e., "from the governance of things" (*ex gubernatione rerum*). In ST I, q. 3, a. 3, Thomas writes:

> We see that things which lack intelligence, such as natural bodies, act for an end, and this is evident from their acting always, or nearly always, in the same way, so as to obtain the best result. Hence it is plain that not fortuitously, but designedly, do they achieve their end. Now whatever lacks intelligence cannot move towards an end, unless it be directed by some being endowed with knowledge and intelligence; as the arrow is shot to its mark by the archer. Therefore some intelligent being exists by whom all natural things are directed to their end; and this being we call God.[7]

---

[4] ST I, q. 1, art. 8, obj. 2, quoting Boethius, *Topics* 6.
[5] ST I, q. 1, art. 8, ad 2.
[6] Prologue to John, 3.
[7] ST I, q. 3, art. 3.

Why does Thomas refer to the fifth way in this prologue? The explanation is likely as simple as this: the word Thomas is presented with by his *thema* verse is *Lord*, and the word "lord" suggests "governance." Thomas tells us as much, saying:

> This authority in governing is shown to be in the Word of God when he says, "Lord." Thus the Psalm (88:10) says: "You rule the power of the sea, and you still the swelling of its waves," as though saying: You are the Lord and govern all things. John shows that he knows this about the Word when he says below (1:11), "He came unto his own," i.e., to the world, since the whole universe is his own.[8]

What this passage suggests is that the so-called "fifth way" fits both the mnemonic device from Isaiah 6:1 and the content of John's Gospel that Thomas wants to emphasize. As we will see in more detail in the text that follows when we get to the comments that Thomas makes related to the word "full," the theological point he wishes to emphasize is that God's power extends to *all* things, and in this way "the whole earth" is said to be *"full* of His majesty." But we will get to this point presently.

Knowing God from His Eternity

The second way of arriving at the knowledge of God, says Thomas, is "from his eternity" (*ex eius aeternitate*), which Thomas associates with the word "seated" in the phrase "I saw the Lord *seated*"; that is, "presiding without any change and eternally" (*idest absque omni mutabilitate et aeternitate praesidentem*).

Those who find the association between "being seated" and "presiding without any change" a stretch – especially those with children who, when seated, are rarely "still" or "unchanging" – should keep in mind that Thomas is not "commenting," he is simply associating. The word "seated" merely has to *suggest* the idea Thomas wants his reader to remember, not *denote* it. The *modus significandi* here is not *direct*, as in the way words regularly denote things; it is *indirect*. The word used as a mnemonic device must call to mind an *image* lively enough and interesting enough to allow it to be associated with a specific chain of ideas to be recalled. The word "seated" may have many other associations in other contexts; the question is whether when the listener hears the phrase "I saw the Lord *seated*," he or she can associate it with "unchanging eternity," and from this recall that one way of coming to know God is "by way of His eternity" (*ex eius aeternitate*).

Once the association has brought about the recollection, there is still the question, "What does it mean to know God *by way of his eternity*?" According to Thomas, we reason from the mutability of things in the created world to the eternity and immutability of their Creator. In the prologue to the Commentary on John, the argument goes like this:

> [Others] saw that whatever was in things was changeable, and that the more noble something is in the grades of being, so much the less it has of mutability. For example, the lower bodies are mutable both as to their substance and to place, while the heavenly bodies, which are more noble, are immutable in substance and change only with respect to

---

[8] Prologue to John, 3.

place. We can clearly conclude from this that the first principle of all things, which is supreme and more noble, is changeless and eternal.[9]

This argument is in certain respects *similar*, but not *identical to*, the first of the "five ways" in Thomas's *Summa*. There, Thomas argued famously for the existence of an "unmoved mover." But in the *Summa*, Thomas is careful to define "motion" as "the reduction of something from potency to act." And since nothing can be reduced from potency to act except by something else already in act, and since there cannot be an infinite series of movers, else "there would be no first mover, and, consequently, no other mover, seeing that subsequent movers move only inasmuch as they are put in motion by the first mover," therefore there must be a "first mover," not moved by another (*primum movens, quod a nullo movetur*); there must be an ultimate act which contains no potency to become anything else. The "first mover" must be the changelesos source of all change in the created realm.[10]

As I stated earlier, this argument in the *Summa*, although similar in certain respects, is not identical to what we find here in the prologue to John's Gospel. In an essay at the back of his translation of *The Commentary of the Gospel of St. John by St. Thomas Aquinas*, Fr. James Weisheipl, points out:

> This argument, it would seem, was never used elsewhere by St. Thomas. It suggests, however, Plato's famous argument that from contemplating "that which is Becoming always and never is Existent" one is led to "that which is Existent always and has no Becoming" (*Timaeus* 27d6–28c4) – an idea Thomas could have read in the translation and commentary by Calcidius (early 4th century). A similar argument from the mutability of all creatures to the absolute immutability of God is also suggested in Malachi (3:6): "I, the Lord, do not change"; while the whole universe constantly changes.[11]

"Some contemporary commentators, however," says Fr. Weisheipl, "have reduced this argument to the 'first' [way] given in the *Summa*," citing as a reference J. A. Baisnée's essay "St. Thomas Aquinas' Proofs of the Existence of God Presented in Their Chronological

---

[9] Ibid., 4.
[10] ST I, q. 3, art. 3.
[11] Weisheipl, *Commentary*, 455. The passage Fr. Weisheipl has in mind from Calcidius's translation of Plato's *Timaeus* reads as follows in the Latin: "Est igitur, ut mihi quidem uidetur, in primis diuidendum, quid sit quod semper est, carens generatione, quid item quod gignitur nec est semper, alterum intellectu perceptibile ductu et inuestigatione rationis, semper idem, porro alterum opinione cum inrationabili sensu opinabile proptereaque incertum, nascens et occidens neque umquam in existendi condicione constanti et rata perseuerans. Omne autem quod gignitur ex causa aliqua necessario gignitur; nihil enim fit, cuius ortum non legitima causa et ratio praecedat." A contemporary English translation of the original Greek text by W. R. M. Lamb (Loeb, 1925) reads as follows (the relevant Greek text is given in parentheses): "Now first of all we must, in my judgment, make the following distinction. What is that which is Existent always and has no Becoming? And what is that which is Becoming always and never is Existent? (γένεσιν δὲ οὐκ ἔχον, καὶ τί τὸ γιγνόμενον μὲν ἀεί, ὂν δὲ οὐδέποτε). Now the one of these is apprehensible by thought with the aid of reasoning, since it is ever uniformly existent, whereas the other is an object of opinion with the aid of unreasoning sensation, since it becomes and perishes and is never really existent. Again, everything which becomes must of necessity become owing to some Cause; for without a cause it is impossible for anything to attain becoming (πᾶν δὲ αὖ τὸ γιγνόμενον ὑπ' αἰτίου τινὸς ἐξ ἀνάγκης γίγνεσθαι· παντὶ γὰρ ἀδύνατον χωρὶς αἰτίου γένεσιν σχεῖν).

Order."[12] "But this view does not seem tenable," argues Weisheipl, "since the argument in the Prologue is cast entirely in terms of temporality and eternity, which is not at all the same as Aristotle's argument from motion (the first way in the *Summa*)."[13] Fr. Weisheipl's point here is well worth considering, especially for those (and there are many) who specialize in parsing out the exact character of each of the "five ways."

Although Fr. Weisheipl claims that "the argument in the Prologue is cast entirely in terms of temporality and eternity, which is not at all the same as Aristotle's argument from motion," Thomas at several points in the Prologue refers to the "mutability" of created things and the "immutability" of God alone. There is a gradation: earthly things are "mutable" regarding both substance and time, whereas heavenly things are "immutable" regarding substance but not regarding time; the First Principle must be "immutable" regarding both. But it is the "immutability" (*immutabilia*) of God as contrasted with the "mutability" (*immutabilia*) of everything else which is at issue, and the conclusion Thomas derives from his argument is: "We can clearly conclude from this that the first principle of all things, which is supreme and more noble, is changeless (*immobile*) and eternal."[14] So it is not as though "motion" in the sense of "mutability" or "change" *isn't* involved here in the Prologue. Moreover, if what Thomas has in mind here is an argument from Plato, as Fr. Weisheipl proposes, then it is odd that Thomas explicitly associates the *next* argument – the one from "dignity" – with "the Platonists," but not this one.

Thomas certainly isn't presenting *Aristotle's* version of the argument for a Prime Mover here in the Prologue; that much is certain. But that's not the question. The question is whether the argument here has at least *some* similarity to the argument *Thomas* makes in the first of the "five ways" in the *Summa*, an argument that, though based on Aristotle's argument for a Prime Mover, is not identical to it. It is, I have suggested, "similar in certain respects." Yet, Fr. Weisheipl is right to point to the differences between the argument here and the first of the "five ways," warning us against too facilely equating the two. Whether the differences between the two are relatively unimportant or whether they are crucial to the very nature of the argument is for the reader to decide. Thomas did not merely "cut-and-paste" his argument from the *Summa* into the prologue, although we know he had the memory to have done so had he wished.

Knowing God from His Dignity

Along with knowing God through his "authority of governing" and through his eternity, one can also come to know God, says Thomas, through his *dignity* or *nobility*, which is suggested by the word "high" in the phrase "I saw the Lord seated on a throne, *high* and lofty." As before, this way of coming to know God corresponds, loosely but identifiably, with one of Thomas's famous "five ways" in the *Summa* – in this case, the fourth way, from participation. Here is how the argument runs in the prologue to Thomas's *Commentary on John*:

---

[12] In *Philosophical Studies in Honor of the Very Reverend Ignatius Smith, O.P.*, ed. J. K. Ryan (Westminster: Newman, 1952), 29–64.
[13] See Weisheipl, *Commentary*, 455.
[14] Prologue to John, 4.

Still others came to a knowledge of God from the dignity of God; and these were the Platonists. They noted that everything which is something by participation is reduced to what is the same thing by essence, as to the first and highest. Thus, all things which are fiery by participation are reduced to fire, which is such by its essence. And so since all things which exist participate in existence (*esse*) and are beings by participation, there must necessarily be at the summit of all things something which is existence (*esse*) by its essence, i.e., whose essence is its existence. And this is God, who is the most sufficient, the most eminent, and the most perfect cause of the whole of existence, from whom all things that are, participate in existence (*esse*).[15]

And here is the famous "fourth way" from the *Summa theologiae*:

> The fourth way is taken from the gradation to be found in things. Among beings there are some more and some less good, true, noble and the like. But "more" and "less" are predicated of different things, according as they resemble in their different ways something which is the maximum, as a thing is said to be hotter according as it more nearly resembles that which is hottest; so that there is something which is truest, something best, something noblest and, consequently, something which is uttermost being; for those things that are greatest in truth are greatest in being, as it is written in Metaph. ii. Now the maximum in any genus is the cause of all in that genus; as fire, which is the maximum heat, is the cause of all hot things. Therefore there must also be something which is to all beings the cause of their being, goodness, and every other perfection; and this we call God.[16]

There are differences between the two, about which I will have more to say shortly. But they share the notion all things which exist merely *participate* in existence (*esse*), as that which is hot *participates* in hotness when it is not itself the source of its own hotness. Since neither we nor anything else we can point to in the created world is the source of its own existence, there must be a *source* of the very *being* (the *esse*) of things: a source of being that does not *participate* in being, but that is the source of its own being.

Thomas's argument here is *similar* to the fourth of the "five ways" in the *Summa*, but it shares even more in common with several arguments he uses in his disputed question *On the Power of God*, q. 3, art. 5, arguments he traces back to Plato, Aristotle, and Avicenna respectively. The question posed in that article is "whether there is anything not created by God?" In his reply, Thomas seeks to show that "reason proves," just as faith holds, "that all things are created by God." Thomas sets out to show that "the philosophers Plato, Aristotle and their disciples attained to the study of universal being, and hence they alone posited a universal cause of things from which all others came into being," which, claims Thomas, "is in agreement with the Catholic Faith." In the three sections that follow, Thomas outlines three arguments for the existence of God: the first of them he attributes to Plato; the second, to Aristotle; and the third, to Avicenna.

The first argument, which he attributes in a guarded way to Plato (*ista videtur ratio Platonis*), involves the notion that "if in a number of things we find something that is common to all, we must conclude that this something was the effect of some one cause,"

---

[15] Ibid., 5.
[16] ST I, q. 3, art. 3.

and since "being (*esse*) is found to be common to all things, which are by themselves distinct from one another, it follows of necessity that they must come into being (*esse*) not by themselves, but by the action of some cause" (*de necessitate eis non ex se ipsis, sed ab aliqua una causa esse attribuatur*).[17]

The second argument, which he attributes to Aristotle (cf. *Metaph.* 2.1), is that

> whenever something is found to be in several things by participation in various degrees, it must be derived by those in which it exists imperfectly from that one in which it exists most perfectly: because where there are positive degrees of a thing so that we ascribe it to this one more and to that one less, this is in reference to one thing to which they approach, one nearer than another: for if each one were of itself competent to have it, there would be no reason why one should have it more than another. Thus fire, which is the extreme of heat, is the cause of heat in all things hot. Now there is one being most perfect and most true: which follows from the fact that there is a mover altogether immovable (*aliquid movens omnino immobile*) and absolutely perfect ... Consequently all other less perfect beings must needs derive being therefrom (*omnia alia minus perfecta ab ipso esse recipiant*).

"This," says Thomas, "is the argument of the Philosopher."[18]

The third argument is based on the principle that whatsoever is through another is to be reduced, as to its cause, to that which is of itself (*illud quod est per alterum, reducitur sicut in causam ad illud quod est per se*).

> Wherefore if there were a *per se* heat, it would be the cause of all hot things, that have heat by way of participation. Now there is a being that is its own being (*quod est ipsum suum esse*): and this follows from the fact that there must needs be a being (*aliquod primum ens*) that is pure act and wherein there is no composition. Hence from that one being all other beings that are not their own being, but have being by participation (*quaecumque non sunt suum esse, sed habent esse per modum participationis*), must needs proceed.

"This is the argument of Avicenna," says Thomas.[19]

I suggest that Thomas's argument "from dignity" in his Prologue to John's Gospel is an amalgamation of all of these. That is to say, Thomas synthesized and condensed for his purposes here in the Prologue to John's Gospel (written probably during the second Parisian period, 1268–1272) the three arguments he had distinguished while writing *On the Power of God* several years earlier (probably sometime during 1265–1266). This little paragraph possesses a rich philosophical background and owes a debt to many sources, all of which have come together here in Thomas's retelling.

I have gone through this rather complicated business of tracing out the sources behind these two paragraphs in Thomas's prologue to suggest that there is some serious intellectual "heavy lifting" going on behind these relatively simple comments in the prologue, all of it

---

[17] *On the Power of God*, q. 3, art. 5. English and Latin quoted from the online version at dhspriory.org/thomas/QDdePotentia.htm, an electronic version of Thomas Aquinas, *On the Power of God*, trans. English Dominican Fathers (Westminster, MD: The Newman Press, 1952, reprint of 1932).

[18] *On the Power of God*, q. 3, art. 5.

[19] Ibid.

tethered to the two words "seated" and "high." Thomas has simplified for his students and condensed into a single paragraph a large and immensely complicated quantity of material.

The reader should not be misled by the ostensible simplicity of these texts. The simplicity here is the result of a superb mind. If the reader scratched the surface and probed more deeply at any point, he or she would unravel a world of interesting detail. The abilities to synthesize and simplify were two of Thomas's great gifts as a master teacher and preacher.[20]

Knowing God from the Incomprehensibility of Truth

The last of the ways of arriving at the knowledge of God, says Thomas, is "from the incomprehensibility of truth," which Thomas associates with the word "lofty" (*elevatum*), because it suggests something "above all the knowledge of the created intellect." Were the reader to ask, "Couldn't Thomas have used the word 'high' (*excelsum*) for this purpose as well?" the answer is yes. Had the verse been written in some other way, or the points he wanted to make somewhat different, then he might have done so. But in this context, *this* was the association he needed to make. And so Thomas adds:

> Still others arrived at a knowledge of God from the incomprehensibility of truth. All the truth which our intellect is able to grasp is finite, since according to Augustine, "everything that is known is bounded by the comprehension of the one knowing"; and if it is bounded, it is determined and particularized. Therefore, the first and supreme Truth, which surpasses every intellect, must necessarily be incomprehensible and infinite; and this is God. Hence the Psalm (8:2) says, "Your greatness is above the heavens," i.e., above every created intellect, angelic and human. The Apostle says this in the words, "He dwells in unapproachable light" (1 Tim 6:16). This incomprehensibility of Truth is shown to us in the word, *lofty*, that is, above all the knowledge of the created intellect.[21]

As there must be an ultimate source of all *being*, so too there must be an ultimate source of all *truth*. J. A. Baisnée reports in his study of Thomas's proofs of the existence of God that he could find no other appearance of this argument anywhere in Thomas's corpus, although it can be traced back ultimately to a comment St. Augustine makes in *The City of God* 12.18 while attempting to refute those who held that God could not comprehend all numbers.[22]

---

[20] My oblique comments about Thomas's departures from strict application of the *sermo modernus* style are not meant to detract from or obscure this truth.
[21] Prologue to John, 6.
[22] J. A. Baisnée, "Thomas Aquinas' Proofs," 64. The original text of Augustine's *City of God* 12.18 reads as follows (in the *Nicene and Post-Nicene Fathers* translation by Marcus Dods): "And thus, if everything which is comprehended is defined or made finite by the comprehension of him who knows it, then all infinity is in some ineffable way made finite to God, for it is comprehensible by His knowledge. Wherefore, if the infinity of numbers cannot be infinite to the knowledge of God, by which it is comprehended, what are we poor creatures that we should presume to fix limits to His knowledge, and say that unless the same temporal thing be repeated by the same periodic revolutions, God cannot either foreknow His creatures that He may make them, or know them when He has made them? God, whose knowledge is simply manifold, and uniform in its variety,

There is admittedly something paradoxical involved in talking about arriving at a *knowledge* of God from the "incomprehensibility of truth" (*ex incomprehensibilitate veritatis*). We usually expect to arrive at "cognition" from comprehension, not from incomprehension. Hence we might describe this manner of arriving at a "contemplation" of God as akin to the famous "way of negation" described in Pseudo-Dionysius's treatise on the *Divine Names*, whereby the human mind proceeds by way of negating the affirmations made in the "way of affirmation." We say "God is *not* good," "God is *not* just," by which we mean that God is not "good" and not "just" in the way *I* comprehend goodness or justice. God's goodness and justice are infinitely beyond what my limited, finite mind can grasp.

Mnemonic Devices and Dilation: Two Benefits of the *Sermo Modernus* Style

Two further observations are in order at this point about the benefits of using the *sermo modernus* style in a prologue such as this. The first has to do with using the style as a mnemonic device to help the listener remember the content of the prologue. Even dedicated Thomists sometimes have trouble keeping track of the "five ways" in the *Summa*. It is easier to keep track of the four proofs Thomas covers in this prologue if one recalls the four parts of the opening *thema* verse: "I saw the Lord" (authority of governance), "seated" (eternity), on a throne "high" (dignity) and "lofty" (above all the knowledge of the created intellect). Remembering the arguments in this way is like remembering the five lines on the treble clef in music by recalling the phrase "Every good boy does fine" (E, G, B, D, F), or remembering the five phases of cell division in mitosis – interphase, prophase, metaphase, anaphase, and telophase – by recalling the phrase: "I propose men are toads."

The second observation has to do with Thomas's remarkable claim that all the complicated and philosophically sophisticated ways of coming to know God described earlier – from the governance of the world, from the necessity of having an eternal first cause, from the participation of all that exists in some first cause whose essence it is to exist, and from the infinite character of the First Truth – were passed on to us in John's Gospel.[23] One has to wonder what he is talking about.

A complete answer to this question would require an analysis of the entire commentary. Yet, consider: What does one learn even from the opening verses of the Gospel? "In the beginning was the Word, and the Word was with God, and the Word was God. He was in the beginning with God." Don't these words seem to suggest the Lord's *eternity*? Then we read: "All things were made through him, and without him was not anything made that was made." Don't these words suggest His *dignity* as the cause of the whole of existence? "He came to his own." According to Thomas, because the whole world here is being called "his own" (*quia totus mundus est suus proprius*), we can understand these words to refer to God's *authority of governing*. Finally, "No one has ever seen God." Don't these words suggest the

> comprehends all incomprehensibles with so incomprehensible a comprehension, that though He willed always to make His later works novel and unlike what went before them, He could not produce them without order and foresight, nor conceive them suddenly, but by His eternal foreknowledge."

[23] Prologue to John, 6.

incomprehensibility of God, who is the First Truth, and who can be made known only by the "true light, which gives light to everyone"? Such are the lessons Thomas thinks we can (and ought to) learn from John's Gospel.

By demonstrating how to "unpack" (by means of *dilatatio*) the *thema* verse of his prologue, Thomas was also teaching his students by example how to "unpack" the Scriptures in order to grasp the intellectual richness hidden beneath the surface simplicity of the text. He was showing them that the Scriptures can be a fruitful source for philosophical reflection and a wise guide – if one learns to read them properly. If any of his students had arrived in his class with the mistaken notion that the Scriptures were "simple" books for "simple people" – that they were "milk" for children, while the books of the philosophers were "meat" for adults – Thomas's remarkable display of erudition in this prologue should have disabused them of this notion.

In four short paragraphs, Thomas was able to sum up layer upon layer of complicated philosophical argumentation, ordering the layers appropriately to direct the mind to the argument's proper end – namely the One who is both Subsisting Being Itself and Truth. And he was able to associate all of this material with four simple words in one biblical verse: "Lord," "seated," "high" and "lofty." *That* is the power of the *sermo modernus* style, and *that* is what can be accomplished when a master teacher makes use of it.

John's Contemplation Was "Full" and "Perfect"

Having gotten everything he wished out of the phrase "I saw the Lord seated on a throne high and lofty" (likely more than most of us would have thought possible) – Thomas then moves on to the next phrase in his *thema* verse, "and the whole house was full of his majesty." John's contemplation was *full*, says Thomas, in the sense that it extended to all things. Contemplation is *full* "when someone is able to consider all the effects of a cause." John, having been raised up to the contemplation of the divine Word when he says "In the beginning was the Word, and the Word was with God," immediately adds that the power of the Word extends to all things, saying: "Through him all things came into being." That John's contemplation was *full* is suggested by the phrase "and the whole house was *full* of his majesty." Thomas writes:

> And so after the prophet [in the text from Isaiah 6:1] had said, "I saw the Lord seated," he added something about his power, "and the whole house was full of his majesty," that is, the whole fullness of things and of the universe is from the majesty and power of God, through whom all things were made, and by whose light all the men coming into this world are enlightened.[24]

With this, we have arrived finally at the last of the three phrases that makes up the opening *thema* verse from Isaiah 6:1: "and the things that were under him completely filled (*replebant*) the temple." As the reader may recall, Thomas associates the Latin word *replebant* (to fill up) with completion or perfection, saying the contemplation of John was

[24] Ibid., 7.

"perfect" (*perfecta*), since he was "led and raised to the height of the thing contemplated (*perducitur et elevatur ad altitudinem rei contemplatae*).[25]

But John's contemplation is "perfect" not only because *he* was raised up to enjoy the height of the thing contemplated, but also because he sees that by which we are *all* raised up – that by which humankind is sanctified and made perfect: that is, by the grace which Christ "pours into us" (*nobis infundit*), especially by means of the *sacraments*.

Note the Eucharistic imagery made possible by Thomas's association of words. As a cup becomes "filled" as wine is poured into it from above, so too we are "filled" with the grace of Christ. "The things ... under him," says Thomas – that is, the sacraments of his humanity – "filled the temple," i.e., the faithful, "who are the holy temple of God (1 Corinthians 3:17) insofar as "through the sacraments of his humanity all the faithful of Christ receive from the fullness of his grace." As John tells us, "Of his fullness (*plenitudine*) we have all received – indeed, grace upon grace" (John 1:16).

Thomas may have had in mind here the iconography that pictures blood and water flowing from Christ's pierced side on the Cross down into a communion chalice. As the chalice is *filled* with wine, so we are *filled* with the grace of Christ. As the priest then takes the cup and raises it up to heaven to become Christ's own body and blood, so too we are "raised up" and made into Christ's Body.

God's love is a "perfect" love precisely because it *perfects* that which God loves. When we accept it, that love does not leave us in our sin. It is a "complete" love that does not fall short, even when we do, because it *completes* us by sanctifying us and bringing us to the fullness of our end. On Thomas's account, it was precisely because John saw how God's love perfects us that we can say John's contemplation was "perfect."

With this, Thomas has finished "unpacking" the three kinds of "contemplation" he set out to associate with the three phrases in the verse from Isaiah 6:1: John's contemplation was "high" ("I saw the Lord seated on a throne high and lofty"); "full" ("and the whole earth was full of his majesty"); and "perfect" ("and the things that were under him completely filled the temple"). And yet, Thomas is not finished with his Prologue, nor is he finished with ideas he wants to associate with his opening *thema* verse. For what Thomas will do now is to associate each of the three kinds of contemplation he distinguished above with a threefold division of the sciences, although not the division made famous by Thomas's account in his *Commentary on Boethius's De Trinitate*.

The Threefold Division of the Sciences

The three characteristics of contemplation "belong to the different sciences in different ways," writes Thomas.

> The perfection (*perfectionem*) of contemplation is found in Moral Science, which is concerned with the ultimate end. The fullness (*plenitudinem*) of contemplation is possessed by Natural Science, which considers things as proceeding from God. Among the physical [natural] sciences, the height (*altitudinem*) of contemplation is found in Metaphysics. But

[25] Ibid., 8.

the Gospel of John contains all together what the above sciences have in a divided way, and so it is most perfect (*perfectissimum*).²⁶

Although the division between mathematics, natural philosophy (or physics), and metaphysics is more well known from Thomas's *Commentary on Boethius's De Trinitate*, q. 5, the division he mentions here between *ethics*, natural science, and metaphysics dates to the early Greek Stoics was well known among Thomas and his contemporaries.²⁷ Thomas's challenge was to figure out how to associate all three sciences with *contemplation* and then how to associate each of these with the basic terms from his *thema* verse: "high" (*alta*), "full" (*ampla*), and "perfect" (*perfecta*).

Consider first how Thomas deals with *contemplation*. Those with knowledge of the ancient Greek tradition might have assumed that Thomas would associate contemplation only with the highest of the three sciences: metaphysics and the contemplation of being *qua* being. But on Thomas's account, a contemplative perfection can be achieved in each of the three sciences. And in each case, John's Gospel provides that perfect vision.

What happens in natural science? The answer John's Gospel provides (because his contemplation has the "fullness" (*plenitudenm*) sufficient to see that the power of the Word extends to all things) is that the study of nature is, ultimately, a reflection on how God works in and through creation. What is the principle that metaphysics seeks? John's Gospel shows (because his contemplation has the "height" (*altitudinem*) sufficient to arrive at the knowledge of God) that the goal of metaphysics ultimately must be Subsisting Being

---

²⁶ Ibid., 9.
²⁷ Zeno (c. 330 BC–c. 230 BC), founder of the Stoic school in Athens, insisted that the didactic order that ought to be observed when teaching students was: logic, ethics, and physics. Cleanthes (c. 330 BC–c. 230 BC), the second head of the Stoic school in Athens, expanded the list, pairing dialectic and rhetoric, adding ethics and politics, and finally physics and theology. Chrysippus (c. 279 BC–c. 206 BC), third head of the school, sometimes called "The Second Father of Stoicism," was even more concerned that theology serve as both the source and the summit of the Stoic course of studies. Plutarch quotes him and describes his view in *De Stoicorum repugnantiis*, 9 (1035a) thus: "Chrysippus is of the opinion, that young students should first learn logic, secondly, ethics, and after these, physics, and likewise in this to meddle last of all with the disputes concerning the Gods. Now these things having been often said by him, it will suffice to set down what is found in his *Fourth Book of Lives*, being thus word for word: 'First then, it seems to me, according as it has been rightly said by the ancients, that there are three kinds of philosophical speculations, logical, ethical, and physical, and that of these, the logical ought to be placed first, the ethical second, and the physical third, and that of the physical, the discourse concerning the Gods ought to be the last." See *Plutarch's Morals, translated from the Greek by several hands, corrected and revised by William W. Goodwin, with an introduction by Ralph Waldo Emerson*, 5 vols. (Boston: Little, Brown, and Co., 1878), vol. 4. It is not entirely clear from what source Thomas knew this particular division. He repeats this threefold hierarchy – similarly without attribution – in his *Commentary on Boethius' De trinitate*, q. 5, art. 1, obj. 10: "The ancients are said to have observed the following order in learning the sciences: first logic, then mathematics, then natural science, after that moral science, and finally ... divine science." Thomas has taken the liberty here of leaving aside the first two – logic and mathematics and of eliding "divine science" and "metaphysics." This identification of the two was not uncommon among Aristotelians: in some places, Thomas will distinguish them carefully; in other circumstances, he will not. Thomas's basic point, however, is that one will find most perfectly in the Gospel of John instruction in those things traditionally considered "highest" in the order of pedagogy set forth by the philosophers – natural philosophy, moral philosophy, and metaphysics.

Itself (*Ipsum Esse Subsistens*), the Source of All Being. What is the ultimate goal of moral science? John's Gospel reveals (because his contemplation has the "perfection" [*perfectionem*] made possible by God's grace) that our minds and hearts must be perfected by grace and reception of the sacraments in order to be raised up to achieve our ultimate end: a loving vision of and union with God.

It may help to compare Thomas's point here with Bonaventure's discussion in *On the Reduction of the Arts to Theology*.[28] Bonaventure's "reduction" does not involve "lessening" the arts and sciences so theology can become preeminent; nor does it involve a violation of the methods proper to each discipline. Rather, it involves showing how each discipline, while retaining its proper rules and autonomy, has its proper end and goal revealed to it by theology. So too here, in his prologue, Thomas suggests that "what the above sciences have in a divided way," the Gospel of John "contains all together," and so is "most perfect." By this he does not mean that we can learn natural science, metaphysics, and ethics simply from reading the Gospel. Rather, what we learn from the Gospel is the proper place of each science within the didactic order that leads us to the highest truth and our ultimate end. Understanding how the disciplines can be conducive to this end is what keeps them from becoming nothing more than disconnected bits of knowledge and prevents them from being used in ways destructive of human flourishing – say, for example, simply to achieve greater power, wealth, or status.

One presupposition of modernity is that each specialized discipline can be judged only according to its own inherent ends or goals – that is, according to the ends or goals of the technē. The excellence of the artist, the lawyer, or the businessperson is judged only by whether he or she exhibited excellence in the skill or craft, not whether he or she employed the craft for "good" or "bad" ends.

Yet, given the damage that can result from the actions and practices of unscrupulous politicians, businessmen, lawyers, and doctors, societies sometimes decide that the practitioners of the sciences of politics, business, law, or medicine should get some training in "ethics." But what that often does is simply introduce extraneously a different set of goals and principles into the usual considerations of the discipline. If business is about maximization of profit, then the "other-regarding" concerns of ethics will often enough seem not only extraneous to the discipline but, in important ways, contrary to it. If politics is the science of gaining and wielding power, then the ethical concerns of those who think others should be treated as rational agents of equal dignity with oneself will likely seem naive: pleasant enough for the Sunday homiletics of priests or the musings of academic moralists, but not anything for serious politicians.

In the medieval view represented by Bonaventure's *reductio* and Thomas's Prologue to John's Gospel, each discipline is understood as pointing the way toward the Creator. The old medieval adage that "grace doesn't violate nature, but perfects it" applies here. On this understanding, recognizing that all the arts and sciences find their ultimate source and summit in God will not violate the order of the sciences, but perfect them. Unlike modern "reductions" of the human person to, say, pure biology or pure physical causality, which often end up negating a great deal of human experience (the value of love and aesthetic

---

[28] Cf. Bonaventure, *On the Reduction of Arts to Theology*, trans. Zachary Hayes, The Works of St. Bonaventure, vol. 1 (Franciscan Institute: St. Bonaventure University, 1996). I will have more to say about Bonaventure's notion of *reductio* in Chapter 11 on Bonaventure's *resumptio* address.

experience to name two), the "reduction" that Bonaventure and Aquinas have in mind doesn't *negate* the importance of the other disciplines; rather, it reveals how divinely important they are precisely by showing how they can be understood as a foretaste of our eternal beatitude and an important means to that end.

Settling in Advance on the Terms for Interpreting the Gospel: John's Prologue – and Thomas's

In his prologue to John's Gospel, Thomas set out to achieve many of the same goals traditionally associated with John's own prologue. So, for example, reading the Gospel of John in light of its prologue means reading the Gospel not merely as the story of a wise and interesting first-century AD prophet, but as the story of the incarnate Word who was "in the beginning with God" and who was responsible for the *being* of all that exists. This, I submit, is the perspective Thomas adopts and expresses in his prologue.

Consider, for example, Thomas's claim that what the sciences of natural philosophy, ethics, and metaphysics have "in a divided way," the Gospel of John "contains all together," and so is "most perfect." What makes a comment like this one possible is precisely the Christocentric perspective from which Thomas approaches all the books of sacred Scripture. There is a natural and understandable tendency to think of "Christocentric" readings of Scripture solely as the basis for viewing events and characters of the Old Testament as "types" or "figures" of Christ. This is one "Christocentric" reading. But there is another.

Here in the New Testament, John's narration of Jesus's life can be called "Christocentric" precisely because John is writing to show that Jesus is "the Christ." What on John's view it means to be "the Christ," however, is not only that Jesus is the long-awaited Messiah but also that He is the Word incarnate, uniting in Himself both divinity and humanity. And through his humanity, He has united Himself physically to all of creation.

Pope John Paul II states the truth of the matter nicely in his encyclical *Dominum et vivificantem* when he says: "The Incarnation of God the Son signifies the taking up into unity with God not only of human nature, but in this human nature, in a sense, of everything that is 'flesh': the whole of humanity, the entire visible and material world. The Incarnation, then, also has a cosmic significance, a cosmic dimension."[29] We find the same notion again in Cardinal Avery Dulles's *The Catholicity of the Church* where he writes: "The Word of God, in assuming a full human existence, entered into a kind of union with the [entire] cosmos."[30]

Thomas's prologue shares this same fundamental premise and applies it to the debates of his own time, thereby clarifying for his readers why the Gospel can, and indeed must, be taken as seriously by philosophers as by the uneducated. The paradoxical claim is that the supreme cause of the Being of everything that exists, the ultimate end of the contemplative searches of Plato and Aristotle, is "revealed in" the words and deeds of this man from

---

[29] *Dominum et vivificantem*, 50.
[30] Avery Dulles, S.J., *The Catholicity of the Church* (Oxford: Clarendon Press, 1985), 54.

Galilee. He is not merely a "religious" figure, not merely a "mythic" figure, not merely "the god of the philosophers"; He is the Word made flesh, God incarnate.

This is the Person to whom Thomas wishes to introduce his readers. This is the Person he believes his students must meet when they read John's Gospel. Without this perspective, what are his readers left with? Without the reality of "the Word made flesh," the Gospel is a very different story. It is the picture of a man pretending to be god-like – a great prophet, perhaps, but one who might rightly be charged with some serious delusions of grandeur – or of a god merely *pretending* to be a man: pretending to be hungry, pretending to be thirsty, pretending to cry at the death of a friend, pretending to suffer and die on a cross, when in reality, as God, he can really do none of these things. Without the belief in "the Word made flesh," the deeds recounted in the Gospel of John would not be outward manifestations of the inner mystery" of Christ's being; they would be nothing more than an outward show, an illusion – something to entertain the crowds perhaps, but not the fit object of study for scholars, whether modern or medieval. If Jesus is not the Word who was in the beginning and without whom nothing was made; if He is not the Way, the Truth, and the Life, then neither Thomas nor anyone else could say that in Him, natural philosophy, ethics, and metaphysics find their source and crown.

The Four Aristotelian Causes

It is clear from this Prologue and the others we have examined that the expectations Thomas's audience brought to reading a prologue differed greatly from ours. We moderns have learned to expect the writers of prologues to provide biographical, historical, intellectual, and/or literary background. Such were not the expectations of Thomas's audience.

Thomas's audience understood how the processes of *divisio* and *dilatio* worked in the medieval *sermo modernus*, and they were not averse to reading a prologue written in this style. His audience was used to hearing such sermons – it was an efficient way of delivering a good amount of information in an ordered, memorable format – so, unlike the members of a modern audience, they clearly did not find this an odd way of introducing a text.

Another commonplace among Thomas's audience of students at the University of Paris would have been knowledge of the four "causes" of Aristotelian natural philosophy: formal, final, material, and efficient. As we saw in the previous chapter, Thomas organized the prologue to his commentary on the Psalms entirely around these four causes.[31] But in other prologues, he sometimes identifies only one or two of the four – as, for example, in his prologue to the commentary on Ephesians, in which he mentions only the efficient cause (Paul) or in his prologues to the commentaries on Colossians and First Corinthians, where he mentions only the *materia* (the subject matter) of the text. Here in his prologue to John's Gospel, Thomas touches upon all four Aristotelian causes, but only briefly.

Thomas begins this final section of the prologue with the "matter" (the *materia*) of the Gospel of John, concerning which he professes that "while the other Evangelists treat

---

[31] For a good treatment, see Alistair J. Minnis, *Medieval Theory of Authorship: Scholastic Literary Attitudes in the Later Middle Ages* (London: Scholar Press, 1984), 75f.

principally of the mysteries of the humanity of Christ, John, especially and above all, makes known the divinity of Christ in his Gospel" – although, adds Thomas, "he does not ignore the mysteries of his humanity either."[32]

From this statement, we can understand why modern translators translate *materia* in this context as "subject matter." Yet, it's important to note that *materia* in Latin has connotations missing in the English term "subject matter." The *materia* – the "subject matter" of the text – must still be given *form*. The author (the efficient cause) must still give his topic a particular shape, size, and order with the words he uses and how he makes use of them.

So too here, after identifying the "subject matter" of the text (the underlying *materia*), Thomas's next step is to identify the *form* of the text – that is, "the order of the Gospel" (*ordo istius Evangelii*). To get his point across, Thomas returns again to his opening *thema* verse from Isaiah 6:1. The order of the Gospel is suggested by this verse, says Thomas, because in his Gospel,

> John first shows us *the Lord seated on a high and lofty throne*, when he says, "In the beginning was the Word" (Jn 1:1). He shows secondly how *the house was full of his majesty*, when he says, "through him all things came into being" (Jn 1:3). Thirdly, John shows how the *things that were under him filled the temple*, when he says, "the Word was made flesh" (Jn 1:14).

Thomas's comment here on the "order of the Gospel" corresponds nicely with his discussion above, where he said that John's contemplation was "high" because it arrived at the height of the Godhead Itself ("the Word," who was "in the beginning"; John 1:1); it was "full" because John possessed a vision of how God's power filled the entire world ("through Him all things came into being"; John 1:3); and John's contemplation was "perfect" because it was of that which "sanctified" and "perfected" man (by "the Word" being "made flesh"; John 1:14).

The "order" Thomas identifies here in this prologue also corresponds with what we find later in the body of his commentary. If we turn to the *Commentary* chapter 1, lecture 1, section 23 (hereafter *In Ioh.* 1.1.23), we find Thomas repeating his claim that about the subject matter of John's Gospel, saying John "intends principally to show (*intendit principaliter ostendere*) the divinity of the Incarnate Word." What, then, is the *order* by which John shows this? Thomas proposes that the Gospel can be divided into two main parts: in the first, John "declares (*insinuat*) the divinity of Christ"; in the second, he "shows it (*manifestat eam*) by the things Christ did in the flesh." Where does the "first part" end and the second part begin?

Thomas's answer is that the second part of the Gospel begins at John 2:1, with the words, "And on the third day there was a wedding at Cana." And if we glance ahead at Thomas's comments on John 2:1, we find: "Above, the Evangelist showed the dignity of the incarnate Word... Now he begins to relate the effects and actions by which the divinity of the incarnate Word was made known to the world" (*In Ioh.* 2:1:335). First, says Thomas, John "tells the things Christ did while living in the world that show his divinity." Second, "he tells how Christ showed his divinity while dying; and this from chapter twelve on." And if we glance ahead again, this time to Thomas's comments at the beginning of his first lecture on chapter 12 (*In Ioh.* 12.1.1589), we find this: "So far the Evangelist has been showing the

---

[32] Prologue to John, 10.

power of Christ's divinity by what he did and taught during his public life. At this point, he begins to show the power of his divinity as manifested in his passion and death."

Putting Thomas's statements in the prologue together with what we find in the *Commentary*, we can describe the "order" of the Gospel this way. It begins with a vision of the divinity of Christ, the Word of God made flesh. It quickly moves on to show how the Lord's power filled the entire world: how Christ manifested His divinity, showing forth His divine power over the natural world (for example, by the miracle at Cana, walking on water, healing of the sick, the multiplication of the loaves and fishes, raising Lazarus from the dead), and by the authority of His teaching. Finally, the Gospel concludes by showing how Christ manifested His divinity in and through His death and resurrection – the sacrifice by mean of which our salvation is won and we are "perfected."

Thomas understands that the early Christians did not proclaim Jesus "the Christ" (the long-awaited Messiah) *in spite of* His death on the cross, but precisely *because* of His death on the cross and resurrection from the dead. It is by His sacrificial death and resurrection that the Word incarnate reveals itself most fully as the perfect Love that conquers both sin and death. This is "perfect" love both in the sense that it is complete (nothing else need be added) and in the sense that it is perfecting. Christ's sacrificial death and resurrection from the dead reveals the truth about God's will to reconcile man to Himself and is also *the means by which* that reconciliation is brought about.

Once the *form* of the Gospel has been clarified, the *end* or *purpose* becomes clear. "The end of this Gospel" (*finis huius Evangelii*), says Thomas, "is that the faithful become the temple of God, and become filled (*repleantur*) with the majesty of God," which Thomas's students can more easily remember from the opening *thema* verse which ends: "and the things that were under him filled (*replebant*) the temple." By "seeing the Lord" as John saw the Lord, with a contemplation that was "high," "full," and "perfect," we are made into "the temple of God" built of living stones and are "filled up to completion with" or "perfected by" (*repleantur*) the majesty of God.[33]

The Author and His Authority

Thus far we have considered Thomas's use of three of the four Aristotelian causes: the material, formal, and final causes of the Gospel. What remains to be examined is the efficient cause, the book's author. And so in section 11, the final section of the Prologue, Thomas says that his final task is to describe "the condition of the author" (*conditio auctoris*) – and this in four ways: his name, his virtue, his symbol, and his privilege. It would have been convenient for us had Thomas managed to map each topic onto his opening *thema* verse. But there are limits to what even an imaginative genius such as Thomas can do with one set of words.[34] And so, instead of trying to wring more blood out

---

[33] On this, cf. also 1 Corinthians 3:16 ("Do you not know that you are God's temple and that God's Spirit dwells in you?") and 1 Peter 2:5 ("And you are living stones that God is building into his spiritual temple.").

[34] By the same token, in the prologue to his *Commentary on the Gospel of St. Luke*, Bonaventure was able to craft three different associations for the words in his *thema* verse. See my discussion of this text in Chapter 13.

of this particular turnip (Isaiah 6:1), Thomas finds another set of mnemonic images to help his readers remember the details he wants to communicate about the author of the Gospel, St. John the Evangelist.

Unfortunately, understanding this final section on the "condition of the author" depends on some elements not plainly in view to the contemporary reader. In medieval editions of the text, Thomas's Prologue would have been printed beneath Jerome's prologue, with a short commentary by Thomas on Jerome's prologue. This was a common practice of the day, as we have seen above – a clear testament to Jerome's abiding influence as an authority on the Scriptures. If we forget that Jerome's prologue would have preceded Thomas's, this may leave the reader wondering what Thomas is referring to in his own Prologue.[35]

Regarding the name of the author, for example, Thomas tells us in his Prologue that "John" is interpreted as "in whom is grace," since "the secrets of the divinity cannot be seen except by those who have the grace of God within themselves." Where, we might wonder, did Thomas get the idea that "John" means "in whom is grace"? One source is the famous Alcuin of York, whom Thomas cites in the *Catena Aurea* in a comment on John 1:6–8. Another is the Venerable Bede, whom Thomas quotes giving this same interpretation of the name "John" in the *Catena Aurea* at Luke 1:11–14. But more immediately, we can also trace this interpretation of John's name to Jerome's prologue. Thomas writes: "For he [that is, Jerome] describes the author from his name, saying, '"This is John," in whom there is grace – 1 Cor 15:10: 'By the grace of God I am what I am.'" And yet, this reference to 1 Corinthians 15:10 as evidence that the name "John" means "in whom there is grace" is odd, since the First Letter to the Corinthians was written by Paul, not John. So the person who utters the phrase "By the grace of God, I am what I am" is not John; it is Paul. Thomas was clearly aware of this fact. So what was he doing here?

We know from the references in the *Catena Aurea* that Thomas had read in other sources – namely, Bede and Alcuin – that the name "John" means "in whom there is grace."[36] Thomas's refers to 1 Corinthians 15:10 not to prove his point about the origin of John's name; he does so, rather, to support his point that it was through God's gracious gifts and not through his own merit or unaided efforts that John possessed whatever wisdom he possessed about God. And this is the key point Thomas wished to make about "the condition of the author" (*conditio auctoris*).

---

[35] Jerome's prologue is missing, for example, from the 1980 Magi Press volume containing Weisheipl's translation. One can find an English translation of Jerome's prologue with Thomas's commentary on it done by Fr. Joseph Kenny, O.P. at http://dhspriory.org/thomas/SSJohn.htm#02. These have been placed *below* the Prologue we are discussing in this chapter, however, an arrangement that makes less sense when it becomes clear that one needs information from Jerome's prologue to understand Thomas's. Jerome's prologue has also been restored in the 2010 Catholic University of America edition. See Aquinas, *Commentary on the Gospel of John, Books 1–5*, trans. J. Weisheipl and F. Larcher (Washington, DC: The Catholic University of America Press, 2010).

[36] Thomas and his medieval sources may indeed be correct about this derivation of the name "John," as it turns out. Some modern commentators suggest that the name "John" (in English), which is derived from the Latin *Ioannes*, which is in turn a form of the Greek *Iōánnēs* ('Ιωάννης), might be a form of the Hebrew name Yôḥanan (יוֹחָנָן), which means "Graced by Yahweh." It would not have been at all uncommon in the ancient Jewish world, of course, to have had a symbolic name of this sort.

Those who understand the resonances that accompany the medieval use of the word *auctor* and its related close cousin *auctoritas* (from which we get our English word "authority") know that, in this context, describing the "condition of the author" has nothing to do with describing the psychological or biographical background of the author; it has to do, rather, with the source of the author's authority to speak on the topic at hand. On Thomas's account, John's name reveals the nature of his relationship to God, and his relationship to God establishes the authority of his writings: because by the grace of God, he is what he is. And this is the essential point.

The same consideration about the source of John's authority underlies Thomas's next comment, about John's *virtue*. "As concerns his virtue," says Thomas, "John *saw the Lord seated*, because he was a virgin; for it is fitting that such persons see the Lord: 'Blessed are the pure in heart' [for they shall see God] (Matthew 5:8)." Thomas inherited this notion that John was a virgin from the exegetical tradition he inherited; more on that in a moment. But the point here isn't merely a biological or psychological one about John's background, as it likely would be if this were a modern prologue. Thomas's point is about John's worthiness to write about God. Although it was Isaiah who originally uttered the phrase: "I saw the Lord seated on a throne high and lofty, and the whole house was full of his majesty . . .," Thomas considers it appropriate to attribute it to John because John was the one who most truly "saw the Lord." John "saw the Lord" *in person*. He saw how "the whole house was *full* of his majesty" by hearing his words and seeing his deeds. And at the foot of the cross, he saw how God's majesty "filled completely the temple," perfecting all those "living stones" that God was "building up into his spiritual temple" (cf. 1 Peter 2:5). But as the Beatitude tells us, it is the "pure of heart" who "see God."

The detail about John being a virgin is something else Thomas got from Jerome's prologue. "This is John, the Evangelist, one of the disciples of the Lord, a virgin chosen by God," says Jerome in the first sentence of that prologue. This is an odd reference, however, not so much because we think that John had a wife – there is no mention of one in the Gospels – but because elsewhere Jerome suggests that the wedding at Cana where Jesus performed his first miracle was *John's* wedding. But according to Jerome, Jesus called him away from the wedding "when he wanted to marry," so he remained a virgin. It is unclear where Jerome got this odd little story.

Wherever Jerome got the story, he passed it on to later exegetes in his prologue to John's Gospel, and Thomas repeated it to make a theological point. When he quotes St. Jerome describing John the Evangelist as "a virgin chosen by God," Thomas's audience would know that the original "virgin chosen by God" was Mary. Indeed, later in his prologue, Jerome writes: "The Lord, hanging on the cross, commended His Mother to him [John], so that a virgin might look after the Virgin." As the Holy Spirit came upon Mary so she could give birth to the Word-made-flesh, so too the Holy Spirit came upon John so he could "enflesh" the Word in written words. The point about the wedding at Cana makes more sense in this context. As Mary was to be married to Joseph, but was married more fully to God, so too John, although he intended to marry at Cana, was instead married more fully to Christ.

Regarding the "condition of the author," Thomas has covered John's name and his virtue – both of which, as we have seen, bear upon his authority. The final two items on the list – John's "symbol," and his "privilege" – will similarly bear upon that authority.

It was a commonplace by Thomas's day to represent the four Evangelists with the four "living creatures" that surround God's throne in Revelation 4:7 and that show up earlier in a vision in Ezekiel 1:1-14: a man, an ox (or bull), a lion, and an eagle. John's symbol is the eagle, says Thomas, because he in a special way among the Evangelists expresses the divinity of Christ.

> The other three Evangelists, concerned with those things which Christ did in his flesh, are symbolized by animals which walk on the earth, namely, by a man, a bull calf, and a lion. But John flies like an eagle above the cloud of human weakness and looks upon the light of unchanging truth with the most lofty and firm eyes of the heart. And gazing on the very deity of our Lord Jesus Christ, by which he is equal to the Father, he has striven in this Gospel to confide this above all, to the extent that he believed was sufficient for all.[37]

This brings us finally to John's "privilege" (*privilegium*). John is repeatedly called "the disciple whom Jesus loved" (cf. John 21:20). "And because secrets are revealed to friends ... Jesus confided his secrets in a special way to that disciple who was specially loved." In Job 36:32, we read that "from the savage," that is, from the proud, "he hides his light," that is, He (Christ) hides the truth of his divinity. But John, as we know from what Thomas has said earlier in the prologue, was "pure of heart." He was like the bride awaiting the bridegroom – like the Virgin Mary awaiting the Spirit.

There is no "seeing" here without loving. Consider again the images Thomas has been using to describe John: a virgin like the Virgin Mary, a bride "pure of heart" prepared for the divine bridegroom, the disciple whom Jesus loved. The implication is that, what the proud and arrogant scribes and Pharisees of Jesus's day could not see, John, the simple youth, who was loved by Jesus and loved him in return, did. Superior human wisdom did not reveal the fullness of Christ's divinity to John; it was his receptivity to Christ's love. John did not demand first that his intellect be satisfied as a precondition to his love of Christ; he loved first, and only then was his vision made high, full, and perfect.

The fundamental question Thomas's prologue poses for his audience is, how will they approach reading the Gospel? Will they approach God's Word with the same level of receptivity as that which animated the author? Will they be "pure of heart" like John, the one whom Jesus loved and who loved Jesus in return, and who as a consequence was granted a special contemplative vision of His divinity? Or will they be savage, proud, and arrogant – like those from whom God hides His light (cf. Job 36:32)?

Thomas sets before his students a clear choice between two distinctly different approaches toward pursuing the highest Wisdom. In the first approach, they sit in judgment of Wisdom; in the other, they allow it to sit in judgment of them. On this view, the choice readers make about *how* to read the biblical text will make all the difference whether they can read it well and understand what it has to teach or remain blind to its deeper wisdom.

Communicating such background information was not alien to the intentions behind Thomas's prologue, but it was not his primary aim, and we will misjudge him if we think he was attempting to do what a modern prologue does, but doing it badly. Thomas's prologue was an exhortation to enter into a practice and a tradition of

---

[37] Prologue to John, 11.

philosophical. And it was precisely in this way that Thomas's prologue served the purposes of the classic philosophical protreptic.

Thomas's Prologue as a Protreptic to *Sacra Doctrina*

Recall the goals of the classical protreptic described in the Introduction to this volume, one of which was to compare the claims to knowledge of the other schools or disciplines with those of the true philosopher in such a way as to show that "every other form of knowledge is found lacking."[38]

In this light, consider what Thomas achieves in the prologue to his *Commentary on the Gospel of John*. First, he subtly challenges the claims to knowledge of the other philosophical schools, showing that John expresses, in a more complete and unified way, the truth they sought imperfectly. Was this not the point of going through all the different approaches to the existence of God – to show that John's Gospel encompasses them all "more perfectly"? So too, was this not the reason Thomas introduced the classic Stoic division of the disciplines – natural philosophy, ethics, and metaphysics – namely, to show how "the Gospel of John contains all together what the aforementioned sciences have in a divided way, and so it is most perfect"? John's contemplation was "high" because it rose to a knowledge of God; it was "full" because he saw how God's power extended throughout all of creation; and it was "perfect" because it is this knowledge that brings us to our ultimate goal and thus "perfects" us. Arguing in this way, Thomas's Prologue sets out to achieve what all protretpics aim to do: namely, to show the superiority of a certain knowledge as the highest form of wisdom – one with the capability of bringing the prospective apprentice, if he or she will enter into the discipline required, to his or her ultimate goal: a life of blessedness and true human flourishing.

Most students for whom Thomas was writing this prologue would already have gone through a strict regimen of philosophical study with the members of the Arts faculty at the University of Paris.[39] Thomas's biographer Fr. James Weisheipl describes the setting:

> The study of the liberal arts and the acquisition of philosophy were functions of the Arts Faculty in the university or *studium*. Approximately eight years were devoted by medieval students to acquiring these tools – roughly equivalent to our four years of high school and four years of college. After the full course had been completed in "the humanities," the young man, generally in his mid-twenties, would begin his study of the Sacred Text, having already heard many sermons in Church and having received much instruction at home.[40]

---

[38] See Mark D. Jordan, "Ancient Philosophic Protreptic and the Problem of Persuasive Genres," *Rhetorica: A Journal of the History of Rhetoric*, 4, no. 4 (Autumn 1986): 321.

[39] Both Weisheipl and Torrell date the *Lectura super Ioannem* to Thomas's second regency at the University of Paris, probably during the years 1270–1272. See Torrell, *St. Thomas*, 339, and James Weisheipl, "An Introduction to the Commentary of the Gospel of St. John of St. Thomas Aquinas" in the Magi Press edition of his translation of Thomas's *Commentary on John*, 9. There is little doubt, therefore, about the audience for these lectures.

[40] James Weisheipl, "An Introduction," 6.

Contemporary professors of theology would immediately recognize the problem and sympathize with the challenge Thomas faces here. Before him would have been students who had spent eight years reading sophisticated and intellectually rigorous philosophical texts. Many would have undoubtedly been proud of these accomplishments and their newly acquired abilities in the arts – educational achievements which would not have been available to most of the rest of the population. And yet likely the only introduction these same students would have had to the Bible might have been the simple, pious interpretations they had heard from their parents or a local parish priest, whose education both theological and otherwise may well have been spotty at best. When such students compared the simple, pious stories they knew from the unschooled preaching they had been accustomed to hearing over the years, they could have been forgiven for thinking the Bible might lack intellectual firepower.

The classic example of a gifted young scholar so proud of his intellectual prowess it led him to imagine he could dispose of the business of Scriptural commentary with little trouble was young Abelard who, in his *Historia calamitatum*, tells the story of how, when studying at the school of Anselm of Laôn, he insisted that, because of his skill in dialectic, in just one night he could write a better commentary on the Scriptures than the master who was lecturing. He writes:

> I, who had as yet studied only the sciences, replied that following such lectures seemed to me most useful in so far as the salvation of the soul was concerned, but that it appeared quite extraordinary to me that educated persons should not be able to understand the sacred books simply by studying them themselves, together with the glosses thereon, and without the aid of any teacher. Most of those who were present mocked at me, and asked whether I myself could do as I had said, or whether I would dare to undertake it. I answered that if they wished, I was ready to try it. Forthwith they cried out and jeered all the more. 'Well and good,' said they; 'we agree to the test. Pick out and give us an exposition of some doubtful passage in the Scriptures, so that we can put this boast of yours to the proof.' And they all chose that most obscure prophecy of Ezekiel. I accepted the challenge, and invited them to attend a lecture on the very next day.[41]

So too at the University of Paris during the 1260s and early 1270s – precisely the time when Thomas would have been writing this prologue – "a radical form of Aristotelianism was being developed by certain Masters in the Faculty of Arts at Paris (by now really a faculty of philosophy)," writes John Wippel. Two of the major figures in this new movement were Siger of Brabant and Boethius of Dacia. "Often if not accurately referred to as Latin Averroism," writes Wippel, "this movement was marked by the total dedication of its leaders to the pursuit of the purely philosophical life. In some cases, some of these scholars were not concerned if their philosophical conclusions were at odds with orthodox Christian belief."[42] It is not difficult to imagine, then, that some of the students trained by

---

[41] Peter Abelard, *Historia calmitatum*, trans. Henry Adams Bellows (St. Paul: T. A. Boyd, 1922), chapter 3.
[42] John F. Wippel, *The Metaphysical Thought of Thomas Aquinas: From Finite Being to Uncreated Being* (Washington, DC: Catholic University of America Press, 2000), xv. The classic study of Siger and his colleagues in the Arts faculty at Paris and their disputes with the likes of Thomas and

these members of the Arts faculty might have arrived in Thomas's lectures on the Bible harboring the assumption that the Bible was for simple folk, whereas the high-level education they had received in the Arts faculty studying the philosophical texts of Aristotle and his commentators was for the more "enlightened."

Thomas's challenge would have been to convince such students that the books of the Bible were worthy of their highest, deepest, and fullest intellectual explorations and labors; that in the pages of this supposedly "simple" book, they would find the fullness of that for which their previous studies in philosophy had only begun to prepare them; and that John's Gospel offered them access to the highest wisdom and the surest path to beatitude.

Note, however, that in formulating his protreptic on behalf of the wisdom of sacred Scripture, Thomas did not seek to negate the potential pedagogical value of all other approaches to wisdom or all other forms of philosophy. It was simply that whatever truth was found elsewhere would be found "most perfectly" or "most completely" (*perfectissima*) in sacred Scripture. Thomas's vision was broad enough to include the Arts and grant them their proper autonomy within a course of education that had *sacra doctrina* at its summit serving an architectonic role regarding the rest.

Thus it is noteworthy that Thomas included explicitly arguments from natural philosophy and metaphysics in a *biblical* prologue. Such an inclusion would not have occurred to someone like Bernard of Clairvaux. The cultural context within which Thomas's commentaries were written had clearly changed since the time when Bernard wrote his. The change must be accounted for not only in terms of a different institutional setting (university rather than monastery), but also in terms of a new set of intellectual challenges from the reception of Aristotle's texts. These challenges prompted Thomas to judge there was a need to preface his commentary on the Gospel of John with a new kind of protreptic appeal to his students that Bernard, as a monk preaching to monks in a monastery, would have felt no need to make.

Thomas's protreptic was crafted for the purposes of exhorting students who might have been tempted to make the mistake St. Augustine had made centuries before of failing to see the true profundity and deeper significance of the biblical texts.[43] Thomas's students would not have been the first, nor would they be the last, to imagine that the Scriptures were "of a

---

Bonaventure is Fernand Van Steenberghen, *Thomas Aquinas and Radical Aristotelianism* (Washington, DC: Catholic University of America Press, 1980). "Radical Aristotelianism" was the name Van Steenberghen gave to those who favored the wisdom of Aristotle over "sacred doctrine" (*sacra doctrina*).

[43] See Augustine, *Confessions* 3.5.9, who admits that, when he was younger, he preferred the eloquence of Cicero to what he considered to be the childishness of the Christian Scriptures: "I resolved, therefore, to direct my mind to the Holy Scriptures, that I might see what they were. And behold, I saw something not comprehended by the proud, not disclosed to children, something lowly in the hearing, but sublime in the doing, and veiled in mysteries. Yet I was not of the number of those who could enter into it or bend my neck to follow its steps. For then it was quite different from what I now feel. When I then turned toward the Scriptures, they appeared to me to be quite unworthy to be compared with the dignity of Tully [Cicero]. For my inflated pride was repelled by their style, nor could the sharpness of my wit penetrate their inner meaning. Truly they were of a sort to aid the growth of little ones, but I scorned to be a little one and, swollen with pride, I looked upon myself as fully grown." *The Confessions*, trans. J.G. Pilkington, in *A Select Library of the Nicene and Post-Nicene Fathers of the Christian Church*, vol. 1, ed. Philip Schaff (Edinburgh: T & T Clark, 1886).

sort to aid the growth of little ones," but not something for educated readers – and, "swollen with pride, looking upon themselves as fully grown," decided that the Scriptures had nothing serious to offer them.[44]

Thomas's protreptic was an attempt to convince such students that the Scriptures contained wisdom worthy of their most vigorous intellectual efforts and that both philosophy and the other arts could serve as handmaids to *sacra doctrina*. On this view, the goal the pagan philosophers sought after imperfectly is supplied by John's Gospel in a more perfect fashion. On this view, if one has read and understood John's Gospel, one can then return to the writings of the philosophers and comprehend them more fully because those writings will then be understood finally within their proper context and directed toward their proper end. The philosophical pedagogy of the philosophers (natural philosophy, ethics, metaphysics) is now recast as propadeutic to sacred doctrine, and sacred doctrine becomes the guiding discipline, architectonic with regard to the others.

The philosophical ascent to First Truth now culminates in sacred doctrine, which is taken to be the privileged revelation of the Mind of God Himself. The perfecting Wisdom is the Word made flesh. The key to understanding Nature, Being, and Ethics is found in the Creator's revelation of Himself in Christ. Who better to reveal the true nature of things, our proper place within the created world, and how humans may best flourish than the Creator Himself?

Ancient and medieval scholars schooled in the arts of rhetoric and philosophical protreptic believed that a necessary prerequisite for growth in *wisdom* when reading a text is a preparation of both the mind *and* the heart. An effective protreptic summons the reader into a deeper engagement with the words of the speaker or the text, calling upon the reader to read as though what is being said might be crucially important for his or her life.

These considerations bring us back to the question I posed earlier in the Introduction to this volume: What makes a good prologue to a text? What would prepare a reader for the task of reading and reading *well*? The contemporary practice is to provide the reader with a detailed scholarly apparatus that provides the historical, biographical, and literary background to the text. Thomas's approach, by contrast, was protreptic in nature: it sought to help the reader to understand the value of the text by first understanding what its author valued and by exhorting the reader to enter into the spirit of the text. Good teachers know that students will not remember a text unless they take it *seriously*, and they will not take it seriously unless they consider it *important*. In this area, as in so many others, Thomas was not merely a good, but a great teacher.

---

[44] Ibid.

9

Aquinas, *Sermo Modernus*–Style Preaching, and Biblical Commentary

WE HAVE been examining the development of Aquinas's proficiency using the *sermo modernus* style to compose prologues during his early years as a bachelor of the Bible and bachelor of the *Sentences*. Our examination has shown that Thomas composed prologues using the *sermo modernus* style when he was a bachelor of the Bible in Paris and may have done so even earlier, when he was studying with Albert in Cologne.[1] All inception *principia* had to be given in this style, as did all university sermons. Furthermore, University regulations stipulated that masters had to use the same *thema* verse in their evening *collatio* at vespers that they had used for their morning sermon.[2]

Early in his career after his inception as a master, while still at Paris (1256–1259), Thomas continued writing prologues using the *sermo modernus* style, for example, for the *Contra Impugnantes* and his *Commentary on Boethius's* De Trinitate. After he left Paris in 1259, he did not always compose prologues the way he had been taught to do at Paris, although he continued to employ the *sermo modernus* style when he was preaching. When he returned to Paris for his second regency (1268–1272), he once again composed the prologue to his *Commentary on the Gospel of John* using the formal *sermo modernus* style, and he continued to write prologues this way when he left in 1272 to teach at the University of Naples, where he composed his commentaries on the Pauline epistles and on the Psalms.

What seems clear from this evidence is that composing prologues in the formal, *sermo modernus* style was accepted, either explicitly or implicitly, as a *formal* requirement at the University of Paris. It was understood that this was simply the way first-day lectures and prologues were supposed to be done when one was lecturing at a university. It was not

---

[1] That is, if he gave any of the cursory lectures on Jeremiah, Lamentations, or Isaiah in Cologne, which remains unclear.

[2] For more on this, see R. Smith, *Reading the Sermons of Thomas Aquinas: A Beginner's Guide* (Steubenville, OH: Emmaus, 2016). In the back of that volume is an appendix with an analytical outline of each of Thomas's extant sermons. A quick glance will reveal the sermons in which Thomas broke off in the middle of dilating the words of the opening *thema* verse and then resumed his dilation of the remaining words at the evening's *collatio*.

difficult for Thomas to fall back into the practice when he returned to Paris for his second regency, because he had continued to preach this way during the intervening years. And preaching, as I will show in the text that follows, was always a central concern. Learning to preach well was the goal of the pedagogical program, whether one was engaged in disputation or biblical commentary.

By the time Thomas was a student at Paris, all bachelors of theology were required to preach several times a year, and being able to preach capably in the *sermo modernus* style was considered an essential skill for any prospective master. It is not clear how instruction in preaching was done, but proficiency in preaching was required.

The master's inception ceremonies required a public display of all three duties of the master. He had to determine four disputed questions over the course of two days. And on the second day, he also had to deliver a sermon in praise of sacred Scripture – the so-called *principium in aula* in the hall of the bishop. Then, on a subsequent day before the commencement of classes, he had to preach yet another sermon in praise of Scripture, at the end of which he had to set out a *divisio textus* of all the books of the Bible – a skill, as we will see, that was essential to the thirteenth-century practice of *lectio*. This last inception address – sometimes called a "second *principium*" – was a model of the addresses masters were required to give on the first day of the term, which was also called a *principium*. If the master's lectures on that book of the Bible were published, that first-day address, the *principium*, became the prologue of the volume. Every such *principia* – whether it was the master's inception address or the first lecture of the term or the written prologue to a biblical commentary – was delivered as a sermon using the *sermo modernus* style.

These requirements, especially those requiring bachelors to preach regularly and write prologues using the *sermo modernus* style, display the importance placed on preaching by those responsible for the educational program in theology at the University of Paris. *Lectio* and *disputatio* were meant to bear fruit in *praedicatio*. Or, to use Peter Cantor's famous analogy between the three duties of the master and three parts of a house, *lectio* was to be foundation, *disputatio* the walls, and *praedicatio* the roof supported by the other two.[3]

Lectio, *Disputatio*, and *Praedicatio*: The Dynamic Interrelationship among Three Culturally Established Practices

One way of characterizing the three duties of the medieval master would be to describe them as social "practices" in the sense defined by Alasdair MacIntyre. A "practice," writes MacIntyre, is

> any coherent and complex form of socially established cooperative human activity through which goods internal to that form of activity are realized in the course of trying to achieve those standards of excellence which are appropriate to, and partially definitive of, that form of activity, with the result that human powers to achieve excellence, and human conceptions of the ends and goods involved, are systematically extended.[4]

---

[3] *Verbum Abbreviatum*, 1.
[4] Alasdair MacIntyre, *After Virtue*, 2nd ed. (Notre Dame, IN: University of Notre Dame Press, 1985), 187.

Our concern in this volume has been primarily with the practice of *praedicatio*, and what we have seen is that the skills necessary to achieving excellence in this practice were systematically developed in the medieval university and took a well-defined form.

Practices of this sort, especially when they play a key role in social, cultural, or intellectual movements, will also often be instrumental in forming certain habits of mind, shaping intellectual expectations and setting standards of excellence. In 4th century BC Athens, excellence in the art of public disputation was a valued skill and something expected of those who wanted to succeed in public life. In modern-day America, one can rise to the highest offices with only the most rudimentary skill in oration. Great public speeches, like those that allowed men such as Cicero to gain preeminence in the 1st century BC, are not only no longer required, but they are also practically nonexistent. At other points in history, such as eighteenth- and nineteenth-century England, writing superb prose was accepted as a highly valued practice within the culture.

The habits of mind needed by those whose goal is to be able to declaim orally, whether one is Homer relating the stories of the epics or Pericles giving his great funeral oration for the fallen Athenian soldiers, differ from those needed by those whose goal is to produce a superb piece of written prose, whether it is Thomas Paine writing *Common Sense* or Jane Austen writing *Pride and Prejudice*. A culture in which it is important to deliver long orations from memory necessitates among its members who wish to succeed in that culture the development of a very particular set of intellectual skills and habits of mind. The members of a culture in which memorizing long speeches is important will develop a different set of skills and habits of mind from those in a culture in which success working out long algebraic equations is valued. To put this simply, the forms of our culture form us.

As we have seen, preaching had become a culturally valued practice by the mid-thirteenth century. The form thirteenth-century preaching employed – the *sermo modernus* style – was not the same form preaching took in St. Augustine's day, when excellence in preaching was judged against the standards of Ciceronian rhetoric. Nor was it the same as when John Henry Newman was preaching at Oxford.[5]

In Chapter 1 I argued that preaching was a central concern at the University of Paris, especially for justifying the University's program of theological education against critics of this new academic institution. In this chapter, my principal goal is to show, using examples from Thomas's biblical commentaries, how significant and influential the arts of preaching were to the thirteenth-century practice of *lectio*. A secondary goal is to show how engaging repeatedly throughout his career, from student to master, in the practice of *sermo modernus* style preaching helped Aquinas develop certain skills and habits of mind he was able to employ profitably when engaged in his other duties as a master.

I do not wish to claim too much for preaching. It is primarily because the importance and relevance of the preaching arts in thirteenth-century scholastic life have too often gone

---

[5] For a variety of interesting historical reasons, Newman's sermons too were inspired by and judged according to the standards of Ciceronian rhetoric, and yet Newman's sermons also were "thematic" rather than line-by-line exegeses of biblical texts. Newman's sermons began, as did medieval sermons, with a single Bible verse. They differ from medieval sermons, however, in that Newman did not divide and dilate that verse to develop his points. In Newman's sermons, the Bible verse merely suggested a topic; it did not serve to structure the entire sermon, as was the practice in thirteenth-century preaching.

unnoticed by modern scholars that I have focused on those arts – and in particular, how those arts were developed and expressed in the composition of *sermo modernus*-style prologues. The point is not to emphasize preaching to the detriment of the other duties of the master. Our ultimate goal should be to envision *lectio*, *disputatio*, and *praedicatio* as three interrelated practices that mutually influenced one another.

Masters such as Aquinas preached regularly – something we too often forget. But this preacher, renowned for his ability to appeal to the common people, was the same man who produced long, sophisticated commentaries on the Gospel of John and epistles of St. Paul, dictated the *Disputed Questions on Truth*, and composed the monumental *Summa theologiae*. Because of the relative popularity in modern times of Thomas's *Summa theologiae* and his commentaries on Aristotle, there has been a tendency to think of him primarily as a "systematic theologian." But "systematic theologian" is a contemporary category derived from contemporary disciplinary divisions. Thomas was a "master of the sacred page" and a member of the Order of *Preachers*. We need to understand him in those terms or we risk misunderstanding him.

Although a full account of the interrelationships among the three arts of *lectio*, *disputatio*, and *praedicatio* is beyond the scope of the present work, in what follows I will sketch out several important connections, the first and most important of which is the connection between preaching and biblical commentary. As we will see, masters of the sacred page lecturing on the Bible in the thirteenth century repeatedly used the methods of *dilatatio* that were used in *sermo modernus*-style preaching. And when these masters lectured, they frequently included material they knew would be useful for preaching in *sermo modernus*-style.

Dilatatio in Thomas's *Commentary on the Gospel of John*

When we examine Thomas's biblical commentaries with an eye to the contemporaneous arts of *sermo modernus*-style preaching, we repeatedly find long passages that could be fit into one of the eight basic methods of "dilating" a word or words from a *thema* verse in a sermon. All eight are listed in Chapter 2, but for ease of reference, I will list them again here.[6]

1. Proposing a discussion based on a noun as it occurs in definitions or classifications
2. Making subdivisions of the original *divisio*
3. Reasoning or argumentation
4. "Chaining" together concordant authorities
5. Setting up a series running from the positive through the comparative and arriving finally at the superlative in the manner of "good, better, best"
6. Devising metaphors through the properties of a thing

---

[6] My source for this list, as I mentioned in Chapter 2, is Robert of Basevorn's *Forma praedicandi*; it can be found in the Latin original in Thomas Charland, *Artes Praedicandi*, 233–323, and in English translation in Robert of Basevorn, *The Form of Preaching*, trans. Leopold Krul, O.S.B., in *Three Medieval Rhetorical Arts*, ed. James J. Murphy (Berkeley: University of California Press, 1971).

7. Expounding the *thema* in diverse ways according to the literal, allegorical, tropological, and/or anagogical senses
8. Consideration of causes and their effects[7]

Thomas employs all of these methods in his sermons. And, more to the point, he employs them repeatedly in his *biblical commentaries* as well. Indeed, in his biblical commentaries, he switches back and forth from one method of *dilatatio* to another just as he does in his sermons. Throughout Thomas's biblical commentaries, we repeatedly find passages that employ one or more of these methods of dilation that could have been lifted directly out of one of his sermons. We begin in this section with several examples from Thomas's *Commentary on the Gospel of John*. Then, in the next section, we turn to some examples from his *Commentary on the Epistles of Paul*.

Consider, for example, "proposing a discussion based on a noun as it occurs in definitions or classifications" – Method 1 listed earlier. Much of the content in Thomas's commentaries is generated by distinguishing the different uses of words. In his *lectio* on the phrase "In the beginning was the Word" (*in principium erat Verbum*) from his *Commentary on the Gospel of John*, Thomas notes that "according to Origen, the word *principium* has many meanings." Thus when the Gospel says, *In the beginning was the Word*, this can be taken in three ways. In one way, *principium* is understood as the person of the Son. In a second way, it can be understood as the person of the Father, "who is the principle not only of creatures, but of every divine process." And in a third way, *principium* can be taken as the beginning of duration, so that the phrase *In the beginning was the Word* means that the Word is eternal and before all things.[8]

How about allegory and the other spiritual senses? By the late thirteenth century, they had become a method of dilation among the others. So, for example, near the beginning of Chapter 2, where Thomas discusses the marriage at Cana, he spends several pages laying out an elaborate allegory about marriage signifying the union of Christ with His Church, complete with "chained" biblical authorities as would be found in a sermon.

> In the mystical sense, marriage signifies the union of Christ with his Church, because as the Apostle says: "This is a great mystery: I am speaking of Christ and his Church" (Eph 5:32). And this marriage was begun in the womb of the Virgin, when God the Father united a human nature to his Son in a unity of person. So, the chamber of this union was the womb of the Virgin: "He established a chamber for the sun" (Ps 18:6). Of this marriage it is said: "The kingdom of heaven is like a king who married his son" (Mt 22:2), that is, when God the Father joined a human nature to his Word in the womb of the Virgin. It was made public when the Church was joined to him by faith: "I will bind you to myself in faith" (Hos 2:20). We read of this marriage: "Blessed are they who are called to the marriage supper of

---

[7] For more on each method of *dilatatio* and examples of each from Thomas's sermons, see R. Smith, *Reading the Sermons*, esp. chapter 4.
[8] *Super Ioan.*, 1.1.23. Latin: Roberto Busa, *Thomae Aquinatis Opera Omnia : Ut Sunt in Indice Thomistico, Additis 61 Scriptis Ex Aliis Medii Aevi Auctoribus* (Stuttgart-Bad Cannstatt: Frommann-Holzboog, 1980), available at corpusthomisticum.org. English translation: James A. Weisheipl and Fabian R. Larcher, trans., *Commentary on the Gospel of John* (Albany: Magi Books, 1980). E-text, https://aquinas.cc/la/en/~Ioan.

the Lamb" (Rev 19:9). It will be consummated when the bride, i.e., the Church, is led into the resting place of the groom, i.e., into the glory of heaven.⁹

Two paragraphs later, Thomas proposes a discussion based on a noun as it occurs in a definition. The *place* for the marriage is appropriate, says Thomas, because "Cana" means "zeal" and "Galilee" means "passage."

> So this marriage was celebrated in the zeal of a passage, to suggest that those persons are most worthy of union with Christ who, burning with the zeal of a conscientious devotion, pass over from the state of guilt to the grace of the Church. "Pass over to me, all who desire me" (Sirach 24:26). And they pass from death to life, i.e., from the state of mortality and misery to the state of immortality and glory: "I make all things new." (Revelation 21:5)¹⁰

Throughout his commentary, Thomas repeatedly makes use of all eight of the methods of *dilatatio*, often in quick succession. Commenting on the scene in John 8:6–7, where Jesus was challenged to pass sentence on a woman caught in adultery and bent down to write with his finger in the dust, Thomas says:

> We can see from this that there are three things to be considered in giving sentences. First, there should be kindness in condescending to those to be punished; and so he says, Jesus was bending down: "There is judgment without mercy to him who does not have mercy" (James 2:13); "If a man is overtaken in any fault, you who are spiritual instruct him in a spirit of mildness" (Galatians 6:1). Secondly, there should be discretion in determining the judgment and so he says that Jesus wrote with his finger, which because of its flexibility signifies discretion: "The fingers of a man's hand appeared, writing" (Daniel 5:5). Thirdly, there should be certitude about the sentence given; and so he says, Jesus wrote.¹¹

In this one passage we find a threefold *divisio*, a series of concordant authorities, and an exegesis based on the properties attributed to (a) the act of bending down, (b) the motion of a finger, and (c) the product of writing, and as we have seen, *divisio*, inserting concordant biblical authorities, and dilating based on the properties of a thing are all methods characteristic of *sermo modernus* style preaching.

In our own day, it is not uncommon for scholars lacking any acquaintance with thirteenth-century preaching to claim that the methods of thirteenth century biblical commentary had their origins in the thirteenth century *quaestiones disputatae*. While there is plenty of material in the biblical commentaries that has been "chewed over" by disputation (to use Peter Cantor's lively image), the *methods* are derived from *sermo modernus*-style preaching.¹²

---

⁹ *Super Ioan.*, 2.1.338.
¹⁰ Ibid.
¹¹ Ibid., 8.1.1131.
¹² Peter Cantor, *Verbum abbreviatum*, 6: "Reading is, as it were, the foundation and basement for what follows, for through it the rest is achieved. Disputation is the wall in the building of study for nothing is fully understood or faithfully preached, if it is not first *chewed by the tooth of disputation*. Preaching, which is supported by the former, is the roof, sheltering the faithful from the heat and

To illustrate, let's compare a distinction Thomas makes in his *Summa theologiae* with his use of that distinction in his commentary on the marriage at Cana story in the Gospel of John. In ST I-II, q. 98, a. 6, for example, Thomas argues that it was fitting that "the Old Law should be given between the law of nature and the law of grace." During "the time of the natural law," man was left to His own devices without the teaching of the law or the help of God's grace, and so he "fell headlong into idolatry and the most shameful vices."[13] Because of the Fall, man needs the written law to teach him what he could and should know by his reason alone, but often doesn't, having been blinded by sin. But as Thomas says in the prologue to ST I-II, q. 90, after God has "taught us by means of His law," it remains for him to "assist us by means of His grace. This threefold distinction helps set up Thomas's discussion in the long sections on the Old Law (qq. 98–105) and the New Law (qq. 106–108) that follow.

So how is this material presented in a biblical commentary? In Thomas's comments on the marriage at Cana, he says that the fact that the marriage is said to have taken place "on the third day" is significant because "the first day is the time of the law of nature; the second day is the time of the written law; but the third day is the time of grace, when the incarnate Lord celebrated the marriage: 'He will revive us after two days: on the third day he will raise us up'" (Hosea 6:3).[14]

The association in this passage of "the third day" of the wedding with the resurrection of Christ would been common enough, but the reference to the three ages of man – the time of the natural law, the time of the written law, and the time of grace – although not unknown, would have been more obscure.[15] And yet, the point would not have been merely to repeat an obscure distinction, but to show his students how one passage could be dilated in several ways. The "three days" of the wedding can refer to three literal days; it can refer to the resurrection of Christ "on the third day"; and/or it can refer to the three ages of man which culminate in the time of grace. It would not be difficult, having made these textual connections, to connect the marriage at Cana with Christ's marriage to His people or His marriage with each person's soul, especially in the gift of grace whereby He spreads charity abroad in our hearts (cf. Rom 5:5) so that acting in accord with God's law is no longer burdensome for us (cf. 1 John 4:1).[16]

The Preaching Arts and the Commentaries on the Pauline Epistles

Although we cannot examine examples from every one of Thomas's biblical commentaries, at least a few from one of his other major commentaries would undoubtedly be in order. Even more extensive than his *Commentary on John* was Thomas's series of

---

wind of temptation. We should preach after, not before, the reading of Holy Scripture and the investigation of doubtful matters by disputation" (emphasis mine).

[13] ST I-II, q. 98, a. 6.
[14] *Super Ioan.*, chapter 2, lecture 1, 338.
[15] Thomas was far from being the only one to make this threefold distinction; proximately, it can be traced back at least to the time of Anselm of Laon (d. 1117), but its ultimate origins go back as far as St. Augustine.
[16] Compare these comments with Thomas's discussion in ST I–II, q. 105, esp. aa. 1 and 3.

commentaries on all the epistles of St. Paul, which he likely undertook toward the end of his life, during his last year as master at Paris (1271–1272) or his first year teaching at Naples (1272–1273).[17] There is abundant material in these commentaries that seems perfectly suited for use in a thirteenth century "modern sermon."

Let us say that a young preacher had come upon the word "judgment" (*iudicium*) in his *thema* verse, as in Psalm 71:2: "Give to the king thy judgment (*iudicium*), O God." How would this young preacher dilate the words of that *thema* verse into an entire sermon? The preacher might want to warn against making the wrong kinds of judgments and exhort his listeners to make good ones. Or he might wish to distinguish between the just judgment God makes on a wicked king who makes evil judgments and the good judgment God bestows in His grace to make kings good. He could easily use this threefold distinction Thomas makes commenting on Romans 2:1: "For wherein you judge another, you condemn yourself." According to Thomas:

> This does not mean that every judgment is a cause of condemnation. For there are three kinds of judgment: one is just, i.e., made according to the rule of justice: *love justice, you rulers of the earth* (Wis 1:1); another is not just, i.e., made contrary to the rule of justice: *although servants of his kingdom, you did not rule rightly* (Wis 6:4); the third is rash judgment against which it is said: *be not rash with your mouth.* (Eccl 5:2)[18]

He continues:

> A rash judgment is made in two ways: in one way, when a person passes judgment on a matter committed to him without due knowledge of the truth, contrary to what is stated: *I searched out the cause of him whom I did not know* (Job 29:16). In another way, when a person presumes to judge about hidden matters, of which God alone has the power to judge, contrary to what is stated: *do not pronounce judgment before the time, before the Lord comes, who will bring to light the things now hidden in darkness.* (1 Cor 4:5)[19]

Here Thomas has supplied not only the necessary distinctions but also the associated, "chained" biblical authorities to use with them.

So too, a distinction Thomas employs in one place can do service elsewhere. Consider, for example, Thomas's discussion of the different senses of the word "servant" made while commenting on Paul's salutation in Romans 1:1: "I, Paul, a servant of Jesus Christ." In his commentary, Thomas distinguishes between the servitude of fear and the servitude of love.

> But one should say that there are two kinds of servitude: one is the servitude of fear, which does not befit saints: *you have not received the spirit of slavery again in fear: but you have received the spirit of adoption of sons* (Rom 8:15); the other is that of humility and love, which does befit saints: *say: we are unworthy servants* (Luke 17:10). For while a free man is one who exists for his own sake, a servant is one who exists for the sake of another, as moving by

---

[17] Jean-Pierre Torrell, *Saint Thomas Aquinas*, vol. 1: *The Person and His Work*, rev. ed. (Washington, DC: The Catholic University of America Press, 2005), 340.
[18] *Super Rom.*, chapter 2, lecture 1, 174. English quoted from the translation by Fr. Fabian Larcher available online at aquinas.cc. [more specifically https://aquinas.cc/la/en/~Rom].
[19] *Super Rom.*, chapter 2, lecture 1, 174.

reason of another's moving him; if then a person acts for the sake of another as though moved by him, the service is one of fear, which forces a man to act in opposition to his own will. But if he acts for the sake of another as an end, then it is the servitude of love; because a friend serves and does good to his friend for the friend's own sake, as the Philosopher says in the ninth book of the *Ethics*.[20]

Thomas employs a similar distinction when he comments on a passage in John 15:15 that might seem contradictory, where Jesus says to his apostles: "I no longer call you servants but friends." In his commentary in the Gospel of John, rather than distinguishing the "servitude of fear" from the "servitude of love," Thomas begins by distinguishing two kinds of fear: servile fear and filial fear. What differentiates them, however, is the presence or absence of love. Whereas "servile fear" is cast out by charity, filial fear is generated by charity, "since one fears to lose who he loves." Hence, the distinction found in Thomas's *Commentary on Romans* 1:1 between the *servitude of fear* and the *servitude of love* can be found in his *Commentary on John* 15:15 as a slightly more complicated distinction between the *servitude of servile fear*, which is the fear of punishment, and the *servitude of filial fear*, which, although it is called filial *fear*, is generated by charity, since one fears to lose who one loves.[21]

A young preacher coming upon either text could pose the same question – are we servants or friends? – and answer using the same distinction between fear and love, which he might then associate with the Old Testament's written law, which Thomas calls a "law of fear" and the New Testament's law of grace, which Thomas calls a "law of charity." We are "servants" in one sense and "friends" in another.

One final example from the *Commentary on Romans*. In Romans 1:24, Paul claims that "God gave them up to the desires of their heart, unto uncleanness." Consider how theologically valuable and broadly useful Thomas's comments on this passage could be, not only to future masters of theology, but also to simple preachers required to address the thorny topic of how God could "give men over" to impurity and sin. The answer, according to Thomas, is that

> God does not give men over to impurity directly, as though inclining a man's affection toward evil, because God ordains all things to himself: *the Lord has made everything for himself* (Prov 16:4), whereas something is sinful through its turning from him. But he gives men over to sin indirectly, inasmuch as he justly withdraws the grace through which men are kept from sinning, just as a person would be said to cause another to fall, if he removed the ladder supporting him. In this way, one's first sin is a cause of the next, which is at the same time a punishment for the first one.[22]

This explanation does not completely resolve the problem, however, since it might still seem as though by withdrawing His grace, God is *causing* man to fall, just as the man who

---

[20] *Super Rom.*, chapter 1, lecture 1, 21.
[21] Cf. *Super Ioan.*, chapter 15, lecture 3, 2015. In both commentaries, Thomas also similarly distinguishes between those who are moved by another – these are "slaves" – and those who move as their own cause in cooperation with the master.
[22] *Super Rom.*, chapter 2, lecture 7, 139.

removes the ladder supporting someone else clearly seems to cause the man's fall. And so Thomas adds:

> To understand this it should be noted that one sin can be the cause of another directly or indirectly: directly, inasmuch as from one sin he is inclined to another in any of three ways. In one way, when it acts as a final cause; for example, when someone from greed or envy is incited to commit murder. Second, when it acts as a material cause, as gluttony leads to lust by administering the material. Third, when it acts as a moving cause, as when many repetitions of the same sin produce a habit inclining a person to repeat the sin. Indirectly, when the first sin merits the exclusion of grace, so that once it is removed, a man falls into another sin. In this way the first sin is the cause of the second indirectly or incidentally, inasmuch as it removes the preventative.[23]

Hence God is not the *cause* of man's sin *directly*, only indirectly. True, God has "given man over to his uncleanness" by withdrawing the grace that would prevent man's sin. But this withdrawal of grace was the result of man's turning away from God. And so, rather than seeing *God* as the cause of man's sin – a "cause" that is only indirect – man should look to himself and focus on how from one sin he is inclined to others. We often imagine that human acts are distinct events, and that when they are complete, we are left as we were before. Thomas forces us to confront the truth that God does not cause our sin, although He allows it, rather *we* cause our sin, not only by the choice we make now, but also by the choices we made earlier. Sin builds upon sin. This is an invaluable lesson that preachers everywhere might profitably have offered to their congregations. If they had, it would have been an example of *praedicatio* supported by both *lectio* and *disputatio*.

Indeed all these bits of biblical commentary, with their distinctions and embedded arguments, provide us with good examples of how later thirteenth-century scholars understood Peter Cantor's admonition that "nothing is understood fully or preached faithfully" unless it is based on sacred Scripture and "chewed by the tooth of disputation." "We should preach after, not before, the reading of Holy Scripture and the investigation of doubtful matters by disputation," declared Peter.[24] Thomas was preparing future preachers by providing them, in his *lectiones* on Scripture, the fruits of his own informed reading, illuminated by his study of the commentaries of the Fathers of the Church and the wisdom gained through disputation.

Supplying Material for *Sermo Modernus*– Style Preaching

Even in those sections of his biblical commentaries that do not sound as if they were lifted directly out of a sermon (and there are many that do), Thomas is almost always communicating material helpful for preaching. Consider a few examples where Thomas's

---

[23] Ibid.
[24] *Verbum Abbreviatum*, 1: "nihil plene intelligitur, fideliterve praedicatur, nisi prius dente disputationis fangatur.... Post lectionem igitur sacrae Scripturae, et dubitabilium, per disputationem, inquisitionem, et non prius, praedicandum est."

parsing of a word might be useful for preachers employing the *sermo modernus* style, should they come upon that word in a *thema* for a future sermon.

In chapter 1, lecture 3 of his *Commentary on John*, Thomas says of the phrase "And that life was the light of men" that,

> according to Augustine and many others, light is more properly said of spiritual things than of sensible things. Ambrose, however, thinks that brightness is said metaphorically of God. But this is not a great issue, for in whatever way the name "light" is used, it implies a manifestation, whether that manifesting concerns intelligible or sensible things. If we compare sensible and intelligible manifestation, then, according to the nature of things, light is found first in spiritual things. But for us, who give names to things on the basis of their properties as known to us, light is discovered first in sensible things, because we first used this name to signify sensible light before intelligible light; although as to power, light belongs to spiritual things in a prior and truer way than to sensible things.[25]

And again in a later *lectio*, Thomas provides another set of distinctions among various senses of "darkness" that might be useful to the aspiring preacher.

> In one way, we can take "darkness" for punishment. For any sadness and suffering of heart can be called a darkness, just as any joy can be called a light. "When I sit in darkness and in suffering the Lord is my light," i.e., my joy and consolation (Micah 7:8)... Secondly, we can take "darkness" to mean the devils, as in Ephesians (6:12), "Our struggle is not against flesh and blood; but against principalities and powers, against the rulers of the world of this darkness"... Thirdly, we can take "darkness" for the error or ignorance which filled the whole world before the coming of Christ, "You were at one time darkness".[26]

Having provided various senses of "darkness," Thomas later provides some sermon material on the several senses of "light."

> Before the Word came there was in the world a certain light which the philosophers prided themselves on having; but this was a false light, because as is said, "They became stultified in their speculations, and their foolish hearts were darkened; claiming to be wise, they became fools" (Rom 1:21); "Every man is made foolish by his knowledge" (Jer 10:14). There was another light from the teaching of the law which the Jews boasted of having; but this was a symbolic light, "The law has a shadow of the good things to come, not the image itself of them" (Heb 10:1). There was also a certain light in the angels and in the holy men in so far as they knew God in a more special way by grace; but this was a participated light, "Upon whom does his light not shine?" (Job 25:3), which is like saying: Whoever shine, shine to the extent that they participate in his light, i.e., God's light.[27]

And so with the coming of Christ, "the light shined in the darkness" (John 1:5) because he enlightened "the men of the world, who are blinded by the darkness of error and ignorance"; as it says in Luke 1:79: He came "to enlighten those who sit in darkness and in the

---

[25] *Super Ioan.*, chapter 1, lecture 3, 96.
[26] Ibid., chapter 1, lecture 3, 105–107.
[27] Ibid., chapter 1, lecture 5, 125.

shadow of death" and Isaiah 9:2: "The people who were sitting in darkness saw a great light." Note that in each instance Thomas has provided the attentive student with the appropriate biblical verses to include using the words "light" or "darkness" from various books of the Bible, should the young preacher wish to use them in a future sermon on this passage or any others which include the words "darkness" or "light."

Let us say that a young preacher found the word "sent" in his *thema* verse. Consider how the following material might have been incorporated into his sermon to dilate that division of the verse.

> Note that there are three ways in which we see men sent by God. First, by an inward inspiration. "And now the Lord God has sent me, and his spirit" (Is 48:16). As if to say: I have been sent by God through an inward inspiration of the spirit. Secondly, by an expressed and clear command, perceived by the bodily senses or the imagination. Isaiah was also sent in this way; and so he says, "And I heard the voice of the Lord saying, 'Whom shall I send, and who will go for us?' Then I said, 'Here I am! Send me'" (Is 6:8). Thirdly, by the order of a prelate, who acts in the place of God in this matter. "I have pardoned in the person of Christ for your sake" as it says in 2 Corinthians (2:10). This is why those who are sent by a prelate are sent by God, as Barnabas and Timothy were sent by the Apostle.[28]

Similarly, let us say the preacher encounters the word "true"; these considerations would undoubtedly be helpful.

> [W]e should note that in Scripture the "true" is contrasted with three things. Sometimes it is contrasted with the false, as in "Put an end to lying, and let everyone speak the truth" (Eph 4:25). Sometimes it is contrasted with what is figurative, as in "The law was given through Moses; grace and truth have come through Jesus Christ," because the truth of the figures contained in the law was fulfilled by Christ. Sometimes it is contrasted with what is something by participation, as in "that we may be in his true Son" (1 Jn 5:20), who is not his Son by participation.[29]

So too with the word "world," should the *thema* verse be taken from John 15:19: "If you were of the world, the world would love you as its own; but because you are not of the world, but I chose you out of the world, therefore the world hates you"; or from Psalm 96:13: "For he comes to judge the earth. He will judge the world in righteousness"; or from any of the many condemnations of "the world" in St. Paul's epistles, the dutiful preacher might profitably employ these three distinctions:

> [W]e should know that "world" is taken in three ways in Scripture. Sometimes, from the point of view of its creation, as when the Evangelist says here, "through him the world was made" (John 1:10). Sometimes, from the point of view of its perfection, which it reaches through Christ, as in "God was, in Christ, reconciling the world to himself" (2 Cor 5:19). And sometimes it is taken from the point of view of its perversity, as in "The whole world lies under the power of the evil one" (1 John 5:19).[30]

---

[28] Ibid., chapter 1, lecture 4, 112.
[29] Ibid., chapter 1, lecture 5, 125.
[30] Ibid., chapter 1, lecture 5, 128.

Or, if the preacher wanted to speak about what it means to be "in the world but not of the world," he might employ the threefold distinction in Thomas's later remark:

> We should remark that something is said to be "in the world" in three ways. In one way, by being contained, as a thing in place exists in a place: "They are in the world." In another way, as a part in a whole; for a part of the world is said to be in the world even though it is not in a place. For example, supernatural substances, although not in the world as in a place, are nevertheless in it as parts: "God ... who made heaven and earth, the sea, and all things that are in them" (Ps 145:6)... [And] in a third way, i.e., as an efficient and preserving cause: "I fill heaven and earth" as said in Jeremiah (23:24).[31]

Consider, finally, how a preacher might use this material from Thomas's *Commentary on the Gospel of John* dealing with Mary Magdalene:

> Notice the three privileges given to Mary Magdalene. First, she had the privilege of being a prophet (*propheticum*) because she was worthy enough to see the angels (*meruit angelos videre*), for a prophet is an intermediary between angels and the people. Secondly, she had the dignity or rank of an angel (*angelorum fastigium*) insofar as she looked upon Christ (*per hoc quod vidit Christum*), on whom the angels desire to look. Thirdly, she had the office of an apostle (*officium apostolicum*); indeed, she was an apostle to the apostles (*immo facta est apostolorum apostola*) insofar as it was her task to announce our Lord's resurrection to the disciples. Thus, just as it was a woman who was the first to announce the words of death, so it was a woman who would be the first to announce the words of life.[32]

How would a preacher use this material in a dilation? Let's say it was Mary Magdalene's feast day, and the message is that Mary Magdalene is as "high" or as "holy" as the angels. Why? Because God's grace granted three privileges to Mary. She received, first, a "prophetic" grace by which merited to see the angels. Second, an "angelic" grace by which she was able to see Christ, on whom the angels desire to look. And third, an "apostolic" grace by which she bore the message (as a "messenger" or *angelus*) of our Lord's resurrection to the apostles.

One might have organized these three by finding a *thema* verse that would allow a threefold *divisio* of prophets, angels, and apostles. One possibility would be the famous passage in Revelation 12:1: "And a great sign appeared in heaven: a woman clothed with the sun, with the moon under her feet, and on her head a crown of twelve stars." The woman could be Mary Magdalene, who is "clothed with the sun" because she has achieved the height of the angels. The sun is above her, and the moon is "under her feet" because she, like the prophets, is an intermediary between angels and the people. And the twelve stars are the twelve apostles to whom she announces Christ's resurrection.

The woman "with the moon under her feet" was commonly understood to be Mary the Mother of God. But Thomas's final comment, "just as it was a woman who was the first to announce the words of death, so it was a woman who would be the first to announce the words of life," would certainly have brought to mind to mind Mary, the Mother of God, whose "yes" to God was always contrasted with Eve's choice to eat the forbidden fruit.

---

[31] Ibid., chapter 1, lecture 5, 133.
[32] Ibid., chapter 20, lecture 3, 2519.

Comparisons between Mary Magdalene and Mary the Mother of Jesus abound: both were devoted to Christ, both stood at the foot of the cross, and a sword pierced both their hearts when they saw Christ upon the cross. Mary Magdalene saw the resurrected Christ among the tombs; Mary the Mother of God saw the resurrected Christ after her death when she was assumed bodily into heaven. Both had an experience of death transformed into life because of their love for Christ.

Alternatively, a preacher could have made a simple threefold division according to "good, better, best." At the tomb, Mary was "good" in that she saw angels. She was "better" in that she saw the resurrected Christ. And she was "best" in that she delivered the news of Christ's resurrection and ascension to the disciples. The possibilities for dilation were nearly endless.

Or let us say that a sermon called for some comment on the apostle Thomas. Here is more material ready-made for a sermon:

> The disciple who was absent is first identified by his name, Thomas, which means a "twin" or an "abyss." An abyss has both depth and darkness. And Thomas was an abyss on account of the darkness of his disbelief, of which he was the cause. Again, there is an abyss – the depths of Christ's compassion – which he had for Thomas. We read: "Abyss calls to abyss" [Ps 42:7]. That is, the depths of Christ's compassion calls to the depths of darkness [of disbelief] in Thomas, and Thomas' abyss of unwillingness [to believe] calls out, when he professes the faith, to the depths of Christ.[33]

Note how, once Aquinas has interpreted the Apostle Thomas's name as "abyss," he can connect Thomas's name to the passage from Psalm 42:7 about the abyss calling to the abyss, which he then figuratively relates back to Christ's calls to Thomas to put his hand in His side. As a species of biblical commentary, using Psalm 42:7 in this way to elucidate a passage in John's Gospel might seem unwarranted. But it provides a beautiful image for preaching.

So too, Thomas can take a traditional biblical *figure* and dilate it in a new way using *sermo modernus*–style methods. Consider, for example, Thomas's comments on Galatians 4:25, where Paul speaks figuratively of the Old Testament and the New in terms of the contrast between Abraham's two sons, "one by a bondwoman" (Hagar) and "the other by a free woman" (Sara). Note how Thomas develops his reader's understanding of the distinction between the Old Testament and the New by distinguishing three types of "bondage" that afflict the Old Testament: a bondage of understanding (*intellectum*), of feeling (*affectum*), and of fruit (*fructum*). The Old Testament "endangers unto bondage," says Thomas:

> As to understanding ... because in man is a twofold knowledge. One is free, when he knows the truth of things according to themselves; the other is servile, i.e., veiled under figures, as was the knowledge of the Old Testament.
>
> As to feeling, the New Law engenders the feeling of love, which pertains to freedom: for one who loves is moved by his own initiative. The Old, on the other hand, engenders the feeling of fear in which is servitude; for one who fears is moved not by his own initiative but by that of another: "You have not received the spirit of bondage again in fear; but you have received the spirit of adoption of sons." (Romans 8:15)

---

[33] Ibid., chapter 20, lecture 5, 2546.

But as to the fruit, the New Law begets sons to whom is owed the inheritance, whereas to those whom the Old Law engenders are owed small presents as to servants: "The servant abideth not in the house forever; but the son abideth forever." (John 8:35).[34]

As before, this is material ready-made for a sermon.

Thirteenth-century biblical commentaries have often been compared to scholastic *quaestiones disputatae*. Although there is plenty of material in these *lectiones* that owes its origins to the master's practice of engaging in disputation, the presentation of the material and the choice of what to include owes just as much, if not more, to the master's judgment about what could be used creatively and imaginatively by young preachers in a *sermo modernus*–style sermon.

The Early Cursory Commentary on Isaiah

Thomas himself was a young preacher once. Thus far, we have been looking at his later biblical commentaries. How about those he did much earlier – for example, when he was giving only "cursory" biblical commentaries as a bachelor of the Bible? Does Thomas show a similar concern for preaching in these early commentaries?

We already know one answer. He was required to write a *sermo modernus*–style prologue – a sort of mini-sermon – so the arts of preaching could not have been far from his mind. But there is more: evidence of a bachelor still in formation, at work on a series of standard, university-level exercises meant to help train his students and hone his own skills – evidence that can be found only in the original manuscript of Thomas's *Commentary on Isaiah*.

Thomas's early "cursory" *Commentary on Isaiah* was composed while he was still a bachelor of the Bible, perhaps in Cologne while he was still working with Albert, but more likely after he left to finish his degree in Paris.[35] As with his other commentaries, sections of the Isaiah commentary could have been copied directly out of a sermon or inserted directly into one.

Consider Thomas's commentary on Isaiah 1:2: "Hear, O ye heavens, and give ear, O earth, for the Lord hath spoken. I have brought up (*enutrivi*) children, and exalted (*exaltavi*) them: but they have despised (*spreverunt*) me." How did God "nourish" (*nutrivit*) the Jewish people? In five ways, says Aquinas.

> First, by restoring the promises made to the fathers (*reficiens promissis in patribus*): *to Abraham were the promises made*. (Gal 3:16)

> Second, by governing with judgments by means of the lawgivers (*gubernans judiciis in legislatoribus*): *he did not do thus with all nations, and he did not manifest his judgments to them*. (Ps 147:20)

> Third, by defending them with assistance by means of the judges and the kings (*defendens auxiliis in judicibus et regibus*): *their God defends them, and we will be a reproach to the whole earth*. (Jdt 5:25)

---

[34] *Super Gal.*, chapter 4, lecture 8, 260.
[35] For the dating, see my discussion of this work in Chapter 7.

Fourth, he taught them through the oracles of the prophets (*erudivit monitis in prophetis*): *and the Lord has been a witness between you and the wife of your youth.* (Mal 2:14)

Fifth, by correcting them with the lash, by means of their enemies (*correxit flagellis in hostibus*): *for it is a token of great goodness, when sinners are not suffered to go on in their ways for a long time, but are presently punished.* (2 Macc 6:13)[36]

This list with its "chained" biblical authorities is characteristic of *sermo modernus*–style preaching, as are the parallel constructions in Latin.[37]

Although this was to be a *literal* commentary on Isaiah, the association with the New Testament and Christ was never far from his mind. So having first commented upon how God "nourished" his people in the time of the law (*nutrivit tempore legis*), Thomas contrasted this with the way God exalted them in the time of grace (*exaltavit in tempore gratiae*). How? Once again, in five ways:

First, by taking on flesh (*secundum carnis assumptionem*): *for nowhere does he take hold of the Angels, but he takes hold of the seed of Abraham.* (Heb 2:16)

Second, by his own preaching (*per personalem praedicationem*): *I am not sent except to the sheep which have been lost from the house of Israel.* (Matt 15:24)

Third, by his own way of life (*per suam conversationem*): *many good works I have worked among you.* (Jn 10:32)

Fourth, by the working of miracles (*per miraculorum operationem*): *for a great prophet has arisen among us, and because God has visited his people.* (Lk 7:16)

Fifth, through the proclamation of the disciples (*per discipulorum praedicationem*): *instead of your fathers, sons have been born to you: you shall establish them princes over all the earth.* (Ps 44:17)[38]

Note again, the "chained" biblical authorities and the parallel Latin phrases.

The tragedy, according to Isaiah, is that even though God had "nourished" (*nutrivit*) His children in the time of the law and "exalted" (*hexaltavit*) them in the time of grace, "they have despised" Him (*spreverunt*) in four ways:

They rejected his teaching (*doctrinam improbant*): *from Galilee all the way to here, we have found this one to be subverting our people.* (Lk 23:5)

---

[36] *Super Is.*, chapter 1, lecture 2. Original Latin text and English translation by Joshua Madden available at aquinas.cc. I have altered the translation in some instances.

[37] I have included the Latin text to indicate that Thomas has, roughly speaking, maintained the structure of each parallel phrase, as was stipulated by the preaching manuals as the proper practice for sermons. It would be difficult to tell from the English text alone that he had maintained the parallelism. Strictly speaking, to maintain the parallelism, Thomas should have written "erudiens monitis in prophetis" and "corrigens flagellis in hostibus." This was still early in Thomas's career. But even later, he was never a stickler for these rules.

[38] *Super Is.*, chapter 1, lecture 2.

> They reviled his way of life (*vitam blasphemant*): *why does your teacher eat with publicans and sinners?* (Matt 9:11)
>
> They perverted his miracles (*miracula pervertunt*): *by the prince of demons he casts out demons.* (Matt 12:24)
>
> They killed his disciples (*discipulos occident*): *I am sending you out as sheep in the midst of wolves.* (Matt 10:16)[39]

Strictly speaking, Thomas should have made all four clauses parallel, writing *doctrina improbant* ("they rejected his teachings") rather than *doctrinam* (sing.) *improbant*, to match the third and fourth items on his list, and changing the singular *vitam blasphemant* to something that could have been made plural. Even so, Thomas took three terms from his original biblical verse – *enutrivi*, *exaltavi*, and *speverunt* – and dilated a list of points based on each to develop coherent points precisely in the way this would have been done in a *sermo modernus*–style sermon.

This practice continues throughout the commentary, but two more examples must suffice. In Isaiah 62:1, Thomas found these words: "For Sion's sake I will not hold my peace, and for the sake of Jerusalem, I will not rest till her just one come forth as brightness (*egrediatur ut splendor*), and her savior be lighted as a lamp" (*salvator ejus ut lampas accendatur*). Although this was to be a "literal" commentary, Thomas could not resist identifying the "just one" who would "come forth as brightness" with Christ, the "savior" who would enlighten the people "as a lamp." This makes sense. What is interesting is the word on which Thomas chose to focus all his attention: *splendor*. What does Isaiah mean when he says that the "just one" will "come forth as brightness" (*ut splendor*)? Thomas writes, "Christ is brilliant" (*Christus splendet*):

> first as the image of the Father (*patris imagine*): *he is the brightness of his glory* (splendor gloriae), *and the figure of his substance* (Heb 1:3);
>
> second, as the light of the saints (*sanctorum lumine*): *in the brightness of the saints* (splendoribus sanctorum), *before the day star I have begotten you* (Ps 109:3);
>
> third, as the fullness of glory (*gloriae plenitudine*): *his face shone* (resplendit facies) *like the sun* (Mt 17:2);
>
> fourth, as upright teaching (*doctrinae rectitudine*): *the nations shall walk in your light, and kings in the brilliance* (splendore) *of your rising.* (Isa 60:3)[40]

Note that here Thomas has managed to get each parallel phrase to match the others, a genitive followed by an ablative, and found biblical verses with some form of the Latin word *splendor* in each. Thomas may not have been a stickler for the rules, but he clearly knew them.

---

[39] Ibid.

[40] *Super Is.*, chapter 62. Note that as Thomas's commentary progressed, the number of *lectiones* in each chapter became fewer. In later chapters, there is just one, as is the case here. So for these later chapters, there is only a chapter number and not a *lectio* number.

One final example. Commenting upon the verse in Isaiah 63:1, "Who is this that cometh from Edom, with dyed garments from Bosra, this beautiful one (*formosus*) in his robe, walking in the greatness of his strength. I, that speak justice, and am a defender to save," Thomas takes the passage once again as applying to Christ and says that "Christ is beautiful" (*formusus*) in four ways:

> first as glowing with the splendor of divinity: *being the splendor of his glory, and the figure of his substance* (Heb 1:3);
>
> second, as formed with the conformity of union: *you are beautiful beyond the sons of men* (Ps 44:3);
>
> third, as distinct by the various shades of virtue: *my beloved is white and ruddy* (Song 5:10);
>
> fourth, as clothed with an honest way of life: *[clothe yourself with nobility, and set yourself up on high,] be glorious, and put on beautiful garments.* (Job 40:5)[41]

None of these distinctions is necessary for a literal interpretation of the text of Isaiah. Nor does Thomas expand at any length on any of them in his commentary. So why does Thomas craft these lists? As it so happens, we possess unique and invaluable manuscript evidence as to their origin and purpose.

Making *Distinctiones*: Guides for Good Preaching

By an amazing stroke of luck, one manuscript we possess of the Isaiah commentary was written in Thomas's own notoriously illegible handwriting. In the margins of this manuscript, Thomas added a series of interesting marginal annotations, which Fr. Torrell, in his biography of Thomas, describes this way:

> There are short, marginal annotations in a telegraphic form that accompany the text proper... They appear in the form of outlines, in the *illegibilis* hand like the rest of the text, and they are linked, assembled, by fanlike lines. Starting with a word from the text of Isaiah, Thomas hastily notes suggestions that he has about it for a spiritual or pastoral expansion of his literal commentary.[42]

Torrell notes that there were reportedly similar annotations in the margins of the *Super Ieremiam* manuscript, but unfortunately that autograph copy has been lost.

Jacobinus of Asti, the first transcriber of Thomas's autograph, called these marginal notes *collationes*. "The word *collationes* makes us think immediately of notes for preaching," says Fr. Torrell, not only because a *collatio* was the name for a sermon given at vespers, but also

---

[41] *Super Is.*, chapter 63.
[42] Torrell, *Saint Thomas*, 29–30. See also P.-M. Gils, "Les *Collationes* marginales dans l'autograph du commentaire de S. Thomas sur Isaïe," *Revue des Sciences Philosophiques et Théologiques* 42 (1958): 253–264. For an excellent commentary on each of these marginal notes, see J.-P. Torrell and Denise Bouthillier, "Quand saint Thomas méditait sure le prophète Isaïe," *Revue thomiste*, 90 (1990): 5–47.

because the primary sense of the word means simply 'things put together' or 'assemblies.'"[43] Another term, more commonly used in the thirteenth century, however, would be *distinctiones*.

Collections of biblical *distinctiones* were preaching aids that had become available only in the thirteenth century. These reference works supplied for a given scriptural term "several figural meanings, and for each meaning provided a passage of scripture illustrating the use of the term in the given sense."[44] The *Summa Abel* of Peter Cantor (so-called because its first entry was "Abel") was one of the most famous of these reference works, and in Chapter 1, I gave an example of the entries in that work for *avis* (bird).

Another of the most popular works in this genre was the *Distinctiones Super Psalterium* of Peter of Poitiers (d. 1215). In Psalm 6:7, one finds the word *lectus* ("bed"), in the sentence "I have labored in my groanings, every night I will wash my bed: I will water my couch with my tears" (*Laboravi in gemitu meo; lavabo per singulas noctes lectum meum: lacrimis meis stratum meum rigabo*). In the *Distinctiones Super Psalterium*, next to the word *lectus* ("bed"), one would find the following list.

"Bed" is [said]:

literally in Scripture; as in the Song of Songs: "Our bed is flourishing, the beams of our houses are of cedar (Song 1.15-16);

of *contemplation*, as "There will be two men in one bed, one will be taken, and the other left (Luke 17:34);

of *the Church*, as: "In the bed of Solomon are sixty brave men" (Song 3:7);

of conscience, as: "I will wash my bed every night" (Ps 6:7);

of *carnal pleasure*, as in the same place according to another reading; or again: "You who sport on beds of ivory" (Amos 6:4); also: If I shall go up into the bed wherein I lie" (Ps 131:3);

of *eternal damnation*, as: "In darkness I have made my bed" (Job 17:13);

of *eternal beatitude*, as: My children are with me in bed." (Luke 11:7)[45]

---

[43] Torrell, *Saint Thomas*, 30.
[44] See Richard and Mary Rouse, *Preachers, Florilegia and Sermons* (Toronto: Pontifical Institute of Mediaeval Studies, 1979), 68. See my discussion of these lists of biblical *distinctiones* in Chapter 1.
[45] "Est lectus scripture ut in Cantico: *Lectus noster floridus, tigna domorum nostrarum cedrina* (Cant. I, 15-16); contemplationis, ut: *Erunt duo in lecto uno, unus assumeter et alter relinquetur* (Luke 17, 34); ecclesie, ut: *Lectum Solomonis ambiunt LX (a) fortes* (Cant. 3.7); conscientie, ut: *Lavabo per singulas noctes lectum meum* (Ps 6.7); carnalis voluptatis, ut ibidem secundum aliam lectionem; item,: *Qui lascivitis in lectulis eburneis* (Amos 6.4); item: *Si ascendero in lectum strati mei* (Ps 131:3); eterne dampnationis, ut: *In tenebris stravi lectulum meum* (Job 17:13); eterne beatitudinis, ut: *Pueri mei mecum sunt in cubili* (Luke 11:7)." Latin quoted from Philip S. Moore, *The Works of Peter of Poitiers: Master in Theology and Chancellor of Paris (1193–1205)* (Notre Dame, IN: University of Notre Dame Press, 1936), 79, which is his transcription of Paris, Bibl. nat., lat. 425, fol. 5rb/LXXXta. The English translation is mine. For a good comparison of the *distinctiones* in the works of Peter of Poitiers, Peter the Chanter, and Prepositinus of Cremona, see Moore, *Peter of Poitiers*, 92–96.

Lists of *distinctiones* were not always published separately, as in the *Summa Abel*. They also often showed up in biblical commentaries. Indeed, as we will see Chapter 13, Bonaventure's *Commentary on the Gospel of Luke* included over thirty such lists, many of which he borrowed from the *Commentary on Luke* by the Dominican Hugh of St. Cher (d. 1263).⁴⁶

Lists of *distinctiones* were often printed in a fan-like fashion with the key term, e.g., *avis* (bird) or *lectus* (bed), at the left and the *distinctiones* spread out to the right. This, significantly, is what we find in Thomas's marginalia: the original word, for instance, "saints" (*sancti*), on the left, with all the uses to which that word might be put fanning out to the right. In other words, Thomas was creating his own lists of biblical *distinctiones* while preparing his *Commentary on Isaiah*.

Let's look at just a few examples. As an illustration, consider this list in which Thomas lays out the ways in which the saints can be compared to eagles.

The saints are compared to eagles:

- Because of the height of their flight (*propter volatus altitudinem*): *shall not the eagle mount up at your command* (Job 39:27), wherein is the eminence of contemplation (*in quo eminentia contemplationis*): *[he shall dwell on high ...] his eyes shall see the king in his beauty, they shall see the land far off* (Isa 33:16-17);
- Because of the pervasiveness of their odor (*propter odoris subtilitatem*): *wheresoever the body shall be, there shall the eagles also be gathered together* (Lk 16:37), wherein is the fervor of love (*in quo fervor dilectionis*): *draw me after you, to the odor of your ointments* (Song 1:3);
- Because of the loftiness of their place (*propter loci sublimitatem*): *three things are hard for me, and the fourth I am utterly ignorant of: the way of an eagle in the air ...* (Prov 30:18), wherein is the study of heavenly conversation (*in quo studium caelestis conversationis*): *our conversation is in heaven* (Phil 3:20);
- Because of the swiftness of their movement (*propter motus velocitatem*): *our persecutors were swifter than the eagles of the air* (Lam 4:19), wherein is their haste in good works (*in quo promptitudo bonae operationis*): *have you seen a man swift in his work? He shall stand before kings and shall not be before those who are obscure* (Prov 22:29);
- Because of their renewal (*propter renovationem*): *your youth shall be renewed like the eagle's* (Ps 102:5), wherein is the fondness for guidance and progress (*in quo studium emendationis et profectus*): *though our outward man is corrupted, yet the inward man is renewed day by day* (2 Cor 4:16);
- Because of the beauty of their members (*propter membrorum pulcritudinem*): *a large eagle with great wings, full of feathers, and of variety* (Ezk 17:3), wherein is the adornment of virtues (*in quo decor virtutum*): *you are all fair, my love, and there is not a spot in you* (Song 4:7);

---

⁴⁶ The numbers are these, as reported by Robert J. Karris: "St. Bonaventure utilizes thirty-six *distinctiones* in his Commentary on the Gospel of St. Luke. Sixteen are his creation. Twenty he has adapted from the Commentary on St. Luke's Gospel by Hugh of St. Cher (d. 1263). Bonaventure has not seen fit to work with sixteen other *distinctiones* that Hugh of St. Cher employs." See Robert J. Karris, "St. Bonaventure's Use of *Distinctiones*: His Independence of and Dependence on Hugh of St. Cher," *Franciscan Studies*, vol. 60 (2002), 209.

- Because of their concern for their children (*propter filiorum sollicitudinem*): *as the eagle entices her young to fly, and hovering over them, spreads its wings, and has taken them and carried them on his shoulders* (Dt 32:11), wherein is the concern of the saints (*in quo sollicitudo sanctorum*): *my daily instance, the concern for all the churches.*] *Who is weak, and I am not weak? Who is scandalized, and I am not burning?* (2 Cor 11:28–29)[47]

Note the strict parallelism. In each item, we get a *propter* clause followed by an *in quo* clause. The *propter* is always followed by a genitive and then an accusative (e.g., *propter membrorum pulcritudinem*), whereas the *in quo* clause is made up of a nominative followed by a genitive (e.g., *in quo decor virtutum*). Such parallelism was required by the *sermo modernus* style.

Now let's consider another passage, also dealing with saints – this time comparing them to lilies not eagles.

The saints are compared to lilies:

- Because of the height of their stem, whereby they are constant in adversity (*propter stipitis altitudinem, ex quo constantia in adversis*): *as the lily among thorns* (Song 2:2);
- Because of their sweet smell, whereby they are well known (*propter odoris suavitatem, ex quo bona fama*): *send forth flowers as the lily, [and yield a smell, and bring forth leaves in grace]* (Sir 39:19);
- Because of the strength of the humors, whereby they are strong of mind (*propter humoris virorem, ex quo virtus mentis*): *as the lilies that are on the brink of the water* (Sir 50:8); and
- Because of their adherence, whereby is the charity of the saints (*propter connexionem, ex quo sanctorum caritas*): *your belly is like [a heap of wheat, set about by lilies].* (Song 7:2)[48]

Note the parallelism: in each case a *propter* clause followed by an *ex quo* clause. This strict parallelism isn't always so clear in English translation, but once you notice it in the Latin, it is hard to miss.

Thomas immediately adds another set of *distinctiones*, expanding upon the image of saints as "lilies" by showing how these lilies can be related to Christ.

> Christ clothes these lilies [says Thomas] as to the gifts of the virtues: *consider the lilies of the field, [how they grow: they do not labor, nor do they spin].* (Matt 6:28)

> He gathers them, for everlasting rewards: *my beloved has gone down into his garden, [to the bed of aromatic spices, to feed in the gardens, and to gather lilies].* (Song 6:1)

> He rests in them through tranquil delight: *my beloved is mine, and I am his, [who feeds among the lilies].* (Song 2:16)

> And he is, himself, a lily: *I am the flower of the field, [and the lily of the valley].* (Song 2:1)[49]

---

[47] *Super Is.*, 40, "collations." Although in the original manuscript, these *distinctiones* would have been written in the margins, in the English and Latin texts published by the Aquinas Institute, the "collations" appear at the end of the chapter. The "collations" for chapter 40, for example, can be found right before chapter 41.
[48] *Super Is.*, 35, "collatio."
[49] Ibid.

Note that all of this marvelous imagery about the saints and Christ is generated by the single word "lily" which appears at the end of Isaiah 35:1, which reads: "The land that was desolate and impassable shall be glad, and the wilderness shall rejoice, and shall flourish like *the lily*" (*quasi lilium*).

Thomas can also string together a series of complex images. In Isaiah 38:14, for example, the prophet cries out: "my eyes are weakened looking upward" (*attenuati sunt oculi mei, suspicientes in excelsum*). In the margin of the manuscript, Thomas wrote:

The eyes are lofty (*oculi excelsi*):

- by the vanity of the heart (*per cordis elationem*): *Lord, [my heart] is not exalted, [nor are my eyes lofty; neither have I walked in great matters, nor in wonderful things above me].* (Ps 130:1)

And they are brought low (*attenuantur*) by God:

- by being pressed down (*a Deo per depressionem*): *the lofty eyes [of man are humbled, and the haughtiness of men shall be made to stoop].* (Isa 2:11)

[They are lifted up]:

- by the curiosity of seeking answers (*per inquisitionis curiositatem*): *[why does your heart elevate you, and why do you stare with your eyes,] as if they were thinking great things?* (Job 15:12)

And they are brought low:

- by the harshness of light (*per luminis oppressionem*): *he that is a searcher [of majesty shall be overwhelmed by glory].* (Prov 25:27)

[They are lifted up]:

- by contemplation (*per contemplationem*): *lift up [your eyes] on high, [and see who has created these things]* (Isa 40:26);

And they are brought low:

- because of the smallness of their knowledge (*propter cognitionis parvitatem*): *all men see him, [every one beholds him afar off; behold, God is great, exceeding our knowledge].* (Job 36:25–26)[50]

This complex set of *distinctiones* is based on only two words in the biblical verse, contrasting the eyes that are "lofty" or "lifted up" (*excelsi*) with those "brought low" or "weakened" (*attenuati*). This sort of contrast was a characteristic way of dilating in a *sermo modernus* sermon.

Here is another example of a multilayered set of *distinctiones*. Isaiah 44:3 contains the verse: "For I will pour out waters upon the thirsty ground, and streams upon the dry land: I will pour out my spirit upon thy seed, and my blessing upon thy stock." Thomas has written in the margin:

---

[50] *Super Is.*, 38, "collations."

The Spirit is given to beginners (*incipientibus*):

- at the start of their being made alive (*in principium vivificationis*): *the spirit came into them, and they lived, and they stood upon their feet* (Ezek 37:10);
- in the bath of restoration (*in lavacrum renovationis*): *by the bath of regeneration and restoration of the Holy Spirit* (Tit 3:5);
- in the privilege of adoption (*in privilegium adoptionis*): *you have received the spirit of adoption of sons.* (Rom 8:15)

[The spirit is given] to the advanced (*proficientibus*):

- for the instruction of the intellect (*ad instruendum intellectum*): *the Holy Spirit, the advocate, whom the Father will send in my name, he will teach you all things and bring all things to your mind, whatsoever I shall have said to you* (Jn 14:26);
- to refashion the passions (*ad reficiendum affectum*): *my spirit is sweet beyond honey* (Sir 24:27);
- to assist activity (*ad adiuvandum actum*): *the spirit helps our infirmity* (Rom 8:26).

[The Spirit is given] to the perfect (*perfectis*):

- as a benefit of freedom (*quasi beneficium libertatis*): *where the spirit of the Lord is, there is freedom* (2 Cor 3:17);
- as a bond of unity (*quasi vinculum unitatis*): *careful to keep the unity of the spirit in the bond of peace* (Eph 4:3);
- as a pledge of inheritance (*quasi pignus haereditatis*): *you were signed with the Holy Spirit of promise* (Eph 1:13).

Having made his way from "beginners" up to "the perfect," which was itself a method of *dilatatio* (proceeding from good to better to best), Thomas adds that,

The saints are

- chosen by predestination (*electi per praedestinationem*): *he chose us in him before the foundation of the world* (Eph 1:4);
- formed by the infusion of grace (*formati per gratiae infusionem*): *the Lord God formed man from the slime of the earth, and breathed into his face the breath of life, and man became a living soul* (Gen 2:7);
- righteous by love (*recti per dilectionem*): *the righteous love you* (Song 1:3);
- servants by the debt of service (*servi per debitum operationis*): *we are unprofitable servants, we have done that which we ought to do.* (Lk 17:10)[51]

I have included the Latin in parentheses throughout so that, as before, the reader can appreciate the parallelism of the phrases in the list. Note also that all of this extensive theological content, nicely organized for easy incorporation into a sermon, was generated by dilating just one word: *spirit*.

Not all of Thomas's *distinctiones* are multi-layered, and often they express fairly straightforward moral or spiritual material. So, for example, in the margin next to the verse "Come near (*accedite*), ye Gentiles, and hear" (Isaiah 34:1), Thomas wrote:

---

[51] Ibid., 44, "collations."

Man approaches God (*Accedit homo ad Deum*):

- by the reception of grace (*per susceptionem gratiae*): *we have access through him [into this grace wherein we stand, and glory in the hope of the glory of the sons of God]* (Rom 5:2);
- by contemplation of divine wisdom (*per contemplationem divinae sapientiae*): *approach him [and be enlightened]* (Ps 33:6);
- by the service of obedience (per ministerium oboedientiae): *the sons of Zadoc, [who are among the sons of Levi,] who approach the Lord, [to serve him]* (Ezek 40:46);
- by the expectation of firm faithfulness (*per expectationem firmae fiduciae*): *[approach her] as one who plows, and sows, [and waits for her good fruits]* (Sir 6:19); and
- by a spirit of harmony (*per spiritum concordiaea*): *you have access in one spirit [to the Father].* (Eph 2:18)[52]

So too, next to Isaiah 37:4, where the prophet exhorts the people to "lift up thy prayer" (*leva ergo orationem*) for the remnant left in Jerusalem, Thomas writes:

Prayer is lifted up (*levatur oratio*):

- by the eminence of contemplation (*per eminentiam contemplationis*): *I have lifted up my eyes [to the mountains, from whence help shall come to me]* (Ps 120:2);
- by the fervor of affection (*per fervorem affectionis*): *let us lift up our hearts [with our hands to the Lord in the heavens]* (Lam 3:41);
- by the tears of compunction (*per lacrimas compunctionis*): *every night I will lift up [upon my bed]* (Ps 6:6); *lift up weeping* (Joel);
- by the practice of good works (*per studium bonae operationis*): *[let my prayer be directed as incense in your sight,] the lifting up of my hands, as evening sacrifice.* (Ps 140:2)[53]

These images can be very creative, as when Thomas, prompted by Isaiah 37:29 – "When thou wast mad against me, thy pride came up to my ears: therefore I will put a ring in thy nose, and a bit (*frenum*) between thy lips" – lists in the margin next to the word *frenum* ("bridle" or "bit") the following:

[We speak of] the bridle (*frenum*):

- of human discretion: *if any man offend not in word, [the same is a perfect man; he is able also with a bridle to lead about the whole body]* (Jas 3:2);
- of divine governance: *for my praise I will bridle you, [lest you perish]* (Isa 48:9);
- of diabolical deception: *the bridle of error* (Isa 30:28);
- of temporal affliction: *[he has opened] his quiver [and has afflicted me, and has put a bridle into my mouth]* (Job 30:11);
- of eternal damnation: *with bit and bridle [bind fast] their jaws.* (Ps 31:9)[54]

Or, having read in Isaiah 41:18 "I will open rivers in the high hills, and fountains in the midst of the plains: I will turn the desert into pools of waters, and the impassable land into streams of waters," Thomas makes this note:

---

[52] Ibid., 34, "collations."
[53] *Super Is.*, 37, "collations."
[54] Ibid.

Water:

- as of tears poured out (*effusae lacrimae*): *who shall give water to my head, and a fountain of tears to my eyes? And I shall weep day and night* (Jer 9:1);
- of baptismal cleansing (*baptismalis munditiae*): *unless a man be reborn, he cannot see the kingdom of God* (Jn 3:3);
- of spiritual grace (*spiritualis gratiae*): *he who believes in me, [as the Scripture says,] rivers of living water shall flow from his belly; now this he said of the spirit* (Jn 7:38-39);
- of divine wisdom (*divinae sapientiae*): *I, wisdom, have poured out rivers* (Sir 24:40);
- of internal joy (*internae laetitiae*): *drink water out of your own cistern, and the streams of your own well.* (Prov 5:15)[55]

Finally there is this series, inspired by Isaiah 41:10, "Fear not, for I am with thee: turn not aside, for I am thy God: I have strengthened thee, and have helped thee, and the right hand of my just one hath upheld thee" (*suscepit te*).

Christ upholds us (*suscepit*):

- as a victor, [who leads] captives to deliverance (*quasi victor captivum ad liberandum*): *to the prey, my son, you have gone up* (Gen 49:9); *bring my soul out of prison, that I may praise your name* (Ps 141:8);
- as a physician, [who leads] the sick to health (*quasi medicus infirmum ad sanandum*): *he who forgives all your iniquities, and who heals are your diseases* (Ps 102:3);
- as an advocate, [who leads] a defendant to acquittal (*quasi advocatus reum ad excusandum*): *we have an advocate with the Father, Jesus Christ the just* (1 Jn 2:1);
- as a strong man, [who leads] the weak to a stronghold (*quasi fortis debilem ad defendendum*): *I, that speak justice, and am a defender to save* (Isa 63:1); *the Lord shall fight for you* (Ex 14:14);
- as a husband, [who leads] his bride to rejoice with him (*quasi sponsus sponsam ad congaudendum*): *I will espouse you to me forever, and I will espouse you to me in justice, and judgment, and in mercy, and in commiserations; and I will espouse you to me in faith, and you shall know that I am the Lord.* (Hos 2:19-20)[56]

Fr. Torrell says that these *marginalia* allow us "to grasp in a very direct way the personal preoccupations of the young Dominican."[57] They are therefore, suggests Torrell,

> as important as the commentary itself for grasping how, from the beginning of his career, Thomas allowed the main traits of his style as a commentator on Scripture to emerge decisively. If the commentary gives the primacy to literal exegesis, the *collationes* show – and simultaneously confirm – the spiritual concern that animates the literal analysis.[58]

I would simply add that these *collationes* or *distinctiones* show Thomas's overriding concern as a Dominican for preaching. They reflect a culture and an educational program dedicated to preaching, especially preaching in the *sermo modernus* style, because this was precisely the sort of preaching these sets of biblical *distinctiones* were meant to foster. Even in a "cursory"

---

[55] *Super Is.*, 41, "collations."
[56] Ibid.
[57] Torrell, *Saint Thomas*, 33.
[58] Ibid., 30.

biblical commentary, Thomas was constantly on the lookout for the verbal associations he might make and how he might use them to illuminate or enliven his preaching. That these sets of *distinctiones* exist in the margins of Thomas's course notes suggests either (a) he wanted to be prepared in each class to give his students a few good examples for preaching, or (b) he was simply making notes for himself as an aid to his own preaching. The two options are not mutually exclusive. What emerges in either case is the concern to provide resources for effective preaching.

Divisio and the Commentary on the Gospel of John

Along with *dilatatio*, the other fundamental skill required for preaching in the *sermo modernus* style was the ability to make a suitable *divisio* – first, of one's opening biblical *thema* verse, and then, of the material within the body of the sermon. The first sort of *divisio* – of the *thema* verse into three or four parts – preceded the *dilatatio* of the various parts. The second sort of *divisio* by which the preacher made further subdivisions and subsubdivisions within the various parts was another means of dilation.

I have proposed several times that crafting a thirteenth-century *divisio textus* required skills and a habit of mind similar to those needed to produce a thirteenth-century "modern sermon." In a medieval *divisio textus*, writes John Boyle, "a commentator states some theme that serves as an interpretive key for this commentary... With the theme stated, the commentator begins to divide the text, dividing each division in turn into smaller and smaller parts down to the verse or even smaller."[59] This sounds very much like what happens in a thirteenth-century "modern sermon" and in a thirteenth-century prologue. One begins by stating a theme (a *thema*), which one then divides and subdivides to develop in a sensible and orderly fashion the parts of the whole sermon. The finished literary product is different – a finished sermon as contrasted with a *divisio textus* – but the same skills are needed for both. And as we saw in Chapter 5, preaching a *sermo modernus*–style sermon in praise of sacred Scripture and crafting a suitable *divisio textus* of all the books of the Bible were required parts of the inception ceremony of every master at the University of Paris.

Why develop the skill of making a good *divisio textus*? An important clue can be found in the first chapter of Thomas's *Summa Contra Gentiles*, where he says, following Aristotle, that "it belongs to the wise man to order" (*quod sapientis est ordinare*) and "they are to be called wise who order things rightly" (*sapientes dicantur qui res directe ordinant*).[60] On this view, crafting a suitable *divisio*, whether for a sermon or for a commentary, demonstrated one's ability to "order things rightly." It was a sign of wisdom. The point of the *divisio*, however, as Prof. Boyle rightly notes, was not merely to break things down into their constituent parts; the goal was to lay out the parts in all their variety and complexity in such a way as to show how each stands in relation to the whole and to each part. When the

---

[59] John Boyle, "Authorial Intention and the *Divisio Textus*," in *Reading John with St. Thomas Aquinas*, ed. M. Levering and M. Dauphinais (Washington, D.C.: The Catholic University of America Press, 2005), 7.
[60] *Summa Contra Gentiles*, Bk 1, chapter 1.

divisio has been done properly, "No part stands in isolation, but rather each stands in a rich and organic set of relations to the rest..."[61]

Consider, for example, the habits of mind Thomas would have needed to produce his *Commentary on the Gospel of John*. Thomas's first task in the commentary is to make a suitable *divisio* of the text. Immediately after finishing his prologue, the first lines Thomas writes are these: "John the Evangelist, as already indicated, makes it his principal object to show the divinity of the Incarnate Word. Accordingly, his Gospel is divided into two parts. In the first he states the divinity of Christ; in the second he shows it by the things Christ did in the flesh" (*In Ioh.* 1.1.23). John's discussion of "the divinity of Christ" encompasses the whole first chapter of the Gospel. If we go to Thomas's first lecture on chapter 2 of John, we find Thomas repeating the division he had made earlier and then extending it:

> Above, the Evangelist showed the dignity of the incarnate Word and gave various evidence for it. Now he begins to relate the effects and actions by which the divinity of the incarnate Word was made known to the world. First, he tells the things Christ did, while living in the world, that show his divinity. Secondly, he tells how Christ showed his divinity while dying; and this from chapter twelve on.
>
> As to the first he does two things. First, he shows the divinity of Christ in relation to the power he had over nature. Secondly, in relation to the effects of grace; and this from chapter three on.[62] (*In Ioh.* 2.1.335)

He repeats this process throughout the *Commentary*, moving from division to division.[63]

Since the last passage stated that the next division would be in chapter three, we turn to the first lines of chapter three. Thomas, once again, repeats the structure he laid out above and extends it further:

> Above, the Evangelist showed Christ's power in relation to changes affecting nature; here he shows it in relation to our reformation by grace, which is his principal subject. Reformation by grace comes about through spiritual generation and by the conferring of benefits on those regenerated. First, then, he treats of spiritual generation. Secondly, of the spiritual benefits divinely conferred on the regenerated, and this in chapter five. (*In Ioh.* 3.1.423)

Since the next major division is in chapter five, we turn to chapter five, at the beginning of which Thomas writes:

> Above, our Lord dealt with spiritual rebirth; here he deals with the benefits God gives to those who are spiritually reborn. Now we see that parents give three things to those who are physically born from them: life, nourishment, and instruction or discipline. And those who are spiritually reborn receive these three from Christ: spiritual life, spiritual nourishment,

---

[61] Boyle, "Authorial Intention," 7–8.

[62] In this part of the chapter, we will be tracking the progression of the *divisio* from one part of a commentary to the next. To make it easier for the reader to see the progression without having to look down at the footnotes, I have inserted the textual citations in parentheses in the body of the text.

[63] It might help the reader working his or her way through these prologues to refer to the outline I have provided in the text that follows.

and spiritual teaching. And so these three things are considered here: first, the giving of spiritual life; secondly, the giving of spiritual food . . .; third, spiritual teaching . . . . (*In Ioh.*, 5.1.699)

After reading about the gift of the spiritual life in chapter 5, the gift of spiritual food in chapter 6, and spiritual teaching in chapter 7, we turn next to the beginning of chapter 8, where Thomas writes:

After having treated of the origin of the doctrine [spiritual teaching] of Christ, the Evangelist here considers its power. Now the doctrine of Christ has the power both to enlighten and to give life, because his words are spirit and life. So first, he treats of the power of Christ's doctrine to enlighten; secondly, of its power to give life (10:1). He shows the power of Christ's doctrine to enlighten, first by words; and secondly, by a miracle (9:1). (*In Ioh.*, 8.1.1118)

At the commencement of chapter 10, he writes: "After our Lord showed that his teaching had power to enlighten, he here shows that he has power to give life. First, he shows this by word; secondly, by a miracle" (*In Ioh.*, 10.1.1364).

In his division of the text at the beginning of chapter 2, Thomas says that John, first, "tells the things Christ did, while living in the world, that show his divinity," and that, second, he "tells how Christ showed his divinity while dying; and this from chapter twelve on." And indeed, if we turn to the beginning of chapter twelve, we find: "So far the Evangelist has been showing the power of Christ's divinity by what he did and taught during his public life. Now he begins to show the power of his divinity as manifested in his passion and death. First, he treats of Christ's passion and death; secondly, of his resurrection" (*In Ioh.*, 12.1.1589). And finally, at the beginning of chapter 20, we find this: "Having related the mysteries of the passion of Christ, the Evangelist now speaks of the resurrection" (*In Ioh.*, 20.1.2470).

In these little prologues, Thomas set forth a *divisio textus* of the entire Gospel. Were we to outline the basic structure of the Gospel according to Thomas's account, it would look something like that shown in Box 9.1.

This outline contains only the most basic structure. Each chapter of Thomas's commentary contains a more detailed *divisio* of its own. So, for example, Thomas tells his students in the first lecture of chapter 1 that John "states the divinity of Christ" (e.g., "In the beginning was the Word . . . and the Word became flesh.") But then Thomas immediately adds another series of divisions and subdivisions.

Regarding the first [stating the divinity of Christ], he does two things. First he shows the divinity of Christ; secondly he sets forth the manner in which Christ's divinity is made known to us (1:14). Concerning the first he does two things. First he treats of the divinity of Christ; secondly of the incarnation of the Word of God (1:6).

Because there are two items to be considered in each thing, namely, its existence and its operation or power, first he treats the existence of the Word as to his divine nature; secondly of his power of operation (1:3). Regarding the first he does four things. First he shows when the Word was: *In the beginning was the Word*; secondly where he was: *and the Word was with God*; thirdly what He was: *and the Word was God*; fourthly, in what way he was: *He was in the beginning with God*. (*In Ioh.*, 1.1.23)

> **Box 9.1** Principal Object of the Gospel: To Show the Divinity of Christ
>
> I. He states the divinity of Christ (chapter 1)
> II. He shows it by the things Christ did in the flesh
>   A. While living
>   1. By showing his power over nature (chapter 2)
>   2. In relation to the effects of grace: primarily our reformation by grace, which comes about:
>   a. Through spiritual generation (chapters 3 and 4)
>   b. By the conferring of benefits on those regenerated
>   i. Spiritual life (chapter 5)
>   ii. Spiritual nourishment (chapter 6)
>   iii. Spiritual teaching:
>   α. origin (chapter 7)
>   β. power:
>   1. to enlighten:
>   a. by words (chapter 8)
>   b. by a miracle (chapter 9)
>   2. to give life:
>   a. by words (chapter 10)
>   b. by a miracle (chapter 11)
>   B. While dying: passion and death (chapter 12 to the end)
>   1. Passion (chapters 12–19)
>   2. Resurrection from the dead (chapter 20)

These divisions and subdivisions continue down to the smallest fragment of text, sometimes (but not always) to individual words or phrases. Thus we can say that dividing and subdividing a text was a habit of mind that united thirteenth-century biblical commentary and preaching.

Much of the content of Thomas's *Commentary on John* is generated by setting forth distinctions. In 1.1.25, for example, Thomas affirms that "intellectual natures are of three kinds: human, angelic and divine; and so there are three kinds of words." Section 26 begins: "We should note that this Word differs from our own word in three ways." After listing and describing these three in sections 27 through 29, in section 30, he writes: "There are four questions on this point, two of them from Chrysostom." In section 34, in his consideration of the meaning of the phrase, *In the beginning*, Thomas notes that "according to Origen, the word *principium* has many meanings." Thus when the Gospel says, *In the beginning was the Word*, "this can be taken in three ways," says Thomas. In one way, so that *principium* is understood as the person of the Son. In a second way, it can be understood as the person of the Father, "who is the principle not only of creatures, but of every divine process." In a third way, *principium* can be taken as the beginning of duration, so the phrase *In the beginning was the Word* means that the Word was eternal and before all things. If this were a sermon, we would describe this as "proposing a discussion based on a noun as it occurs in definitions or classifications." As I mentioned earlier in this chapter, this would be method 1 in the list of eight methods of *dilatatio* described in chapter 2 of this book. As I have suggested several times, a great deal of overlap existed in the uses that were made of these basic skills.

Prologues in the *Summa Theologiae*

In the final part of this chapter, I wish to examine another example of that overlap. We have been examining the role prologues played in helping prepare readers to read a text well. As we have seen, one skill needed to craft a good prologue in the *sermo modernus* style was the ability to make suitable divisions of the text. Making a suitable division of the *thema* was a necessary first step and making further subdivisions of each division was a frequently used method of dilating the parts of the sermon. So too, in biblical commentaries, providing students with a suitable *divisio textus* was also considered an essential task. As we have seen, masters often set forth their divisions of the text in mini-prologues scattered throughout their commentary. If you read from prologue to prologue, as we did with Thomas's *Commentary on the Gospel of John* – you can get a good idea of how the master conceived of the structure of the whole.

When we think of the skills needed to produce a work such as Thomas's *Summa theologiae*, it might seem as though only *disputatio* would be relevant. But is this really so? In the remainder of this chapter, I wish to direct our attention to the structural prologues that often go unnoticed scattered throughout the *Summa*. In these prologues, Thomas lays out, *in seriatim*, a *divisio textus* of the *Summa* in a fashion similar to the progression of *divisiones* we traced in Thomas's *Commentary on John*. The skills and habits-of-mind Thomas brought to bear to craft the elaborate architecture of his *Summa of Theology* were many of the ones developed over years of reading and outlining the books on which he lectured.

As is widely known, the *Summa* is divided into four parts, the *prima pars*, *prima secundae*, *secunda secundae*, and *tertia pars*, each of which is divided into questions and articles. Some modern editions will contain entries such as "The Treatise on Happiness," "The Treatise on Man," or "The Treatise on Law." Sometimes these "treatises" are sold separately in a stand-alone volume. There is nothing objectionable about this practice if readers understand these treatises do not represent the divisions Aquinas made of his own text.[64] Thomas's own analytical divisions are expressed in the prologues scattered throughout the *Summa*.[65]

---

[64] Readers of the popular 1947 Benziger Brothers edition of the *Summa* may have noticed the analytical outlines or "synoptical charts" (as they call them) scattered throughout. If readers have ever wondered how the editors came up with these extremely detailed analytical outlines, the answer is they simply followed the information Thomas himself provides in the prologues scattered throughout the *Summa*. See Thomas Aquinas, *Summa Theologica*, 1st complete American ed., trans. by Fathers of the English Dominican Province, with Synoptic Charts (New York: Benziger Bros., 1947).

[65] The "prologues" to which I refer do not include the brief prologue at the very beginning of the *Summa*, which begins: "Because the Master of Catholic Truth ought not only to teach the proficient, but also to instruct beginners ..." The first of the structural prologues comes at the beginning of ST I, q. 2. Not all on-line versions of the *Summa* include these prologues. The version at New Advent does not, nor does the one at Catholic Primer. One can find them, however, in the excellent facing-Latin version at https://isidore.co/aquinas/summa/index.html. All quotations from the *Summa* have been taken from this source.

Allow me to provide several examples for the sake of illustration. After ST I, q. 1 of the *Summa* – a famous question in which Thomas discusses the nature and character of "sacred doctrine" (*sacra doctrina*) – and before he begins the first article of ST I, q. 2, Thomas, in this little prologue, informs his reader what is coming:

> Because the chief aim of sacred doctrine (*sacra doctrina*) is to teach the knowledge of God, not only as He is in Himself, but also as He is the beginning of things and their last end, and especially of rational creatures, as is clear from what has been already said, therefore, in our endeavor to expound this science, we shall treat: (1) Of God; (2) Of the rational creature's advance towards God; (3) Of Christ, Who as man, is our way to God.

Let's stop here for a moment. Most readers will recognize this threefold division as the one that describes the contents of the rest of the *Summa*: the *prima pars* deals with God, the *secunda pars* deals with the rational creature's advance toward God, and the *tertia pars* deals with Christ, "our way to God."

The prologue continues:

> In treating of God [the subject of the *prima pars*] there will be a threefold division, for we shall consider: (1) Whatever concerns the Divine Essence; (2) Whatever concerns the distinctions of Persons; (3) Whatever concerns the procession of creatures from Him.

Now we have the basic threefold division of the *prima pars*: Thomas first treats of matters pertaining to the divine essence (qq. 2–26); second, of matters pertaining to the distinction of Persons in the Trinity (qq. 27–43); and third, of each part of creation – angels, the six days, man – and of their divine government (qq. 44–119).

The same prologue (still to ST I, q. 2) continues:

> Concerning the Divine Essence [subject of the *prima pars*, qq. 2–26], we must consider: (1) Whether God exists? [q. 2]; (2) The manner of His existence, or, rather, what is not the manner of His existence [qq. 3–13]; and (3) Whatever concerns His operations – namely, His knowledge, will, power [qq. 14–26].

This prologue ends, finally, with this:

> Concerning the first [namely whether God exists, the subject of q. 2], there are three points of inquiry: (1) Whether the proposition "God exists" is self-evident? [q. 2, a. 1] (2) Whether it is demonstrable? [q. 2, a. 2] And (3) Whether God exists? [q. 2, a. 3]

In one short prologue, therefore, Thomas has taken us from the basic division of the whole of the *Summa* – the first, second, and third parts – down to the specific divisions within this one question.

From this point, we go to the next place where Thomas has stated in his prologue there will be another important transition. According to the division Thomas set forth above, we should expect the next prologue to come at the beginning of ST I, q. 3, the place where Thomas begins his discussion of the *manner* of God's existence. And indeed, before we get to the first article of q. 3, we find the next prologue:

> When the existence of a thing has been ascertained [God's existence was discussed in q. 2], there remains the further question of the manner of its existence, in order that we may know its essence [the divine essence is the subject of qq. 3–13]. Now, because we cannot know what God is, but rather what He is not, we have no means for considering how God is, but rather how He is not. Therefore, we must consider: (1) How He is not [qq. 3–11]; (2) How He is known by us [q. 12]; (3) How He is named [q. 13].
>
> Now it can be shown how God is not, by denying Him whatever is opposed to the idea of Him, viz. composition, motion, and the like. Therefore (1) we must discuss His simplicity [q. 3], whereby we deny composition in Him; and because whatever is simple in material things is imperfect and a part of something else, we shall discuss (2) His perfection [qq. 4–6]; (3) His infinity [qq. 7–8]; (4) His immutability [qq. 9–10]; (5) His unity [q. 11].
>
> Concerning His simplicity [q. 3], there are eight points of inquiry...

Once again, we have gone from a consideration of a larger sub-section down to the level of the eight articles in ST I, q. 3. The rest of the *prima pars* can be divided in the same way. There are important structural prologues before ST I, qq. 27, 44, 50, 75, and 103.

Ignoring Thomas's structural prologues can lead to poor interpretation. One notorious example is in the prologue to ST I–II, q. 90. Having finished his consideration of the *intrinsic* principles of human acts (passions, habits, and virtues), he turns next to the *extrinsic* principles, saying:

> We have now to consider the extrinsic principles of acts. Now the extrinsic principle inclining to evil is the devil, of whose temptations we have spoken in the First Part. But the extrinsic principle moving to good is God, Who both instructs us by means of His Law, and assists us by His Grace: wherefore in the first place we must speak of law; in the second place, of grace.

Following this structure, we know that the "questions on law" continue all the way up to the "questions on grace." The questions on grace begin with ST I–II, q. 109. This means that the "questions on law" continue from q. 90 all the way through q. 108. One wonders, then, why books with the title *Thomas Aquinas: The Treatise on Law* contain only the material in qq. 90 through 97, as though the material in qq. 98 through 108 on the Old Law and the New Law were not part of Thomas's discussion of law. If we listen to Thomas himself, we know that it is.

The pattern should be clear by now. The point is that Thomas's prologues are invaluable guides that can help us understand how he himself conceived of the basic divisions of his text. These prologues are an invaluable resource, and they show us that what Thomas learned at Paris was not only how to do a *divisio textus* of someone else's text, but also how to use the same skill to organize his own.

The Arts of Preaching in a University Culture in Love with Logic

There is no doubt that the chance to get training in logical argumentation and the arts of *disputatio* was one of the primary factors that had lured students to study at Paris since the time of Abelard and John of Salisbury in the mid-twelfth century.[66] The protreptic character of the prologues Thomas wrote to preface his biblical commentaries may suggest that at least some students trained by the Arts faculty at Paris valued certain kinds of logical disputation a bit *too* much, especially when that culture of logical disputation became highly competitive and caused its devotees to become arrogant, looking down upon the study of sacred Scriptures as though it were a crazy half-uncle to serious philosophy. On such a view, serious thinking was what one did reading Boethius, Aristotle, or Avicenna. For such students and masters, the Scriptures were thought to be pious books for simple folk, constraining the keys to some important doctrines, but reading them would not advance university education to its highest level of intellectual excellence and sophistication.

And yet even if dialectic and disputation were key motivating factors drawing students to Paris, as the historical analysis in Chapter 1 shows, there were many within the Church and at the University of Paris who viewed the emergence of this new educational institution, the medieval university, as an excellent opportunity to train theologically well-formed and rhetorically well-trained preachers for the laity. In the School of Theology, the result was the institutionalization of practices whose aim was the education and formation of just such preachers.

Once such practices are institutionalized and become habitual, it is hard for them *not* to influence the other practices within the institution and the habits-of-mind members of the community bring to bear on other tasks. The goal of the chapters in this section has been to show how the preaching and prologue culture at the University of Paris influenced both the student work and the more mature work of Thomas Aquinas. In the next section, we will carry out a similar examination to see whether we can trace influences of the preaching and prologue culture at Paris on the work of the other great light of the thirteenth century, a person whose philosophical views were, on certain key questions, quite different from Aquinas's, the Franciscan Bonaventure of Bagnoregio.

---

[66] On Abelard, John of Salisbury, and the "lure of logic" at Paris, see Ian P. Wei, *Intellectual Culture in Medieval Paris: Theologians and the University, c. 1100–1330* (Cambridge: Cambridge University Press, 2012), 17–33.

PART THREE

Bonaventure
The Scholastic with the Soul of a Poet

10

Bonaventure's Inception
Principium
Omnium Artifex

WE HAVE been concerned thus far primarily with prologues of Thomas Aquinas. The reason for focusing on the work of one master was to examine how he developed his proficiency in using the *sermo modernus* style over his student years and how engaging in the practices of preaching and writing prologues influenced him over the course of his entire career from a young *cursor biblicus* to a mature "master of the sacred page." The prologues of other masters were introduced only for comparative purposes and to show that this emphasis on the arts of preaching and writing prologues was not something peculiar to Thomas, the Dominicans, or the middle decades of the thirteenth century.

In the next few chapters, we will be taking a similarly detailed look at the development of another master: the Franciscan Bonaventure of Bagnoregio. Bonaventure's road to becoming regent master at Paris differed somewhat from Thomas's, and not merely because he was a Franciscan, not a Dominican. Bonaventure had been at Paris for years before his inception, having entered the University as a layman to study the Arts in 1235 at age fourteen. He became a bachelor of the Arts in 1241, lectured on them for two years, entered the novitiate as a Franciscan in 1243, and began his studies as an *auditor theologiae*. He was licensed as a *lector biblicus* by John of Parma, the minister general of the Franciscans, in 1248 and, after two years as a *baccalarius biblicus*, began his studies as a *baccalarius sententiarius* in 1252–1253. The disputes between the seculars and regulars at Paris had broken out anew in 1250, and this made both Thomas's and Bonaventure's inceptions more complicated. After a truce arranged between John of Parma and the University authorities, which stipulated that the Franciscan William of Middleton would step down as regent master, William was replaced in his position by Bonaventure, who likely incepted in the spring of 1254, two years before Aquinas.[1]

---

[1] I am following the dating from Jay M. Hammond's scrupulously researched and argued article "Dating Bonaventure's Inception as Regent Master," *Franciscan Studies*, 67 (2009): 179–226.

Comparing Two Medieval Masters: Similar Training, Different Results

We will approach his development much as we did with Aquinas, beginning in this chapter with an analysis of the *principium in aula* Bonaventure delivered when he incepted as a master. In the next chapter, we examine the *resumptio* he delivered several days later. There are several reasons we begin with the master's *principium* address. First, it was the culmination of the master's student years. Comparing Thomas's *principium* with Bonaventure's is a bit like comparing Thomas's *Commentary on Peter Lombard's Sentences* with Bonaventure's. Our concern is with how two masters of distinctive genius approached the same assignment. How were the two products of their labors similar in some ways and different in others?

The two men had traveled different paths to their inception as master. Bonaventure had spent some fourteen years training at Paris, whereas Thomas had come to Paris from the University of Naples and left before long to study with Albert in Cologne. He had returned several years earlier to finish his *Commentary on the Sentences*, but he was not a long-time resident in Paris the way Bonaventure had been. So too, each man had different paths after his inception. Bonaventure became master general of the Franciscans within the year, whereas Thomas went on to teach at universities and *studia generale* across Europe. Yet, at the moment of their inception, they were, in one sense at least, at the same stage of their academic careers.

What makes the comparison even more *apropos* is that Thomas and Bonaventure incepted at roughly the same time and under similar circumstances. Both were opposed by the secular faculty of arts, and both were only admitted fully to the faculty by order of the pope. Thus it will be interesting to compare how each man addressed the political and cultural challenges facing the mendicant orders at the University of Paris at that time.[2]

Our study of Bonaventure's development has been designed very intentionally to be as similar as possible to the one we did with Aquinas. They had similar training and education. Both were trained to write prologues in the *sermo modernus* style. Both became proficient at the skill. For both, this early training and the continual practice of preaching in the *sermo modernus* style lent a distinctive character to their later work. And yet they were far from being carbon copies of one another. Similar training bore fruit in two very different ways. Bonaventure's works, even from early on, show evidence of a superb literary education. Thomas, though a clear and penetrating thinker, rarely showed the literary skills we will see in evidence in Bonaventure's works.

---

[2] Perhaps a rough analogy will make the nature of the comparison clearer. Let us imagine a comparison of the development of two poets who had been great friends during their student days at the University of Oxford: Gerard Manley Hopkins and Robert Bridges. Neither was recognized as a great poet early on, but Bridges was eventually appointed Poet Laureate of England (1913 to 1930). Hopkins, who is better known now, only gained renown after his death because of the efforts of his friend Bridges, who is nearly unknown now. They had many of the same influences at Oxford and had undergone similar educational formation. It would be fascinating to see how similar and yet how different their poetry was when they graduated from Oxford and how their work developed in the years that followed: Hopkins as an unknown Jesuit pastor and Bridges as someone in a post of high renown.

Bonaventure was so proficient at the *sermo modernus* style, his peers took his preaching to be a model of the style at its best. The wonderful collection of sermons for each Sunday of the liturgical year, found in English translation in *The Sunday Sermons of St. Bonaventure*, were likely collected to serve as a manual of "model sermons" for other preachers to learn from.[3]

In the chapters on Aquinas, by contrast, I identified several places where Thomas deviated (or ignored) the rules of the *sermo modernus* style. In Thomas's *principium in aula*, for example, which we analyzed in Chapter 2, Thomas says that the students of sacred doctrine should be, like the earth, "low" in humility (*infimi per humilitatem*), "firm" in the rectitude of sense (*firmi per sensus rectitudinem*), and "fecund," so the words of wisdom they hear may bear fruit in them (*fecundi, ut percepta sapientiae verba in eis fructificent*). According to the strictures of the *sermo modernus* style, those three Latin clauses should be parallel. Thomas *mostly* observes this rule, but on occasion, he does not.[4] Although Thomas's content is always edifying, according to the standards of the *sermo modernus* style, there are places where his preaching technique lacks polish and precision.

Bonaventure, by contrast, never makes this mistake. He never fails to make his clauses match, even though they are often quite complicated. Consider, for example, how Bonaventure in his *principium in aula* divides his opening *thema* verse from Wisdom 7.21: *Omnium artifex docuit me sapientia* ("The maker of all things taught me wisdom"). These words, he says, show "the fourfold cause" [of the Scriptures]: namely, "the excellence of the author from the sublimity of the principle" (*auctoris excellentiam ex sublimitate principia*); "the contents of the matter from the utility of the sign" (*materiae continentiam ex utilitate signi*); "the evidence of the form from the singularity of the mode" (*formae evidentiam ex singularitate modi*); and "the sufficiency of the end from the uncommon teachability of the good" (*finis sufficientiam ex docibilitate boni*). Note the complexity of the parallel constructions as compared to Thomas's.

R.-A. Gauthier once described the difference between Bonaventure's style and Thomas's as moving "from the luxuriance of a virgin forest to a French garden."[5] A better image might be the comparison between an elaborate, well-sculpted French palace garden (Bonaventure) and a somewhat disorganized, but beautiful Italian garden. Either way, Bonaventure would have been recognized at the time as having a very "high" style; Thomas's was much simpler.

Consider, for example, Bonaventure's use of authorities. Thomas mentions Pseudo-Dionysius and Augustine in the first paragraph of his *principium in aula* but makes not one non-biblical reference thereafter. Bonaventure, by contrast, often considered less "scholastic," begins the first paragraph of his *principium* with a complex series of references to Aristotle's *Physics*, *Metaphysics*, and the *Prior Analytics*, after which the breadth of the authorities he "chains" together as he dilates each section is simply exhausting: Augustine, Ambrose, Aristotle, Seneca, Cicero, Gratian, Cassiodorus, Jerome, Gregory the Great,

---

[3] *The Sunday Sermons of St. Bonaventure*, trans. Timothy J. Johnson (St. Bonaventure, NY: The Franciscan Institute, 2008).

[4] One *might* attribute this problem to a failure of the scribe doing the *reportatio*, except that it happens too often to be attributed solely to that difficulty.

[5] *Sancti Thomae de Aquino Opera Omnia*, 25.1, *Quaestiones quodlibetales* (Paris: Edita Leonis XIII, 1984), 81. Translated from the French original.

Pseudo-Dionysius, Fulgentius, an author he thinks is John Chrysostom, Avicenna, Boethius, and Richard and Hugh of St. Victor.

Not only is the number of authors he cites astounding, the breadth of the works cited is similarly impressive. His favorite authority by far other than the Bible is St. Augustine, whom he cites some forty times in a text with twenty-nine sections. The list of Augustine's works from which he cites includes: *De trinitate*, *De libero arbitrio*, *Contra Faustum*, *De civitate dei*, *De vera religione*, *De genesi ad litteram*, *De baptismo*, *De doctrina christiana*, *Contra Academicos*, *Enarrationes in Psalmos*, *Confessiones*, *In Iohannis evangelium tractatus* and a wide selection from Augustine's letters. The breadth is simply amazing.

University regulations stipulated that the *principium in aula* address was to be delivered "briefly" and "quickly terminated." As we will see, Bonaventure's understanding of those terms differed from Thomas's. Thomas finished his *principium* in roughly ten minutes. Bonaventure's *principium* is, by my reckoning, four of five times as long, requiring something like 45 or 50 minutes to deliver orally. "Brief," it seems, can be said in many ways.

Bonaventure's *Principium*: *Omnium Artifex*

The *thema* Bonaventure chose for his *principium* was from Wisdom 7.21: *Omnium artifex docuit me sapientia* ("Wisdom, the maker of all things, taught me").[6] After a brief introduction in which he reaffirms the Aristotelian notion that to know a thing is to know it in its principles or causes, Bonaventure makes a fourfold *divisio* of his opening *thema* in order to associate each part with one of the four Aristotelian causes.[7]

A. *artifex* ("maker"): author, or efficient cause;
B. *omnium* ("of all things"): subject matter or material cause;
C. *sapientia* ("wisdom"): form;
D. *docuit me* ("taught me"): end.[8]

---

[6] I have provided an English translation of this text in the accompanying website. As of this writing, it is the only translation available. The Latin text of Bonaventure's *principium* I have used is, to my knowledge, the only one currently available. See Joshua C. Benson's invaluable article "Bonaventure's Inaugural Sermon at Paris: *Omnium artifex docuit me sapientia*, Introduction and Text," *Collectanea franciscana* 82 (2012): 517–562. According to Prof. Benson, "The most important manuscript of Bonaventure's inaugural sermon remains (at present) Vatican Burghesiani 157... a manuscript that dates "from roughly the first quarter of the fourteenth century, and was largely copied by the Parisian theologian Pierre Roger, who later became Pope Clement VI." "This manuscript was known to the Quaracchi fathers," says Benson, "who utilized it in their edition of the *De reductione*." Why, then, did it take until 2012 for us to have a copy of Bonaventure's *principium*? As Benson tells it, the problem seems to have been that the Vatican manuscript's presentation of the *De reductione* confused the Quaracchi editors: "They could not understand why the text seemed to have an 'introduction' which they did not recognize as a work of Bonaventure." Prof. Benson has done us the invaluable service of identifying it as Bonaventure's *principium*.

[7] Cf. my comments in Chapter 7, n. 34. On the thirteenth development of the "Aristotelian" ("Type C") prologue, see Alastair J. Minnis, *Medieval Theory of Authorship: Scholastic Literary Attitudes in the Later Middle Ages* (Philadelphia: University of Pennsylvania Press, 1984; 2nd ed. 1988), esp. chapter 1

[8] I will be referring to the *principium* by the section numbers in Benson's Latin text: e.g., *Omnium art.*, 2.

Characteristically, Bonaventure associates this first fourfold division with two others. The excellence of the author, he says, is related to the sublimity of the principle (*auctoris excellentiam ex sublimitate principii*); the content of the material is related to the utility of the sign (*materiae continentiam ex utilitate signi*); the evidence of the form is related to the uniqueness of the mode (*formae evidentiam ex singularitate modi*); and the sufficiency of the end is related to Scripture's superior ability to teach the good. The first of these, the sublimity of the principle, shows the "height" of the authority (*altitudinem auctoritatis*) of Scripture; the fullness of the subject-matter shows the "breadth of its generality" (*latitudinem generalitatis*); the evidence of the form shows the "certitude of its truth" (*certitudinem veritatis*); and the sufficiency of the end shows the "fullness of its utility" (*plenitudinem utilitatis*).[9]

Beginning in section 3 Bonaventure dilates each element of the *divisio* in turn, beginning with the first: the efficient cause or author of the Scriptures, a topic he has associated with the word *artifex* ("maker"). In each case, after brief introductory comments, Bonaventure supplies four subdivisions for each of his four primary divisions (Box 10.1).

Box 10.1 Outline of Bonaventure's *Divisio*

A. *Artifex* ("maker"): excellence of the author, or efficient cause shows "height" of authority
   1. Superiority of reason
   2. Priority of edition
   3. Majority of correction
   4. Stability of adhesion
B. *Omnium* ("of all things"): utility of the subject matter or material cause shows "breadth" of generality
   1. Utility of comprehension
   2. Totality of perfection
   3. Principle of attribution
   4. Uniformity of consideration
C. *Sapientia* (wisdom): evidence of the form shows the certitude of its truth
   1. Highest in principles
   2. Most certain in opinions
   3. Most profound in mysteries
   4. Most plain in necessary things

D. *Docuit me* (teach me): sufficiency of the end shows the fullness of its utility
   1. Cognition of the truth
   2. Argumentation against falsity
   3. Reproof of iniquity
   4. Building up of charity

---

[9] *Omnium art.*, 2.

Efficient Cause: "The Maker"

The author or "maker" of the Scriptures, says Bonaventure, is the "highest" (*summa*): the eternal Father expresses Himself in the eternally begotten Word, and through His Word, the Father makes all of creation. The distinction between the "Book of Nature" and the "Book of Scripture" is fairly well known. Bonaventure takes this idea a step further and says that the Father has written his art "in this book" – namely Christ.[10] Creation is, as it were, a "mirror" of this first writing. But the first (Christ) is eternal and immutable, while the second (creation) is produced in time and is mutable. The highest Maker also expresses himself in the word of revealed Scripture. Hence there are three "books": the eternal book in which God the Father has written, expressing His Word; the Book of Creation, which is a mirror of this first "book"; and the Book of Scripture, an authoritative guide to the first two, because expressed by the same divine author and supreme "maker" (*artifex*).

Although for Bonaventure the *author* of Scripture, properly speaking, is God, he does not deny the role of "secondary makers" (*artifices secundarios*). Aquinas quoted Pseudo-Dionysius's *Celestial Hierarchy* in his *principium* to make a similar point – namely, that "the gifts of God's providence come to the lower through intermediaries," although for Aquinas, the masters were the intermediaries. Bonaventure quotes, first, Ephesians 4:11–12 and, second, Augustine's *City of God* 11 to say something, not about masters, but about the human authors God employed to produce the Scriptures.

> And he gave some apostles, and some prophets, and other some evangelists, and other some pastors and doctors, for the perfecting of the saints, for the work of the ministry, for the edifying of the body of Christ. (Ephesians 4:11–12)

> This Mediator, having spoken what He judged sufficient first by the prophets, then by His own lips, and afterwards by the apostles, has besides produced the Scripture which is called canonical, which has paramount authority, and to which we yield assent in all matters of which we ought not to be ignorant, and yet cannot know of ourselves.[11]

In Thomas's *principium*, these intermediaries were said to be directed by "the most sacred law" of divine providence; this gave them their ultimate authority over the works of other human authors. So too in Bonaventure's *principium*, the Scripture's inspiration by God gives them their preeminence over other works. As Augustine attests, "the Scriptures ... have gained dominion over every branch of human genius, not by virtue of any random activity of men's minds but by the decree of Providence Most High, surpassing every literary work of every nation because of their divine authority."[12] It is their divine authorship that provides the Scriptures with what Bonaventure describes as their "height."[13]

---

[10] *Omnium art.*, 4: "*Haec ars in illo libro scribitur, immo est Christus liber ille* ..."

[11] *Omnium art.*, 7; cf. Augustine, *City of God* 11.3.

[12] *Omnium art.*, 7; cf. Augustine, *City of God* 11.1.

[13] Recall that Thomas also associated height with the Scriptures. In his *principium*, he affirmed that the "mountains," which he associated with the masters, had to be watered from "the places above."

From this "height," a fourfold privilege (*privilegium*) follows: the Scriptures possess a "superiority of reason" (*superioritatem rationis*) because they contain clear, certain truth; a "priority of edition" (*prioritatem editionis*) because this law is eternal and thus prior to all other laws; a "majority of correction" (*maioritatem correctionis*) – that is to say, it has a higher rank when it comes to correction because it serves as an "architectonic principle" (*principalis architectonica*) for all other texts; and it has a "stability of adhesion" (*stabilitatem adhensionis*), not merely from the certitude of reason, but from Scripture's supreme authority.[14]

The Material Cause: "Of All Things"

Bonaventure associates the material cause of the Scriptures with the next word in his *thema*: *omnium* ("of all things"). In accord with the image of the three "books" he set out in the first section – the Book of Christ, the Book of Creation, and the Book of Scripture – he declares that the Scriptures mirror the fullness found in Christ and in creation. They contain "every truth": all of physics, ethics, and logic, the three classic branches of philosophy. And not only every truth, but all good. The Scriptures, says Bonaventure, are "the mother of all good" because without knowledge of the soul there is no good, and the Scriptures provide knowledge of the soul.

The knowledge that comes through the Scriptures has, according to Bonaventure, a "community of utility" (*communitatem utilitatis*), and something is more useful, he claims, to the degree that it is more singular (*quia aliquid quanto utilius est, aliquid tanto unicius*). So he identifies a fourfold unity (*unitas*) of the Scriptures.

A potential source of confusion here is that Bonaventure associated the word *omnium* from his opening *thema* verse with the "breadth of generality" (*latitudinem generalitatis*) of the Scriptures, because the Scriptures cover every subject. But here he argues for its utility based on its fourfold *unity*. Is it one or many?

It is both. Like the Triune God, whose expression they are, the Scriptures are both "one" and "many." Although they contain and express "all things," the "science" of theology and the Scriptures retain a fundamental "unity." Bonaventure's use of the Latin term *scientia* in a previous sentence, *Habet igitur* **haec scientia**, *quantum ad causam materialem, communitatem utilitatis*, suggests that he has in mind both Scripture and the "science" of theology, the two of which are closely associated in his mind.

However why this emphasis on "unity"? Bonaventure lived and worked during a period when young friars, not exposed to much in the way of formal theological instruction or provided with any systematic introduction to the Scriptures, were being sent off for training at the major universities at Paris, Oxford, and Cambridge. The result for these young friars, says Dominic V. Monti, was that

---

Without this water from on high, the mountains would have nothing with which to water the plains to make them fruitful.

[14] *Omnium art.*, 8–12. Cf. Aristotle's reference to an "architectonic" principle in *Nicomachean Ethics* 1.1. According to Bonaventure, the Scriptures are now "architectonic" to the other disciplines. Bonaventure will develop this idea further in his *resumptio*.

Their exposure to secular learning, both in terms of content and method, thus far exceeded their knowledge of their faith. Furthermore, the standard textbooks in theology – the Bible and Peter Lombard's *Sentences* – did not present the same scientific clarity as textbooks in the arts, with their clear outlines and definite objectives. The Bible appeared to be a confusing and contradictory collection of stories, the *Sentences* a disorganized assemblage of arcane and sterile questions.[15]

In such circumstances, one can imagines some friars asking whether there was any unity and coherence in theology sufficient to make it an actual University discipline, something on par with the unity and coherence of their other studies. The less unified, the more scattered, the less analytic its manner of proceeding, the less theology would seem like something appropriate for study in a university. Bonaventure himself adverts to this problem in the prologue to the *Breviloquium*, his own short *summa* of the Christian faith.

> And because this teaching (*doctrina*) has been transmitted, both in the writings of the saints and in those of the doctors, in such a diffuse manner that those who come to learn about Sacred Scripture are not able to read or hear about it for a long time. In fact, beginning theologians (*novi theologi*) often dread (*exhorrent*) Sacred Scripture itself, feeling it to be uncertain (*incertam*), disordered (*inordinatam*), and uncharted as some impenetrable forest.[16]

It was in response to these same intellectual and spiritual challenges that Franciscan masters Alexander of Hales and John of La Rochelle had earlier produced the monumental *Summa fratris Alexandri* (or *Summa Halensis*).

It is in this context, I would suggest, that we must understand Bonaventure's comments about the unique "utility" of the Scriptures following from its "unity" and "latitude," or what we might call its "expansive-all-inclusiveness-in-one." Where the other sciences treat one subject and make use of a variety of authorities, the Scriptures offer a clear and true perspective about the whole of reality in one book. Bonaventure will argue again later in his *resumptio* that all the arts can be "reduced" to – they ultimately "lead back to" – the Scriptures in which they find their ultimate source and summit: the source of the intellectual light that illumines all other studies and the summit or ultimate end to which all their searching should lead.

In speaking of a "community of utility" (*communitatem utilitatis*) of the Scriptures here, Bonaventure is also likely making reference to Augustine's distinction between *signs* and *things* and between things to be used (*uti*) and the one thing that is to be enjoyed (*frui*). Signs direct us to things; those things can in turn direct us to other things. The chief thing to be enjoyed, however, is God, the Father, Son, and Holy Spirit, which, says Augustine, "is a kind of single, supreme thing, shared in common by all who enjoy it" (*una quaedam summa res communisque omnibus fruentibus ea*). This may well be the source of Bonaventure's "community of utility" (*communitatem utilitatis*). This "community" is, first and foremost, the communion of Father, Son, and Holy Spirit. But this is a communion we are called to

---

[15] Dominic V. Monti, trans., *Breviloquium*, Works of St. Bonaventure, vol. 9 (Saint Bonaventure, NY: Franciscan Institute Publications, 2005), xix–xx.
[16] Prologue to *Breviloquium*, 6.

participate in by loving God and our neighbor. We learn about this Triune God through the Scriptures. But this is not merely a matter of knowing the most certain truth; it is also a matter of desiring the highest good, "the mother of all good things." On this "Augustinian" view, the *signs* of Scripture are singularly *useful*, because they are especially effective at leading us upward to enjoy and share in the one thing to be enjoyed, the one thing in which we are truly at rest, the triune *community* of love.[17]

With this in mind, we can consider the fourfold unity (*unitas*) of the Scriptures upon which, according to Bonaventure, follows its singular utility. The first unity of the Scriptures is a unity of "useful comprehension" (*utilis comprehensionis*); they uniquely contain in one text everything necessary to bring us to our final end, including precepts, counsels, miracles, and examples (*praecepta, consilia, miracula, et exempla*), and accounts of our creation, fall, the manner of our reparation, and the fruit of our redemption.[18] The Scriptures singularly possess, second, a unity of "total perfection" (*totalis perfectionis*); one need not seek for anything beyond them.[19] The Scriptures possess, third, a unity of "principle attribution" (*principalis attributionis*); the content of all these books refers ultimately to the principle of all things, God.[20] And finally, the Scriptures possess a unity of "uniform consideration"; "while other sciences consider singular things with reason according to that which in being they are properly what they are, the Scriptures consider uniformly all things as a 'vestige' and participation in the divine being" (*cum enim aliae scientiae considerent singulas res sub ratione, qua in esse priprio sunt id, quod sunt; haec tamen uniformiter considerat omnia sub ratione vestigii ex participatione esse divini*). And since the sacred Scriptures provides the highest knowledge of the first principle of all things, it can serve as a "measure" (*mensura*) of all the other sciences.[21]

---

[17] On this, see, for example, Augustine, *De doctrina christiana* I.2.4: "All teaching is teaching of either things or signs, but things are learnt through signs." I.3.7: "There are some things which are to be enjoyed, some which are to be used, and some whose function is both to enjoy and use. Those which are to be enjoyed make us happy; those which are to be used assist us and give us a boost, so to speak, as we press on towards our happiness, so that we may reach and hold fast to the things which make us happy." ("Res ergo aliae sunt quibus fruendum est, aliae quibus utendum, aliae quae fruuntur et utuntur. Illae quibus fruendum est nos beatos faciunt; istis quibus utendum est tendentes ad beatitudinem adiuvamur et quasi adminiculamur, ut ad illas quae nos beatos faciunt pervenire atque his inhaerere possimus.") I.4.8: "To enjoy something is to hold fast to it in love for its own sake. To use something is to apply whatever it may be to the purpose of obtaining what you love – if indeed it is something that ought to be loved." ("Frui est enim amore inhaerere alicui rei propter se ipsam; uti autem, quod in usum venerit ad id quod amas obtinendum referre, si tamen amandum est.") And I.5.10: "The things which are to be enjoyed, then, are the Father and the Son and the Holy Spirit, and the Trinity comprised by them, which is a kind of single, supreme thing, shared by all who enjoy it." ("Res igitur quibus fruendum est, pater et filius et spiritus sanctus, eademque trinitas, una quaedam summa res communisque omnibus fruentibus ea.")

[18] *Omnium art.*, 14. To understand the significance of these categories – *praecepta, consilia, miracula,* and *exempla* – see the examples of the various *divisiones textus* of the books of the Bible in the chapter on Thomas's *resumptio*. These are the categories commonly used in those outlines.

[19] *Omnium art.*, 15.

[20] Ibid., 16.

[21] Ibid., 17. By calling the Scriptures the "measure" of the other sciences, Bonaventure was putting the Scriptures in the preeminent place that others would have said was occupied by metaphysics, especially Aristotelian metaphysics.

The Formal Cause: "Wisdom"

Bonaventure associates the formal cause of the Scriptures with the next word in his *thema*: *sapientia* ("wisdom"). Before he gets to his consideration of the fourfold dignity that follows from the excellence of its form, Bonaventure begins with some preliminaries to establish the nature of that excellence. First, he notes that the word in the *thema* is not "science" (*scientia*) but "wisdom" (*sapientia*), which signifies that the Scriptures are "higher in dignity" (*dignitate altior*), "more certain in truth" (*veritate certior*), and "superior in freedom" (*libertate potior*) than other authorities. By "superior in freedom," Bonaventure means that the Scriptures are better than other works at making humans free.[22]

Bonaventure follows this threefold list with another fourfold one. The Scriptures, he says, are "deiform in inspiration" (*deiformis inspiratione*), "luciform in erudition" (*luciformis eruditione*), "multiform in signification" (*multiformis significatione*), and "pulchriform in representation" (*pulchriformis in representatione*). The words "luciform" (*luciformis*) and "pulchriform" (*pulchriformis*) are Bonaventure's creations – they exist nowhere else in Latin – made by joining the roots *lux, lucis* ("light") or *pulchra, pulchris* ("beauty") with *forma* ("form, figure, appearance"). The Scriptures are "formed by God" (*deiformis*) because inspired by God. They are "formed with light" (*luciformis*) because they contain and communicate tremendous learning or erudition. They possess many forms (*multiformis*) because they have multiple means of signification and multiple senses. And so too the Scriptures possess a beautiful form (*pulchriformis*) in their expression. Considering both lists, we see again Bonaventure's rigorous application of the *sermo modernus* rule about strict parallelism; he applies it here even though it means creating words that do not exist and when a different locution might have been clearer.[23]

At this point we get another rumination on the nature of the *wisdom* of the Scriptures based on the description of wisdom in Wisdom 7.25–26, which says that "wisdom" is "a certain pure emanation" (*emanatio ... sincera*) "of the glory of the almighty God ... the brightness of eternal light" (*candor lucis aeternae*), "the unspotted mirror" (*speculum macula*) "of God's majesty, and the image of his goodness" (*imago bonitatis illius*). These descriptive phrases, applied to "wisdom" in their original biblical context, Bonaventure now applies to the Scriptures. The Scriptures are a "pure emanation," he says, because in them there is no mixture of human invention. They are "bright" or "radiant" (*candor*) because they are "the first impression of the divine illumination" (*prima impression divinae illustrationis*). They are a "mirror" (*speculum*), because they are a "certain description of the eternal disposition" (*certa descriptio aeternae dispositionis*); and they are an "image" (*imago*) because they are a "clear expression of future contemplation" (*clara expressio futurae contemplationis*).

Because the Scriptures express uncreated Wisdom, they possess no falsity (because they are pure emanation of God's glory), no duplicity (because they are bright light of truth about God), no dubiety (because they are an unspotted mirror of God's majesty), and no opacity (because they are a clear image and expression of the glory God has in store for mankind). Hence, "in the Scriptures there is most certain and inerrant truth, and so it is certain that whatever does not agree with them is undoubtedly false."[24]

---

[22] *Omnium art.*, 18.
[23] Ibid.
[24] Ibid.

In a *sermo modernus*–style sermon, a little section like this with its own *thema* verse and its own division and dilation would be called a *prothema*. Bonaventure is fond of inserting them into his sermons, where they are commonly found near the beginning of the sermon rather than somewhere in the middle. The *prothema* operates as a mini-*sermo modernus* style sermon of its own right after the statement of the *thema*. It can be confusing because it breaks the flow and continuity between the statement of the *thema*, the declaration of the parts of the *divisio*, and the beginning of the *dilatatio*. (Indeed, the structure of this entire section can be confusing, so readers may wish to consult the outline I have provided below.) Scholars are not entirely sure what the purpose of these *prothemata* were, but whatever the reason, it was a common occurrence. After it had concluded, the preacher would return to the structure he had outlined in his opening *thema* verse, which is precisely what Bonaventure does here.

From the excellence of the form of the Scriptures, says Bonaventure, a fourfold dignity results; they are "highest in principles" (*altissima in principiis*) because they have been inspired by God; "most certain in opinions" (*certissima in sententiis*) because their source is the highest; "most profound in mysteries" (*profundissima in mysteriis* because they express things in mystical figures; and yet "most plain in necessary things" (*planissima in necessariis*). Bonaventure uses the most space dilating the third of these – how the Scriptures are "most profound in mysteries" – because it allows him to describe the multiple senses of Scripture.

The Scriptures express things "in mystical figures" (*sub mysticis figuris*), says Bonaventure, in order to "exclude the unfaithful" (*infideles excludat*), "lead by the hand the faithful" (*fideles manuducat*), "train the seeking" (*quaerentes exerceat*), and "refresh the understanding" (*intelligentes reficiat*) – four categories Bonaventure borrowed from his favorite authority, St. Augustine, who in *The City of God* 15.25 had written: "But the Scriptures use such expressions, to alarm the proud (*terreat superbientes*), arouse the careless (*ecitet negligentes*), exercise the inquisitive (*exercitet quaerentes*) and satisfy the intelligent (*alat intelligentes*)."[25]

There are three causes of this marvelous "profundity" of the Scriptures: the multiplicity of their signification (*significatorum multiplicitas*); the limitlessness of their understanding (*intellectuum infinitas*); and the multiformity of their senses (*sensuum multiformitas*). A word of explanation is in order about each.

Regarding the first, the multiplicity of their signification (*significatorum multiplicitas*), Bonaventure notes that, in the Scriptures, many things signify: not only words, but also things (as the Passover bread signifies the Body of Christ) and properties (as the strength and support of a wall signifies the strength and support of God). On this view, *all* things point ultimately to God their Creator and Redeemer. So Bonaventure quotes the first book of Hugh of St. Victor's *On the Sacraments of the Christian Faith*: "Therefore, it is clear that all the arts serve this wisdom" – namely, the wisdom of the Scriptures.[26] Here Bonaventure

---

[25] Ibid., 22. Bonaventure abbreviated Augustine's original, quoting only four of the five categories.

[26] Once again, Bonaventure appears to be quoting from memory and hasn't gotten the passage quite right. Modern critical editions have: "Ex quo constat quod omnes artes naturales divinae scientiae famulantur." Bonaventure quotes it: "omnes artes huic sapentia famulantur." For a further development of this idea, see Bonaventure's *Reduction of the Arts to Theology*, the first version of which was delivered as his *resumptio* shortly after he delivered this *principium* address. We'll discuss Hugh's influence on that document in due course.

was giving his listeners a foretaste of the hierarchy of the arts which he would provide in his *resumptio* address, a text more commonly known to modern readers under the title *On the Reduction of the Arts to Theology*. We will have more to say on that topic in the next chapter.

The second cause of Scripture's profundity is the limitlessness of their understanding (*intellectuum infinitas*). No matter how much can be elicited by one exegete, there is always more that the Holy Spirit, the ultimate author of the Scriptures, understands – more even than what the human author originally intended. Hence Augustine, in *Confessions* 12.31–32 says of an Old Testament text:

> He [Moses], surely, when he wrote those words, perceived and thought whatever of truth we have been able to discover and whatever we have not been able, nor yet are able, though still it may be found in them. O Lord, if man does see anything less, can anything lie hidden from Your good Spirit, which You Yourself, by those words, were going to reveal to future readers, and if he, through whom they were spoken, amid the many interpretations thought of one alone?[27]

The third cause of the profundity of the Scriptures, related to the first two, is that they contain multiple senses. Bonaventure has quite a lot to say on this topic and develops the parts at some length. It has long been characteristic of exegetes to claim that one of the most profound, beautiful, and unique characteristics of the Sacred Scriptures is that they have multiple senses. In the Scriptures, not only the words signify, but also, since God is their author, and He is the Creator all things and providentially governs them, the things signified by the words can also signify. Just as God has spoken his Word eternally and then revealed Himself in and through Nature, so too He can communicate Himself and His will in and through the events of human history. No other author can do this in the same way. Human authors cannot speak in and through the events of history. By the thirteenth century, this set of presuppositions about the Scriptures was a commonplace among Christian scholars.

It is worth noting briefly here the roots of this tradition, how it developed, and how it was received in the thirteenth century. We can trace the origins of this tradition to the New Testament's account of Jesus and the use the New Testament authors made of Old Testament texts. As is well known, Paul and the other New Testament authors repeatedly cite Old Testament passages as "promises" fulfilled only in Christ. But just as important is the fact that, throughout the New Testament accounts of Christ, He is described as speaking words or doing things that signify. So, for example, in the account of the wedding at Cana, the wine steward tells the bridegroom: "Everyone serves the good wine first, and when people have drunk freely, then the poor wine. But you have kept the good wine until now" (John 2:10). The Gospel itself calls this "the first of Jesus's signs" (cf. John 2:11). The wine served first and the water Jesus transformed into the better wine is meant to *signify* the relationship between the Old Covenant and the New. So too in the accounts of the Last Supper, the *things* Christ employs – the bread and the wine – are meant simultaneously to

---

[27] *Omnium art.*, 24. Cf. Augustine, *Confessions*, 12.31.41 and 12.32.43.

hearken back to the Passover and the Exodus event as well as prefigure Christ's sacrificial death on the cross.

Due to the influence of Augustine's *On Christian Doctrine*, medieval Christian biblical exegetes came to understand the relationship between the words and events in terms of Augustine's distinction between *signs* and *things*. The words of the Scriptures signified certain things (bread and wine, used as part of a meal celebrated during Passover), and yet those things signified other things: Christ's body and blood on the Cross. Thus it was from Christ Himself and from the writings about Him in the New Testament that Christian exegetes learned to interpret the Scriptures *figuratively*. They learned to interpret the Scriptures figuratively from the Scriptures themselves.

But this approach to the Scriptures, this openness and eagerness to discover *figurative* meanings, had been mediated through generations of biblical exegetes so that by Bonaventure's time the general category of "figurative" had been specified into three categories. Along with the literal sense, there were the allegorical, the moral, and the anagogical. And, as we have seen, St. Augustine had analyzed the figurative senses in terms of the distinction between *signs* and *things*.

Words are a kind of *sign* (a conventional sign rather than a natural sign) that signify *things*. But according to Augustine, these *things* can also signify other *things*. In the Scriptures, when we seek to understand the first level of signification – the *things* signified by the *words* – this is the literal sense. When an exegete discovers that the *things* signified by the words signify other *things*, then we have one of the other "figurative" senses. When the word "Moses," for example, signifies the historical person Moses, this is the literal sense. When we come to believe that the person Moses is a prefiguration of Christ, this would be a figurative sense.

All this was common knowledge among theologians of the thirteenth century. The distinction between *signs* and *things* was central to medieval thought and practice. Medieval theologians such as Bonaventure and Thomas engaged in at least one figurative, sacramental act every day of their priesthood when they celebrated the Mass. It is not too much to say that theirs was a sacramental existence in which *signs* signifying *things* and those things signifying (or embodying) deeper realities was a daily experience.

So too, in their academic lives, the standard text on which all masters of theology were required to comment, the *Sentences* of Peter Lombard, was arranged based on this distinction between *signs* and *things*. The first three books dealt with "things" – "things to be enjoyed" (the Trinity), things to be used (creation), and things to be used and enjoyed (man, the angels, the virtues, and Christ) – and the fourth book dealt with *signs*, namely, the sacraments.

So to summarize: the "figurative" character of the Scriptures and the notion that the obscure promises of the Old Testament are revealed finally, most fully, in Christ was a way of thinking that traced its origins back to the Scriptures themselves and which was embodied in the sacramental practice of the Church. It was mediated to medieval theologians by the example of centuries of figurative exegesis and was during the thirteenth century understood primarily in the categories of *sign* and *thing* they had inherited from Augustine's *On Christian Doctrine*.

It is not without significance to our present study, therefore, to note that one of Bonaventure's favorite authors, one of his most influential authorities, along with St. Augustine, was the man sometimes described as *alter Augustinus*, "another

Augustine," the great twelfth-century theologian Hugh of St. Victor. One of Hugh's most prominent works was *On the Sacraments of the Christian Faith*, a book that deals with more than the seven sacraments of the Catholic Church and is, rather, a synthesis of all theology, beginning with chapters on the Sacred Scriptures and how they are to be read and interpreted.[28] It is no surprise, then, that the first authoritative text Bonaventure cites to establish the "excellence of the form" of Scripture because of its multiple senses is from the first book of Hugh of St. Victor's *On the Sacraments*:

> Wherefore, it is apparent how much Divine Scripture excels all other writings in subtlety and profundity, not only in its subject matter but also in its method of treatment, since indeed in other writings words alone are found to have meaning, but in it not only words, but also things are significant. Hence, just as wherever the sense between words and things is uncertain, the knowledge of words is necessary, so in the case of that which exists between things and mystical acts done or to be done, the knowledge of things is necessary.[29]

Traditionally, the four senses are listed as the literal, the allegorical, the moral or tropological, and the anagogical. Bonaventure repeats this traditional division. What is unique is the way he associates each of the four senses with the four creatures from Ezekiel 1: the man, the lion, the ox, and the eagle. These four creatures were traditionally associated with the four evangelists: the man with Matthew; the lion with Mark; the ox with Luke, and the eagle with John. Bonaventure, however, associates the historical sense with the ox, "because of its simplicity"; the allegorical sense with the lion, "because of its authority", the tropological sense with the man "because of its civility" (*propter civilitatem*) – by which I take it he means because of its power to make men civilized; and finally, the anagogical sense, which he associates with the eagle, "because of its sublimity."

Bonaventure finishes his disquisition on the multiple meanings of the Scriptures with this quotation from St. Augustine:

> For such is the depth of the Christian Scriptures, that even if I were attempting to study them and nothing else from early boyhood to decrepit old age, with the utmost leisure, the most unwearied zeal, and talents greater than I have, I would be still daily making progress in discovering their treasures; not that there is so great difficulty in coming

---

[28] See Hugh of St. Victor, *On the Sacraments of the Christian Faith*, trans. Roy J. Deferrari (Medieval Academy of America, 1951; repr. Eugene, OR: Wipf & Stock, 2005), esp. 3–7.

[29] *Omnium art.*, 23. Bonaventure refers to the passage only by quoting a few words, and these he does not quote with complete accuracy, which suggests he is quoting from memory and presupposing that his audience knows the passage to which he is alluding. See Hugh of St. Victor, *De Sacramentis* I.5: "Unde apparet quantum divina Scriptura caeteris omnibus scripturis non solum in materia sua, sed etiam in modo tractandi, subtilitate et profunditate praecellat; cum in caeteris quidem scripturis solae voces significare inveniantur; in hac autem non solum voces, sed etiam res significativae sint. Sicut igitur in eo sensu qui inter voces et res versatur necessaria est cognitio vocum, sic in illo qui inter res et facta vel facienda mystica constat, necessaria est cognitio rerum." It should be no surprise, then, additionally, that Bonaventure based his *resumptio* on another of Hugh's major works: the *Didascalicon*.

through them to know the things necessary to salvation, but when any one has accepted these truths with the faith that is indispensable as the foundation of a life of piety and uprightness, so many things which are veiled under manifold shadows of mystery remain to be inquired into by those who are advancing in the study, and so great is the depth of wisdom not only in the words in which these have been expressed, but also in the things themselves, that the experience of the oldest, the ablest, and the most zealous students of Scripture illustrates what Scripture itself has said: "When a man hath done, then he beginneth."[30]

After this long intervention on the multiple senses of Scripture, Bonaventure arrives finally at his fourth category under "excellence of the form." The Scriptures are, he says, "most plain in necessary things." Why does he leave this point for last, *after* he has provided us with a long discussion of the multiple senses of the Scriptures? His point, I take it, is this: Although the Scriptures can be complex, containing multiple senses and profound meanings, yet they always speak plainly and teach clearly about those things necessary for salvation. The Scriptures are not merely a book of mysteries for the elite. They contain wisdom for the simple. Referring to 1 Corinthians 3:2, Bonaventure concludes: "Hence just as I feed the perfect with solid food, so the simple are fed here with milk, because in a simple style things necessary for salvation are proposed."[31]

The contrast Bonaventure makes here between the *complexity* and the *simplicity* of the Scriptures is analogous to one he made earlier in his discussion of the material cause of the Scriptures between their *breadth* and their underlying *unity*. The *breadth* of the Scriptures, claimed Bonaventure, was wide enough to cover all things and all the disciplines, including physics, ethics, and logic. And not only every truth, but all good. And yet, the Scriptures, as broad and diverse as they are, containing books of all genres written centuries apart, also possess a fundamental *unity*. They are unified, first, because everything in them directs us to our one proper end: namely, God. They are unified, second, because they contain everything we need to achieve that end. Our victory was complete with the sacrifice of Christ. They are unified, third, because all the things contained in them refer ultimately to God. And they are unified, fourth, because the Scriptures consider everything "as vestiges by participation in the divine being" – vestiges meant to lead us back to their Source and ours.

We might say that in affirming both the *complexity* and *simplicity* of the Scriptures, on the one hand, as well as their *breadth* and *unity*, on the other, Bonaventure was claiming for the Scriptures a quality St. Paul claimed for himself when he claimed that he had "become all things to all people" so that "by all possible means" he might save some (cf. 1 Cor 9:19–22). There is material in the Scriptures complex enough to enthrall the students of the Arts limitlessly and yet simple enough to teach the uneducated and lead them to their proper end with God.

On outline of this long and complex section of Bonaventure's *principium* would look like shown in Box 10.2.

---

[30] *Omnium art.*, 26. Cf. Augustine, *Epistula* 137, para. 3.
[31] *Omnium art.*, 27.

> **Box 10.2** Outline of Bonaventure's *Omnium Artifex Sapientia*
>
> *Omnium artifex **sapientia** (wisdom)*: The evidence of the form is shown from the uniqueness of the mode: it possesses the "certitude" of truth.
>
> From the excellence of the form, which we call wisdom itself, a fourfold dignity follows. It is
>
> 1. Highest in principles: which by supernatural light are naturally above things known: articles of faith, inspired and revealed by God
> 2. Most certain in opinions
> 3. Most profound in mysteries, which contains under mystical figures to exclude the infidel, lead faithful by the hand, exercise the seeking, satisfy the intelligent
>   a. The first cause of this profundity is the multiplicity of their signification, namely: "of voices, of things, of properties," as Hugh teaches in the first book of *De sacramentis*; from this he concludes that "all the arts are servants of this wisdom."
>   b. The second cause is the limitlessness of their understanding
>   c. The third cause is the multiformity of their senses:
>   i. Literal: what was done (the ox, which represents its simplicity): contains precepts, counsels, miracles, examples
>   ii. Allegory: what is to be believed (the lion, which represents its authority): deals with our humanity assumed, the glorious Virgin, and the "church militant"
>   iii. Tropology: what bearing one should have (the human person, which represents its bearing on our civility): deals with spiritual grace, the spiritual life, spiritual warfare, and the "church spiritual"
>   iv. Anagogy: for what one should hope (the eagle, which represents its sublimity): deals with uncreated essence, exemplary wisdom, angelic sublimity, and the "church triumphant"
> 4. Most plain in necessary things

The Final Cause: Teaching for Happiness

The last of the four causes is the final cause, or purpose, which, as we saw earlier, Bonaventure has associated with the remaining words in his opening *thema*: *docuit me* ("he teaches me"). Thus, what the reader will find in the first sentences of this final section of the *principium* (section 28) are numerous references to teaching. The final cause of the Scriptures, says Bonaventure, is the final cause of doctrine (or "teaching" from the Latin *doctrinae*). As St. Paul says in Romans 15:4: "For what things soever were written, were written for our doctrine" (*quaecumque enim scripta sunt ad nostram **doctrinam** scripta sunt*). The utility of this teaching, says Bonaventure – its end or fruit – is "happiness of life, to which end all the sciences tend" (*vitae Felicitas, ad quam finem licet tendant omnes scientiae*).

Following the pattern he has established of offering four subdivisions in each section, Bonaventure identifies in the Scriptures a fourfold utility for attaining the end of happiness. They offer "cognition of the truth" (*cognitio veritatis*), "argumentation against falsity" (*argumentatio falsitatis*), "reproof of iniquity" (*correptio iniquitatis*), and the "building up of charity" (*eruditio caritatis*). He has borrowed this fourfold division from a well-known passage in 2 Timothy 3:16–17, in which St. Paul says: "All Scripture, inspired of God, is profitable for teaching (*docendum*), reproving (*arguendum*), correcting (*corrigendum*), and instructing (*erudiendum*) in justice, that the man of God may be perfect, furnished for every good work."[32] Human cognition is perfected when it arrives at truth and excludes every falsity. The Scriptures offer truth and reject every falsity. By extirpating every evil and perfecting the good, the Scriptures help perfect the affections.

Although Bonaventure had spent a great deal of time in previous sections dilating each of his four sub-sections, and although this last section deals with the end or goal of the Scriptures, a subject about which we might have expected him to have a lot to say, this final section is relatively brief. Bonaventure may have run out of time. Whereas his dilation of the word *artifex* ("maker") and the efficient cause of the work fills six full pages of text, his dilation of this final section takes up less than two. After stating the fourfold utility and quoting the passage from 2 Timothy 3:16, he barely has enough time to wrap things up with a quotation from his favorite authority, St. Augustine.

> Wisdom seems to me to be not only knowledge of the human and divine matters that are relevant to the happy life but also the diligent search for it; so that however much he tends more tranquilly to God, also on the final day of his life, he is found to be ready to attain what he desired, and having thoroughly enjoyed human happiness, he deservedly enjoys divine happiness.[33]

And with that, he is finished.

Cutting a sermon or presentation short was not unknown among thirteenth-century preachers.[34] And University regulations stipulated that the *principium* address was to be "brief" and "quickly terminated." Though much longer than Thomas's, Bonaventure's *principium* was not much longer than most other masters. And yet, at a certain point, perhaps he simply had to wrap things up. Bonaventure may have found he had run too long speaking about the multiple senses of Scripture and decided to cut short this final section.

---

[32] I have supplied the Latin terms Bonaventure would have found in his Vulgate Bible.
[33] Bonaventure may be quoting from memory, so he ends up eliding three places in Augustine's original text. See Augustine, *Contra academicos* I.8.23. The original reads: "Wisdom seems to me to be not only knowledge of the human and divine matters that are relevant to the happy life but also the diligent search for it. If you want to split up this account, the first part, which embraces knowledge, belongs to God, whereas the latter, which remains content with the search, belongs to man. God, then, is happy in the former condition. Man is happy in the latter. By the very fact that he is searching, he is wise. He is happy in being wise, since he frees his mind as far as he can from all the wrappings of the body and gathers himself within himself. He doesn't allow himself to be torn to pieces by his desires. Instead, he is always tranquil. He turns toward himself and toward God, so that even here he makes full use of his reason, and we agreed above that this is happiness. And on the final day of his life, he is found to be ready to attain what he desired, and having thoroughly enjoyed human happiness, he deservedly enjoys divine happiness."
[34] See, for example, Thomas Aquinas's Sermon 20 (*Beata gens*). Thomas began by making a fourfold *divisio* of his opening *thema* verse, intending in the morning's sermon and evening *collatio* to commend the saints in four ways: first, for their dignity; second, for their leader (Christ); third, for their virtues; and fourth, for their election. Although he finished the first two divisions in the morning's sermon, he got so caught up describing the virtues of the saints at that evening's vespers, he left himself no time to discuss their election.

But consider what can be recalled by calling to mind the opening *thema*: *Artifex omnium sapientia docuit me*. The *efficient cause* or author of the Scriptures is God, who is the ultimate maker (*artifex*). The *material cause* or subject matter of the Scriptures is "all things" (*omnium*), especially those things necessary for man's salvation. The unique *form* of the Scriptures that allows them to communicate wisdom (*sapientia*) better than all other texts is that they communicate in multiple senses: literal, allegorical, tropological, and anagogical. And the *final cause* – the goal or end – of the Scriptures is to teach mankind (*docuit me*) and, by teaching, to bring them to happiness and eternal life with God.

Although both Thomas and Bonaventure were required by University statute to deliver a "commendation of Sacred Scripture," and both employed the *sermo modernus* style, the results were very different. Thomas's gifts were clarity and conciseness; Bonaventure's were a highly developed style and extraordinary verbal fluency. And although Thomas is often associated with the "scholastic" style and quotations from numerous "authorities" such as Aristotle, Avicenna, Gregory the Great, and Augustine, it was *Bonaventure* who quoted all the non-Scriptural authorities, not Thomas. Both men were still relatively young scholars. Indeed Thomas was younger than the University regulations permitted when he incepted. Both were to have very different futures and write works of a very different character. But their respective *principia* reveal the degree to which both were formed in the same academic culture at the University of Paris – a culture of *disputatio*, no doubt, but also one devoted to forming good preachers for the laity who could, if called upon to do so, write a suitable protreptic prologue when they were required to lecture on a book of the Bible. It was, in short, a culture of the three arts of the master: *disputatio*, *lectio*, and *praedicatio*. For our own reasons, we may have wished to focus exclusively on the first of these: *disputatio*.[35] It is equally important to recognize, however, that the greatest of masters, men like Aquinas and Bonaventure, did not.

---

[35] There is much that could be said about how the origins of the modern recovery of medieval thought brought about by Pope Leo XIII's 1879 encyclical *Aeterni Patris* ended up, for historical reasons and undoubtedly with good intentions, being directed primarily at deriving good *arguments* to defend the faith against post-Enlightenment, nineteenth century rationalism. There was less interest in recovering the heritage of medieval preaching and biblical commentary. An extended discussion of this topic is obviously beyond the scope of the present work.

11

Bonaventure's *Resumptio*

An Early Attempt to Think through the Hierarchy of the Sciences

AFTER THEIR *principium in aula* address, masters incepting at the University of Paris in the thirteenth century were required to give another address the next day. In this second address, the incepting master customarily would set forth a detailed *divisio textus* of all the books of the Bible, usually after another short *sermo modernus* style "commendation" of the Scriptures. Stephen of Besançon, who incepted as master of theology at Paris in 1286, stated at the beginning of his *resumptio* address:

> In the *principium* of a science or a book, the intention of doctors is accustomed to touch on two things. They are accustomed first to commend the science in order to have benevolent listeners (*auditores benevolos*). Also, they are accustomed to treat the causes and offer a general division in order to render them [their listeners] docile and attentive (*dociles et attentos*). Yesterday we showed, from the word proposed [i.e., the *thema* verse], that Sacred Scripture is commendable and surpasses all others [i.e., other sciences]. Now the causes will be treated and the division of the books...[1]

Nancy Spatz comments that "Stephen's inception speech shows that a *principium in aula* typically contained a commendation of Scripture and a comparison of Scripture to other fields of study, while the *principium* at the resumption contained a division of the books of the Bible and an analysis of Scripture."[2]

Stephen was following the usual practice, as had Thomas Aquinas and nearly every other master of theology at the University of Paris since its beginnings. Until Bonaventure. Bonaventure chose a substantially different approach. Instead of comparing Scripture to the other fields of study in his *principium*, he did so in his *resumptio*, and this extended

---

[1] English translation quoted from Nancy Spatz, *Principia: A study and edition of inception speeches delivered before the faculty of theology at the University of Paris, ca. 1180–1286* (PhD diss., Cornell University, 1992), "Galdericus," 136; see also n. 13 for the Latin text. Aquinas made use of the same threefold *divisio* in his *resumptio*.
[2] Spatz, *Principia*, 136.

discussion replaced the traditional division of the books of the Bible. Yet, as we will see, this approach still achieved the ultimate goal of the *resumptio* address, by commending the sacred Scriptures in relation to other fields of study.

The First Version of the *De Reductione Artium ad Theologiam*

The text that Bonaventure used at his *resumptio* was, as Joshua C. Benson has shown, an early version of a work scholars used to think came from late in Bonaventure's career: the *De Reductione Artium ad Theologiam* ("On the Reduction of the Arts to Theology").[3] A quick comparison of the Latin version of the *De Reductione* in the Quaracchi edition with the critical edition of Bonaventure's *resumptio* published by Benson reveals that the sole difference is the first paragraph.[4]

Bonaventure's *resumptio* begins, in proper *sermo modernus* style, with a reference back to the *thema* verse he used for his *principium*: *Omnium artifex docuit me sapientia* ("Wisdom, the maker of all things, taught me"). In his *principium* Bonaventure associated the efficient cause of the Scriptures with the word *artifex* ("maker"), the material cause or subject matter with the word *omnium* ("of all things"), the formal cause with the word *sapientia* ("wisdom"), and the final cause with the word *docuit me* ("teaches me"). Here in his *resumptio*, Bonaventure refers back to that earlier address, saying "I, in my approach to the divine, resume the material cause of the canon, the division of which by the form was noted in the word *omnium* [i.e., in the *thema* verse]."[5]

As we have noted, university regulations required a master to use the same *thema* verse at the evening vespers service that he had preached on earlier that morning. So using a word from an earlier *thema* verse to bridge the transition from one address to the other would not

---

[3] See Joshua C. Benson, "Identifying the Literary Genre of the *De reductione artium ad theologiam*: Bonaventure's Inaugural Lecture at Paris," *Franciscan Studies* 67 (2009): 149–178; and Bonaventure's *De reductione artium ad theologiam* and Its Early Reception as an Inaugural Sermon," *American Catholic Philosophical Quarterly* 85 (2011): 7–24. For a different view, see the Introduction by Zachary Hayes, O.F.M., in *St. Bonaventure's On the Reduction of the Arts to Theology*, Works of St. Bonaventure, vol. 1 (St. Bonaventure, NY: Franciscan Institute, 1996), 3: "J. Bougeral suggests that this may well have been the final work of Bonaventure in which he summarized what he had been attempting to do in much greater detail in the *Collations on the Hexaemeron*. However we try to resolve the question of dating, the fact is that this text hardly seems to be an immature work."

[4] The Quaracchi editors seem to have known of this manuscript, but because the first paragraph was different from nearly all of the other manuscripts of the *De reductione* they had identified, they assumed it was an aberrant copy. It was Prof. Benson's genius to realize that the manuscript contained Bonaventure's *principium* and *resumptio* addresses. In addition to the two articles by Benson cited in n. 3, see Joshua Benson, "Bonaventure's Inaugural Sermon at Paris: *Omnium Artifex Docuit Me Sapientia*: Introduction and Text," *Collectanea franciscana* 82 (2012): 517–562.

[5] The Latin for the first paragraph of Bonaventure's *resumptio* has been taken from the text found in Benson, "*Omnium Artifex*," 552–553. All English translations of the *resumptio* are mine. Throughout the remainder of this chapter, however, although I have checked Prof. Benson's Latin text of the *resumptio* against the Latin text of the *De reductione artium ad theologiam* found in vol. 5 of the Quaracchi edition of Bonaventure's *Opera Omnia*, I have quoted the Latin text from the Quaracchi, and this for two reasons. First, the Quaracchi version is, at this moment, the more standard, critically accepted version of the text. And second, its greater accessibility is a boon to readers who might want to check the Latin.

have been considered odd. When Bonaventure mentioned the word *omnium* in conjunction with "I resume the material cause of the canon," his audience, nearly all of whom would have been present the previous day, would have known that he was referring to his discussion of the material cause or subject matter of the Scriptures in his *principium* address, where he associated the word *omnium* with the subject matter of the Scriptures because the Scriptures deal with "all things." He argued that the Scriptures are superior to the other sciences because, whereas the other sciences treat one subject and make use of a variety of authorities, the Scriptures offer a clear and true perspective about the whole of reality in one book. And whereas the other sciences depend on the principles of being that are proper to them, the Scriptures consider uniformly all things as a "vestige" and "participation" of the divine being (*uniformiter considerat omnia sub ratione vestigii ex participatione esse divini*). For this reason, the sacred Scriptures provide the highest knowledge of the first principle of all things and can serve as a "measure" (*mensura*) of all the other sciences.

It made sense for Bonaventure to hearken back to this particular section of his *principium* for two reasons: first, because the theme just mentioned – the relationship between the Scriptures and the other sciences – will be the subject of his *resumptio*, and second, because in his *principium*, he associated the word *omnium* with the subject matter of the Scriptures, and the *divisio* of that subject matter was ostensibly to be one of the key features of any *resumptio*. Bonaventure had something slightly different in mind, however.

Having recalled the word *omnium* ("of all things") from his previous day's *principium* address, Bonaventure makes use of it repeatedly at the outset of his *resumptio*.

> And I divide **all things** (*omnia*) in the whole canon in two: namely, in two testaments. And so commenting on this verse from The Song of Songs, "The new and the old, I have kept for you," we read in a gloss: "Promises of each testament." But I distinguish the New Testament [sic] into three parts, according to the threefold division the Savior makes in the book of Luke: "It is necessary to fulfill **all things** (*omnia*) which are written in the law and the prophets and the Psalms concerning me. Because **all truth** (*omnis veritas*) is sought in the light of the First Cause."[6]

The Scriptures contain "all things," but they are divided into parts. This would seem to have been the perfect transition into the standard *divisio textus* of the books of the Bible.

And in fact, Bonaventure begins as though just such a *divisio* was what he intended to undertake. As every master before him had done, he first distinguishes the whole of the Bible into two basic parts: the Old and New Testaments. He then seems to divide the *New* Testament into three parts – the *law*, the *prophets*, and the *Psalms* – but we have to imagine he meant the *Old* Testament or *both* Testaments.[7] This distinction among the Old Testament books was well known at the time. One finds it, for example, in John of La

---

[6] Cf. Benson, "*Omnium Artifex*," 552, n. 30. Emphases mine.

[7] See the outlines of the *divisio textus* done by each of these masters in the Appendix. We compared Thomas's *divisio textus* with these masters in Chapter 5. A close reading will reveal that Bonaventure says that this threefold distinction characterizes the *New* Testament. Although most masters applied this distinction primarily to the Old, a quick glance back at the *divisio* of Matthew of Aquasparta reveals that he, among others, found it desirable to envision a parallel between the Old and New Testaments, with some version of law, prophets, and Psalms in both.

Rochelle's *resumptio*, written twenty years before Bonaventure's inception, and in Henry of Ghent's, written twenty years after.

But having signaled that he might be starting the customary *divisio textus*, Bonaventure switches gears abruptly, using a passage from Augustine's *Soliloquies* to facilitate his transition.

> "It is necessary to fulfill all things which are written in the law and the prophets and the Psalms concerning me" – which is the truth. Because all truth is sought in the light of the First Cause, according to what Augustine says in the first book of the *Soliloquies*: "Therefore," he says, "as in this visible sun we may observe three things: that it is, etc." [that it shines, that it illuminates: so in that God most far withdrawn whom you would wish to apprehend, there are these three things: that He is, that He is apprehended, and that He makes other things to be apprehended].[8]

Note that "all that is written in the law, the prophets, and the Psalms" is *fulfilled* in Christ, not merely because He fulfills the prophecies and promises contained therein thereby validating their truth, but also because He is the Truth who illumines all human knowing. Just we can see visible things only when illumined by the light of the sun, so too, on Bonaventure's account, we can only *know* things when illumined by the intellectual "light" of the Son, the Word "through whom all things were made," the First Cause of all created things. Hence "all truth," says Bonaventure, "is sought in the light of the First Cause."

Here Bonaventure is likely once again hearkening back to key elements from his previous day's *principium*, where he affirmed that the "author" or efficient cause of the Scriptures is our "Maker" (*artifex*) and that what the Maker "teaches" us is not merely "science" (*scientia*) but "wisdom" (*sapientia*). In that *principium* address, "wisdom" (*sapientia*) was associated with the excellence of the *form* of the Scriptures, because, according to Bonaventure, they are (1) highest in principles, (2) most certain in opinions, (3) most profound in mysteries, and (4) most plain in necessary things. Under item 3, the *profundity* of the Scriptures, Bonaventure argued that the "first cause" of their profundity is the "multiplicity of their signification." This, he says, is what Hugh of St. Victor teaches in the first book of *De sacramentis*, from which he (Hugh) concluded that "all the arts are servants of this wisdom." As we will see, Hugh's work, especially his understanding of the relationship between the Scriptures and the other disciplines, will play a key role in the remainder of Bonaventure's *resumptio*.

The passage from Augustine's *Soliloquies* about the sun sets up an analogy between the three actions of the physical sun – it exists, it shines, and it illuminates – and three things we can say about God: He exists; He "shines forth," revealing Himself in such a way that He is apprehended; and He "illuminates" other things so they can be apprehended. The

---

[8] I have included the whole passage from Augustine's *Soliloquies*, even though in the original manuscript, Bonaventure provides only the first several words followed by "et cetera," suggesting he could quote the text from memory and needed only those first words to help bring to mind the text he intended to use. "Necesse est impleri omnia quae scripta sunt in lege et prophetis et psalmis de me. Quod est verum. Quoniam omnis veritas quaeritur in lumine primae causae, secundum quod ait Augustinus primo *Soliloquiorum*: 'Sicut – inquit – in isto sole tria quedam licet advertere', et cetera." Although Bonaventure may have known the entire verse by memory, most of us do not, so I have taken the liberty of supplying the missing text in brackets.

only obvious connection between Bonaventure's earlier mention of the threefold distinction between "law, prophets, and Psalms," and the quotation from Augustine's *Soliloquies* is that both involve "three." Yet, this similarity is enough for Bonaventure's purposes. The quotation from Augustine's *Soliloquies* establishes an analogy between material light and intellectual illumination, which is important because Bonaventure intends to show that the Scriptures, which contain "all things" in its two testaments and in the law, prophets, and Psalms, are an essential source of *intellectual* illumination.

Developing this analogy between material and intellectual light, Bonaventure generates another threefold distinction between the different kinds of mental or spiritual light, which he then relates to the "light" of the sacred Scriptures. There is, first, the exterior light of the mechanical arts (*exterius artis scilicet artis mechanicae*), the inferior light of the sensitive cognition (*cognitionis sensitivae*), and the interior light of philosophical cognition (*cognitionis philosophicae*). Above these three is the superior light (*superius*) of sacred Scripture.

We find an interesting textual conundrum in the next sentence, though. Allow me to quote the Latin text in full: "Hoc illuminat nos respectu figurae artificialis, formae naturalis, veritatis intellectualis, veritatis salutaris." Translating literally, we get: "This illuminates us with respect to artificial figures, natural forms, intellectual truth, and saving truth." The question is to what "this" (*hoc*) refers?

In this list, "artificial figures" (*figurae artificialis*) are clearly meant to be associated with the mechanical arts; "natural forms" (*formae naturalis*) with the sensitive cognition; and "intellectual truth" (*veritatis intellectualis*) with philosophical cognition. But the text does not say "these" illuminate us" (*haec illuminant nos*), only "this" illuminates us. By "this," I take it Bonaventure means the "superior" light of the sacred Scriptures which, in addition to illuminating us with regard to artificial figures, natural forms, and intellectual truth, also illuminates us with regard to "saving truth" (*veritatis salutaris*). So although the other lower "lights" illuminate us, each in its own way, the Scriptures illuminate us with respect to all of these *and* regarding our salvation.

Interpreting the singular *hoc* here as referring to the Scriptures makes sense if we recall Bonaventure's dilation of the Latin word *ominium* in his *principium*, to which he himself has referred his listeners already. There he associated *omnium* with the "breadth" of the Scriptures, because they contain "all things." They contain this breadth, however, as the reader may recall, within a unity: one book. And from that unity, a fourfold utility followed: (1) a utility of comprehension, because everything necessary to bring us to our end is contained there; (2) a utility of total perfection, because our salvation and ultimate end is achieved by Christ; (3) a utility and unity of attribution, because everything contained in the Scriptures refers us to God; and (4) a utility in its unity of consideration because the Scriptures consider uniformly all things as a "vestige" and participation in the divine being while other sciences consider only singular things according to the causes that make them to be what they are.

Thus in both his *principium* and his *resumptio*, will find Bonaventure delivering much the same message. Contrary to the view that holds that the Scriptures tell us about salvation but have nothing of importance to say about any of the other branches of knowledge, Bonaventure insists that the Scriptures can illumine us regarding *all things*. It is the "measure" of the other disciplines. One "sees" the objects of these other disciplines fully and properly only when they are "seen" in – when they are "illumined" by – the light of the sacred Scriptures.

Why Did Bonaventure Change His Opening Paragraph?

These four "lights" – the exterior, inferior, interior, and superior lights – corresponding to the mechanical arts, sensitive cognition, philosophical knowing, and the light of divine revelation – are exactly the ones we find in the standard editions of the *De Reductione*. Why, then, did Bonaventure revise this opening paragraph when he published it later as an independent treatise?

Let's look first at the later, revised opening of the treatise. Here is the first paragraph of the standard text of the *De Reductione* translated from the critical edition in volume 5 of the Quaracchi edition:

> *Every good gift and every perfect gift is from above, coming down from the God of Lights*, writes James in the first chapter of his epistle. This text speaks of the source of all illumination; but at the same time, it suggests that there are many lights which flow generously from that fontal source of light. Even though every illumination of knowledge is internal, still we can reasonably distinguish what may be called an *exterior* light, or the light of mechanical art; an *inferior* light, or the light of sense perception; an *interior* light, or the light of philosophical knowledge; and a *superior* light, or the light of grace and of Sacred Scripture. The first light illumines with respect to the *forms of artifacts*; the second, with respect to *natural forms*; the third, with respect to *intellectual truth*; the fourth and last, with respect to *saving truth*.[9]

Note what Bonaventure has done. First, he added an entirely new *thema* verse. In his *resumptio*, the first paragraph referred back to the *thema* verse had used in his earlier *principium* address, in particular to his comments about the "material cause" of the Scriptures, which he associated with the word *omnium*. In the original version of his *resumptio*, Bonaventure was simply "resuming" a train of thought from a previous address the way a university preacher was required, at the evening vespers service, to resume his train of thought from the morning Mass using the same *thema* verse. When he published his *resumptio* separately, as the text we have come to know as *On the Reduction of the Arts to Theology*, Bonaventure knew that his readers would not have already heard his *principium* address, so they would lack the context necessary to understand his references to the word *ominium* in the first paragraph when he used this text as his *resumptio*.

So he revised his opening paragraph, which also solved several unfortunate problems in his original. In the first paragraph of his *resumptio*, Bonaventure used the quotation from

---

[9] *Omne datum optimum et omne donum perfectum desursum est, descendens a Patre luminum*, Iacobus in Epistolae suae primo capitulo (James 1:17). In hoc verbo tangitur origo omnis illuminationis, et simul cum hoc insinuatur multiplicis luminis ab illa fontali luce liberalis emanatio. Licet autem omnis illuminatio cognitionis interna sit, possumus tamen rationabiliter distinguere, ut dicamus, quod est lumen *exterius*, scilicet lumen artis mechanicae; lumen *inferius*, scilicet lumen cognitionis sensitivae; lumen *interius*, scilicet lumen cognitionis philosophicae; lumen *superius*, scilicet lumen gratiae et sacrae Scripturae. Primum lumen illuminat respectu *figurae artificialis*, secundum respectu *formae naturalis*; tertium respectu *veritatis intellectualis*, quartum et ultimum respectu *veritatis salutaris*. English translations of the *De reductione* (and thus of all sections of the *resumptio* after the first paragraph) are taken from Zachary Hayes, O.F.M., trans., *St. Bonaventure's* On the Reduction of the Arts to Theology, Works of St. Bonaventure, vol. 1 (St. Bonaventure, NY: Franciscan Institute, 1996). Italics are in the original.

Augustine's *Soliloquies* to suggest that there is a "threefold light" (*triplex lumen*), but then proceeded to list *four* lights: exterior, inferior, interior, and superior. One might argue that the *superior* light of sacred Scripture is the "sun" from which the other lights are derived, but this interpretation won't work, because, as Bonaventure himself made clear in his *principium* address, the sacred Scriptures are a reflection of the Word of God. As such, they cannot be the originating light or "the sun." Only the Son can be "the sun" in this analogy. And even if we could find some pretext for justifying the extension from three lights to four, it seems legitimate to expect a good preacher to signal to his audience why he made the shift. Preaching manuals of the day insisted that good preachers were not to leave listeners guessing in this way. Once you said "three," you were supposed to give a list of three. If you stopped after two, then this was considered a mistake.[10] The four "lights" – exterior, inferior, interior, and superior – were likely tied in Bonaventure's mind to his theory of illumination, but that connection was not made explicit in his *resumptio*. So there were good reasons for Bonaventure to revise the first paragraph of his first version.

In the revised version, Bonaventure inserted an entirely new *thema* verse from James 1.17: "Every good gift and every perfect gift is from above, coming down from the God of Lights." This verse, a favorite of one of Bonaventure's heroes, Hugh of St. Victor, does better service for him. As Bonaventure himself points out, this verse suggests that "there are many lights which flow generously from one fontal source of light." And although Bonaventure does not do the customary *divisio* of this verse, he dilates it in a common way, by taking the word "light" and distinguishing a fourfold subdivision: exterior, inferior, interior, and superior. Having gotten to this fourfold list, he was able to leave out everything else he had used in the opening paragraph of his *resumptio*. Gone is the passage from Aristotle's *De anima*; gone is the verse from the Song of Songs and the gloss on it; gone is the quotation from Augustine's *Soliloquies*. He replaced all of this complicated apparatus with a single verse from the New Testament. It was an elegant solution to his problem.

The Question of the Hierarchy of the Sciences

Bonaventure's substitution – from setting forth a *divisio textus* of the books of the Bible to a discussion of the division of the arts and sciences and their relationship to Sacred Scripture – was a bold move and may have been unprecedented. We know of two masters who within the next five years took a similar approach in their inception addresses: Guy of Aumône, the first Cistercian master of theology at Paris, who incepted in 1256, and Galdericus, the first Cluniac master at Paris, who incepted in 1259. But Bonaventure may have been the first.[11]

[10] So too, for example, if you used the image of a house and said that the house had foundation, roof, and walls, you weren't supposed to comment only on "the foundation" and "the walls," leaving your listeners to guess, "What happened to the roof?" On this, see Robert Baesevorn, *Forma praedicandi*, 33, and R. Smith, *Reading the Sermons of Aquinas: A Beginner's Guide* (Steubenville, OH: Emmaus, 2016), 60–61.

[11] For a brief description of Guy of Aumône, see Spatz, 103–107; for Galdericus, see Spatz, 111–117. For a longer description of Galdericus's *principium* address, see Nancy Spatz, "A Newly Identified Text: The Inception Speech of Galdericus, First Cluniac Regent Master of Theology at the University of Paris," *Archives d'histoire doctrinale et littéraire du moyen âge* 61 (1994): 133–147. For the text of

There is abundant evidence that the hierarchy of the sciences was much on the minds of masters at the time. Not only did Bonaventure, Guy, and Galdericus, each from a different religious order, pursue the same question in their inception addresses, but Thomas Aquinas, in one of his earliest treatises as a master, his *Commentary on Boethius's De Trinitate* (1257–1258), attempted to set forth his own vision of the hierarchy of the sciences.[12]

Boethius exerted a major influence on these discussions in the thirteenth century. Fr. James Weisheipl, one of the greatest modern authorities in this area, reports the three sources with the greatest influence on the development of the classification of the sciences in the thirteenth century were (1) "the Greco-Roman heritage of a liberal arts education"; (2) "the profound influence of Manlius Boethius"; and (3) the twelfth- and thirteenth-century translations from the Greek and Arabic, which helped make this schema intelligible to the Latins."[13]

The earliest Latin classification and exposition of the liberal arts seems to have been Terence Varro's *Disciplinarum libri IX* (116–27 BC). Varro's list of the arts included these nine: grammar, dialectics, rhetoric, geometry, arithmetic, astrology, music, medicine, and architecture. As a pragmatic Roman, Varro envisioned the liberal arts as preparations for the study of the more practical arts of medicine and architecture. These more pragmatic arts were dropped from later lists, leaving the classic seven liberal arts of the *trivium* (grammar, rhetoric, and logic) and *quadrivium* (geometry, arithmetic, astronomy, and music).

By the time Bonaventure composed his *resumptio*, the twelfth-century theologian Hugh of St. Victor (1096–1141) had added the more pragmatic, "mechanical" arts back into the mix in his *Didascalicon*. But instead of being the goal to which the other studies were to lead, the mechanical and pragmatic arts were now considered "lower" disciplines leading to the "higher studies" contained in the liberal arts, philosophy, and theology.

This revaluation of values which resulted in the elevation of philosophy and theology had largely been accomplished during the Patristic period, when the classic tradition of the liberal arts was mediated through early Christian sources. The third-century Eastern Father of the Church Clement of Alexandria (c. 150– c. 215) insisted, for example, that young people should study all the liberal disciplines as a foundation for the higher study of

---

Galdericus's *principium*, see Jean Leclercq, "Un témoignage du XIIIe siècle sur la nature de la théologie," *Archives d'histoire doctrinale et littéraire du moyen âge* 15–17 (1940–1942): 301–321. We do not, however, possess anything like a complete collection of the *principium* and *resumptio* addresses of all the thirteenth-century masters who incepted at the University of Paris. Nancy Spatz suggests, both in her 1992 dissertation, "Principia," and in her 1994 article "A Newly Identified Text," that Guy and Galdericus were the first to make the substitution of a hierarchy of sciences discourse for a complete *divisio textus* of the Scriptures. Bonaventure's inception was earlier than either Guy or Galdericus's, but since Joshua Benson did not identify Bonaventure's *principium* and *resumptio* until 2009, Spatz would not have been aware of it.

[12] Indeed, the English translation of the first part of Thomas's commentary by Armand Maurer was titled *The Divisions and Methods of the Sciences* (Toronto: Pontifical Institute of Mediaeval Studies, 1986).

[13] See James A. Weisheipl, O.P., "Classification of the Sciences in Medieval Thought," *Mediaeval Studies* 27 (January 1, 1965): 54–90, esp. 54. My discussion throughout this section is indebted to Fr. Weisheipl's article. Those interested in more than the very general outline I am offering here merely as a preface to Bonaventure's *De reductione* would be well served by consulting Fr. Weisheipl's article directly.

philosophy, which was itself to be a preparation for the reception of Christian wisdom.[14] So too in the Latin West, Augustine was a proponent of students studying the seven liberal arts, but he viewed them, as had Clement before him, as preparatory for the reception of Christian doctrine and as an aid to its interpretation.[15] In the Early Middle Ages in the West, the knowledge of the seven liberal arts was kept alive in works such as Donatus's *Ars grammatica* (mid-fourth century AD), Martianus Capella's *De nuptiis Philologiae et Mercurii* (*On the Marriage of Philology and Mercury*, mid-fifth century AD), and Priscian's *Institutiones grammaticae* (late fifth, early sixth century AD).

The work of the sixth-century Roman Christian Boethius, however, was to be of special significance for Christian authors, especially Christian theologians, in the twelfth and thirteenth centuries. Boethius, like many before him, divided philosophy into two kinds: theoretical and practical. But he was distinctive in maintaining there were three subdivisions of each. In his treatise *On the Trinity* – the work on which Thomas Aquinas was later to make a famous commentary – Boethius conceived of a new threefold division of speculative philosophy elegant in its clarity and simplicity. The first division of speculative philosophy he called *naturalis*, or physics; the second, *mathematica*; and the third, *theologica*. The first, said Boethius, deals with forms that cannot exist or be considered apart from matter and motion. The second, *mathematica*, deals with forms that, although they can never actually exist separate from matter, can be considered apart from matter. The third, *theologica*, finally, deals with forms that exist apart from matter and motion.

According to Boethius, each branch of speculative philosophy had its own proper method. The method proper to physics and the other natural sciences (*naturalia*) he called *rationalibiliter*, by which Boethius had in mind the demonstrative process of reasoning that Aristotle had used in his works of natural science. The method proper to *mathematica* he called *disciplinaliter*, "disciplinary," a word derived from the Latin *disco, discere*, "to learn." It had long been held that mathematics was especially "teachable" because of the precision its abstraction from matter and motion afforded it. The method needed in *theologica*, finally, Boethius described as *intellectualiter*, by which he meant that "theology" involves a contemplation and intellectual grasp not merely of "forms" but of that form that is pure *esse*.

This tradition of reflection on the liberal arts was further mediated to the Middle Ages through the *Institutiones* of Cassiodorus (562 AD) and the *Etymologiae* of Isidore of Seville (c. 600–625 AD) who, along with Boethius and Augustine, "served as the principal sources for all later discussions of the seven liberal arts and the tripartite division of philosophy."[16] Isidore divided philosophy into physics, ethics, and logic; he then subdivided each of these further, with physics subdivided according to the four arts of the quadrivium: arithmetic, geometry, music, and astronomy; ethics subdivided according to the four cardinal virtues: prudence, justice, fortitude, and temperance; and logic subdivided into rhetoric and dialectic.

There were a large number of important medieval thinkers who took up the question of the order and hierarchy of the sciences in the late twelfth and early thirteenth centuries – among them Clarenbaud of Arras (c. 1110–c. 1187), Gilbert de la Porrée (1085–1154), Thierry of Chartres (c. 1100–1150, Robert Grosseteste (c. 1175–1253), Robert Kilwardby (c. 1215–1275),

---

[14] See, e.g., Clement of Alexandria, *Stromata* I.5–7.
[15] See, e.g., Augustine, *De doctrina christiana*, II.27–39.
[16] Weisheipl, "Classification," 64.

Roger Bacon (c. 1220–1292), Albert the Great (1193–1280), and Thomas Aquinas (1225–1274).[17] The fact that all these highly regarded thinkers wrote important and widely circulated treatises on the divisions, methods, and hierarchy of the sciences indicates that the topic was of great interest and likely had generated no small amount of controversy in academic circles such as those at the University of Paris by the time Bonaventure incepted there in 1254.

Hugh of St. Victor and the *Didascalicon*

The man with the most profound and direct influence on Bonaventure's account of the hierarchy of the sciences, however, was Hugh of St. Victor, the man who in the *Didascalicon* had reintroduced the mechanical arts back into the schema of the liberal arts. In place of medicine and architecture, the two arts Varro had listed, Hugh listed *seven* mechanical arts, likely to provide a nice sense of symmetry and balance with the seven liberal arts. These seven make for an interesting list: fabric making, armament, commerce, agriculture, hunting, medicine, and theatrics. Bonaventure simply reproduced Hugh's list in his *resumptio* and provided a broad enough description of each of the seven to establish why the list was all-inclusive. "Hunting," for example, on Bonaventure's account, was not merely about hunting for animals, but included "every conceivable way of preparing foods, drinks, and delicacies." "Armour-making" included not merely armor, but also "the production of every instrument made of iron or of any other metal, or of stone or wood."[18]

Hugh divided philosophy into theoretical, practical, mechanical, and logical. The *theoretical* branch of philosophy he subdivided according to Boethius's threefold schema: physics or natural philosophy, mathematics, and theology. Although Hugh was a Christian author, "theology" in this context should not be mistaken for the discipline of "sacred doctrine." "Theology" here meant, as it did for Boethius and Aristotle before him, the study of forms separated from matter and motion. It is more akin to what we today would call "metaphysics." Hugh divided *practical* philosophy in a Boethian manner, distinguishing ethics, economics (or domestics), and politics. Hugh divided the *mechanical* arts into the seven we discussed above: fabric making, armament, commerce, agriculture, hunting, medicine, and theatrics. And *logical* philosophy, finally, he distinguished into the classic three arts of the trivium: grammar, rhetoric, and dialectic. Bonaventure reproduced nearly all the elements of Hugh's complex schema in his *resumptio*. (See Box 11.1.)

Bonaventure's account of the hierarchy of sciences in his *resumptio*, although not original, having drawn heavily from Hugh's *Didascalicon*, was not without a certain bravado. Bonaventure had not only foregone the traditional practice of providing a *divisio textus* of all the books of the Bible, but he had also substituted in its place an address hitting upon what was undoubtedly still a contentious issue at the university: namely the proper order of study and the place of theology within the university's curriculum.

---

[17] For more on the thought of these men, I refer the reader again to Fr. Weisheipl's excellent article, esp. 66–94.
[18] See Hugh of St. Victor, *Didascalicon of Hugh of St. Victor: A Medieval Guide to the Arts*, trans. Jerome Taylor (New York: Columbia University Press, 1991).

Bonaventure's *Resumptio* *261*

> **Box 11.1** Hugh's Fourfold Division of Knowledge
>
> 1. Theoretical (*naturalis*)
>   a. Theology: deals with forms separated from matter
>   b. Mathematics: deals with forms of bodies considered apart from matter
>   i. Arithmetic
>   ii. Music
>   iii. Geometry
>   iv. Astronomy
>   c. Physics: deals with forms in matter
> 2. Practical (*moralis*)
>   a. Ethics
>   b. Economics
>   c. Politics
> 3. Mechanical: fabric making, armament, commerce, agriculture, hunting, medicine, theatrics
> 4. Logical (*sermocinales*)
>   a. Grammar
>   b. Dialectics
>   c. Rhetoric

Zachary Hayes has suggested that Bonaventure's accomplishment in the *De reductione* consists in the fact that

> he incorporates all the familiar and new forms of knowledge in the arts and sciences into an all-embracing, theological framework and integrates them into the journey of the human spirit into God. All must be situated in the context of the going-forth from and the return of creation to God. . . . He argues, in effect, that spirituality and theology do not have to bypass or bracket the so-called secular disciplines in order to find God elsewhere; for the entire world is drenched with the presence of the divine mystery. It is a world that bears at least the vestiges (=foot-prints) of God, and at some levels even the image and similitude of God. It is the task of the human person situated in such a world to learn how to detect the symptoms of that mysterious, divine presence.[19]

This is a beautiful summary of Bonaventure's accomplishment, to which I would add only that, for Bonaventure, learning how to detect "the symptoms of that mysterious divine presence" in the world in its various manifestations involved mastering the methods appropriate to each discipline. This was not a mysticism of the mountaintops; it was, rather, a very Franciscan reaffirmation of the truth and holiness to be sought and achieved in everyday life, study, and work.[20]

---

[19] Hayes, *Reduction*, 11.
[20] Franciscans have gotten the reputation for being especially concerned with nature and animals. This reputation is not undeserved, but it is worth recalling that the Franciscans were founded to do work in the developing medieval towns. So, for example, in in his first version of the rule, the so-

From Hugh's Classification to Bonaventure's Dilation

We reviewed in the preceding text the basic structure of Hugh's schema in the *Didascalicon* and discussed briefly some of its ancient and medieval precursors. Bonaventure borrowed much of this material when he wrote his *resumptio*, but the literary structure of his text differs greatly from the *Didascalicon*. Hugh's work has the characteristics of a *treatise*; Bonaventure's reads more like a *sermo modernus* style sermon. Here, for example, is Hugh on the origin of logic:

> Having demonstrated the origin of the theoretical, the practical, and the mechanical arts, we must now therefore investigate as well the derivation of the logical; and these I have left to the end because they were the last to be discovered. All the other arts were invented first; but that logic too should be invented was essential, for no man can fitly discuss things unless he first has learned the nature of correct and true discourse.[21]

By way of contrast, here is Bonaventure on "rational philosophy," the part of philosophy that includes logic as one of its subdivisions along with grammar and rhetoric:

> Considering speech in the light of its *delivery*, we shall see there a pattern of *human life*, for three essential qualities work together for the perfection of speech: namely, *fittingness*, *truth*, and *style*. Corresponding to these three qualities, all acts of ours should be characterized by *measure*, *beauty*, and *order* so that they may be *measured* by reason of modesty in external works, *rendered beautiful* by purity of affection, and *ordered* and adorned by uprightness of attention.[22]

The patterns of parallel phrasing we find in Bonaventure's text – "measured by reason of modesty of works" (*modificata per modestiam in exterior opera*), "rendered beautiful by purity of affection" (*speciosa per munditiam in affectione*), "ordered and adorned by uprightness of attention" (*ordinata et ornata per rectitudinem in intentione*) – are characteristic of the *sermo modernus* style. One can see in the original Latin just how similar the phrasing is. Note how the simple word *modum* ("measure") becomes *modificata*; *speciem* ("beauty") becomes *speciosa*; and *ordinem* ("order") becomes *ordinata*. And because the words sound so similar, Bonaventure cannot restrain himself from adding *ornata* to *ordinata*. Such attention to the sound and beauty of the words betrays in Bonaventure the sensibility of a poet.

---

called *Regula non bullata* ("Rule without papal approval"), Francis envisioned that his friars would work in and among the townspeople, using the skills and in the occupations for which they had been trained before entering the order. After finishing their work, they were not to accept money, but they were allowed to accept food and a place to sleep. This, it seems, was to be their primary way of preaching. Cf. "Earlier Rule," chapter 7: "Let the brothers who know how to work do so and exercise that trade they have learned, provided it is not contrary to the good of their souls and can be performed honestly... and *Let everyone remain* in that trade and office *in which he has been called*. And for their work they can receive whatever is necessary excepting money... And it is lawful for them to have the tools and instruments suitable for their trades."

[21] Hugh of St. Victor, *Didascalicon of Hugh of St. Victor: A Medieval Guide to the Arts*, trans. Jerome Taylor (New York: Columbia University Press, 1991), I.II, pp. 57–58.

[22] *De reductione*, 17.

Bonaventure did not merely write a treatise on the divisions and methods of the sciences, he preached a sermon. It was a sermon of the sort a master would give during a *principium* address, but a sermon nonetheless, one that employed in abundance the arts of the *sermo modernus* style of preaching. To use the language of the medieval preaching manuals of the day, we could say that Bonaventure didn't merely "develop" his points as in a treatise, he "dilated" them – *dilatatio* being the term for how a preacher would "expand" the content of his sermon by "chaining" together biblical authorities, creating subdivisions, setting up a series according to good, better, best, or creating metaphors based on the properties of a noun.[23] Examining how Bonaventure transformed the hierarchy he found in Hugh's *Didascalicon* in his own *resumptio* by means of these *sermo modernus* style "dilations" is the task to which we must now turn our attention.

The Four Lights

As mentioned earlier, Bonaventure appears to have changed the first paragraph of his *resumptio* after his inception so the text no longer depended upon the *thema* verse from his previous day's *principium*: "Wisdom, the maker of all things, taught me" (Wisdom 7.21). When he revised his *resumptio* address into the text we now know as the *De reductione artium ad theologiam* ("On the Reduction of the Arts to Theology"), he substituted a new *thema* from James 1.17: "Every good gift and every perfect gift is from above, coming down from the God of Lights." The usual practice in a *sermo modernus* style sermon would have been to make a division of this *thema* verse into three or four parts, each with a key word or words that would prompt the comments in the following sections. In this instance, however, because Bonaventure had already written the treatise *before* he appended the new *thema*, the process was reversed: he needed to find a biblical verse with a key word in it corresponding to the sermon he had already written.[24]

Since he had structured the first part of his *resumptio* around the fourfold division of light – interior, exterior, inferior, and superior – he needed a biblical verse with the word "light" in a prominent place. He might have used any number of passages, such as "In him was life, and the life was the light of men" (John 1:4) or "And the light shone in darkness, and the darkness did not comprehend it" (John 1:5), or something even more basic, such as "And God said, 'Let there be light'" (Gen 1:3). This passage from the first Genesis creation account would have worked especially well given that Bonaventure shifts in the middle of his *resumptio* from the "four lights" image with which he began to a second section structured around the "six days" of creation.

But the passage from James 1:17 had been a favorite of Hugh of St. Victor's, and since the basic conception of the hierarchy of the sciences in the *resumptio* (later, the *De reductione*) owes much to Hugh's influence, it may have seemed fitting.

---

[23] For the major methods of *dilatatio*, see my brief descriptions in Chapter 2.
[24] Although Bonaventure does not make the customary *sermo modernus* style *divisio* of the *thema* verse into its constituent parts, he does make a common *sermo modernus* style *dilatatio* of the word "light" into four senses. In other words, although Bonaventure does not observe the sermon style per se , he does use contemporary sermon methods in developing his points.

Bonaventure had also already made reference to the "God of Lights" in a later section of his *resumptio*, where claims that the light of sacred Scripture should be called "superior," first, because it leads to higher things by revealing truths that transcend reason, and second, because it is not acquired by human investigation but is sent down to us from "the God of Lights." So when he changed the opening *thema* verse after his inception to prepare the text for publication, he may have had this later reference in mind as well.[25]

As we have seen, when Bonaventure delivered the address we now know as the *De reductione* as his inception *resumptio*, he used a quotation from Augustine's *Soliloquies* to introduce the notion of "light" in order to introduce his discussion of the "four lights": exterior, inferior, interior, and superior. He had to add this passage from Augustine because the word "light" did not show up anywhere in the original *thema* verse he had used for his *principium*: *Artifex omnium docuit me sapientia*. When he later revised the text of his *resumptio* and added the new first paragraph based on the *thema* from James 1:17, he no longer needed the passage from the *Soliloquies*, which unfortunately mentioned only three lights instead of four anyway, so he dropped it. The passage from James 1:17, with its mention of gifts "coming down from the God of *Lights*," fulfilled what was needed by providing the word "Lights," thereby setting up the fourfold division of light into exterior, inferior, interior, and superior that dominates the first half of the treatise that follows.*

This fourfold division of light allowed Bonaventure to creatively retrofit Hugh's fourfold hierarchy into a new schema with the sacred Scriptures more clearly at the top. In Bonaventure's new schema, the *inferior* light is the light of sense knowledge – called "inferior" because it begins with an inferior object and requires the aid of corporeal light. The *exterior* light is the knowledge of the mechanical arts, which produce things "external" to us. The *superior* light is the light of the sacred Scriptures, the light that, by revealing truths transcending human reason, leads to higher things, the light sent down from on high by "the God of lights" (cf. James 1:17). The *interior* light is the light of philosophical knowledge by which we inquire into inner and hidden causes through principles in the recesses of the human mind.[26]

Note the nice *sermo modernus* style verbal associations. The "inferior" light deals with the inferior sense objects. The "exterior" light deals with the external objects created by the mechanical arts. The "superior" light leads us above. And the "interior" light is the light by which we inquire *inwardly*, in our minds, into the *inner* principles of things.

---

[25] Compare *De reductione*, 5 with *Omnium art.*, 40.

* NB: Since the remainder of Bonaventure's *resumptio* is identical to the text of the *De reductione artium ad theologiam* – the only change being the first paragraph – and since the English translation I will be using and citing hereafter is that of Zachary Hayes, O.F.M., trans., *St. Bonaventure's* On the Reduction of the Arts to Theology, therefore, in an attempt to avoid confusion, especially if the reader glances at the footnotes, I will henceforth be referring to Bonaventure's *resumptio* as the *De reductione*. See n. 9, where I provided the full citation to the Hayes translation and gave the reader the first warning that this shift was coming.

[26] A reader interested in a modern example of this sort of "dilation" should consult Avery Cardinal Dulles's book *The Catholicity of the Church* (Oxford: Clarendon Press, 1987), in which the author structures his discussion around this fourfold distinction: "Catholicity from Above," "Catholicity from Below," "Catholicity in Breadth," and "Catholicity in Length."

The Interior Light and Hugh's Hierarchy of the Sciences

Bonaventure then places Hugh's entire hierarchy of the sciences (minus the mechanical arts) under the heading of the "interior" light. His schema reduces Hugh's hierarchy to these three divisions: (1) "natural" philosophy (theoretical), which includes both the mathematical disciplines (arithmetic, geometry, music, and astronomy) and physics; (2) "moral" philosophy (practical), which includes ethics, economics, and politics; and (3) "rational" philosophy (logical), which includes grammar, dialectic, and rhetoric. Compare the outline of Bonaventure's divisions under "interior" light in the *De reductione* in Box 11.2 with the outline of Hugh's division of the sciences in Box 11.1.[27]

In the first half of section 4 of the *De reductione*, Bonaventure sets forth this basic threefold division between rational, natural, and moral by describing it in three ways. The problem with his discussion is that he does not always keep the same order: in his first account, he lists "rational" philosophy first; in his second, "natural" philosophy comes first; and in his third, "moral." If one fails to notice this, the lists can be confusing.

In his first account, he distinguishes the truth of *speech*, the truth of *things*, and the truth of *morals*. *Rational* philosophy considers the truth of *speech*; *natural* philosophy, the truth of *things*; and moral philosophy, the truth of *conduct*.

In his second account, he states that "since 'God is the cause of being, the principle of intelligibility, and the order of human life,' so we may find these in the illumination of philosophy."[28] When the illumination of philosophy enlightens the mind to discern the

---

Box 11.2 Bonaventure's Divisions under "Interior" Light in the De Reductione

1. Theoretical Knowledge (Natural Philosophy)
   A. Mathematics: deals with forms of bodies considered apart from matter
      i. Arithmetic
      ii. Music
      v. Geometry
      vi. Astronomy
   B. Physics: deals with forms in matter
2. Practical Knowledge (Moral Philosophy)
   A. Ethics
   B. Economics
   C. Politics
3. Logic (Rational Philosophy)
   A. Grammar
   B. Dialectic
   C. Rhetoric

---

[27] Cf. *De reductione*, 4. Allow me to remind the reader again that from here to the end of the chapter, I will be making reference to the standard edition of Bonaventure's text, the *De reductione* artium ad theologiam, because it is (1) identical to the *resumptio* from this point on, and (2) because for most readers, it is easier to access than Joshua Benson's text of the *resumptio*.

[28] *De reductione*, 4.

Table 11.1 Bonaventure's Divisions of Philosophy

Category of Philosophy	Deals with:	Which explores:	Intellect directs:	Category of Truth:
Natural Philosophy a. Mathematics b. Physics	Truth of things	Causes of being	Intellect directs itself (to understand the truth of things)	Truth of knowledge
Moral Philosophy a. Ethics b. Economics c. Politics	Truth of conduct	Principles of understanding	Intellect directs the interpretive power (to interpret the truth of speech)	Truth of doctrine
Rational Philosophy a. Grammar b. Dialectic c. Rhetoric	Truth of speech	Order of living	Intellect directs the motive power (to move one to act in accord with the truth)	Truth of Life

causes of being, it is physics. When we are enlightened to know the principles of understanding, it is logic. And when the illumination involves the order of living, this is moral philosophy. Notice in this second list that the first and second categories have been reversed: he lists physics first, which would correspond to "natural" philosophy in the first list, and logic second, which would correspond to "rational" of "discursive" philosophy, the first item in the first list.

In his third account of this same threefold division, Bonaventure takes an entirely different approach, stating that "the light of philosophical knowledge illumines the intellect itself and this enlightenment may be threefold."[29] If it directs the *motive power*, it is *moral* philosophy, which enlightens us regarding the truth of life; if it *directs itself*, it is *natural* philosophy, which enlightens us regarding the truth of knowledge; and if it directs *the interpretive power*, it is *discursive* philosophy, which enlightens us regarding the truth of doctrine.

Since the terms can be confusing, I have attempted to diagram the various lists together in one chart in Table 11.1.

The Superior Light of the Scriptures

The "superior" light, the light that is the "highest," is the light that illuminates respect to saving truth: this is the "light" of Sacred Scripture. This conclusion is unsurprising, not only because Bonaventure is a Christian theologian, but also because, as we have noted, the *De reductione* was originally Bonaventure's *resumptio* address, and that address was by University statute required to be a "commendation" of sacred Scripture.

[29] Ibid.

This light is called "superior," says Bonaventure, for two reasons: first, because it leads to higher things by revealing truths that transcend reason, and second, because it is not acquired by human investigation but is sent down to us from "the God of Lights."[30]

But note, these gifts *come down* from the God of Lights. What about the return? The "God of Lights" *illumines* us in various ways – through sense perception, the mechanical arts, the liberal arts, and sacred Scripture – but this illumination is not merely an end unto itself. We are illumined so that we can achieve our ultimate end, which is union with Him. So after he has described in the first part of his text the ways in which God illumines us, it remains for Bonaventure in the second part to describe how they *lead us back to* God. This change of focus required a change of Bonaventure's governing image: from the "four lights" to the "six days."

From the Four Lights to the Six Days

Up to this point, Bonaventure has been dealing with a fourfold schema of the four lights: exterior, inferior, interior, and superior. He was able to fit Hugh of St. Victor's entire division of the sciences into this fourfold schema with room to spare for insights of his own. But starting in section 6, Bonaventure shifts from the image of the four "lights" to the six "days" of creation. Rather than trying to describe this rather startling transition, it will be best simply to quote Bonaventure's text in full. After finishing his discussion of the last of the four "lights," the *superior* light of the sacred Scriptures, Bonaventure says this.

> From what has been said up to now it can be concluded that, according to our primary division, the light coming down from above is *fourfold*; nonetheless there are six differentiations of this light namely, the light of *sacred Scripture*, the light of *sense perception*, the light of the *mechanical arts*, the light of *rational philosophy*, the light of *natural philosophy*, and the light of *moral philosophy*. Therefore, in the present life there are six illuminations; and they have their evening, for all *knowledge will be destroyed*. And therefore they will be followed by a seventh day of rest, a day which knows no evening, namely, *the illumination of glory*.

> Therefore these six illuminations may very fittingly be traced back to the six days of formation or illumination in which the world was made, so that the knowledge of sacred Scripture would correspond to the creation of the first day, that is, to the formation of light, and so on with the rest, one after the other in proper order. And as all those lights had their origin in a single light, so too all these branches of knowledge are ordered to the knowledge of sacred Scripture; they are contained in it; they are perfected by it; and they are ordered to the eternal illumination by means of it. Therefore all our knowledge should come to rest in the knowledge of sacred Scripture, and particular in the *anagogical* understanding of Scripture, through which any illumination is traced back to God from whom it took its origin. And there the circle is completed; the pattern of six is complete, and consequently there is rest.[31]

---

[30] Cf. n. 25.
[31] Hayes, trans., *Reduction*, 6–7.

But why make this switch from the image of the four lights to the six days? It is potentially confusing and lacks Bonaventure's usual elegance and continuity. Well, first, it is not without scriptural warrant, since "light" is the first thing created on the first day – "And God said, 'Let there be light'" – and since in the Gospel of John's recapitulation of the creation story in Genesis – "In the beginning was the Word" – he declares that the Word is "the true light, which gives light to everyone" (John 1:9). Moreover Bonaventure's audience would have known that St. Augustine, in his *Literal Commentary on Genesis*, had identified the "morning" and the "evening" of each of the six "days" with the "light" of the angelic intelligence, seeing the thing to be created first in the mind of God (morning intelligence) and then as it is in its own created nature (evening intelligence).[32] For these reasons, taking the structure of lights from the first part of his *resumptio* into the second part on the six days would likely not have seemed odd to Bonaventure's audience.

Yet, even though the *image* may not have seemed odd or out of place, why the need for the transition at all? My supposition is that, having in the first section settled upon an image that would allow him to make a suitable "division" of the sciences – one corresponding, as we have seen, with the schema set forth by Hugh of St. Victor in his *Didascalicon* – Bonaventure needed another image to communicate more clearly the idea that the sciences should culminate in a goal beyond themselves. His goal, after all, wasn't merely to *classify* the sciences, as a scientist or metaphysician might. Bonaventure set out to show how all human knowing was a reflection of the divine image meant to lead back to (*reducit*) union with God. The "four lights" image couldn't communicate this idea well enough, so he switched it. Using the image of the "six days" of creation allowed Him to continue to use the image of light, which was the first thing created on the first day. But it also allowed him to picture the movement of the days *toward* the Sabbath – a movement of the disciplines leading mankind back to God, the source and summit of all things. The six "days" imagery allowed Bonaventure to picture more adequately the "lights" of the various sciences as *flowing forth from* God (since "light" is created on the first day) and *flowing toward* God (who is our "rest" on the seventh day).

Wayne Hellmann has suggested that, for Bonaventure, *reductio* involves the notion of order, but in two senses. "In the first sense," says Hellmann, "the 'reduction' means the resolution of knowledge by which the ultimate and basic principles of metaphysics are seen and understood. In the second sense, the *reduction* means the completion of the order of salvation in which the person is brought into unity with God, who is the *primum* and the *ultimum*."[33] In his *resumptio*, the imagery of the four "lights" in the first half allowed Bonaventure to emphasize *reductio* in the first sense: the resolution of knowledge into its basic principles. The imagery of the six "days" in the second half, then, allowed him to connect *reductio* in this first sense with *reductio* in the second: how by this knowledge we are *led back to* God.

To put this another way, he begins with an academic, pedagogical point about the relationship between theology and the other arts and sciences, something evidently relevant to the disputes going on in and around the University of Paris during the twelfth and

---

[32] Cf. Augustine, *De genesi ad litteram*, esp. Bk 1, chapter 10.
[33] Cf. J. A. Wayne Hellmann, *Divine and Created Order in Bonaventure's Theology*, trans. Jay Hammond (St. Bonaventure, NY: The Franciscan Institute, 2001), esp. 18–22; the quotation cited is on p. 18.

thirteenth centuries. But then, in the second half of the *resumptio*, he connects this "academic" point about the structure of the curriculum with a properly "theological" point about human salvation, as if to say: Getting the order of the arts and sciences right is the way we in the university set up the proper sort of "ladder" of ascent up the Platonic "divided line" so our students can raise their minds from the knowledge they gain in any of the disciplines to achieve an ever greater knowledge of, and relation to, God. Bonaventure's message to his confreres at the University of Paris was that what they were studying in their academic classrooms was meant to bear fruit in greater union with God.

And so Bonaventure begins the second half of his treatise – the "six days" section – with a description of the light of the first day, which he associates with Sacred Scripture. In the four "lights" schema, sacred Scripture was the "superior" light at the top. Here the Scriptures are the primary light which illumine all the rest.[34] The second light is the light of sense perception; the third, the light of the mechanical arts; the fourth, the light of rational philosophy; the fifth, the light of natural philosophy, and the sixth, the light of moral philosophy. These six "days" are followed by a seventh day of rest, a day that has no evening. Bonaventure associates this day of rest with the light of eternal glory we will enjoy in union with God. Note how the disciplines merely listed and divided in the earlier "four lights" schema are here set within a dynamic hierarchy, with sense perception at the bottom (since we come to know through sense perception) and moral philosophy, the knowledge of how to live one's life well, near the top, and with the "lights" of the various "days" leading ultimately to the seventh "day," union with God.

The material from the four lights section gets reapportioned into the six days in the following way:

Superior Light: Light of Sacred Scripture: First Day
Inferior Light: Light of Sense Perception: Second Day
Exterior Light: Light of Mechanical Arts: Third Day
Interior Light: Light of Philosophical Science (threefold division)
Light of Rational Philosophy: Fourth Day
Light of Natural Philosophy: Fifth Day
Light of Moral Philosophy: Sixth Day
Illumination of Glory (New Culmination): Seventh Day

On this account, sacred Scripture is the first light that illumines all the rest, and it does so by keeping them directed to their primordial Source, which is also their ultimate End: the Triune God. Bonaventure's account of the three mystical senses of Scripture helps him make this transition from the "four lights" part of the treatise to the second part structured around

---

[34] As mentioned earlier, Bonaventure may have in mind Augustine's *Literal Commentary on Genesis* where the "light" created on the first day are the angels. Their intellection of creation, first in the mind of God and then in created reality, is what produces the "morning" and the "evening" of each "day." Thus the "light" of the first day suffuses all the rest. Cf. Augustine *De genesi ad litteram*, esp. book I. In addition, we might profitably view the discussion that follows as an early application of Bonaventure's concept of divine illumination. We cannot delve into that theory in any detail here, but for a good, short introduction, the reader should consult the article on "Bonaventure" at the on-line "Stanford Encyclopedia of Philosophy": Tim Noone and R. E. Houser, "Saint Bonaventure," *The Stanford Encyclopedia of Philosophy* (Winter 2014 edition), Edward N. Zalta (ed.), https://plato.stanford.edu/archives/win2014/entries/bonaventure.

the six days. The allegorical sense, he says, is concerned with *faith*; the moral sense with *morals*; and the anagogical sense with the ultimate goal of both, namely union with God. Therefore, claims Bonaventure, the whole of sacred Scripture teaches these three truths: the eternal generation of the Son and His incarnation in the person of Jesus Christ (the subject of the allegorical sense), the pattern of human life (the subject of the moral sense), and the union of the soul with God (the subject of the anagogical sense). Moreover, these three truths, claims Bonaventure, can be found "reflected in" or "illumined by" the lights of each of the following five "days" leading up to the light of eternal glory on the seventh day.

Just as all the lights of creation "had their origin in a single light – that is, the light created on the first day – so too all the "lights" of the various branches of knowledge "are ordered to the knowledge of sacred Scripture."

> [T]hey are contained in it; they are perfected by it; and they are ordered to the eternal illumination by means of it. Therefore all our knowledge should come to rest in the knowledge of Sacred Scripture, and particularly in the *anagogical* understanding of Scripture through which any illumination is traced back to God (*refertur in Deum*) from whom it took its origin (*unde habuit ortum*). And there the circle is completed; the pattern of six is complete, and consequently there is rest.[35]

In Table 11.2, I have diagrammed how, according to Bonaventure, the three basic truths of Sacred Scripture illuminate the other sciences, which in turn "lead back to" God. I suggest the reader take a quick look at the diagram before getting into the details below and/or refer back to it if the details get confusing.

This threefold schema is consistent across all the "days." Bonaventure's challenge is to see whether he can identify "vestiges" or "echoes" of (1) the generation and incarnation of the Word, (2) the moral pattern of human life, and (3) the union of the soul with God in *all* the various arts and branches of knowledge. To see how he accomplishes this monumental task, we will need to get into the details of the "light" of each "day": sense perception (day 2), the mechanical arts (day 3), rational philosophy (day 4), natural philosophy (day 5), and moral philosophy (day 6).[36]

Emanation, Exemplarity, and Consummation in Sense Perception

We begin with sense knowledge. In sense knowledge, says Bonaventure, there are three elements to be considered: namely the *medium* of knowing (*cognoscendi medium*), the *exercise* of knowledge (*cognoscendi exercitium*), and the *delight* of knowledge (*cognoscendi oblectamentum*). Note the parallelism here. This, as I've mentioned before, is a characteristic requirement of the *sermo modernus*-style.

---

[35] *De reductione*, 7.
[36] In the sections that follows, I have borrowed three terms – emanation, exemplarity, and consummation – from Zachary Hayes's introduction to his translation of *On the Reduction of the Arts to Theology*. "Emanation" is shorthand for "generation and incarnation of the Word." "Exemplarity" is shorthand for the "moral pattern of human life." And "consummation" is shorthand for the final union of the soul with God.

Table 11.2 The Lights of Each of the Six Days

First Day: Light of Sacred Scripture	Second Day: Light of Sense Perception	Third Day: Light of the Mechanical Arts	Fourth Day: Light of Rational Philosophy	Fifth Day: Light of Natural Philosophy	Sixth Day: Light of Moral Philosophy	Seventh Day: Illumination of Glory
Allegorical Sense: Generation and incarnation of the Word	Medium of knowledge	Production (skill of the artist)	Person speaking (mental concept)	Relation of Proportion	"Right": middle between extremes	
Moral Sense: Pattern of human life	Exercise of knowledge	Effect (quality of the effect produced)	Delivery (fittingness, truth, style)	Effect of Causality	"Right": guided by regulations of divine law	
Anagogical Sense: Union of the soul with God	Delight	Fruit of the work (usefulness of the product)	Purpose (express, instruct, persuade)	Medium of Union	"Right": when one's summit is raised upward (e.g., upright posture)	

How Sense Knowledge Is Related to the Eternal Generation of the Son

Bonaventure's account of how sense knowledge "leads us back to" the eternal generation and incarnation of the Word depends a great deal, as one might expect, on his underlying notion of sense knowledge. This is not the place to delve deeply into the details of Bonaventure's epistemology, so we must let it suffice simply to say that Bonaventure seems to have accepted the view, common among the Franciscans, that we come to know material objects only indirectly.[37] According to Bonaventure, "no sense object can stimulate the cognitive faculty except by means of a similitude which proceeds from the object as a child proceeds from its parent."[38] Once that similitude comes into contact with a sense organ, "the mind is led back to the object by means of that similitude." Hence even when the object is absent, the similitude can still be present to the mind. We perceive the "similitude" (*similitudo*) with our senses, and it is what inheres in our knowing power. When we know "That is a dog," we know the "similitude" of the dog which leads our mind back to the actual dog. But even when the dog has run away, we still have that "similitude" of the dog in our minds can knowingly say, "That was a dog."[39]

Bonaventure believes that an object (in our example above, the dog), as long as it exists, always generates this similitude, and he sees this perpetual generation of a similitude as a clue to and a "vestige of" the eternal generation of the Son from the Father. Just as (on Bonaventure's account) an object is always generating the similitude that makes it possible for us to know it, in an analogous way, "from the supreme Mind" – that is from God the Father – "there has emanated from all eternity a Similitude, an Image, and an Offspring," the eternal Word, the Son of God, that, when He becomes incarnate in human form, makes it possible for us to know God. Just as the similitude generated by the object leads our minds back to the object when it comes into contact with our senses, so the Eternal Similitude of God, expressed in His eternal Word, leads our minds back to Him when we come into contact with His incarnate presence. Hence the "medium" of knowledge – the

---

[37] There is not space here to provide anything like an adequate account of Bonaventure's epistemology. My limited goal in what follows is simply to provide the reader the bare minimum needed to understand how Bonaventure finds "vestiges" or "echoes" of the three key teachings of Scripture (eternal generation, exemplarity, and consummation with God) in each subdivision. For more on Bonaventure's epistemology and account of sense perception, see Noone and Houser, "Saint Bonaventure," section 3.7.

[38] *De reductione*, 8.

[39] I have left aside any extended discussion of how Bonaventure's position here accords with his famous "theory of illumination," which Étienne Gilson has summarized thus: "If, therefore, the human intellect possesses intellectual certitudes, it is because the divine Ideas themselves, which are immutable intelligibles, illumine the human intellect in its knowledge of such objects." See Étienne Gilson, *History of Christian Philosophy in the Middle Ages* (New York: Random House, 1955), 337. For Aquinas, by contrast, this "similitude" of the dog would be something generated, not by the dog, but by the active intellect, which does the work of grasping the essence of the thing in the particular. I am seeing or smelling *this particular dog*: Bowzer. But my mind can sometimes discern in that particular sense impression the "dog-ness" of Bowzer, so that when I see another dog, even one of a different breed, I can still recognize it as a "dog." Granted it may take several such experiences with dogs to refine my knowledge of what makes a dog a dog and distinguishes a dog from a small horse, but our minds seem quite capable of making these distinctions all the time. Whether Bonaventure's or Thomas's epistemology is more accurate is not at issue at the moment.

similitude that mediates between the object and the knower – reveals to us something important about God's eternal generation and incarnation in the Word made flesh.⁴⁰

How the Exercise of Sense Knowledge Suggests the Proper Order of Human Life

What about the "exercise of sense knowledge"? Each sense acts in relation to its proper object, says Bonaventure. The sense of smell acts in relation to odors and aromas, not in relation to sounds; and vice versa. We do not hear sounds with our eyes. Each sense "shrinks from what may harm it, and does not claim what is foreign to it." I am drawn to good aromas by my sense of smell. I am repelled by bad ones. I am drawn to good flavors by my sense of taste. But I am repelled by bad ones. Such is the case, at least, when the sense is in good working order. In a similar way, claims Bonaventure, the sense of the heart (*sensus cordis*) is in good working order when it directs our life in ways proper to its nature: when it is not negligent in seeking the good nor does it seek what is harmful due to concupiscence or claim what does not belong to it out of pride.⁴¹ Therefore, in this way, in the *exercise of sense knowledge*, we see the proper pattern of human life (*ordo vivendi*).

What the Delight of Sense Knowledge Teaches about Our Union with God

Despite centuries of warnings from Christian ascetics about the dangerous allure of the senses drawing us away from God, Bonaventure claims that "if we consider the *delight* of sense knowledge, we shall see here the union of the soul with God." Is the "delight" Bonaventure praises here (as an image of the union of the soul with God) a purely *spiritual* delight? It seems not, for he says: "Every sense seeks its proper sense object with longing, finds it with delight, and never wearied, seeks it again and again." Bonaventure cites as a biblical authority this passage from Ecclesiastes 1.8: "The eye is not filled with seeing, neither is the ear filled with hearing." Those who know the stern warnings of "the Preacher" of Ecclesiastes would be right to imagine that, in that verse's original context, the failure of the senses to be satisfied was what made them worthy of condemnation. Here, by contrast, is Bonaventure's comment on that verse from Ecclesiastes:

---

⁴⁰ This may seem to some like a long way to go to get to the truth about the emanation of the Son and His incarnation as "the Word made flesh." And yet we should remember that Bonaventure was writing in the wake of Anselm's fascinating "ontological argument" based purely on an a priori analysis of our concept of God – or at least it seemed so to Anselm. And in the spirit of Augustine's *De trinitate*, with its host of analogies meant to help us grasp the three-in-oneness of God, Bonaventure has at least provided an interesting intellectual image to help his readers understand better how God can remain one and yet still "project" (as it were) perpetually, indeed eternally, a perfect "image" of Himself out into the world – an image *by means of which* we come to know Him. We should also undoubtedly keep in mind that all such analogies, no matter how good, will by their limited nature still be highly imperfect.

⁴¹ *De reductione*, 9.

In the same way, our spiritual senses must seek with longing, find with joy and time and again experience the beautiful, the harmonious, the fragrant, the sweet, or that which is delightful to the touch. Behold how the divine wisdom lies hidden in sense knowledge and how wonderful is the contemplation of the five spiritual senses in the light of their conformity to the bodily senses.[42]

We might be able to spiritualize our experiences of "the beautiful" and "the harmonious," but how about "the fragrant, the sweet, and that which is delightful to the touch"?

Whatever dangers others may have seen in these experiences, Bonaventure says that, rather than avoid them completely, we should learn from them. We should *learn* from the eagerness with which our senses seek out and enjoy the finite pleasures proper to them how much more our hearts and souls should be united to the only object that will satisfy them: the infinite goodness of God. In a similar spirit, St. Paul had argued in 1 Corinthians 9.25 that Christians should learn from the discipline that athletes show in training to win a laurel wreath that soon fades how much more Christians should work to win a crown that lasts forever!

Emanation, Exemplarity, and Consummation in the Mechanical Arts

Just as in the "light" of sense perception, Bonaventure found "vestiges" of (1) the generation and incarnation of the Word, (2) the right ordering of human life, and (3) the union of the soul with God, so too he will find vestiges of the same three truths in the "light" of the mechanical arts. We find evidence of the first – the generation of the Son – in the production (*egressum*) of work; of the second – the right order of human life – in its effect (*effectum*); and of the third – the union of the soul with God – in its fruit (*fructum*). We can also find clues in the skill of the artist (*artem operandi*), the quality of the effect produced (*qualitatem effecti*) and the usefulness of the product that results (*utilitatem fructus eliciti*).

"Production" (Egressus) in the Mechanical Arts

Note that Bonaventure has already "stacked the deck in his favor" linguistically, we might say, by using the Latin term *egressum*, which our English translator renders as "production," but which really means a "going out." When the idea in the mind of the artist "exits" or "goes out" *into* an external work, this is an *egressus*. Bonaventure draws an analogy between this *egressus* of the work from the mind of the artisan and the eternal *egressus* of the divine Word from the mind of the Father. If we recall that this text served as Bonaventure's *resumptio*, this point about the *egressus* accords nicely with what Bonaventure had argued the previous day in his *principium* under the heading of *artifex* ("the maker"), where he maintained that the Father had written his art, first, "in this book," namely Christ.[43] On

---

[42] Ibid., 10.
[43] *Omnium art.*, 4: "*Haec ars in illo libro scribitur, immo est Christus liber ille . . .*" See my discussion of this passage in Chapter 10.

this view, the creation of the world is a "mirror" of this first writing, even though the first is eternal and immutable and the second produced in time and mutable. When we come to understand how the artisan produces an external work resembling the interior exemplar he had in his mind when he set out, we are grasping a "vestige" or hearing an "echo" of the way the Creator produces nothing except through the eternal Word and Wisdom expressed eternally in the mind of God.[44]

But what about the incarnation? Bonaventure's claim was that both the generation *and* the incarnation of the Word are revealed in the mechanical arts. We have seen an echo of the generation of the Son; what about His *incarnation*? Consider again the act of making, says Bonaventure. If it were possible for a human artisan to produce an object that could know and love him, he might do this. (The obvious example would be the story of Geppetto and Pinocchio.) But if the object he produced did know and love him, it could only be because the artist possessed the skill and power to make an object similar to himself in this way. So although human artists do not have this power or skill, God does, and so He has created beings with the ability to know and love Him.

And yet what if the intellects of these creatures were darkened (as ours is) by sin so they could not rise from the knowledge of things to the knowledge of their Maker? What then? Then, argues Bonaventure, it would be "necessary for the similitude according to which the effect was produced to lower itself to that sort of nature which the effect could grasp and know," and for this reason, "it was most fitting that the eternal and invisible should be visible and assume flesh in order to lead us back to God."

If, to use my own example, Geppetto were able by his own skill to make Pinocchio capable of knowing and loving him, but if, by his own fault, Pinocchio could no longer see beyond his own materiality to know and love his maker, then on Bonaventure's account, the maker "Geppetto" would have to *become wood* to show Pinocchio that he had been made in the "image and likeness of" his maker and that, although Pinocchio was wood, his material woodenness did not exhaust the fullness of his essence, but rather was meant to point beyond itself to the possibility of a deeper communion with a *person* – one whose nature transcended mere woodenness. Bonaventure does not use the specific example of Geppetto and Pinocchio – I have inserted them here because they are generally well known to modern readers – but Bonaventure does mention a maker uniting himself with the thing he has made to reveal to his creation that it has been made in the maker's image.

Bonaventure believes that reflections such as these on the "illumination of the mechanical arts as regards the production of the work" can help us come to understand more fully "the Word begotten and incarnate."[45] It should be clear by now, however, that the "illumination" involved operates in two directions. Although Bonaventure finds throughout creation "vestiges" of the eternal generation and incarnation of God, these vestiges would likely not be evident apart from divine revelation in the Scriptures. Given the diminished capacity of man's reason, they are often not known or admitted. We would not *know* what the production of artificial things was *analogous to* unless the generation of the Son from the Father and the incarnation had been revealed to us in the Scriptures. So, on the one hand, insofar as the lesser "lights" of the first six "days" are participations in the one divine light,

---

[44] *De reductione*, 12.
[45] Ibid.

they can illumine us about their Source and ours. Yet, these lesser lights do not illumine as they were meant to – as they were created to do – unless they are seen in the light of divine revelation, especially as illumined by the light of the sacred Scriptures.

So there is a twofold movement here. While the other disciplines and ways of knowing are meant to "lead us back to" sacred Scripture, so too sacred Scripture can help "illumine" our understanding of those other disciplines. When understood in the light of sacred Scripture, the other disciplines "speak" to us in the way they were originally intended, since, on Bonaventure's account, all creation is meant to reveal God to us and to invite us into a loving relationship with Him, living our lives in this world according to the pattern he laid down in the law and the Gospel, so that later, after this life, we may know and love Him eternally.[46]

The Effect and Fruit of the Mechanical Arts

After considering the *production* of the mechanical arts, Bonaventure next discusses their *effect* and *fruit*. Considering the *effect* of the work of art reveals to us truths about how we ought to order our lives. "Every artisan aims to produce a work that is beautiful (*pulcrum*), useful (*utile*), and enduring (*stabile*)," says Bonaventure. So too our goal should be to produce a human life that is beautiful, useful, and enduring. Just as *knowledge* is what allows us to make a work that is beautiful, *will* is what allows us to make it useful, and perseverance is what allows us to make it enduring, so too our goal should be to know the truth, to will the good, and to persevere in both. This is done by perfecting, first, our rational powers; second, our concupiscible appetite; and third, our irascible appetite.[47]

Artisans who produce something do so, says Bonaventure, in order to derive praise, benefit, or delight from it. These are the three "fruits" of one's labor. So too in the labor of our lives, there ought to be three objects of our appetites: first, to achieve the noble good (for which we would deserve praise); to possess the useful good (from which we would derive benefit); and to enjoy the agreeable good (which would give us delight). Thus the soul is meant to praise God (a noble good), serve God (a useful good), and find delight in God (an agreeable good).[48] Such are the ways in which the mechanical arts can lead us back (*re-ducere*) to the truths of Sacred Scripture and, ultimately, to union with God Himself.

---

[46] Let me suggest again that Bonaventure's discussion here should be read in the light of his theory of divine illumination. Indeed, I would suggest that this text is perhaps the best example of what Bonaventure has in mind. I have not gone into the details of Bonaventure's account of divine illumination, because there are other, fuller accounts available to the interested reader. Earlier, I suggested the short online article on Bonaventure by Noone and Houser in the Stanford Encyclopedia of Philosophy. Other good resources include Étienne Gilson, *The Philosophy of St. Bonaventure*; Andreas Speer, "Illumination and Certitude: The Foundation of Knowledge in Bonaventure," *American Catholic Philosophical Quarterly* (Special Issue: Bonaventure), 85: 127–141; and J. A. Wayne Hellman, *Divine and Created Order in Bonaventure's Theology*.

[47] *De reductione*, 13.

[48] Ibid., 14.

Emanation, Exemplarity, and Consummation in Rational Philosophy

Can divine wisdom be found in rational philosophy? Answers to this question have varied over the centuries. Some have believed that rational philosophy simply leads people astray and should be forsaken for divine wisdom. Others have been convinced that rational philosophy can lead us at least part of the way to divine wisdom – it can be, in this sense, "preparatory" – but it must admit when it has reached the limit of its proper objects, after which it must allow a higher science to lead the way. Still others have argued that the only way to achieve divine wisdom is through rational philosophy.

Bonaventure argues a position most like the second of these; but if we stopped there, we would miss much of what Bonaventure has to offer. For what we get in this section are not arguments about the relative merits of faith versus reason. What we are offered instead is a discussion of how one can find in rational philosophy the three teachings on emanation, exemplarity, and consummation – at least as Bonaventure understands rational philosophy.

The principal concern of rational philosophy, claims Bonaventure, is *speech* (*sermonem*), a comment that might make one wonder whether he is expressing a rhetorician's view of philosophy as something primarily directed to making speeches and speaking persuasively – a view one associates with the classic fifth-century BC sophists Gorgias and Protagoras.[49] Although Bonaventure is concerned ultimately with speech – especially the speech with which his young friars would preach and teach the lay faithful – his attitude toward the importance of the other elements of rational philosophy is more subtle than some of his interpreters have been willing to allow, especially those who prefer to characterize Bonaventure as "anti-scholastic."

in the earlier "four lights" section of the *De reductione*, Bonaventure described rational philosophy, which he associated with the "interior" light, as "discursive or rational philosophy" (*sermocinalis sive rationalis philosophia*). Here too the focus on giving "speeches" or "sermons" was apparent. Under this heading, Bonaventure included, as Hugh of St. Victor had before him, the classic three arts of the trivium: grammar, logic, and rhetoric. The first of these, grammar, is concerned, he said, with expressing through appropriate speech (*per sermonem congruum*) what reason apprehends; the second, logic, with teaching by means of true speech (*per sermonem verum*); and the third, rhetoric, with persuading by means of eloquent speech (*per sermonem ornatum*). The inclusion of all three shows that Bonaventure's concern was not merely with persuasive speech, but with persuasive speech that moved its listeners by expressing *the truth of things* and *right judgments* about how to live. Bonaventure would have been aware of the threats to orthodoxy presented by the spirited-but-misdirected preaching of groups such as the Albigensians in southern France and the Joachimites of Italy. We should recall as well that one of the goals of the Fourth Lateran Council was to provide not only *more* sermons for the laity, but also *more rhetorically effective* and *doctrinally sound* sermons.[50]

With this concern for rhetorically effective and doctrinally sound sermons in mind, Bonaventure accepted Hugh of St. Victor's categorization of grammar, logic, and rhetoric as the three major divisions of "rational philosophy," envisioning "rational philosophy,"

---

[49] *Sermo* can, of course, also refer to a written word, but it is primarily oral, a "discussion" or "conversation." The relationship between the spoken word and the written word is a complicated one that I will not be examining here.

[50] See my discussion in Chapter 1.

thereby, as three means of perfecting *speech*. Far from expressing an un-scholastic or anti-scholastic rhetorician's view of philosophy, Bonaventure is expressing here, I would suggest, a distinctively *scholastic* concern that "logic" and "disputation" should bear fruit in doctrinally sound preaching that can both satisfy the mind's desire to know the truth and move the heart's desire to live in the truth.[51]

In this earlier "four lights" section of the *De reductione*, Bonaventure's primary concern was the classification of the various disciplines within a coherent hierarchy. In the present "six days" section, he wants to show how these arts can dynamically "lead us back to" the knowledge and love of God. Regarding speech, the theological perspective Bonaventure would have learned from Augustine's discussion of *signs* and *things* in the *De doctrina christiana* was that *signs* point to *things*, both of which are meant to point ultimately to God. The perfection of speech, on this view, would be realized by using words in the proper way – for the purpose God intended, which is to lead people back to Him to embrace Him in truth and love.

Since, according to Bonaventure, rational philosophy's principal concern is "speech," then we should consider the three elements of every speech: (1) the person speaking, (2) the delivery of the speech, and (3) the situation of the hearer, or the goal of the speech. In the sections that follow, Bonaventure's analysis of the speaker leads us back to the generation and incarnation of the Word; the delivery of the speech has lessons about the pattern of human life; and the purpose of a speech tells us about the union of the soul with God.

The Person Speaking

Regarding the first, the person speaking, Bonaventure holds, following the teaching of St. Augustine in *De doctrina christiana*, that a verbal word is an outward expression of an inward, mental word. This inner, mental word can be made known to another person only if the speaker "clothes" the inner, intelligible word in sensible speech and utters it externally where it can be received into the ear of a listener. Yet, when the word is uttered outwardly in this way, the inner mental word does not depart from the mind of the person speaking. If it did, the person would immediately forget what he said the moment he said it. If the internal word disappeared from my mind whenever it appeared in yours, there could be no real communication or sharing of ideas.

We find something analogous in God's utterance of His eternal Word, says Bonaventure. God conceives the Word by an eternal act of generation. But in order that this eternal Word might be known by humans who are endowed with senses, the Word assumed the form of flesh. Yet, although "the Word was made flesh and dwelt among us,"

---

[51] If we understood "scholastic" in the traditional way, as implying something dry and dialectical, lacking pastoral concern for the laity, then Bonaventure should certainly not be considered "scholastic" in this sense. What I have been attempting to show throughout this volume, however, is that this traditional view of "scholasticism" and the culture of "the schoolmen" is too narrow. If it is true that the founders and officials at the University of Paris were as interested in producing good preachers and preaching as the evidence seems to suggest they were, then Bonaventure would not have been expressing here an "anti-scholastic view" of the relationship between philosophy and preaching, but precisely a representative *scholastic* concern for good preaching as the goal of one's academic training.

He also remained eternally "in the bosom of God." Both can be true, says Bonaventure, in a way analogous to the way a speaker with a mental word who "incarnates" his mental word in speech and expresses it outwardly, retains the mental word inwardly. The word can exist simultaneously in one way in the mind of the speaker and, after its expression ("incarnation") as outward speech, also become present to the listener. In this way, rational philosophy helps us understand the incarnation.

The Delivery of a Speech

How, then, does considering the *delivery* of a speech shed light on the order of human life? According to Bonaventure, three essential qualities work together for the perfection of speech: its fittingness (*congruitas*), its truth (*veritas*), and its style (*ornatus*). Note how similar Bonaventure's discussion in this short paragraph is to a characteristic form of *dilatatio* one finds in *sermo modernus*-style preaching: "proposing a discussion based on a noun as it occurs in definitions or classifications" (*proponendo orationem pro nomine, sicut fit in diffinitionibus seu quibuscumque notificationibus*).[52]

Here the three characteristics of a good speech – fittingness (*congruitas*), truth (*veritas*), and style (*ornatus*) – are associated with a morally upright human life. As a good speech should be characterized by measure (*modum*), beauty (*speciem*), and order (*ordinem*), so too our acts should be "measured" (*modificata*) by modesty in exterior works, "made beautiful" (*speciosa*) through the purity of affection, and ordered or adorned (*ordinata*) by rightness of intention. The parallelism Bonaventure maintains among those three clauses is also characteristic of the *sermo modernus* style, as is the modification of the nouns in the second list – measure (*modum*), beauty (*speciem*), and order (*ordinem*) – into the adjectives in the third: *modificata*, *speciosa*, and *ordinata*.

Note as well the "fittingness" of Bonaventure's speech: a speech characterized by a "measure," "beauty," and "order" of its own. The result is a speech in which form and message harmonize. Bonaventure does not merely speak *about* measure, beauty, and order, his speech *possesses* and *expresses* measure, beauty, and order. And that measure, beauty, and order were not merely for the sake of show, but were intended to lead listeners back to God.

The Goal or Purpose of a Speech

This brings us to what we can learn if we consider speech in relation to its purpose. As he did in the previous section on the *delivery* of a speech, Bonaventure here creates a threefold subdivision – subdivision, as have seen, being another key element of the *sermo modernus* style. The three purposes of a speech, he says, are to express (*ad exprimendum*), to instruct (*ad erudiendum*), and to persuade (*ad movendum*). These three are in accord with what he had maintained earlier in the "four lights" section of his address, where he described the three arts of grammar, logic, and rhetoric, saying that the first expresses what

---

[52] See Robert of Basevorn, *Forma praedicandi*, 33; and my discussion in Chapter 2, where this is the first of the eight methods of *dilatatio*.

reason apprehends through appropriate speech, the second instructs through true speech, and the third persuades with eloquent speech.

Here, Bonaventure adds that speech never expresses except by means of a "type" or "likeness" [to the inner thought or word] (*nunquam exprimit aliquid nisi mediante specie*); never teaches except by means of a convincing light (*nunquam docet nisi mediante lumine arguente*); and never persuades except by means of virtue (*nunquam movet nisi mediante virtute*). Therefore, the only true teacher is someone who can impress a likeness (*speciem imprimere*), infuse light (*lumen infundere*), and give virtue (*virtutem dare*) to the heart of the listener. Since Christ is the only one who can achieve all three, Christ is the one teacher of all (*Christus unus omnium magister*), the one who brings us back to God.[53]

The goals of speech, therefore, are on this view fully realized only in Christ. And the "expressing," "teaching," and "persuading" that one can attain through the human arts of grammar, logic, and rhetoric should be understood as participations in the more fundamental "expressing," "teaching," and "moving" that God achieves through His Word. Indeed, according to Bonaventure's theory of divine illumination, there would be no human "expressing," "teaching," and "moving" *without* the divine illumination of the mind by the Word.

Emanation, Exemplarity, and Consummation in Natural Philosophy

As we have seen, the "light" of the fourth "day" is the light of natural philosophy. Earlier in the "four lights" section, Bonaventure listed under "natural philosophy" the three sciences made famous by Boethius: physics, mathematics, and metaphysics. *Physics* he described as involving "a consideration of the generation and corruption of things according to natural powers and seminal principles"; *mathematics*, he said, is a "consideration of abstract forms in terms of their intelligible causes"; and *metaphysics*, "the knowledge of all beings according to their ideal causes, tracing them back to the one first Principle from which they proceeded, that is, to God, insofar as He is the Beginning, the End, and the Exemplar."[54] Bonaventure's discussion in what follows will be clearer if we keep in mind these descriptions of the three sciences.

In *De reductione*, 19, Bonaventure declares that "the wisdom of God is to be found in the illumination of *natural philosophy*, which is concerned chiefly with the *formal principles in matter*, in the *soul*, and in the *divine wisdom*. From Bonaventure's previous discussion, we know that he is talking about physics (formal principles in matter), mathematics (formal principles in the soul), and metaphysics (formal principles in the divine Wisdom and Eternal Exemplar). But we must take care, because the "three perspectives" that will serve as the structuring principle around which he will organize his discussion in this section apply to all three sciences. The "three perspectives" from which the three sciences should be

---

[53] For Augustine's development of this idea, see *De magistro* I.11.38, and for a longer development of the idea in Bonaventure's works, see *Sermo IV, Christus unus omnium magister* (Quaracchi 5:567). For an English translation, see Zachary Hayes, O.F.M., trans., *What Manner of Man? Sermons on Christ* (Chicago: Franciscan Herald Press, 1974).

[54] *De reductione*, 4.

considered,[55] says Bonaventure, have to do with (1) the relation of proportion (*habitudinem proportionis*), (2) the effect of causality (*effectum causalitatis*), and (3) the medium of union (*medium unionis*).[56]

Relation of Proportion

"If we consider the formal principles in terms of their *relation of proportion*," says Bonaventure, "we shall see there the *Word Eternal* and the *Word Incarnate*."[57] What Bonaventure has in mind here may not be immediately apparent. So we must recall the three sciences of physics, mathematics, and metaphysics. According to Bonaventure, "the *intellectual* and abstract principles are, as it were, midway between the *seminal* and the *ideal* principles." In other words, mathematics, which is a "consideration of abstract forms in terms of their intelligible causes," is midway between physics, a "consideration of the generation and corruption of things according to natural powers and seminal principles," and metaphysics, "the knowledge of all beings according to their ideal causes." So far so good. But how do we get from these basic descriptions of the three sciences to the *Word Eternal* and the *Word Incarnate*?

The answer is that Bonaventure reasons his way from the bottom up, from physics to mathematics to theology, all three of which in his view involve some kind of *generation*. *Seminal* principles cannot exist in *matter* without generation and the production of form; neither can *intellectual* principles exist in the *soul* without the generation of a word in the mind. Therefore, by extension, *ideal* principles cannot exist *in God* without the generation of the Word from the Father in due proportion. "This is a mark of dignity," says Bonaventure, "and if it is true of the creature, how much more so must it be true of the Creator."[58]

Yet, we might wonder about the soundness of this argument. Simply because it is true of the creature, must it also be true of the Creator, even if it is "a mark of dignity" in the creature? It might help if we recall that this is not meant to be an argument of the Anselmian sort with the goal of providing "necessary reasons" for the eternal generation of the Word from the Father. Rather, it is an exercise in leading the mind back to God by seeking "vestiges" of the Creator in all of creation, especially in the human sciences. What is clear to Bonaventure is that the science of physics depends upon understanding the generation and production of form, because "form" is what underlies all accidental changes, as the "form" of the man persists even as he changes from black haired to gray haired. So too, mathematical knowledge depends upon forms, generated by the mind, which are abstracted from all matter and motion. On Bonaventure's account, both sorts of form can help "lead our mind back" to the Word being generated eternally by the Father.

---

[55] I am using the terminology in the English translation. The Latin text has simply: "*Quas tripliciter contingit considerare ...*"
[56] *De reductione*, 19. As before, the reader should take note of the *sermo modernus*-style parallelism Bonaventure maintains between the clauses.
[57] *De reductione*, 20.
[58] Ibid.

"By similar reasoning," says Bonaventure, we come to the conclusion that the highest and noblest perfection cannot exist in this world unless that nature in which the seminal principles are present (i.e., the forms in material things, such as rocks, plants, trees, dogs, and humans), and that nature in which the intellectual principles are present (i.e., the abstracted forms of mathematics present in the human mind), and that nature in which the ideal principles are present (i.e., in the Mind of God) "are simultaneously brought together in the unity of one person, as was done in the incarnation of the Son."

Keep in mind that this *reductio* is not meant as a "proof." Bonaventure is not claiming that he can *prove* – reasoning from the characteristics of physics, mathematics, and metaphysics – that the Word of God became incarnate. The truth about the Incarnation can be known only by the light of divine revelation in the sacred Scriptures.

What Bonaventure seeks to help us see, rather, is how – from physics, mathematics, and metaphysics – we can come to understand, under the guidance of sacred Scripture, that Christ, since He is the Word Incarnate, is also "the "Beginning, the End, and the Exemplar" of all creation. Thus, although it is sometimes claimed that "Christ" and "the Incarnation" are subjects only for theology, on Bonaventure's account, all the sciences, whether they realize it explicitly or not, presuppose Him as their first cause, their exemplar cause, and their ultimate goal.

Effect of Causality

Following the pattern he has set up from the beginning, wherein the first subdivision always deals with the generation and incarnation of the Word, the second with the right ordering of human life, and the third with the union of the soul with God – the subjects respectively of the allegorical, the moral, and the anagogical senses – Bonaventure turns in this second sub-division to how the *effect of causality* can reveal important truths about the right ordering of human life.

He begins by declaring that "generation by means of seminal principles cannot take place in generative and corruptible matter except by the beneficial action of the light of those heavenly bodies that are most remote from generation and corruption; namely, the sun, the moon, and the stars."[59] Just as plants and trees cannot live and grow unless they receive light and heat from the sun, "so too the soul can perform no living works unless it receive from the sun, that is, from Christ, the gift of a gratuitous light." And just as the moon and the stars receive their light from the sun, and then play their own role in governing physical changes on earth, so too we must "seek the protection of the moon, that is, of the Virgin Mary, Mother of Christ" and should imitate the motion of the stars, that is, "the example of the other saints."[60]

---

[59] Cf. *Itinerarium* 2.2: "In the world of sense object, some things generate, some are generated, and some govern both of these. Those that generate are simply bodies such as the heavenly bodies and the four elements. For anything that is generated or produced through the operation of a natural power must be generated or produced from these elements by means of the power of light that harmonizes the contrary qualities of the elements in mixed things." For more, see also *Breviloquium* II,3–4 and the discussion in Étienne Gilson, *The Philosophy of Saint Bonaventure*, 245–264. The validity of this theory is not crucial for our purposes.

[60] *De reductione*, 21.

Let me remind the reader again that Bonaventure is not setting out to demonstrate by means of a logical argument that "the soul can perform no living works" unless it receives from Christ "the gift of gratuitous light." What he is trying to show, rather, is how the insights from the other disciplines can illuminate one's understanding of sacred Scripture. An additional benefit of the image her uses here, comparing Mary and the saints to the moon and the stars, is that this is an image the friars in his audience might remember and use in their own preaching.

Medium of Union

Bonaventure takes the same approach in the next paragraph, where he discusses the third subdivision under "natural philosophy," namely, the "medium of union." According to Bonaventure's physical theory, "the corporal nature can be united to the soul only through the medium of moisture, breath, and warmth: three conditions which dispose the flesh to receive life from the soul." The validity of this physical theory is not relevant to our present concerns. Bonaventure takes himself merely to be repeating the best Aristotelian biology of his day. It would not have seemed unreasonable to conclude that the soul is united to the body by the medium of moisture, breath, and warmth, since these are precisely the things bodies lack when they are dead. But getting all the details right would not have been as important to Bonaventure as helping his listeners gain the habit of doing the *reductio*. The students listening to his *resumptio* would be learning a host of interesting and important facts and theories in their studies in the different disciplines. The skill Bonaventure wished to impart to them was the ability to use that knowledge, whatever its source, to lead their minds and hearts back to God.

As the body needs moisture, breath, and warmth to unite to the soul, says Bonaventure, "so too we may understand that God gives life to the soul and is united to it only on the condition that it be *moistened* with tears of compunction and filial love, that it be made *spiritual* by contempt of every earthly thing, and that it be *warmed* by desire for its heavenly home and its Beloved."[61] This threefold image sounds like something right out of preaching, and there is no reason to think Bonaventure didn't intend for his audience to think of it that way. Not every *reductio* we have examined would have supplied the proper material for preaching, but this one certainly did, just as did the previous analogy comparing Mary and the saints with the moon and stars.

Let us suppose for a moment that the underlying physical theory Bonaventure is presupposing about mediation were to change, as in fact it has. We no longer believe that the corporal nature is united to the soul through the medium of moisture, breath, and warmth. What then? Those who have developed the habit of doing the *reductio* would find resources in the new theory for leading the mind back to God. The "medium" we use might not be moisture, breath, and warmth, we might instead think of the relationship between photosynthesis, chlorophyll, and the sun giving life to plants. Bonaventure's key point is that everywhere, in all true knowledge of the world and of the human person, one will be

---

[61] Ibid., 22.

able to find "vestiges" of the Creator that can help us understand Him better and provide resources (such as resources for preaching) that can lead our minds and hearts back to Him.

Emanation, Exemplarity, and Consummation in Moral Philosophy

The last "day" of the six before the seventh day of rest is occupied by moral philosophy, and in it, like the others, the threefold light of Sacred Scripture is to be found. Given that the three truths of Sacred Scripture that have been consistent across the days so far are (1) the generation and incarnation of the Word, (2) the right order of human life, and (3) union of the soul with God, one might have imagined that *moral philosophy* dealt solely with the second of these, the right order of human life. But Bonaventure is nothing if not consistent, so he will identify vestiges of all three in moral philosophy, a task he accomplishes here by creatively applying one of the eight methods of dilating a *sermo modernus*-style sermon: "by proposing a discussion based on a noun as it occurs in definitions or classifications" (*proponendo orationem pro nomine, sicut fit in diffinitionibus seu quibuscumque notificationibus*).[62] The noun Bonaventure chooses for this purpose is the word "right" (*rectum*). And after he has distinguished three sense of "right," Bonaventure associates the first with emanation, the second with exemplarity, and the third with consummation. We begin with the first: "right" as the "middle between extremes."

"Right": Middle between Extremes

In one sense of the word, something is said to be "right," says Bonaventure, if its middle is in line with its extreme points. Even in English, a carpenter might look along the line of a board or across the flat surface of a table and say, "it is right as a rule," by which he means it does not dip or bow anywhere in the middle; the middle is precisely in line with the two ends. How do we get from this sense of "right" to the emanation and incarnation of the Son?

Bonaventure argues that, since God has perfect rectitude ("rightness"), and since God is the Beginning and End of all things, it is necessary to posit within God an intermediate person of the divine nature. This is the Son. Let us say that God is the Principle and Source of all things and the End or Goal of all things. Now we must ask: How is this *going forth from* God and this *returning to* God mediated to creatures? Bonaventure's answer: As creatures went forth from God through the Word of God who is co-eternal with the Father, so too for their perfect return to God, it was necessary for the Word to become flesh. In this way, says Bonaventure, Christ is the "perfect middle" between the two extremes, God and mankind.[63]

---

[62] This is the first of the eight methods of *dilatatio* listed in Chapter 2.
[63] *De reductione*, 23.

"Right": Guided by Regulations of the Divine Law

In a second sense, something is called "right" when it is conformed to that by which it is ruled and measured. This is the moral sense of "right." We say that a person lives "rightly" if his conduct is in accord with the law or fundamental moral principles. Bonaventure says that a person lives rightly "who is guided by the regulations of the divine law" (*dirigitur secundum regulas iuris divini*), whether these are the "necessary precepts" (*praeceptis necessariis*), the "salutary warnings" (*monitis salutiferis*), or the "counsels of perfection" (*consiliis pefectis*). In other words, a person's acts should be in accord with the will of God. When they are, we say that he or she is acting "rightly" or "with rectitude."

"Right": Head Raised Upward ("Upright")

The final sense of "right" is when something's top is facing up. In English, we use the term "upright," but we also say, for example: "he righted the capsized boat." This sense of "right" expresses the union of the soul with God, says Bonaventure, for since God is above, the mind must be raised upward to reach Him. "And indeed this is what happens," he adds, "when our *rational nature* assents to the first truth, our *irascible nature* strives after the highest generosity, and our *concupiscible nature* clings to the [supreme] good."[64]

Bonaventure's conclusion here is strikingly similar to the one he reached earlier when he was considering the threefold effect of the *mechanical arts*. There, in *De reductione* 13, Bonaventure suggested that, as every artisan aims to produce a work that is beautiful, useful, and enduring, so too we should aim to produce a human life that is beautiful, useful, and enduring. Since knowledge makes a work beautiful, will makes it useful, and perseverance makes it enduring, so our goal should be to know the truth, will the good, and persevere in both. We accomplish these three goals, argues Bonaventure, by perfecting, first, our rational powers; second, our concupiscible appetite; and third, our irascible appetite.[65]

It is unsurprising that Bonaventure reaches the conclusion human flourishing involves the perfection of the rational, irascible, and concupiscible powers. What is perhaps surprising is that one can be led to this conclusion not only by moral philosophy but also by the mechanical arts. That these diverse sciences can lead us to similar conclusions has a lot to do with the underlying unity Bonaventure believes exists between the two: both are vestiges of the Creator meant to lead us back to Him. As we should understand our work in the mechanical arts to be a reflection of the work of the Creator, so too we should understand the "work" of our lives to be a reflection of the divine nature. The mechanical arts teach us that we are to be "images" of our Creator by working always in accord with the God's original design for His creation. So too moral philosophy teaches us that we are to be "images" of our Creator by striving to bring our minds, hearts, and appetites in accord with God's design for our lives.

---

[64] Ibid., 25.
[65] Ibid., 13.

The Summit of Human Learning

In the first book of the *Metaphysics*, Aristotle famously declared that "all men by nature desire to know" and to know the "highest" things. The "highest" knowledge, thought Aristotle, would be the knowledge of first principles and the causes of things, "for by reason of these, and from these, all other things come to be known."

> And the science which knows to what end each thing must be done is the most authoritative of the sciences, and more authoritative than any ancillary science; and this end is the good of that thing, and in general the supreme good in the whole of nature. Judged by all the tests we have mentioned, then, the name in question falls to the same science; this must be a science that investigates the first principles and causes; for the good, i.e. the end, is one of the causes.[66]

Aristotle called that the "highest science," which provides knowledge of the first principles, causes, and the good of all things, "first philosophy," or "first science," sometimes "wisdom," or "theology." To pursue this knowledge, thought Aristotle, was to pursue the highest wisdom of which human beings are capable.

In his *resumptio*, Bonaventure shifted the summit of human learning upward – to God Himself. And although God is in His essence unknowable, Bonaventure accepted that He had made Himself known through the revelation of Sacred Scripture. And so he argued that all the disciplines in the Arts curriculum at the University of Paris, including the study of Aristotle's *Metaphysics*, needed to be illumined by the knowledge gained by reading sacred Scripture to be "seen" fully. To read and study these texts apart from divine revelation would be like trying to see the woman you intend to marry only in the dark.[67] Without seeing her in the light, you will fail to see and appreciate her true beauty, and failing to appreciate her beauty, your heart may fail to be drawn to her as it ought and as she deserves. So too, when the objects of the other sciences are "illumined" by the light and wisdom shining forth from the sacred Scriptures, it is only then that we finally see them in their full truth and beauty, and our hearts should be drawn to the Source of all Truth, Beauty, and Goodness – the First Cause, Highest Principle, and Complete Good of all things. When studied properly, all the sciences should lead us back to the Creator who has revealed Himself in and through the sacred Scriptures.

For in those Scriptures, we find to our amazement that the First Cause, Highest Principle, and Complete Good of all things reveals Himself to be a loving Father who has sent His eternally begotten Son into the world to redeem it from sin. He further extends this loving gift of Himself and His eternal Son to us by sending us His own Spirit whose loving gifts of grace help perfect our rational powers and even our baser, "earthier" powers: our irascible and concupiscible appetites. Our *irascible nature* is perfected, claims Bonaventure, "when it strives after the highest generosity," and our *concupiscible nature* is perfected "when it clings to the good." When we are angry, when we are motivated by wrath or fear, it is a wise counsel that advises: "Turn your mind to generosity." And when

---

[66] Aristotle, *Metaphysics* I.2 (981a 1–25), trans. W. D. Ross.
[67] This image is mine, not Bonaventure's.

we are motivated by lust or greed or the desire for power and prestige, should we not consider whether the things we desire are truly for our good?[68]

Principia and Protreptic

At the heart of this *reductio* of the other arts to theology is not only a clarity of the mind and a perfection of the rational powers – although these are important – but also a perfection of the will through the gift of charity. For Bonaventure, what should animate all one's studies in the disciplines is the conviction that we can find God in them – a conviction borne of the faith that God, out of His love, has revealed Himself to us, and that we are creatures He made capable of both knowing and loving Him.[69] So we realize the highest potential and perfection of each discipline when we see in them a revelation of the God who loved us so much He became flesh for us, sacrificed Himself for us on the cross, and rose to the right hand of the Father to send His Holy Spirit that we might be brought into a fuller union, a deeper communion with Him.[70]

In earlier chapters, I proposed that we view these prologues and *principia* as having a *protreptic* purpose; they were *exhortations* to the kind of study being proposed to the students. Bonaventure's *resumptio* fits this model of the classical *protreptic* by showing not only how the Scriptures were superior to other forms of wisdom, but also how all the other disciplines lead back to the truths contained in them.

Allow me, if I may, to suggest a modern analogue. In the first edition of Mortimer Adler's best-selling volume *How to Read a Book*, Adler's advice on "how to read" comes only after a long, introductory section in which Adler seeks to interest his audience in the analytically engaged reading of the sort he has in mind by describing the structure and character of the classical liberal arts curriculum.[71] He returns to the *goals* of reading at the

---

[68] Cf. Plato's *Gorgias*, in which one of Socrates's primary goals is to show each of his interlocutors that many of the things men desire as good are merely apparent or illusory goods and are not in fact truly good.

[69] Étienne Gilson has written: "Saint Bonaventure's doctrine can be characterized as an 'itinerary of the soul toward God' ... It teaches 'how man goes to God through other things.' Accordingly, his outlook on man and things will be dominated by a twofold tendency: first, to conceive the sensible world as the road that leads to God; next, to conceive man as a creature naturally open to the divine light and God as revealing himself to man through the whole gamut of his illuminations." See *History of Christian Philosophy in the Middle Ages* (New York: Random House, 1955), 332.

[70] Gilson, *History*, 333: "It is possible to find God by considering his creature, because the truth of things consists in their representing the primary and supreme truth. In this sense, all creatures are so many ways to God. Their resemblance to him is not a sharing in his own being; it is but a resemblance or imitation which can be a faithful one only to the extent that the finite can resemble the infinite. To describe it by a technical term, let us say that it is a resemblance of "expression," as a spoken word expresses its meaning. Considered from this point of view, therefore, what we call creatures, or things, constitute a sort of language, and the whole universe is only a book in which the Trinity is read on every page. And if one were to ask why God created the world on this plan, the answer would be very simply: the world has no other reason for being that to give utterance to God; it is a book which was written only that it might be read by man and be the unceasing reminder of its Author's love."

[71] Mortimer Adler, *How to Read a Book: The Art of Getting a Liberal Education* (New York: Simon & Schuster, 1940).

end of the book in a section entitled "Free Minds and Free Men." Clearly the purpose of these sections was to interest students in reading by considering the art of reading within the broader perspective provided by an account of the nature and goals of an education meant for freedom.[72]

Although Bonaventure did not give the standard *divisio textus* of the Scriptures in his *resumptio*, his decision to provide a broad outline of all the disciplines then understood to make up a liberal arts education, showing how they culminated in the knowledge provided by Sacred Scripture and theology, fulfilled the same protreptic purpose, perhaps better than just another *divisio textus* would have done.

For Bonaventure, the truths of the Scriptures help to illumine the other disciplines, while the lesser lights of the other disciplines can, in turn, help us understand the truths of sacred Scriptures more fully. "It is for this reason," says Bonaventure, "that theology makes use of illustrations and terms pertaining to every branch of knowledge" because every branch of knowledge can build up faith, hope, and love, if we see them as containing self-revelations of the God of love in whom is our ultimate faith and hope.

Bonaventure's message was that one should study as a lover studies his beloved; the more love he has, the more he notices, and the more he notices, the more it inspires the increase of his love. When one's studies are illumined by the light of the Holy Spirit and the sacred Scriptures, each discipline, each science, becomes a potential means of building up charity. Hence "the fruit of all the sciences," says Bonaventure, is

> that in all, faith may be strengthened, God may be honored, character may be formed, and consolation may be derived from the union of the Spouse with the beloved, a union which takes place through charity: a charity in which the whole purpose of Sacred Scripture, and thus of every illumination descending from above, comes to rest – a charity without which all knowledge is vain because no one come to the Son except through the Holy Spirit who teaches us *all the truth, who is blessed forever*. Amen.[73]

---

[72] I am not asking the reader to accept Adler's vision. Nor am I *comparing* Adler's view of education with Bonaventure's. The analogy is simply meant to illustrate why Bonaventure might have chosen to go into these details about the nature and purpose of a liberal arts education.

[73] *De reductione*, 26.

12

Searching the Depths of the Lombard

The Prologue to Bonaventure's Sentences *Commentary*

IN PART I, we examined several of the early prologues Thomas Aquinas crafted during his student years at Paris. In the next several chapters, we will examine several of Bonaventure's early prologues, specifically to his commentaries on the Gospel of Luke and John, written, scholars think, while he was still a *lector biblicus* at St. Jacques, the Franciscan house of study in Paris. In this chapter, however, we will examine the general prologue to Bonaventure's *Commentary on the Sentences of Peter Lombard*, just as in a previous chapter we examined Thomas's general prologue to his *Sentences* commentary.

It is not entirely clear how we should date these early prologues to Luke and John in relation to the prologue to his *Sentences* commentary. Did he write them before, at the same time, or later? We don't know with any certainty. Some have suggested that Bonaventure revised these biblical commentaries shortly after his inception as a master. If so, did he revise the prologues? Again, we don't know.

Since I am not proposing that any of the prologues influenced the others, it is not crucial that we establish the correct chronological order. What we know is that all three – the prologues to John and Luke and the general prologue to his *Sentences* commentary – were *early* productions, and we are treating them as such. We also know that Bonaventure in his *Sentences* commentary would have been required to meet some fairly strict University protocols for the production of such a text, so we can consider this prologue, in conjunction with Thomas's, as evidence of what those requirements were and, more particularly, as evidence of Bonaventure's early proficiency using the *sermo modernus* style.

Searching the Depths of the Rivers and Bringing Hidden Things to Light

As I mentioned in Chapter 1 and again in Chapter 4, after the University of Paris expelled and excommunicated the friars in 1254, university officials circulated a letter in which they boasted that "the fount of wisdom" that rose from Paris and its four faculties – theology, jurisprudence, medicine, and philosophy – were "like the four rivers of Paradise" watering and irrigating the whole earth.¹ It is noteworthy, therefore, that both Thomas and Bonaventure chose for the general prologues to their respective *Sentences* commentaries biblical *thema* verses that made reference to "rivers." Thomas began his prologue with this verse from Ecclesiasticus (Sirach) 24:40–42: "I, wisdom, have poured out rivers. I, like a brook out of a river of a mighty water; I, like a channel of a river, and like an aqueduct, came out of paradise. I said: I will water my garden of plants, and I will water abundantly the fruits of my meadow."² Bonaventure, for his part, chose as the *thema* for his general prologue this verse from Job 28:11: "The depths of rivers he hath searched, and hidden things he hath brought forth to light" (*profunda quoque fluviorum scrutatus est et abscondita produxit in lucem*).³ And although Bonventure begins his prologue developing points he associates with the four characteristics of a river – perpetuity, spaciousness, circulation, and cleansing – he shortly thereafter turns his attention to the same four rivers of paradise mentioned in that infamous 1254 letter. If Bonaventure did in fact have in mind the "four rivers" of that letter when he wrote his prologue, then his use and re-interpretation of the image might well have been a reminder to the other faculty at Paris that the source of wisdom was not the four faculties at Paris, but Christ.

Bonaventure structured his prologue around a fourfold *divisio* of his opening *thema*, but not, as one might have expected, in order to associate each part with one of the four books of the *Sentences*.⁴ Instead, Bonaventure made use of what A. J. Minnis has called "the Aristotelian prologue," structured around the four Aristotelian causes: material, formal, final, and efficient.⁵ Bonaventure associates the material cause with the word *fluviorum* ("rivers"); the formal cause with the word *profunda* ("depths"); the final cause with the word *abscondita* ("hidden things"); and the efficient cause with the words *scrutatus est* ("he has searched") and *produxit in lucem* ("he has brought forth to light"). The image that suffuses the whole is of Peter Lombard, "the *Magister*," having searched out (*scrutatus est*) the depths (*profunda*) and the hidden things (*abscondita*) of the rivers – of which there are four, corresponding to the four books of the *Sentences* – in order to bring these "hidden things" forth into the light (*produxit in lucem*).

As we will see, Bonaventure makes especially creative use of the subject matter and form of the four books of the *Sentences* by using various senses of "depth" and "hidden." Because of the complexity of Bonaventure's imagery, I have supplied an outline of the prologue below (see Box 12.1). The reader may wish to consult it while progressing through each stage of the prologue. In my subheadings, I have indicated the sections dealing with the material, formal, and final causes. There is no section heading for the efficient cause because

---

¹ This letter can be found in the *Chartularium universitatis Parisiensis*, I, 252–258; and in English translation in *University Records and Life in the Middle Ages*, ed. and trans. Lynn Thorndike (New York: Norton, 1975; repr. of New York: Columbia University Press, 1944), 56–64. See esp. 57. Cf. also my discussion above in Chapter 4 of the possible influence of this letter on Thomas's *principium*.
² See my discussion in Chapter 6.
³ The Latin text of Bonaventure's prologue to his *Sentences Commentary* can be found in *Opera Omnia S. Bonaventurae* (Ad Claras Aquas (Quaracchi): Collegii s. Bonaventurae, 1882–1901), vol. 1, pp. 1–6.
⁴ This is what Thomas had done. See my discussion in Chapter 6.
⁵ For the basic idea, see Alastair J. Minnis, *Medieval Theory of Authorship: Scholastic Literary Attitudes in the Later Middle Ages* (Philadelphia: University of Pennsylvania Press, 1984; 2nd ed. 1988), 5–6 and 28–29.

> **Box 12.1** Outline of Bonaventure's Prologue to Peter Lombard's *Sentences*
>
> *Thema*: "The depths of rivers he hath searched, and hidden things he hath brought forth to light" (*profunda quoque fluviorum scrutatus est et abscondita produxit in lucem*) – Job 28:11.
>
> **Book 1: The Trinity**
> 1. First characteristic of rivers: perpetuity = timeless emanation of Persons
> 2. First river of paradise: Phison: change of mouth = emanation of Persons
> 3. Depth of the river searched: sublimity of the divine being
>   a. Trinity
>   b. Divine properties
> 4. Hidden thing revealed: magnitude of the divine substance
>
> **Book 2: On Creation**
> 1. Second characteristic of rivers: spaciousness = the whole world
> 2. Second river of paradise: Gehon: sand = the world
> 3. Depth of river searched: emptiness of the created being, esp. because of sin
>   a. Creation
>   b. Sin
> 4. Hidden thing revealed: order of divine wisdom
>
> **Book 3: On the Incarnation of the Word**
> 1. Third characteristic of rivers: circulation = *exitus* and return of Christ; God united to man
> 2. Third river of paradise: Tigris: arrow = Christ (iron and wood; destroys enemies)
> 3. Depth of river searched: bottomlessness of Christ's love and humiliation on the cross
>   a. Passion
>   b. Action: virtues, gifts, and precepts
> 4. Hidden thing revealed: fortitude of divine power
>
> **Book 4: Sacraments**
> 1. Fourth characteristic of rivers: cleansing = the sacraments cleanse us from sin and make us fruitful
> 2. Euphrates: fruit-bearing = sacraments as medicinal fruit
> 3. Depth of river searched: profound (beyond human mind) medicinal efficacy of the sacraments
>   a. The illnesses they cure
>   b. The renewed health they offer
> 4. Hidden thing revealed: sweetness of divine mercy

the whole prologue presumes the reader knows the author of the *Sentences* is Peter Lombard. He is the person who "searched the depths of the [four] rivers" and "brought hidden things to light."

From the examination of the four depths in the four books is elicited *the end*, namely the bringing to light of the four *hidden things*. The one doing the "searching the depths" and "bringing the hidden things to light" – the author of the work – is Peter Lombard.

Material Cause: The Four Properties of a River and the Four Books of the *Sentences*

Bonaventure associates the material cause of the *Sentences* with the word *fluviorum* ("of rivers") from the opening *thema* verse. Dilating according to the properties of this noun, Bonaventure identifies the four properties of a river as (1) perpetuity (*perennitatem*), since rivers are always flowing; (2) spaciousness (*spatiositatem*), which distinguishes a river from a brook or a stream; (3) circulation (*circulationem*), for as it says in Ecclesiastes 1.7: "All the rivers run into the sea, yet the sea doth not overflow: unto the place whence the rivers come, they return, to flow again"; and (4) cleansing (*emundationem*), for the waters cleanse the earth through which the river runs.

From these four properties of a material river, we can discern the four properties of what Bonaventure calls a "spiritual river." This spiritual river is *perpetual* because it involves an emanation of Persons, and this emanation is without beginning or end. Concerning this river, the prophet Daniel (7.9–10) says: "the Ancient of Days sat ... [and] a swift river of fire issued forth from his face" (*fluvius igneus rapidusque egrediebatur a facie ejus*). This Ancient of Days is the eternal Father, says Bonaventure, whose antiquity is eternal. The Ancient *sits* because He is both eternal and immutable. From "his face," a "swift river of fire issued forth"; that is, from the sublimity of his divinity, a plenitude of love and virtue issues forth. The plenitude of virtue issued forth in the Son, which made the river *swift*, and the plenitude of love issued forth in the Holy Spirit, hence the river was *of fire*. Hence we can remember that the subject matter of the first book of the *Sentences* is the *Trinity*.

The second property of a material river is its *spaciousness*, and this Bonaventure associates with *creation*, the subject matter of the second book of the *Sentences*. Bonaventure will have his work cut out for him in his attempt to associate the spaciousness of the river with the production of worldly things, but he finds the biblical texts to do it. He begins by associating a spacious river with a sea, and then quotes Psalm 103:25: "How great are thy works, O Lord? thou hast made all things in wisdom: the earth is filled with thy riches. So is this great sea, which stretcheth wide its arms." And so too, concerning this river, he points to this passage in Ezekiel 29:3–4: "Behold, I come against thee, Pharaoh, king of Egypt, thou great dragon that liest in the midst of thy rivers, and sayest: The river is mine, and I made myself (*ego feci memetipsum*). But I will put a bridle in thy jaws" (*ponam frenum in maxillis tuis*).[6]

According to Bonaventure, this great dragon to whom the Lord speaks and whom he threatens in the figure and person of Pharaoh, is the devil, who reigns among those whom he blinds in the shadows of error; as he does the heretics to whom he says: "The river is mine, and I made it for myself," as if he, the devil, had made this world, and it did not have

---

[6] There is a small confusion in the Latin translation of the Greek Septuagint. The Greek has the Lord saying that He will put a "hook" (παγίδας) in the jaws of the great dragon to pull him out of the sea. This is a nice fishing image. But for some reason, this was translated into Latin using the Latin word *frenum*, meaning "bit" or "bridle." Bridles and bits are used on horses, not fish, and thus we have here something of a mixed metaphor. In accord with his Latin text, however, Bonaventure says that the Lord "bridles" (*infrenabit*) the jaw of the dragon (*huius draconis maxillas*). Strictly speaking, the piece one puts in the mouth of the horse is the bit. But the bridle includes both the bit and the reins, so we get the point. The fishing image, however, has been lost.

another prince. Such is the error of the Manicheans, for example, who argue that the whole world of visible things was made by an evil God. But the Lord bridles the jaw of the dragon and shows He is the maker of this river and can say: "Let all the inhabitants of Egypt know, that I am the Lord" (Ezekiel 29.6).

The third property of a material river is its *circulation*, which suggests to Bonaventure the subject matter of the third book of the *Sentences*: the incarnation. Just as in a circle, the beginning is joined to the end, so in the incarnation, the highest is joined to the lowest; God to man; the first to the last; the eternal Son of God to man made on the sixth day.

Concerning this river, we read in Ecclesiasticus 24:41: "I, like a brook out of a river of a mighty water; I, like a channel of a river and like an aqueduct, came out of paradise." The reader might recall this passage from Thomas's prologue to the *Sentences*, and if so, might also recall the textual difficulty. The Latin that Thomas and Bonaventure were reading seems to have had this: *ego quasi tramis aquae inmensae de fluvio; ego quasi fluvius* **Doryx** *et sicut aquaeductus exivi a paradiso*. Modern critical editions have something slightly different: *ego quasi fluvii* **dioryx**. The Greek word *diōrux* (διωρυξ) means "channel," "canal," or "trench." This is its meaning in Latin as well, since the Greek word was simply taken over into Latin without change. In the version of the Vulgate Thomas and Bonaventure both were using, however, one finds, instead of *dioryx*, the word *doryx* or *dorix*, so both read the passage to say: "I, like the river Dorix and like an aqueduct, came out of paradise."

No one has ever identified a river in the ancient world named "Dorix." And yet if one imagined that it "came out of paradise," then all sorts of special properties could be attributed to it. In this instance, Bonaventure tells us that the river Dorix should be interpreted as a river that "generated medicine." Bonaventure might have been associating this "river Dorix" with the river mentioned in Apocalypse 22:2, beside which is said to have grown the Tree of Life, whose leaves were medicinal.

If so, it seems that for the purposes of this prologue, Bonaventure associated the properties of this special medicinal river with the incarnation of the Son of God, declaring that the incarnation of the Son of God was nothing other than the generation of medicine, for as we read in Isaiah 53.4: "Surely he hath borne our infirmities and carried our sorrows" (Is 53.4). Thus Christ rightly says of himself: "I am, as it were, the river Dorix," that is, the medicinal river.

Whether the text has Dorix or *doryx* (a canal), Bonaventure knows that it contains water; further, he has been informed by Ecclesiastes 1:7 it is in the nature of water to *circulate*, ascending back to the height from which it came. And so the *exitus* of the incarnation is followed by a *reditus* to the Father. As Christ says in John 16:28: "I came forth from the Father, and am come into the world: again I leave the world, and I go to the Father." And so, like the water in the river, Christ completes the circle.

However, the river can also be understood, says Bonaventure, as Christ's egress from his mother. He quotes Esther 10:6: "The little fountain which grew into a river, and was turned into a light," and says that this "little fountain" is the humble virgin, who "grew into a river when she gave birth to Christ." In its original context, the whole verse in Esther 10:6 says, "The little fountain which grew into a river, and was turned into a light, and into the sun, and abounded into many waters, is Esther, whom the king married, and made queen."

If a reader struck by the oddness of this image of a river being turned into light and into the sun were to check a modern English translation such as the Revised Standard Version, he or she would find this: "The tiny spring which became a river, and there was light and the sun and abundant water – the river is Esther, whom the king married and made queen."

This is admittedly less odd, but there is no escaping the fact that Bonaventure's Latin has *Parvus fons, qui crevit in fluvium, et in lucem, solemque conversus est,* which does seem to say that the "little fountain" (*parvus fons*) was "converted" (*conversus est*) into light and the sun (*lucem solemque*).

Bonaventure would have accepted the notion that, in its original context, the "little fountain" that grew into a river and became a light for her people was Esther, who, though she began life as a captive among the Jewish exiles in Persia, eventually became a "light" shining forth and giving hope to her people as queen. It would not have been odd, then, for him or for any medieval preacher to envision Esther as an Old Testament "type" or "figure" of Mary.

Note, however, what Bonaventure has added here to account for the odd Latin phrase he found in the Vulgate. The "little fountain" is the humble virgin who "grew into a river" when she gave birth to Christ, but Christ is the real "river" because through Him flows an abundance of grace. He is also called "light" because He is the "light of wisdom" and "the sun" because He is the "sun of justice." So on Bonaventure's account, instead of Mary being the "little fountain," the river, the light and the sun, Mary is the little fountain that became a river, but Christ is the river that is also the light and the sun.

The fourth property of a material river is *cleansing*, which Bonaventure associates with the subject of the fourth book of the *Sentences*, namely the sacraments. The sacraments are like a river because they cleanse us "from the pollution of sin." Concerning this river, we read in Apocalypse 22:1: "And he shewed me a river of water of life, clear as crystal, proceeding from the throne of God and of the Lamb." As I mentioned above, this was "the medicinal river" that Bonaventure associated with the "River Dorix" mentioned in his Latin version of Ecclesiasticus 24:41. The reference back to that earlier discussion is especially significant. Allow me to explain why.

Consider for a moment the concern expressed by twentieth-century Dominican theologian Edward Schillebeeckx that the discussion of the sacraments has too often been divorced from the reality of Christ and his incarnation, passion, death, resurrection, and ascension to the right hand of the Father. Schillebeeckx, by contrast, exhorted Catholics to remember that the "primordial sacrament" is Christ, who in His incarnate presence in the world is "the sacrament of the encounter" with the invisible God.[7] In a similar spirit, Bonaventure's mention of the "medicinal river" in connection with the third book of the *Sentences*, which deals with the incarnation, and the fourth, which deals with the sacraments, communicates an important truth about the connection between the sacraments and Christ. Bonaventure insists that "sacramental grace proceeds from God as from its author and efficient cause and from Christ as from the mediator and one meriting." Hence, solely because of the passion of Christ can the sacraments be said to be efficacious.

Switching from the Four Properties of a River to the Four Rivers of Paradise

Bonaventure has indicated the subject matter of each of the four books of Lombard's *Sentences*, associating each with one of the four properties of a river, so it might seem as

---

[7] Cf. Edward Schillebeeckx, *Christ, the Sacrament of the Encounter with God* (Lanham, MD: Rowman & Littlefield, 1963).

though he would soon be finishing his prologue. But in fact, he had only just begun. For in the second half of his prologue, he sets out an even more complicated description of the four books of the *Sentences* using the image of the four rivers that in Genesis 2:10-14 are said to "water paradise": the Phison, the Gehon, the Tigris, and the Euphrates.

The name "Phison," says Bonaventure, means "the change of the mouth," and this signifies the emanation of the persons of the Trinity. For just as from the material mouth come word and spirit, so from the mouth of the Father come the Son and the Holy Spirit. And so, from the River Phison, we can remember that the subject of the first book of the *Sentences* is the Trinity.

"Gehon" means "sand," and this signifies the production of worldly things, for just as the universe of creatures is compared to the sea because of the sea's spaciousness, so too the universe is compared to the sands because of their being numerous; as it says in Ecclesiasticus 1.2: "Who hath numbered the sand of the sea, and the drops of rain, and the days of the world?" And so, he associates the River Gehon with the subject of the second book of the *Sentences*, namely creation.

"Tigris" means "arrow," and so this river, according to Bonaventure, signifies the incarnation of the Son of God. For just as in an arrow, iron is joined to wood, so in Christ the strength of divinity is conjoined to the weakness of humanity.[8] And just as an arrow from a wooden bow flies to pierce one's adversaries, so Christ flies from the cross to crush his enemies. So the Tigris River can remind us that the subject of the third book of the *Sentences* is the incarnation.

"Euphrates," finally, according to Bonaventure, means "fruit-bearing." This signifies the dispensation of the sacraments, which not only "purge the soul from blame," but also "make fertile in grace." This is signified in the final book of the Apocalypse 22:2, where it is said that next to the crystalline river, "there was a tree bearing fruit, whose leaves were for medicine" (a passage we've seen before). Thus the subject of the fourth book of the *Sentences* is the sacraments.

It is not clear where Bonaventure got these specific interpretations of the names of the four rivers of paradise. But switching as he does here from a discussion based on the four properties of a river to one based on the four rivers of paradise allows him to discuss the "depths" and the "things hidden" in each of the four "rivers," that is to say, in each of the four books of the *Sentences*. Using this imagery, he can say that the "formal cause" of the *Sentences* involves "searching the depths" of each of the four rivers, and the "final cause" – the reason why Lombard wrote the *Sentences* – was precisely to bring to light the "things hidden" in those depths. Logic dictates, therefore, that we begin with the formal cause, the "depths" or "profound things" (*profunda*) that, according to Bonaventure, Peter Lombard explored in each of the four "rivers" of the *Sentences*.

Formal Cause: The Depths (*Profunda*) in Each of the Four Rivers

According to Bonaventure, the *depth* the Lombard explores in the first river – that is, the first book – is the sublimity of the divine being (*divini esse*), which consists in two

---

[8] Bonaventure likely also has in mind the passage from Isaiah 49.2-3, one of the so-called "Servant Songs" regularly interpreted by Christians as applying to Christ: "He made me a polished arrow; in his quiver he hid me. You are my servant, he said to me, Israel, through whom I show my glory."

things: first, in the most noble emanations, which are generation and procession; and second, in the most noble conditions, which are the highest wisdom, omnipotence, and perfect will. And so in the first part of Book One, the Lombard treats of the divine unity and trinity; and in the second part, he treats of the threefold properties of God: wisdom, omnipotence, and perfect will.

The "depth" he explores in the second book is the "vanity of created being" (*vanitas esse creati*), for creatures vanish if they tend into depths of sin, blame, and punishment. And thus in Psalm 68:2 it is said of a man who lapsed into sin that he is "stuck fast in the mire of the deep." And later in the same Psalm (68:16), the Psalmist prays, "Let not the tempest of water drown me, nor the deep swallow me up," lest he be "swallowed up" by the punishments for his sins. The Lombard explores this "depth" in the second book of the *Sentences*, says Bonaventure, for the vanity of created being consists in two things: namely, in change from non-being into being, and again in reverse, from being into non-being. And although no creature wholly descends into non-being by nature, nevertheless sinners tend toward non-being through their fault. And this twofold depth of the second river is what the Lombard explores in the second book, for in the first part, he treats of the existence of things, and in the second part, he treats of the Fall, the temptation of the devil, and original and actual sin.

Attentive readers may have noticed that the "depths" (*profunda*) explored in the first river was something "high" and "profound": the "sublimity of the divine being" (*sublimitas esse divini*). But the "depths" explored in the second river is something "low" and "deep," as in the "depths" of sin. In *sermo modernus*-style preaching, words could take on different connotations depending upon the verbal association the preacher wished to make. Thus it would not have seemed odd to Bonaventure's audience for the word "*profunda*" to suggest "high" and "sublime" in one sentence, but "deep" and "unsavory" in the next.[9]

In the next or third river, "depth" (*profunda*) will take on another, more ambiguous connotation, for Bonaventure will claim that "the depth of the incarnation is the merit of the humanity of Christ" (*profundum incarnationis est meritum humanitatis Christi*) and that its "depth" is so great it cannot be said to have an end or source. And yet this "bottomlessness" refers not only to the *merit* of Christ, but also to the depth of *humiliation* he suffered. Since Christ was "despised" and "rejected" (cf. Isaiah 53:3), the passage in Jonah 2:4 can be applied to Him: "And thou hast cast me forth into the deep in the heart of the sea, and a flood hath compassed me." The passion of Christ is compared to the sea in this passage, says Bonaventure, because of the harshness of the penalty he suffered on the cross. But His passion is compared also to the flood, because of the overflowing sweetness of love He showed. The depth of this love was so great it was "bottomless," says Bonaventure, both because it was infinite and because Christ descended so fully into the human condition he agreed to suffer the cruelest, "lowest" death on a cross, a just man punished as a criminal, so we might be rescued from sin.

This third "depth" that Lombard examines in the third book of his *Sentences* is twofold. The merit of Christ consists in two things, claims Bonaventure: in his *passion*, through which he redeemed us, and in his *action*, by which he informs us. His action consists in the

---

[9] Recall, in this connection, the thirteenth-century reference works containing lists of *distinctiones* such as those found in Peter Cantor's *Summa Abel* discussed in Chapter 2. One could associate the word avis or "eagle" with angels, demons, or prelates – or all three.

Prologue to Bonaventure's Sentences Commentary 297

works of the virtues, gifts, and precepts. And so in the third book of the *Sentences*, the Lombard treats, first, of the incarnation and Christ's passion, and second, of the virtues, gifts, and precepts.

The fourth "depth" the Lombard investigates, finally, is the depth of the efficacy of the sacraments. For so great is the efficacy of sacramental medicine, says Bonaventure, that it exceeds the human mind, and in this sense can be called "profound." We have now a fourth sense of *profunda* – as something that exceeds human comprehension – just as we have a fourth river. Concerning this fourth "depth," Isaiah 51:10 says: "who made the depth of the sea a way [a road] that the delivered might pass over?" (*qui posuisti profundum maris viam ut transirent liberati*). The reference here is to the Exodus event, when God parted the sea to allow the Israelites to cross dry shod, which Bonaventure describes as a "type" of the Christian sacraments. He writes:

> This depth, in which the Egyptians sunk and the sons of Israel crossed over liberated and saved, is the efficacy of the Sacraments, in which the works of darkness are destroyed and the arms of light and the gifts of the graces are conferred and by which man is transferred from the power of darkness into the kingdom of the sun of the love of God.

What connects (textually) the "depth" of the fourth river and the passage in Isaiah 51:10 about "depth of the sea" is simply the word *profundum*. It was not uncommon in the *sermo modernus* style for a preacher to move from passage to passage – a process sometimes called "chaining" authorities – based solely on the same word showing up in each passage. The process of "chaining" biblical authorities is sometimes dismissed as "preaching by means of a biblical concordance," but I have argued elsewhere that this is to make a category mistake. Were the preacher doing exegesis, the rather tenuous connection between the texts based solely on sharing a single word might be dubious. But Bonaventure is not doing exegesis here; he is weaving a tapestry of images designed to help the reader remember the points he is making.[10]

I have proposed elsewhere that the craft involved here, especially its use of words, should be likened to the art of the poet.[11] Consider, for example, the various meanings and connotations of the words "dark" or "darkness" in this passage from T. S. Eliot's poem "East Coker."

> *O dark dark dark. They all go into the dark,*
> *The vacant interstellar spaces, the vacant into the vacant,*
> *The captains, merchant bankers, eminent men of letters,*
> *The generous patrons of art, the statesmen and the rulers,*
> *Distinguished civil servants, chairmen of many committees,*
> *Industrial lords and petty contractors, all go into the dark,*
> *And dark the Sun and Moon, and the Almanach de Gotha*
> *And the Stock Exchange Gazette, the Directory of Directors,*
> *And cold the sense and lost the motive of action.*

---

[10] For a more detailed discussion of "chaining" authorities, see my *Reading the Sermons of Aquinas*, esp. 131–141.

[11] See *Reading the Sermons of Aquinas*, 223–225.

> *And we all go with them, into the silent funeral*
> *Nobody's funeral, for there is no one to bury.*

In these lines, the word "dark" suggests emptiness and death. But now consider the lines that immediately follow in the poem: "I said to my soul, be still, and let the dark come upon you / Which shall be the darkness of God." This darkness is not entirely unrelated to the first, but it suggests an emptiness that allows for the entry of God's grace and peace.

> Here, then, are the final lines:
>
> *I said to my soul, be still, and wait without hope*
> *For hope would be hope for the wrong thing; wait without love*
> *For love would be love of the wrong thing; there is yet faith*
> *But the faith and the love and the hope are all in the waiting.*
> *Wait without thought, for you are not ready for thought:*
> *So the darkness shall be the light, and the stillness the dancing.*

Here, the "darkness" has become "light"; emptiness and death have opened up to "hope" and new life." We need not go into the particularities of how this change comes about; I merely wish to note that, even in English, we recognize and accept these changes in the use and connotations of words all the time.

The unity that holds these lines together in Eliot's poem is neither the narrative unity of a story nor simply the thematic unity of an essay. What holds the passage together, if anything, is the intricate and interesting way Eliot plays with the words and images. My claim is that Bonaventure's use of words and images is no less flexible and no less complex.

But to recap, Bonaventure has deftly moved us from the "depth" of a river to the deep sea that Moses parted to allow the Israelites to pass through dry shod. And this image is used to signify the efficacy of the sacraments. Just as Moses liberated the Israelites from their slavery in Egypt and cleared the way for their entry into the glory of the Promised Land, so too the sacraments both liberate us from sin and make it possible for us to enjoy the sweetness of God's glory. And so the Lombard examines the sacraments in the fourth book of the Sentences. For the efficacy of the perfect medicine consists in two things, says Bonaventure: in being cured from a variety of depressing illnesses and in being freed from all aggravating miseries. And so in the first part of Book Four, the Lombard treats the multiple cleansings brought about by the seven sacraments; and in the second, he treats of the glory of the revival that the sacraments of the Church truly and faithfully secure for us and the punishment of evils that the sacraments keep far away.

In these sections on the "depths" explored in each of the four books of the *Sentences*, which as we should recall, is also a discussion of the formal cause of each book, Bonaventure is presupposing an interesting relationship between matter and form. The subject matter of Book One of the *Sentences* is the Trinity. The *form* of the book is bipartite. In the first part of Book One, the Lombard discusses the unity and trinity of God; in the second, he treats the properties of God: wisdom, omnipotence, and divine will. The subject matter of Book Two is creation. The form of this book is also bipartite. In the first part, the Lombard treats created being; in the second, the privation of the being of things due to sin. The subject matter of the third book is the incarnation. Once again, the *form* of the book is bipartite. In the first part, the Lombard he treats the incarnation and Christ's passion; in the second, he discusses our participation in Christ's redemptive sacrifice by means of the virtues, gifts, and precepts. The subject matter of the fourth book of the *Sentences*, finally, is the sacraments. The form of the book, as before, is bipartite. In the first part, the Lombard treats the multiple ways we are cleansed by the sacraments (i.e., the illnesses they cure); in the second, he discusses the glory of the revival the sacraments offer (i.e., the renewed health they restore). To modern readers, it might seem as though specifying the two parts of each book would be merely a further specification of the subject matter of that book. But Bonaventure considers these divisions under the heading of the formal cause. The two subsections are the "form" within which the subject matter of the book is treated.

The Final Cause: Bringing to Light the Four Hidden Things

As Bonaventure moved earlier from the four properties of a river to the four rivers in his discussion of the material cause or subject matter of each book of the *Sentences*, and from the four rivers to the "depth" of each river in his discussion of the formal cause of each book, so now in this third section he will build on the image of "depth" to show that Lombard's goal or purpose (the final cause) is to reveal the "hidden things" (*abscondita*) hidden in the depths of each river. It will be useful, therefore, to recall briefly each of these "rivers" and its "depth."

The first property of a river is perpetuity, and the first river is the Phison, which means "change of mouth." And so the first book of the *Sentences* has as its subject matter the timeless emanation of Persons in the Trinity. The "depth" of this river is the sublimity of the divine *esse*.

The second property of a river is spaciousness, and the second river is the Gehon, which means "sand." And so the second book of the *Sentences* has as its subject matter the creation of all worldly things, which are as numerous, but also as empty, as sand. The "depth" of this river is the emptiness of created being, especially sin.

The third property of a river is circulation, and the third river is the Tigris, which means "arrow." And so the third book of the *Sentences* has as its subject matter the incarnation, a conjoining of God and man similar to the conjoining of wood and iron that is an arrow. And just as an arrow strikes down the enemy, so Christ's sacrifice on the cross struck down the devil. The "depth" of this river is the bottomlessness of Christ's love and of His humiliation.

The fourth property of a river is cleansing, and the fourth river is the Euphrates, which means "fruit-bearing." And so the fourth book of the *Sentences* has as its subject matter the efficacy of the sacraments, the medicine made from the fruit of the Tree of Life by which our illness is cured and our health is restored.

To these four, we can now add the things "hidden" (*abscondita*) in the "depths" of each river. In the first book of the *Sentences*, the mystery "hidden" in the "depths," says Bonaventure, is the "magnitude of the divine substance" (*magnitudo divinae substantiae*), about which Isaiah says (45:15): "Verily thou art a hidden God (*Deus absconditus*), the God of Israel, the savior." Hence,

> the Teacher, filled with the wisdom of the heavens, brought into light the investigation of this hiddenness in the first book. For having seen and understood the most noble

emanations and most noble properties, he made known to us (as much as is possible for those *in via*) the magnitude of the divine substance.

The mystery "hidden" in the "depths" of the second book, then, is "the order of divine wisdom" (*ordo divinae sapientiae*) according to which the world was made. This is the wisdom of which Job speaks when he asks (28.12): "But where is wisdom to be found, and where the place of understanding?" and answers (28:21): "It is hid (*abscondita*) from the eyes of all living." Although we cannot know this wisdom in itself, God makes it known to us in His works, in which His wisdom shines forth. This hiddenness is what the Lombard discloses in the investigations of the second book.

The mystery "hidden" in the "depths" of the third book is "the fortitude of the divine power" (*fortitudo divinae potentiae*), a power that lay hidden under a cloak of infirmity when Christ, though strong, put on the arms of our infirmity and hung on the cross for us, something unheard of through all the ages. A powerful man does not allow himself to be put to death. Yet, says Bonaventure, if Christ still conquers in infirmity, how much more is His divine power shown in this way. It should be clear, therefore, that "his fortitude is unwavering whose infirmity is so strong" (*inenarrabilis fortitudo eius, cuius tam fortis infirmitas*).

The mystery "hidden" in the "depths" of the fourth book, then, is "the sweetness of divine mercy" (*dulcedo divinae misericordiae*), about which we read in Psalm 30:20: "O how great is the multitude of thy sweetness, O Lord, which thou hast hidden (*abscondisti*) for them that fear thee!" This sweetness is manifested in the investigations of the fourth book, for in it, the Lombard considers the way God dismisses sins in the present, applies medicines to our wounds, and gives awards, revealing to us the sweetness of His divine mercy.

The publishing of these four "hidden" things is the end or purpose of the whole work, says Bonaventure. Hence:

> the Teacher of the *Sentences*, wishing to lead and be led, investigated the depths of the rivers, led by the grace of the Holy Spirit. For he especially investigated the secrets (*secretorum*) and the depths (*profunda*), according to what is said in 1 Corinthians 2:10: "For the Spirit searcheth all things, yea, the deep things of God" (*profunda Dei*).

And with this, Bonaventure has begun his transition into the last, and shortest, section of his prologue: namely the one dealing with the efficient cause or author of the work.

The Efficient Cause or Author of the Work

After nearly ten columns in the Quaracchi volume dealing with the material, formal, and final causes of the *Sentences*, Bonaventure expends barely one paragraph – some four sentences – talking about the author, the man he calls simply "the Teacher" (*Magister*), the way Thomas Aquinas called Aristotle simply "the Philosopher." If we have been following the steps of Bonaventure's opening *divisio*, we know that the material cause was associated with the word *fluviorum* ("rivers"); the formal cause with the word *profunda* ("depths"); the final cause with the word *abscondita* ("hidden things"); and the efficient cause, finally, with the words *scrutatus est* ("he has searched") and *produxit in lucem* ("he has brought forth to light"). The divisions with the most words do not always result in the longest dilation, however. Here is how Bonaventure finishes his prologue:

> Stirred in love by this Spirit and illumined by clarity and by light, the Teacher composed this work and "searched the depths of the rivers." With the help of the same Spirit, he was made the revealer of hidden things. For he is the one concerning whom it is written in Daniel 2.22: "He revealeth deep and hidden things, and knoweth what is in darkness." And this was the intention and end of the Teacher.

And with this, it seems that Bonaventure has finished. He finished dilating each section of his opening *thema* verse; he covered all four Aristotelian causes: the material, formal, final, and efficient; and he provided a clear picture of the topics covered in each of the four books of the *Sentences*. He clarified how the diverse topics of each book might be fitted together into a theologically coherent whole, and he accomplished all this with creative imagery and in perfectly parallel Latin phrases. All in all, the prologue has probably done about as much as a prologue can do to make Peter Lombard look smart and the *Sentences* seem impressive. So, is he finished? Not quite.

The Four Disputed Questions

Bonaventure finishes his prologue with four "disputed questions" that further elaborate the author, subject matter, form, and purpose of the book. Bonaventure will similarly append several disputed questions to the end of the prologue to his *Commentary on the Gospel of John*. He did not always add disputed questions to the end of his prologues, but he did so here.

The four questions Bonaventure poses are these:

Question 1: What is the subject of this book, that is, of theology?
Question 2: What is the way of proceeding in this book?
Question 3: Is this book, or theology, for the sake of contemplation, or for the sake of making us good; i.e., is it a speculative or a practical science?
Question 4: What is the efficient cause or author of this book?

These are standard questions about the subject matter, the manner of proceeding, the purpose, and the author of the book – in other words, the material cause, the formal cause, the final cause, and efficient cause of the book – topics that Bonaventure covered already in the *sermo modernus* section of the prologue. It is difficult to know why he chose to review the material he had already covered in this different format. Perhaps he thought he could make certain points clearer this way. Whatever his reasons, the pairing allows us to compare the treatment of what is basically the same material in these two different, modes of scholastic discourse.

Question 1: What Is the Subject of this Book, That Is, of Theology?

In the earlier *sermo modernus* section of the prologue, Bonaventure discussed the subject matter of the four books of the *Sentences* by associating them with the four qualities of a river and the four rivers of paradise, both of which he interpreted figuratively to show that the first book of the *Sentences* dealt with the Trinity, the second book with creation, the third with the incarnation, and the fourth with the sacraments.

Here, in the disputed questions section of his prologue, Bonaventure argues, in good scholastic fashion, that "the subject in any science or doctrine can be understood in three ways." In one way, the subject of a science is understood as something to which all things are reducible (*reducuntur*) as to their root principle (*principium radicale*); in a second way, as something to which all things are reducible as to an integral whole (*totum integrale*); and in a third way, as something to which all things are reducible as a universal whole (*totum universale*).

"A clear example," he says, "is provided in grammar." In grammar, its *subject* in the first sense (that to which all things are reducible as to their root principle) is "letter" (*littera*). The subject of grammar in the second sense (that to which all are reducible as to an integral whole) is "perfect and well-rounded speech" (*oratio congrua et perfecta*). The subject of grammar in the third sense (that to which all are reducible as a universal whole) is "literate speech, articulated in an orderly fashion for signifying something in itself or in something else" (*vox litterata, articulata ordinabilis ad significandum aliquid in se vel in alio*).

If we ask, "What is the subject of grammar?" one way of answering that question would be to say: "The subject of grammar is letters." Letters are the building blocks of language. Since Latin is an inflected language, Bonaventure may also have had in mind the fact that Latin uses letters to indicate different parts of speech (nouns, verbs, adjectives) and to make plurals and possessives. These are the "principal roots," the "building blocks," of grammar.

And yet rarely do people study the "root principles" of grammar for their own sake. We study the building blocks of grammar so we can learn to speak and write clearly, to produce what Bonaventure describes as "perfect and well-rounded speech" (*oratio congrua et perfecta*) – what we might describe as speaking and writing "in complete sentences." This is what Bonaventure would call the "integral whole" to which the study of the parts is ordered.

But there is more. All people want to speak clearly and make their thoughts known to others. The "subject" of grammar in this sense – that whole to which the parts (the letters and words) are ordered – would be "literate speech" (*vox litterata*): articulate sentences, delivered in an orderly fashion, so people can understand what you are saying. In contemporary discourse, we might describe this as the ability to "make a speech" (or in writing, write a coherent paragraph or essay). The person not only forms words and complete sentences; he forms those sentences into a coherent whole that communicates a message. This would be the "universal whole" to which the study of the parts of grammar is ordered.

Bonaventure's second example is taken from geometry. If we ask, "What is the subject of geometry?" and if what we mean is, "What is the root principle of everything in geometry?" the answer, says Bonaventure, is "the point" (as in points, lines, and planes). If we are asking, "What is the subject in the sense of that to which all things are reduced as to an integral whole?" the answer would be "body," which "contains in itself every genus of dimension." If we are asking, "What is the subject to which all things are reduced as to a universal whole?" the answer would be "continuous, immobile, quantity" (*quantitas continua, immobilis*).

From these examples, we move to the subject matter of the *Sentences* and of theology – which, says Bonaventure, we can also assign according to a triple sense. The subject to which all things can be reduced as to their "root principle" or origin is God Himself. And so, in this sense, the "subject" of theology is God. The "subject" of the *Sentences* in the sense of "that to which all things can be reduced as to an *integral whole*" is Christ, says Bonaventure, since he contains within Himself both divine and human natures, created and uncreated. And so the subjects of the first two books of the *Sentences* are the uncreated God (Book One) and creation (Book Two). Or we might consider Christ as head and members, and these are the subjects of the final two books: Christ's incarnation (Book Three) and the sacraments (Book Four).

The "subject" of the *Sentences* in the sense of "that to which all things can be reduced as to a *universal whole*," finally, is "sign" and "thing." The sign here is called a "sacrament." But we can also say that the "subject" of theology (and thus of the *Sentences*) in this sense is the "credible" (in the sense of "that which is believed") insofar as the credible becomes intelligible through the addition of reason (*credibile, prout tamen credibile transit in rationem intelligibilis, and hoc per additionem rationis*). We might put this more simply and say that theology involves an "understanding of faith." Or, to use Bonaventure's terminology, we can say that the "subject" of the *Sentences* is "the credible," signs pointing to things proposed for belief as they can be understood by reason. This third dimension of Lombard's *Sentences* is not entirely absent from the *sermo modernus* part of the prologue: it is covered under the notion that the Lombard is the one who "searched" (*scrutatus est*) the depths and "brought forth to light" (*produxit in lucem*) the hidden things.

The disputed question mode allows Bonaventure to affirm that the subject of the book (and of theology) ultimately is God – God as we know Him through creation and as He has revealed Himself in and through Christ, the Scriptures, and the sacraments, which are signs that point in various ways to deeper realities. How we understand the nature of the signification in each case (the Book of Nature, the Book of Scripture, the Incarnation, and the sacraments) is crucial to how we come to understand the things proposed for our belief.

Question 2: What Is the Formal Cause or Manner of Proceeding in This Book of Sentences?

We come now to Bonaventure's second question, which deals with the formal cause or the manner of proceeding in the book. In the *sermo modernus* part of the prologue, Bonaventure discussed this topic by associating it with a "thorough examination" of the "depths" of the rivers. He repeatedly used some form of *perscrutor, perscrutari, perscrutatus sum* there, clearly suggested to him by the words *scrutatus est* in his opening *thema*, in conjunction with various meanings of the Latin word *profunda* (depth). The four "depths," as the reader may recall, were: (1) the sublimity of the divine being; (2) the emptiness of created being, especially the emptiness caused by sin; (3) the bottomlessness of Christ's love and humiliation on the cross; and (4) the profound efficacy of the sacraments. Each of these four was then divided into two subsections: Trinity and divine properties in the first; creation and sin in the second; incarnation and passion, and then virtues, gifts, and precepts in the third; and the illnesses the sacraments cure, and then the health they supply in the fourth.

Here in the disputed question section, Bonaventure reiterates what he had established in that earlier section: "It has been said" that it (the manner of proceeding) is "by a thorough examination and inquiry of mysteries" (*quod est perscrutatorius et inquisitivus secretorum*).

The "ratiocinative" (*ratiocinativus*) or "inquisitive" (*inquisitivus*) mode of theology is effective in promoting the faith, says Bonaventure, in three ways for three sorts of men. Some men are opposed to the faith, and for these, such reasoning as we find in the *Sentences* is effective for refuting them (*ad confudendum adversaries*). Those of the second group are merely weak in their faith, and for these, theology is effective in strengthening them (*ad fovendum infirmos*). For those whose faith is perfect, however, theology is effective in pleasing them (*ad delectandum perfectos*) because "the soul delights in understanding what it believes with perfect faith."

If we combine the categories discussed in Question 2 with the imagery found in the *sermo modernus* part of the prologue earlier, we could say that a "thorough examination" of the "depths" is valuable in order to "bring to light" things "hidden" there because (1) some people will deny that the things hidden in the depths exist at all; (2) others will be only weakly convinced of the existence of the hidden things unless they see at least some evidence of them; and (3) still others will delight to see what they, without seeing, knew by faith was there.

Question 3: Whether This Book, or Theology, Is for the Sake of Contemplation, or So That We May Be Made Good, That Is, Whether It Is a Speculative or a Practical Science

This long question is merely another way of asking, "What is the final cause of the text?" Earlier, in the *sermo modernus* section of the prologue, Bonaventure stated that the final cause was "examining" and "bringing to light" the things "hidden" in the "depths" of the rivers. In the first river, the hidden thing revealed was the magnitude of the divine substance; in the second, the order of divine wisdom; in the third, the fortitude of divine power; and in the fourth, the sweetness of divine mercy. And sure enough, at the beginning of this third question, Bonaventure reiterates that "it has been said that this book is for the purpose of revealing hidden things" (*ad revelandum abscondita*).

Yet there is something more involved here – the classic question that divided the medieval Dominicans and Franciscans: whether theology should be seen as a speculative or a practical science. Does our love of God help propel us to the end of *knowing* Him, or does *knowing* God help direct us to the end of *loving* Him? Thomas Aquinas's answer was that the ultimate end of man consists in the contemplation of God.[12] Bonaventure stakes out a different position.

He begins by agreeing that what is perfected by any science is our intellect (*quod perfectibile a scientia est intellectus*). Yet, he adds, in characteristic scholastic fashion, that the intellect can be considered in three ways: namely, (1) in itself (*in se*), (2) insofar as it is extended to the affections (*prout extenditur ad affectum*), or (3) insofar as it is extended to work (*prout extenditur ad opus*). The intellect extends itself by dictating and regulating (*dictantis et regulantis*), and thus it has a threefold directive habit (*habitum directivum*). If we consider the intellect *in se*, it is properly speculative and is perfected by the *habitus* which is for the sake of contemplation, which is called "speculative science" (*scientia speculativa*). But if we consider it as by nature extended to some work, it is perfected by a *habitus* that makes

---

[12] See SCG III.37 and ST I–II, q. 3, esp. aa. 5, 6, and 8.

us good; and this is the practical or moral science (*scientia practica sive moralis*). But if the intellect is considered in some middle way as naturally extended to the affections, it is perfected by a *habitus* midway between the purely speculative and the purely practical that embraces both. This *habitus* is called "wisdom," and it simultaneously expresses cognition and affection. Developing this third cognitive *habitus*, namely wisdom, is the goal of the *Sentences*, claims Bonaventure, as it should be the goal of all studies.

For faith, says Bonaventure, is a cognition that by nature moves the affections. There are things we know that do not move the affections, such as trivial facts or unused theorems. Merely knowing *that* "Christ died for us" is not the aim of theology. The point of knowing this fact is to move us to love. "Therefore it ought to be conceded," says Bonaventure, "that theology is for making us good." As for the objection that the purpose of theology is to reveal hidden things – a conclusion Bonaventure's own earlier prologue would have done much to support – this is not so, he says here, "because that revelation is ordered to affection."

Question 4: What Is the Efficient Cause or Author of This Book?

Bonaventure spent only one, short paragraph in the *sermo modernus* part of his prologue on the author of the *Sentences*. Question 4 will provide him room to say more. We might have expected him to concentrate on praising Peter Lombard and admiring his virtues both intellectual and moral, just as it was customary in prologues to biblical commentaries to praise the sacred author. Instead, Bonaventure spends his time defending the Lombard as an authentic "author" because so much of the *Sentences* had been culled from earlier Patristic sources.

Bonaventure distinguishes four ways of making a book. One way would be to write out the words of someone else without adding or changing anything. Such a person would be called a scribe, not an author. Another way would be to copy the words of a number of other writers, merely putting them together in a certain order. Such a person should be called a compiler. A third way would be to copy the words of several other writers while adding some of one's own, but the words of the other writers comprise the principal part, whereas one's own are added merely to clarify the arguments of the others. Such a person should be called a commentator, not an author. A fourth way of making a book would be to copy the words of others and then add one's own, with one's own words forming the principal part of the book and the words of others being added merely as a confirmation. This last person, says Bonaventure, is rightly called an author (*auctor*), and the Lombard falls into this category, for he sets forth his own positions (*sententiae*) and then confirms them with the sayings of the holy Fathers.

As we have seen, a young bachelor of the Bible commonly would copy out St. Jerome's prologue to whatever book of the Bible he was commenting upon and would append it to his own prologue when he was lecturing. Here, after having resolved Question 4, Bonaventure in like manner copied out Peter Lombard's own prologue to the *Sentences* and then provided a short commentary on it, mostly by way of a *divisio textus*. And with this, he brought his prologue to a close, an admirable schoolroom project preparing him for the kinds of prologues it was assumed he would soon be writing each term after he had been incepted as a master. However, the Franciscans would soon call Bonaventure to a different future – as Minister General of the Order.

13

Exalting Our Understanding
The Prologue to Bonaventure's Commentary *on the Gospel of John*

Bonaventure's *Commentary on the Gospel of John* was revised, scholars tell us, when he was an early master, but it was based on materials he had prepared several years before as a *baccalarius biblicus*.[1] An interesting characteristic of this prologue is that, unlike his later prologue to his *Commentary on the Gospel of Luke* in which Bonaventure spent very little time talking about St. Luke, in this prologue, the figure of St. John dominates. The praise of the Gospel is carried out primarily by praising its author because, as Bonaventure comments, "the commendation of the author redounds upon the work."

The structure of this prologue is also much simpler than the sprawling and complicated structure of the prologue to his *Commentary on the Gospel of St. Luke*. Bonaventure makes a simple threefold *divisio* of his opening *thema* verse and then subdivides each of these into three subdivisions, the sole exception being the last of these. After the last subdivision of the words "exceedingly sublime," Bonaventure makes a further threefold sub-subdivision related to the "sublimity" of the Gospel. In this section, he adds comments about the material, formal, and final causes of the Gospel.

Bonaventure chose as his *thema* for this prologue a selection from Isaiah 52.13: "Behold, my servant will understand, and he will be exalted and elevated and will be exceedingly sublime" (*Ecce intelleget servus meus exaltabitur et elevabitur et sublimis erit valde*). He begins by making a threefold division of the verse: Behold my servant / will understand / and he will be exalted and elevated and will be exceedingly sublime. "In these words," says Bonaventure, St. John is praised for three things: for his "holiness of life" (*sanctitate vitae*), where it says "Behold my servant"; for his "clarity of understanding" (*claritate intelligentiae*),

---

[1] English: Bonaventure, *Commentary on the Gospel of John*, trans. Robert J. Karris, Works of St. Bonaventure, 11 (St. Bonaventure, NY: The Franciscan Institute, 2007), esp. 1–3. Latin: St. Bonaventure, *Opera Omnia* (Ad Claras Aquas Quaracchi: Collegii s. Bonaventurae, 1882–1901), vol. 6. Since the section numbers in the English translation follow those in the Quaracchi edition, references to Bonaventure's text will be given by these section numbers, i.e., "*In Ioan. prol.* 3."

> **Box 13.1** Outline of Bonaventure's Prologue to *Commentary on John*
>
> "Behold, my servant will understand, and he will be exalted and elevated and will be exceedingly sublime" (*Ecce intelleget servus meus exaltabitur et elevabitur et sublimis erit valde*). Isaiah 52:13
>
> 1. "Behold my servant": sanctity of life, shown by:
>   a. His fidelity (*obsequium*)
>   b. His office (*officium*)
>   c. His benefit (*beneficium*)
> 2. "he will understand": clarity of understanding, arose in him due to:
>   a. Anointing of the Holy Spirit (he understood useful matters)
>   b. Angelic revelation (he understood hidden things)
>   c. Christ's teaching (he understood sublime things)
> 3. "and he will be exalted and elevated and will be exceedingly sublime": excellence of doctrine (of teaching), by a threefold dignity of instruction"
>   a. Exalted (to the apostolic chair): Canonical Epistles (authentic preacher)
>   b. Elevated (to prophetic pronouncement): Book of Revelation (illustrious prophet)
>   c. Exceedingly sublime (in his evangelical teaching): Gospel (most learned author)
>   i. The Gospel deals with sublime matters: Incarnate Word according to two natures (material cause)
>   ii. Proceeds in a sublime manner: manner of certitude though narrative (formal cause)
>   iii. Leads to sublime things: believe in Jesus and have eternal life (final cause)

where it says "will understand"; and for his "excellence in teaching" (*excellentia doctrinae*), where it says "he will be exalted and elevated and will be exceedingly sublime"[2] (Box 13.1).

I have suggested already that Bonaventure's use of language resembles that of a poet more than a scholastic logician. Listen to how he words his categories: *sanctitate vitae*, *claritate intelligentiae*, and *excellentia doctrinae*. All three together roll off the tongue sonorously. I have argued in several places already that the thirteenth-century use of the *thema* verse to lend structure to a sermon was done as a mnemonic device to help the audience remember and recall the points in the sermon. The preaching manuals all insist that the phrases in such lists should be parallel. Bonaventure takes this art a step further, having realized that making the phrases rhyme and the meter of the phrases match also aid the memory. People can often memorize poems more readily than they do prose because the sounds of the words and the rhythm of the phrasing help them remember, much as the rhythm and melody of music help people memorize song lyrics more easily.

Whereas Thomas always had the spirit of a logician who sought clarity of argument first, and who only later became adept at the *sermo modernus* style, Bonaventure, although he learned logic and how to make divisions and distinctions, always had the soul of a poet. He clearly loved the sounds of words and the evocative play of imagery they could invoke in people's minds. I ask the reader to notice as we proceed how Bonaventure's celebration of the sounds of words is manifested time and again.

---

[2] *In Ioan. prol.* 1.

Sanctity of Life

John's "sanctity of life" is suggested by the words "Behold my servant." John was God's servant par excellence, says Bonaventure, and this was shown three ways: first, because of his fidelity (*obsequium*); second because of his office (*officium*); and third because of the benefit (*beneficium*) he received as a gift from the Spirit.[3] The order here is relevant, as Bonaventure comments: "For this is the order in these matters, holiness of life merits the gift of understanding, and the gift of understanding disposes a person to excellence in teaching."[4] And yet, if someone is worried whether Bonaventure is suggesting that John *earned* God's gifts because he "merited" them, quite the contrary, as we will see, Bonaventure understands all three as the result of God's predestined will for John.

John's sanctity of life was shown, first, by his fidelity (*obsequium*). John was the most faithful of all the apostles, claims Bonaventure. Although he does not mention it, Bonaventure likely has in mind that John was the only apostle to come to the site of the crucifixion. What he does mention is that Christ "committed to [John's] care that most noble treasure, namely, the virginity of his Mother." This took place, as Bonaventure's audience would have known, at the foot of the cross.

John's sanctity was shown in a second way by the office (*officium*) that God bestowed upon him: that is, the office of preaching – an office he did not receive for his own glory, but for God's, and for which he was predestined from eternity.

John's sanctity was shown, third, by the benefit (*beneficium*) God bestowed upon him, "for he was elected and chosen beforehand and beloved by God and gifted with a special bestowal of grace." John was Christ's *servant* ("Behold my servant") because of his fidelity, office, and God's benefit.[5]

Gift of Understanding

Because of his holiness of life, which as we have said, was due to the gift of God's grace, John merited "the gift of understanding" (*donum intelligentiae*), which is suggested by the word *intelleget* ("will understand") in the opening *thema*: "Behold my servant will understand . . ." According to Bonaventure, this gift of understanding arose in John, first, from the *anointing of the Holy Spirit*, through which he came to understand *useful* matters, since the Spirit of truth is the spirit of salvation. It arose also from *angelic revelation*, through which he came to understand *hidden things* which would come to be. And by means of *Christ's teaching*, John came to understand *sublime things*.[6] Note the precise relationships mapped out here:

---

[3] Ibid., 2.
[4] Ibid., 1.
[5] See ibid., 2. I have changed Robert Karris's translation of *beneficium* here from "graciousness" to "benefit" because it is closer to *beneficium*. The Latin word can also mean "graciousness," it is true, but Karris is right that Bonaventure probably also has in mind a medieval *benefice*. This would be the gift of an office, generally bestowed by a medieval lord on a faithful servant. This meaning of the word would make the most sense in the context.
[6] See *In Ioan. prol.* 3.

Anointing of the Holy Spirit: useful things (*utilia*)
Angelic revelation: hidden things (*abscondita*)
Christ's teaching: sublime things (*sublimia*)

Does Bonaventure have something specific in mind here, or is he merely tossing about these categories arbitrarily? The answer can be found in the next section on the excellence of teaching.

Excellence of Teaching

Section 4 begins:

> Thus Blessed John understood useful and hidden and sublime matters, and by reason of this threefold understanding was exalted to the triple dignity of instruction. Therefore the text [the opening *thema* verse] says: "He will be exalted," that is, to the apostolic chair. He will be "extolled" to prophetic pronouncement." And he will be "exceedingly sublime" through his evangelical teaching. For this reason he produced three writings, namely, the canonical Epistles as authentic preacher; Revelation as illustrious prophet; and the Gospel, as most learned author.[7]

With this, Bonaventure is transitioning from his second division, based on the words "he will understand," to his third, with its dilation of the words: "and he will be exalted and elevated and will be exceedingly sublime." As he linked the first section with the second, saying that John's sanctity of life merited the gift of understanding, so too here, he links John's special "gift of understanding" that made possible what he described above as an "excellence of doctrine" (*excellentia doctrinae*) with what he calls here a threefold "dignity of instruction" (*dignitatem doctrinae*).[8]

Matching the three categories from this section with the three from the previous one gives us this:

Anointing of the Holy Spirit	Useful things	Exalted to apostolic chair	Canonical epistles
Angelic revelation	Hidden things	Elevated to prophecy	Revelation
Christ's teaching	Sublime things	Sublime in Gospel teaching	Gospel

John, having been "anointed by the Holy Spirit," was "exalted to the apostolic chair" (the position of bishops and the pope as the successors of the apostles) and in that position, with that apostolic authority, he wrote the canonical epistles which expressed "useful" things to the early Church. But John also is said to have written the Book of Revelation. These visions were revealed to him on the island of Patmos by an angel. Because of this angelic revelation, he was

---

[7] *In Ioan. prol.* 4.
[8] Ibid.

"elevated" – raised up to see the heavens – where the angels reveals to him "hidden things," things to come, which he reveals as a New Testament prophet in the Book of Revelation.

We come finally to the book Bonaventure is setting out to comment upon, namely the Gospel. Where did John learn the things he teaches here? Bonaventure's answer: from Christ himself. Why is its teaching not only "sublime" but "most sublime"? Because John, according to Bonaventure (following nearly every other commentator in the Middle Ages), is the Gospel writer who sees most clearly and expresses most profoundly the divinity of Christ.[9]

Three Ways for a Teaching to Be Sublime: The Material, Formal, and Final Causes

Thus far we have seen paragraph after paragraph noting the special gifts and blessings God lavished upon John to prepare him for writing. He is "the most learned author" and thus the "efficient cause" of the Gospel marked with his name. What of the other three Aristotelian causes? Bonaventure tucks them in at the very end of this prologue, claiming that "since the sublime nature of the teacher is manifested in the sublimity of the teaching, he rightly seems to be exceedingly sublime, if an explanation is given for the sublimity of this Gospel."[10] Under the heading "exceedingly sublime," then (the final two words in his opening *thema* verse), Bonaventure sneaks in another threefold subdivision.

A teaching is sublime, says Bonaventure, for any of three reasons: first, because it deals with sublime matters; second, because it proceeds in a sublime manner; or third, because it leads to sublime things. It is likely no surprise to discover that, according to Bonaventure, John's Gospel is sublime in all three ways.[11] It *deals* with sublime matters: that is, with the Incarnate Word in its two natures, which is most sublime subject and the subject matter of the Gospel. It *proceeds* in a sublime manner: the manner of certitude, which is its formal cause. And it *leads to* sublime things: namely eternal life, which is its final cause, as John himself says at the end of his Gospel (20.31): "These things have been written, so that you may believe that Jesus is ... the Son of God, and that believing you may have life in his name." This single verse from John 20:31 provides everything Bonaventure needs to establish the final cause of the Gospel. The elaborate biblical imagery John uses to establish the first two points, however – that the Gospel deals with a sublime subject matter and proceeds in a sublime manner – are worthy of further examination.

The Cedar Tree and the Eagle

The elaborate allegory Bonaventure uses to discuss the subject matter of the Gospel is of special interest because it presents a good example of Bonaventure incorporating allegory into a *sermo modernus*–style prologue.[12] His goal is to make the fairly simple point

---

[9] See ibid. One could compare Bonaventure's comment about John's especially clear vision of Christ's divinity with those in nearly any medieval commentator. But for our present purposes, the reader might simply compare Bonaventure's affirmation with the same notion found in Thomas's prologue to John described in Chapter 8. The idea had by this time become commonplace.
[10] *In Ioan. prol.* 4.
[11] Ibid., 5.
[12] The entire allegory can be found in *In Ioan. prol.* 5.

that the Gospel of John deals with the Incarnate Word in His two natures, human and divine. The way he illustrated this point, however, was by means of a complex and fascinating set of biblical images.

He begins with a passage from Ezekiel 17.22–23: "The Lord God says this: I myself will take the finest part of the high and sublime cedar... And I will plant it on a mountain high and eminent, on the high and sublime mountain of Israel..." There is a clear division here between the first verse and the second. What is not so obvious is the way Bonaventure dilates them. "The finest part of the high and sublime cedar," says Bonaventure, is the hidden divinity of the Word. God the Father planted it "on the high and sublime mountain of Israel," since he united it to the human nature in Christ. Interpreting this cedar planted on the mountain of Israel as an image of the incarnation was creative, but the allegory is about to get more complicated still.

According to Bonaventure, "the Gospel of Blessed John flows from the finest part of this high and sublime cedar." If we recall that "the finest part of this high and sublime cedar" is the incarnate divinity of Christ, then we realize he is saying figuratively that the Gospel of John "flows" from the divinity of Christ. He undoubtedly has in mind the first verses of John's Gospel, which states: "In the beginning was the Word, and the Word was with God, and the Word was God." Everything else in the Gospel "flows forth" from this. We are meant to understand the significance of the events of Christ's life in light of the central affirmation of faith that "the Word became flesh and dwelt among us" (John 1.14) in the person of Jesus of Nazareth. His teachings, His miraculous deeds, and His death on the cross were not merely those of a prophet, a great teacher, or a wise and holy man; rather, they all must be understood in light of His incarnate divinity, as God "speaking" to us, revealing Himself, His love, and His salvific will to us so we might be reconciled to Him and enjoy eternal life with Him.

And yet Bonaventure is still not finished, for he has yet to work into his prologue the iconic image of John as the eagle. Bonaventure's listeners would have known that among the four creatures mentioned at the beginning of the Book of Ezekiel (the lion, the ox, the man, and the eagle), the eagle always, even from the time of the earliest Church, was taken to represent John the Evangelist.[13] And in Ezekiel 17:3–4, Bonaventure found this verse:

> The large eagle with great wings, long pinions, full of thick plumage of many colors, came to Lebanon and took away the finest cedar. He cropped off the summit of this cedar and carried it away into the land of Canaan.

He applies the imagery he finds here to elucidate the author and subject matter of the Gospel. "The large eagle," he says, which we know is John the Evangelist, is large "with the breadth of charity" (*per latitudinem caritatis*). The eagle also has "great wings" with which to reach "the height of contemplation" (*per altitudinem contemplationis*).[14] He also has "long pinions," representing "the length of expectation" (*per exspectationis longitudinem*). The

---

[13] Cf. Ezekiel 1, esp. 4–5, and 10: "And I saw, and behold a whirlwind came out of the north: and a great cloud, and a fire infolding it, and brightness was about it: and out of the midst thereof, that is, out of the midst of the fire, as it were the resemblance of amber: And in the midst thereof the likeness of four living creatures ... And as for the likeness of their faces: there was the face of a man, and the face of a lion on the right side of all the four: and the face of an ox, on the left side of all the four: and the face of an eagle over all the four."

[14] Aquinas also associated John with the height of contemplation in the prologue to his commentary.

eagle's thick full plumage of many colors represents his "multitude of virtues" (*per virtutum multitudinem*). This eagle "came to Lebanon," to "the mountain of mountains," Christ (*montem montium Christum*)[15] and "took away the finest cedar," that is, the hidden divinity of the Word (*latentem Divinitatem Verbi*). This eagle "cropped off the summit of this cedar," then, in the sense that "he depicted the excellence of his [Christ's] divine works, such as his outstanding miracles and most exalted teaching, which the other Evangelists had not mentioned."

So let's review the entire set of images. God says: "I myself will take the finest part of the high and sublime cedar... And I will plant it on a mountain high and eminent, on the high and sublime mountain of Israel..." In other words, God takes His "high and sublime" divinity and plants it (incarnates it) in the man Jesus who lives in Galilee, a district in the northern part of David and Solomon's kingdom known for centuries as "Israel" to distinguish it from "Judah" in the south. The "large eagle with great wings, long pinions, full of thick plumage of many colors" who "cropped the summit of this cedar and carried it away to Canaan," was John, who wrote in his Gospel with special brilliance of Christ's divinity.

If this seems a long way to go to make a fairly simple, straightforward point, it is. But it is also extraordinarily creative. Bonaventure saw the chance to craft a beautiful allegory tying together Christ's incarnation with the iconic image of John as the eagle, and he couldn't resist.

The Eagle Speaks Like God: With Certitude

But there is more. Bonaventure returns to the same source one more time in the next section, where he maintains that John not only treated sublime matters, he also proceeded in a sublime manner (*non tantum de sublimibus agit, sed etiam sublimiter procedit*). Those branches of knowledge are more sublime, says Bonaventure, which are more certain (*illae scientiae dicuntur sublimiores, quae certiores*).[16] The "exceedingly sublime" manner of proceeding in the Gospel of John, therefore, is the "mode of certitude" (*modus certitudinalis*).[17]

We might wonder what Bonaventure is referring to here, since as he himself later admits, "the formal cause or manner of proceeding" of the Gospel is "the form of a narrative."[18] With justification, we think of the Gospels as a story, not as a series of dogmas asserted "with certitude." Has Bonaventure succumbed to an overly dialectical, "scholastic" way of looking at the Gospel? I suggest not.

Although Bonaventure would have been concerned to show his students trained in the Arts at the University of Paris that the Scriptures were as "certain" as the other sciences, that they were worthy not only of pious admiration, but also serious academic study, he is

---

[15] Bonaventure is not thinking of the modern country of Lebanon, but Mount Lebanon, a high mountain range often covered in snow on whose slopes grew the famed "cedars of Lebanon." It is not without significance here either that the Temple of Jerusalem was built of just such cedars.

[16] Thomas similarly claimed that all the ways of knowing God that were found in philosophy were found, and were found more clearly, in the Gospel of John.

[17] See *In Ioan. prol.* 6.

[18] Ibid., 8.

likely making a further point here as well. Had Bonaventure's sole purpose been to convince his students of the intellectual superiority of the Gospels, we would expect to find this same argument about "certitude" in his prologue to the Gospel of Luke. But we do not find it there. Rather, in his discussion there of the "form" of the Gospel, he argues that since "the application of the form is in accord with the disposition of the matter," and since the subject matter of the Gospel is one, namely Christ, but considered under a fourfold description, therefore the book must have four parts. In the first part, the Gospel focuses on the mystery of the incarnation (chapters 1–3); in the second, on Christ's magisterial teaching (chapters 4–21); in the third, the "medicine of the passion" (chapters 22 and 23); and in the fourth, the triumph of the resurrection (chapter 24).

This is a common way of understanding the "form" or "manner of proceeding" of a text: in terms of the order in which the topics are treated. However, when Bonaventure says that the "way of proceeding" in John's Gospel is the "mode of certitude," this seems to involve a rather different sense of "form." In one sense, we can describe the "form" of the book as having four parts. In another sense, however, we can say that its "form" is "narrative." In yet another sense, we can say that its "form" is characterized by the certitude of its proclamation.

In his discussion of this point, Bonaventure returns to the biblical imagery he has been employing from the book of the prophet Ezekiel and claims that John's "sublime way of proceeding is described in Ezekiel 1:24, where the text says that the prophet beheld the famous four winged creatures with the faces of the man, the lion, the ox, and the eagle and "heard the sound of their wings, like the sound of many waters, as it were (*quasi*) the voice of the sublime God.'"[19] If the voice of the Gospel writers is "like" the voice of God, what can we say about the voice of God? Bonaventure's answer: "The voice of the sublime God is the voice of certitude, not variableness." How do we know? Because Jesus said about Himself in John 3.11: "We speak of what we know, and we bear witness to what we have seen." And John spoke in a similar way, as he says of himself in John 19.35: "The one who saw it has borne witness, and his witness is true. And he knows that he tells the truth." In this way, the eagle's voice is like God's.

At the beginning of John's Gospel, instead of an infancy narrative, we get this famous proclamation:

> In the beginning was the Word, and the Word was with God, and the Word was God. The same was in the beginning with God. All things were made by him: and without him was made nothing that was made. In him was life, and the life was the light of men. And the light shineth in darkness, and the darkness did not comprehend it. (John 1.1-5)

And again shortly thereafter, we find the affirmation that Jesus

> was the true light, which enlightens every man that cometh into this world. He was in the world, and the world was made by him, and the world knew him not. He came unto his own, and his own received him not. But as many as received him, he gave them power to be made the sons of God, to them that believe in his name. Who are born, not of blood, nor of the will of the flesh, nor of the will of man, but of God. And the Word was made flesh, and

---

[19] Ezekiel 1.24.

dwelt among us (and we saw his glory, the glory as it were of the only begotten of the Father,), full of grace and truth. (John 1.9-4)

Bonaventure likely had such texts such in mind when he claimed that the Gospel of John employs "the mode of certitude."

These "certain" proclamations characterize not only the words of John's prologue, but also in the way Christ addresses himself to His listeners. Consider, for example, the many places where Jesus describes Himself using the revealing phrase "I AM." "I am the bread of life... Truly, truly, I say to you, unless you eat the flesh of the Son of Man and drink his blood, you have no life in you. Whoever feeds on my flesh and drinks my blood has eternal life, and I will raise him up on the last day" (John 6.48, 54–55). "I am the light of the world" (John 8:12). "I am the resurrection and the life; he who believes in Me will live even if he dies" (John 11:25). "I am the way, and the truth, and the life; no one comes to the Father but through Me" (John 14:6). "I am the vine, you are the branches; he who abides in Me and I in him, he bears much fruit, for apart from Me you can do nothing" (John 15:5). And in what is perhaps the most dramatic example: "Before Abraham was, I AM." (John 8:58). There is little of the reserve of Mark's "Messianic secret" in John's Gospel.

Furthermore, the *certitude* to which Bonaventure refers can also be found in the certitude John expresses about his own witness. As he says at the conclusion of his Gospel: "He who saw it has borne witness, and his witness is true. And he knows that he tells the truth." Bonaventure likely has all these expressions of certitude in mind. This certitude of its expression is a "formal" element that distinguishes John's Gospel from the others.

The Disputed Questions: Usefulness, Certitude, and Sublimity

After he completed the *sermo modernus*-part of his prologue, Bonaventure added several disputed questions, something he did at the end of the prologue to his *Sentences* commentary as well.[20] The four questions he posed at the end of his *Sentences* prologue were these:

Question 1: What is the subject of this book, or theology?
Question 2: What is the way of proceeding in this book of *Sentences*?
Question 3: Is this book, or theology, for the sake of contemplation, or for the purpose of us becoming good, i.e., is it a speculative or a practical science?
Question 4: What is the efficient cause of author of this book?

These were all issues he had covered in the *sermo modernus* section of that prologue. In his prologue to the *Commentary on John*, however, the three questions he poses are not items he had covered earlier; rather, they are questions about (1) the usefulness of the text (whether it was necessary for John's Gospel to be added to the other three); (2) the certitude of the text (since it uses arguments from authority rather than ones based on reason); and (3) the sublimity of the text (whether John employed the proper rhetorical style).

---

[20] This was not a constant practice, however. Bonaventure did *not* add disputed questions to the end of his prologue to the *Commentary on Luke*.

Usefulness: Why Multiple Gospels?

Bonaventure's first question at the end of his prologue deals with a set of fairly well known objections. First, why are there four Gospels rather than just one, especially if the "divine science" is supposed to have a unique unity? Second, what about the problem that different Gospels don't tell the same story? And finally, if John did nothing but repeat what the other Evangelists said, and if the other Gospels were sufficient – indeed, if each is sufficient in itself – then why was there a need for John to write his Gospel, especially since he is reported to have written it so many years after the other three?[21]

Bonaventure's answer is that there are four Gospels, not because of any lack of clarity on God's part, but because of human weakness. We humans have trouble believing in one witness alone, so God arranged for multiple witnesses. If they all said precisely the same thing, then more than one would be superfluous. And yet if they said entirely different things, they would diminish trust rather than bolstering it. Therefore, argues Bonaventure, the Holy Spirit arranged it so that, in some instances, an event would appear in only one Gospel; in others, it would appear in them all; but in no instance would they contradict each other.

Regarding each Gospel being sufficient in itself, Bonaventure argues that there are two ways of treating something "sufficiently." In one way, no human writing or series of writings could ever treat of Christ sufficiently. And yet, in a second way, sufficient material might be provided to attain a goal. And in this sense, each of the Evangelists provides the substance of the faith in a sufficient way for us to attain our salvation.[22]

Certitude: What Kind of Certitude Should a Gospel Provide?

As we saw earlier, Bonaventure claims that a formal characteristic of John's Gospel is its certitude. But what kind of certitude? It is not the certitude of logical demonstration. And yet a certain certitude is needed to ground one's act of faith. In his resolution of the question, Bonaventure argues that certitude is of four kinds: the certitude of logical demonstration, the certitude of authority, the certitude of interior illumination, and the certitude of external persuasion. When certitude results from logical demonstration, then the person is forced to assent; this certitude eliminates faith. Another kind of certitude is based on authority. And since the authority of the Scriptures is based on the authority of the Holy Spirit, which is the highest authority, this certitude can be the basis of faith.[23] A third kind of certitude results from interior illumination, and this, says Bonaventure, perfects faith. The fourth kind of certitude results from persuasion and occurs when believers formulate reasons of fittingness and efficacy in order to help them understand

---

[21] *In Ioan. prol.* 9.
[22] See ibid.
[23] As Josef Pieper suggests, "faith" is always faith in a person. Or to be more precise, it is faith in a message because of the faith one has in the person delivering the message. In the case of the Scriptures, one's faith in the message is bound up with one's faith in the Scriptures being inspired by the Holy Spirit. See Josef Pieper, "On Faith: A Philosophical Treatise," in *Faith, Hope, Love* (San Francisco, CA: Ignatius Press, 1997).

what they believe. Rational explanations of this kind are most helpful and effective for believers, says Bonaventure, "but for non-believers they are wholly useless and weak."[24]

Thus faith does not result from logical demonstration, for logical demonstration would remove the freedom of the believer. Nor is the faith derived from authority the same as interior illumination, although interior illumination can help perfect faith. Nor is faith the same as the understanding of faith derived from theological reflection on the truths of faith.

It is worth noting how this discussion of "certitude" differs from, but also adds to, Bonaventure's previous comments about certitude in the earlier, *sermo modernus* section of the prologue. In that earlier section, he claimed that John's way of proceeding was the way of certitude. John says what he knows, and what he knows is true. Here Bonaventure adds that "what John knows" he knows based on the authority of the Holy Spirit, and so John's testimony provides a certain and sure foundation for faith.

Sublimity: Was John Seeking Things Too High?

Earlier in his prologue, Bonaventure had made a point of emphasizing that, as the last two words in his *thema* had indicated, "exceedingly sublime" (*sublimis . . . valde*). The "waters of wisdom lifted him up," says Bonaventure of St. John, "to a sublime height, above all mountains, since in his Gospel he spoke in a more exalted way than everyone else."[25] John's teaching was sublime because it dealt with sublime things, in a sublime manner, and led to a sublime end.[26]

So now Bonaventure poses this question: Did John violate the prohibition in Ecclesiasticus 3:22: "Do not seek the things that are too high for you, nor investigate matters above your ability?" And in 1 Corinthians 2:1, St. Paul says that when he first came to the Corinthians, he did not come "proclaiming the testimony of God in lofty words or wisdom." Were John's sights set too high and his speech too lofty?[27]

Bonaventure replies that an investigation of sublime matters can be carried out with three different intentions. The first stems from malice, he says, and is found among the heretics. The second is based purely on curiosity and is the sort found among the philosophers. The third, however, results from a devoted love and is the sort found among the apostles and prophets.

One gets the sense in this section and the next that although the direct object of inquiry is John the Evangelist, the second object of concern is the teachers and students of sacred doctrine. Just as John, "the Beloved Disciple," was motivated by a devoted love of Christ and was free from malice or mere curiosity, so too should the teachers and students of John's words be. They are called upon to ask themselves what intentions motivate their studies and with what spirit they approach their reading of the Gospel.

Consider in this light the next section about the sublimity of speech. Sometimes, argues Bonaventure, sublime speech should be censured or curbed because it is motivated by an

---

[24] *In Ioan. prol.* 10.
[25] Ibid., 4.
[26] See ibid., 5–7.
[27] See ibid., 11.

evil intention – say, for example, solely for the intention of drawing applause.[28] Bonaventure likely had in mind the popular preachers of his day who preached unorthodox doctrines, but got public acclaim. In other instances, sublime speech needs censure because of its subject matter – as for example if one's speech is about trivial matters blown out of proportion or if matters are being obfuscated by pompous speech. Here, Bonaventure likely had in mind the practice of certain philosophers who, in his view, blew out of proportion some small point or obfuscated the issue with technical jargon. And sometimes sublime speech needs to be curbed because one's listeners lack the capacity understand it. It was for this reason that Paul told the Corinthians in 1 Corinthians 2:1 that he did not come to them "in sublimity of speech." John, by contrast, had a subject-matter that was lofty, good intentions in writing, and listeners who were advanced in the faith, for by the time he was writing his Gospel, says Bonaventure, the Church had flourished for several decades.

What is most marvellous and sublime about John's words, says Bonaventure, is that they provide both milk for infants and meat for adults (cf. 1 Corinthians 3.2). He ends his prologue, therefore, with this wonderful image from Gregory the Great: "In its public nature the divine word nourishes infants, while in private its nature is to suspend minds in admiration of its sublime matters. I would describe it this way: It is like a river that is broad and deep and in which both a lamb may wade and an elephant swim."[29]

Prologue as Protreptic

Bonaventure's prologue to his *Commentary on John* possesses the same protreptic character as Thomas's prologue to his *Commentary on John*. Both were delivered to much the same audience: students trained in the Arts at Paris or elsewhere whose knowledge of the Scriptures may have been rather sketchy and incomplete. After getting their teeth into Aristotle, Boethius, and Pseudo-Dionyisus, the Scriptures might have seemed a bit thin – worthy of pious regard, but not serious intellectual study. It may have seemed to them, as it often seems to many of our contemporaries, that the Scriptures could not provide a solid foundation on which to build a "science."

The attendant danger is that those who are convinced of Scripture's inability to ground a proper "science" or academic "discipline" also may conclude that theology is not a kind of "knowing" (a *scientia*), nor something that can be "taught" (which is at the root of our word "discipline"). On this view, what can be derived from the Scriptures never passes much beyond the realm of what Plato would have called *doxa* or "opinion." On this view, "faith" would no longer be a mode of knowing, as it is for both Bonaventure and Thomas, but merely a way of feeling: an attitude or an emotional "leap" into the unknown.

---

[28] Augustine too spoke of the problems of giving speeches solely for praise; cf. *Confessions* 1.15–17.

[29] This saying has been attributed to Augustine, Jerome, and a host of Protestant writers. It is actually found in Gregory the Great's preface to the *Moralia in Job* (Epistola, chapter 4): "For as the word of God, by the mysteries which it contains, exercises the understanding of the wise, so usually by what presents itself on the outside, it nurses the simpleminded. It presenteth in open day that wherewith the little ones may be fed; it keepeth in secret that whereby men of a loftier range may be held in suspense of admiration. It is, as it were, a kind of river, if I may so liken it, which is both shallow and deep, wherein both the Lamb may find a footing, and the elephant float at large" (*in quo et agnus ambulet, et elephas natet*).

The protreptic approach Bonaventure takes in this prologue to his *Commentary on John* is different from the approach Thomas took in his prologue – although we should remember that Thomas wrote his prologue at the end of his career during his second Parisian regency, while Bonaventure wrote his at the beginning of his career, perhaps even before his inception as a master at Paris. But they touch on many of the same points. Both argue that the unity, excellence, intellectual clarity, and utility of the Scriptures made them superior to other texts. And both made use of the *sermo modernus* style to lend structure and eloquence to their words. What should be clear by now is that this was simply the "form" expected in a prologue at the University of Paris.

14

The Spirit of the Lord Is Upon Me

The Prologue to Bonaventure's Commentary on the Gospel of Luke

ONE OF Bonaventure's most sophisticated prologues is the prologue to his *Commentary on the Gospel of Luke*.[1] Although it is likely that the text of this commentary underwent several revisions between its first version and the final one found in the Quaracchi edition, Bonaventure most likely undertook the first version of the work in 1248 while he was a *lector biblicus* in the Franciscan *studium* at Paris but not yet a master at the University.[2] Scholars agree that the text shows remarkable proficiency; indeed Theodore Crowley has claimed that "a mere *baccalarius biblicus*" could not have produced the *Commentary on Luke*. "The Commentary in its present state is undoubtedly the work of a master and not a beginner."[3] Jay Hammond's suggestion, though, seems most reasonable: that Bonaventure composed the earliest version while he was still a *lector biblicus*, a position above a *cursor biblicus* (who could give only a cursory reading of the text) but below a *magister* (the position needed to "determine" a question arising within the text). Even so, the sophistication of this early prologue is still quite remarkable.

---

[1] English: *St. Bonaventure's Commentary on the Gospel of Luke*, trans. Robert J. Karris, Works of St. Bonaventure, 8, pt. 1 (St. Bonaventure, New York: Franciscan Institute Publications, 2001). Latin: St. Bonaventure, *Opera Omnia* (Ad Claras Aquas Quaracchi: Collegii s. Bonaventurae, 1882–1901), vol. 7. Hereafter, simply "*Super Lucam*, prol." with the section numbers from the "preface" in the Karris English translation.

[2] This, according to both an early chronicler (Salimbene) and a recent scholar (Hammond). See Jay M. Hammond, "Dating Bonaventure's Inception as Regent Master," *Franciscan Studies* 67 (2009): esp. 186–190. See also J. Guy Bougerol, *Introduction to the Works of Bonaventure*, trans. José de Vinck (Paterson, NJ: St. Anthony Guild Press, 1964), 94–95: "Brother Salimbene tells us, in his *Chronicle*, that 'Brother John of Parma gave formal license to Brother Bonaventure of Bagnorea to 'read' in Paris, which was not done heretofore as he was a bachelor not yet installed in his Chair: and so he 'read' a very beautiful and perfect commentary on the whole Gospel of Saint Luke: this was in 1248." Cf. also Salimbene, *Chronica* 1, 299.

[3] Theodore Crowley, "St. Bonaventure Chronology Reappraisal," *Franziskanische Studien* 56 (1974):320; quoted from Hammond, *Dating*, 189.

The *Thema* Verse

Bonaventure chose as the *thema* for this prologue the text of Isaiah 61:1: "The Spirit of the Lord is upon me, because the Lord has anointed me. He has sent me to preach to the meek, to heal the contrite of heart, and proclaim freedom to the captives, and release those shut up" (*Spiritus Domini super me, eo quod unxerit Dominus me. Ad annuntiandum mansuetis misit me, ut mederer contritos corde et praedicarem captivis indulgentiam et clausis apertionem*). This text shows up in a slightly different version in Luke 4:18, where Jesus notably applies it to Himself. According to Luke's Gospel, when Christ finally came out of the desert after the forty days, he returned to his home town of Nazareth in Galilee where, entering the synagogue on the Sabbath, he read out this passage from Isaiah 61:1 and said to the gathered congregation: "Today this Scripture has been fulfilled in your hearing." Luke reports that the reaction among Jesus's neighbors was not positive. They led Jesus to the brow of a hill intending to throw him off. But according to Luke's account, "Jesus walked through their midst" and escaped that fate.

According to Luke's Gospel, the passage Jesus read from Isaiah on this occasion that so infuriated his Nazarene neighbors was this one (in the Latin Vulgate Bonaventure was using): *Spiritus Domini super me propter quod unxit me evangelizare pauperibus misit me praedicare captivis remissionem et caecis visum dimittere confractos in remissionem praedicare annum Domini acceptum et diem retributionis*: "The Spirit of the Lord is upon me. Wherefore he hath anointed me to preach the gospel to the poor, he hath sent me to heal the contrite of heart, to preach deliverance to the captives, and sight to the blind, to set at liberty them that are bruised, to preach the acceptable year of the Lord, and the day of reward" (cf. Luke 4:18). Note that Luke's version of the passage, just quoted, differs slightly from the original in Isaiah 61:1. It is not clear why Bonaventure chose not to use the version in Luke's Gospel, even though he was setting out to comment on that Gospel, and chose instead the original version found in Isaiah 61:1. It may have simply been that the words in Isaiah's version fit his intended themes better.

Whatever his reason for the choice, Bonaventure accomplishes something astounding in this prologue. He uses the same biblical verse in three ways to lend structure to three mini-sermons within the same prologue. He proposes that Isaiah 61:1 can be understood in three ways. According to a "general understanding" (*generalem intellectum*), the verse applies to any teacher of sacred Scripture. According to a "special understanding" (*specialem intellectum*), it applies to Luke the Evangelist. But according to a "unique understanding" (*singularem intellectum*), it applies to Christ himself.[4] Bonaventure then divides and dilates this single *thema* verse in three different ways in order to be able to comment upon three separate topics. The result is an amazing literary tour de force (Box 14.1).

---

[4] *Super Lucam*, prol. 2.

Box 14.1 Outline of the Threefold Dilation Bonaventure Makes of His *Thema* Verse in the Prologue to His *Commentary on the Gospel of Luke*

Thema: "The Spirit of the Lord is upon me, because the Lord has anointed me. He has sent me to preach to the meek, to heal the contrite of heart, and proclaim freedom to the captives, and release those shut up"

I. According to a general understanding, this *thema* verse applies to any teacher of sacred Scripture and any student.
   A. A good teacher must be:
      1. Anointed with divine grace: **The Spirit of the Lord is upon me because the Lord has anointed me.**
      2. Educated with genuine obedience: **He has sent me to preach to the meek.**
      3. Inflamed with fraternal love: **that I might heal the contrite of heart and proclaim freedom to the captives and release those shut up.**
   B. A good student should be:
      1. "meek in speech": **He has sent me to preach to the meek.**
      2. "humble in affection": **that I might heal the contrite of heart.**
      3. "faithful in assent": **and proclaim freedom to the captives and release those shut up.**
II. According to a special understanding, the *thema* applies to Luke the Evangelist.
   A. The *efficient cause* of the Gospel: The Spirit of the Lord is upon me, because the Lord has anointed me.
      1. Who is the primary author of the Gospel? The Holy Spirit: **The Spirit of the Lord**
      2. Who is the secondary author? Luke: [The Spirit of the Lord] **is upon me**: i.e., Luke
      3. Why was Luke able to write? **because the Lord has anointed me.**

   All three causes are presupposed whenever we refer to Luke as the author of the Gospel.

   B. The *final cause* (why Luke wrote the Gospel): **He has sent me to preach to the meek, to heal the contrite of heart, and proclaim freedom to the captives, and release those shut up.**
      1. The first purpose of the Gospel is the "manifestation of truth": **He has sent me to preach to the meek.**
      2. The second purpose is the "cure of our infirmity": **to heal the contrite of heart.**
      3. A third goal of the Gospel is the "revelation of eternity": **and proclaim freedom to the captives and release to those shut up.**
III. According to a unique understanding, the *thema* applies to Christ Himself.
   A. The *material cause* of the Gospel: The entire Gospel concerns Christ as:
      1. Mediator (because of His Incarnation): **The Spirit of the Lord is upon me because the Lord has anointed me.**
      2. Preacher (because of His magisterial teaching): **He has sent me to preach to the meek.**

> 3. Restorer (because of the remedy of His passion): **to heal the contrite of heart.**
> 4. Conqueror (because of the triumph of the resurrection): **and proclaim freedom to the captives and release those shut up.**
>
> B. The *form* of the Gospel:
> 1. The first part of the Gospel focuses on the mystery of the incarnation (chapters 1–3).
> 2. The second focuses on Christ's magisterial teaching (chapters 4–21).
> 3. The third deals with the "remedy of the passion" (chapters 22–23).
> 4. The fourth describes the triumph of the resurrection (chapter 24).

A "General" Understanding of the *Thema* Verse: Good Teachers and Listeners

If we take the words of the *thema* to apply generally (*generaliter*), says Bonaventure, it can apply to any teacher of Sacred Scripture. By "generally," here, he doesn't mean the way the verse would be understood "generally" by most people. Most people would not likely interpret this passage as referring to teachers of Sacred Scripture. What he means rather is that, if we apply it generally to a broad category of persons, we can take it as referring to any teacher of Sacred Scripture.

Contrary to modern assumptions that good teachers can teach anyone no matter how recalcitrant the student or how lazy the audience, Bonaventure believes that a good teacher needs good listeners. So he describes not only the type of person he thinks the teacher of sacred Scripture should be, but also the type of characteristic the students should have.[5] He provides a threefold subdivision to characterize each.

A good teacher of the Scriptures, he says, must be "anointed with divine grace" (*inunctus divina gratia*), "educated with genuine obedience" (*institutus mera obedientia*), and "inflamed with fraternal love" (*inflammatus benevolentia fraterna*). As is the custom of the *sermo modernus* style, he associates each of these with a word or phrase from his opening *thema*. The words "The Spirit of the Lord is upon me because the Lord has anointed me," he associates with being anointed with divine grace. "He has sent me to preach to the meek," he associates with being instituted with genuine obedience. And "to heal the contrite of heart and proclaim freedom to the captive and release those shut up," he associates with being inflamed with fraternal love.[6]

Good students, on the other hand, should be "meek in speech" (*mitis in affatu*), "humble in affection" (*humilis in affectu*), and "faithful in assent" (*fidelis in assensu*). The first of these, meekness of speech, he associates with the phrase "He has sent me to preach to the meek." The second, humility in affection, he associates with the phrase "to heal the contrite of

---

[5] Thomas would make a similar point about teachers and students several years later in his *principium in aula* address. Thomas discusses the characteristics teachers should have under the heading of "mountains" and those that students should have under the heading of the "plains" watered by rain coming from those mountains. See my discussion of Thomas's *principium* in Chapter 4.

[6] See *Super Lucam*, prol. 3, 4, and 5.

heart." And the third, fidelity in assent, he associates with the words "and proclaim freedom to the captive and release those shut up."[7]

Teachers must be "anointed with divine grace," claims Bonaventure, just as Elijah, Elisha, and David were anointed so they might receive the Spirit of the Lord "through whom the divine mysteries are revealed to us." We understand why the writers of the Scriptures, like Luke, must be divinely anointed, but why must the *teachers* of the Scriptures be similarly anointed? Because, answers Bonaventure, "the Scriptures are to be interpreted by the same Spirit through whom they were written," and so it is necessary that the teacher be anointed with the same Spirit as the writer "so that he might be an apt teacher of the things propounded by Christ and written by the Holy Spirit."[8]

A good teacher must also be "educated with genuine obedience," claims Bonaventure, a point he associates with the phrase "The Lord sent me to preach to the meek." Although we might have expected Bonaventure to associate "genuine obedience" with the phrase "The Lord sent me," he focuses rather on the word "meek," even though "the meek" are the ones being preached to, not the ones doing the preaching. He makes the connection by reference to the most famous Old Testament figure described as "meek": Moses. Just as Moses led the sons of Israel out of Egypt, so also a teacher should lead his students "out of the darkness of ignorance." Moses is an exemplar for teachers of Sacred Scripture in several other ways too. Moses did not seek his office; he was called. He did not procure his office; he refused it, accounting himself unworthy of it. Moses accepted the office only because the Lord spoke to him "in his heart" (*ad cor*). The teacher who believes the Lord has spoken to him in this way should also feel in himself, as did Moses, "the effect of having a speech impediment and being slow in speech;" in other words, the teacher of Scripture should not be too quick or too sure to presume he knows how to express the divine mysteries the Lord has revealed to him unless they follow from his being "instituted by genuine obedience" to God and God's word.[9] This lesson, derived from the story of Moses and his speech impediment, is a classic bit of figurative exegesis. More precisely, it is a tropological or moral interpretation of the Moses story. Moses shows us that teachers should not speak excessively about the divine mysteries because they probably know less than they assume they do and they might create unnecessary misunderstandings among the faithful. As I have pointed out several times, figurative exegesis did not disappear from thirteenth-century preaching; it was simply incorporated as another method of dilation along with many others.[10]

---

[7] See ibid., 6, 7, and 8. Strictly speaking, Bonaventure has violated one of the rules of the *sermo modernus* style here. When he ran through his list of characteristics of the good student, he should have used all the parts of his opening *thema* verse. Instead, he failed to associate the first part of the *thema* – "The Spirit of the Lord is upon me because the Lord has anointed me" – with anything in his list. The canons of the *sermo modernus* style dictated that he should have either used the first part of the *thema* verse to discuss teachers and the second part to discuss students, or he should have used the entire verse again to associate each part with the points he intended to make about students. We might mark this down as a novice misstep in an otherwise brilliant prologue.

[8] *Super Lucam*, prol. 6. Bonaventure's view here is obviously very different from the modern presumption that someone is qualified to teach a biblical book as long as he or she knows enough of the relevant scholarship about the text.

[9] *Super Lucam*, prol. 4.

[10] On this, see for example, *Forma praedicandi*, 33, or the list of methods of *dilatatio* and descriptions of them in *Reading the Sermons of Aquinas*, 113–180.

Third, good teachers of Scripture should also be "inflamed by fraternal love." This love, says Bonaventure, should be like that of a preacher who sets out to "heal the contrite of heart, proclaim freedom to captives and release those shut up." Without this concern for his brothers, the teacher will fail.

So much for teachers; what about the students? For the evangelical doctrine to have an effect, the teacher must have students who are meek, humble, and faithful. Why meek? Because "quarrelling and disputations do not befit disciples of the Gospel, but disciples of Aristotle," says Bonaventure, an obvious jab at some of his colleagues at Paris and their students.[11] But along with external quarreling, internal quarreling ought to be avoided as well. To support this view, he quotes his favorite authority, St. Augustine, who says:

> We must become meek through piety. We ought not to protest against Sacred Scripture, either when we understand it and it is attacking some of our vices, or when we do not understand it and think that we ourselves could be wiser and give better advice. In this latter case we must rather reflect and believe that what is written there is more beneficial and more true.[12]

The good student must also be "humble in affection" (*humilis in affectu*) through "contrition of the spirit" – a comment suggested by the phrase "to heal the contrite of spirit" from the opening *thema*. Students must be "humble," says Bonaventure, for as Matthew 11:25 tells us, "God has hidden his mysteries from the wise and the prudent and revealed them to children."[13]

Finally, the good student should be "faithful in assent" (*fidelis in assensu*) "through captivity of the understanding" (*per captivitationem intellectus*) to the truth. This beneficial "captivity" of the intellect was suggested by the phrase "and proclaim freedom to the *captives*" in Bonaventure's opening *thema*. Note, however, that text in Isaiah 61:1 proclaims *freedom* from this captivity, not the benefits of it. Sometimes the repetition of a single word is all a preacher needs to make the association he wants. In faith, our intellects are captivated by the truth, and the captivity of the intellect to the truth is beneficial. Quoting a line made famous by St. Augustine, Bonaventure adds: "If you do not believe, you will not understand."[14]

Before moving on to our consideration of Bonaventure's next two uses of the same *thema* verse, it is worth noting how pertinent these words would have been to the students to whom Bonaventure first delivered this *principium*.[15] He would have been telling them, in effect: "If we are to be successful in what we are setting out to do in this course, namely, to read and understand the Gospel of Luke, here is what I must be like as a teacher and what you must be like as students." It is an exemplary bit of self-reflection, especially for students who might themselves become teachers someday.

---

[11] *Super Lucam*, prol. 6.
[12] Cf. Augustine, *On Christian Doctrine* II.7.
[13] *Super Lucam*, prol. 7.
[14] *Super Lucam*, prol. 8. Bonaventure calls this "another translation," showing that he knows this verse is not in his Vulgate version of Isaiah 7:9, which has "If you do not believe, you will not remain" (*permanebitis*); this is an alternative translation based on the Septuagint.
[15] I am using the word *principium* here to indicate the first class a master would give before he began his lectures on a biblical book in earnest.

I have suggested at several points that these prologues served a "protreptic" purpose: they set out for students a clear choice about the person they would have to become and the life they would have to lead to read well and learn what the Scriptures had to teach. These protreptic discourses were also often related to some description of the life and death of a great teacher.

I suggest the first part of this prologue exhibits just such a protreptic dimension. A teacher who admits up front that a teacher should be "anointed with divine grace," "instituted with genuine obedience," and "inflamed with fraternal love" is asking his students to challenge him to show (1) that he has read and interpreted the Scriptures in the same Spirit in which they were written, (2) that he is genuinely obedient to the Scriptures and to the Church and to the office with which he has been entrusted, and (3) that he teaches with a real love for his brethren. And yet such a teacher is also warning his students that he expects them to (1) avoid quarrelsomeness, (2) learn humility, and (3) realize that their minds need to be formed and molded by the Scriptures, not presume that the Scriptures must meet their expectations and answer all their objections.

A "Special" Understanding of the *Thema* Verse: Efficient and Final Cause

In the next two sets of divisions and dilations of the opening *thema*, Bonaventure will discuss the four Aristotelian causes. In sections 9 through 16, he takes up issues related to the *efficient* and *final* cause of the Gospel; thereafter, in sections 17 through 22, he deals with the *material* and *formal* causes. We begin here with the first two: the *efficient* and *final* causes. Or to put this more colloquially, Bonaventure will consider in this section who wrote the Gospel and why.

Note the order of topics. Bonaventure first considers his opening *thema* verse as it applies "generally" to all teachers and students, as if to say to his students: "Before we read and study this Gospel together, before we even get into the usual considerations about the author, purpose, form, and subject-matter, we need to consider what is required of me as a teacher and you as a student." Having discussed those questions, Bonaventure now moves on to deal with the authorship and purpose of the Gospel. He does this by going back to his *thema* verse and considering it "specially" (*specialiter*) as it applies to Luke the Evangelist rather than "generally" (*generaliter*) as it would apply to all teachers and students.

Here, Bonaventure uses a twofold *divisio* rather than the threefold *divisio* he used before. He considers the *efficient cause* of the Gospel in association with the first part of the *thema* verse – "The Spirit of the Lord is upon me, because the Lord has anointed me" – and considers the *final cause* (why Luke wrote the Gospel) in association with the remainder of the verse: "He has sent me to preach to the meek, to heal the contrite of heart, and proclaim freedom to the captives, and release those shut up."

Bonaventure identifies three subdivisions in the first *divisio*: "The Spirit of the Lord / is upon me / because the Lord has anointed me." Who is the efficient cause of the text? Bonaventure's first answer is: "the Spirit of the Lord." The Holy Spirit is the supreme (*suprema*) cause of the text. The second answer, however, is Saint Luke, who is a lower and more humble cause. On this interpretation, Luke is the one who says (in the *thema* verse) "the Spirit of the Lord is *upon me*." Luke was enabled to write the Gospel because the Lord "anointed" him. "For anointing by grace disposes the soul to receive the teachings of truth from God."[16] All three causes are presupposed, says Bonaventure, whenever we refer to Luke as the "author" of the Gospel. He is the author, but only in a secondary sense and only because he has been inspired by the Holy Spirit.

The *final* cause of the work is expressed in the remainder of the *thema* verse: "He has sent me to preach to the meek, to heal the contrite of heart, and proclaim freedom to the captives, and release those shut up." The first purpose of the Gospel is the "manifestation of truth" (*manifestatio veritatis*), which is suggested by the phrase "He has sent me to *preach* to the meek" [emphasis mine].[17] The second purpose is the "cure of our infirmity" (*medicatio nostrae infirmitatis*), which is suggested by the phrase "to heal the contrite of heart." Putting the first and second goals together, we can say that Luke manifests the truth so that we might possess a cure for our infirmity.[18] A third goal of the Gospel, then, is the "revelation of eternity" (*reseratio aeternitatis*), which is suggested by the phrase "and proclaim freedom to the captives and release to those shut up" because our ultimate "release" and "freedom" are achieved, says Bonaventure, only when we achieve eternal life in and through Christ.[19]

A "Unique" Understanding of the *Thema* Verse: Material and Formal Cause

Having interpreted the opening *thema* verse "generally" as applying to all teachers and listeners and then "specially" as applying specifically to St. Luke, Bonaventure turns finally to the person to whom the verse applies "uniquely" (*singulariter*): Christ. The *thema* verse is "properly" (*proprie*) attributed to Christ, claims Bonaventure, because, in the Gospel, Christ attributes it to Himself. Recall, this was the passage from Isaiah 61:1 Jesus read in the synagogue and announced that it had been "fulfilled" in Him.

The subject matter (the *materia*) of the Gospel, therefore, is Christ, and the multiple ways the Gospel considers His life, death, and resurrection constitutes the *form* of the Gospel. Bonaventure specifies four ways the Gospel considers Christ: as mediator (*mediator*), as preacher (*praedicator*), as restorer (*reparator*), and as conqueror (*triumphator*). Each of these is associated with the elements of a fourfold *divisio* of the opening *thema*:

> The Spirit of the Lord is upon me, because the Lord has anointed me. / He has sent me to preach to the meek, / to heal the contrite of heart, / and proclaim freedom to the captives, and release those shut up"

Jesus indicates that he is "mediator" when he says: "The Spirit of the Lord is upon me because the Lord has anointed me." He becomes *mediator* between God and man in the incarnation because He is by nature both fully God and fully man.

He indicates that he is *preacher* when He says "the Lord has sent me to preach to the meek." He is a preacher of "magisterial erudition" (*eruditionis magisterium*) because His words are a "teaching" (*doctrinam*).

---

[16] *Super Lucam*, prol. 12.
[17] Ibid., 14.
[18] Ibid., 15.
[19] Ibid., 16.

He indicates that He is a *restorer* when He says "to heal the contrite of heart," for He restores in the sacrifice of His passion.

And He refers to himself, finally, as *conqueror* when He speaks of proclaiming "freedom to the captives and release to those shut up," a freedom and release He wins for us through the triumph of His resurrection.[20]

Summarizing, we say that the material cause or "subject matter" of the Gospel is Christ as an object of faith under a fourfold description as mediator, preacher, restorer, and conqueror; as one who was mediator because of the mystery of the incarnation (*mysterium incarnationis*), preacher because of His magisterial teaching (*magisterium eruditionis*), restorer because of the remedy of the passion (*remedium passionis*), and conqueror because of the triumph of the resurrection (*tropaeum resurrectionis*).

What, then, is the *form* of the Gospel? Since "the application of the form is in accord with the disposition of the matter" (*inductio formae est secundum dispositionem materiae*) and since the subject matter of the Gospel is Christ, considered under a fourfold description, it follows the Gospel must have four parts, one for each of the four ways of considering Christ. Hence the first part of the Gospel focuses on the mystery of the incarnation (chapters 1–3); the second, on Christ's magisterial teaching (chapters 4–21); the third deals with the "medicine of the passion" (chapters 22–23);[21] and the fourth describes the triumph of the resurrection (chapter 24).

Note, in retrospect, that Bonaventure has divided and dilated the same *thema* three different ways (with a threefold, twofold, and fourfold *divisio*). Doing so has allowed him to make some protreptic comments about the dispositions needed to be a good teacher and good students and to cover the customary questions about the efficient, material, formal, and final causes of the Gospel. Bonaventure certainly got his money's worth out of that single Bible verse. In short, this prologue is, with one minor misstep, a carefully crafted and supremely skillful expression of a high style of *sermo modernus*-style preaching. The phrases are not only parallel; they are also long and elegant. In places, the phrases rhyme and scan (*mitis in affatu / humilis in affectu / fidelis in assensu*).

A quick look back at Thomas's capable, but brief, prologues to his commentaries on Jeremiah, Lamentations, and Isaiah suggests there is simply no comparison between Bonaventure's skill using the *sermo modernus* style at this point in his career and Thomas's at a roughly similar point. Bonaventure already showed the rhetorical polish of a Paris-trained preacher. Thomas showed the rhetorical polish of a Naples-trained logician. To Thomas's credit, later efforts show he was a quick study.

---

[20] See ibid., 17–20.

[21] Having described this section as dealing with the "medicine of the passion," Bonaventure can now make the comment that this subject was "most fittingly" treated by the physician Luke. This association is merely another mnemonic device to aid the memory. Noting this verbal relation would also provide good material for a *sermo modernus*–style sermon.

15

Bonaventure, *Sermo Modernus*–Style Preaching, and Biblical Commentary

WE HAVE been examining the culture of preaching and prologues at the University of Paris in the thirteenth century using the works of two of that century's greatest masters of sacred theology, Thomas Aquinas and Bonaventure. One goal has been to show how the three arts of the master – preaching, disputation, and lecturing on the Bible – though distinct, ran together and influenced each other in important ways.

It was not without reason that prospective masters had to display their proficiency in all three arts during the various stages of their inception ceremony. They had to resolve a series of disputed questions on two consecutive days and preach a sermon praising sacred Scripture on the second day. Several days later the newly incepted master had to deliver another praise of the Scriptures that was to be accompanied by a *divisio textus* of all the books of the Bible.

Scholars have long known that being able to craft a suitable *divisio textus* was a crucial skill among thirteenth-century biblical commentators. What has not been examined sufficiently is the extent to which thirteenth-century biblical commentary borrowed methods from contemporary *sermo modernus* style preaching. Nor have scholars appreciated the degree to which thirteenth-century biblical commentaries were formulated with an eye to providing students with material suitable for preaching – specifically, preaching in the *sermo modernus* style.

In Chapter 9, I traced out some of these connections in several of the biblical commentaries of Aquinas. In this chapter, I will make a similar analysis of some passages from Bonaventure's biblical commentaries. In Chapter 9, I proposed that thirteenth-century preaching in the distinctive *sermo modernus* style could be considered a culturally established "practice" (in Alasdair MacIntyre's sense of that term) that required of preachers – and helped develop in them – distinctive habits of mind. Contemporary preaching manuals show that there were common methods and formulas for preaching. These methods of *divisio* and *dilatatio* were well known and widely used. A comparison of Bonaventure's and Aquinas's *use* of those methods shows how the same methods could produce very different results when employed by two scholars. Yet, however different the final products, the biblical commentaries of both Bonaventure and Aquinas exhibit how important it was to the community of scholars in theology at Paris to prepare young preachers to be able to preach doctrinally sound, memorable sermons.

In the first part of this chapter, we will examine some representative texts from Bonaventure's *Commentary on the Gospel of Luke* that exhibit Bonaventure's use of the *sermo modernus* style. Next, we will examine Bonaventure's frequent use of *distinctiones*: those lists of the various senses of a word accompanied by representative biblical passages, lists of the sort we found Thomas had sketched in the margins of his Isaiah commentary. Finally, in the last part of the chapter, we will examine Bonaventure's use of *divisio* in his *Commentary on the Gospel of John*.[1]

A Preacher's Commentary for Preachers

We begin with Bonaventure's *Commentary on the Gospel of Luke* and his employment of the arts of *sermo modernus*–style preaching, now not in the prologue, but in the body of the commentary itself. Consider, for example, his comments on Luke 1:8–17. Zechariah goes into the Temple and encounters an angel who promises him a son; Zechariah is struck dumb. Bonaventure begins by making a standard *sermo modernus*–style *divisio*. Three things are involved in this scene with Zechariah, he says: first, the "fulfillment of his priestly office" (*executio sacerdotalis officii*), the "appearance of the heavenly messenger" (*apparitio caelestis nuntii*), and "the annunciation of the future conception" (*denuntiatio conceptus futuri*). Note the *sermo modernus*–style parallel constructions in Latin, which are difficult to render into English. In English, we normally cannot capture the rhyming sound made by the triad *executio sacerdotalis officii*, *apparitio caelistis nuntii*, and *denuntiatio conceptus futuri*.[2]

Having established this threefold *divisio*, Bonaventure proceeds – again in good *sermo modernus* style – to associate each member of the *divisio* with a different part of the biblical text with which he is dealing. The "fulfillment of his priestly office" he associates with the verse "Now it came to pass as he was officiating ... as priest"; the "appearance of the heavenly messenger" he associates with the verse "Now the angel of the Lord appeared to him"; and the "annunciation of the future conception" he associates with the verse beginning "But the angel said to him."[3]

Dividing the verses in this way, then associating each with a topic, allows Bonaventure to expand upon each using the methods of *dilatatio* common to medieval preachers, including making subdivisions, creating a good–better–best series, or incorporating the three figurative senses. Here, he takes the first member of the *divisio* – fulfillment of priestly office – and

---

[1] I have arranged the topics in this chapter to mirror the discussion of Thomas's work in Chapter 9, where we first dealt with Thomas's use of the arts of *dilatatio* in his biblical commentaries, then examined the *distinctiones* in his Isaiah commentary, and finally discussed the various ways in which he employed the skills of *divisio*.

[2] See *Super Lucam*, 1:12. English: *St. Bonaventure's Commentary on the Gospel of Luke*, trans. Robert J. Karris, Works of St. Bonaventure, vol. 8, pt. 1 (St. Bonaventure, New York: Franciscan Institute Publications, 2001). Latin: St. Bonaventure, *Opera Omnia* (Ad Claras Aquas Quaracchi: Collegii s. Bonaventurae, 1882–1901), vol. 7.

[3] *Super Lucam*, 1:12.

subdivides it into three. The "fulfillment of priestly office," he says, "is depicted in the fitting manner of harmonious order (*congruentiam ordinis*), the demands of custom (*exigentiam consuetudinis*), and the attendance of a devout multitude (*assistentiam devotae multitudinis*)."[4] Note again that the translator was not able to preserve Bonaventure's parallel Latin phrases in his English translation. The result preserves the clarity of thought, but loses the poetic beauty of the sound.

Now that he has made this subdivision, Bonaventure can "dilate" each of these in turn: "harmonious order" in section 13, "demands of custom" in section 14, and "attendance of a devout multitude" in section 15. In each case, he develops or "dilates" the points he wishes to make by "chaining" biblical authorities to each point as he proceeds.

Consider, for example, his discussion of the first subdivision, "harmonious order," in section 13.

> Therefore, the interpretation that it is a fitting fulfillment according to *harmonious order* is found in: "And it came to pass, when he executed the priestly function in the order of his course before God" (*Factum est autem cum sacerdotio fungeretur in ordine vicis suae ante Deum*).[5] Whence it was incumbent upon him to do what is said of Aaron in Sirach 45:19: "The Lord gave him to function as priest, to have a position of honor, and to bless his people in his name," etc. And it says *in order* (*in ordine*) because this of all things must be done in an orderly manner (*ordinate*), as 1 Corinthians 14:40 has: "Let all things be done properly and in order (*secundum ordinem*) among you." But order (*ordo*) is rightly observed when the mind of the priest worthily attends to the divine presence. And therefore, it says *in order* (*in ordine*) according to what we read about Christ in Hebrews 9:24: He went into heaven in order that (*ut*) he might appear now in the presence of God on our behalf."[6]

Here we have a fascinating series of biblical passages "chained" together as various iterations of the word "order."[7]

Although the bulk of his commentary is based on the literal sense of Luke's text, Bonaventure incorporates the mystical senses when it suits his purposes. As I have mentioned several times, the mystical senses are not abandoned in thirteenth-century preaching; they merely become one of several ways of dilating a text. Consider, for example, Bonaventure's commentary on the story of the faithful centurion (in Luke 7:1-10) who sends for Jesus to ask for healing for his servant, the same man who tells Jesus: "Lord . . . I am not worthy that you should enter under my roof. . . but only say the word, and my servant shall be healed." Jesus marvelled at the man's faith, and his servant was healed.

---

[4] Ibid., 1:13.

[5] I have altered the English translation of the biblical verse in Fr. Karris's translation of Bonaventure's commentary. Most modern translations of this biblical verse do not include any rendering of the Latin words "*in ordine*," preferring to translate it as "custom," "he was exercising his priestly office," "his section was on duty," or "according to the practice of the priestly service." The Greek original, ἐν τῇ τάξει, appears ten times in the New Testament and every time is translated with the Latin word *ordo* in the Vulgate. (I am grateful to Susan Needham for this insight.) Without this reference to *ordo*, the reader is hard-pressed to know what Bonaventure is referring to when he talks about the "harmonious order."

[6] *Super Lucam*, 1:13.

[7] "Chaining" was listed as Method 4 in my review of the methods of *dilatatio* in Chapter 2.

In his commentary, Bonaventure makes a threefold *divisio* that provides him with categories he can dilate afterward. Regarding the miraculous cure of the sick servant boy, there are "three points pertinent to the explication of the miracle," says Bonaventure. The first is "the opportunity to perform the miracle" (*opportunitas faciendi miraculum*). The second is "the dignity of the person requesting the cure" (*dignitas impetrandi remedium*). And the third is "the congruity of hastening the bestowal of the benefit" (*congruitas accelerandi beneficium*).[8] Note again the *sermo modernus*–style parallelism.

What follows this is a *sermo modernus*–style series of subdivisions. Regarding the first, "the opportunity of performing the miracle," Bonaventure comments that this opportunity arises because (1) "the time is right" (*temporis commoditate*), (2) "the place is fitting" (*loci congruitate*), and (3) "the sickness provides the necessity for action" (*morbi necessitate*). This threefold subdivision affords Bonaventure the occasion to "dilate" each of these three subdivisions in the following two paragraphs.[9]

After dilating each of these three subdivisions, he takes up the second member of his original *divisio*: "the dignity of the person requesting the cure." This, he says, is shown in three ways: the first is the reverence of the centurion in making the request (*ex centurionis reverentia in supplicando*), the second is the confidence of the elders in entreating Jesus (*ex seniorum confidentia in postulando*), and the third is the clemency of the Savior in condescending (*ex Salvatoris clementia in condescend*).[10]

Bonaventure expands upon these topics in sections 4 through 8 of chapter 7, which brings him in section 9 to the final member of the original threefold *divisio*: "the congruity of hastening the bestowal of the benefit" – in other words, Jesus heals the centurion's servant immediately. According to Bonaventure, the healing is bestowed quickly because of the excellence of the centurion's faith, which is shown in three ways: first, from the humility of his devout confession (*ex humilitate confessionis devotae*); second, from the authority of divine testimony (*ex auctoritate testificantionis divinae*); and third, from the quickness of the desired cure (*ex celeritate curationis optatae*).[11] Bonaventure dilates each of these subdivisions in sections 9 through 16 of chapter 7, with an interesting aside in sections 14 and 15 on how Christ can say that He had "not found such great faith even in Israel" when the Blessed Virgin Mary and the Apostles were from Israel. Was their faith less than the centurion's? Christ made the comment, says Bonaventure, "not because the faith of the centurion is greater *in an absolute sense*, but in consideration of the nature of the person." While others had the law and the prophets, he, though a Gentile, believed of his own accord with no one to teach him. And with this, Bonaventure concludes the discussion he began in section 1 of chapter 7, saying: "And in this manner the Evangelist gives sufficient expression to the wondrous cure of the servant."[12]

But Bonaventure is not finished with the centurion and his servant quite yet. In sections 17 through 19 of chapter 7, he offers his audience two more interpretations of the passage: one allegorical, the other tropological. "*Spiritually* and according to *the allegorical sense*," says Bonaventure, "the miracle [of the healing of the sick servant] is to

---

[8] *Super Lucam*, 7:1.
[9] See ibid., 7:2–3.
[10] Ibid., 7:4.
[11] Ibid., 7:9.
[12] Ibid., 7:16.

be understood as *the cure of the Gentile people*." Bonaventure then guides his listeners through the spiritual senses in the customary *sermo modernus* style, beginning with a threefold *divisio*, each part of which has a role to play in his allegory. There is (1) the sick person (i.e., the servant boy) who was of servile standing, just as were the Gentile people before the coming of Christ, because they were enslaved to sin; (2) the persons acting as intermediaries (i.e., the elders of the Jews) who interceded on the centurion's behalf, just as the Apostles are sent out to convert the Gentiles; and (3) the sequence of the cure (i.e., its quickness), which shows, according to Bonaventure, that "the greatness of Gentile faith is preferred to Israelite faith."[13]

Allow me to quote in full Bonaventure's description of the sick boy, to give the reader a flavor of how close these sections are to a thirteenth-century sermon, especially with regard to the "chaining" of biblical authorities.

> For the sick person was of *servile standing*. And so it was also with the Gentile people before the coming of Christ, for they were in thralldom to sin, according to what John 8:3-4 says: "The one who commits sins is a slave to sin." And the reason for this is given in 2 Peter 2:19: "A person is the slave of whatever overcomes him." And this sin especially revolves around idolatry, for whose sake they were slaves of the weak elements. Galatians 4:3 has: "When we were children, we were slaves under the elements of the world." And Galatians 4:9 continues: "How is it that you turn to the weak and beggarly elements, whose slaves you again desire to be?" The Apostle is speaking to the Galatians, who were Gentiles.[14]

It is worth remembering that Thomas was commenting here on a passage *in the Gospel of Luke*; the references to other Scriptural books might cause us to forget this. What drives the "chaining" of these authorities is pretty much the repetition of one word: "slave." I ask the reader the keep this in mind when we get to the next section on Bonaventure's use of *distinctiones*.

What about the tropological sense? According to Bonaventure, the *tropological sense* of the text is that, in the cure of the sick boy, we see the cure of sinful man. Bonaventure creates a threefold *divisio*, spelling out three things that contribute to this cure: first, "the recognition of one's own sickness" (*recognitio infirmitatis propriae*), because one must first acknowledge one's sin before one can be forgiven; second, "the intervention of Apostolic authority" (*interventio auctoritatis apostolicae*), for as it was said in Matthew 16:19: "And I will give you the keys of the kingdom of the heavens, and whatever you bind on earth, will be bound also in heaven"; and third, "the condescension of divine compassion" (*condescensio pietatis divinae*), "which draws near to the house of the sick person by the infusion of grace."[15]

Although it was a commonplace to consider *three* figurative senses – the allegorical, the tropological, and the anagogical – note that Bonaventure, for whatever reason, chose in this instance not to supply an interpretation according to the anagogical sense.

These figurative interpretations of the slave as representative of the Gentiles, or of the cure of the sick boy as the cure of sinful man, were not uncommon among medieval and patristic exegetes. What is distinctive here, however, is the repeated use of the threefold

---

[13] Ibid., 7:17.
[14] Ibid.
[15] Ibid., 7:18.

divisio followed by a pattern of parallel phrases, a style characteristic of Bonaventure's preaching. Listening to Bonaventure deliver these *lectiones* on the Gospel of Luke, or reading them afterward, would have been as valuable an introduction to *sermo modernus*-style preaching as any collection of model sermons.

Creating *Distinctiones* for Young Friars

Further evidence that the commentary on Luke was intended to benefit aspiring preachers can be found in Bonventure's insertion, in various places, of lists of biblical *distinctiones*, either his own or those he borrowed from the Dominican master Hugh of St. Cher.[16] "*Distinctiones*," as the reader may recall, was the name given in the thirteenth century to a certain type of preaching aid that provided for a given scriptural term "several figural meanings, and for each meaning provided a passage of scripture illustrating the use of the term in the given sense."[17] We encountered biblical *distinctiones* in Chapter 9 in our examination of Thomas's handwritten marginalia in the manuscript of his *Commentary on Isaiah*. The example I provided there was drawn from the *Summa Abel* of Peter Cantor; it provided a series of possible associations that could be made with the word *avis* or "bird." The *Summa Abel* was the most famous of these sets of *distinctiones*, but it was just one of many. Another prominent source was Alan of Lille's *Liber in distinctionibus dictionum theologicalium*. There one finds this list of *distinctiones* related to the word *denarius*.

> *Denarius* is a type of coin having the value of ten regular coins in circulation. Thus in the Gospel: Why this waste? For it could have been sold for three hundred denarii (John 12:5).
>
> It is said to be everlasting life. Thus in Matthew: Did you not agree with me for a denarius (20:13)? Note that everlasting life is said to come from the tenfold number on account of the fulfillment of the Decalogue.
>
> Or from the denarius coin, since on it are two sides, namely, the image of the king and his name. Thus too the saints will bear in everlasting life the image of Christ with respect to nature and his likeness with regard to grace. And the saints will have the name of Christ and will be called by Christ's name.
>
> It is said to be Christ's passion or Christ. Thus in Revelation (6:6): A measure of wheat for a denarius, that is, the sacred Old and New Testaments, which are signified by wheat, are bought with a denarius, that is, by the passion of Christ or by Christ.
>
> So it is fitting that the saints are signified by grain, for just as grain is first ground, then formed into pasta, afterwards cooked in the oven, and finally put on the table, so too the saint is ground by tribulation, cooked by suffering, and finally placed at the table of everlasting happiness.
>
> It signifies sin. Thus in the Gospel it is read that one owed five hundred denarii, another fifty. And since they did not have the wherewithal to repay, he forgave each one (Luke

---

[16] See Robert J. Karris, "St. Bonaventure's Use of *Distinctiones*: His Independence of and Dependence on Hugh of St. Cher," *Franciscan Studies* 60 (2002): 209–250.

[17] For this definition and a fuller account of the use of *distinctiones*, see Richard and Mary Rouse, *Preachers, Florilegia and Sermons* (Toronto: Pontifical Institute of Mediaeval Studies, 1979), 68.

7:41–42). This is to be understood of sin. So the devil is said to be the tax collector, who gave the first parents a denarius together and daily demands it of us.[18]

In his article "St. Bonaventure's Use of *Distinctiones*: His Independence of and Dependence on Hugh of St. Cher," Prof. Robert J. Karris notes that "Bonaventure utilizes thirty-six *distinctiones* in his *Commentary on the Gospel of St. Luke*," sixteen of which are his creation, and twenty he has adapted from Hugh of St. Cher's *Commentary on the Gospel of St. Luke*.[19] For our purposes, their presence is noteworthy for what they suggest about the commentary. *Distinctiones* are preaching aids; they really have no other purpose. So the fact that Bonaventure included them in his commentary suggests strongly that he intended it to be of use to prospective preachers.

We will examine first several examples of lists written just the way they would have been found in a reference book. Then we will examine other places with material that resemble these.

Consider, for example, this set of *distinctiones* (which Bonaventure borrowed from Hugh of St. Cher) concerning the possible uses of the word "lamp." I have listed these below, separated and numbered for clarity.

1. "For it is the property of a lamp to illumine, and therefore, the word of God is said to be *a lamp*, according to the Psalmist: 'Your word is a lamp to my feet and a light to my paths' (Ps 118:105)."
2. "With regard to *things to be believed*, 2 Peter 1:19 has: "We have the word of prophecy, surer still, to which you do well to attend, as to a lamp shining in a dark place."
3. "With regard to *things to be done* because of commandments." Proverbs 6:23: "the commandment is a lamp, and the law a light."
4. "*The preacher* is said to be *a lamp*. John 5:35 says: 'He was the lamp, burning and shining.' Philippians 2:15 states: 'Among these you shine like stars in the world.'"
5. "It is said to be *the gift of the Holy Spirit*. Exodus 25:37 has: 'You shall also make seven lamps and set them upon the lamp stand,' that is, the seven gifts of the Holy Spirit upon Christ."
6. "It is also said to be *a work*. Luke 12:35: 'Let your loins be girt about and your lamps burning.'"
7. "It is also said to be *the intention*, which if it is *deceitful*, is extinguished, according to what Job 18:6 states: 'The light will be dark in his tabernacle, and the lamp that is over him, will be extinguished.' But if it is *just*, it illumines the entire body of good works."[20]

Another example can be found in Bonaventure's comments on Luke 23:43, where the thief crucified with Jesus asks, "Remember me, Lord, when you come into your kingdom," to which Christ replies: "Amen I say to you, this day you shall be with me in paradise." Bonaventure's first comment is straight commentary: "In this Christ show wondrous mercy ... for he did not reject the repentance of the thief, no matter how tardy it was."[21]

---

[18] Quoted from Karris, "*Distinctiones*," 209–210. I have added spacing to help distinguish the various senses of *denarius* and made slight alterations of punctuation.
[19] Karris, 209.
[20] See *Super Lucam*, 11:72.
[21] Ibid., 23:51.

But after a brief discussion of this point, he plunges in the next section into a list of the possible uses of the word "paradise."²²

> And note here that *paradise* in Scripture is first said to be a *garden of delight*. Genesis 2:8: "And the Lord god planted a paradise of delight from the beginning."
>
> And *the heavenly homeland*. Revelation 2:7: "To the person who overcomes I will give to eat of the tree of life, which is in the paradise of my God."
>
> And *a vision of splendor*. 2 Corinthians 12:4: "He was caught up into paradise and heard there words of mystery," etc.
>
> *Allegorically* paradise is said to be *the Church*. Genesis 2:10: "A river went out of the place of delight to water paradise."
>
> It is said to be the *Blessed Virgin*. Song of Songs 4:12–13: "A garden enclosed, a fountain sealed up; your fruit is paradise."
>
> *Sacred Scripture*. Sirach 24:41: "I, like an aqueduct, have come out of the paradise of God."
>
> *Tropologically*, paradise is said to be *grace*." Sirach 40:17: "Grace is like a paradise in blessings."
>
> It is said to be *the soul filled with fear*. Sirach 40:28: "The fear of the Lord is like a paradise of blessing."
>
> It is also said to be *religious life*. Genesis 13:10: "All the country about the Jordan was watered ... like the paradise of the Lord."
>
> Therefore, paradise stands here [in Christ's comment to the thief] for *the beatific vision*, since as it is said in John 17:3: "This is everlasting life that they may know you, the only true God, and him whom you have sent, Jesus Christ."

Note that none of these meanings of "paradise" except the last have anything to do with Christ's comment to the repentant thief, "Today you will be with me in paradise," which is the text upon which Bonaventure is commenting. Christ is not saying to the repentant thief that they will be in the paradise of delight in Genesis (the first meaning in the foregoing list), nor obviously is he promising him that they will enter religious life together (the seventh meaning in the foregoing list). Bonaventure *could* have made these associations in his commentary, but he doesn't. The word "paradise" in the text is simply the occasion for Bonaventure to lay out this series of *distinctiones* for his students, not because the alternative meanings of "paradise" will help them understand this verse in Luke's Gospel better, but because the list will help them use this verse to preach on many different topics or to preach whatever is needed on any verse containing the word "paradise."

Note also that Scripture passages Bonaventure supplies with each entry are not meant to *prove* the validity of the use of the word in the sense specified. Take the third sense of "paradise," which refers to the Church. The passage from Genesis 2:10, "A river went out of the place of delight to water paradise" is hardly a "proof-text" for that interpretation of paradise. It is merely a text the prospective preachers in his audience might use to refer to the Church at some point in the future in one of their own sermons.

---

²² See *Super Lucam*, 23:52. I have altered Karris's English translation, but only to make it more like the Latin original.

An interesting feature of these lists is that the same word can take on completely opposite connotations depending on the context and the way the preacher wishes to use it. Bonaventure himself reflects on this fact in his comments on the text in Luke 13:21, where Christ compares the Kingdom to leaven. At first, he comments that "since love and joy expand the heart and warm it from the inside, they find an external analogy in leaven." But *leaven* can also refer to the corruption of peace and unity, as in Luke 12:1: "Beware of the leaven of the Pharisees, which is hypocrisy." This is appropriate, claims Bonaventure, because leaven is "old dough, corrupted by age and turning sour, which corrupts the remainder of the matter and turns it sour."[23] Thus it is said in 1 Corinthians 5:7: "Purge out the old leaven." In other circumstances, however, *leaven* can imply ardor and love: "for leaven warms the dough and induces a certain fire into it, as if from the hidden interior," says Bonaventure. "So it is not incongruous that *leaven* is love."[24]

There is an interesting lesson here. A word like *leaven* can be treated in different ways because of its diverse properties. As Augustine says in *De doctrina christiana* III.25.35, there is no law stipulating that, because a thing has a certain analogical meaning in one place, it must always have this same meaning elsewhere. As an example, Bonaventure supplies two opposite connotations of the word *lion*. The word *lion* can signify Christ, as it does in the Book of Revelation 5:5: "The lion of the tribe of Judah has conquered." But it can also signify the devil, as in 1 Peter 5:8: "Your adversary, the devil, is prowling around like a roaring lion, looking for someone to devour." In the first instance, it is the pride and nobility of the lion that is applied to Christ; in the second, it is the lion's ravenous appetite and destructive man-eating ability that is associated with the devil. "The cause of this diversity," says Bonaventure, "is the multiplicity of properties, from which a diversity of analogies and representations arise in figures" (*Cuius diversitatis similitudinum et repraesentationum oritur in figuris*).[25]

Bonaventure makes other lists that seem especially suited for preaching. Consider, for example, Bonaventure's comments on Luke 7:22. There, in answer to the question, "Are you the one who is to come; or should we look for another?" posed by the disciples of John the Baptist, Jesus proclaims: "Go and relate to John what you have heard and seen: the blind see, the lame walk, the lepers are made clean, the deaf hear, the dead rise again, to the poor the gospel is preached." Perhaps because he himself was a mendicant who had taken a vow of poverty and was lecturing to young friars who had taken the same vow, Bonaventure took the occasion of that one phrase, "to the poor the gospel is preached," to list "the "ten most excellent merits" (*decem excellentissimas dignitates*) of poverty. The first is the "understanding of its own weakness" (*intelligentiam infirmitatis propriae*); the second, "the excellence of the virtue granted" (*excellentiam virtutis gratuitae*); the third, "the affluence of internal joy" (*affluentiam iucunditatis internae*); the fourth, "the wealth of its abundant sufficiency" (*copiam abundantis sufficientiae*); the fifth, "the custody of supernal protection" (*custodiam protectionis supernae*); the sixth, "the pleasure of divine acceptance" (*complacentiam acceptationis divinae*); the seventh, "the condescension of paternal kindness" (*condescendentiam pietatis paternae*); the eighth, "the eminence of judiciary authority" (*eminentiam auctoritatis iudiciariae*); the ninth, "the evidence of proven perfection" (*evidentiam perfectionis probatae*); and the tenth,

---

[23] *Super Lucam*, 13:43.
[24] Ibid.
[25] Ibid., 13:43.

"the excellence of regal precedence" (*excellentiam regalis praesidentiae*).²⁶ Note the "poetic" nature of the list: the phrases are parallel, rhyme, and scan – just as in a sermon.²⁷

Preaching, Commenting, and Disputing: Examining Bonaventure's *Divisio Textus* of the Gospel of John

Although Bonaventure's *Commentary on Luke* and his *Commentary on John* differ in style, I will argue in what follows that the *Commentary on John* was equally directed to an audience of prospective preachers and that it too exhibits many of the distinctive characteristics of the prologue and preaching culture at Paris. Recall that the three parts of the inception ceremony of the medieval master of theology were (1) a series of disputed questions, (2) two sermons in praise of sacred Scripture, and (3) a *divisio textus* of all the books of the Bible. A distinctive feature of Bonaventure's *Commentary on the Gospel of John* is the way Bonaventure provides in each section a running *divisio textus* of the Gospel, followed by a short series of divisions and dilations, culminating in three or four disputed questions provoked by the text (Box 15.1). Several examples of this progression must suffice.²⁸

> **Box 15.1** An Outline of Bonaventure's *Divisio Textus* in the Early Chapters of His *Commentary on the Gospel of John*²⁹
>
> Part I: The Word *in se* (John 1:1-5)
>   Section 1: In relationship with the speaker ("the speaker" being God, who speaks the Word)
>   A. Unity in essence: "In the beginning was the Word"
>   B. Dissimilarity in person: "The Word was with God"

---

²⁶ Ibid., 7:42–43.
²⁷ I am not alone in arguing that Bonaventure's Commentary on the Gospel of Luke had preachers in mind. Robert Karris points out (*"Distinctiones,"* 243) that "scholars have been contending for decades" that "Bonaventure's Commentary on Luke's Gospel has preachers as its target audience". Prof. Karris cites also the prologue to the Quaracchi edition of the sermons, vol. 7, p. ix: "Haec omnia, sicut minus praelectionibus scholasticis convenient, sic optime ei scopo, quem supposuimus, scilicet quod liber sit in usum praecipue praedicatorum destinatus." See also Thomas Reist, *Saint Bonaventure as a Biblical Commentator: A Translation and Analysis of His Commentary on Luke, XVIII,34– XIX,42* (Lanham, MD: University Press of America, 1985); and Barbara Faes Mottoni, "Introduzione," in *Commento al Vangelo di San Luca/1 (1–4)* (Rome: Città Nuova, 1999), 7–26.
²⁸ A fuller accounting of Bonaventure's *divisio textus* of the whole Gospel can be found in the introduction to Bonaventure, *Commentary on the Gospel of John*, tr. Robert J. Karris, O.F.M., vol. 11, Works of Saint Bonaventure (St. Bonaventure, NY: Franciscan Institute, 2007), 23–26. It too, however, is far from complete.
²⁹ This outline is meant to aid the reader's understanding of the parts of Bonaventure's commentary discussed in this section. The outline of the later parts of the commentary (sections 2 and 3 of part II) have not been filled in because (1) the outline would be too long and (2) that material is not directly relevant to the discussion here. Note, however, that the outline includes both the main divisions of the text (part 1, section 1, section 2, part 2, section 1, section 2, etc.) as well as the divisions within the verses that Bonaventure will develop (or "dilate upon") in his commentary ("In the beginning was the Word" is associated with "unity of essence"; "The Word was with God" is associated with "dissimilarity in person"; etc.).

     C. Equality in majesty: "And the Word was God"
     D. Co-eternity in duration: "He was in the beginning with God"
   Section 2: In relationship with the things that are spoken through the Word
     A. Sufficient principle of creation: "All things were made through him"
     B. Unfailing principle: "And without him was made nothing"
     C. Foreknowing principle: "What had been made in him was life"
     D. Principle that bestows understanding: "And the life was the light for men"
Part II: The Word United to the Flesh (John 1:6–21:25)
   Section 1: The Incarnation (John 1:6–11:46)
     A. The Advent of the Precursor (John 1:6–8)
       1. His nature: "There was a man"
       2. His authority: "sent by God"
       3. His name: "his name was John"
       4. His office: "This man came as a witness"
     B. The Advent of Christ (John 1:9–14a)
       1. The reason for His coming: "He was the true light that enlightens every person coming into this world."
       2. The disdain shown the one coming: "He was in the world, and the world was made by him, and the world knew Him not. He came unto his own, and His own received Him not."
       3. The usefulness or fruit of the coming: "But as many as received Him, He gave them power to be made the sons of God."
       4. The manner of coming: "And the Word was made flesh and dwelt among us"
     C. The Manifestation of the Incarnation (John 1:14b–11:46)
   Section 2: The Passion (John 11.47–19.42)
   Section 3: The Resurrection of Christ (John 20:1–21:25)

Bonaventure begins his *Commentary on St. John* with this *divisio textus*.

This book, which deals with the incarnate Word, in whom a twofold nature, namely, divine and human, is considered, is divided into two parts. The first part concerns the Word *in se*, while the second deals with the Word in as far as it is united to flesh. That part commences with the words: *There was a man sent by God* (*Super Ioan.*, 1:1).[30]

---

[30] English: Bonaventure, *Commentary on the Gospel of John*, trans. Robert J. Karris, Works of St. Bonaventure, vol. 11 (St. Bonaventure, NY: The Franciscan Institute, 2007), esp. 1–3. Latin: St. Bonaventure, *Opera Omnia* (Ad Claras Aquas Quaracchi: Collegii s. Bonaventurae, 1882–1901), vol. 6. Since the section numbers in the English translation follow those in the Quaracchi edition, references to Bonaventure's text will be given by these section numbers; i.e., *Super Ioan.* 3:1 refers to chapter 3, section 1 of Bonaventure's commentary. These citations to the chapter and section in Bonaventure's commentary should not be confused with the chapter and verse in the Gospel. Since we are examining a progression in the text, I have left citations in the body of the text so that the reader can more easily note the progression.

According to Bonaventure's division, the "first part" of the Gospel dealing with "the Word in itself (*in se*)" includes John 1:1–5 (in our modern numbering system), and the "second part" dealing with the Word united to flesh includes everything else: John 1:6–21:25. It was not uncommon among thirteenth-century commentators to make this sort of lopsided division, in which the first part was short and the second part much longer. Modern commentators will generally say of John 1:1–5 that it is a "prologue."

According to Bonaventure, this first part (John 1:1–5) on "the Word in itself" has two sections. The first section concerns the Word in relationship to the speaker (John 1:1–2); the second focuses on those things spoken by the Word, starting at the words: *All things were made through him* (John 1:3–5). In what follows, Bonaventure first comments on the four "small sentences" (*clausulae*) in John 1:1–2 – "In the beginning was the Word; the Word was with God; the Word was God; He was in the beginning with God" – and then answer questions that arise about them (sections 2–8), after which he takes up the *clausulae* in John 1:3–5 and answers questions about them. Thus we begin each major section with a *divisio textus*, then move to what I will call a *sermo modernus* style section, after which we get a few *quaestiones*. This pattern is repeated throughout the commentary.

So, for example, commenting on the four *clausulae* in John 1:1–2, Bonaventure states that they "describe the incarnate Word relative to four qualities: first, "unity in essence" (*in essentia unitas*); second, "dissimilarity in person" (*in persona alietas*); third, "equality in majesty" (*in maiestate aequalitas*); and fourth, co-eternity in duration (*in duratione aeternitas*). Note the *sermo modernus* style fourfold parallel construction. Bonaventure dilates each member of this fourfold division in the sections that follow. The first, "unity in essence," he associates with the words "In the beginning was the Word" and dilates them in section 2. The second, "dissimilarity in person," he associates with the words "The Word was with God" and dilates them in section 3. The third, "equality in majesty," he associates with the words "and the Word was with God" and dilates them in section 4. And finally, "co-eternity in duration," he associates with the words "He was in the beginning with God" and dilates them in section 5.

After this *sermo modernus*–style section, Bonaventure poses and answers several questions. These do not all follow the "disputed question" style faithfully – there are not always "objections" and "replies" – but Bonaventure begins his response with the characteristic formula, known to all readers of Thomas's *Summa of Theology*: "*Respondeo: Dicendum quod* ...." In this first group, there are three questions:

1. Since the term Son expresses a characteristic that is most distinctive, why does John describe the Son of God with the term *Word* rather than the term *Son*? For it seems that it should be the other way around (*Super Ioan.*, 1:6).
2. Furthermore, it is asked what is described by the word *was*. For if "was" refers to past time, such a meaning is wholly contrary to eternity, because eternity has no past (*Super Ioan.*, 1:7).
3. But a heretic objects: If the Word proceeds from the speaker as a son from a father and the son is posterior to the father, then the Word was not in the beginning with God (*Super Ioan.*, 1:8).

Most questions in Bonaventure's commentary are similar to these in that they tend to involve clarifications of potential theological confusions regarding John's Gospel.

After the questions, we move to the next section in Bonaventure's *divisio textus*. In this instance, we move to the passage in John 1:3–5, which Bonaventure describes as dealing with the Word "in relationship with the things that are spoken through the Word" (*Super Ioan.*, 1:9). As before, we get a short *sermo modernus* style section in which Bonaventure distinguishes four qualities of the Word in relationship to "the things spoken through the Word" – that is to say, in relationship to created things. These are, first, that the Word is a "sufficient principle" (*principium sufficiens*) of creation; second, an "unfailing principle" (*principium indeficiens*); third, a "foreknowing principle" (*principium praecognoscens*); and fourth, a principle "bestowing understanding" (*cognitionem praebens*) on others. Note again the *sermo modernus* style parallelism in a fourfold distinction that allows him to dilate each member in a subsequent section. The first claim – that the Word is a "sufficient principle" – he associates with the words "All things were made through him" and dilates these words in *Super Ioan.*, 1:9. The second claim – that the Word is an "unfailing principle" – he associates with the words "And without him was made nothing that was made" and dilates them in *Super Ioan.*, 1:10. The third claim – that the Word is a "foreknowing principle" – he associates with the words "What had been made in him was life" – they existed in him before they came to be – and dilates these words in *Super Ioan.*, 1:11. And the fourth claim – that the Word is a principle "bestowing understanding" – he associates with the words, "And the life was the light of men" and dilates these in *Super Ioan.*, 1:12.

One question that naturally arises when comparing this fourfold *divisio* and the verses from the Gospel that Bonaventure pairs with each is whether the distinctions came first or the texts from the Gospel of John. So, for example, when one sees Bonaventure claiming that the words "What had been made in him was life" show that the Word is a "foreknowing principle," one wonders whether the words of John's Gospel aren't being stretched to fit the categories Bonaventure created in the *divisio*.

A study of Bonaventure's sermons reveals that the influences can run in both directions. The categories of the *divisio* are often suggested by the words of the biblical text, but Bonaventure won't allow an odd biblical verse to hinder a nice, neat *divisio*. His presumption seems to be that there is a logic in the text, and that the statements of the author ultimately follow this logic, even if "following this logic" entails taking certain words in a metaphorical sense or stretching their meaning.

After this fourfold *divisio* and *dilatatio*, we get another section of three *quaestiones*. The first deals with John 1:3, which says, "Without him was made nothing that was made." The objection is that the person who steals is doing and making something; therefore, it seems stealing is from God. Bonaventure's reply is the classic one given by St. Augustine: that sin is a privation, a "deprivation of the due order towards which the good should tend." So while the existence of the person and his freedom are good and from God, the deformity of his action is not (*Super Ioan.*, 1:14). The next question concerns the statement in John 1:3–4, "What has been made in him was life." Since all things were made in him, it seems that all things are life, even a stone. Bonaventure interprets this passage as saying that all things made pre-existed in God (*Super Ioan.* 1:15). And the third and final question deals with the meaning of John 1:5: "The light shone in the darkness, and the darkness did not comprehend it." There are two objections. The first is that corporeal light, when it shines and is present, cannot *not* be seen. Similar reasoning concludes that the same would hold of spiritual light and the intellect. The second objection runs in the opposite direction, asking why the text limits itself to darkness: "For not even a good person comprehends this light, for it is incomprehensible" (*Super Ioan.*, 1:16).

Bonaventure replies to the first by pointing out that there is a threefold difference between corporeal light and spiritual light: first, corporeal light shines forth naturally, whereas spiritual light does so voluntarily; second, people can see things with their physical sense of sight, but still be blind (that is to say, ignorant) about God. And third, whereas there is a proper proportion between our physical eyes and corporeal light, spiritual light exceeds our senses in a disproportionate way (*Super Ioan.*, 1:16).

Thus far we have reviewed the first part of a two-part text. Part one dealt with the Word *in se* and had two sections. We move on now to part two, in which, according to Bonaventure, St. John moves from his consideration of the Word *in se* to a consideration of the Word united to the flesh. Part two, as we saw earlier, includes the entire remainder of the Gospel (John 1:6-21:25). Unsurprisingly, Bonaventure begins his commentary on part two with another *divisio textus*, subdividing this second part of the Gospel into three major subdivisions. In the first, he says, John focuses on the incarnation (John 1:6–11:46); in the second, on the passion (John 11:47-19:42); and in third, on Christ's resurrection (John 20:1–21:25).

In the first lines of the first subdivision – the section dealing with the *incarnation* – Bonaventure comments that "since the coming of Christ in the flesh was the coming of a King, he sent someone ahead to announce his coming, a precursor." This precursor is of course John the Baptist. Bonaventure lays out a brief *divisio textus* of the verses of the Gospel, then sets forth a fourfold *divisio* in the *sermo modernus* style by means of which he informs his reader that four characteristics are used to describe John the Baptist. He is identified by his nature (*a natura*), his authority (*ab auctoritate*), his name (*a nomine*), and his office (*ab officio*): his nature, when the Gospel says, "There was a man"; his authority, when it says "sent by God"; his name, when it says "his name was John"; and his office or function, when it says "This man came as a witness" (*Super Ioan.*, 1:18–19).

After dilating each of these four characteristics in *Super Ioan.* 1:18 through 20, he proposes three questions. In the first question, regarding John 1:7, "He came to bear witness," he asks why, if as Christ says in John 5:34, "I do not accept human testimony," he should have sent John the Baptist for this purpose. Furthermore, since light does not need illumination, so too the greatest Truth needs no witness. Why, then, was John sent to "bear witness to the Truth" (*Super Ioan.*, 1:21)? The second question deals with the meaning of John 1:7, "so that all might believe through him." If God sent John the Baptist to accomplish this purpose, both God and John the Baptist would be prevented from attaining it, since John was not the Christ (*Super Ioan.*, 1:22). So what does the Gospel mean? And finally, regarding John 1:8, "He was not the light," the objection might be made that, as Ephesians 5:8 reads, "You were once darkness, but now you are light in the Lord," therefore should we not say that all good people are the light? (*Super Ioan.*, 1:23).

In good thirteenth-century style, Bonaventure resolves these questions by making several key distinctions. In reply to the first question, about why God sent a human messenger, Bonaventure distinguishes between those who need the witness of another because they are weak as contrasted with those who send a witness because their *audience* is weak. In reply to the second question – what the Gospel means when it says John the Baptist was sent "so that all might believe through him" – Bonaventure distinguishes between achieving an end by oneself (which can be said of Christ) and achieving it through another (which is why John was sent). And finally, in reply to the third question, why the Gospel says of John the Baptist that "he was not the light," Bonaventure distinguishes between light that illuminates and light that is illuminated by another. John the Baptist is not the light that illuminates; rather he is a light illuminated by another, as the moon and stars are illuminated by the sun.

The Scholastic Habits of Mind

In Chapter 9, we examined examples of Thomas's use of the methods of the *sermo modernus* style in his biblical commentaries. In the present chapter, we have similarly examined examples of Bonaventure's use of the same methods in his biblical commentaries. Our examination showed that not only were these commentaries crafted using contemporary methods of preaching, they were also made with an eye to training and assisting future preachers to preach in that style. We noted, for example, that both men incorporated lists of *distinctiones* in these early commentaries. Each master created a distinctive rhetorical style, but for those who recognize the forms that characterized their education at Paris, the roots of their similar training becomes apparent.

In the latter half of Chapter 9, I noted that, although the section numbers and question numbers helped lend structure to the *Summa of Theology*, a reader who wanted to understand Thomas's own *analytical* structure of the text should read the brief prologues he included at key points in the text. In these prologues, Thomas set out a running *divisio textus* of his own work; a skill he would have learned during his training at Paris doing *divisiones textus* of books of the Bible.

Thomas's *Summa of Theology* and Bonaventure's *Commentary on the Gospel of St. John* represent two different genres. But comparing the divisions and subdivisions in the prologues from Thomas's *Summa* with the divisions and subdivisions we have examined in this chapter from Bonaventure's *Commentary on the Gospel of John*, we can say that similar habits of mind produced both texts – the habits of mind both men learned during their training at the University of Paris when they were drilled in the skills of *divisio*, *dilatatio*, and *disputatio*. Evidence of all three skills can be found in the work of both authors.

These skills were applied in all three of the duties of the master: *lectio*, *disputatio*, and *praedicatio*.[31] These were three distinct tasks, and yet our examination shows that the connections between and among them was extensive. I suggest that it was this particular marriage of skills and habits of mind that gave the products of these thirteenth-century masters the distinctive character they enjoyed: their preference for clarity, grounded both in the logic of their argumentation and in the order of topics addressed; their sense of order in which the parts were always seen in relation to the whole; their insistence that their lectures be well grounded in an authoritative text; their continual referencing of biblical passages no matter what the text or subject-matter; their special sensitivity to the various meanings of

---

[31] Note that I am referring to *disputatio* here as a duty. In the previous paragraph, I referred to *disputatio* as a skill. What is the difference? The duty of the master was to engage in public *quaestiones disputatae*. To be able to do this well, he had to develop the skill of *disputatio*.

words in different contexts; their partiality toward the use of divisions, distinctions, and lists of categories, always with an eye to their completeness.[32]

All of these rhetorical practices and habits of mind were, I would argue, the product of an educational culture that valued preaching – preaching that was based on the firm foundation of Scripture and whose theological assertions had met the test of questioning through rigorous disputation.

---

[32] Regarding "completeness," it was, for example, a set rule of *sermo modernus*-style preaching that a preacher who began a metaphor mentioning the foundation and walls of the house had to finish the metaphor with some discussion of the roof, or else his listeners would be left feeling that the analogy was incomplete, asking "What about the roof?" So too, the lists of attributes in a sermon did not have to be exhaustive, but they always had to give the impression of being complete. It was understood to be a *faux pas* to mention the matter without discussing the form, or vice versa. You were not to mention the head and the arms without mentioning the body and the legs. And you were not to make a list with "head, ears, arms, body, legs, and toes," because "ears" would overlap with "head," and "toes" could not be listed without feet (otherwise what are the toes attached to?) and/or fingers.

16

A Master's Praise of Scripture
The Prologue to Bonaventure's Breviloquium

IT HAS been a guiding hypothesis of this study that a major impetus for the educational reforms at universities such as those at Paris, Oxford, and Cambridge, and at a host of *studia generalia* across Western Europe, was the concern for good, clear, doctrinally sound preaching and teaching. Good preaching and teaching had been called for at the Fourth Lateran Council, and the new mendicant orders in particular heeded that call.

The prevailing educational curriculum when both Thomas and Bonaventure incepted as masters involved attending lectures on the Bible, participating in "disputed questions," and completing a commentary on all four books of Peter Lombard's *Sentences*. Contemporary evidence suggests, however, that there was widespread interest in producing simpler, more concise, and more logically coherent introductions to theology. Such was the purpose of the many *summae* of theology produced during this period. In Bonaventure's own Franciscan order, there was the monumental *Summa fratris Alexandri*, also known at the *Summa Hallensis*, produced by Alexander of Hales, Jean of La Rochelle, Eudes Rigaud, William of Middleton, and perhaps several others over the span of almost two decades between 1238 and 1257.

The *Breviloquium*, written likely in 1257, was a product of Bonaventure's early years as a master at Paris. Yet this was also the year Bonaventure was elevated to master general of the Franciscan order. For this reason, the *Breviloquium* has been described as a "turning-point text or a border-line text" at the intersection of two worlds.[1] The text displays the training and skill of a master of sacred doctrine at Paris. But it is also a work directed to the wider needs of the Franciscan order and represents Bonaventure's attempt to provide a good introductory text, a "brief discourse" (*breviloquium*), on the basic elements of theology to help prepare his young friars to enter into a course of rigorous study.

---

[1] See Emmanuel Falque, *Saint Bonaventure et l'entrée de Dieu in théologie*, Études de philosophie médiévale (Paris: Librairie philosophique J. Vrin, 2000), 25: "un texte charnière ou un texte frontière." Quoted from Dominic Monti's "Introduction" to Bonaventure, *Breviloquium*, Works of St. Bonaventure, vol. 9 (St. Bonaventure, NY: The Franciscan Institute, 2005), xv.

The *Summa*, the *Breviloquium*, and the Search for a Simpler Introduction to Theology

Emmanuel Falque has proposed that Thomas's goal in writing his *Summa of Theology* and Bonaventure's goal in writing the *Breviloquium* were "remarkably similar": they both came out of a "concern with beginners" and "the desire to achieve a brief and coherent synthesis."[2]

Thomas Aquinas gave as one of his reasons for writing the *Summa theologiae* the desire to "present those things that pertain to the Christian religion in a manner befitting the education of beginners." "Students in this science," wrote Thomas, "have not seldom been hampered by what they have found written in other authors, partly on account of the multiplicity of useless questions, articles, and arguments; partly also because the things they need to know are not taught according to the order of learning, but according as the plan of the book might require or the occasion of disputing might offer."[3] Because of these difficulties, Thomas described himself as "anxious, therefore to overcome these and other obstacles" and declared his goal was to "present those things pertaining to sacred doctrine briefly and clearly insofar as the matter will permit."[4]

In a similar spirit, Bonaventure explains near the end of his prologue to the *Breviloquium* that

> This teaching [of theology] has been transmitted, both in the writings of the saints and in those of the doctors, in such a diffuse manner that those who come to learn about Sacred Scripture are not able to read or hear about it for a long time. In fact, beginning theologians often dread Sacred Scripture itself, feeling it to be confusing, disordered, and uncharted as some impenetrable forest. That is why my colleagues have asked me, from my own modest knowledge, to draw up some concise summary of the truth of theology (*breve in summa dicerem de veritate theologiae*). Yielding to their requests, I have agreed to compose what might be called a brief discourse (*breviloquium*). In it I will summarize not all the truths of our faith, but some things that are more opportune [for such students] to hold.[5]

---

[2] See Falque, *Saint Bonaventure*, 34–35; quoted from Monti, Introduction, *Breviloquium*, xxi.

[3] Thomas Aquinas, *Summa Theologiae*, general prologue. Those who make use of the many online versions of the *Summa* may wish to be warned that very few of these prominent online versions contain the general prologue. This unfortunate practice demonstrates how little the importance of such prologues is appreciated.

[4] Ibid.

[5] *Brev. prol.* 6.5, quote from Monti, xx. Throughout this chapter, I have used the English translation of the *Breviloquium* by Dominic Monti in the Franciscan Institute "Works of St. Bonaventure" series. For the full reference, see note 1. I have taken the Latin text from the standard Quarrachi edition, vol. 5, 201–208. Note however that, although in other volumes of "The Works of St. Bonaventure" series, the English translator normally followed the numbering of the text of the Quaracchi editors, the problem with which our translator was faced in this case was that the numbering of the prologue provided by the Quaracchi editors was rather sparse. So he wisely added some paragraph numbers to the section numbers proposed by the editors. I will report the section and paragraph numbers as they appear in the English translation (e.g., *Brev. prol.* 5.1, which refers to the prologue, section 5, paragraph 1). Another difficulty is that the Quaracchi editors did not begin "section 1" until six paragraphs into the prologue. So references up to section 1 will be made only with paragraph numbers; e.g., *Brev. prol.* 3, which would refer to the third paragraph of the prologue, which occurs *before* "section 1" in the Quaracchi edition.

One sees in the Latin of this passage not only the term that has become the title of the work, "*breviloquium*," but also the words "*summa*" and "*theologiae*." It would be right to see this work, therefore, as Bonaventure's attempt to provide for his young Franciscan friars in formation a similar resource of the sort Thomas would seek some years later to provide for the young Dominican friars in his order: a concise, orderly introduction to the truths of the faith to replace the sprawling jumble of distinctions, questions, and articles found in contemporary *summae* and in Peter Lombard's *Sentences*.[6]

The goals may have been similar, and much of the content, but the methods and approach were strikingly different. As is well known, Thomas's *Summa of Theology* is divided into four major sections: the *prima pars*, the *prima secundae*, the *secunda secundae*, and the *tertia* pars. In the "first part," he deals with God (one and three), creation, the angels, the nature of man, and divine government of the cosmos. In the "first part of the second part," he deals with beatitude, habits, passions, virtue, law, and grace. In the "second part of the second part," he treats each of the three theological and four cardinal virtues. And in the third part, he deals with the Incarnation and the sacraments. Bonaventure, by contrast, divides his *Breviloquium* into seven major sections. In part one, he deals with the Trinity; in part two, with creation; in part three, with the corruption of sin; in part four, with the incarnation of the Word; in part five, with the grace of the Holy Spirit; in part six, with the sacraments; and in part seven, with the final judgment.

The most obvious difference between the *Breviloquium* and Thomas's *Summa* is the emphasis Thomas places on the habits, passions, and virtues – all of the material in the *prima secundae* and *secunda secundae* that makes up the immense middle section of the *Summa* – most of which is missing from the *Breviloquium*. The absence of this immense middle section allows Bonaventure's *Breviloquium* to be "brief" and its presence makes Thomas's *Summa* much less so. Something else that makes Thomas's *Summa* somewhat longer is his use of the "disputed question" style, albeit a stripped down version, including usually no more than three or four objections and responses. Bonaventure's style in the *Breviloquium* is more like Thomas's style in the *Summa contra Gentiles*: in both, the arguments are laid out in sequential paragraphs, not in disputed question-style questions and articles.

Some scholars have questioned whether the prologue to the *Breviloquium* was written separately, perhaps earlier in Bonaventure's career, and joined later to the *Breviloquium* after it was finished. There is no manuscript evidence to support this theory; rather, the theory is based on the belief that the prologue does not fit stylistically with the rest of the *Breviloquium*. "It is much too lengthy when compared with the body of the text," it is claimed, and "it reads like a lyrical narrative in comparison to the tightly organized arguments that follow."[7] Pedro Bordoy-Torrents, the originator of this theory, argued that the prologue "was probably a revision of a university sermon Bonaventure gave earlier in his career, probably the 'praise of Sacred Scripture' required when he was installed as a Biblical bachelor."[8] Other Bonaventure

---

[6] The *Breviloquium* was one of Bonaventure's most popular works. It survives in some 227 manuscripts, outstripping the second most popular of Bonaventure's works, the *Itinerarium mentis in Deum*, which survives in 138.

[7] See Pedro Bordoy-Torrents, "Técnicas divergentes en la redaccion del *Breviloquio* de S. Bonaventura," *Cientia Tomista* (1940): 442–451. The summary quoted in the foregoing text is from Dominic Monti, xxxix.

[8] Quoted from Monti, Introduction, *Breviloquium*, xxxix.

scholars such as Jacques Bougerol followed Boroy-Torrents' judgment, but more recent scholars have disputed it, among them Francisco Chavero Blanco, Camille Bérubé, and Emmanuel Falque.[9] I have no final judgment on whether the prologue might have been written earlier, but Joshua Benson's discovery of Bonaventure's *principium* puts to rest the theory that this prologue was the "commendation of Sacred Scripture" at Bonaventure's inception as a master.

Our examination of this prologue will show, moreover, that it is actually quite similar to the other prologue we have seen up to this point. Hence there is really no *textual* reason to conclude that it was written later in Bonaventure's career. Given what we have seen about the ubiquity of such prologues, it is not surprising to find Bonaventure writing a complex prologue of this sort as a preface even to a treatise filled with "tightly organized arguments." It would have been more surprising if he hadn't.

Dividing the *Thema*

At the outset of his prologue, Bonaventure lays out as his *thema* this long passage from St. Paul's Letter to the Ephesians (3:14–19):

> For this reason I bow my knees before the Father of our Lord Jesus Christ, from whom every fatherhood in heaven and on earth takes its name, that he would grant you, according to the riches of his glory, to be strengthened through his Spirit with power in your inner being, and that Christ may dwell in your hearts through faith; that being rooted and grounded in love, you may be able to comprehend, with all the saints, what is the breadth and length, height and depth, and to know the love of Christ that surpasses all knowledge, so that you may be filled with all the fullness of God.

In this passage, Bonaventure finds material he can associate with the three topics he wants to discuss: (1) the source or origin of the Scriptures, (2) their manner of proceeding, and (3) their purpose or fruit. The result is a threefold *divisio* (Box 16.1). The *source or origin of the Scriptures*, says Bonaventure, is the "inflowing of the Most Blessed Trinity." This he associates with the first part of his *thema*. Next is their distinctive *manner of proceeding* (*progressus*), which he associates with the next section of his *thema*, especially the four terms "breadth, length, height, and depth." Dilating these four terms will occupy the bulk of the prologue. Finally there is the purpose or fruit of Sacred Scripture, which is expressed by the last words in the *thema* verse: "to know the love of Christ that surpasses all knowledge, so that you may be filled with all the fullness of God." "For these are writings," says Bonaventure, "whose *words* are *of eternal life*, recorded "not only that we might believe, but also that we might possess that life everlasting, in which we shall see and love and our desires will be completely satisfied."[10]

---

[9] Francisco Chavero Blanco, *Imago Dei: Aproximacion a la Antropologia Teologica de San Buenaventura* (Murcia: Publicaciones del Instituto Teologico Franciscano, 1993), 210–221; Camille Bérubé, *De la philosophie a la sagesse chez Saint Bonaventure et Roger Bacon* (Rome: Istituto Storico dei Cappuccini, 1976), 91–162; Emmanuel Falque, *Saint Bonaventure et l'entrée de Dieu in théologie*, 31–52.

[10] *Brev. prol.* 4.

> **Box 16.1** Outline of the Threefold *Divisio* of the *Thema* from Ephesians 3:14–19
>
> 1. The origin (*ortum*) of Scripture (the inflowing of the Trinity):
>   "For this reason I bow my knees before the **Father** of our Lord **Jesus Christ**, from whom every fatherhood in heaven and on earth takes its name, that he would grant you, according to the riches of his glory, to be strengthened through his **Spirit** with power in your inner being, and ***that Christ may dwell in your hearts*** through faith"
> 2. The manner of proceeding (*progressum*) of sacred Scripture:
>   "that being rooted and grounded in love, you may be able to comprehend, with all the saints, what is the **breadth and length, height and depth**, and to know the love of Christ that surpasses all knowledge
> 3. The purpose or fruit (*statum sive fructum*) of sacred Scripture (a superabundance of overflowing happiness):
>   "so that you may be filled with all the fullness of God."

After briefly previewing the three categories of *ortum*, *progressum*, and *statum* in the first several paragraphs of the prologue, Bonaventure quickly moves on in the main body of the prologue to his much longer discussion of the breadth, length, height, and depth of the Scriptures — that is to say, his discussion of the modes of discourse in the Scriptures and the basic rules for expounding them. He does not return to the "purpose or fruit" at the end.

Indeed, the reader who consults either the Latin text in the standard Quaracchi edition or the English translation in the Franciscan Institute's "Works of St. Bonaventure" series will find that these early paragraphs where Bonaventure lays out the threefold distinction between *ortum*, *progressum*, and *statum* are all considered preliminary and are not given section numbers. Given this approach, "section 1" begins with the breadth of Scripture, and the editors divide up the rest of the prologue into these six sections:

Section 1: The Breadth of Holy Scripture
Section 2: The Length of Holy Scripture
Section 3: The Height of Holy Scripture
Section 4: The Depth of Holy Scripture
Section 5: The Mode of Procedure of Holy Scripture
Section 6: The Mode of Expounding Holy Scripture

It is worth noting in passing that, at the conclusion of section 6, Bonaventure tells his reader that he has "taken the trouble to set down in advance the particular chapter headings [of the main body of the text] to aid the memory and give a clearer prospect of what will be treated." Some might see this as a precursor of the modern Table of Contents. But those who have been studying these prologues would likely see it as a stripped down, simpler version of what all masters of theology were trained to provide at the end of a prologue: namely, a good *divisio textus*.

As already mentioned, the main section of the prologue is organized the four terms *length*, *breadth*, *height*, and *depth*. It may interest the reader to know that there is a contemporary book by a highly-respect theologian that uses the same literary device. *Divisio* is not just for medieval authors, it seems.

In his 1987 book *The Catholicity of the Church*, the late Cardinal Avery Dulles quoted the *same passage* from Ephesians 3:18–19 to set up the four categories of height, depth, breadth, and length, which he then used to structure his discussion of what he took to be the four essential characteristics of the "catholicity" of the Church. In his Introduction to that book, Cardinal Dulles writes:

> As we read in the Letter to the Ephesians, Paul prays that his readers may be enabled to comprehend "the breadth and length and height and depth" of the love of Christ, even though this "surpasses knowledge" (Eph. 3:18–19). Like the love of Christ, the Church may be viewed as a mystery with four dimensions: height, depth, breadth, and length. In this and the three following chapters we shall consider this fourfold catholicity. In the present chapter we shall reflect on the divine component of catholicity [its height], as the gift of the Father who communicates himself through his incarnate Word and the Holy Spirit. In Chapter 3 I shall turn to the depth dimension of catholicity, its rootedness in the natural and the human. In the following two succeeding chapters I shall discuss the spatial universality of the Church, which may be called catholicity in breadth, and its temporal extension, or its catholicity in length.[11]

One thing to notice here is that Dulles's use of Ephesians 3 is no more justified by the actual content of the verse than Bonaventure's. He quotes the verse merely as an occasion to use its four terms: breadth, length, height, and depth. Dulles associates *height* with the Godhead in Whom the Church has her origin, *depth* with Christ's taking on the fullness of our humanity in the incarnation, *breadth* with the geographical spread of the Church throughout the world, and *length* with its extension over time. Bonaventure, by contrast, associates the *breadth* of Scripture with "the variety of its parts," the *length* with "its description of times and ages," its *height* with "its account of the ordered levels of hierarchies," and its *depth* with "the multiplicity of its mystical senses and interpretations." The similarity is that, for both authors, "height" is associated with the divine realm and "length" is associated with extension over time and through history. In both instances, the author's use of the fourfold *divisio* was intended to lend structure the work by making use of a visually significant set of images that would aid the process of recollection.

Breadth: Scripture's Many Parts

In his extended section on the *breadth* of the Scriptures, Bonaventure provides a *divisio textus* of the Bible similar to the *divisio* masters in theology gave during their *resumptio* address. As the reader may recall, Bonaventure did not give the standard *divisio textus* in his *resumptio*. He chose instead to lay out a hierarchy of the sciences to show how they all could

---

[11] Avery Dulles, S.J., *The Catholicity of the Church* (Oxford: Clarendon Press, 1987), 31. When I first read Cardinal Dulles's book some years ago, I found that the author's use of these four spatial terms to organize his points not only added clarity, it has in the years since also helped me more easily recall the contents of the book.

"lead back to" (*re-ducere*) theology and sacred Scripture. It is intriguing to find, therefore, that in one of his earliest works as Master General of the Franciscans, Bonaventure chose to set forth the *divisio textus* of the Bible that he had spared himself in his *resumptio*.

The *divisio textus* he supplies here is fairly standard and resembles in many respects the *divisiones* we examined in Chapter 5 on Thomas's *resumptio*.[12] There are two Testaments, Old and New. In the Old Testament, he distinguishes five "legal" books, ten historical, five sapiential, and six prophetic books, for a total of twenty-six books in the Old Testament. Bonaventure then maps out the customary structural correlation between the books of the Old Testament and the New. Just as the Old Testament contains legal books, historical books, sapiential books, and prophetic books, so too the New Testament contains "legal" books (the Gospels), a "historical" book (Acts of the Apostles), sapiential literature (the epistles), and a prophetic book (the Apocalypse), resulting in what Bonaventure describes as a "wondrous concordance" between the Old Testament and the New, "not only in the consistency of meanings, but also in their fourfold division."[13] As we saw in the chapter on Thomas's *resumptio*, both Henry of Ghent and Matthew of Aquasparta would some years later follow Bonaventure's lead and map out a similar series of correlations in their *resumptio* addresses between the books of the Old Testament and the books of the New.

Indeed, Bonaventure simplifies Augustine's famous comment that "the New Testament lies hidden in the Old, and the Old becomes manifest in the New," to say that "the Old is contained in the New and the New in the Old."[14] The image he uses to express the relationship between the two is the famous one from Ezekiel 10 of the wheel within a wheel. This is the same passage in which the famous four creatures appear: the lion, the ox, the man, and the eagle.

Instead of associating the lion with Mark, the ox with Luke, the man with Matthew, and the eagle with John, as was customary, Bonaventure associates the "legal" and "evangelical" books (the books of Old Testament law and the Gospels) with the lion, because the lion represents authority; the historical books of the Old and New Testaments with the ox, because the ox represents strength; the sapiential books with the man, because the man represents wisdom; and the prophetic books with the eagle, because the eagle possesses a "penetrating vision."[15]

---

[12] It is this similarity between Bonaventure's *divisio textus* here and those found in the *resumptio* addresses of other masters that undoubtedly led some scholars to conclude that this prologue might have been a recycled version of Bonaventure's own *resumptio*. Even if Joshua Benson had not identified Bonaventure's *principium* and *resumptio* addresses, however, one could still conclude that this prologue does not exhibit the usual characteristics of a *resumptio*.

[13] Comments such as this, repeated by numerous masters, along with the fact that numerous masters during this period wrote long treatises on the Old Law – Thomas Aquinas's questions on the Old Law are, for example, the longest in the entire *Summa* – should finally put to rest the old notion that the scholastics of the thirteenth century didn't care about the Old Testament. To the contrary, thirteenth-century masters quite often quote the Old Testament in sermons and use verses from the Old Testament as *thema* verses. For a good introduction to these treatises on the Old Law, see Beryl Smalley, "William of Auvergne, John of La Rochelle and St Thomas Aquinas on the Old Law," in *St Thomas Aquinas (1274–1974): Commemorative Studies* (Toronto: Pontifical Institute of Mediaeval Studies, 1974), vol. 2, 1–71.

[14] *Brev. prol.* 1.1.

[15] Ibid. Both Thomas and Bonaventure in their commentaries on the Fourth Gospel associate John with the eagle. Note, however, that in Bonaventure's current scheme, John's Gospel would be associated with the lion and his epistles with the man; only the Book of Revelation would be associated with the eagle.

Unlike modern biblical scholars who distinguish the Old Testament from the New in terms of the difference between "law" and "faith" – a tendency especially popular among certain nineteenth-century Protestant exegetes that often had the effect of deemphasizing the law – Bonaventure insists that we "cannot segregate in Scripture the knowledge of things we should believe from the knowledge of morals." Faith, he declares, "is the foundation that supports us, the lamp that directs us, the door that lets us enter." Both the Old Testament and the New provide us with knowledge that moves us to do good and avoid evil. The difference between the two, on Bonaventure's account, has to do with two different ways of motivating compliance: fear or love. "Thus it follows," says Bonaventure, that the Scripture "is divided into two Testaments which, to put it briefly, differ as fear does from love."[16]

How does Bonaventure get from the twofold division of the Scriptures into Old and New Testaments to the fourfold division of each Testament into legal, historical, sapiential, and prophetic books? In a master's *resumptio*, often the *divisio textus* was merely stated, without justification. Here, Bonaventure justifies the fourfold division, saying that there are four ways a person may be prompted toward goodness and drawn away from evil: "by the precepts of a most powerful authority (*per praecapta maiestatis omnipotentissimae*), contained in the legal books; by the examples and benefits of a most innocent goodness (*per exempla bonitatis innocentissimae*), contained in the historical books; by the teachings of a most wise truth (*per documenta veritatis providentissimae*), contained in the sapiential books; and finally, by a combination of all three," by recalling the legal and doctrinal wisdom of the others, which is found in the prophetic books.[17] Hence the Holy Scripture is like a "vast river," says Bonaventure, which continually grows in size by the addition of many tributaries.[18]

Length: God's Governance of the Whole Course of History

St. Bonaventure analyzes the "length" of Scripture in terms of its temporal extension: its description of times and ages from the beginning of the world until the Day of Judgment. To fill out this section, Bonaventure proposes two different schemata for dividing all of history, both of which can be traced ultimately to the works of St. Augustine. The first schema is threefold: it divides history into the time of the law of nature; the time of the written law, and the time of grace.[19] The time of the natural law extended from Adam to Moses; the time of the written law from Moses to Christ; and we live now in the time of grace. This does not mean that the precepts of the natural law no longer apply, merely that we cannot fulfill its precepts on our own without grace. This threefold schema can be traced back to Hugh of St. Victor's *On the Sacraments of the Christian Faith*, one of Bonaventure's favorite sources, and from there back to the famous eleventh-century theologian Anselm of Laon, about whom Odo Lottin has written:

---

[16] *Brev. prol.*1.2, quoting Augustine, *Contra Adimantum* 17.2.
[17] *Brev. prol.* 1.3.
[18] Ibid., 1.4. The image of a river vast and deep, containing "hidden" things," was one Bonaventure had used previously in his prologue to the *Sentences* commentary (see Chapter 15), where he used the image to praise, not the Scriptures, but Lombard's *Sentences*.
[19] *Brev. prol.* 2.1.

The school of Anselm of Laon spread, on the subject of the natural law, a conception that exercised a profound influence. Before the epoch of the Mosaic Law, humanity was subject to the reign of the natural law, which *naturalis ratio* dictated to him. It was condensed into this principle: Do not do to another that which you would not want for him to do to you. But this natural reason was soon obfuscated by sin, to the point that few men remained faithful to the true God. The Mosaic Law, thus, became necessary to revive the natural law in the heart of man.[20]

The ultimate source for this view can be traced to a brief comment in St. Augustine's *On the Trinity*, where he refers to a "time before the Law; a second, under the Law; and a third, under grace."[21]

As Augustine had done before him, Bonaventure combined this threefold schema with another six-fold schema that more closely reflected the Scriptural account of salvation history. The "six ages" of history (in both Augustine and Bonaventure) are these: the first runs from Adam to Noah; the second from Noah to Abraham; the third from Abraham to David; the fourth from David to the Babylonian Exile; the fifth from the Babylonian Exile to the coming of Christ; and the sixth runs from Christ until the end of the world. There is also a seventh age, says Bonaventure, which runs from the time when Jesus was laid in the tomb until the general resurrection.[22] There is some confusion here, since there seems to be an overlap between the sixth and seventh ages, and Bonaventure himself says that "the full compass of time" reaches its "consummation at the end of the sixth." In the source text from Augustine's *De trinitate*, there are only six ages.[23] Bonaventure's sixth age includes the Day of Judgment; the seventh age involves the "everlasting rest of souls" corresponding to the seventh day of creation, on which God rested.

There is another interesting wrinkle here. The threefold schema of salvation history – the age of the natural law, the age of the written law, and the age of grace – seems to correspond chronologically to the time before Moses, the time between Moses and Christ, and the time after Christ. And yet attempting to unify the two schemata, Bonaventure claims "the full compass of time" runs "according to a triple law" – the first is "innately given" (the natural law); the second is "externally imposed (the written law); and the third is infused from above (the law of grace). This threefold law runs through all seven ages, he says, although it reaches its consummation at the end of the sixth.[24] What this suggests is that all humans,

---

[20] Cf. Dom Odon Lottin, *Le droit naturel chez Saint Thomas d'Aquin et ses prédécesseurs*, 2me ed. (Bruges: Beyaert, 1931), 27: "L'école d'Anselme de Laon a répandu, au sujet de la loi naturelle, une conception qui a exercé une profonde influence. Avant l'époque de la Loi mosaïque, l'humanité était soumise au règne de la loi naturelle que lui dictait la *ratio naturalis*. Elle se condensait en ce principe: Ne fais pas à autrui ce que tu ne voudrais pas qu'on te fît. Mais cette raison naturelle fut bientôt obnubilée par le péché, au point que peu d'hommes restèrent fidèles au vrai Dieu. La Loi mosaïque devenait ainsi nécessaire pour faire revivre la loi naturelle au coeur de l'homme." The translation is my own. One finds this same threefold schema of history in Thomas's *Summa of Theology* I-II, q. 98, a. 6. See also Hugh of St. Victor, *De sacramentis*, 1.8.3.

[21] Augustine, *De Trinitate* 4.4.7.

[22] *Brev. prol.* 2.1.

[23] One can also find the same sixfold division of history in Augustine's *De catechizandis rudibus*, esp. chapter 6.

[24] *Brev. prol.* 2.2.

no matter what "age" they live in, participate in the threefold law. There are times even now in the sixth age when we are left to our own devices to figure out moral questions according to the natural law. Yet, since we are fallen beings, we are often confused about what is good and what is evil. Even when we can figure out the right thing to do, we often find ourselves saying, with St. Paul, "the good which I will, I do not; but the evil which I will not, that I do" (Romans 7:19). For these reasons, we need the guidance of the written law and the enabling power of grace to do the good. We each live out in our own way the movement from the age of the natural law to the age of the written law to the age of grace. "For in this way," says Bonaventure, "the course of the macrocosm corresponds with that of the microcosm – namely, of the human being, for whose sake the larger world was created." In understanding the threefold order of salvation history, therefore, we come to understand an important truth about our own moral development.

The Sacred Scriptures offer something else that helps us in our moral and spiritual growth: a sense of perspective, a sense of the whole, and of God's providence. "Just as no one can appreciate the loveliness of a song unless one's perspective embraces it as whole," writes Bonaventure, "so none of us can see the beauty of the order and governance of the world without an integral view of its course. But since no mortal lives long enough to see all this with bodily eyes, nor can any individual foretell the future, the Holy Spirit has provided us with the book of Sacred Scripture, whose *length* corresponds to God's governance of the universe."[25]

Height: Hierarchies Leading "Down From" and "Back To" God

In his book *The Catholicity of the Church*, Cardinal Dulles speaks of the *height* of the Church as linked hierarchically with the Triune God through the mediation of the incarnate Son. So too in Bonaventure's prologue, the *height* of the Scriptures is linked to "the one Hierarch, Jesus Christ, who, by reason of the human nature he assumed, is Hierarch in the ecclesiastical hierarchy, but also in the angelic hierarchy, and is the middle person of that supercelestial hierarchy of the Blessed Trinity. Through him, from the very height of God, the grace of unction descends . . ."[26] Bonaventure begins the section declaring:

> Sacred Scripture, as it unfolds, also possesses a height, which consists of the description of the hierarchies in their ordered ranks. These hierarchies are the ecclesiastical, the angelic, and the divine – or in other words, the sub-celestial, the celestial, and the supercelestial. The first is described clearly, the second somewhat more indirectly, and the third more obscurely still. From its description of the ecclesiastical hierarchy, we can see that Scripture is lofty, and from its description of the angelic, loftier still, and from its description of the divine, most exalted.[27]

One sees in this passage the influence of Pseudo-Dionysius's *Celestial Hierarchy* and *Ecclesiastical Hierarchy*. But we also find in its final sentence evidence of the preacher's art:

---

[25] Ibid., 2.4.
[26] Ibid., 3.2.
[27] Ibid., 3.1.

setting up a series based on a positive, comparative, and superlative (good, better, best): lofty (*alta*), loftier (*altior*), loftiest (*alitissima*). If this were a sermon, we would now expect Bonaventure to "dilate" this threefold distinction by describing how the first is lofty, how the second is loftier, and how the third is loftiest and most exalted. This is essential what he does, but to the threefold hierarchy of Church, angels, and Triune God, he adds creation and human learning with the result that he can reiterate the point he made in his *resumptio* address (the *De reductione artium ad theologiam*) about all creation and all learning leading back to God.

Created things exist in matter, but they also have existence in the Eternal Art, that is, in God's eternal Word through Whom He created everything that is. Human beings gain knowledge of created things in three ways: either through acquired knowledge, through grace, or in glory. Philosophy deals with the knowledge of things gained by innate or acquired knowledge; theology, because it is knowledge gained by faith and revealed by the Holy Spirit, deals with things which concern grace and glory, and even eternal Wisdom. Theology, therefore, says Bonaventure, "subjects philosophical knowledge to itself, borrowing from the nature of things what it needs in order to construct a mirror for the representation of divine realities. Thus, it erects a ladder, as it were, *set upon earth* but whose *top touches heaven*."[28] This image of the ladder between heaven and earth hearkens back to the famous ladder Jacob sees in Genesis 28:12: "And he saw in his sleep a ladder standing upon the earth, and the top thereof touching heaven: the angels also of God ascending and descending by it."

The shifts here have been ingenious. He began with a threefold hierarchy: celestial, angelic, and the three Persons of the Trinity. In the middle section, he introduces material creation and human knowing to make the point that these can lead back to their ultimate Source, God, but they must be put under the discipline of theology, which is based on divine revelation and eternal Wisdom. He illustrates this point with the image of Jacob's ladder, upon which, as was well known to his listeners, *angels* ascended and descended between heaven and earth.

Bonaventure introduced this middle *reductio*-section into what began as a threefold hierarchy, so that when it came time for him to reiterate his "good-better-best" progression to tie things up at the end of this section, he now has four terms instead of three. Although there is "great beauty" in the world machine," he says, there is "far greater beauty" in the Church, which is "adorned with the splendor of the gifts of holiness." After the positive and comparative, we fully expect him to give us the superlative: the thing of "greatest beauty." But he hasn't mentioned the angels yet, so after "great beauty" (*pulcritudo magna*) and "far greater beauty" (*longe maior ... pulcritudine*), he adds that there is "an even greater beauty" (*maxima*) in the heavenly Jerusalem of the angels. The "greatest beauty of all" (*supermaxima*), however, is found in the supreme and most blessed Trinity.[29] In Latin, the third term in the progression is the superlative: *maxima*. What do you do when you need to indicate something beyond the best? You call it "super-best." Bonaventure creates the term *supermaxima*. This might be seen as linguistic cheating, but

---

[28] Ibid., 3.2.
[29] Ibid., 3.3.

Bonaventure's addition of the fourth term left him no other option but to create this fourth, "super-superlative."³⁰

Depth: A Plurality of Mystical Meanings

The "depth" of Scripture has to do with the multiplicity of its senses: allegorical, moral, and anagogical. But why do the Scriptures have senses that other texts lack? Bonaventure answers that this is "appropriate" due to (1) the subject matter of the text, (2) its hearers, (3) its origin or source, and (4) its end or purpose.³¹

Often with lists such as these, each term represents a separate argument. In this instance, however, I wish to argue that these four terms – subject matter, hearers, source, and end – represent the four interrelated stages of a longer argument. If we read each stage in isolation from the others, we are likely to conclude each is intolerably weak.³² So we will first examine each stage individually before seeing how they can be fitted together as parts of a larger whole.

Appropriate to the Subject Matter

Bonaventure's first claim is that the multiplicity of senses is appropriate to the subject-matter of the Scriptures because the Scriptures deal with God, Christ, the works of redemption, and the content of belief.³³ By itself, this is not an especially convincing argument for the multiplicity of senses in Scripture because clearly one can have a book covering multiple topics and not have multiple senses. Peter Lombard's *Sentences* and modern catechisms deal with all the topics Bonaventure listed – God, Christ, the works of redemption, and the content of belief – and yet they do not possess multiple senses.

Bonaventure's next claim is that God is three and one: one in essence and three in person. "Therefore, Scripture, which is concerned with God, contains within the unity of the letter a threefold understanding."³⁴ This too is not an especially convincing argument, since many books deal with the Triune God – St. Augustine's *On the Trinity* was one of Bonaventure's favorites – but don't possess multiple senses.

So too, if Bonaventure reasoned from the dual nature of Christ the way he has reasoned from the triune character of God, he would be forced to say that there is within the unity of the letter a *twofold* understanding of the Scriptures corresponding to the two natures in Christ's one person. Instead Bonaventure argues that, although the works of redemption are many, "all look toward the one principal offering of Christ."³⁵ This is a better argument

---

³⁰ Bonaventure might also have thought the term was justified by the "supernatural" goodness of God. This would be true of the angels as well, but they are not *supermaxima*. In the final analysis, the problem is how we can refer to God at all, given how far He surpasses all our concepts.
³¹ Cf. *Brev. prol.* 4.2.
³² Indeed some readers may conclude that they simply *are* weak. In what follows, I give the best construal I can.
³³ *Brev. prol.* 4.2.
³⁴ Ibid.
³⁵ Ibid.

for the allegorical sense and for viewing all the senses – moral, anagogical, and allegorical – as essentially "Christological." But we still lack a separate reason for the moral and anagogical senses.

Why not, in conjunction with his earlier claim that the Scriptures consider *God* and *the works of redemption*, simply associate *union with God* with the anagogical sense and the *works of redemption* with the moral sense? This would have run him into several difficulties. First, we learn a lot about God and Christ's work of redemption from the literal sense of the text. And second, it would not have been theologically sound to associate "redemption" solely with the results of the moral sense. We learn a great deal about what how we ought to act from a literal reading of the Ten Commandments and from the teachings of the Sermon on the Mount, as we also learn a great deal about the need for grace and repentance.

So, let me repeat my contention that, although we do not yet have a solid argument for the three figurative senses of Scripture, we must wait and see all the parts in tandem.

Appropriate to the Hearers

The "content of belief," says Bonaventure, "sheds its light in different ways according to the differing states of believers. Scripture, responding to all these circumstances, "gives us many-faceted meanings in the one text."[36] In the next paragraph, Bonaventure argues that the multiplicity of sense is appropriate to the hearer, "for no one is a suitable hearer of Scripture without being humble, pure, faithful, and attentive" (*humilis, mundus, fidelis, studiosus*). Note the fourfold *divisio*, which Bonaventure will echo shortly thereafter when he declares that the depth of meaning lying within the humble letter of the biblical text "abashes the ignorant" (thereby keeping them humble), "keeps out the unclean" (thereby ensuring those who enter are pure), "drives away the deceitful" (thereby ensuring those who remain are faithful), and "arouses the idle to an understanding of the mysteries" (by piquing their interest to become more attentive).[37] On this view, the Scriptures have multiple meanings to "win over every mind, meeting each at its own level while remaining superior to all, illuminating and setting afire with shafts of love every mind that searches it with care."[38]

The difficulty with this argument is that Bonaventure has not provided a sufficient account of the primacy of the *literal* sense. How is it important? Does speaking of the "depth of meaning lying within the humble letter of the text" mean that one should quickly get past the literal sense in order to get on to one of the "higher" senses? If Bonaventure were not a scholastic theologian of the thirteenth century, this might have been the message. But since scholastic theologians of the thirteenth century affirmed that the literal sense was primary and that all the other senses should be based on it, this hardly seems likely. So once again we need to move to the next stage of the argument.

---

[36] Ibid.
[37] Ibid., 4.3: "superbi comprimantur," "immundi repellantur," "fraudulenti declinentur," and "negligentes excitentur" (ad intelligentiam mysteriorum).
[38] *Brev. prol.* 4.3.

Appropriate to Its Source

Next Bonaventure argues that the multiplicity of senses of Scripture is appropriate to its source because its source is God, and God can communicate in both words and deeds. God alone, as Creator and Provident Caretaker of all things, can communicate in and through creation and through the events of history. And so in the Scriptures, says Bonaventure, "deeds no less than words have meaning."[39] I believe that this is the core of Bonaventure's argument: the Scriptures possess spiritual meanings because, whereas human writers can signify with words alone, God can write with words and *things* – with the very events of history.

But why force exegetes to search for deeper meanings at all? And by a reverse logic, why aren't the Scriptures *nothing but* deeper meanings? When I give my students poems to read and ask them in class what they mean, they will often say something like this: "It *says* this, but I know it doesn't *mean* that because poems never mean what they say." Some people have the same view about the Scriptures. Whatever the surface meaning of the text seems to be, the text *can't* mean *that*. We must look for a *deeper meaning*. But why, then, do Christians read some biblical texts – such as those narrating the death and resurrection of Christ – and refuse to interpret them merely "spiritually"? Why not say that he merely *spiritually* "rose" from the dead, not *physically*? Why not grant that his birth from Mary of Nazareth was merely a "spiritual" birth? Plenty of Gnostics in the early Church claimed that "ordinary" Christians did not understand the *real* story hidden behind the outward, simple meaning of the text.

Bonaventure's answer is that, by becoming incarnate, God condescended to the level of human understanding. "Christ the teacher, lowly though he was in the flesh," says Bonaventure, "remained exalted in his divinity." It was fitting, therefore, that he and his teachings should be humble in words yet profound in meaning, so that "just as Christ was wrapped in swaddling clothes, so the wisdom of God in Scriptures should be enveloped in humble images."[40] Hence, while the mystical senses are appropriate to the height of Christ's divinity, the simplicity of the literal sense is appropriate to Christ's humanity. In this way, Bonaventure accounted for both the plain understanding of the literal sense and the more complex interpretations of the mystical senses.[41]

The incarnation reveals that God wills to speak directly to men in human fashion. But it also shows that, behind the plain vision of the flesh – as important and valuable as this is for us humans who depend upon our five senses to come to know things – there are deeper meanings. Christ is fully human, but He is also fully divine. Since He is Word made flesh, it is in and through the "flesh" that we must come to know "the Word." So too in the

---

[39] Ibid., 4.4.
[40] Ibid.
[41] We find a similar approach in the Second Vatican Council's Dogmatic Constitution on Revelation, *Dei Verbum*, 13: "In Sacred Scripture, therefore, while the truth and holiness of God always remains intact, the marvelous 'condescension' of eternal wisdom is clearly shown, 'that we may learn the gentle kindness of God, which words cannot express, and how far He has gone in adapting His language with thoughtful concern for our weak human nature.' For the words of God, expressed in human language, have been made like human discourse, just as the word of the eternal Father, when He took to Himself the flesh of human weakness, was in every way made like men."

Scriptures, it is in and through the literal sense that we must come to know the deeper mysteries of Christ, and it is in relation to the clear passages of Scripture that we must interpret those that are more mysterious.

Appropriate to Its End

This brings us to the question of how the multiplicity of senses helps to realize the purpose of Scripture. One hears this question posed in various ways depending upon the audience. Simple believers ask: "Why did God put all these difficult passages in the Scriptures? Why not just speak plainly?" Others, by contrast, ask: "Why all the odd stories with these ancient Jewish people? Why not write a sophisticated spiritual treatise? Wouldn't something more spiritual leading our minds and spirits upward be more appropriate to the transcendent deity?"[42]

Bonaventure answers that the goal or purpose of the Scriptures is that we might (1) know and love Christ, (2) live as we ought, and (3) come at last into union with the Triune God. "But we will not be guided to eternal life," says Bonaventure,

> unless our intellect knows the truth we should believe, unless our will chooses the good that we should do, and unless our affections yearn to see God and to love and enjoy him. Thus Sacred Scripture, given to us by the Holy Spirit, takes up the book of creation, making it [creation] relate to its end [God] through a threefold manner of understanding. The tropological meaning lets us know what we should resolutely do; the allegorical meaning, what we should truly believe; the anagogical meaning, what we should desire for our eternal delight. In this way, cleansed by virtuous deeds, illumined by radiant faith, and made perfect by burning love, we may come at last to the prize of eternal happiness.[43]

The Four Stages of the Argument

Now, if we trace back the sections from *purpose* to *source* to *hearer* to *subject-matter*, we see that Bonaventure has laid out the stages of an argument, but he has structured it in a fourfold manner around these four terms. Moving in reverse order from *purpose* to *subject-matter*, we see that the **purpose** of the Scriptures is to help us to know and love God and to know how we ought to live and for what we ought to hope. The **source** of the Scriptures is Christ. In and through the incarnation of Christ, God reveals to us that His will is to speak to humans in human fashion and to draw all people, no matter what their level of learning, to Himself. Since the One who is the *source* of the Scripture is both Creator and Redeemer, He can speak in Scripture in both words and deeds, in and through created things and in the events of history. Yet, just as the "fleshiness" of Christ through which He revealed His divinity kept some people from recognizing his divinity – either because their pride caused them to refuse to see divinity in Christ's humility or because

---

[42] I have posed these questions in an attempt to clarify the issue for a modern audience. They are not quotations from Bonaventure's text.
[43] *Brev. prol.* 4.5.

Christ's message was not to their liking – so too with the words of Scripture: some cannot accept them because of the plainness of their language, others because the message is not to their liking or not sophisticated enough. Although they are intended to reveal God's mysteries to people of every type, their style prevents some people from appreciating their divine source. The plainness of the literal meaning of Scripture ensures humility, purity, faithfulness, and attentiveness among the **hearers** of the Word. Although there are three mystical senses of Scripture, it is essential to remember that the **subject matter** of the Scriptures is always the Triune God and the redemption won for us by the incarnate Son of God, Jesus Christ.

If we summarized this argument in its original order, we would say that, (1) because the **subject matter** of the Scriptures is God, but not just any "god," rather the God who became incarnate, fully God and fully man; (2) because its *hearers* are not all philosophers (although some are) but have manifold dispositions with which they approach the text; (3) because the *source* of the Scriptures is God the Creator of all things, who can reveal Himself in both words and deeds, in created things and the events of history; and (4) because the *purpose* of the Scriptures is to help us know and love God, live rightly, and reach our final end with him; *therefore*, the Scriptures contain, in addition to the literal sense, three mystical senses: an allegorical sense (directing us what to believe), a moral sense (directing us how we should act), and an anagogical sense (providing us a vision of what we should hope for). Bonaventure's argument is complex, but the order can be more easily recalled if one remembers these four terms: subject-matter, hearers, source, and end.

Mode of Proceeding in Sacred Scripture

Bonaventure fit quite a lot into his fourfold *divisio* of breadth, height, length, and depth. But Bonaventure (being Bonaventure) isn't quite finished. Because he wasn't able to fit absolutely everything he wanted into his fourfold schema, he simply added two disquisitions at the end to communicate the points he still wanted to make. Bonaventure's practice here is not unlike the way he appended material at the end of the prologues to his *Commentary on the Gospel of John* and his *Commentary on the* Sentences *of Peter Lombard*. Bonaventure did not hesitate to add several disputed questions when he thought he had not covered all the necessary material within the confines of his division and dilation of the opening *thema* . So too here, after he had finished dilating his fourfold *divisio* of breadth, height, length, and depth, he added two sections: one on the mode of proceeding in sacred Scripture and another on the method of expounding sacred Scripture.

In the first of these, the "mode of proceeding" (*modo procedendi*), Bonaventure claims: "Among all the many kinds of wisdom that are contained in the breadth, length, height, and depth of Sacred Scripture, there is one common way of proceeding: that of authority."[44] Although there are a number of literary forms in Sacred Scripture – narration, precept, prohibition, exhortation, instruction, threat, promise, supplication, and praise – yet all of them, he insists, operate by *authority*. But why authority, rather than reason or argumentation or example?

[44] Ibid., 5.1.

Bonaventure reminds us that the purpose of the Scriptures is to make us good and bring us to our final end. These goals cannot be achieved by speculation alone; they require an "inclination of the will." "Now the affection is moved more strongly by examples than by arguments," says Bonaventure, "more by promises than by reasoning, more by devotions than by definitions," which is why the Scripture adopts various modes to appeal to people in many ways.

> Thus if some are not moved to heed precepts and prohibitions, they may be moved by the examples narrated; if they are not moved by these, they may be moved by the benefits held out to them; and if they are not swayed by these, they may be moved by wise admonitions, trustworthy promises, or terrifying threats, and thus be stirred to devotion and the praise of God, thereby receiving grace which will guide them in virtuous deeds.[45]

Yet, as valuable and necessary as these various literary modes are, the problem with them is that they do not proceed "by way of certitude based on reasoning." Narrated examples and wise admonitions may help motivate us, but they do not bring the certitude a scientific demonstration brings. But if the Scriptures lacked certitude, says Bonaventure, they would lose their power to move us. It follows, therefore, that the Scripture must have another kind of certitude – a certitude based on an authority so great it surpasses the keenest of human minds.[46] Underlying whatever certainty or motivation we might derive from the biblical texts themselves, it is the authority of their divine author that gives them sufficient weight and us adequate motivation to pattern our lives in accord with what they command and teach.

The Mode of Expounding Sacred Scripture

Having spent a good deal of time in his section on "depth," arguing for the existence and importance of the "mystical" senses of Scripture, Bonaventure proceeds in the last section of his prologue to impart several important lessons about their application and use. So, for example, he recommends that exegetes not look for figurative senses everywhere, because not everything should be given a mystical interpretation.[47] So too, a basic principle of interpretation dictates that, when one reaches a difficult passage in Scripture, the way to clarify the meaning is by using another, more evident passage.[48] A related principle is that one must never try to clarify the meaning of a difficult passage using the figurative or mystical sense of some other passage. Bonaventure also summarizes from Book 3 of Augustine's *On Christian Doctrine* these three rules:

> 1. Where the primary signification of the words denotes created realities or individual acts of human behavior, in the first instance they refer to the facts signified by these words, but then secondly to the mysteries of our redemption. But where the primary signification of

---

[45] Ibid., 5.2.
[46] See ibid., 5.2–3.
[47] Ibid., 6.2.
[48] Ibid., 6.1.

the words expresses some aspect of faith or love, then one has no need to look for any allegorical meaning.

2. When the words of Scripture signify created realities or an aspect of the life of the people of Israel, there the interpreter must use some other part of Scripture to find what each thing signifies, and then elicit the meaning of that passage using words which plainly signify some truth of our faith or of some correct principle of morality.

3. When a certain Scriptural passage possibly has a literal *and* spiritual meaning, the interpreter ought to judge whether that passage relates better to the literal or to a spiritual meaning – if, that is, it cannot be accepted in both senses. For if it can be accepted in both senses, then it ought to be given both a literal and a spiritual interpretation. But if it is capable of only one interpretation, then it must be taken in the spiritual sense alone.[49]

Along with these rules for dealing with the figurative senses, he mentions another, even more basic, rule that goes back to the earliest Church and is a precursor to the others. It hold that, to read the Scriptures properly, one must begin with the *regula fidei* or "rule of faith," the basic teachings of the creed and the Church.[50] The notion was (and is) that an unmediated reading of the Scripture is not possible; that all readers bring certain presuppositions to their reading; and that the basic statements of the faith are the presuppositions that *Christians* should bring to their reading of the Scriptures.

Note, however, that, after this prologue, with its extended praises of sacred Scripture in terms of its "height," "length," "breadth," and "depth," and after these discussions of how Scripture proceeds and how it is to be interpreted, the *Breviloquium* itself is not a commentary on a book of the Bible, as is the case with most of Bonaventure's other prologues. What, then, is the relationship between the prologue we've been examining and the text it prefaces?

The *Breviloquium* was written to provide its readers with a "concise summary of the truth of theology" (*breve in summa dicerem de veritate theologiae*). Near the end of this amazing prologue, Bonaventure says this:

> Scripture, then, deals with the whole universe: the highest and the lowest, the first and the last, and everything that comes between. In a sense, it takes the form of an intelligible cross on which the entire world machine can be described and in some way seen in the light of the mind. To understand this cross, one must know about God, the First Principle of all things, about the creation of those things, about their fall, about their redemption through the blood of Jesus Christ, about their reformation through grace, about their healing through the sacraments, and finally about their remuneration through punishment or everlasting glory.[51]

And yet, in order to draw out of the Scriptures all the wondrous things Bonaventure promises above – "the highest and the lowest, the first and the last, and everything that

---

[49] Ibid., 6.3. I have numbered the three rules for easier reference.
[50] For an early statement of this basic principle, see Irenaeus, *Against Heresies* 1.1.1 and 3.2.2. For a modern statement of it, see *Catechism of the Catholic Church* section 1, chapter 2, art. 3 "Sacred Scripture," III, "The Holy Spirit, Interpreter of Scripture," esp. 114.3 on the "analogy of faith."
[51] *Brev. prol.* 6.2.

comes between" – one must first have acquaintance with the basic teachings of the Church handed down from the apostles and the Fathers and Doctors of the Church.

The question is how. Bonaventure laments, "This teaching has been transmitted, both in the writings of the saints and in those of the doctors, in such a diffuse manner that those who come to learn about Sacred Scripture are not able to read or hear about it for a long time." The sad result is that "beginning theologians often dread Sacred Scripture itself, feeling it to be as confusing, disordered, and uncharted as some impenetrable forest."[52]

What was to be the answer to this problem? Bonaventure's answer was this "brief discourse" (*breviloquium*) wherein he attempted to summarize the basic teachings concisely but fully enough to prepare them to begin a well-grounded study of the Scriptures. The *Breviloquium* was not a text meant to *replace* the Scriptures; it was meant, rather, to be a propaedeutic to them. It was intended as a preparation for a lifetime's worth of fruitful reading and study of the Scriptures. It is likely for this reason that Bonaventure judged that a prologue in praise of sacred Scripture, in the style of a master's *principium* address, would serve here as a suitable introduction to what is essentially a *summa* of the doctrines of the faith. It was a form he knew, one for which his training had prepared him and at which he had become marvelously adept. He employed those skills here in this early work, even though the *Breviloquium* itself differed significantly from the texts he had been assigned to produce as part of his university education.

---

[52] Ibid., 6.5.

17

The Union of Paris and Assisi
The Prologues to Bonaventure's Later Collations

IT HAS been claimed that, after his elevation to the position of Minister General of the Franciscan Order, Bonaventure developed a mode of expression "wholly alien to the language of the schools."[1] The noted Bonaventure scholar Jacques-Guy Bougerol, in his *Introduction to the Works of Bonaventure*, still a standard reference work, declares that, as Minister General, Bonaventure set himself "free from the patterns of the Schools, that is, free to develop a form for his thought more concordant with his vision."[2] There is no denying Bonaventure's creativity. And works such as the *De Reductione Artium ad Theologiam*, the *Breviloquium*, and the *Collations on the Six Days of Creation* do not resemble the standard "disputed question" format such as one finds in Thomas Aquinas's *Summa theologiae*.

Yet, the "disputed question," as important as it was to the education and work of any thirteenth-century medieval master, was not the only rhetorical form that characterized the schools. As we have seen, along with *lectio* and *disputatio*, the medieval master was trained in the arts of *praedicatio*. I have no wish to deny that Bonaventure's advanced style owed much to his training in *lectio* and *disputatio*. But our present concern is with how his early training in the arts of *sermo modernus*-style preaching continued to exhibit itself throughout his career, even in late works such as the *Collations on the Ten Commandments*, the *Collations on the Seven Gifts of the Holy Spirit*, and his last work, *The Collations on the Six Days of Creation*. As we will see, Bonaventure did not develop a mode of expression "wholly alien to the language of the schools" or "free from the patterns of the Schools"; rather he adapted that language and those patterns in creative ways.

---

[1] Kent Emery, "Reading the World Rightly and Squarely: Bonaventure's Doctrine of the Cardinal Virtues," *Traditio*, vol. 39 (1983): 183–218. I think Prof. Emery is quite right about Bonaventure's doctrine of the cardinal virtues. Where I think he is mistaken is in this off-hand comment about Bonaventure developing a mode of expression "wholly alien to the language of the schools" – a comment which I take it has little or no bearing on the substance of the rest of his article.

[2] Jacques-Guy Bougerol, *Introduction to the Works of Bonaventure*, tr. José de Vinck (Paterson, NJ: St. Anthony Guild Press, 1964), 123.

Delivering the *Collationes*

As we have seen, in October 1256, Pope Alexander IV ordered the secular masters at Paris to admit Bonaventure and Thomas into the *consortium magistrorum* at the University, but it was not until the following August, 1257, that this was done. Six months earlier, Bonaventure had been appointed Minister General of the Franciscan Order. Bonaventure had been performing all the tasks of a master of theology from 1254 to 1257. Now that his appointment was finally official, he was already being called away to deal with the many challenges facing the Franciscan Order. Although he set up his headquarters in Paris, Bonaventure had to spend much of the time between 1257 and 1266 traveling by foot across France and Italy attempting to mediate and reconcile divisions between the two factions among the Friars, the *spirituales*, who insisted upon a rigorous observance of the original rule, especially regarding poverty, and the *relaxati*, who wished to allow some innovation and adaptation of the rule to changed circumstances.

The Order's General Chapter of 1257 was held in Rome, where it was agreed that Bonaventure would undertake to write a new life of St. Francis. The Chapter of 1260 was held in Narbonne, France, where Bonaventure's new edition of the general constitutions were approved, and he reported on his progress writing a new, definitive biography of Francis. The final draft of that biography, the *Legenda maior*, was approved three years later at the General Chapter of Pisa in 1263.

The year 1266 found Bonaventure back in Paris, where for several years, the friars had been under attack both from the radicals in the arts faculty and the conservatives in the theology faculty, such as Gerard of Abbeville and William of Saint-Amour. William had been banished from Paris by Pope Alexander IV, but he returned after Alexander's death in 1266. In that same year, Siger of Brabant, the most influential of the "radical Aristotelians," was admitted to the arts faculty at Paris. Hence it is likely no coincidence that in 1267, Bonaventure began a series of public lectures – we are told that his audience consisted of "some masters and bachelors of theology, along with other friars, numbering 160"[3] – which have come down to us under the label "*collationes*" or, in English, "collations." There were the *Collations on the Ten Commandments* (*Collationes de decem praeceptis*), delivered during the weeks of Lent in 1267 and the *Collations on the Seven Gifts of the Holy Spirit* (*Collationes de septem donis Spiritus sancti*), which he delivered during the weeks of Lent the following year, 1268. The duties of his office kept him busy for the next several years,[4] so he was not

---

[3] "Legabatur et componebatur hoc opusculum Parisiis, anno Domini MCCLXXIII, a Pascha usque ad Pentecosten, praesentibus aliquibus magistris et baccalauris theologiae et aliis fratribus centum sexaginta." Quoted from Kevin L. Hughes, "St. Bonaventure's *Collationes in Hexaëmeron*: Fractured Sermons and Protreptic Discourse," *Franciscan Studies*, vol. 63 (2005): 109–110 n. 4, who is quoting the Quaracchi critical edition, 5:449–450, *additamentum*.

[4] What might have delayed the third and final installment? In 1269, Bonaventure had convened his fourth general chapter in Assisi and soon after delivered his Defense of the Mendicants (Apologia pauperum) directed against Gerard of Abbeville, who had been anonymously slandering the mendicants. The next year brought a series of condemnations in which Étienne Tempier, bishop of Paris, condemned what he took to be certain erroneous propositions in the works of Aristotle and forbade certain of his works to be taught at the University of Paris. The year 1271 found Bonaventure in Viterbo, Italy, where he was instrumental in reconciling the differences among the cardinals who had been unable to elect a new pope after the death of Clement IV who had died nearly three years

able to give the next series of collations, his monumental *Collations on the Six Days of Creation* (*Collationes in Hexaëmeron*) until 1273.[5]

These were not *collationes* of the sort that a master of theology would have delivered in the evening at vespers; those *collationes* were a continuation of a sermon the master had begun earlier in the day at mass. *Collationes* of this sort can be found in many of Thomas's and Bonaventure's sermons.[6] The Latin word "*collatio*" simply means a "gathering together," although it is sometimes translated into English as "sermon conference." This is unfortunate, because it fails to distinguish between the *collationes* that were not delivered in a liturgical setting, such as these by Bonaventure, and the *collationes* that were delivered in a liturgical setting, in which the master would preach using the *sermo modernus* style very strictly; indeed, he was required by university regulation to use the same *thema* verse in the evening *collatio* that he had used in the morning's sermon.

The nonliturgical *collatio* was more of a conference address than a sermon strictly speaking. So, for example, when Thomas Aquinas delivered his *collationes* on the Ten Commandments, on the Creed, and on the Hail Mary, he did not employ the *sermo modernus* style, even though he always used it when preaching. This is because they were not homilies; they were "talks," which is why they have been so much more accessible to modern audiences than Thomas's sermons. Bonaventure's approach in these collations was to modify the *sermo modernus* style creatively. (This is what has made them so much less accessible to modern audiences than Thomas's collations.) So the translation "sermon conference" would be appropriate for these works – not because Bonaventure was delivering a sermon, but because the rhetorical structure and many of the rhetorical devices he used were derived from the contemporary arts of preaching.[7]

Bonaventure's purposes in writing these collations were undoubtedly many, and there have been scores of proposals by scholars over the years. I will not propose anything new on that score. Even the brief biography of Bonaventure sketched out earlier shows he might have had a good many things on his mind. There were the academic debates at Paris between the conservatives in the theology faculty and the radical Aristotelians in the arts faculty, the difficulties occasioned by the condemnations of Archbishop Tempier, the continuing slew of criticisms the mendicants were suffering at the hands of theology faculty members at the University, the passionate disagreements that continued to wrack the factions in the Franciscan Order, and of course there were the divisions that beset the

---

before. Largely on Bonaventure's advice, the cardinals chose Theobald Visconti of Piacenza to become Pope Gregory X. In 1272 Bonaventure convened a general chapter again at Pisa. Hence it was not until Easter of 1273 that Bonaventure was able to deliver the *Collationes in Hexaëmeron*.

[5] In June of that year, Bonaventure was appointed Cardinal-Bishop of Albano, against his wishes but at the insistence of Pope Gregory X. Bonaventure continued to govern the Franciscans until May 20, 1274, when at the General Chapter of Lyons, Jerome of Ascoli, the later Pope Nicholas IV, was elected to succeed him. Meanwhile Bonaventure had been charged by Gregory X to prepare the questions to be discussed at the General Ecumenical Council which opened at Lyons in May of 1274. And it was there that Bonaventure died suddenly the following July, 1274. So the *Collationes in Hexaëmeron* was not only a mature work, but Bonaventure's last major work of academic theology.

[6] Cf. *The Sunday Sermons of St. Bonaventure*, trans. Timothy J. Johnson, The Works of St. Bonaventure, vol. 12 (St. Bonaventure, NY: Franciscan Institute, 2008).

[7] We don't, for example, call thirteenth-century biblical commentaries "sermon commentaries," even though many of their methods were derived from the arts of *sermo modernus*–style preaching.

entire Church which had been without a pope for nearly three full years. But whichever of these conflicts Bonaventure took himself to be addressing in the *collationes* – whether one or more or perhaps all of them – he did so in his characteristic manner: by getting right to the heart of Christian revelation and doctrine. How does one address the intellectual challenges at Paris and the religious challenges in Assisi at the same time? If you're Bonaventure, you offer a series of sophisticated lectures on the basic tenets of the faith: the Ten Commandments, the Seven Gifts of the Holy Spirit, and the six days of creation – the last of which set forth a comprehensive view of reality as a guide to the revitalization of university education for the next generation.

This is not to say that Bonaventure avoided the more pastoral, spiritual approaches to the challenges of his time. He had by this time published his "Life of St. Francis" (the *Legenda maior*) in addition to *The Tree of Life* (*Lignum vitae*), *The Triple Way* (*De triplici via*), *A Soliloquy about Four Mental Exercises* (*Soliloquium de quatuor mentalibus exercitiis*), and the *Itinerarium ad Mentis Dei*, with its profound allegory of the six-winged seraph representing the six stages of spiritual enlightenment. But in his collations, Bonaventure was addressing a university audience with intellectual pretensions and expectations. He needed to show that he had an undeniable command of the most advanced intellectual currents of the day, but also that he knew how to direct those intellectual gifts to serve the moral and spiritual goals of his Christian faith and the Franciscan Order.

Leading Bonaventure scholar Kevin Hughes has written this about the *Collationes in Hexaëmeron*:

> Taken as a whole, the *Collationes in Hexaëmeron* are an invitation to seek this union of Paris and Assisi, of intellectual rigor and holy desire, of wisdom and understanding, in the midst of almost insurmountable opposition. Bonaventure preaches these last collations in a highly contested environment about issues he believed absolutely vital to the future of the church. Above all his concern is to "distinguish in order to unite": the very goods that set brother against brother, secular against mendicant, arts faculty against theology faculty, can be held together if they are properly ordered, and he sets about in the *Collationes in Hexaëmeron* to order them rightly. It represents Bonaventure's *scholastic mystagogy*, wherein academic work is an instrumental part of a spiritual discipline. The *Collationes* are Bonaventure's offering of an exemplary occasion to practice that spiritual discipline, to follow the lines of the scholastic reasoning within each collation, all the while moving with the general movement into deeper and deeper vision, into the scriptural logic of Genesis 1 and the full flowering of human wisdom.[8]

Elsewhere, Hughes affirms that the *Collationes in Hexaëmeron* can be described as "a masterpiece of symbolic and mystical theology."[9] I suggest these are apt descriptions we can apply to all three sets of collations: each is in its own way "a masterpiece of symbolic and mystical theology" and a work of "scholastic mystagogy, wherein academic work is understood to be an instrumental part of a spiritual discipline."

---

[8] Hughes, "Fractured Sermons," 128–129.
[9] Ibid., 107, quoting Bernard McGinn, *The Flowering of Mysticism: Men and Women in the New Mysticism – 1200–1350* (New York: Crossroad, 1998), 97.

The Collations as "Fractured Sermons and Protreptic Discourse"

The article by Kevin Hughes I just quoted, "St. Bonaventure's *Collationes in Hexaëmeron*: Fractured Sermons and Protreptic Discourse," is to my mind one of the best guides to this work.[10] Hughes claims that people have not yet been able to read the *Collationes* well "because we have paid insufficient attention to its literary form."[11] What, then, is the nature and character of that literary form? Here is Professor Hughes:

> In brief, my argument is as follows: The *Collationes in Hexaëmeron* are best understood as sermons adapted to the mode of *protreptic*. Protreptic is a mode of discourse that aims to exhort readers to pursue a particular form of life and provides exemplary instances for the practice of that form, even in the exhortation. Bonaventure's protreptic exhorts his Franciscan audience to pursue a life of Franciscan holiness even as they pursue their academic study in Paris, for it is only in the integration of holiness and insight that one may find the Wisdom of God. Given room to exist as protreptic discourse, the *Collationes* emerge as a very nuanced but passionate exhortation to an integrated life of study and holiness, of scholastic discipline and Franciscan piety, of Paris and Assisi. They present what I will call Bonaventure's scholastic mystagogy.[12]

"Sermons adapted to the mode of *protreptic*": this, to my mind, has it exactly right. But let's examine this claim more fully.

One objection to the idea that the *collationes* should be thought of as sermons is simply that, in them, Bonaventure did not strictly follow the rules of the *sermo modernus* style. As Prof. Hughes rightly notes, "the *Collationes*, along with their sister series, the *Collationes on the Ten Commandments* and the *Collationes on the Gifts of the Holy Spirit*, are more like sermons than like theological treatises, *and yet they are not quite sermons either*" [emphasis mine].[13] A more precise accounting of the ways in which the *collationes* are *like* sermons, but not *quite* like them either, must await our more extended treatment below. So perhaps it will suffice for now to point out that, although the Quaracchi editors placed the *Collationes* in volume V of Bonaventure's *Opera Omnia*, with the *Opuscula varia theologica*, and not in volume VI, the works *In Sacram Scripturam* ("regrettably," comments Prof. Hughes), Jacques Guy Bougerol in the second edition of his *Introduction to the Works of Bonaventure* moved his discussion of the *collationes* into the section on Bonaventure's sermons.[14]

---

[10] *Franciscan Studies*, vol. 63 (2005): 107–129. When I was finishing the final draft of this work, the new translation of the *Collationes in Hexaemeron* by Jay Hammond had just become available. His introduction to that volume, along with Prof. Hughes' article, are the two best resources for understanding this famously difficult text. See Jay Hammond, trans., *Collations on the Hexaemeron: Conferences on the Six Days of Creation: The Illuminations of the Church*, Works of St. Bonaventure, vol. 18 (St. Bonaventure, NY: Franciscan Institute, 2018).
[11] Hughes, "Fractured Sermons," 107.
[12] Ibid., 108–109.
[13] Ibid., 110.
[14] Compare the first American edition of Jacques Guy Bougerol, *Introduction to the Works of Bonaventure* (Paterson, NJ: St. Anthony Guild Press, 1964), with the second French edition, *Introduction à Saint Bonaventure* (Paris: J. Vrin, 1988).

Professor Hughes's claim is that the *Collationes in Hexaëmeron* "integrate the structure of a sermon with arguments that are both more detailed and more comprehensive than common contemporary sermons, creating an expanded form of persuasive discourse."[15] "The *Collationes*, when taken as a whole," says Hughes, "bear all the elements of the sermon structure, but it is difficult to find them all in one particular conference. Rather, Bonaventure stretches the sermonic structure across several individual collations..."[16] – hence the first part of the title of Hughes's article is "*Fractured* Sermons." What this "fracturing" looks like awaits our more detailed analysis in the text that follows, but as we will see, the description is apt.

I will argue, moreover, that even when the collations depart from the strict *structural* rules of the *sermo modernus* style – that is to say, even when Bonaventure does not strictly apply the rules of *divisio* – he continues to make use of the *sermo modernus*-style methods of *dilatatio*. A useful comparison here would be with Bonaventure's adaptation and use of the methods of *sermo modernus*–style *dilatatio* in his biblical commentaries.[17]

So, my claim is that the collations should be seen as an adaptation of the *sermo modernus* style. What about Prof. Hughes' claim that they should be seen as a "protreptic discourse"? Although I am sympathetic to the claim, I am not sure how far to extend it.

I have argued repeatedly in this volume that prologues written in the *sermo modernus* style commonly served a protreptic purpose.[18] As we have seen, a "protreptic" was an exhortation to a particular kind of study and a specific way of life. The presupposition was that one had to strive to become a certain kind of person with a specific character to be capable of undertaking the proposed course of study. And all this was proposed as the necessary path to true wisdom and human flourishing. I argued earlier, for example, that the master's inception addresses in praise of sacred Scripture were meant to serve the purposes of a classical protreptic. These "first lectures" of the master were, however, merely a "first installment" of what was to come: a career of delivering *principia* sermons of this sort (printed as a "prologue") for each biblical text on which he would lecture each term. It should not be surprising, therefore, to find that Bonaventure had something similar in mind when he was composing his *Collationes*.[19]

Yet, should the entire series of collations be considered "protreptic"? Perhaps. But in my view, it would be helpful to distinguish the "protreptic" character of the early, "introductory" collations in each of the three works and the subsequent collations making up the "body" of the text. In the *Collations on the Ten Commandments* and the *Collations on the Seven Gifts of the Holy Spirit*, the first collation serves as a "prologue" to the rest. In the *Collations on the Six Days of Creation*, the first *three* collations serve that purpose.

As Professor Hughes notes, Professors Mark Jordan and Kent Emery have both argued that we should see the first three collations of the *Collations on the Six Days of Creation* as an *accessus* (Jordan) or *principium* (Emery), that is to say, as a version of the standard medieval

---

[15] Hughes, "Fractured Sermons," 110.
[16] Ibid., 111.
[17] See my discussion in Chapter 15.
[18] See in particular, my discussion of the purposes of classical protreptics in the Introduction to the book and in Chapter 8.
[19] For an excellent discussion of the "protreptic" character of the *Collationes in Hexaëmeron*, see Hughes, "Fractured Sermons," 113–117.

form used to introduce a commentary on an important text, usually biblical.[20] My practice has been to call this medieval form a *principium* (as does Emery) or a "prologue." Unless I am mistaken, I believe we are all three describing the same thing. As the reader will see, I am in essential agreement with the view that the first three collations of the *Collations on the Six Days of Creation* should be viewed together as an *accessus* or "prologue" to the whole work.[21] So too, it is fairly clear that the first collation of the *Collations on the Ten Commandments* as with the first collation of the *Collations on the Seven Gifts of the Holy Spirit* are similarly to be understood as an *accessus* or "prologue," serving a "protreptic" purpose. Whether we should describe the remaining collations as also having a "protreptic" purpose is not entirely clear. There is likely a sense in which it can be considered true, but we would want to distinguish the "protreptic" character of these later chapters from the protreptic purpose more commonly associated with the prologue.

The *Collations* are notoriously complex works – several volumes could be written on each – so we don't have the space for a serious analysis of even one of them. In what follows, therefore, we will focus our analysis on the prologue of each work and then examine several exemplary sections. The goal of this analysis is to show how the *Collations* are similar to *sermo modernus*–style sermons or can be seen as a creative adaption of them. I will argue that the categories of the "protreptic" prologue apply to the first collation in each work, or in the case of the *Collations on the Six Days*, the first three collations, which together serve as the prologue.

We will take up the three *Collations* in chronological order, starting with the *Collations on the Ten Commandments* (1267), moving to the *Collations on the Seven Gifts of the Holy Spirit* (1268), and finishing with the *Collations on the Six Days* (1273). Since Bonaventure mentions the earlier works at the beginning of the later works, it is clear that in his mind, they were meant to express a certain topical order. There was also, as we will see, a certain development of style. The shortest and least complicated with the clearest structure is the first, the *Collations on the Ten Commandments*. The next, the *Collations on the Seven Gifts of the Holy Spirit*, is somewhat longer and more complex. And the *Collations on the Six Days of Creation* is by far the longest and most complicated of the three – so complicated and developed, in fact, that Bonaventure was not able to finish it. His original plan was to write several collations on each of the six days and then something on the seventh day. As it turned out, he got through only the fourth day before he was called away. This does not concern us here because our goal is not to give an interpretation of the whole. We are merely sampling sections to get a sense of their style and to see how that style resembles and/or differs from that of his prologues, sermons, and biblical commentaries.

---

[20] Cf. Mark D. Jordan, *The Care of Souls and the Rhetoric of Moral Teaching in Bonaventure and Thomas*, in *Spirit and Life: A Journal of Contemporary Franciscanism* 4 (St. Bonaventure, NY: The Franciscan Institute, 1993); Kent Emery, Jr, "Reading the World Rightly," 183–218. I had the honor of studying with both men and owe much to both.

[21] Prof. Hughes similarly announces himself to be "in substantial agreement" with Emery and Jordan, but differs from them somewhat. In his opinion, their views tend to focus on the "textuality" of the *Collations*, whereas he sees their "orality as performed discourse" as essential to understanding "their method and effect." See Hughes, "Fractured Sermons," 112, n. 8.

Prologue to the *Collations on the Ten Commandments*: Why Should I Obey?

We turn first to the earliest of the three *Collations*, the *Collations on the Ten Commandments*, delivered during the weeks of Lent in 1267, and to the first collation, the prologue (or *principium* or *accessus*) to the rest, which begins with a *thema* verse from Matthew 19:17: "If you wish to enter into life, keep the commandments."[22] It made sense for Bonaventure to begin his *Collations on the Ten Commandments* with this verse from the Gospel of Matthew because it was in these words that Jesus replied to the "rich young man" who asked him, "Master, what should I do to have eternal life?" Answer: "If you wish to enter into life, keep the commandments." Hence we have it from the mouth of the Lord Jesus Himself that the commandments are crucial.

But note, this verse does not operate here the way a '*sed contra*" would in a medieval *Summa*. It is not merely a stand-alone authority. It *is* an authority, but it serves another purpose as well. Bonaventure divides the verse and dilates it to help fill out the content in the collation. "In these words," he says, "the entire substance of our salvation is explained as it relates to two things: our eternal salvation and the merit of human actions. The goal of achieving our salvation is communicated by the words, "If you wish to enter into life," says Bonaventure; the merit of human action is communicated by the words, "keep the commandments."[23]

Hence there will be two main parts of the collation. In the first, Bonaventure describes the motives that lead us to observe God's commandments, and in the second, he discusses the commandments themselves. Recall that in the master's *resumptio* address, the master would begin with a sermon in praise of sacred Scripture, which was followed by a *divisio textus* of all the books of the Bible.[24] In a similar way here, Bonaventure begins with a list of positive characteristics of the commandments that motivate us to pattern our lives on them and follows with a *divisio* of the commandments. By "*divisio*" here, I mean he organizes them into their proper categories so we can more easily see the relationships between the parts and the whole. We will see the similarity between what Bonaventure does here and a standard *divisio textus* shortly.

We begin, however, with the four reasons that the commandments motivate us to pattern our lives on them. First, says Bonaventure, because of the authority or dignity of the one commanding (*auctoritas sive dignitas mandantis*), who is God. Second, because of the benefits of observing them (*utilitas observationis*). Third, because of the perils of transgressing them (*pericula transgressionis*). And fourth, because of the faultless character

---

[22] *Collations on the Ten Commandments* 1.1. English translation: *St. Bonaventure's Collations on the Ten Commandments*, trans. Paul J. Spaeth, Works of Saint Bonaventure, 6 (St. Bonaventure, NY: The Franciscan Institute, 1995). Latin from the standard Quaracchi edition, vol. 5, 507–532. Hereafter "*Coll. de decem.*" NB: When I use the singular "collation," I am referring to one of the collations – what in English we might call one of the "chapters" of the work. It is only when I use the plural, "collations" or "*Collations*" that I am referring to the whole work, e.g., the *Collations on the Seven Gifts of the Holy Spirit*.

[23] *Coll. de decem.* 1.1.

[24] Bonaventure did not deliver the customary *divisio textus*, preferring to deliver an early version of the *De reductione artium ad theologiam*. See my comments on this in Chapter 11. For a general discussion of the master's *divisio textus*, see my discussion in Chapter 5.

of the commandments (*irreprehensibilitas mandatorum*).[25] Note the parallel phrases. This is a dilation based on causes and effects.

Bonaventure makes a further threefold subdivision of each of these four. Why does the one commanding (namely, God) have great authority? First, because He creates us with great power (*quia ipse sua magna potentia nos creat*). Second, because He rules and governs us with marvelous wisdom (*quia sua mira sapientia nos regit et gubernat*). Third, because He saves us with generous kindness (*quia sua munifica benevolentia nos salvat*).[26]

What benefits are derived from observing the commandments? The first is reception of the divine gifts (*impetratio divinorum charismatum*). The second is the revelation of the sacred Scriptures (*revelatio sacrarum Scripturarum*). And the third is the gaining of the heavenly reward (*assecutio caelestium praemiorum*).[27]

What are the perils of a person transgressing the commandments? The first is he loses many good things (*multa bona perdit*). The second is he plunges into unspeakable evils (*nefanda flagitia ruit*). And the third is he merits eternal punishment (*aeterna supplicia meretur*).[28]

Why are the commandments "faultless"? First, because they contain nothing impossible (*impossibile*). Second, because they contain nothing burdensome (*onerosum*). And third, because they contain nothing unjust (*iniquum*).[29]

Note in these examples the parallel Latin clauses and the complex descriptions. Bonaventure does not simply say that God's authority comes from His (1) power, (2) wisdom, and (3) kindness; single-word descriptions of this sort were frowned upon in the *sermo modernus* style. When making such a list, a preacher would always write "with great power," or better yet, "with great, creative power." Longer constructions of this sort were a hallmark of the *sermo modernus* style.

Another hallmark of the *sermo modernus* style was the "chaining" of biblical authorities. Topical outlines such as the one I have provided earlier fail to give the reader a sense of the actual oral delivery. Allow me to quote a section of the collation to give the reader a sense of how "chaining" biblical authorities into the text alters its character. As we saw earlier, the first benefit to be derived from keeping the commandments is the reception of the divine gifts; the second is the revelation of the sacred Scriptures. Here is how those two points were actually delivered orally.

> The first benefit to be derived from keeping the commandments of God is the reception of the divine gifts. So, in *John* it says: "If you love me keep my commandments, and I will ask the Father and he will give you another paraclete." (Jn 14:15–16)
>
> The second benefit is the understanding (*intelligentia*) of Sacred Scripture. The *Psalms* say: "I have sought your commandments" (Ps 118:100). Gregory shows how we come to an understanding of the Sacred Scriptures. He does this by citing the incident when the disciples saw Jesus and did not know him. But when they heard him speaking, then they

---

[25] *Coll. de decem.* 1.2.
[26] Ibid., 1.3.
[27] Ibid., 1.6.
[28] Ibid., 1.10.
[29] Ibid., 1.14.

knew him. And so Gregory says the following: "The disciples were not enlightened by hearing the commandments of God, but were enlightened by doing them" (Pope Gregory, *Hom. in Ev.* II.23.n.2). Because: "It is not those who merely hear the Law but those who carry out the Law who are justified" (Rom 2:13). And James says in his epistle: "Be doers of the Word of God and not hearers only, deceiving yourselves; because if anyone is a hearer of the Word of God only and not a doer, he will be like a man looking at his own face in a mirror" (James 1:22–23). If a person sees his own face in a mirror ten times, he still will not know his face well. But if sees the face of another person apart from the mirror, he will know the other well. This is because of the strong and direct impression of the image on the eye, while in the mirror the perception is not true. Similarly, when a person hears the Word of God, it seems to him that he understands it well. But immediately that understanding leaves. However, when he puts it into practice by acting correctly, then he comes to understand it.[30]

"Chaining" not only lengthens the text; it also makes the collation profoundly biblical in character. Indeed, these are not merely "proof texts" of the sort we sometimes associate with disputed questions. Rather these biblical verses have been woven into the very verbal fabric of the collation.

Divisio of the Commandments

Recall that when masters crafted their *divisio textus* of all the books of the Scriptures, the most basic was the twofold division between the Old Testament and the New.[31] Similarly, the most common division among the Ten Commandments was a twofold division based on Jesus's comment that the "first and greatest" commandments which "sum up the Law and the prophets" are the two commandments to "Love the Lord your God with all your heart and with all your soul and with all your mind" and to "Love your neighbor as yourself."[32] And so the Ten Commandments have classically been divided into two groups associated with the "two tablets" Moses brought down from the top of Mt. Sinai.[33] The "first tablet" commandments include the first three: you shall not have strange gods; you shall not take the name of the Lord in vain; remember to keep holy the Sabbath. These commandments direct us in our relationship with God. The "second tablet" commandments include the next seven: honor your father and mother; you shall not kill; you shall not commit adultery; you shall not steal; you shall not bear false witness; you shall not desire your neighbor's wife; and you shall not covet your neighbor's goods. These commandments direct us in our relationship with our neighbor.[34] This twofold division

---

[30] Ibid., 1.7–8.
[31] See my discussion in Chapter 5.
[32] See Matthew 22:36–40.
[33] See Exodus 19–20.
[34] There are two ways of numbering the commandments. Aquinas mentions both in the *Summa* (cf. ST I-II, q. 100, a. 4). The first he associates with Origen; the second with Augustine. The first way of numbering them divides the first commandment into two, "have no other gods before me" and "make no graven images." Numbered this way, the final commandment, then, is a combination of "you shall not desire your neighbor's wife" *and* "you shall not desire your neighbor's possessions."

between "the two tablets" was basic, everyone at the time made it, so Bonaventure would not have been saying anything new or unusual when he used it here.

What is unique is how each master characterizes and subdivides the commandments *after* having made the first, basic twofold division. Bonaventure argues that the first tablet commandments order us to God, but God is Triune: Father, Son, and Holy Spirit. To the Father, we attribute "the highest majesty"; to the Son, truth; and to the Holy Spirit, goodness. In the Father, the highest majesty is to be humbly adored; in the Son, the highest truth is to be faithfully confessed; in the Holy Spirit, the highest goodness is to be sincerely loved. Hence the first, humble adoration of God's "highest majesty" (*humilis adoratio divinae maiestatis*) is commanded by the first commandment, "You shall not have strange gods." The second, faithful confession of the highest truth (*fidelis assertio divinae veritatis*), is commanded by the second commandment, "You shall not take the name of the Lord in vain." And the third, sincere love of the highest goodness (*sincera dilectio divinae bonitatis*), is commanded by the third commandment, "Remember to keep holy the Sabbath."[35]

How else might this *divisio* been done? For the sake of comparison, allow me to quote three passages from an article in Aquinas's *Summa* in which he proposes three other ways of distinguishing the first three commandments.[36] I will quote them in full because they are already so compact, any attempt to paraphrase them would only lengthen them. Here is his first *divisio*.

> Now man owes three things to the head of the community: first, fidelity; secondly, reverence; thirdly, service. Fidelity to his master consists in his not giving sovereign honor to another: and this is the sense of the first commandment, in the words "Thou shalt not have strange gods." Reverence to his master requires that he should do nothing injurious to him: and this is conveyed by the second commandment, "Thou shalt not take the name of the Lord thy God in vain." Service is due to the master in return for the benefits which his subjects receive from him: and to this belongs the third commandment of the sanctification of the Sabbath in memory of the creation of all things.

After setting forth his division of the commandments of the second tablet according to whether the harm done to another is by deed, word, or thought, he returns to the commandments of the first tablet and divides them according to deed, word, and thought. He says:

> The three precepts that direct man in his behavior towards God may also be differentiated in this same way. For the first refers to deeds; wherefore it is said, "Thou shalt not make ... a graven thing": the second, to words; wherefore it is said, "Thou shalt not take the name of the Lord thy God in vain": the third, to thoughts; because the sanctification of the Sabbath, as the subject of a moral precept, requires repose of the heart in God.

According to this way of numbering the commandments, there would be four commandments on the first tablet and six on the second. In the modern world, Origen's system is often thought of as the "Protestant" numbering system and Augustine's as the "Catholic" system. The truth is, both go back to the early Church. Aquinas mentions both, but in the thirteenth century, it was more common to follow the numbering system associated with Augustine.

[35] *Coll. de decem.* 1.22.
[36] All three can found in ST I–II, q. 100, a. 5.

This desire to find a symmetry between both tablets is not unrelated to the desire we saw in Chapter 5 whereby thirteenth-century masters sought to find a symmetry between the categories they applied to the Old Testament and the New Testament: e.g., law, history, and prophecy.

Yet there is still another way of dividing the first tablet commandments, says Aquinas, which was proposed by St. Augustine, who claimed that "by the first commandment we reverence the unity of the First Principle; by the second, the Divine truth; and by the third, His goodness whereby we are sanctified, and wherein we rest as in our last end." This threefold distinction, which he traces back to St. Augustine, was clearly the source for the same threefold distinction in Bonaventure's *Collations on the Ten Commandments*.

Let's examine now how Bonaventure divides the seven commandments on the second tablet that order us to our neighbor. These seven can be understood as expressions of the two precepts of the natural law: do to others what you would wish done to you (the principle of beneficence) and do not do to others what you do not wish done to you (the principle of innocence).³⁷

According to Bonaventure, among the Ten Commandments, the sole commandment commanding that we do to others what we would wish done to us is "honor your father and mother," not only by acts of reverence, but also by acts of kindness and obedience. And this commandment applies, adds Bonaventure, not only to our parents, but to all those with a similar authority over us.³⁸

The commandments bidding us *not* to do to others what we would *not* wish done to us include the remaining six. But they can be distinguished according to the three ways we can offend our neighbor: in thought, word, or deed.

Offenses in deed can be of three kinds, says Bonaventure, because a person can offend his neighbor in any of three ways: by violating the person himself (hence the commandment "You shall not kill"), by violating a person related to that person (hence the commandment "You shall not commit adultery"), or by violating the person's possessions (hence the commandment "You shall not steal).

We are forbidden to offend our neighbor *in word* by the commandment "You shall not bear false witness." And offenses against one's neighbor *in thought* can have two sources: it can originate in the flesh or in the eyes. To guard against the concupiscence of the flesh, we have the commandment "You shall not desire your neighbor's wife." And to guard against the concupiscence of the eyes, there is "You shall not desire your neighbor's possessions."³⁹

Second Tablet: Ordering us to our neighbor

A. Do unto others as you would wish done to you (benevolence): "Honor your father and mother."
B. Don't do to others what you would not wish done to you (innocence):
   1. Offenses in deed:
      a. Against the person himself: "You shall not kill."
      b. Against someone related to the person: "You shall not commit adultery."
      c. Against the person's possessions: "You shall not steal."
   2. Offenses in word: "You shall not bear false witness."

---

³⁷ *Coll. de decem.* 1.23. Cf. Mt 7:12, Luke 6:31, Tobias 4:16.
³⁸ *Coll. de decem.* 1.23.
³⁹ Ibid., 1.24.

3. Offenses in thought:
   a. Related to the flesh: "You shall not desire your neighbor's wife."
   b. Related to the eyes: "You shall not desire your neighbor's possessions."

In his division of the commandments of the second tablet, Thomas also distinguishes the commandments according to deed, word, and thought. But the division is stated rather differently. Here is Thomas:

> To his neighbors a man behaves himself well both in particular and in general. In particular, as to those to whom he is indebted, by paying his debts: and in this sense is to be taken the commandment about honoring one's parents. In general, as to all men, by doing harm to none, either by deed, or by word, or by thought. By deed, harm is done to one's neighbor – sometimes in his person, i.e. as to his personal existence; and this is forbidden by the words, "Thou shalt not kill": sometimes in a person united to him, as to the propagation of offspring; and this is prohibited by the words, "Thou shalt not commit adultery": sometimes in his possessions, which are directed to both the aforesaid; and with this regard to this it is said, "Thou shalt not steal." Harm done by word is forbidden when it is said, "Thou shalt not bear false witness against thy neighbor": harm done by thought is forbidden in the words, "Thou shalt not covet."[40]

After this introductory collation, Bonaventure begins his comments on the first commandment in the next collation. We will not examine the subsequent collations in this work in any detail. Our goal has been merely to show how this first collation bears undeniable marks of the *sermo modernus* style and the master's *principia*. But it is worth noting before we move on that the remaining collations also retain some of these characteristics. For our purposes, I will focus on just one.

Each collation states as its opening *thema* the commandment on which Bonaventure will be commenting. But in each collation, Bonaventure also adds something characteristic of many sermons: a *prothema*. Not every sermon had a *prothema*, but when they did, it came right after the *thema* and served as the structuring device for its own introductory section to the sermon. Some historians have theorized that this "introductory" *prothema* section of a sermon was intended to give the congregation time to settle down before getting into the body of the sermon, especially since these introductory *prothema* sections were often finished with a prayer. This theory is not entirely convincing since some of these introductory *prothema* sections went on for pages. But whatever their purpose, they were a common introductory feature of *sermo modernus*–style sermons, and we find them here at the beginning of each collation.

Bonaventure does not always develop his *prothemata* in much detail, but he still proceeds by way of the customary *divisio* and *dilatatio*. Consider, for example, his *prothema* at the beginning of Collation 3 (on the second commandment): "I am your servant; give me understanding that I may know your decrees" (*Servus tuus sum ego: da mihi intellectum, ut sciam testimonia tua*). "Therefore I have loved your commandments above gold and topaz. Therefore I was directed to all your commandments, I have hated every sinful path" (*Ideo dilexi mandata tua super aurum et topazion. Propterea ad omnia mandata tua dirigebar;*

---

[40] ST I–II, q. 100, a. 5.

omnem viam iniquam odio habui).[41] In these three verses, says Bonaventure, David shows three reasons we should speak about God's commandments: first, "that we may be inflamed with love for the divine commandments," which he associates with the words "Therefore I have loved your commandments of gold and topaz." Second, "so that we may know the commandments better," which he associates with the words "Give me understanding that I may know your decrees." And third, so that we will gain a "hatred of sin," which he associates with the words "Therefore I was directed to all your commandments, I have hated every sinful path."[42] "Therefore we should speak of the commandments," concludes Bonaventure, "so that we might love and understand them, and so that we might move on the way to heaven and have a hatred for sin. And so, in order that we might be able to accomplish these three things let us pray to the Lord at the start. . ." And here he would have inserted his own prayer or led the group in some commonly known prayer, such as the Hail Mary or Our Father. This was standard *sermo modernus* style. And yet these collations were not sermons. They were a hybrid of various styles and a product of Bonaventure's own genius.

Prologue to the *Collations on the Seven Gifts of the Holy Spirit*: Grace and the Moral Life

Bonaventure delivered his *Collations on the Seven Gifts of the Holy Spirit* during Lent in 1268, the year after he delivered his *Collations on the Ten Commandments*. The topical progression is apparent. In the *Collations on the Ten Commandments*, the topic was the Law. In the *Collations on the Seven Gifts of the Holy Spirit*, the topic is the grace that perfects the Law. The *thema* verse of the first collation is taken from 2 Corinthians 6:1: "We exhort you not to receive the grace of God in vain (*exhortamur ne in vacuum gratiam Dei recipiatis*).

The First Collation: A Protreptic Prologue with a Prothema

As with the first collation of the *Collations on the Ten Commandments*, the first collation of the *Collations on the Seven Gifts* serves as a protreptic prologue to the entire work.[43] After stating his *thema*, "We exhort you not to receive the grace of God in vain," Bonaventure immediately introduces another verse from Psalm 44:3 which serves as a *prothema*: "Grace has poured out upon your lips. Therefore, God has blessed you forever."[44] This second text, the *prothema*, refers to Christ, says Bonaventure, "who is the blessed one in whom all the peoples of the earth are blessed." Note the interesting and important shift:

---

[41] Bonaventure is quoting here from Psalm 118:125 and 127–128. It is not clear why he skipped verse 126. It could be because he was quoting from memory, because the scribe who copied his version of the Psalms missed it, or because it just did not fit the three points he intended to make.

[42] *Coll. de decem.* 3.1.

[43] I have quoted throughout this section from the English translation by Zachary Hayes in *Collations on the Seven Gifts of the Holy Spirit*, The Works of St. Bonaventure, 14 (St. Bonaventure, NY: The Franciscan Institute, 2010). References will be given to "conference" and section; e.g., *Coll. de sept.* 1.3 refers to *Collations on the Seven Gifts of the Holy Spirit*, "conference" 1, section 3. The Latin text has been quoted from the version of the *Collationes de septem donis Spiritus Sancit* in the Quarrachi edition of Bonaventure's *opera omnia*, vol. 5.

[44] *Coll. de sept.* 1.1.

in a treatise on the seven Gifts of the Holy Spirit, he begins, properly enough, with *grace*. But immediately he makes a biblical reference that causes us to trace this grace back to its ultimate source: not the Holy Spirit per se, but Christ. It is the grace of Christ that is imparted with the Gifts "of the Holy Spirit." We move from an abstract consideration of *grace* right back to the person of Jesus Christ: to receive the Gifts is to receive Christ.

In section 2, Bonaventure explicitly relates this series of collations on the seven Gifts of the Holy Spirit to the series of collations he had delivered the year before on the Ten Commandments as though they were two parts of a single pedagogical project. "Two things are necessary for salvation," he tells his audience, "namely knowledge of truth and practice of virtue."[45] Knowledge of truth comes through "the Law" – that is, the Mosaic or "Old Law" – but the practice of virtue comes about through grace.[46]

Bonaventure describes the relationship between "law" and "grace" using the image of a bird with the power to see the heavens but without the power in its wings to fly.

> The Law is related to grace as the power to know is related to the ability to do, and as a tool is related to the power of the one who uses it. It as though a bird had the power to see the heavens, but did not have strength in its wings. It would not be able to fly and hence could not reach the heights... So it is clear that the grace of God is far more excellent than the Law itself. I have spoken to you at another time about the Law of the Decalogue, and now I will speak to you about grace. Grace is more necessary for us than the Law.[47]

As a feature of the "protreptic" dimension of this early collation, Bonaventure is telling his audience, in effect: "If you thought my *Collations on the Ten Commandments* last year were worthwhile, these collations on the Gifts of the Spirit are even more important, because grace is what makes adherence to the commandments possible."

Both Thomas and Bonaventure share the notion that the Law instructs us in the truth we could and should know by reason alone; often, though, we do not, because our reason and will have been damaged by sin. Even once we are taught by the Law, the full realization of the moral life and the perfection of the virtues depend upon the gift of God's grace. Although they share the notion, each man expresses this view in his own characteristic fashion.

At the conclusion of this brief introductory section, Bonaventure finishes with a feature characteristic of sermons that had a *prothema*: he ends with a prayer that God may give him the grace to speak well on the topic he has proposed. In his sermons, these prayers concluding the *prothema* section can sometimes be long. So, for example, in Sermon 5 of *The Sunday Sermons of Bonaventure*, Bonaventure concludes his *prothema* this way:

> Before all else it is necessary to ask God with a prayer, so that with his word of grace and piety, he wash the net, that is, our sermon, and ennoble it with the clarity of truth by

---

[45] Ibid., 1.2.
[46] Similarly, Thomas Aquinas's prologue to *Summa Theologiae* I–II, q. 90 reads, in part, that God "both instructs us by means of His Law, and assists us by His grace." Thomas's discussion of the "Old Law" includes several questions (qq. 98–105) and some of the longest articles in the *Summa*. It is followed by questions on the New Law, which is the law of grace, the law by which "charity is spread abroad in our hearts." It is this charity that informs the other virtues which Thomas discusses in more detail in the *secunda secundae*.
[47] *Coll. de sept.* 1.2. Compare Bonaventure's use of the image of the bird flying up to heaven with Peter Cantor's list of *distinctiones* related to the word "*avis*" or "bird" in Chapter 1.

removing the obscurity of error, with the delight of rest by removing the gravity of labor, and with the usefulness of charity by removing the unfruitfulness of the works, so that with clear understanding, delighted affections, and beneficial works, we might be able to say some things to the praise and glory, etc.[48]

So too, early in the first collation of his *Collations on the Seven Gifts of the Holy Spirit*, Bonaventure asks the Lord's blessing in these words:

So to begin, we shall ask the Lord that our words may serve the cause of grace and that the intention of our mind, if it finds favor with the Lord, may find powerful expression in words so that we might be able to say something that will be for the glory of God and the salvation of souls.[49]

Prayers of this sort, imploring God's help to speak worthily, were an essential part of academic sermons of the day. Its presence here suggests strongly that the genre in which Bonaventure sees himself writing is that of the sermon.

Origin, Use, and Fruit: From a General Description of Grace to the Seven Gifts

In a sermon, after the *prothema*, we would expect a restatement of the *thema* verse. And sure enough, at the beginning of the third section of Collation 1, after the prayer, we find a restatement of his opening biblical verse from 2 Corinthians 6:1: "We exhort you not to receive the grace of God in vain." Bonaventure comments: "In this brief text, the apostle Paul encourages us to be receptive to divine grace, and once we have received that grace, that we preserve it, and as we preserve it, that we seek to guard it and let it increase."[50] Had Bonaventure been following the *sermo modernus* style strictly, he would have divided up his *thema* verse in such a way as to associate each of its parts with the three topics he intended to discuss. He might, for example, have associated "receiving" with the word "receive," "preserving" with the words "not in vain," and "increasing" with the words "we exhort you."

Instead, Bonaventure quickly transitions from receiving (*suscipiendam*), preserving (*custodiendam*), and increasing (*multiplicandam*) grace to a consideration of its origin (*ortus*), use (*usus*), and fruit (*fructus*). This threefold distinction between origin, use, and fruit will govern his analysis in each of the remaining collations on the seven gifts.[51]

---

[48] *The Sunday Sermons of St. Bonaventure*, trans. Timothy J. Johnson, The Works of St. Bonaventure, vol. 12 (St. Bonaventure, NY: The Franciscan Institute, 2008), 100.
[49] *Coll. de sept.* 1.2.
[50] Ibid., 1.3.
[51] For a nice guide to the basic threefold divisions in each of the collations, see the fine introduction by Robert Karris to his English translation of the *Collations on the Seven Gifts of the Holy Spirit*, especially the diagram on p. 17, where he outlines the basic threefold structure of "origin, "use," and "fruit" Bonaventure employs with each of the seven gifts.

How does Bonaventure verbally transition from the first three categories to the next three? He provides no overt justification, but merely adds this:

> Therefore, he [St. Paul] urges us to be prompt in receiving, in preserving, and in increasing the grace of God. Three points come to mind that we must consider if this exhortation is to be realized in us. First, what is the origin of this grace; second, what is its use; and third, what is its fruit."[52]

Bonaventure simply assumes his audience will see the connection between receiving, preserving, and increasing grace and the origin, use, and fruit of grace. To make the connection more explicit, we might say that we *receive* grace from its origin, we *preserve* it when we use it properly, and we *increase* it (that is to say, it *increases* us) when we bear the fruit it is supposed to bring us. We do not *receive* it if we mistake its *origin*; we do not *preserve* it if we squander it and do not use it properly; and we do not increase it if we bear the wrong fruit: if we assume, for example, that grace is supposed to "bear fruit" in greater power, pleasure, status, or wealth.

Here again, had this been a sermon of the strict *sermo modernus* style, Bonaventure would have associated each of his three categories with words in his opening *thema* verse: "We exhort you not to receive the grace of God in vain." He might, for example, have associated the *origin* of grace with the words "grace of God"; its *use* with the word "receive"; and its *fruit* either with "exhort" or "not in vain" or both. Although Bonaventure does not make the standard divisions and associations here characteristic of the *sermo modernus* style, the methods he employs in the collation are clearly drawn from preaching. He is especially fond of making threefold lists of divisions and subdivisions into which he inserts or "chains" biblical authorities.

We have already seen him create the first threefold *divisio* by distinguishing the origin, use, and fruit of grace (Box 17.1). In what follows, he will take each of these and dilate it by

---

Box 17.1 Bonaventure's Origin, Use, and Fruits of Grace

Origin of Grace: Christ
a. Incarnate Word
b. Crucified Word
c. Inspired Word

Use of Grace – becoming:
a. Faithful regarding God
b. Strong in relation to oneself
c. Generous in relation to one's neighbors

Fruits of Grace:
a. The remission of guilt ⟶ healing grace (7 sacraments)
b. The fullness of justice ⟶ strengthening grace (7 virtues and 7 gifts of the Holy Spirit)
c. The endurance of a happy life ⟶ perfecting grace (7 beatitudes and 7 endowments)

---

[52] *Coll. de sept.* 1.3.

first making a further threefold subdivision. So, for example, the *origin* of grace he traces back, unsurprisingly, to Christ, the Word of God, but then makes a threefold subdivision, distinguishing (1) the incarnate Word (*Verbum incarnatum*); (2) the crucified Word (*Verbum crucifixum*); and (3) the inspired Word (*Verbum inspiratum*).[53]

Under the heading the *use* of grace, he distinguishes three components, becoming (1) faithful with respect to God (*fidelis respectu Dei*); (2) strong in relation to oneself (*virilis in se*); and (3) generous in relation to one's neighbor (*liberalis in proximum*).[54]

Under the "fruits" of grace, he lists (1) the remission of guilt (*remissio culpae*), (2) the fullness of justice (*plenitudo iustitiae*), and (3) the endurance of the happy life (*perpetuatio vitae beatae*).[55] Note in each list the *sermo modernus* style subdivisions and parallelism. It may be eleven years since Bonaventure's inception, but he hasn't lost his touch. This is precisely how he created content in his sermons, prologues, and early writings: by *divisio* and *dilatatio*. He begins with a threefold division, which becomes, with a threefold subdivision of each, nine headings in which to develop content with comments and "chained" biblical texts. By devoting one or two sections to each subdivision, he fills sections 5 through 16 with his discussion of these nine categories.

In section 17, he formulates another *divisio* to help him transition from his discussion of the origin, use, and fruit of grace (with its series of "threes") to the sevenfold division he needs to discuss the seven gifts of the Holy Spirit. Corresponding to the three "fruits" of grace – the remission of guilt, the fullness of justice, and the endurance of a happy life – Bonaventure identifies three types of grace: "healing grace" (*gratia curans*), "strengthening grace" (*gratia corroborans*), and "perfecting grace," the "grace that brings one to completion" (*gratia consummans*).[56] The "remission of guilt" results from God's "healing grace"; the "fullness of justice" results from God's "strengthening grace"; and "the endurance of the happy life" results from "a grace that brings one to completion" (*gratia consummans*).[57]

"Healing grace" (*gratia currans*) is given in the seven sacraments. "Strengthening grace" (*gratia corroborans*) is associated with the seven virtues (the four cardinal and three theological virtues) and the seven gifts of the Holy Spirit. And "perfecting grace" (*gratia consummans*), the grace that brings to completion, is associated in this life with the seven beatitudes mentioned in Matthew 5:3–11 and in the next life with seven endowments – three that relate to the soul: vision (the fulfillment of faith), enjoyment (the fulfillment of hope), and possession (the fulfillment of charity); and four that overflow into the body from the joy of the soul: clarity, subtlety, agility, and impassibility. With this, Bonaventure has transitioned nicely from his series of "threes" to a series of "sevens," and from his general

---

[53] Ibid., 1.5.
[54] Ibid., 1.9.
[55] Ibid., 1.13.
[56] I am largely following the fine translation by Robert Karris. But it is very difficult to translate into English all of Bonaventure's parallel constructions in Latin. Karris made the very reasonable decision to make these two words in Latin into a noun with a relative clause in English. My goal throughout has been to make clear to the reader that these would have been parallel constructions in the original Latin and the similarity of their sound would have given the collations what I have described as a "poetic" quality.
[57] *Coll. de sept.* 1.17.

discussion of grace in the first collation to his more particular descriptions of each of the seven gifts of the Holy Spirit in the collations discussed in the text that follows.

Divisio of the Gifts

Bonaventure has deftly made the transition from his general threefold division of grace in terms of *origin*, *use*, and *fruit* – a threefold distinction he will apply to each gift of the Holy Spirit in the subsequent collations – to the seven gifts of the Holy Spirit. But he has done something else as well. Just as the first collation of Bonaventure's *Collations on the Ten Commandments* contained a useful *divisio* of the commandments, so here in the first collation of his *Collations on the Seven Gifts*, Bonaventure has provided another useful *divisio*. He has located his discussion of the seven gifts within a broader context that includes Christ at its origins (Christ incarnate, crucified, and sender of the Holy Spirit) and the Christian moral life animated by the sacraments, virtues, and beatitudes as its fruit.[58] Hence were we to ask, "Where do the seven gifts of the Holy Spirit fit into the moral life?" or "What role do they play?" Bonaventure has provided a clear picture of where we can locate them. On this view, the gifts of the Holy Spirit are considered auxiliary to the three theological and four cardinal virtues. The gifts help complete in us the work of the virtues.

How are we transformed by the incarnation, crucifixion, and resurrection of Christ? Those are evens in the past. How do they affect us *now*? How do we "put on Christ," as Paul says? (cf. Rom 13:14, Gal 3:27). Answer: Christ sends His Holy Spirit to bring to fruition in each of us the salvation He won for us in His salvific death on the cross.

But what does the Holy Spirit *do*? And how does it relate to the elements of the Christian moral life, such as faith, hope, and love; the four cardinal virtues of prudence, justice, temperance, and fortitude; the seven beatitudes mentioned by Christ in the Sermon on the Mount; and the seven sacraments of the Church? Friars who listened to Bonaventure's *Collations on the Seven Gifts* would have known that the "healing grace" that brings about the remission of guilt comes through the sacraments and the "strengthening grace" that brings the fullness of justice comes through the seven virtues and the seven gifts of the Holy Spirit. Both of these were preparatory for the "perfection" or fullest realization of the moral life, namely the happiness achieved in this life by living out the beatitudes and in the next life by enjoying the seven endowments: vision, enjoyment, possession, clarity, subtlety, agility, and impassibility. Bonaventure has identified a hierarchy of graces, and he has fit the seven gifts of the Spirit into that hierarchy. Are the seven gifts meant solely for the next life? No. Are they necessary to heal us from our sin? No. But they *are* needed if we are to achieve the fullness of justice.

Fitting these various elements into a meaningful whole has long been a challenge for moral theologians. Many of us simply put these various elements into separate "boxes,"

---

[58] Cf. Thomas's discussion of the relationship between the virtues, gifts, beatitudes and fruits in ST I-II, qq. 55–67 (virtues), q. 68 (gifts), q. 70 (beatitudes), and q. 71 (fruits). Thomas affirms that carrying out the beatitudes is made possible by the virtues and gifts.

often failing to consider how they might come together into a meaningful whole.[59] Such was not the case for masters of theology such as Thomas and Bonaventure. Providing a meaningful catalogue and hierarchy of the virtues, gifts, sacraments, and beatitudes was considered an important goal. Indeed, the habits of mind of the master that produced these catalogues and considered them invaluable guides were not unrelated to those that insisted on producing a *divisio textus* for books of the Bible. The medieval genius was the ability to see the order in diverse things and to find the interrelations and order among them.

Consider again the challenges Bonaventure was facing at Paris and in the Franciscan Order. He was addressing a group of brothers many of whom were being educated at the University of Paris. Likely they would be influenced by the intellectual disputes occurring there. By the year this series of collations was being composed, zeal for the works of Aristotle was rampant at Paris, especially among masters in the Arts faculty. For devotees of Aristotle's *Ethics*, the virtues would have been a prominent topic. It would have been Bonaventure's task to remind his audience of the human need for grace without which we cannot overcome our sinful human nature, become just, or reach our ultimate end, which is attained only in union with God in heaven, not merely exercising the political virtues or in a life devoted to contemplation.

Hence this first collation served a protreptic purpose as an exhortation to its listeners to follow a particular path to wisdom and embrace a specific way of life. It called its audience to embrace a Christian wisdom about the world and a scripturally based understanding of human nature and human flourishing. An important goal was to convince its listeners that, although Aristotle could teach them much that is valuable about the virtues and the moral life, without grace, we humans are like birds that can see the sky but have no power in our wings to rise upward.[60] For that upward ascent, we need God's grace.

It seems clear that Bonaventure's training in preaching in the *sermo modernus* style influenced his writing throughout his career. The benefit of recognizing this fact is that, once readers have accustomed themselves to the way the *sermo modernus* style works, they can better navigate what might otherwise be confusing bits of text. It sometimes happens, for example, that one will finish a section that is third in a list and find that the next section begins "second." To the reader keeping track of the overall structure, it will be clear that the "third" section is the third member of a subdivision, and the "second" is the second member of the original division. Such tracking of the divisions and subdivisions helps turn what can become a confusing jumble into a meaningfully ordered set of parts within a whole. Keeping clear on this order of parts-to-whole is helpful when reading Bonaventure's *Collations on the Ten Commandments* and *Collations on the Seven Gifts of the Holy* Spirit. It is an essential survival skill, however, when it comes to Bonaventure's *Collations on the Six Days of Creation*. And it is to that notoriously complex text that we turn in the next chapter.

---

[59] The Dominican Servais Pinckaers has pointed out that considerations of the gifts and the beatitudes and their importance in the moral life were often simply left out of modern manuals of the moral life. Such was not the case with thirteenth century masters such as Thomas and Bonaventure. See Servais Pinckaers, *The Pinckaers Reader: Renewing Thomistic Moral Theology* (Washington, DC: The Catholic University of America Press, 2005), 93–129. For an even fuller presentation of Aquinas's treatment of the beatitudes, see Anton ten Klooster, *Thomas Aquinas on the Beatitudes: Reading Matthew, Disputing Grace and Virtue, Preaching Happiness*, Thomas Instituut Utrecht, 18 (Leuven: Peeters Publishers, 2018).

[60] Cf. *Coll. de sept.* 1.2 and note 24.

18

The *Reduction of the Arts to Theology* Redux
The Prologue to the Collations on the Six Days of Creation

BONAVENTURE'S COLLATIONS *on the Six Days of Creation* were delivered during the weeks of Easter, 1273, some five years after the *Collations on the Seven Gifts of the Holy Spirit.* These collations, composed near the end of his life and much more complex than its predecessors, signaled a return to a subject with which Bonaventure had begun his career: the hierarchy of the sciences and the proper order of study. In his *resumptio* – an early version of the text most readers know as *On the Reduction of the Arts to Theology* – Bonaventure depended largely upon the hierarchy in Hugh of St. Victor's *Didascalicon*.[1] In the *Collations on the Six Days,* Bonaventure set out his own, more developed view.

In his original plan of the work, Bonaventure intended to distinguish seven levels of "vision" corresponding to the seven days of creation. He finished comments only on the first four days, up through the creation of the "greater light" to rule the day and the "lesser lights" to rule the night. We are missing anything on the fifth, sixth, and seventh days. In May of that year, 1273, Bonaventure was appointed cardinal by Pope Gregory X, who bid him to come immediately to the Second Council of Lyons, convened in March of 1272 in an attempt to heal the schism between the Eastern and Western Churches. Whether Bonaventure was simply too busy with his new duties and obligations as a cardinal to finish the *Collations on the Six Days* or whether, as happened occasionally in sermons, he simply ran short of time before he had to leave Paris, we don't know. What we do know is that the work was left unfinished when Bonaventure fell ill and died suddenly on July 15, 1274 at the Council.

Transitions Signaled by a Change in *Thema* Verse

What help do we get from reading the *Collations on the Six Days* from the perspective of the *sermo modernus* style? For one thing, it provides a useful guide to the work's structure. Recall that when we examined the prologues in Aquinas's *Summa of Theology* in

---

[1] See my discussion in Chapter 11.

Chapter 9, we discovered that, behind the obvious division of the text into questions and articles, Thomas had in mind another, deeper, logical structure of divisions and subdivisions into which he had conceptually divided the whole. We found, moreover, that the places in the *Summa* where Thomas delineates this deeper, logical structure was in prologues scattered throughout the text.

In a similar way, although the *Collations on the Six Days* is divided into "collations" numbered 1 through 23, and these numbers are valuable for reference purposes, they do little more than indicate the time Bonaventure was able to speak on a particular day. To discern the logical structure of the text, the reader should pay attention to the *thema* verse of each collation. When Bonaventure starts a new collation, he is not necessarily beginning an entirely new topic. If the *thema* verse at the beginning of the collation is the same as the one that prefaced the previous collation, then Bonaventure is still addressing the same topic. If there is a new *thema* verse, he is taking up a new topic.

So, for example, Bonaventure uses the same *thema* verse from Ecclesiasticus 15:5 for the first three collations: "In the midst of the Church the Lord shall open his mouth, and shall fill him with the spirit of wisdom and understanding and shall clothe him with a robe of glory."[2] These three collations serve as a prologue to the rest.

At the beginning of the fourth collation, he introduces a new *thema* verse from Genesis 1:4–5: "God saw that the light was good. God separated the light from the darkness," and he continues using this verse at the beginning of Collations 4 through 7. In these, he is dilating upon the first "vision," the "light" given on the first day, which is "the light of understanding naturally given" (*quae est intelligentiae per naturam inditae*).

At the beginning of Collation 8, we find a change – a new *thema* verse from Genesis 1:8: "God called the firmament heaven. And there was evening and morning, the second day." This signals the change from a discussion of the "light" of the first day to the "vision" of the second day, in which the understanding is lifted up by faith (*intelligentiae per fidem sublevatae*). Bonaventure continues to use this same *thema* verse for Collations 8 through 10.

We will come back to what he does in Collations 11 and 12 in a moment.

At the beginning of Collation 13, he switches the *thema* verse again to signal that he is beginning the "vision" of the third day. He quotes Genesis 1:9–11: "'Let the waters below the heavens be gathered into one place and let the dry land appear.' And so it was. God called the dry land Earth and the assembled waters Seas. And God saw that it was good. Then God said, 'Let the earth bring forth vegetation: seed-bearing plants and all kinds of fruit trees that bear fruit containing their seed,'" etc. He continues using this same *thema* at the beginning of Collations 13 through 19.

At the beginning of Collation 20, he changes to a new *thema* to signal the transition into the "vision" of the fourth day: "And God said: "Let there be lights in the firmament of the heavens to separate day from might; let them serve as signs and for the fixing of seasons,

---

[2] I have quoted from the wonderful new translation of the *Collations on the Six Days* by Jay Hammond, trans., *Collations on the Hexaemeron: Conferences on the Six Days of Creation: The Illuminations of the Church*, Works of St. Bonaventure, vol. 18 (St. Bonaventure, NY: The Franciscan Institute, 2018). References will be given to collation and section; e.g., *Coll. in Hex.* 1.3 refers to *Collations on the Six Days*, Collation 1, section 3. The Latin text has been quoted from the version of the *Collationes in Hexaemeron* in the Quarrachi edition of Bonaventure's *opera omnia*, vol. 5.

days and years ..." And he continues using this *thema* verse at the beginning of Collations 20, 21, and 23, which is as far as he got before he was called away.

Here is a diagram of the basic structure so far:

Thema of Collations 1–3: "In the midst of the Church the Lord shall open his mouth, and shall fill him with the spirit of wisdom and understanding and shall clothe him with a robe of glory (Eccli. 15:5). **Prologue**

Thema of Collations 4–7: "God saw that the light was good. God separated the light from the darkness." **Vision of the First Day**

Thema of Collations 8–10: "God called the firmament heaven. And there was evening and morning, the second day." **Vision of the Second Day**

Thema of Collations 13–19: "'Let the waters below the heavens be gathered into one place and let the dry land appear.' And so it was. God called the dry land Earth and the assembled waters Seas. And God saw that it was good. Then God said, 'Let the earth bring forth vegetation: seed-bearing plants and all kinds of fruit trees that bear fruit containing their seed.'" **Vision of the Third Day**

Thema of Collations 20, 21, and 23: "And God said: "Let there be lights in the firmament of the heavens to separate day from might; let them serve as signs and for the fixing of seasons, days and years ..." **Vision of the Fourth Day**

There are two variations to the basic structure I just laid out above: the first occurs at the beginning of Collation 11, and the second occurs at the beginning of Collation 22. What happens in Collations 11, 12, and 22? Let me suggest that, in each case, the change in *thema* verse suggests an important shift. So, for example, at the beginning of Collation 11, Bonaventure shifts from using the *thema* verse he used in Collations 8–10, "God called the firmament heaven," and introduces a new verse from 2 Corinthians 3:18: "But we all, with faces unveiled, reflecting as in a mirror the glory of the Lord, are being transformed into His very image from glory to glory, as through the Spirit of the Lord." He uses this new *thema* to mark the transition from his discussion in Collation 10 of God considered as "universal first Cause" of all things – a knowledge of God available to reason alone – to his discussion in Collation 11 of the triune God – a knowledge of God requiring divine revelation. In Collation 12, he continues with a discussion based on the images on that passage from Revelation.

There is another shift of *thema* at the beginning of Collation 22. Rather than using the Genesis passage about "lights in the firmament of the heavens" with which he begins Collations 20, 21, and 23, he substitutes the famous passage from Revelation 12:1, often interpreted as referring to the Virgin Mary: "And a great sign appeared in heaven: a woman clothed with the sun, and the moon was under her feet, and upon her head a crown of twelve stars." This verse marks his extended discussion in Collation 22 of the hierarchy in the Church and in the soul.

The First Three Collations as a "Fractured" Prologue

Since even a cursory consideration of all the *Collations on the Six Days* is beyond the scope of the present chapter – an entire volume would barely scratch the surface – we will restrict our focus to the first three collations that together constitute a prologue to the rest of the work. In the previous chapter, I quoted Kevin Hughes's comment, "The

Collationes, when taken as a whole, bear all the elements of the sermon structure, but it is difficult to find them all in one particular conference. Rather, Bonaventure stretches the sermonic structure across several individual collations..."[3] This is exactly right. So, for example, whereas in his other two *Collations*, Bonaventure finished his prologue in one collation and nearly all the separate sections in his original plan fit into one collation, in the *Collations on the Six Days*, Bonaventure spreads his treatment of each "day" out over several collations. He signals the major transitions when he switches his *thema* verse.

Consider the first three collations. We know that the first three are to be read as a group because they all share the same *thema* verse: "In the midst of the Church the Lord shall open his mouth, and shall fill him with the spirit of wisdom and understanding and shall clothe him with a robe of glory" (Ecclesiasticus 15:5). "In these words," says Bonaventure at the beginning of Collation 1, "the Holy Spirit teaches the prudent man to whom he should address his speech, from where he should begin it, and finally where he should end it."[4] To whom should the prudent man address his speech? *In the midst of the Church*. From what source should his speech take its origin? Who should "open his mouth"? *The Lord*. And what should be the goal of the prudent man? *To be filled with the spirit of wisdom and understanding* so that God may *clothe him with a robe of glory*. Bonaventure treats the first two questions in Collation 1, and the third question in Collations 2 and 3. The goal of the prudent man is that the Lord would "fill him with the spirit of wisdom and understanding." Hence "wisdom" is the topic of Collation 2 and "understanding" of Collation 3. We will consider each in turn.

Collation 1: "In the Midst of the Church the Lord Shall Open His Mouth"

According to Bonaventure, the prudent man should address his message *in the midst of the Church*. But what is the Church? It is, says Bonaventure, "a union of rational men living in harmony and uniformity" through (1) harmonious and uniform observance of the divine law (*per concordem et uniformem observantiam divinae legis*); (2) harmonious and uniform adherence to divine peace (*per concordem et uniformem cohaerentiam divinae pacis*); and (3) harmonious and uniform consonance of divine praise (*per concordem et uniformem consonantiam divinae laudis*).[5] Note the wonderful parallel phrases. After dilating each of these in sections 3, 4, and 5, Bonaventure uses a common *sermo modernus* technique and considers the contraries of each.

How is a man *snatched away* from the Church? Carnality and cupidity turn a man away from the *divine law* (section 6); malice and cruelty are opposed to one's adherence to *divine peace* (section 7); and the spirit of presumption and curiosity are opposed to the *concelebration of divine praise* (section 8). The prudent man should address himself to those in the Church in the first three ways, but not to those working *against* the Church in the second three ways.

So the prudent man should speak "in the midst of the Church." But what should be the source of his speech? What is its *origin*? Where should the prudent man *begin*? Answer: He

---

[3] Kevin L. Hughes, "St. Bonaventure's *Collationes in Hexaëmeron*: Fractured Sermons and Protreptic Discourse," *Franciscan Studies*, vol. 63 (2005): 111.
[4] *Coll. in Hex.* 1.1.
[5] Ibid., 1.2.

should begin at the beginning – that is to say, the beginning of everything. The source of the prudent man's wisdom and understanding should be the creative source of all things. Since it is impossible to understand a creature except through that by which it was made, it is necessary to begin with the Word through whom all things were made.[6]

Recall that in the *De reductione artium ad theologiam*, Bonaventure showed how all the disciplines could be "reduced" to theology, in the Latin sense of the word *re-ducere*, meaning "to lead back to." In the *De reductione*, his approach was determined by the context in which the address was originally given. It was originally a *resumptio* address, and such addresses were by university regulation to be in praise of sacred Scripture. Here his goal is even more ambitious. In these *Collations*, he set his own guidelines, and instead of approaching his topic by arguing that all the disciplines should "lead back to" and thus be guided by the divine revelation contained in the sacred Scriptures, here he argues that all knowledge should be seen as having its origin *in Christ*. Why? Precisely because He is the Word "through whom all things were made" – the Word that "became flesh" to raise us up to union with God. As such, he is the *mediator* between God and man – between God the Father and the whole of creation.

"Our purpose then," says Bonaventure, "is to show that in Christ *are hidden all the treasures of God's wisdom and knowledge* (scientiae), and that [Christ] himself is the center (*medium*) of all the sciences (*scientiarum*)."[7] Note the subtle shift of metaphor. We *begin* from the *center*.[8] All such metaphors are limited, but if we add Bonaventure's claim in the *De reductione* that the culmination of all the disciplines is Christ to his claim here that Christ is the "beginning" and the "middle," he is claiming that Christ is the beginning, the middle, and the end of all knowledge.

But it is important that we make some necessary distinctions. He is the "beginning" in the sense that He is the source of all creation. He is the "end" in the sense that He brings all of creation to its proper end or goal. He is, as the Book of Revelation tells us, the alpha and the omega.[9] Yet he is also the mediator between God and man. What it means for Christ to be the "center" in this way, the "mediator" of all true wisdom and knowledge, is the subject of the remainder of the collation.

Christ as Sevenfold Center

On Bonaventure's account, Christ is the "center" in a sevenfold way. To understand Bonaventure's teaching in these sections, one must keep clear in one's mind the remarkable seven-tier structure he maps out in section 11. Allow me to quote it in full.

---

[6] Cf. *Coll. in Hex.* 1.10.

[7] Ibid., 1.11.

[8] Ibid.: "Concerning the second point [where to begin], it should be noted that the beginning (*incipiendum*) is from the center (*medio*), who is Christ. For, [Christ] himself is the *mediator between God and humans* (cf. 1 Tim 2:5) holding the center (*medium*) in all things, as will be explained. Hence, it is necessary to begin from him if anyone wishes to reach Christian wisdom, as shown in Matthew: *for no one knows the Son except the Father; nor does anyone know the Father except the Son, and those to whom the Son wishes to reveal Him* (Mt 11:27).

[9] Rev 22:13.

And the center (*medium*) is sevenfold, namely: of essence, nature, distance, teaching, moderation, justice, [and] concord. The first is the concern of the metaphysician, the second the physicist/physician, the third the mathematician, the fourth the logician, the fifth the ethicist, the sixth the politician or jurist, and the seventh the theologian. The first center (*medium*) is primary by eternal origin (*aeternali origine primarium*), the second strong by diffusion of power (*virtuali diffusione pervalidum*), the third deep by central position (*centrali positione profundum*), the fourth clear by rational demonstration (*rationali manifestatione praeclarum*), the fifth foremost by moral choice (*morali electione praecipuum*), the sixth high by the compensation of justice (*iudiciali compensatione praecelsum*), [and] the seventh peaceful by universal union (*universali conciliatione pacatum*). Christ was the first center (*medium*) in eternal generation, the second in the incarnation, the third in the passion, the fourth in the resurrection, the fifth in the ascension, the sixth in the future judgment, [and] the seventh in everlasting retribution or beatification.[10]

I have made a point throughout this book that one of the benefits of the *sermo modernus* style was that its series of associations served as a mnemonic device to help listeners recall the material after the original presentation was finished. Medieval theologians understood the difference between "memory" (*memoria*) and "recollection" (*reminiscentia*).[11] One reason the *sermo modernus* style developed as it did, with sections keyed to the words of an opening *thema* verse, is that after the sermon was finished, the words of the opening *thema* verse would help listeners recollect the points in the sermon. Since many in Bonaventure's audience would have had large portions of the Scriptures memorized, remembering a single verse would not be as difficult as it would be for many people today.

In Table 18.1, the list with Christ's generation, incarnation, passion, resurrection, ascension, judgment, and beatification would undoubtedly have been the easiest to remember. If he made the associations with the items on the other lists clear and convincing enough, this would help his listeners recollect the items on the rest of the chart. It was not by accident, for example, that the entire list in column four contains words beginning with the letter "p". Bonaventure's listeners and readers would have been schooled in the memory arts, so making these mnemonic connections would have been more natural to them. I will begin each heading below with the event from Christ's life, death, and resurrection (which I put in the final column above) because these are the easiest to remember, and remembering them can spur the reader's recollection of the rest.

Christ's Eternal Generation/Primary (Primarium) by Eternal Origin/Essence/Metaphysician

We begin with the primary way Christ can be called the "center" (*medium*). Christ is the "center" (*medium*) in the order of essence by reason of His eternal generation from the Father. The Son is "the middle" of the three Persons because He is eternally

---

[10] *Coll. in Hex.* 1.11.
[11] One source was Aristotle's work *De memoria et reminiscentia*. On the importance of memory in the Middle Ages, see Mary Carruthers, *The Book of Memory: A Study of Memory in Medieval Culture* (Cambridge: Cambridge University Press, 2008).

Table 18.1 *The Seven "Centers"*

The "center" (*medium*) of the science –	Which is the concern of the:	The "center" (*medium*) is:	Christ is the *medium* by:
Essence	Metaphysician	Primary (*primarium*) by eternal origin	Eternal generation
Nature	Physicist/physician	Strong (*pervalidum*) by diffusion of power	Incarnation
Distance	Mathematician	Deep (*profundum*) by central position	Crucifixion
Teaching	Logician	Clear (*praeclarum*) by rational demonstration	Resurrection
Moderation	Ethicist	Foremost (*praecipuum*) by moral choice	Ascension
Justice	Jurist/politician	High (*praecelsum*) by the compensation of justice	Future judgment
Concord	Theologian	Peaceful (*pacatum*) by universal union	Eternal beatification

generated by the Father while also participating with the Father in the generation of the Holy Spirit.

So too, the Son is the "middle" – the mediating center – between God and His creation. God creates *in and through* the Son, as He also redeems His creation in and through the Son. Note, however, that in saying this, we are not saying that Christ is *other than* God, which would be to make the Arian mistake. We do not say that Christ is a *created thing* and receives His existence "from another." According to Bonaventure, "'to Be' (*esse*) exists in only two ways: either 'to Be' (*esse*) that is from itself, according to itself, and because of itself, or 'to Be' (*esse*) that is from another, according to another, and because of another," then we must put Christ on the first side rather than the second, as having "to Be" from Himself."[12]

Yet there is still a distinction between the Persons in God. We can consider the "to- Be"-that-is-from-itself-and-not-from-another "under the notion of originating" principle (*in ratione originantis*); this is the Father. Or we could consider the "to-Be"-that-is-from-itself-and-not-from-another "under the notion of exemplifying" principle (*in ratione exemplantis*); this is the Son. Or, finally, we could consider the "to-Be"-that-is-from-itself-and-not-from-another as the goal or terminating principle (*in ratione finientis vel terminantis*); this is the Holy Spirit. "These three Persons are equal and equally noble," says Bonaventure, "because it is of equal nobility for the Holy Spirit to complete (*terminare*) the divine Persons, just as it is for the Father to originate them (*originare*), or for the Son to represent them all (*omnia repraesentare*)."[13]

How does all this relate to the work of the metaphysician? As the metaphysician raises his mind from the particular to the universal – from this particular man, Socrates, to "man," and from this particular city, Athens, to "city" – and from thence to the notion of Being itself, the exemplary cause and final end of all things, by considering (1) what makes

---

[12] *Coll. in Hex.* 1.12.
[13] Ibid.

Socrates or anything *exist* (exemplary cause) and (2) what Socrates or any man must become in order to reach their fullest perfection as "man" (final end), in this "raising of the mind," he or she begins to grasp, if only inchoately, some of the essential principles that help us understand God the Father, Son, and Holy Spirit. In this way, metaphysics becomes the means of a *reductio*, leading our minds back to God, Christ, and other truths necessary for our salvation.

Note that the "illumination" operates in both directions. In one way, the notion of a three-person God in whom the Father eternally generates the Son, and the Son and Father eternally generate the Spirit, challenges metaphysics to reach beyond itself, to grasp principles that are not merely principles, but Persons with freedom and love. On the other hand, however, the Church developed its mature teaching on the Triune God – three Persons subsisting in One Being; the exemplary Cause and Supreme Good of all created things – with the insight gained from the tradition of classical Greek metaphysics.

At the heart of classical metaphysics are essence and existence and, according to Bonaventure's account, these lead us ultimately to (because they have their origin in) the eternal generation of the Son, who is the Word through whom all things were created. Since it is through the Word that all things were created, and since, according to Bonaventure, "to know" in the strict sense (*scire*) means knowledge in and through the "forms" of things in the Mind of God, which are the source of the "to Be" (the *esse* or *essentia*) of the thing, *therefore*, the *medium* making things known (*faciens scire*) is Christ, the Truth. Christ, the Word made flesh, says Bonaventure, "is the metaphysical center (*medium metaphysicum*) leading us back (*reducens*), and this is the whole of our metaphysics: emanation, exemplarity, and consummation, that is to be illumined (*illuminari*) by spiritual rays of light (*radius spirituales*) and to be led back (*reduci*) to the Most High (*summum*). And in this way [that is to say, being led back this way by means of this spiritual illumination] you will be a true metaphysician (*verus metaphysicus*)."[14] A "true" metaphysician on this view is one who knows that the essence and existence of all things comes from the Father through the Son and who is led by his knowledge of whatever exists in the world back to the Source of All Being and Goodness; that is to say, he is led by the Son who mediates back to the Father who is the Source.

Christ's Incarnation/Strong (Pervalidum) by Diffusion of Power/Nature/Physicist

We turn now to the order of nature. Christ is the "center" (*medium*) in the order of nature by reason of His physical incarnation and strong (*pervalidum*) by the diffusion of power. Recall that Bonaventure's goal is "to show that in Christ 'are hidden all the treasures of wisdom and knowledge,' and that He Himself is the central point of all understanding."[15] How do we find in Christ "the central point of understanding" when it comes to the physical world? The concern of the physical scientist, says Bonaventure, is studying "motion and generation according to the influence of heavenly bodies on the

---

[14] Ibid., 1.17.
[15] Ibid., 1.11.

elements, and the ordering of elements."[16] So, for example, the sun stands in the center (in the "middle," *medium*) of the planets and the diffusion of its rays on the earth brings about the generation of life. In a similar way, the heart is the "center" (*medium*) of the human person, and the diffusion of its "spirits" throughout the body generates life.[17]

What do these teachings of physical science teach us, inchoately, about Christ? Like the sun and the heart, Christ is both Head and Center of the Church. Whatever power exists in Nature, just as whatever power exists in the Church, has been diffused into it by Christ. And just as in the human body there is no diffusion from the head to the members unless the members are united to the head, so too in the Mystical Body, all its members must be united to Christ as the Head. All grace and love flow from Him, which he diffuses into all the members of His Mystical Body.[18]

Christ's Passion/Deep (Profundum) by Central Position/Distance/Mathematician

The third center is in the order of distance. This is the "center" with which mathematics deals: the centrality of position, as in the center of a circle or the center of the earth. The "center" in this sense is the lowest or deepest point.[19] Likewise, the Son of God, in the deepest humility, assumed "our earth" (*humum*) and "made of earth (*humo factus*), came not only upon the surface of the earth, but indeed to the depth of its center ..., because after the crucifixion his soul descended into hell and restored the heavenly thrones."[20] So we too must have humility (*humilitas*) – be "of the earth" – because our salvation is from Christ, our mediator. If we pull away from this our "center," the "means" of our salvation won through Christ's crucifixion, then we are left condemned.[21]

To keep the basic outline clear, I have not quoted or mentioned the "chained" biblical verses that appear in each section of the *Collations*. But they would have been a prominent feature in the oral delivery of the collation. Allow me to mention a few examples from this section of the collation. Bonaventure declares that "Christ was this center (*medium*) in the crucifixion," then immediately quotes Psalm 73:12: "Our king before ages has worked salvation in the midst (*medio*) of the earth."[22] Several lines later, referring back to this passage from the Psalm, he says that Christ "has worked salvation 'in the midst (*medio*) of the earth,' because after the crucifixion his soul descended into hell and restored the heavenly thrones."[23] "This center (*medium*) is salvific," declares Bonaventure, and "whoever

---

[16] Ibid., 1.18.
[17] Ibid., 1.19.
[18] Ibid., 1.20.
[19] Ibid., 1.21.
[20] Ibid., 1.22. The reader should not miss the implicit word-play. *Humum* sounds similar to *humanum*. And *humo* is close to *homo*, Latin for "man." Christ was not only *homo factus est*. He was *humo factus*. And so we must have *humilitas*, a word built on the root *humo*. The connection would have been clear in Latin when the collation was delivered orally. This sort of play on words was very popular in thirteenth-century sermons.
[21] *Coll. in Hex.* 1.23.
[22] Ibid., 1.22
[23] Ibid.

withdraws from it is damned, namely, withdrawing from the center (*medio*) of humility. And this the Savior shows: 'I am in your midst (*medio*) as he who serves' (Luke 22:27). And in Matthew: 'Unless you turn and become like little children, you will not enter into the kingdom of heaven' (Mt 18:3). In this center (*medio*) he has worked salvation, namely, in the humility of the cross."[24] This entire section could have been copied directly out of sermon or inserted into a sermon.

Christ's Resurrection/Clear (Praeclarum) by Rational Demonstration/Doctrine/Logician

The fourth center is in the order of doctrine (*doctrina* or teaching) which is most clear when manifestly rational and logical.[25] If a teacher or an interlocutor's speech makes no sense, then we cannot learn from him or her. If a speaker's arguments are invalid, then they will not be convincing. In a syllogistic argument, that which connects the major premise with the conclusion is called "the middle term." At first, the relationship between the major premise and the conclusion may not be clear; it is the "middle term" that makes this relationship manifest. I can say "This is a whale," and "This animal feeds its young with milk." The connection between the two statements is made manifest by the middle term "All whales are mammals; that is, animals who feed their young with milk."

Christ is such a "center," metaphorically speaking, in His resurrection, says Bonaventure. The resurrection helps us see the connection between the eternal divinity of the Son of God and the horrendous suffering of his crucifixion.

"The major proposition [the divinity of the Son] was from eternity," says Bonaventure, "and the [minor] assumption (*assumtio*) is the cross; and truly, the conclusion is the resurrection."[26] The scribes and Pharisees taunted Christ, saying: "If you are the Son of God, come down from the cross." But Christ, in His death and resurrection, confounded this reasoning.[27] It is as if the reasoning of those taunting Christ was:

> *If you are the Son of God, come down from the cross.*
> *Hidden middle term: The Son of God cannot suffer death.*

Hence the "logic" of Christ's sacrifice went something like this instead:

> *Although I am the eternal Son of God, I will endure even death on a cross.*
> *Hidden middle term: The Son of God will rise from the dead*
> *(and ascend to the right hand of the Father).*

The reasoning of those taunting Christ was similar to the reasoning of the devil when he tempted our First Parents in the Garden.

For the devil deceived (*paralogizavit*) the first human and placed a certain proposition into the heart of the human, as if it were known as self-evident (*per se*), that is: the rational

---

[24] Ibid., 1.23.
[25] Ibid., 1.25.
[26] Ibid., 1.28.
[27] Ibid.

(*rationalis*) creature must desire (*appetere*) a likeness (*similitudinem*) to its Creator precisely because it is an image."[28] There is a certain "logic" here: If we are "like" God, shouldn't we be "equal to" God? But this is, says Bonaventure, a "sophistic and destructive argument," whereas the reasoning of Christ is "constructive and reparative."[29] What the devil did was to make man different from God while promising to make him similar. So Christ made Himself similar to man in order to make man similar to Himself.[30] We must, therefore, use the logic of Christ against the devil who is constantly arguing with us. If we refuse to suffer with Him in his crucifixion, then we will not rise with Him in His resurrection.[31] The "logic" of the resurrection indicates we must embrace "the middle," Christ, if we are to unite the Father's divinity with our fallen humanity.

Christ's Ascension/Foremost (Praecipuum) by Moral Choice/Moderation/Ethicist

The next group, which includes "moderation" and the "ethicist," is fairly straightforward, especially in an Aristotelian context, because virtues for Aristotle are a mean between two extremes. What is more challenging is how this relates to Christ's *ascension*. Bonaventure's account is that, as Christ ascended in the cloud, so too the Christian must rise from strength to strength and not rest content in his virtue, for a person who did so would cease to be virtuous.[32]

Moreover, the foundation of virtue, says Bonaventure, is faith. This would have been news to Aristotle, but while "right reason" is what discovers "the middle" in ethical judgments – that which is neither too much nor too little – for Bonaventure and the Christian tradition of which he is a part, *faith* guides "right reason" to discern reality truly.

Owing to certain fideistic tendencies in modern thinking, we sometimes forget that medieval thinkers considered faith to be a kind of *knowing*. And as a kind of knowing – indeed, a higher form of knowing – they assumed that it could and should guide prudent action. This view is accurately expressed by Josef Pieper, one of the foremost scholars of the virtues in the twentieth century, who describes prudence as a quality of "clearsightedness." "The prudent man," says Pieper, "approaches each decision with his eyes open, in the full light of knowledge and faith. He discerns reality objectively, sizes up a factual situation for what it is, and weighs the real value of things."[33] Note Pieper's qualification: "in the full light of knowledge *and faith*."

Bonaventure does not provide any examples in his text of faith informing prudence but allow me to suggest one. When the Protestant inhabitants of the little French mountain town of Le Chambon were ordered by officials of the Vichy government to hand over the Jews they knew to be hiding in the town, the entire town, under the leadership of their

---

[28] Ibid., 1.26.
[29] Ibid.
[30] Ibid., 1.27.
[31] Ibid., 1.30.
[32] Ibid., 1.31.
[33] Josef Pieper and Heinz Raskop, *What Catholics Believe* (New York: Pantheon Books, 1951; repr. Providence, RI: Cluny Media, 2019), 73.

pastor, André Trocmé, refused and continued to hide Jewish refugees throughout the war. One might have thought this the least "prudent" act possible. Yet, their faith told them that these Jews were not a "disease," but God's "chosen people," with an infinite dignity and worth that revealed the regulations of the Vichy government to be unjust. So they disobeyed the government's orders and quietly hid and supported as many Jewish refugees as they could.[34]

From one perspective, their actions could be seen as rash, foolish, and extreme. The entire town might have been deported to concentration camps along with the Jewish refugees they were harboring. Yet from the perspective of faith in a God who rose from the dead and ascended to God's right hand, this act might be seen as "Christ-like" and thus "just" or "righteous" in the best and most proper sense of the word; that is to say, acting *like* Christ thanks to the grace *of* Christ. With Christ as both the model and the end, the "mean" of the virtuous act informed by charity may shift, along with one's understanding of what is "prudent."

Future Judgment/High (Praecelsum) by the Compensation of Justice/Justice/Judge

The terms in the sixth row are the most easily associated: "justice," "judges," and divine "judgment." On Bonaventure's account, Christ's final judgment offers the fullest realization of justice in the sense of "repayment made according to merit." We know that perfect justice is not possible in this world. The guilty sometimes go free and the innocent are sometimes punished unfairly. Only in the final judgment of Christ will all these injustices be "set right"; only then will persons be judged on their true merit.[35]

Bonaventure dilates this point with an elaborate allegory on the classic text in Ezekiel 1:4 in which one finds the famous "four living creatures": the man, the lion, the ox, and the eagle. "I looked, and behold, a whirlwind came from the North, a huge cloud with flashing fire, enveloped in brightness, from the midst of which, the midst of the fire, something gleamed like electrum. Within it were figures resembling four living creatures."[36] Here Bonaventure does not take these four creatures to signify, as was commonly done, the Evangelists Matthew, Mark, Luke, and John. Nor does he follow his practice in the prologue to the *Breviloquium* of associating the "legal" and "evangelical" books (the books of Old Testament law and the Gospels) with the lion, because the lion represents authority; the historical books of the Old and New Testaments with the ox, because the ox represents strength; the sapiential books with the man, because the man represents wisdom; and the prophetic books with the eagle, because the eagle possesses a "penetrating vision."[37] Rather he claims that Ezekiel is describing the final judgment. The "whirlwind" (*ventus turbinis*) represents the disturbance of the powers of nature that will occur at the final judgment, and the "huge cloud

---

[34] For a good account of the villagers and their village-wide conspiracy to rescue Jewish refugees, see Philip Hallie, *Lest Innocent Blood Be Shed: The Story of the Village of Le Chambon and How Goodness Happened There* (New York: Harper & Row, 1979).

[35] *Coll. in Hex.* 1.34.

[36] *Vidi, et ecce, ventus turbinis veniebat ab aquiline et nubes magna et ignis involens; et splendor in circuitu eius, et de medio eius quasi species electri, scilicet de medio ignis. Et in medio eius similitude quatuor animalium.*

[37] See *Brev. prol.* 1.1.

with flashing fire" (*nubes magna et ignis involens*) suggests the conflagration of fires that will accompany it. The word "brightness" (*splendor*) suggests the examination of consciences at the judgment, since then all consciences must be clear. Christ in his twofold nature is referred to by the word *electri*, and the four orders of the Church are designated by the four living creatures: the order of pontiffs by the lion, the martyrs by the ox, the confessors by the man, and the virgins by the eagle because they are devoted to contemplation.[38]

Why would Bonaventure insert an allegory into an otherwise technical theological account of the ways in which Christ is at the "center" of all the various disciplines from metaphysics to mathematics, and from the natural sciences to ethics? The answer is that it was not uncommon in thirteenth-century sermons for a preacher to dilate several sections based on the definition or classification of a word and/or by a consideration of causes and effects (with the result that these sections sound very "scholastic") but then to follow these with a section dilated using one or several of the mystical senses. This was standard *sermo modernus*–style practice, and from that perspective, it is not surprising that we should find an elaborate allegory inserted into a dialectical section filled with definitions and distinctions.

Eternal Beatification/Peaceful (Pacatum) by Universal Union/Concord/Theologian

This brings us to the terms in the seventh and final row. Christ is the "center" in this way because he is the bringer of "peace and the concord of universal reconciliation" (*concordiae universali conciliatione pacatum*).[39] Just as no complete or perfect justice can be delivered by human institutions, so too there is no complete or lasting peace among all people. The peace we can establish in this world is merely a foretaste of the peace Christ will bring at the final reconciliation at Christ's Second Coming. Moreover, the peace we can establish imperfectly in this world is always a participation in the peace Christ brings. Rulers concern themselves with a certain kind of peace, but it is usually a "concord" brought about by the threat of external force. Theologians, says Bonaventure, deal with "the salvation of the soul (*animae*): how it is begun in faith, advanced in the virtues, and consummated in the gifts [of the Holy Spirit].[40] This is a deeper sort of peace, not brought about by external force; this peace begins interiorly and spreads outwardly by degrees to one's neighbors and one's community.

Recalling the Associations and Enacting the *Reductio*

Now that we have reviewed the associations Bonaventure makes among the terms in the three columns – associations made in several creative ways – it is time to think back on the list. I will begin with list that includes Christ's life, death, and resurrection.

---

[38] *Coll. in Hex.* 1.35.
[39] Ibid., 1.37.
[40] Cf. my discussion of the relationship between the virtues, gifts, and beatitudes in the section on Bonaventure's *Collations on the Seven Gifts of the Holy Spirit*.

The eternal generation of the Son
Incarnation
Crucifixion
Resurrection
Ascension
Judgment
Eternal beatification

The question is whether we can recollect the items on the other two lists based on the associations Bonaventure established in the collation. Consider:

1. The *eternal generation* of the Son concerns being and *essence* and is thus *metaphysical*.
2. The *incarnation* is the Son's entry into the *physical* realm of *nature*, in particular, human nature.
3. The *crucifixion* and descent to the dead are Christ's lowest point. He descended to the "center" of the earth and reestablished God's reign even there. This sense of "center" is *equidistant* from all points on the sphere. It is a *mathematical* center.
4. Christ's refusal to "come down from the cross" and instead suffer death and rise again in the *resurrection* from the dead is the ultimate argument against the devil's logic that creatures made in God's likeness must be God's equal. This argument is *logical* in the best sense, as all *doctrine* should be.
5. Just as Christ *ascended* in the cloud, so too the Christian in his *ethical* life must rise from strength to strength and not rest content in his virtue, for a person who did so would cease to be virtuous. Virtues are determined by *moderation*, but also according to the knowledge gained by faith.
6. Christ's *final judgment* is the perfect realization of *justice*, not in the sense of personal virtue, but justice in the *juridical* sense.
7. Christ will bring *eternal beatification* and universal concord to all the blessed. *Theologians* deal with the salvation of the soul: how it begins with faith, moves forward through the virtues, and is consummated in the gifts. Only in this way do we get true reconciliation, *concord*, and peace.

Alternatively, one could begin with the items in the second list and in a similar way generate the others.

1. Metaphysics suggests essence, which suggests eternal generation.
2. Physics suggests nature, which suggests Christ's incarnation.
3. Mathematics suggests a geometric "center," equidistant from all points on the circle of a sphere, and this center suggests Christ's death on the cross and descent to the center of the earth.
4. Logic suggests arguments and "teaching" (or doctrine), which suggests Christ's ultimate argument against those who tempt him to come down from the cross, which is shown in His resurrection from the dead.
5. Ethics suggests virtues, which suggest moderation, but also suggests constant growth in virtue, which suggests Christ's ascension.
6. Judging suggests justice, which suggests Christ's final judgment.
7. Theological suggests salvation, which suggests peace, reconciliation, and eternal beatification at the end of time.

If one can remember the seven items on just one list, one can generate by recollection the items on the others.

I am not claiming that that the underlying associations are *only* for the sake of memory and recollection. Bonaventure believes he has shown that "in Christ are hidden all the treasures of wisdom and knowledge, and that He Himself is the central point of all understanding." My point is simply that the *way* Bonaventure chose to dilate upon this point involved skills – such as the skill of making memorable associations – that he learned at Paris when he was taught the *sermo modernus*–style of preaching.

It is that training, for example, that allowed Bonaventure at the end of this first collation to associate the seven categories he has set forth in such detail with the seven golden lampstands in the Book of Revelation (1:12–13) and the seven days of creation in Genesis (1:1–2:3). These associations helped his audience remember the seven items in each list. In the original Latin, provided below (whose poetic diction our English translation cannot communicate), Bonaventure's Paris training is evident in the strictly parallel *sermo modernus*–style constructions he uses to describe each "center":

1. Primum medium est essentiae aeternali generatione primarium
2. Secundum medium est naturae virtuali diffusione pervalidum
3. Tertium medium est distantiae centrali positione profundum
4. Quartum medium est doctrinae rationali manifestatione praeclarum
5. Quintum medium est modestiae morali electione praecipuum
6. Sextum medium est iustitiae iudicali recompensatione perpulcrum seu praecelsum
7. Septimum medium est concordiae universali conciliatione pacatum.[41]

Collation 2: "With the Spirit of Wisdom"

I have spent a good deal of time reviewing the material in Collation 1 to show how Bonaventure's style in the *Collations*, despite having been described as "free from the patterns of the Schools" and "wholly alien to the language of the schools," is in fact rooted in the *sermo modernus* style of preaching taught at the University of Paris.[42]

If we look back at the very beginning of Collation 1, Bonaventure begins with this *thema* verse: "In the midst of the Church the Lord shall open his mouth, and shall fill him with the spirit of wisdom and understanding and shall clothe him with a robe of glory." "In these words," says Bonaventure, "the Holy Spirit teaches the prudent man to whom he should address his speech, from where he should begin it, and finally where he should end it" (i.e., to what end it should be directed). In Collation 1, Bonaventure dilated the first two of these: to whom the prudent man should address his speech ("In the midst of the Church") and

---

[41] The great medieval scholar Étienne Gilson, in an article on *sermo modernus*–style preaching, commenting upon its parallel phrases and their "constantly rhythmic nature and the assonance of their divisions," declared that "In this respect, St. Bonaventure is a master of the genre." Étienne Gilson, "Michel Menot et la Technique du Sermon Médiéval," *Les Idées et Les Lettres* (Paris: Vrin, 1932), 122. Translation mine. It is because Bonaventure not only possessed this skill, but also exercised it continuously throughout his writing, that I have described him as "a scholastic with the soul of a poet."

[42] For the source of the judgments that Bonaventure developed a mode of expression "wholly alien to the language of the schools" and "free from the patterns of the Schools," see notes 1 and 2.

where he should begin it (Christ, "the Lord" who "shall open his mouth"). He has yet to expand upon the third, the end to which it should be directed, hence it is significant that he begins Collations 2 and 3 with the same *thema* verse. He associates the "end" to which the prudent man's speech should be directed as being "filled with the spirit of wisdom and understanding." It should come as no surprise, then, that Collation 2 deals with "wisdom" and Collation 3 with "understanding."

Regarding the first, the "spirit of wisdom," Bonaventure makes a fourfold division in his second collation: wisdom's origin (*ortus*), its dwelling (*domus*), its door (*portus*), and its form (*forma*).[43] Its origin, he says, is a topic he covered in his earlier *Collations on the Seven Gifts of the Holy Spirit* where he said, quoting James 1:17, that wisdom came down "from the Father of Lights" into the soul where it takes up its dwelling. He spends less than one section here discussing both.

Bonaventure identifies the "door to wisdom," the third item in his list of four, as an eager desire for it, which gives birth to love and makes a person observant of authority and *exempla*. Dilating this topic (with all the "chained" biblical authorities inserted appropriate to the *sermo modernus* style) takes up sections 3 through 6 of Collation 2. So, for example, he says:

> Therefore, yearning (*concupiscentia*) and vehement desire (*desiderium*) is the door to wisdom. Wisdom 7 (7–12): I wished (*optavi*) and sense was given to me; and I called, and the spirit of wisdom came into me. And I preferred her before kingdoms and thrones, and considered riches nothing in comparison to her, up to: I rejoiced in them all, because wisdom itself was before me, and I knew not that she is the mother of all these." But [the author] says that he possessed this [wisdom] by wishing (*optando*) and calling. For if she is the highest good, she must be loved (*amanda*) supremely. And if she is all good, she must be sought (*appetenda*) universally and above all else. The same is clear in the example of Solomon, who did not request gold and silver, but for a teachable heart; thus it came to him (cf. 1 Kgs 3: 9ff.). Hence James: "If any of you lack wisdom, let him ask for it from God who gives generously and ungrudgingly to all, and it will be given to him. But he must ask in faith without hesitation" (James 1:5–6). For the one who hesitates is not disciplined. This is, therefore, the door. And this desire extinguishes all other yearning (*concupiscentia*) and makes a person lifted up from the world. Hence he says: "I loved (*amavi*) and sought her from my youth; I sought to take her as my bride, and I was made to be a lover (*amator*) of her form" (Wis 8:2).[44]

This last sentence provides a transition into the next section, because the remainder of the second collation, from sections 7 through 27, is given over to dilating the final topic: the "form" of wisdom.

The Four Forms of Wisdom

The "form" of wisdom is wondrous, says Bonaventure, because at times it is uniform (*uniformis*), at others multiform (*multiformis*), at still others it can assume every form

---

[43] *Coll. in Hex.* 2.1.
[44] Ibid., 2.6.

(*omniformis*) or none at all (*nulliformis*).⁴⁵ Hence wisdom "clothes itself" in a fourfold light (*quadriformi igitur se vestit lumine*). It is "uniform" in the rules of the divine laws (*in regulis divinarum legum*). It is "multiform" in the mysteries of the divine Scriptures (*in mysteriis divinarum Scripturarum*). It can have "every form" (*omniformis*) "in the vestiges of the divine works" (*in vestigiis divinorum operum*). And it can be "without-form" (*nulliformis*) in the "elevations of divine excess (*in suspendiis divinorum excessuum*).⁴⁶ Note the customary parallel phrases. Let's consider each of these briefly.

Wisdom Is Uniform in the Rules of the Divine Law

Wisdom appears "uniform" and "immutable" (*immutabilis*) in the rules of the divine laws, says Bonaventure, which, "shining in rational minds (*mentibus rationalibus*), are all of those ways by which the mind knows (*mens cognoscit*) and judges that which could not be otherwise." What are these laws that the mind knows and judges could not be otherwise? The first is "that the supreme principle must be supremely venerated"; the second, "that the supreme truth must be supremely believed and assented to"; and the third, "that the supreme good must be supremely desired (*desiderandum*) and loved (*diligendum*)." "And these," say Bonaventure, "are on the first tablet; and in them wisdom appears, for they are so certain, that they cannot be otherwise."⁴⁷

Some explanation is in order. By "the first tablet," Bonaventure is referring to the first tablet of the Ten Commandments. Recall from our discussion above that, in his *Collations on the Ten Commandments*, Bonaventure argued that the first tablet commandments order us in our relationship to God. He then associated each of the first three commandments with one of the three Persons of the Trinity. To the Father, to whom should be attributed "the highest majesty," we are ordered by the commandment "You shall not have strange gods" that "the supreme principle must be supremely venerated." To the Son, to whom should be attributed supreme truth, we are ordered by the commandment "You shall not take the name of the Lord in vain" that "the supreme truth must be supremely believed and assented to." And to the Holy Spirit, to whom should be attributed supreme goodness, we are ordered by the commandment "Remember to keep holy the Sabbath" that "the supreme good must be supremely desire and loved."⁴⁸

It was common in the thirteenth century to associate the two "great commandments" to love God and love one's neighbor as oneself and the Ten Commandments with the fundamental principles of the natural law.⁴⁹ There was disagreement among theologians over which commandment should be considered "self-evident" (*per se nota*) and which were "simple judgments" of which every person was capable, but nearly everyone associated the commandments in one way or another with the natural law.⁵⁰ In this passage, Bonaventure

---

⁴⁵ Ibid., 2.8.
⁴⁶ Ibid.
⁴⁷ Ibid., 2.9.
⁴⁸ Cf. *Coll. de decem.* 1.22.
⁴⁹ Cf., for example, Aquinas's discussion of the Old Law, esp. in ST I–II, q. 100.
⁵⁰ Thomas argued that only the two great commandments to love God and neighbor were *per se nota*. The Ten Commandments, on Aquinas's view, were "simple judgments of which even the

makes clear that he considers all three of the commandments of the first tablet to be "so certain that they cannot be otherwise." He describes these rules as "infallible, indubitable, and unjudgeable because judgment is by them, and not about them." They are also "unchangeable, unrestricted, and unending" and so their wisdom "never fades." For they are "so certain that there is no way to contradict them."[51] The only way to contradict them would be by a higher reason. But since they represent the very highest reason and most certain truth, other truths must be judged in their light and not vice versa. We judge the truth of a proposition in the light of Truth itself, as we judge the goodness of an act in light of Goodness itself.

Wisdom Is Multiform in the Mysteries of the Divine Scriptures

So one form of wisdom, as we have seen, can be found in the divine law, especially the commandments of the first tablet. This association between wisdom and the law was common in the Old Testament, but it was expressed perhaps nowhere more beautifully than in the "wisdom" literature, especially in many of the Psalms, the Proverbs, the Book of Wisdom, Sirach, and the Song of Songs (cf. esp. Psalms 19 and 119).

Whereas, on Bonaventure's account, the many parts of the divine law express a uniform wisdom, the divine Scriptures also contain multiple senses. Along with the literal sense, there were the allegorical, anagogical, and tropological senses. The wisdom of the Scriptures was so great, says Bonaventure, it was necessary that the wisdom be revealed "in many figure, many Sacraments, and many signs."[52] Yet, while multiple senses were needed to *reveal* Christ, they also *veiled* Him from the proud. Just as the Son revealed Himself in and through Christ's flesh, but that flesh also veiled Him from the proud who refused to accept that God could lower Himself to become fully human, so too the multiple senses of Scripture both reveal Christ to the humble, but also veil Him from the proud.

Why *three* senses? Because, says Bonaventure, following a common medieval tradition, the Scriptures teach what is to be believed, what is to be expected, and what is to be done. Allegory teaches what is to be believed in faith; anagogy teaches what is to be expected in hope; and tropology teaches what is to be done in charity.[53] And as importantly, there is a certain *beauty* in all this – a beauty meant to draw us to itself in love as the beauty of the bride draws her spouse. God's wisdom appears "most beautifully" in these divine mysteries, says Bonaventure, "even more than the first way" of uniform wisdom.

> Just as, for example, I wish to praise the bride because she is beautiful, she is truthful; if I simply say, 'she is beautiful, she is truthful,' my heart is not affected much. But when I say: 'Your cheeks are beautiful as the turtledove's, your neck like jewels' (Song 1:9), I commend her wonderfully, provided I understand. For I commend her not only as chaste and honest, but because, on account of the love (*amorem*) for the bridegroom, she is chaste and loveable (*amorosa*). For the turtledove is a chaste and loving (*amorosa*) bird, because, out of love (*amorem*) for her mate, she does not conjoin with another while he is living, nor after his

unlearned were capable." See ST I–II, q. 100, esp. aa. 1, 3, and 11. For more, see also my article, "What the Old Law Reveals about the Natural Law according to Thomas Aquinas," *The Thomist*, vol. 75, no. 1 (January 2011): 95–139.

[51] *Coll. in Hex.* 2.10.
[52] Ibid., 2.8 and 2.11–19.
[53] Ibid., 2.13.

death. Thus, a bride is honorable not because she is chaste, but because she is chaste on account of love (*amorem*) for her spouse.[54]

We might take this argument as an explanation of why Bonaventure feels justified inserting lively images and metaphors into his works at various points. His goal is not merely to illuminate the mind, but to move the heart. The beauty of the images is meant to inspire a loving desire in the reader. These too are meant to serve the "protreptic" aims of the text: to draw its readers to the wisdom it proclaims and move their hearts to embrace the discipline required to attain it.

Wisdom Is Omniform in the Vestiges of the Divine Works

Because it is "diffused in everything" (*diffusa est in omni re*), and since "everything possesses a rule of wisdom and displays divine wisdom," those earnestly searching for wisdom can find it in many places – potentially everywhere.[55] Bonaventure sets out to show that wisdom can be found in the "vestiges of the divine works" by setting out three divisions, each of which will have its own threefold subdivision. (I have provided an outline in Box 18.1.)

"Now the work of God is expressed in three ways," says Bonaventure: first in terms of "essence" (*essentia*), whatever a thing is, in whatever genus; second in terms of "completed essence" (*essentia completa*), namely substance alone (*sola substantia*); and third in terms of "essence made in the image of God" (*essentia ad imaginem Dei facta*). This last is the mode of essence one finds in spiritual creatures, such as human beings.[56] Some explanation is in order regarding each.

We consider, first, "essence" (*essentia*). There is a certain order in things, says Bonaventure, for God creates every essence according to *measure, number, and weight* (Wisdom 11:20). By "measure" is meant a thing's "mode" (*modum*) or "that by which it exists" (*quo constat*); by "number" is meant a thing's "species" (*speciem*) or "that by which it is distinct" (*discernitur*); and by "weight" is meant its "order" (*ordinem*) in the sense of "that to which it is ordered" or "that with which it is 'fitting'" (*congruit*).[57] So everything that exists has (1) that by which it exists, (2) that which distinguishes it from other things, and (3) that end to which by its nature it is ordered. It is in this threefold character of existing things that Bonaventure finds "vestiges" leading to the highest Wisdom: knowledge of the Triune God.[58]

So too, one finds another vestige of this Wisdom in "completed essence" (*essentia completa*) or "substance alone" (*sola substantia*). If we consider a substance in and of itself (rather than its mode, species, and order, as we did earlier), we can consider the substance, its power, and its operation, since power depends upon substance, and operation upon both substance and power. A thing receives its being (*esse*) from substance, its survival from power, and its efficacy from operation.[59] And these too can teach us something important about the Triune God. As Bonaventure writes:

---

[54] Ibid., 2.18.
[55] Ibid., 2.21.
[56] Ibid., 2.22.
[57] I have altered the English translation slightly here.
[58] *Coll. in Hex.* 2.23.
[59] Ibid., 2.26.

> **Box 18.1** An Outline of the Discussion of Wisdom in Collation 2
>
> I. To whom he should address his speech? Church [covered in Collation 1]
> II. From where he should begin it? Its origin: Christ [covered in Collation 1]
> III. Where he should end it? Its purpose: Wisdom
>   A. Origin: the Father of Lights
>   B. House: wisdom makes the soul the house of God
>   C. Door: an eager desire for wisdom
>   D. Form
>   1. Uniform: the divine laws
>   2. Multi-form: the multiple senses of Scripture
>   3. Every-form: vestiges in the divine works
>   a. *Essentia*
>   i. Matter ⎫
>   ii. Form ⎬ Trinity
>   iii. Composite
>   b. *Essentia Completa*
>   i. Substance ⎫
>   ii. Power ⎬ Trinity
>   iii. Operation
>   c. *Essentia ad imaginem Dei facta*:
>   i. Likeness of nature
>   (a) Memory
>   (b) Understanding ⎬ Trinity
>   (c) Will
>   ii. Likeness of grace
>   (a) Immorality
>   (b) Understanding ⎬ Trinity
>   (c) Joy
>   4. No Form: Negative Theology

Now in substance there is a higher vestige that represents the divine essence. For every created substance has matter, form, and composition; the original principle or foundation, the formal complement, and the bond (*glutinum*). It has substantial existence (*substantiam*), power (*virtutem*), and operation (*operationem*). And in these the mystery of the Trinity is represented: the Father as the origin (*origo*), the Son as the image (*imago*), and the Holy Spirit as the bond (*compago*).[60]

---

[60] Ibid., 2, 23. Étienne Gilson provides a nice exposition of Bonaventure's position in *The Philosophy of St. Bonaventure*, trans. Trethowan and Sheed (Paterson, NJ: St. Anthony Guild Press, 1965), 193–194: "Whatever corporeal body we consider, its essence will show immediately that God has created everything according to the triple law of measure, order, and weight ... For the body possesses a certain external dimension which is it measure, a certain internal order of parts which is its number and a certain movement resulting from an inclination which impels it as weight impels the body. But we can penetrate more deeply into the very substance of this body; before possessing

Yet, Bonaventure is careful to distinguish between the "vestige" leading us back to God and God Himself. Although the threefold division "matter," "form," and "composite" is a "vestige" of the Trinity, Bonaventure carefully distinguishes this threefold distinction in things from the very different threefold distinction between the Father, Son, and Holy Spirit. In created things, matter, form, and composite are three *principles*, not three *hypostases* or *persons*, as in the Triune God. The threefold principle we find in things are *vestiges* of the Trinity, but they still fall infinitely short of God as He is in His fullness.[61]

We turn, finally, to *essentia ad imaginem Dei facta*, the essence of those beings made in the image or likeness of God. This likeness can be a likeness human beings have either by nature or by grace. By nature, human beings made in the likeness of God have memory, intelligence, and will: the three powers of the mind that St. Augustine had famously used in *De trinitate* as an image of the Triune God.[62] According to Bonaventure, when the soul receives likeness not only by nature, but also by grace, it receives immortality, understanding, and joy: immortality, in that eternity is held in memory; wisdom, in that truth shines forth in understanding; joy, in that goodness gives pleasure to the will. And in these two sets of three, Bonaventure believes he has found yet more "vestiges" of the Triune God.[63]

Summing up Bonaventure's position so far, we can say that the cosmos, since it was made by God, is imbued in the very fabric of its being with a Trinitarian character. Bonaventure's metaphysical and physical claims about the cosmos being a "mirror" of the Trinity are in accord with the biblical notion that human creation and human redemption are deeply intertwined with the creation and redemption of the whole cosmos. On this view, human beings are not totally *separate from* nature and the natural order. Rather, we are fundamentally *united to* it and in our own way *responsible for* it. The order of the cosmos should teach us and lead us to God. What often happens, however, is that our disordered souls bring about disorder not only within ourselves and in our relations with other humans, but also in our relationship with nature. With grace, however, the proper order of our souls can be

---

weight, number, and measure, which are so many vestiges of God corresponding to appropriate attributes, this body possesses being or substance, considered under their most general and least determinate aspect, shadows of the primary Being from Whom they derive. Now if we allow the light of faith to illumine our reason, with what richness will this distant shadow seem to us to be filled! Every being is defined and determined by an essence; and every essence in its turn is constituted by the concurrence of three principles: matter, form, and the composition of matter with form. What is corporeal creation necessarily constituted to this type? There would seem to be no *a priori* reason, and the internal structure of the beings which made up the universe would remain unexplained unless we remembered what faith teaches us about the primary essence, the origin of all the essences and the model which they are constituted to imitate. It is in God first of all that this unity in trinity appears. An original principle or foundation of being, a formal complement to this principle and a bond that unites them (God, Who is the origin, the Son, Who is the image, the Holy Spirit, Who is love and intercourse between Them), this internal order which constitutes the divine essence has become the very law which controls the internal economy of created bodies."

[61] On this, see my comments below about the importance of apophatic or "negative" theology in sections 28 through 34 of the second collation.
[62] Cf. Augustine, *On the Trinity* 10.8–12.
[63] *Coll. in Hex.* 2.27.

restored, so that with our memory, we can be mindful of the immortality to which we are called; with our intelligence, we can attain the understanding of truth that brings wisdom; and with our will, we can do the good that bring lasting joy.

"No Form" and Negative Theology

Bonaventure has dilated up to this point only three of the four subdivisions under the "form" of wisdom: uniform, multiform, and omniform. He still must say something about "no form at all" (*nulliformis*). According to Bonaventure, this fourth face of wisdom, "without form," is the most difficult and yet is "the highest state of achievement of Christian wisdom."[64] To open himself up to this wisdom, man must free himself of all the categories he uses in normal life because the Trinity is above any substance or knowledge our intelligence can perceive. So too, it transcends every power of the soul, whether sensitive, imaginative, estimative, or intellective.[65]

This contemplation comes about through grace and results in a supreme union of love which divides, puts to sleep, and lifts up. It *divides* because it cuts a person away from any other love because of the single love for the Spouse. It *puts to sleep* because it appeases all the intellective and imaginative powers and imposes silence. And it *lifts up* because it leads to God.[66] In this union the mind is joined to God whereby in a certain sense it sleeps, while in another it keeps vigil. The affective power keeps vigil, and imposes silence upon all the other powers.[67] Then man becomes foreign to his senses, and he enters into an ecstatic union with God above words or conceptions.[68] Carried above all words and conceptions, all sense and imagination, one enters what Bonaventure describes as "the radiance of darkness" (*tenebrarum radium*), a state we call "darkness" because the intellect cannot grasp it, even though "the soul is supremely illumined (*anima summe illustratur*).[69]

Like Pseudo-Dionysius before him, Bonaventure claims that this ascent of the mind to God comes about both by affirmation and negation.[70] Yet, after all of Bonaventure's dedicated efforts to show how, by way of affirmation, one can find the "vestiges" of the Trinity spread throughout all of creation, it is interesting to find him here proclaiming that the way of negation is superior.[71] "Love is always preceded by negation," he tells his young

---

[64] Ibid., 2.28–29.
[65] Ibid., 2.29. We might describe this as Bonaventure's version of the "dark night of the soul."
[66] *Coll. in Hex.* 2.31. Bonaventure also suggests that this sleep signifies the death of Christ, the burial of Christ, the passage of the Red Sea, and the entrance into the Promised Land. *Coll. in Hex.* 2.34.
[67] *Coll. in Hex.* 2.30.
[68] Ibid.
[69] Ibid., 2.32.
[70] Ibid., 2.33. Cf. Pseudo-Dionysius, *Mystical Theology*, esp. chapter 3.
[71] It is worth noting the difference between Bonaventure's approach and Thomas's. Thomas also affirms the way of affirmation and negation, but then offers the way of analogy as well. Cf., for example, Aquinas, I *Sent.* d. 19, q. 5 and ST I, q. 13. Bonaventure's notion of "analogy," however, is very different from Aquinas's; it is related to his notion that one can find hidden "vestiges" of the Trinity spread throughout creation. On this, see the chapter in Gilson's *Philosophy of St. Bonaventure* on "Universal Analogy," pp. 185–214.

friars. This for Bonaventure is signified by Moses separating himself from the elders before going up the mountain to meet God; it can be understood by analogy with a sculptor lovingly crafting an image by taking away bits of stone until the sculpture is just as he conceived of it in his mind.[72]

Bonaventure shows himself here to be a faithful proponent of apophatic or "negative" theology of the sort usually associated with John of the Cross's *Dark Night of the Soul* or the fourteenth-century *Cloud of Unknowing*. But two passages in this section provide important correctives. In the first, he notes that, although this fourth "face of wisdom" (the "nulliform") is the highest, it does not destroy the other faces of wisdom he elaborated earlier. In the second, he relates the legend that "Dionysius wrote many books" but stopped (*consummavit*) with the *Mystical Theology*. The conclusion he draws from this story is not that the other approaches to wisdom are unimportant. Rather "it is necessary that a man be instructed in many things and in everything that comes before."[73] So although Bonaventure here lauds the supreme value of negative theology, he does not do so at the expense of positive theology. On Bonaventure's account, a person must possess a firm grasp of what can intelligently be affirmed before he can "negate" it intelligently.[74]

Collation 3: "and Understanding"

The third collation begins with the same *thema* verse as the first two: "In the midst of the Church the Lord shall open his mouth, and shall fill him with the spirit of wisdom and understanding and shall clothe him with a robe of glory" (Eccli. 15:5), indicating to the listener or reader that we are still in the "prologue" section of the *Collations*. Thus far, Bonaventure has dilated these words from his opening *thema*:

In the midst of the Church: To whom should the prudent man address himself? The Church (Collation 1)

the Lord shall open his mouth: Where should the prudent man begin? With Christ (Collation 1)

and shall fill him with the spirit of wisdom: origin, dwelling, door, and forms of wisdom (Collation 2)

---

[72] *Coll. in Hex.* 2.33.
[73] Ibid., 2.29.
[74] One can, therefore, affirm of St. Bonaventure what Thomas Merton says of Saint John of the Cross" in *The Ascent to Truth* (New York: Harcourt, Brace & Company, 1951), 144–146: "It is clear, then, that if Saint John of the Cross was severe in criticizing incompetent teachers and directors it was precisely because he realized the importance of sound teaching and spiritual direction. It is true that God Himself, and God alone, forms contemplatives and makes men saints. It is true that the mystic is guided in a sacred, personal, and intimate way by the inspirations of the Holy Ghost. Nevertheless, God does not normally teach us the ways of interior prayer without making use of other men... No matter how solitary a man may be, if he is a contemplative his contemplation has something of a social character. He receives it through the Church. The teaching of the Church is therefore not an evil which the contemplative must bear patiently as a test of his humility. It is the solid nourishment of his whole interior life..."

The key word left in the opening *thema* he has not yet dilated is *understanding*. And sure enough, here in Collation 3, Bonaventure discusses how "understanding" is a key to achieving "wisdom" (the subject of Collation 2). As before, Bonaventure will proceed by making a series of divisions and distinctions. And as before, it is important to keep the order of things clear in one's mind in order to keep Bonaventure's discussion from becoming a disconnected series of unrelated categories.

Bonaventure explains at the beginning of this collation that the "understanding" to which he is referring is the understanding that comes as the gift of the Holy Spirit, of which he had spoken previously in his *Collations on the Seven Gifts of the Holy Spirit*.[75] The remainder of the collation is governed by a basic threefold division. According to Bonaventure, wisdom is fostered by a threefold understanding: (1) of the Uncreated Word by whom all things are brought forth; (2) of the Incarnate Word by whom all things are restored; and (3) of the Inspired Word by whom all things are revealed.[76] As is customary, there are several subdivisions under each.

In his consideration of the wisdom gained by understanding *the Uncreated Word by who all things were brought forth*, Bonaventure argues:

1. That "God's everlasting power and divinity are understood through their effect, since God is the Cause of things, and all things are made by this power" (section 3).
2. That the Uncreated Word represents the Father's power, which is one, but infinite; hence this likeness properly represents infinite things. If, therefore, you understand the Word, you understand all understandable things (section 4).
3. That because the first intellect is an active principle, it is necessary that it dispose and express all things in the likeness of itself (section 5).
4. That all temporal things proceed from an Eternal Being (section 6).
5. That possible or material things are made by the "most actual" (*actualissimo*) (section 7).
6. That a thing is true in so far as there is a correspondence (*adequatio*) between one's understanding (*intellectus*) and the thing understood (*intellectae*), but in the case of something *caused* by God, a thing is true insofar as it corresponds to the understanding (*intellectui*) causing it (section 8).

Bonaventure's summary and conclusion is this: "And so it is clear that possible things are from the most actual, changeable things from the most stable, and the lowest from the highest. And just as the shining sun produces a variety and multiformity of colors, so from this Word there is a variety of things. Hence one does not come to understand (*intelligere*) except through the Word" – that is to say, we come to *understand* through the Uncreated Word by whom all things were made (section 9).

Next, Bonaventure considers the understanding we gain from considering *the Incarnate Word by whom all things are restored*. To achieve this cosmic restoration of all things, Christ must:

1. Be preeminent in power (section 13)
2. Be endowed with a threefold awareness according to the threefold wisdom within Him: the *innate*, by which he knows all things which we are able to know by mental habit; the

---

[75] *Coll. in Hex.* 3.1.
[76] Ibid., 3.2.

infused, by which he comprehends gloriously and infinitely because his wisdom has no limit; and the *eternal*, by which he comprehends all things (sections 14–16)
3. Be acceptable to God (section 17)
4. Be totally victorious (section 18)
5. Be most generous (sections 19–20)
6. Be supremely just (section 21)

Finally, near the end of this collation, Bonaventure considers "the third key," which is the understanding which comes from considering *the Inspired Word through whom all things are revealed*, "for there is no revelation (*revelatio*) except through the inspired Word."[77] Revelations usually come through words or visions, notes Bonaventure. And generally speaking, there are three kinds of vision: the bodily (*corporalis*), the imaginary (*imaginaria*), and the intellectual (*intellectualis*).[78] The first two have no value without the third. So the corporal vision of the handwriting on the wall was of little value to Belshazzar (Daniel 5:1–31), nor was the imaginary vision in a dream of the statue of gold, silver, brass, and clay of value to Nebuchadnezzar (Daniel 2:1–46, without Daniel to interpret for them. What, then, of the third vision, the "intellectual" vision, the vision of "understanding" (*intelligentiae*)? This is where the plot thickens.

Recall that at the end of many prologues, one finds a *divisio textus* of the book to be commented upon. So too, as we have seen, it was not uncommon for an author to provide a *divisio textus* of his own work. Bonaventure provides just such a *divisio textus* of the remaining collations at the end of this three-collation "prologue." Having completed his protreptic exhortation to Christian wisdom and understanding in which he showed that in Christ "are hidden all the treasures of God's wisdom and knowledge" (*scientiae*), and that Christ himself is the center (*medium*) of all the sciences (*scientiarum*),"[79] Bonaventure's task now was to provide his audience with a suitable outline of what was to come.

As we have seen, Bonaventure liked making lists – divisions and subdivisions filled with terms he could dilate in the sections following. Sometimes those lists were threefold lists, especially when Bonaventure wanted to associate the items on the list with the Trinity. But it would be a mistake to claim, as some have done, that Bonaventure *always* used threefold lists. He would use lists of two, three, four, or more depending on the context. So, for example, here, Bonaventure will make a sixfold *divisio* of this third type of vision, the "intellectual" vision or vision of "understanding" (*intelligentiae*).

There is, first, "the vision of understanding (*intelligentiae*) implanted by nature" (*per naturam inditae*); second, the vision of understanding "lifted up by faith" (*per fidem sublevatae*); third, the vision of understanding "taught by Scripture" (*per Scripturam eruditae*); fourth, the vision of understanding "suspended by contemplation" (*per contemplationem suspensae*); fifth, the vision of understanding "enlightened by prophecy" (*per prophetiam illustratae*); and sixth, the vision of understanding "absorbed into God by rapture (*per raptum in Deum absorptae*). Following these six, there is a seventh vision of the glorified soul (*animae*)..."[80] The first two kinds of understanding – the kind implanted by nature and the kind lifted up by

---

[77] Ibid., 3.22.
[78] Ibid.
[79] Ibid., 1.11.
[80] Ibid., 3.24.

faith – are found among the many. The next two – the kind taught by Scripture and the kind suspended by contemplation – are found among only a few. And the final two – the kind of understanding enlightened by prophecy and absorbed into God by rapture – are found among only a very few. Organizing the list this way – in order of "good, better, best" – was a characteristic method of *sermo modernus*–style preaching.[81]

So where does Bonaventure dilate these six subdivisions? Answer: in the remaining twenty collations. Such was Bonaventure's rather ingenious transition from his extended three-collation "protreptic" prologue into the body of the text. In the remaining collations, Bonaventure intended to associate each of these "visions of understanding" with one of the six days of creation – a nice mnemonic device. We will have more to say about this association with the "six days" in a moment. But two comments are in order at this point.

The first is simply to remind the reader that Bonaventure did not finish dilating all six subdivisions, all six "days." The *Collations on the Six Days* was left unfinished when Bonaventure was called away to the Second Council of Lyon. He only got as far as the fourth "day."

The other detail perhaps worth mentioning is this. One might have expected Bonaventure to associate these six "visions" he associates with each of the six "days" of creation with the understanding we get from *the Uncreated Word by whom all things are created* rather than, as he does here, the understanding we get from *the Inspired Word by whom all things are revealed* (see *Coll. in Hex.* 3.2). One way of accounting for this anomaly would be to claim that, yes, this was an error, but a minor one in what is obviously a complex schema of divisions and subdivisions. This is possible, but I prefer another explanation. Bonaventure's choice here makes more sense if we remember that the biblical account of the "six days" of creation are part of divine revelation. They are "signs" needing to be "interpreted" just as the visions given to Belshazzar and Nebuchadnezzar had to be interpreted by Daniel. The role of Daniel here is filled by Bonaventure, who interprets the signs for his audience and show them the deeper meaning to be found in the *visions* of the six "days."

The "Visions" of the Six "Days"

When Bonaventure begins with the vision of the first "day," the locution he uses is "through the first [day], we understand ..." (*per primam intelligitur ...*). With all such associations, their value is based upon the order and structure they provide to help the audience retain in their memory all the categories Bonaventure introduces. The trick is to make associations that help listeners use the bits of the creation account they have memorized to recollect the points he makes in the collations.

So, for example, according to Bonaventure's schema, the "vision" of the first day represents the light of understanding we are given by nature, a "light" that he associates with the light of the first day of creation when God says, "Let there be light."[82] Just as the light created on the first day is in the foundation for all the days that follow – there being no

---

[81] See method 5 of the eight methods of *dilatatio* listed in Chapter 2.
[82] *Coll. in Hex.* 3.24.

possibility of "evening" and "morning" to distinguish the "days" without it – so too, without this light of understanding imparted to man naturally, there would be no possibility of any further, more developed understanding by faith, grace, or the illumination of wisdom.[83]

On the second day, God made a firmament in the midst of the waters, dividing the waters above from the waters below. "This firmament is faith," says Bonaventure, and it "divides the waters from the waters." What does this mean? As "the firmament" is a foundation supporting the waters above, separating them from the waters below, so also faith is "the origin of wisdom and the origin of knowledge, whether of eternal or of temporal things." And just as the firmament "divides" and, by distinguishing, makes the distinct existence of the waters above and waters below, so too faith distinguishes authentic wisdom and knowledge from illusory because, insists Bonaventure, "neither knowledge nor wisdom can disagree with faith."[84]

The third day is when the waters were gathered together and dry land appeared. The land is Sacred Scripture, says Bonaventure, which has spiritual meanings that bring forth *living vegetation* and *the tree of life*. And yet everyone should also beware the other tree, the tree of pride that brings our downfall, "the tree of curiosity of knowledge" (*a ligno curiositatis scientiae*).[85]

On the fourth day, God created the sun, the moon, and the stars: the "greater light to rule the day" and "the lesser lights to rule the night." These "lights" represent the wisdom gained through contemplation: the sun, the contemplation of the super-heavenly hierarchy; the moon, the contemplation of the sub-heavenly hierarchy; and the stars, the contemplation of the heavenly hierarchy.[86]

On the fifth day, God created the birds of the air and the fish of the sea. The fifth vision comes about, says Bonaventure "through understanding enlightened by prophecy" (*per prophetiam illustratae intelligentiae*).[87] Enlightened in this way, the true prophet can see even contingent matters infallibly and with certainty. One can associate this sort of vision with the fifth day, because birds were created on the fifth day, and when the understanding is enlightened by prophecy, the soul is carried upward to God as birds are carried upward by the breeze under their wings.[88]

The sixth day saw the creation of mankind when God said: "Let us make mankind in Our image and likeness." The sixth vision, says Bonaventure, is that of understanding absorbed by rapture in God (*intelligentiae per raptum in Deum absorptae*), a lifting up of the soul that makes it as similar to God as is possible in our present state of pilgrimage. As mankind is said to have "dominion over the fish of the sea, the birds of the air ... and every creature that crawls upon the earth," so too "a man who has attained such a state may order and command other men, as did Paul." Yet, the higher a man is lifted up, warns Bonaventure, the humbler he must be, which is why Paul was given a "thorn in the flesh"

---

[83] Ibid., 3.25.
[84] Ibid., 3.26.
[85] Ibid., 3.27.
[86] Ibid., 3.28.
[87] A more faithful translation might be "through the prophecy of an illumined intelligence."
[88] *Coll. in Hex.* 3.29.

to keep him humble. For had he become proud, even Paul would have "lost grace and fallen into a reprobate sense" (*amittere gratiam et cadere in reprobum sensum*).[89]

The seventh day was the day of God's rest. And as this day had no evening, so it corresponds to man's eternal rest after death.

So let's review, recalling that Bonaventure would have been speaking to an audience that would have had committed to memory the items created on each of the "days" of creation mentioned in Genesis 1.

1. "Light" was created on the first day, so the first "vision" is the light of understanding we are given by nature.
2. The firmament was created on the second day, dividing the waters above from the waters below. This firmament is faith, which is the origin of both wisdom and knowledge, whether of eternal or temporal things.
3. The dry land and its vegetation were created on the third day. The land is Sacred Scripture, which has spiritual meanings that bring forth *living vegetation* and *the tree of life*.
4. The sun, the moon, and the stars were created on the fourth day. The sun represents the contemplation of the super-heavenly hierarchy; the moon, the contemplation of the sub-heavenly hierarchy; and the stars, the contemplation of the heavenly hierarchy.
5. The fish and birds were created on the fifth day. And just as birds are carried upward by the breeze under their wings, from which vantage point they can see more widely and yet with "eagle eyes" notice a small mouse in a field, so too, in this fifth "vision," understanding, enlightened by prophecy, is carried upward toward God, from which height of understanding one can see even contingent matters infallibly and with certainty within the context of the divine truth.
6. On the sixth day, mankind was created in God's image and likeness, so the sixth "vision" is that of understanding absorbed by rapture in God. As mankind is granted dominion over all the other creatures, so too a man who has attained this state may order and command others as St. Paul did; albeit, such a person must also remain humble.

In this manner, a complex hierarchical schema of different categories of understanding can be recalled simply by associating each category of understanding with one of the days of creation.

Now, as we have said, Bonaventure did not finish developing his thoughts on all six "days." He discussed the vision of the first day in Collations 4 through 7; the second vision of the second day in Collations 8 through 12; the third vision of the third day in Collations 13 through 19; and the fourth vision of the fourth day in Collations 20 through 23. After Collation 23, we find an epilogue by the compiler of the manuscript, who admits: "There still remains the fifth vision proposed in the beginning of the work, namely, the vision of understanding elevated by the spirit of prophesy, and "there is also the sixth vision proposed in the beginning, that is, the vision of understanding absorbed into God through the mind's rapture (*raptum mentis*)." To these was to be added "the final vision, the "vision of understanding consummated in the state of glory, when there comes about a return of the soul (*animae*) to the body, covering what and how it will see in this state of glory."

---

[89] Ibid., 3.30.

"These three visons would have exceeded the first four," writes the author of this epilogue, "but alas, alas, as a higher state and an excess of life overcame the lord and master, they did not permit him to continue this work."[90]

As we have seen, Bonaventure never lost his expertise in the use of the *sermo modernus* style, nor his mastery at writing protreptic prologues. Quite the contrary, he continued the practice of crafting complex prologues throughout his career. Indeed, in this his final work, we find what in many ways is his longest and most complex prologue, extending over three full collations. Hence it would not be accurate to say that Bonaventure "freed himself" from the patterns of his university education and developed a mode of expression "wholly alien to the language of the schools." If by this one meant only that, later in his life, Bonaventure no longer composed treatises in the style of the "disputed question," then this is certainly true. But the "disputed question" was not the only "language" or "pattern" of the schools. The language and patterns of the *sermo modernus* style were also a characteristic element of the training at Paris, and Bonaventure was one of its most adept and creative practitioners.

---

[90] Ibid., Epilogue.

19

Summary and Concluding Remarks

WHAT, IN my view, has this study shown? And what conclusions may we draw? There are several but allow me to gather them under five separate headings. In the first section below, I recapitulate the evidence showing the importance attached to the practice of *sermo modernus*–style preaching in the thirteenth-century Latin Church and how the educational program that arose at the University of Paris supported and sustained it.

In the second section, I review the habits of mind that would have been inculcated in thirteenth-century students by their need to compose *sermo modernus*–style prologues and sermons. These skills were not *contrary to* the skills they brought to the practice of disputation, but they were not the same. Preachers were warned not to sound like a disputation. Rather the two practices worked in tandem, sometimes supporting each other, sometimes the one modifying the other.

In the third section, I summarize how the examples of Bonaventure and Aquinas show us that a single university curriculum can produce two very different scholars, exhibiting many similar *formal* habits, but very different theological styles.

At the end of this chapter, I make some comments about how an increased understanding and appreciation of thirteenth century preaching can and should help us reconsider certain narrow, outdated notions of "scholasticism."

And finally, I make some comments about how difficult it is to achieve the proper balance between the sometimes rarefied, "academic" concerns that animate the practice of disputation and the more "popular," "pastoral" concerns that must animate the practice of preaching.

In Addition to Disputation, a Culture of Preaching, *Principia*, and Biblical Commentary

The thirteenth century saw a tremendous increase of interest in preaching; this much is clear from the tremendous increase in model sermon collections and in the production of materials to aid preachers during the century. The major center of this reform and the place that produced the most preaching material was Paris. The recently founded Dominican and Franciscan orders played a major role in this "homiletic revolution" of the thirteenth century, especially in preaching to the newly educated class of lay men and women increasingly populating the towns of western Europe.

The *sermo modernus* or "modern sermon" style arose in and around Paris but became popular and dominant throughout the Western Latin Church. Indeed, it became the standard style for preaching for the next 150 to 200 years. Instead of a line-by-line exegesis of the text, the "modern sermon" was based on a single Bible verse, a *thema*, which the preacher would "divide" into several parts and then associate each part with the subjects he wished to address. The process by which each word or sentence fragment from the original *thema* verse was expanded into the content of the sermon was called "dilation" or *dilatatio*. There were many methods of dilating a word or phrase, and medieval preachers used them all. In these "modern sermons," identifying the allegorical, tropological, or anagogical meaning of a text became just another mode of dilating a word or phrase along with the many others.

The *sermo modernus* style, by associating the content of the sermon with the words in a single phrase, helped the listeners recall the content of the sermon. If they called to mind the original *thema* verse, they could recall the points the preacher had associated with each word or phrase. This style of preaching was a concrete expression of how important the arts of memory were considered during the Middle Ages.

Learning to preach in the *sermo modernus* style and doing so repeatedly helped develop and strengthen within the preacher certain mental habits, especially the ability to make sensible and meaningful divisions and sub-divisions of a text, and a special sensitivity to the possible meanings and uses of a word. Since dividing and subdividing was the bread-and-butter of medieval biblical commentary, young bachelors at the University of Paris would have had extensive lessons in how to divide and subdivide in each course they took on a book of the Bible and in each course they taught as a *lector biblicus*. Collections of biblical *distinctiones* cataloguing ten, fifteen, or twenty possible uses of a word would have helped train them to distinguish continually various possible meanings of words and the connotations they can take on; as when the same word, "lion," can refer either to the nobility of a king or to a ravenous and dangerous man-eater, or when the flight of birds can refer to angels or to the tumult of evil thoughts.

The University of Paris envisioned itself as a place for training thoughtful, orthodox theologians and interesting, articulate preachers. Preaching was considered important at Paris, and students had to prove they were improving in the skill to progress in their studies. The three duties of the master were said to be preaching, lecturing, and disputing, with preaching often considered the end or goal of the other two: the "roof" of the house sitting on the walls and foundation. The inception ceremony for masters of theology at Paris required them to demonstrate all three skills of the master, but at the heart of the ceremony was a sermon in praise of Sacred Scripture called the master's *principium*.

The word *principium* was used for (1) this inception address; (2) the first lecture of the term; and (3) the prologue of a commentary, mostly biblical, but prologues were also written for other important texts, such as Peter Lombard's *Sentences* and Boethius's *De Trinitate*. The "prologues" or "proemia" that appeared with the published version of the commentary was a written version of the *principium* lecture from the opening day of class, and the inception *principium* was modeled on this first lecture of the term.

The *principium* delivered verbally to students at the commencement of the term (and the written version of the same that appeared thereafter at the university stationers for copying), was meant to serve the purposes of the classical philosophical protreptic. It was an exhortation to the listener, arguing for the superior wisdom of the text and urging the reader to prepare himself not only intellectually, but morally and spiritually to become a worthy vessel to receive the wisdom of the text. The master or *lector biblicus* would also commonly provide a *divisio textus* of the book upon which he was commenting to help the students begin the process of analytical reading. Since the master's inception *principium* was not on a particular book of the Bible, the assignment was to craft an encomium to the Scriptures as a whole and provide a *divisio textus* of the books in both the Old and New Testaments.

There is plenty of evidence in these Parisian biblical commentaries to suggest that they were composed with an eye toward training future preachers. We do not know exactly how preaching was taught at Paris, although there is evidence that some early instruction in preaching was given in the convent to those in religious orders. We know that bachelors were required to preach at least one sermon and one *collatio* per year, but we have no evidence that the university sponsored specific instruction in preaching to help students meet this requirement. And yet preaching in the *sermo modernus*-style seems too complex a task and too important a university duty to have been entrusted to the caprices of the bachelor himself to learn on his own.

I have argued that a key method used to train bachelors to preach in the *sermo modernus* style (besides regular attendance at the sermons of other preachers) included requiring them to write numerous *principia* using the *sermo modernus* style. Bachelors were required to compose a *principium* for every course they taught as a *lector biblicus*. And even though they were not required to preach during the years they were working on their *Sentences* commentary, they continued to write prologues for each book of their commentary. Writing *sermo modernus*–style prologues was a regular practice, one that would have helped prepare them for the educated and well-formed sermons they would be asked to deliver to the increasingly educated congregations the friars were encountering in the towns and cities of Europe.

Because so much of the curriculum at Paris – whether lecturing on the Bible or engaging in disputations – was directed at the goal of producing good preachers and preaching, I have described the University of Paris as having a "culture of preaching." Listening to preaching was stipulated to be a regular, twice-daily part of the life of the student – at the morning's sermon and at the evening's *collatio*. Bachelors were also required to show their proficiency at preaching at least once per year. And one of the major tests of a master's skill was the delivery at his inception of a good *principium* in the *sermo modernus* style.

All three types of *principia* at Paris – the master's inception address, the protreptic sermon delivered at the beginning of each term, and the written prologue – were all composed in the *sermo modernus* style. Writing *principia* in this manner was a standard university practice and had become by the time Thomas and Bonaventure were bachelors at Paris a "form" or "genre" of its own. Thomas and Bonaventure both used the form and observed its strictures when they were addressing university audiences, both early on their careers at the University of Paris and again years later near the end of their careers. But they did not always use this same form when it wasn't required. Both continued to write prologues that shared many features of the strict *sermo modernus*–style prologues, such as crafting frequent threefold or fourfold lists of divisions and subdivisions and "chaining" together Bible passages, but they did not always follow the practice of starting with a biblical *thema* verse, dividing it, and then associating each subsequent section with a separate part of this opening *thema*.

Preaching Methods Developed Certain Habits of Mind

I have argued that repeatedly wiring prologues and preaching sermons in the *sermo modernus* style developed certain habits of mind that bore fruit in other activities and written works. Note, however, that my argument has *not* been that these habits of mind were formed *only* by writing prologues. Rather, I have claimed that there were certain common habits of mind informing all three skills of the master: preaching, lecturing on the Bible, and disputing. Preaching was by no means the sole factor, but it played its own important role. It helped form the other two duties of the master as it was also formed by them.

The habits of mind a young bachelor or master was likely to gain through the regular practice of preaching and composing *principia* in the *sermo modernus* style would have included

a. *More widespread use of divisions and subdivisions.*

   Thirteenth-century *praedicatio*, *disputatio*, and *lectio* all helped bachelors and masters develop the skill of analyzing texts and arguments into a meaningful set of constituent parts and the ability to see each part in relation to the whole. It also developed in them the predisposition to do so.

b. *Greater attention to the various meanings and potential uses of words in different contexts.*

   The habit of paying attention to the various meanings and potential uses of words, in conjunction with the "subdividing mentality" described earlier, was what enabled an astute master to resolve disputes by cleverly distinguishing one sense of a word from another. Thomas Aquinas is renowned among students of medieval thought for repeatedly using phrases such as "The word 'necessity' is said in many ways" (*necessitas dicitur multipliciter*).[1] A good resolution of a dispute in a *respondeo* often depended upon distinguishing the use and meaning of a word in one context from its use and meaning in another. *Sermo modernus*–style preaching helped form this habit of attending closely to the possible meanings and uses of words because the method entailed dilating long sections of a sermon based on possible uses of a single word or phrase.

c. *Greater awareness of how a creative use of imagery could communicate a doctrinal point more powerfully.*

   We rarely associate the creative and imaginative use of visual imagery with the "scholastics." When we venture beyond the arena of disputed questions, however, to include sermon material and biblical commentary, we find that thirteenth-century masters had lively imaginations and made creative use of imagery. Bonaventure's skill

---

[1] This particular example is taken from ST I, q. 82, Art. 1, but the examples could be multiplied endlessly, so much so that a common joke about Thomas's claim that he wrote the *Summa of Theology* for "beginners" involves the reply, "*beginner* can be said in many ways." This "habit of mind" so characterized the thirteenth century that this intellectual "rule of thumb" seems to have arisen: "Never deny; rarely affirm; always distinguish" (*Numquam negare, raro affirmare, semper distinguere*).

at crafting and manipulating images to communicate theological and doctrinal truths equaled the skill of such twelfth-century notables as Bernard of Clairvaux and Richard of St. Victor. And Thomas Aquinas – not known for writing "imaginative" texts such as Bonaventure's *Itinerarium in Mentis ad Deum*, with its complex image of the six-winged seraphs – even he, when he wrote sermons and prologues, made abundant use of ingenious mnemonic associations and remarkably creative images.[2]

d. *More advanced skill at crafting categories and word associations to allow greater recall.*

As Mary Carruthers has shown in her book on memory in medieval culture, the memory arts were highly valued in the Middle Ages, and trained memory played an important role across the arts: in the composition of music and literature, in architecture and building, the production of manuscripts, and, as we have seen, in preaching and lecturing.[3] It also would have been essential in disputation for keeping mental track of the various objections and responses. The ability to make sensible and meaningful divisions and a decided cleverness at making creative associations were both crucial to the arts of memory, and both featured prominently in *sermo modernus*– style preaching and in university-style *principia*.

Sermo modernus preaching and prologues were structured, organized works, crafted with an eye toward memory and recollection. These habits, skills, and practices of reading and writing in which masters were trained at Paris would bear fruit in Thomas's and Bonaventure's later works, albeit in very different ways.

Bonaventure and Thomas: One University Education, Two Different Styles

In his sermons and prologues, Bonaventure wrote in what I have described as a very "high" literary style, one that his student prologues show he possessed even early-on in his career. By saying his was a "high" literary style, I mean he was able to (and often did) craft lengthy parallel constructions with similar rhythms and which often rhymed. For this reason, I have described him as "the scholastic with the soul of a poet."

Thomas's skill at this art was, by comparison, more rudimentary, especially in his early years as a bachelor. Even dedicated lovers of St. Thomas can admit that his early prologues as a *lector biblicus* pale in comparison to Bonaventure's. And rarely, even in his later prologues, does Thomas exhibit the "high" literary style, with the intricate structure and complex parallel clauses, at which Bonaventure was so adept.

---

[2] For an example of an ingenious set of mnemonic associations, I suggest glancing at the way Thomas was able to associate the four "advents" of Christ with the four uses of the word "*Ecce*" ("Behold") in Sermon 5 (*Ecce rex tuus*). See *Reading the Sermons of Aquinas*, 4–7. And for an example of a creative use of imagery, read Sermon 18 (*Germinet terra*). In it, Thomas takes a single *thema* verse from Genesis 1:11, "Let the earth sprout forth the green plant that brings forth seed, and the fruit tree that bears fruit," and uses the image of the "green plant" in his morning's sermon to praise the Virgin Mary and the image of "the fruit tree that bears fruit" in his evening *collatio* at vespers to speak about Christ's sacrifice on the cross. His use of the imagery in both morning and evening services is both ingenious and beautiful. See *Reading the Sermons of Aquinas*, 70–89.

[3] Mary Carruthers, *The Book of Memory: A Study of Memory in Medieval Culture*, 2nd ed. (Cambridge: Cambridge University Press, 1990, 2008).

Yet, although Thomas never developed the complex, "high" style that Bonaventure enjoyed using, he developed a style of admirable clarity with its own flashes of imaginative genius. (For a good example, see note 2 earlier.) Thomas's special talent was his ability to take complex ideas, concepts, and arguments and present them in a clear, orderly fashion using mostly common terms and basic, sensible distinctions. He had the precision of thought of a great logician, but also the clarity of expression of a great teacher. I have characterized him, therefore, as "the logician who learned to preach."

These two Parisian masters were like two varieties of Italian grapevines grown in the same soil at the University of Paris. That soil in which they both grew imparted to them a distinctive character that distinguished them from similar grapes grown in Naples, Bologna, or Salamanca. And yet, the wine each vine eventually produced was distinctive and unique, each excellent in its own way.

Their educations, as similar as they were, led Thomas and Bonaventure to preach in a certain style, to write prologues of a certain kind, and to engage in disputation using similar methods. And yet, even as they composed texts of the same sort and form, according to the same university statutes, and during the same period in history, those practices served as a common foundation for two remarkably distinctive approaches to theology, natural philosophy, and metaphysics.

The Delicate Balance: Preaching and Disputation

The thirteenth century was an age different in most ways from our own, but it had at least one important feature in common with ours: the challenge presented by increasing numbers of educated laity, many of whom had advanced training in secular disciplines but little theological understanding of their faith. Many students coming to the recently established but rapidly expanding universities spent a great deal of time studying disciplines other than theology, and their moral formation was often not what it ought to have been. So Paris was often the setting for student drunkenness and riots.

In this historical and cultural context, there were some who were convinced that an earlier century's ways of dealing with the laity – fostering a simple piety, often "monastic" in its origins, not burdening them with much if any preaching, and certainly nothing too "intellectual" – no longer did justice to the laity's increased intellectual sophistication. It was in response to these challenges that scores of dedicated bishops and members of the two new religious orders of friars, the Dominicans and Franciscans, pioneered a new approach to preaching, one that would bridge the divide between the fiery sermons of a new class of wandering preachers that had spread out across Europe – men who preached with passion, but without an equal degree of wisdom and theological understanding – and the new intellectual class of scholars in the Arts, many of whom were convinced that trying to preach anything intellectually serious to the laity was a fool's errand.

It was providential, therefore, that Paris possessed at the same time and in the same city:

a. A tradition of dedicated preaching spearheaded in many instances by the city's powerful bishops
b. A large number of secular clerics with first-rate intellects who were also excellent preachers, willing to devote the time and energy to the production of preaching aids

c. Members of two, new, energetic religious orders dedicated to the goal of preaching and teaching this newly educated laity who were also willing to dedicate the time and resources to training their younger members to excel at the skills needed to bring this about
d. The benefit of a first-rate educational institution to help bridge the gap between the demands of this new style of preaching and the rudimentary knowledge of the students

As historian Ian Wei has argued, "The thirteenth century marks a turning-point in the history of medieval preaching, not just because of the proliferation of preaching aids but because there were for the first time organizations – the mendicant orders – whose members were properly trained to make use of these tools." With the mendicants, "the gulf between preaching aids and their users was bridged."[4]

I would not wish for readers to get the impression that I consider thirteenth-century Paris to have been some kind of blessed paradise – certainly not of the sort that the University of Paris officials seem to have associated with their own institution, with "the four rivers of paradise" flowing out to the four corners of the earth. Paris and its university were in constant ferment; disputes broke out regularly threatening to tear the entire educational institution apart. Often enough, an uneasy relationship persisted between the arts of preaching and disputation, with disagreements over which of the two was "the most important."

What appears to have persisted for a time, however, was an uneasy but fruitful balance between and among the three arts of the master: preaching, commentary, and disputation. Preaching was expected to be edifying and thoughtful, the fruit of serious and repeated intellectual engagement with authorities and arguments.[5] Yet these rarefied arguments and disputes were not to dominate the message. Those who engaged in disputation were given the responsibility of preaching and teaching those who had not attained high levels of specialized training, whether it was the younger friars or lay people in parishes. In these settings, preachers had to express the results of their theological reflections in language comprehensible to plain persons. Such imposed discipline, which kept them from indulging in the more outlandish extremes to which a philosophical "system" or an ideology can sometimes lead, often proved a valuable corrective.

---

[4] Ian Wei, *Intellectual Culture in Medieval Paris: Theologians and the University, c. 1100–1330* (Cambridge: Cambridge University Press, 2012), 20–21.

[5] See, for example, Humbert of Romans' book of instructions to young thirteenth-century Dominican friars on preaching, the *Liber de eruditione praedicationis* (trans., *Treatise on the Art of Preaching*, Westminster, MD: Newman Press, 1951). In section 2.2 on the "knowledge required by a preacher," he tells them, "We must not overlook the high degree of learning that is necessary for preachers, who are commissioned to instruct others." Among the things he says they must possess are "a firm grasp of Holy Scripture"; "after the study of the Holy Books should follow the study of creatures, for the Creator has placed in these many profound lessons"; a firm knowledge of "the laws of the Church"; an ability to "penetrate the meaning hidden in words and figures"; "knowledge gained by experience"; and an "ability to judge souls." In section 4.4, he lengthens the list, adding: "Also of advantage in this office, is a knowledge of all that the profane sciences have to offer for use for the composition of sermons. As a builder gathers from many sources whatever he needs for his edifice, so too the preacher has recourse to many sources for his material" – materials such as "the holy doctors" and the "writings and lectures on physics, ethics, logic, and so forth." It is not without reason, therefore, in section 2.5, that he also tells them, "The preacher must also have sufficient strength for long hours of study."

This uneasy balance was bound to break up before long, with advanced skill at disputation becoming a more specialized and rarefied practice of the academic elite who showed themselves less and less concerned that the fruit of their disputations should inform preaching with the kind of wisdom that would make sense in the lives of ordinary lay men and women. Preaching often became less and less "academic," giving way to the temptation to become more "popular" with expressions of "simple piety."

Examples of the former – increasingly rarefied discussions directed primarily at one's colleagues in the academic elite – are well known to anyone who has had the occasion to study the scholarly ruminations of many of the fourteenth century nominalists. Evidence of the latter – preaching as a popular expression of simple piety – can be found in the increased use in late thirteenth- and early fourteenth-century preaching of *exempla*: pious little stories meant to exemplify the moral lesson of the sermon. There seem to have been immense volumes cataloguing these *exempla* and indexing them for the preacher's use.[6]

There was, for example, the popular story of the prostitute who happened upon a church, and venturing inside out of curiosity to see "what this folke do there," was converted upon the hearing of the hymns and the solid Christian preaching of the pastor. There was also the story of the Dominican who heard the tale of a lady's pet monkey that escaped into the church and swallowed the host. Forthwith the monkey was burned by its mistress, but the host was rescued from the animal's stomach unharmed. There were other stories, somewhat less fantastical, such as the one about the Franciscan friar who, near death, begged that the lector be brought to his bedside quickly. When asked why, he replied: "Innumerable devils have just come in by window and door and have filled the house, and as I have very little learning they are posing me with hard questions on the Trinity and the Catholic Faith, so run and ask the lector to help me and to answer for me." The sick man's Franciscan confrère hurriedly took the cross and put it into the sick man's hands, saying, "Do not be afraid if you cannot answer; this will answer for you till I return." When the young friar turned to go for the lector as requested, the sick brother broke into loud laughter. When asked why, he replied: "As soon as you gave me this champion, all the devils took to flight, and they are crowding out of the windows and doors in such a hurry and confusion that I think they are breaking each other's necks and backs."[7] Such tales were rarely first-person narratives and were frequently introduced with formulaic pronouncements such as: "This is a story which I learnt from the lips of a certain very truthful and holy man, who asserted that he had himself witnessed the fact which he narrated"; or "A certain trustworthy man of religion, a great preacher and a

---

[6] Charles Smyth, *Art of Preaching: A Practical Survey of Preaching in the Church of England, 747–1939* (New York: Macmillan, 1940), 58, playfully compares these medieval collections of *exempla* to modern compositions such as "A Thousand and One Things to Say in Sermons." One of the best known of these catalogues, the *Tactatus de diversis materiis praedicalibus* (ca. 1250–1261) by the Dominican Stephen of Bourbon, contains nearly 2,900 *exempla*, not counting the Bible stories and interesting "facts" (often enough wrong) from natural history. A key secondary source on medieval *exempla* is J.-Th. Welter, *L'Exemplum dans la littérature religieuse et didactique du moyen age* (Paris: Occitania, 1927), but see also, for its wonderful examples, G. R. Owst, *Literature and Pulpit in Medieval England* (Cambridge: Cambridge University Press, 1933).

[7] See ibid., 62, referencing A. G. Little, *Studies in English Franciscan History* (New York: Longmans and Green, 1917), 145–146.

dependable witness, who learnt this same story from the priest who heard the confession of the woman mentioned in her last infirmity, related it to me."[8]

Illustrating sermons with these little stories seems to have become increasingly popular during the thirteenth century and after. Richard and Mary Rouse did a study of three separate collections of sermons preached at various churches in and around Paris during the years 1230–1231, 1272–1273, and 1274–1302.[9] They noted a shift in the preferred methods of dilation. In the earliest sermons, preachers "displayed a near single-minded enthusiasm for the *distinctio*," that is, for providing several figurative meanings for a scriptural term, and for each meaning providing a passage of scripture illustrating the use of the term in the given sense. Later in the century, one finds more use of the "chaining" of biblical authorities, accompanied by the "near disappearance of the *distinctio*." The sermons of 1272–1273 contain many more *exempla* than do the sermons of forty years earlier, and those of the latest period, 1274–1302, even more. Since the sermons studied by the Rouses were intended primarily for university audiences, they speculate that the use of *exempla* would have been even greater in sermons intended for less educated audiences, given that, even Thomas's contemporaries in Paris, such as the French cardinal Jacques de Vitry (ca. 1160/70–1240) and his Dominican confrère Humbert of Romans (ca. 1200–1277) considered them valuable devices.[10]

Given their later popularity, it is noteworthy that neither Thomas nor Bonaventure ever used *exempla* in their preaching. Indeed, Thomas remarked in a response to Gerard of Besançon, that "it is not proper for the preacher of truth to be diverted to unverifiable fables" (*ad fabulas ignotas divertere*).[11] As Thomas biographer Fr. Jean-Pierre Torrell comments: "Thomas believes orators need an art that can move feelings, but he refuses

---

[8] See ibid., 60, referencing Owst, *Literature and Pulpit*, 171–172.

[9] See Richard and Mary Rouse, *Preachers, Florilegia and Sermons: Studies on the "Manipulus Florum" of Thomas of Ireland*, Studies and Texts 47 (Toronto: Pontifical Institute of Mediaeval Studies, 1979), 69–74.

[10] Humbert warned, however, that they should be used in moderation: no more than one or two per sermon. And the preacher should always have care that the stories he selects are suited to his listeners, be kept short, supported by reference to acceptable authorities, and *true*. A preacher should never use an *exemplum* he suspects is untrue, the one exception being an animal fable presented as a fiction and not a fact, lest more credulous audiences get the wrong idea. See Humbert of Romans, *De eruditione praedicatorum* 1.6, found in Latin in *B. Humberti de Romanis opera de vita regulari*, ed. J. J. Berthier (Rome: Typis A. Befani, 1888–1889), and in English in *Treatise on Preaching*, ed. Walter M. Conlon, O.P. (Westminster, MD: Newman Press, 1951); this English translation can also be found online at www.op.org/sites/files/public/documents/fichier/treat_on_preaching_humbert_en.pdf. On Jacques de Vitry, see T. F. Crane's study: *The Exempla of Jacques de Vitry* (London: T. F. Crane, 1890).

[11] *Responsi ad lectorem Bisuntinum*, in Leonine edition vol. 42 (1979), 355. The text is also more easily found online at the Corpus Thomisticum website under "Responsio de 6 articulis ad lectorem Bisuntinum," Quaestio 3. The question the lector of Besançon posed to Thomas was what form the star that appeared to the magi took: a cross, a man, or a crucifix. In his reply, Thomas insists the preacher of truth should not be diverted to unverifiable fables. Thomas's attitude was that there is so much truth already revealed in Scripture and contained within the tradition – the stories there are already so good and so nourishing to the spirit – that there is no need to look elsewhere (to be "diverted") in order to use "made-up" material and little "fables." As a general rule, they serve no purpose other than empty entertainments that flatter the prejudices of the listeners (when they hear words that neither teach nor challenge them) and the vanity of the preacher (when his listeners congratulate him for the delight he has provided them).

Summary and Concluding Remarks 421

to reduce that art to the wisdom of this world. That is why we scarcely find in him those little stories (*exampla*) so valued by so many preachers. He warns us, on the contrary, against what he calls 'frivolities' (*frivolitates*)."[12]

There may have been good reasons for this restraint. Michèle Mulcahey reports the marvelous lines Dante puts in the mouth of Beatrice chastising preachers for their often mindless and inane use of these *exempla*.

Christ did not say to his first company:

> 'Go, and preach idle stories to the world';
> but he gave them the teaching that is truth,
> and truth alone was sounded when they spoke;
> and thus, to battle to enkindle faith,
> the Gospels served them as both shield and lance.
> But now men go to preach with jests and jeers,
> and just as long as they can raise a laugh,
> the cowl puffs up, and nothing more is asked.[13]

So too she repeats the criticisms of the early thirteenth-century Florentine Dominican friar Jacopo Passavanti (ca. 1302–1357), who admits that some of his fellow preachers were acting more like "jongleurs and storytellers and buffoons" than like the preachers they were supposed to be.[14]

When it was at its best, the mid-thirteenth century university supported a culture in which there were two distinct but interrelated modes of discourse.[15] The first was the mode

---

[12] See Jean-Pierre Torrell, O.P., *Saint Thomas Aquinas*, vol. 1, *The Person and His Work*, rev. ed., trans. R. Royal (Washington, DC: Catholic University of America Press, 2005), 72–73. Thomas makes this comment on the same page in the *Responsi ad lectorem Bisuntinum* cited earlier (Léonine, t. 42, p. 355 b, line 54): "nec estimo huiusmodi frivola esse predicanda ubi competit tanta copia certissime ueritatis." Both Torrell and Bataillon have made special note of the conspicuous absence of such *exempla* in Thomas's sermons. See Torrell, *Sermons*, 24: "Parmi les caractéristiques externes, le P. Bataillon signale encore que Thomas diffère de la plupart de ses contemporains dans son utilisation parcimonieuse des *exempla*..." See also L. J. Bataillon, "*Similitudines* et *exempla* dans les sermons du XIIIe siècle," in *Prédication*, Étude 10, 192–193.

[13] *The Divine Comedy of Dante Alighieri: Paradiso*, trans. Allen Mandelbaum (New York: Bantam Books, 1984), 29.109–117.

[14] See Michèle Mulcahey, *First the Bow Is Bent in Study: Dominican Education Before 1350* (Toronto: Pontifical Institute for Mediaeval Studies, 1998), 465.

[15] Historian Ian Wei, in an important section on "Means of Communication" in his book *Intellectual Culture in Medieval Paris* writes that "masters had to be able to communicate their rulings to a wide audience. Moreover, they had to do so in ways that conveyed and reinforced their authority. They were not simply passing on neutral information that people could take or leave as they saw fit. On the contrary, the message had to be presented in a form that would command respect. The masters therefore refined and theorized their techniques of communication and spent a great deal of time and effort putting them into practice" (Wei, 228). The two primary techniques by which masters communicated to this wider audience, he maintains, were by means of "quodlibetal disputations" and "preaching." Of preaching, he writes: "Preaching was therefore a key part of the intellectual and moral formation of the men who attended university, and it bound them together in community. Crucially, however, it also provided a point of direct contact between intellectuals and the rest of society... Preaching was therefore a means by which Parisian intellectuals communicated directly with and asserted authority over the rest of society" (Wei, 236–237).

of the "disputed question," by means of which scholars could communicate meaningfully with one another to adjudicate substantive philosophical questions and intellectual disputes. Using this approach, the best arguments on both sides of a question could be brought together in such a way as to maintain the integrity of their voices. The other mode of discourse that characterized the age was preaching. Using this means, the university was able to communicate directly with the laity. At its best, the formation in preaching animated and informed by education at the university produced a discourse that was not "dumbed down" and yet was also not argumentative; it was edifying without being technical, expressive without being saccharine or sentimental.

Achieving this admirable balance of "education" and "eloquence," "disputation" and "preaching," required decades of ecclesiastical support, sometimes at the highest levels. It also required educational institutions devoted to the highest levels of intellectual attainment yet imbued with a sense of their mission to the wider church community and dedicated to a meaningful "spirituality of preaching." These institutions also had available to them a ready source of clerics willing to enter upon the rigorous training needed for this level of intellectual and pastoral engagement. It was a providential coming together of diverse elements that bore fruit in ways that no one of them could have produced on their own.

Thirteenth-Century Preaching and "Scholasticism"

A final word is in order about the connotations people commonly attach to the word "scholastic." David d'Avray poses this question about the characterization of thirteenth-century preaching as "scholastic" in his superb book on *The Preaching of the Friars: Sermons Diffused from Paris before 1300* (Oxford, 1985). As d'Avray points out, this characterization goes back to Rudolf Cruel's 1879 landmark study *Geschichte der deutschen Predigt im Mittelalter* in which he argued that the "new" sermon form of the thirteenth century was the product of scholastic influence, specifically the philosophical transformation of theology in France by the reception of Aristotle's works.

As is so often the case with such complex historical theses, it is necessary to tease out the various strands that make up the intricate weave. Aristotle's works were not always given a welcome reception at Paris and were not really a major factor at all at the beginning of the century when the *sermo modernus* style was being developed and gaining in popularity. It would certainly be true to say that *logic* had gained in popularity in the twelfth century during Abelard's time in Paris. But Abelard's own *History of My Calamities* suggests he too was often not warmly welcomed in Paris. Even the more highly trained theologians at the Abbey School of St. Victor were not early supporters of the "scholastic" style being developed at the University of Paris. So, as I suggested in the previous chapter, the officials at the University of Paris may have embraced the "spirituality of preaching" in Pope Gregory IX's bull *Parens scientiarum* and the mission of training preachers it called for precisely as a way of deflecting the criticisms coming their way from St. Victor and the monastic schools.

Two other major works in German followed Cruel's, both of which traced the origins of the new *sermo modernus* form to the influences of scholasticism, not only with regard to its form, but also its content. In an 1886 book on the history of preaching in Germany from Charlemagne to the beginning of the fourteenth century, Anton Linsenmayer described the influence of scholasticism on preaching in the thirteenth century as "epoch-making."[16] Paul Wilhelm Keppler, in an 1892 article surveying the development of preaching from the thirteenth century on, described the influence of scholasticism on German preaching as "unmistakable."[17]

A somewhat different note was sounded in the twentieth century, however, by the prominent French medievalist, Étienne Gilson who, in an essay entitled "Michel Menot et la technique du sermon medieval," suggested that the origins of the *sermo modernus* technique were originally quite distinct from scholastic argument. The *sermo modernus* style was an entirely original rhetorical technique, argued Gilson, derived neither from the dialectic of Aristotle nor the rhetorical techniques of Cicero, invented not to silence an opponent or win legal cases, but to win souls to God.[18] Summing up what he took to be the medieval attitude, Gilson declared that "The place for disputes is the School; the place for sermons is the church."[19]

"Here, then," declares d'Avray, "are two apparently contrasting interpretations of the relation of preaching to scholasticism in the age of Bonaventura."[20] On the one side are those who claim that thirteenth century preaching was "popularized scholasticism" – a style of preaching that originated within and was driven by scholastic methods. On the other side are those who view preaching and disputation as two very different arts – the one for the church, the other for the schools – each having its own distinctive character, development, and raison d'être.

I will not pretend to resolve this dispute here. Much depends on the meaning one attaches to the word "scholasticism." Thirteenth century preaching was not "popularized scholasticism" if by that one means *sermo modernus* preaching was simply "disputation" turned into preaching. *Sermo modernus* sermons do not use "disputed questions," and preachers were warned against allowing them even to *sound* like "disputed questions."

But disputed question-type arguments were far from the only sort known to thirteenth century scholasticism. In both the thirteenth century *Ars concionandi* and the fourteenth century *Forma praedicand*, including arguments was listed as one of the ways of "dilating" a section of a sermon, and preachers made frequent use of them. Preachers did not want their preaching to *sound* like a disputation, but he same passage in the *Ars concionandi* that warns against using premises and conclusions in a sermon advises the preacher to say instead: "for it is so, and this for multiple reasons" (*nam ita est, et hoc multiplici ratione*).[21]

Nor is *sermo modernus* style preaching merely scholastic biblical commentary turned into preaching. Biblical commentaries never structured their content around the divisions of a single *thema* verse, and the *thema*, as all the preaching manuals agree, was the central feature

---

[16] *Geschichte der Predigt in Deutschland von Karl dem Grossen bis aum Ausgange des vierzehnten Jahrhunderts*, 71: "in formeller Beziehung kann man den Einfluess der Scholastik auf die Predigt geradezu einen Epoche machenden nennen." Quoted from d'Avray, 166, n. 2.

[17] "Beiträge zur Antwicklungsgeschichte der Predigtanlage," *Theologische Quartalschrift* 74 (1892): 52–120, 179–212; esp. 62–63: "Vom 13. Jahrhundert an ist der Einfluss der Scholastik auf die deutsche predigt unverkennbar." Quoted from d'Avray, 166, n. 5.

[18] Gilson, "Michel Menot," 100.

[19] Ibid., 134.

[20] d'Avray, *Preaching*, 168.

[21] *Ars Concionandi*, 3.42. For a discussion of arguments in medieval preaching and a defense of their inclusion, see *Reading the Sermons of Aquinas*, 129–131, 199–207.

of the *sermo modernus* style sermon: the trunk of the tree from which the branches would sprout, to employ a contemporary image used to describe it.

The influence likely ran in the opposite direction: thirteenth-century preaching influenced scholastic biblical commentary. Scholastic biblical commentary used some of the same modes of "dilating" a section of text as found in *sermo modernus*-style preaching – the "chaining" of biblical authorities was especially popular. Whereas sermons were developed around a single theme (e.g., the holiness of Mary, the coming of the Savior during Advent, the power of the sacraments), biblical commentaries followed systematically through an entire book of the Bible, which is why an overarching *divisio textus* was considered necessary: to give the students a vision of the whole.

A scholar's training in biblical commentary and disputation helped provide the content for sermons, and there was certainly overlap in some of the "habits of mind" involved. So perhaps the best way to describe the relationship between commentary, disputation and preaching in thirteenth century is the way they themselves saw it. Using Peter Cantor's famous image, biblical commentary was the foundation of the house, disputation the walls, and preaching the roof. They were seen as distinct, but necessarily related parts of one house, with preaching drawing upon biblical commentary and disputation. It was the roof being "held up" by the walls and the foundation. Disputation provided the walls laid upon the foundation of biblical commentary that connected biblical commentary with preaching.[22]

A "still more watered down version" of the "scholastic interpretation," writes d'Avray, leaves aside the question of influence altogether and simply presents scholasticism as "a form of thought shared by sermons and academic theology, a part of the general intellectual climate at Paris."[23] I find this position to be the most defensible, which is why I have not drawn conclusions about causality or lines of influence, preferring rather to restrict my comments to "habits of mind" that characterized thirteenth-century preaching, pointing out places where there was potential overlap between it and the other two skills of the master. My preference, therefore, would be to expand our common understanding of the term "scholastic" to include sermon material, the biblical commentaries, and these ingenious prologues along with "disputed questions."

Yet, one cannot change the language overnight, and one must generally use words as they are commonly understood, not as one wishes that they might be understood. Therefore, in my view, d'Avray is wise to caution, given the current, common understanding of the term "scholastic," that "[t]he use of the word 'scholastic' to describe thirteenth-century preaching blurs some fundamental differences between it and the disputations, *summae*, and *Sentence* commentaries of thirteenth-century masters, and, indeed, the treatises of Abelard or Anselm." If thirteenth-century preaching is to be called "scholastic," suggests d'Avray, "then we would need to find another word for the intellectual phenomenon which everyone has hitherto called by that name."[24] Fair enough. But this still leaves us with the problem of allowing a false, or at the very least, incomplete, picture of the "scholastic" culture of the thirteenth-century universities to persist.

---

[22] Cf. Peter the Chanter, *Verbum abbreviatum*, 6.
[23] d'Avray, *Preaching*, 164.
[24] Ibid., 169.

I have no desire to deemphasize the undisputed importance of the "disputed question" among medieval theologians of the thirteenth century – it was obviously crucially important – but the "disputed question" was not the only "language" of the schools. The language and patterns of biblical commentary and of the *sermo modernus* style of preaching were also characteristic elements of the culture at the University of Paris and other medieval universities that followed its lead. If we need to banish the word "scholastic" to the dustbin of old history books, then so be it. But no equally good term comes readily to mind with which to replace it. My preference, therefore, would be to broaden our overly narrow conception of "scholastic" to include all the key elements of the intellectual and social culture of the thirteenth-century "schools" and then use this occasion to reexamine some of the assumptions and connotations attached to the word by earlier writers.

Consider, for example, the "scholastic interpretation" of the origin and development of thirteenth-century "modern sermon" that has been advanced by Johannes Baptist Schneyer, whose *Repertorium der lateinischen Sermones des Mittelalters für die Zeit von 1150–1350* still stands as the most extensive *repertorium* of medieval sermons available.[25] Schneyer describes the universities as a "driving force" in the development and spread of the new sermon style, but he is far from considering this an unmixed blessing.[26] It was his view that the scholastic method of teaching and disputation – defining, dividing, arguing, giving examples, raising contradictions – resulted in preaching that could have appealed only to masters and students. This has been a common-enough criticism: that the *sermo modernus* style was for educated elites, not laypeople, and that it was, in a word, too "scholastic," by which the writer usually means "dull," "boring," or "too intellectual to appeal to the laity." This judgment, however, involves not only a prejudiced understanding of "scholastic," it also does a great disservice to the intelligence of the laity.

Recent studies and contemporary historical evidence suggests that the *sermo modernus* style did not appeal only to masters and students; rather, as we have seen, it came to dominate all over in western Europe to such a degree that the older style could only be found in certain rural areas.[27] There is in fact no evidence that the *sermo modernus* style was "forced" on unwilling listeners. Quite the opposite. It seems to have been embraced readily by the newly educated, literate members of the laity.

Thomas Aquinas, for example, was reputed to be an excellent preacher, and when he preached, "many people came to hear him."[28] His confrere Bernardo Gui wrote of him that, "To the ordinary faithful he spoke the word of God with singular grace and power, without indulging in far-fetched reasoning or the vanities of worldly wisdom or in the sort of language that serves rather to tickle the curiosity of a congregation than do it any real good. Subtleties he kept for the Schools." His words, says Gui, "had a warmth in them that kindled in [the ordinary faithful] the love of God and sorrow for sin in men's hearts," and

---

[25] Johannes Baptist Schneyer, *Repertorium der Lateinischen Sermones des Mittelalters für die Zeit von 1150–1350* (Münster Westfalen: Aschendorffsche Verlagsbuchhandlung, 1969–1990).
[26] Schneyer, *Repertorium*, 131.
[27] See my discussion and notes in Chapter 1.
[28] See the testimony of William of Tocco in "From the First Canonisation Enquiry," n. 58 in *The Life of St. Thomas Aquinas: Biographical Documents*, trans. Kenelm Foster, O.P. (London: Longmans and Green, 1959), 97.

the people "heard him with great respect as a real man of God."²⁹ Yet, a glance at any of Thomas's extant sermons will reveal that his style was very much the style of the thirteenth century "modern sermon." Although modern readers may find these sermons strange, perhaps even a bit off-putting, evidence suggests that medieval congregations did not.

Yet even a medievalist as dedicated as Étienne Gilson admitted the "strange impression" he experienced when he first experienced on reading the *sermo modernus*–style sermons of the early sixteenth century Franciscan Michel Menot and asked himself about such sermons, "divided and constructed according to a plan of logic that escapes us, nourished by associations of ideas which seem neither natural nor at all necessary, is it possible for one who has been instructed, engrossed, and moved by the French spirit with the works of Bossuet, Bourdaloue, and Massillon, to be passionate about this way of preaching?"³⁰ I cannot comment on "the French spirit" and its passionate attachments, but as Gilson himself admits, Menot was known in his time as another Chrysostom and given the nickname "Langue d'or" or "Golden tongue."³¹ Perhaps the best we can say is that tastes vary.

To associate the word "scholastic" solely with the medieval practice of disputation is a common, if unfortunate, mistake. But to associate "scholastic" with "dull," "boring," and "too intellectual to appeal to the laity" is simply false.

---

[29] Bernardo Gui, *The Life of St. Thomas Aquinas*, chapter 29, quoted from Foster, *Biographical Documents*, 47–48.
[30] Gilson, "Michel Menot," 94–95.
[31] Ibid., 95.

Appendix 1

Outlines of the *Divisiones Textus* of the Books of the Bible from the Inception *Resumptio* Addresses of Four Thirteenth-Century Masters

John of La Rochelle's *Divisio Textus*

I. Old Testament (signs; wrapped in obscurities and the veilings of figures) – three parts:
A. Law: Christ is shown as mediator of precepts, which pertains to power
 – what ought to be done
  1. Teaching of precepts: five books of Moses
    a. Unwritten: **Genesis** (proemium of Law)
      i. Before sin
        α. Nature
          α1. Conservation of the individual: eat of every tree
          α2. Conservation of the species: increase and multiply
        β. Discipline: do not eat of the tree of good and evil
      ii. After the fall – three ages:
        α. Adam to Noah: resist concupiscence (given to Cain) [moral precept]
        β. Noah to Abraham: do not eat meat with blood: abhor letting blood (to Noah) [judicial precept]
        γ. Abraham to Moses and prophets: circumcision [ceremonial precept]
    b. Written:
      i. First edition – three states of man:
        α. Beginners: receding from evil, approaching good: precepts in **Exodus**
        β. Progressing in the desert (moral, ceremonial, judicial): **Leviticus**
        γ. Perfection: prepare to enter land of promise (signifying the perfection of contemplatives and actives): **Numbers**

ii. Second (explanation): **Deuteronomy** (recap of Law)
      α. Love the Lord your God (affirmative precepts)
      β. Fear God (negative precepts)
2. Teaching of *exempla* (deeds): ten books: Joshua, Judges, Kings, Chronicles, Ezra, Esther, Judith, Tobit, Job, Maccabees – threefold state:
   a. Acting (in accord with law), in state of prosperity: Joshua, Judges, Kings, Chronicles, Ezra, Nehemiah
      i. *Exempla* of perfection to the good (before captivity):
         α. Beginning (entering land): **Joshua**
         β. Progress (in land, people tested): **Judges**
         γ. Consummation:
            γ1. *Exempla* for actives: regal power: **Kings**
            γ2. *Exempla* for contemplatives: priestly: **Chronicles**
      ii. *Exempla* of reparation to the good after the captivity: Ezra, Nehemiah
         α. Contemplative (repair of the temple): **Ezra**
         β. Active (repair of the city): **Nehemiah**
   b. Sustaining, in state of adversity: Esther, Tobit, Job, Judith
      i. Personal adversity: **Job, Tobit**
      ii. General adversity:
         α. Through hidden machination: **Esther**
         β. Through open violence: **Judith**
   c. Persevering (in both): **Maccabees**
3. Teaching of admonitions (words): Proverbs, Ecclesiastes, Songs, Wisdom, Ecclesiasticus.
   a. General admonition: **Proverbs**
   b. Special admonitions:
      i. Contempt for commutable good: **Ecclesiastes**
      ii. Conversion to incommutable good: **Song of Songs**
      iii. To justice: **Wisdom**
      iv. To the benefits of mercy: **Ecclesiasticus**
B. Prophets: Christ is shown as mediator of revelation, which pertains to truth
   – What ought to be believed (both affections and intellect)
   1. Concerning the Head (Christ): four Major Prophets → four Gospels: Christ is God-man
      a. Focus on divinity: **Isaiah** (*Immanuel*) and John (the Word)
      b. Focus on humanity – dignity of Christ; union of:
         i. Power (king): **Daniel** (Dan 7: Son of Man) and **Matthew** (prologue; Sermon on the Mount)
         iii. Wisdom (preaching): **Jeremiah** (preaches to Jews) and **Mark** (begins preaching after baptism by John, focus on preaching)
         iii. Goodness (priest): **Ezekiel** (was a priest) and **Luke** (begins with Zechariah; true priesthood in passion)
   2. Concerning the Body (the Church): twelve Minor Prophets → twelve apostles
C. Psalms: Christ is shown as mediator of prayers, which pertains to goodness
   – Seeking the grace of perseverance in prayers to God: divided into three parts in accord with three rules or *regula* (not specified)

II. Teaching of the New Testament – two parts
A. Evangelical teaching: Four Gospels (treat of the head, Christ; see earlier)
B. Apostolic teaching: Acts, Pauline Epistles, Apocalypse (treat of the Body, the Church)
   – three states:
   1. Beginning: **Acts**
   2. Growth: **Epistles**
   3. Culmination: **Apocalypse**

Matthew of Aquasparta's *Divisio Textus*

Old Testament: four parts

I. Legal precepts: provide ruling precepts
   A. **Genesis**: treats of multiplication of the people and election, to which the law was given
   B. **Exodus**: treats of the legislation
   C. **Leviticus**: treats of rites of sacrifice and divine cult
   D. **Numbers**: treats of the progress and order of that people
   E. **Deuteronomy**: recapitulation of the law
II. Examples (*exempla*) of the fathers: provide moving examples from history
   A. The common state of the whole people
      1. **Joshua**: entry into the promised land and distribution of it
      2. **Judges**: progress of the at people, multiplication in variety of states
      3. **Kings**: promotion and exaltation of a king
      4. **Chronicles**: exaltation of the priesthood
      5. **Ezra–Nehemiah**: reparation after ruin (temple and city)
   B. The state of notable singular persons
      1. **Job**: example of patience under the natural law
      2. **Tobit**: example of the same patience under the written law
      3. **Judith**: example of purity and chastity (merited cutting off the head of Holofernes)
      4. **Esther**: example of clemency and mercy as queen, not elevated by pride
      5. **Maccabees**: example of constancy to the laws of the fathers even to death (prefiguring the martyrs of the Church)
III. Sapiential literature: provide directing warnings and information (switch from opening)
   A. Special information
      1. **Proverbs**: information concerning the exercise and progress of virtue
      2. **Ecclesiastes**: contempt of vanity, making the mind ready for "the embrace of love" (in the Song of Songs) –
      3. Song of **Songs**: the embrace of love
      4. **Wisdom**: the contemplation of truth
   B. Universal information (all higher things): **Ecclesiasticus**
IV. Oracles of the prophets: provide illustrating oracles
   A. Through the medium of prayer (by which the light of grace is obtained by entreaty)
      – **Psalms**: because of the truth of the grace of the Spirit

B. Through the medium of preaching (by which the truth is manifested)
   1. **Isaiah**: principally predicts the mystery of the incarnation (Advent readings)
   2. **Jeremiah**: principally predicts the remedy of the passion (Lamentations: prefigures the passion of the Lord)
   3. **Ezekiel**: principally predicts the resurrection (rededication of the temple)
   4. **Daniel**: principally predicts the judgment [Son of Man coming on the clouds]
C. Through the medium of testifying: 12 prophets = 12 apostles (bound in one volume)

New Testament

I. Lord's precepts (correspond to books of the Law)
   – Christ is God-man, king and priest
   A. **Matthew**: treats of his humanity
   B. **Mark**: treats of his regal power
   C. **Luke**: treats of his priestly dignity
   D. **John**: treats of his divinity
II. Apostolic *exempla* (correspond to historical books)
   – **Acts of the Apostles**: unity of the mystical body and bond of charity commended
III. Canonical literature (correspond to sapiential books)
   A. Special information for the churches and persons to whom they are directed:
      – **Pauline Epistles**
   B. General information, thus common name retained
      – **Canonical Epistles**
IV. Prophetic Oracle (correspond to prophetic books)
   Apocalypse: deals with the final state of the Church, in which is rest and consummation

Henry of Ghent's *Divisio Textus*

Augustine: "signs" and "things"

I. Old Testament: sign; mystical senses; figural with respect to the New
   A. Law: what ought to be done (to be expounded principally with tropological sense)
   1. Preceptive (what ought to be done): Five books of Moses
      Genesis as prologue: rejected
      Genesis provides creation of creatures; other books provide the law for them: rejected because Genesis not part of law; instead:
      a. Remembrance of natural law (not only word, but deeds in history; man was made in natural law; patriarchs observed it; corrupted by sinners; show by deeds): **Genesis**
      b. Coercion to observe the natural law: precepts of written law
         i. Law promulgated:
            α. Moral precepts (man ordered in relation to himself): **Exodus**
               – Pertains to beginners (beginning good): describes the people exiting from Egypt, hastening to sea of baptism and to mountain of divine law)

B. Sacramental (man ordered in relation to God): **Leviticus**
      – Pertains to those progressing and the increase of good: describes the people progressing through the desert of this world to the promised land
      γ. Judicial (man ordered in relation to neighbor): **Numbers**
      – Pertains to the perfect and the consummation of good: describes the people preparing themselves to enter and possess the promised land
    ii. Law explained: Deuteronomy
 2. Directive (how it ought to be done):
   a. *Exempla* through just deeds: historical books
      i. Of doing the good of justice
         α. Entry (beginning): **Joshua**
         β. Progress (against temptation; progress in virtue): **Judges**
            – Annexed: time under one judge: **Ruth**
         γ. Perfect consummation: justice of divine cult
            γ1. Active life (kings and princes): **Kings**
            γ2. Contemplative life (ministers; spiritual matters): **Chronicles**
         δ. Reparation for lost justice – twofold:
            δ1. In the spiritual regimen of the contemplative life: **Ezra** (temple)
            δ2. In the temporal regimen of the active life: **Nehemiah** (city)
      ii. Of sustaining the evil of punishment
         α. Personal:
            α1. Pain of loss: **Tobit** (struck with blind)
            α2. Pain of sense: **Job** (struck with the worst boils: sustained the cross)
         β. Communal
            β1. Through open violence: **Judith**
            β2. Through hidden machinations: **Esther**
      iii. Of persevering in both doing the good of justice and in enduring the evil of punishment: **Maccabees**
   b. Exhortation through words: books of Solomon
      i. Dissuading from doing evil
         α. Flee iniquity: **Proverbs**
         β. Not to love vanity: **Ecclesiastes**
      ii. Persuading to do good
         α. To the contemplative life: **Song of Songs**
         β. To the conservation of the republic: **Wisdom**
         γ. Invocation to divine mercy: **Ecclesiasticus**
 B. Prophets: what ought to be believed (principally w/ allegorical)
   1. Twelve minor prophets: concern the mystic body, the Church
   2. Four major prophets: concern the head, Christ
      a. Nativity and incarnation: **Isaiah** (Virgin will conceive)
      b. Passion and death: **Jeremiah**
      c. Resurrection and ascension: **Ezekiel**
      d. Advent to judgment: **Daniel**
 C. Psalms: For what we ought to hope (principally w/ anagogical): most excellent, preeminent prophet (less involved with images and coverings of words; dreams; more directly inspired by Holy Spirit)

II. New Testament: (New Law divided as was the Old)
  A. Law (what ought to be done from charity)
    1. Preceptive: evangelical doctrine, concerning Christ per se
      a. Principally divinity: **John**
      b. Principally humanity:
        i. His entry into the world and things pertain to human generation and birth:
        Matthew
        ii. His progress in the world and things pertaining to things foretold of him: **Mark**
        iii. His exit from the world and things pertaining to his passion: **Luke**
    2. Directive: Apostolic doctrine, concerning Christ through the apostles and his disciples
      a. Through the example of the just: **Acts**
      b. Through the instruction of words: Epistles of Apostles
        i. For informing the faithful in the time of prosperity: **Pauline epistles** (Grace to you and peace)
        ii. To console the afflicted in the time of adversity: **Canonical epistles** ("Count it joy when you fall into various temptations," James 1:1)
  B. Prophets (how it ought to be done fruitfully): **Apocalypse**

Thomas Aquinas's *Divisio Textus*

The Sacred Scriptures lead to eternal life – and this in two ways:

I. By commanding:
(Old Testament)
  A. Binding: Command of a king who punishes
    1. King who establishes the law
      a. Private: **Genesis** (Adam, Eve, Abraham, etc.)
      b. Public:
        i. Law from Lord to mediator: three ways people need to be ordered:
          α. Equity of judgments: **Exodus**
          β. Establishment of worship: **Leviticus**
          γ. Establishment of offices for community: **Numbers**
        ii. Law from mediator to people: **Deuteronomy**
    2. Heralds who induce its observance (prophets)
      a. Manifest beneficence of the king
        i. Effect of heredity: **Joshua** [see also under "Warning by deed"]
        ii. In destruction of armies: **Judges**
        iii. Exultation of the people
          α. Private: **Ruth**
          β. Whole people: **Kings**
      b. Declare the edict of the law

i. To the whole people for observance of the whole law (major prophets)
      α. By cajoling: **Isaiah** (also foretells Incarnation, read during Advent)
      β. By warning: **Jeremiah** (foretells Passion, read during Passiontide)
      γ. Arguing, scolding: **Ezekiel** (foretells Resurrection: raising of bones)
      δ. **Daniel** spoke of the divinity of Christ
   ii. For special reasons to special tribes (minor prophets), e.g.:
      α. To the ten tribes: **Hosea**
      β. To the Ninevites: **Jonah**
B. Warning: precept of a father who teaches
   1. By deed
      a. Warning about future: **Joshua** (cf. St. Jerome)
      b. Teaches virtues from past
         i. Justice: Paralipomenon (Chronicles)
         ii. Temperance: **Judith**
         iii. Fortitude
            α. To attack: **Maccabees**
            β. To endure: **Tobit**
         iv. Prudence:
            α. To build city and temple with enemies plotting: **Ezra/Nehemiah**
            β. To repel the violent: **Esther**
   2. By word
      a. Asking for gift of wisdom: **Psalms**
      b. Teaching wisdom:
         i. Expose the liar: driving out errors by disputation: **Job**
         ii. Not to lie about what is known:
            α. Wisdom is commended to us: **Wisdom**
            β. Precepts of wisdom are proposed (and virtue)
            – Three grades of virtue (cf. Politinus)
               β1. Political virtues (use things of the world): **Proverbs**
               β2. Purgative virtues (contempt of the world): **Ecclesiastes**
               β3. Virtues of purged soul (wholly cleansed from worldly care; contemplation alone): **Song of Songs**
   3. In word and deed: **Ecclesiasticus**
II. By helping with gifts of grace:
(New Testament)
   A. Origin of grace: Jesus Christ (divine and human: priest, prophet, king)
      1. Divine nature: esp. **John** (Eagle)
      2. Human nature: Synoptics
         a. King: **Matthew** (incarnation: Man)
         b. Prophet: **Mark** (resurrection: Lion)
         c. Priest: **Luke** (passion: Bull)
   B. Power of grace: Pauline Epistles:
   [missing from the *resumptio*; between lines supplied from prologue to Pauline Epistles]
      1. As it is in the Head, namely Christ: **Hebrews**
      2. As it is found in the chief members of the Mystical Body: the letters to the prelates, both spiritual and temporal:

     a. Spiritual prelates instructed about:
          i. Establishing, preserving, and governing ecclesial unity: **I Timothy**
          ii. Resistance against persecutors: **II Timothy**
          iii. Defense against heretics: **Titus**
     b. Temporal lord instructed: **Philemon**
  3. As it is found in the Mystical Body itself, that is, the Church: the letters to the gentiles:
     a. As it is in the Church itself: **Romans**
     b. As it exists in the sacraments of grace:
          i. Nature of the sacraments: **I Corinthians**
          ii. Dignity of the minister: **II Corinthians**
          iii. Superfluous sacraments rejected against those who wanted to join old sacraments to the new: **Galatians**
     c. With regard to the effect of the unity it produces in the Church:
          i. Establishment of ecclesial unity: **Ephesians**
          ii. Consolidation and progress of unity: **Philippians**
          iii. Defense against certain errors: **Colossians**
          iv. Unity during existing persecutions: **I Thessalonians**
          v. Unity uring persecutions to come, especially in time of the anti-Christ: **II Thessalonians**
C. Execution of power of grace: progress of the Church
  1. Beginning: **Acts of the Apostles**
  2. Progress: **Canonical Epistles** (James, 1 and 2; Peter, 1, 2, and 3; John; and Jude)
  3. End: **Apocalypse (Revelation)**

Works Cited

Since even a rudimentary bibliography of works devoted to either Thomas or Bonaventure would take a book of its own, and since such resources already exist, I am going to restrict items on this list to works cited.

Abelard, Peter. *Historia calmitatum*, trans. Henry Adams Bellows. St. Paul: T. A. Boyd, 1922.

Adler, Mortimer. *How to Read a Book: The Art of Getting a Liberal Education*. New York: Simon & Schuster, 1940.

Albertus Magnus. "Principium Biblicum Alberti Magni," edited by Albert Fries. In H. Ostlender, ed., *Studia Albertina: Festschrift für Bernhard Geyer*, 128–147. Münster Westfalen: Aschendorff, 1952.

Armstrong, A. H. *Plotinus: A Volume of Selections in a New English Translation*. New York: Collier, 1963.

Athanasius. *On the Incarnation*, trans. by a religious of C.S.M.V. New York: Macmillan, 1946.

Augustine. Confessions, trans. J. G. Pilkington. In Philip Schaff, ed., *A Select Library of the Nicene and Post-Nicene Fathers of the Christian Church*, vol. 1. Edinburgh: T & T Clark, 1886.

―――. *De doctrina christiana*. Oxford Early Christian Texts. Oxford: Oxford University Press, 1995.

―――. *De doctrina christiana*, trans. James Shaw, Nicene and Post-Nicene Fathers. In Philip Schaff, ed., First Series, vol. 2. Buffalo, NY: Christian Literature Publishing, 1887.

Baisnée, Jules A. "Thomas Aquinas' Proofs of the Existence of God Presented in Their Chronological Order." In J. K. Ryan, ed., *Philosophical Studies in Honor of the Very Reverend Ignatius Smith, O.P.*, 29–64. Westminster: Newman, 1952.

Baldwin, J. W. *Masters, Princes and Merchants: The Social Views of Peter the Chanter and His Circle*, 2 vols. Princeton, NJ: Princeton University Press, 1970.

Bataillon, L. "La diffusione manoscritta e stampata dei commenti biblici de San Tommaso d'Aquino." *Angelicum* 71 (1994): 579–590.

Benson, Joshua C. "Bonaventure's Inaugural Sermon at Paris: *Omnium artifex docuit me sapientia*, Introduction and Text." *Collectanea Franciscana* 82 (2012): 517–562.

―――. "Bonaventure's *De reductione artium ad theologiam* and Its Early Reception as an Inaugural Sermon." *American Catholic Philosophical Quarterly* 85.1 (2011): 7–24.

―――. "Identifying the Literary Genre of the 'De reductione artium ad theologiam': Bonaventure's Inaugural Lecture at Paris." *Franciscan Studies* 67 (2009): 149–150.

Bériou, Nicole. *L'avènement des maîtres de la Parole: La Prédication à Paris au XIIIe siècle*, 2 vols. Paris: Institut d'Études Augustiniennes, 1998.

―――. "Les Sermons Latin après 1200." In Beverly Kienzle, ed., *The Sermon*, 363–447. Turnhout: Brepols, 2000.

Bernardo Gui. "The Life of St. Thomas Aquinas." In *The Life of St. Thomas Aquinas: Biographical Documents*, trans. and ed. Kenelm Foster, O.P., 25–81. London: Longmans, Green, 1959.

Bérubé, Camille. *De la philosophie a la sagesse chez Saint Bonaventure et Roger Bacon*. Rome: Istituto Storico dei Cappuccini, 1976.

Blanco, Francisco Chavero. *Imago Dei: Aproximacion a la Antropologia Teologica de San Buenaventura*. Murcia: Publicaciones del Instituto Teologico Franciscano, 1993.

Blastic, Michael. "Preaching in the Early Franciscan Movement." In Timothy Johnson, ed., *Franciscans and Preaching: Every Miracle from the Beginning of the World Came about through Words*, 15–40. Leiden, The Netherlands: Brill, 2012.

Bloch, Marc. *The Ile-de-France: The Country Around Paris*. Ithaca, NY: Cornell University Press, 1971.

Boethius. *Theological Tractates. The Consolation of Philosophy*. Loeb Classical Library 74. Cambridge, MA: Harvard University Press, 1973.

Bonaventure. *Breviloquium*, trans. Dominic Monti. Works of St. Bonaventure 9. Saint Bonaventure, NY: Franciscan Institute Publications, 2005.

———. *Collationes de decem praeceptis*. In *Opera Omnia S. Bonaventurae*, vol. 5, 507–532. Quaracchi: Collegii S. Bonaventurae, 1882–1901.

———. *Collationes de septem donis Spiritus Sancti*. In *Opera Omnia S. Bonaventurae*, vol. 5, 457–503. Quaracchi: Collegii S. Bonaventurae, 1882–1901.

———. *Collations on the Hexaemeron: Conferences on the Six Days of Creation: The Illuminations of the Church*, trans. Jay Hammond. Works of St. Bonaventure 18. St. Bonaventure, NY: Franciscan Institute, 2018.

———. *Collations on the Seven Gifts of the Holy Spirit*, trans. Zachary Hayes. The Works of St. Bonaventure 14. St. Bonaventure, NY: The Franciscan Institute, 2010.

———. *Commentarius in Evangelium Ioannis*. In *Opera Omnia S. Bonaventurae*, vol. 6, 237–532. Quaracchi: Collegii S. Bonaventurae, 1882–1901.

———. *Commentarius in Evangelium Lucae*. In *Opera Omnia S. Bonaventurae*, vol. 7, 1–604. Quaracchi: Collegii S. Bonaventurae, 1882–1901.

———. *Commentary on the Gospel of John*, trans. Robert J. Karris. Works of St. Bonaventure 11. St. Bonaventure, NY: The Franciscan Institute, 2007.

———. "Prologus." In *Commentaria in quatuor libros Sententiarum Magistri Petri Lombardi*. In *Opera Omnia S. Bonaventurae*, vol. 1, 1–6. Quaracchi: Collegii S. Bonaventurae, 1882–1901.

———. *On the Reduction of Arts to Theology*, trans. Zachary Hayes. The Works of St. Bonaventure 1. Franciscan Institute: St. Bonaventure University, 1996.

———. *St. Bonaventure's Collations on the Ten Commandments*, trans. Paul J. Spaeth. Works of Saint Bonaventure 6. St. Bonaventure, NY: The Franciscan Institute, 1995.

———. *St. Bonaventure's Commentary on the Gospel of Luke*, trans. Robert J. Karris. Works of St. Bonaventure 8, 3 vols. St. Bonaventure, NY: Franciscan Institute Publications, 2001.

———. *The Sunday Sermons of St. Bonaventure*, trans. Timothy Johnson. Works of Bonaventure 12. St. Bonaventure, NY: Franciscan Institute Publications, 2008.

———. *What Manner of Man? Sermons on Christ*, trans. Zachary Hayes, O.F.M. Chicago: Franciscan Herald Press, 1974.

[Bonaventure]. *Ars concionandi*, in *Opera Omnia S. Bonaventurae*, vol. 9, 9–21. Quaracchi: Ad Claras Aquas, Collegii S. Bonaventurae, 1882–1901.

Bonnes, J. P. "Un des plus grands prédicateurs du XIIe siècle: Geoffrey du Louroux, dit Geoffrey Babion." *Revue bénédictine* 56 (1945-1946): 174–215.

Bordoy-Torrents, Pedro. "Téchnicas divergentes en la redaccion del *Breviloquio* de S. Bonaventura." *Cientia Tomista* (1940): 442–451.

Bougerol, Jacques-Guy. *Introduction à Saint Bonaventure*, 2me ed. Paris: J. Vrin, 1988.

———. *Introduction to the Works of Bonaventure*, trans. José de Vinck. Paterson, NJ: St. Anthony Guild Press, 1964.

Boyle, John F. "Authorial Intention and the *Divisio Textus*." In M. Levering and M. Dauphinais, eds., *Reading John with St. Thomas Aquinas*, 3–8. Washington, DC: The Catholic University of America Press, 2005.

———. "The Theological Character of the Scholastic 'Division of the Text' with Particular Reference to the Commentaries of Saint Thomas Aquinas." In J. D. McAuliffe, et al., eds., *With Reverence for the Word: Medieval Scriptural Exegesis in Judaism, Christianity, and Islam*. Oxford: Oxford University Press, 2003.

———. "The Theological Character of the Scholastic 'Division of Text' with Particular Reference to the Commentaries of Saint Thomas Aquinas." In J. McAuliffe, B. Walfish,

and J. Goering, eds., *With Reverence for the Word: Medieval Exegesis in Judaism, Christianity, and Islam*, 276–283. Oxford: Oxford University Press, 2003.
Boyle, Leonard. *The Setting of the Summa theologiae of St. Thomas.* Toronto: Pontifical Institute of Mediaeval Studies, 1982.
Brady, Ignatius. "The *Opera Omnia* of Saint Bonaventure Revisited." In Pascal Foley, ed., *Proceedings of the Seventh Centenary Celebration of the Death of Saint Bonaventure*, 47–59. St. Bonaventure, NY: The Franciscan Institute, 1975.
Brown, Raymond. "The History and Development of the Theory of a *Sensus Plenior*." *Catholic Biblical Quarterly* 15 (1953): 141–162.
——— "The Problems of the *Sensus Plenior*." *Ephemerides Theologicae Lovanienses* 43 (1967): 460–469.
——— *The 'Sensus Plenior' of Sacred Scripture.* Baltimore: St. Mary's University Press, 1955.
Cantor, Peter. *Verbum Abbreviatum Petri Cantoris Parisiensis. Verbum adbreviatum. Textus conflates*, ed. M. Boutry. Corpus Christianorum, Continuatio Mediaeualis 196. Turnhout: Brepols, 2004.
Caplan, Harry. "A Late Medieval Tractate on Preaching." In *Studies in Rhetoric and Public Speaking in Honor of James Albert Winans*, 61–90. New York: Century, 1925.
Carruthers, Mary. *The Book of Memory: A Study of Memory in Medieval Culture.* Cambridge: Cambridge University Press, 1990.
Carruthers, Mary and Jan Ziolkowski. *The Medieval Craft of Memory: An Anthology of Texts and Pictures.* Philadelphia: University of Pennsylvania Press, 2003.
Charland, Thomas. *Artes Praedicandi: contribution à l' histoire de la rhétorique au moyen âge, Publications de l'Institut d'Etudes Medievales d'Ottawa 7* . Paris: J. Vrin/Institute of Medieval Studies, 1936.
Chartularium Universitatis Parisiensis, ed. H. Denifle, O.P., and E. Chatelian, vol. 2. Paris: 1891.
Cicero. *Tusculan Disputations,* trans. J. E. King, Loeb Classical Library 141. Cambridge, MA: Harvard University Press, 1927.
[Cicero]. *Rhetorica ad Herennium*, trans. Harry Caplan, Loeb Classical Library 403. Cambridge, MA: Harvard University Press, 1954.
Comestor, Peter. *Sermo LV primus de adventu domini.* In B. Kienzle, ed. *The Sermon*, 353–362. Typologie Des Sources Du Moyen Age Occidental 81. Turnhout: Brepols, 2000.
Conciliorum Oecumenicorum Decreta curantibus J. Alberigo, et al., 3rd ed. Bologna: Istituto per le scienze religiose, 1973. www.internetsv.info/Archive/CLateranense4.pdf and www.documentacatholicaomnia.eu/01_10_1215-1215-_Concilium_Lateranum_IIII.html.
Crane, T. F. *The Exempla of Jacques de Vitry.* London: T. F. Crane, 1890.
Crowley, Theodore. "St. Bonaventure Chronology Reappraisal." *Franziskanische Studien* 56 (1974): 310–322.
d'Avray, David. *The Preaching of the Friars: Sermons Diffused from Paris before 1300.* Oxford: Oxford University Press, 1985.
Dahan, Gilbert. "Genres, Forms and Various Methods in Christian Exegesis of the Middle Ages." In M. Sæbø, ed., *Hebrew Bible / Old Testament: The History of Its Interpretation I/2*, 196–236. Göttingen: Vandenhoek & Ruprecht, 2000.
Dante. *The Divine Comedy of Dante Alighieri: Paradiso,* trans. Allen Mandelbaum New York: Bantam Books, 1984.
Davy, M.-M. *Les sermons universitaires parisiens de 1230-32: contribution à l'histoire de la prédication médiévale.* Etudes de philosophie médiévale 15. Paris: J. Vrin, 1931.
de Lubac, Henri. *Catholicism: Christ and the Common Destiny of Man.* San Francisco: Ignatius, 1988.
Dulles, Avery, S.J. *The Catholicity of the Church.* Oxford: Clarendon Press, 1985.
Emery, Kent. "Reading the World Rightly and Squarely: Bonaventure's Doctrine of the Cardinal Virtues." *Traditio* 39 (1983): 183–218.
Falque, Emmanuel. *Saint Bonaventure et l'entrée de Dieu in théologie.* Études de philosophie médiévale. Paris: Librairie philosophique J. Vrin, 2000.

Francis of Assisi. "Early Rule" (*Regula non bullata*). In Regis J. Armstrong, et al., eds., *Francis of Assisi: Early Documents*, 63–86. New York: New City Press, 1999.

Fries, Albert, CSSR. "Der Schriftkanon bei Albert der. Grossen." *Divus Thomas* 29 (Feb. 1951): 195–213.

———. "Eine Vorlesung Alberts des Grossen über den biblischen Kanon." *Divus Thomas* 28 (1950): 194–213.

Frischer, Bernard. *The Sculpted Word: Epicureanism and Philosophical Recruitment in Ancient Greece*. Berkeley: University of California Press, 1982.

Giambrone, Anthony, O.P. "The Prologues to Aquinas' Commentaries on the Letters of St. Paul." In P. Roszak and J. Vijgen, ed. *Towards a Biblical Thomism: Thomas Aquinas and the Renewal of Biblical Theology*. Navarre, Spain: Eunsa, 2018.

Gils, P.-M. "Les *Collationes* marginales dans l'autograph du commentaire de S. Thomas sur Isaïe." *Revue des Sciences Philosophiques et Théologiques* 42 (1958): 253–264.

Gilson, Étienne. *History of Christian Philosophy in the Middle Ages*. New York: Random House, 1955.

———. "Michel Menot et la Technique du Sermon Médiéval." In *Les Idées et Les Lettres*, 93–154. Paris: Vrin, 1932.

———. *The Philosophy of St. Bonaventure*, trans. D. I. Trethowan and F. J. Sheed. Paterson, NJ: St. Anthony Guild Press, 1965.

Gregory the Great. *Gregory the Great: Forty Gospel Homilies*, trans. David Hurst, 226–235. Collegeville, MN: Cistercian Publications, 1990.

———. *Homilia XXIX in Evangelia*. In B. Kienzle, ed. *The Sermon*, 248–265. Typologie Des Sources Du Moyen Age Occidental 81. Turnhout: Brepols, 2000.

Hall, Thomas N. "The early medieval sermon." In Beverly Kienzle, ed. *The Sermon*. Turnhout: Brepols, 2000.

Hallie, Philip. *Lest Innocent Blood Be Shed: The Story of the Village of Le Chambon and How Goodness Happened There*. New York: Harper & Row, 1979.

Hammond, Jay M. "Dating Bonaventure's Inception as Regent Master." *Franciscan Studies* 67 (2009): 179–226.

Hayes, Zachary, trans. *Collations on the Seven Gifts of the Holy Spirit*, The Works of St. Bonaventure 14. St. Bonaventure, NY: The Franciscan Institute, 2010.

Hazel, Harry Charles. "A Translation, with Commentary, of the Bonaventuran '*Ars Concionandi*'" PhD diss., Washington State University, 1972.

Hellman, J. A. Wayne. *Divine and Created Order in Bonaventure's Theology*, trans. Jay Hammond. St. Bonaventure, NY: The Franciscan Institute, 2001.

Henry of Ghent (Henricus de Gandavo), *Lectura Ordinaria Super Sacram Scripturam* In Raymond Macken, ed., *Henrici de Gandavo Opera Omni*, vol. 36, 5–27. Leuven: Leuven University Press, 1980.

Hugh of St. Victor. *Didascalicon of Hugh of St. Victor: A Medieval Guide to the Arts*, trans. Jerome Taylor. New York: Columbia University Press, 1991.

———. *On the Sacraments of the Christian Faith*, trans. Roy J. Deferrari. Medieval Academy of America, 1951; repr. Eugene, OR: Wipf & Stock, 2005.

Hughes, Kevin L. "St. Bonaventure's *Collationes in Hexaëmeron*: Fractured Sermons and Protreptic Discourse." *Franciscan Studies* 63 (2005): 107–129.

Humbert of Romans. *Liber de eruditione praedicatorum*. In Joachim Berthier, ed., *B. Humberti de Romanis opera de vita regulari*, vol. 2, 373–484. Rome: A Befani, 1888–1889.

———. *The Formation of Preachers*. In trans. and ed. Simon Tugwell, *Early Dominicans: Selected Writings*. New York: Paulist Press, 1982.

———. *Treatise on the Art of Preaching*, trans. Dominican students of the Province of St. Joseph, ed. Walter M. Conlon, O.P. Westminster, MD: Newman Press, 1951. www.op.org/sites/files/public/documents/fichier/treat_on_preaching_humbert_en.pdf.

Jacques de Vitry. *The Historia Occidentalis of Jacques de Vitry*, ed. J. F. Hinnebusch, O.P. Fribourg: The University Press, 1972.

John of La Rochelle. "Deux leçons d'ouverture de Cours Biblique données par Jean de La Rochelle." ed. F. Delorme, O.F.M., *La France Franciscaine* 16 (1933): 345–360.

Jordan, Mark D. "Ancient Philosophic Protreptic and the Problem of Persuasive Genres." *Rhetorica: A Journal of the History of Rhetoric* 4.4 (Autumn 1986): 309–333.

—— "The Care of Souls and the Rhetoric of Moral Teaching in Bonaventure and Thomas." In *Spirit and Life: A Journal of Contemporary Franciscanism* 4 St. Bonaventure, NY: The Franciscan Institute, 1993.

Karris, Robert J. "St. Bonaventure's Use of *Distinctiones*: His Independence of and Dependence on Hugh of St. Cher." *Franciscan Studies* 60 (2002): 209–250.

Kelly, J. N. D. *Early Christian Doctrines*, rev. ed. New York: Harper Collins, 1978.

Keppler, P. W. "Beiträge zur Entwicklungsgeschichte der Predigtanlage," *Tübinger Theologische Quartalschrift* 74 (1892): 52–120, 179–212.

Kienzle, Beverly. "The twelfth-century monastic sermon." In Beverly Kienzle, ed. *The Sermon*, 271–324. Turnhout: Brepols, 2000.

King, P. D. *Charlemagne: Translated Sources*. Lambrigg, Kendal, Cumbria: P.D. King, 1987.

Kulstad, Mark and Laurence Carlin. "Leibniz's Philosophy of Mind." In *The Stanford Encyclopedia of Philosophy*, https://plato.stanford.edu/archives/win2013/entries/leibniz-mind/.

Leclercq, Jean. "Un témoignage du XIIIe siècle sur la nature de la théologie." *Archives d'histoire doctrinale et littéraire du moyen âge* 15–17 (1940-1942): 301–321.

—— "Le magistère du prédicateur au XIIIe siècle." *Archives d'histoire doctrinale et littéraire du Moyen Age* 15 (1946): 105–147.

Linsenmeyer, A. *Geschichte der Predigt in Deutschland von Karl dem Grossen bis aum Ausgange des vierzehnten Jahrhunderts*. Munich, 1886.

Little, A. G. *Studies in English Franciscan History*. New York: Longmans and Green, 1917.

Lottin, Odon. *Le droit naturel chez Saint Thomas d'Aquin et ses prédécesseurs*, 2me ed. Bruges: Beyaert, 1931.

MacIntyre, Alasdair. *After Virtue: A Study in Moral Theory*, 3rd ed. Notre Dame, IN: University of Notre Dame Press, 1981, 1984, 2007.

—— *Three Rival Versions of Moral Enquiry: Encyclopedia, Genealogy, and Tradition*. Notre Dame, IN: University of Notre Dame Press, 1990.

Mandonnet, Pierre. *St. Dominic and His Work*, trans. Sister Mary Benedicta Larkin, O.P. New York: Herder, 1945). http://laity.stdombenicia.org/stdominicandhisworks.pdf.

Matthew of Aquasparta. *Quaestiones Disputatae Selectae*. Quaracchi: Collegium S. Bonaventurae 1903.

McGinn, Bernard. *The Flowering of Mysticism: Men and Women in the New Mysticism – 1200-1350*. New York: Crossroad, 1998.

McInerny, Ralph. *Thomas Aquinas: Selected Writings*. Harmondsworth: Penguin, 1998.

Meersseman, G. G. *Ordo fraternitatis: confraternite e pietà dei laici nel Medioevo*. Rome: Herder, 1977.

Merton, Thomas. *The Ascent to Truth*. New York: Harcourt, Brace & Company, 1951.

Minnis, Alastair J. *Medieval Theory of Authorship: Scholastic Literary Attitudes in the Later Middle Ages*. Philadelphia, PA: University of Pennsylvania Press, 1984; 2nd ed. 1988.

Moore, Philip S. *The Works of Peter of Poitiers: Master in Theology and Chancellor of Paris (1193–1205)*. Notre Dame, IN: University of Notre Dame Press, 1936.

Mottoni, Barbara Faes. "Introduzione." In *Commento al Vangelo di San Luca/1 (1-4)*, 7–26. Rome: Città Nuova, 1999.

Mulcahey, Michèle. *First the Bow Is Bent in Study: Dominican Education before 1350*. Toronto: Pontifical Institute of Mediaeval Studies, 1998.

Murphy, James J. *Rhetoric in the Middle Ages: A History of Rhetorical Theory from Saint Augustine to the Renaissance*. Berkeley: University of California Press, 1974.

Noone, Tim and R. E. Houser. "Saint Bonaventure." In Edward N. Zalta (ed.), *The Stanford Encyclopedia of Philosophy* (Winter 2014 edition), https://plato.stanford.edu/archives/win2014/entries/bonaventure.

Owst, G. R. *Literature and Pulpit in Medieval England.* Cambridge: Cambridge University Press, 1933.

Pieper, Josef. "On Faith: A Philosophical Treatise." In *Faith, Hope, Love.* San Francisco, CA: Ignatius Press, 1997.

Pieper, Josef and Heinz Raskop. *What Catholics Believe.* New York: Pantheon Books, 1951; repr. Providence, RI: Cluny Media, 2019.

Pinckaers, Servais. *The Pinckaers Reader: Renewing Thomistic Moral Theology.* Washington, DC: The Catholic University of America Press, 2005.

Quintillian. *Institutio Oratoria,* trans. H. E. Butler, 4 vols. Loeb Classical Library. Cambridge, MA: Harvard University Press, 1920–22.

Reist, Thomas. *Saint Bonaventure as a Biblical Commentator: A Translation and Analysis of His Commentary on Luke, XVIII,34–XIX,42.* Lanham, MD: University Press of America, 1985.

Reynolds, Suzanne. *Medieval Reading: Grammar, Rhetoric and the Classical Text.* Cambridge: Cambridge University Press, 1996.

Robert of Basevorn. Forma praedicandi. In T. Charland, ed., *Artes Praedicandi: contribution à l'histoire de la rhétorique au moyen âge,* 233–323. Publications de l'Institut d'Etudes Medievales d'Ottawa, 7. Paris: J. Vrin / Institute of Medieval Studies, 1936.

    The Form of Preaching, trans. Leopold Krul, O.S.B. In James J. Murphy, ed., *Three Medieval Rhetorical Arts,* 109–215. Berkeley: University of California Press, 1971.

Robert, Phyllis B. *Studies in the Sermons of Stephen Langton,* 224–237. Toronto: Pontifical Institute of Mediaeval Studies, 1968.

    Selected Sermons of Stephen Langton. Toronto: Pontifical Institute of Mediaeval Studies, 1980.

Robertson, D. W. "Frequency of Preaching in Thirteenth-Century England." *Speculum* 24.3 (July, 1949): 376–388.

Rouse, Richard and Mary Rouse. "Biblical 'Distinctiones' in the Thirteenth Century." *Archives d'histoire doctrinale et littéraire du moyen age* 41 (1974): 27–37.

    Preachers, Florilegia and Sermons: Studies on the Manipulus florum of Thomas of Ireland. Toronto: Pontifical Institute of Mediaeval Studies, 1979.

Salimbene. *The Chronicle of Salimbene of Adam,* trans. Joseph L. Baird, Giuseppe Baglavi, and John Robert Kane. Binghamton, NY: Medieval & Renaissance Texts & Studies, 1986.

Schillebeeckx, Edward. *Christ, the Sacrament of the Encounter with God.* Lanham, MD: Rowman & Littlefield, 1963.

Schneyer, Johannes Baptist. *Repertorium der Lateinischen Sermones des Mittelalters für die Zeit von 1150–1350* Münster Westfalen: Aschendorffsche Verlagsbuchhandlung, 1969–1990.

Smalley, Beryl. "William of Auvergne, John of La Rochelle and St Thomas Aquinas on the Old Law." In *St Thomas Aquinas (1274–1974): Commemorative Studies,* vol. 2, 1–71. Toronto: Pontifical Institute of Mediaeval Studies, 1974.

    The Study of the Bible in the Middle Ages. Oxford: Blackwell, 1952.

Smith, Randall B. "What the Old Law Reveals about the Natural Law according to Thomas Aquinas." *The Thomist* 75.1 (January 2011): 95–139.

    Reading the Sermons of Thomas Aquinas: A Beginner's Guide. Steubenville, OH: Emmaus, 2016.

Smyth, Charles. *Art of Preaching: A Practical Survey of Preaching in the Church of England, 747–1939.* New York: Macmillan, 1940.

Spatz, Nancy. "A Newly Identified Text: The Inception Speech of Galdericus, First Cluniac Regent Master of Theology at the University of Paris." *Archives d'histoire doctrinale et littéraire du moyen âge* 61 (1994): 133–147.

    Principia: A Study and Edition of Inception Speeches Delivered before the Faculty of Theology at the University of Paris, ca. 1180–1286. PhD diss., Cornell University, 1992.

    "Imagery in University Inception Sermons." In J. Hamesse Kienzle, et al., eds., *Medieval Sermons and Society: Cloister, City, University,* 329–342. Louvain-La-Neuve: Fédération Internationale des Instituts d'Études Médiévales, 1998.

Speer, Andreas. "Illumination and Certitude: The Foundation of Knowledge in Bonaventure." *American Catholic Philosophical Quarterly* 85.1 (2011): 127–141.

Stegmüller, Friedrich. *Repertorium biblicum medii aevi*, 11 vols. (Madrid, 1950–). http://repbib.uni-trier.de/cgi-bin/rebihome.tcl.

Stock, Brian. *The Implications of Literacy*. Princeton, NJ: Princeton University Press, 1983.

Sulavik, Athanasius. "*Principia* and *Introitus* in Thirteenth Century Christian Biblical Exegesis with Related Texts." In Giuseppe Cremascoli and Francesco Santi, eds., *La Bibbia del XIII secolo, storia del testo, storia dell'esegesi*, 269–322. Florence: SISMEL, 2004.

Teeuwen, Mariken. *The Vocabulary of Intellectual Life in the Middle Ages, Études sur le vocabulaire intellectual du Moyen Âge 10*. Turnhout: Brepols, 2003.

ten Klooster, Anton. *Thomas Aquinas on the Beatitudes: Reading Matthew, Disputing Grace and Virtue, Preaching Happiness*, Thomas Instituut Utrecht 18. Leuven: Peeters Publishers, 2018.

Thomas Aquinas. *An Apology for the Religious Orders*, trans. John Procter. London: Sands, 1902; reprint, Westminster, MD: Newman, 1950.

"Hic est liber." In R. A. Verardo, ed. *Opuscula Theologica*, vol. 1, 435–443. Turin: Marietti, 1954,

"Rigans Montes." In R. A. Verardo, ed. *Opuscula Theologica*, vol. 4, 481–496. Turin: Marietti, 1954.

Commentaries on Aristotle's "On Sense and What Is Sensed" and "On Memory and Recollection," trans. Kevin White and Ed Macierowski. Washington, DC: Catholic University of America Press, 2005.

Commentary on the Gospel of John, trans. J. Weisheipl, O.P. Albany, NY: Magi Books, 1980.

Commentary on the Gospel of John, trans. J. Weisheipl and F. Larcher Albany: Magi Books, 1980.

Commentary on the Letter of Saint Paul to the Romans, trans. Fabian Larcher, O.P., ed. John Mortensen and Enrique Alarcón. Lander, WY: The Aquinas Institute, 2012. E-text: aquinas.cc.

Expositio super Isaiam ad litteram. Leonine, 1974, vol. 28. www.corpusthomisticum.org/cis00.html.

In Jeremiam prophetam expositio, vol. 14, 577–667. Parma: Fiaccadori, 1863. www.corpusthomisticum.org/cph.html.

In psalmos Davidis expositio proemium. Reportatio Reginaldi de Piperno, vol. 14, 148–553. Parma: Fiaccadori, 1863. www.corpusthomisticum.org/cps00.html.

In Threnos Jeremiae exposition, vol. 14, 668–685. Parma: Fiaccadori, 1863. www.corpusthomisticum.org/cth.html.

On the Power of God, trans. English Dominican Fathers. Westminster, MD: The Newman Press, 1952.

Quaestiones quodlibetales, vol. 25. Paris: Edita Leonis, 1984.

Responsi ad lectorem Bisuntinum, Leonine 42 (1979), 355. Corpus Thomisticum under "Responsio de 6 articulis ad lectorem Bisuntinum," Quaestio 3.

Summa Theologica, 1st complete American ed., trans. by Fathers of the English Dominican Province, with Synoptic Charts. New York: Benziger Bros., 1947.

Thomas Aquinas: The Academic Sermons, trans. Mark-Robin Hoogland, C.P., The Fathers of the Church: Mediaeval Continuation 11. Washington, DC: The Catholic University of America Press, 2010.

Truth, trans. Robert W. Mulligan, James V. McGlynn, and Robert W. Schmidt. Chicago: Regnery, 1952–54; repr. Indianapolis: Hackett, 1994.

Thomas Waleys (Thomas of Wales). *De modo componendi sermones, in Artes Praedicandi: contribution à l'histoire de la rhétorique au moyen âge*, 327–403. ed. T. Charland. Publications de l'Institut d'Etudes Medievales d'Ottawa, 7. Paris: Institute of Medieval Studies, 1936.

Thorndike Lynn, ed. and trans., *University Records and Life in the Middle Ages* New York: Norton, 1975; repr. of New York: Columbia University Press, 1944.

Torrell, Jean-Pierre, O.P., and Denise Bouthillier. "Quand saint Thomas méditait sure le prophète Isaïe." *Revue thomiste* 90 (1990): 5–47.
    Initiation à saint Thomas d'Aquin: Sa personne et son oeuvre. Paris: Cerf, 2015.
    Saint Thomas Aquinas: The Person and His Work, trans. Robert Royal. Washington, DC: Catholic University of America Press, 1996.
Tugwell, Simon. *Albert and Thomas: Selected Writings*. Classics of Western Spirituality. Mahwah, NJ: Paulist Press, 1988.
Van Steenberghen, Fernand. *Thomas Aquinas and Radical Aristotelianism*. Washington, DC: The Catholic University of America Press, 1980.
Wei, Ian P. *The Intellectual Culture in Medieval Paris: Theologians and the University, c. 1100–1330*. Cambridge: Cambridge University Press, 2012.
Weisheipl, James, O.P. *Friar Thomas d'Aquino: His Life, Thought, and Works*. Washington, DC: Catholic University of America Press, 1974, 1983.
    Review of *Expositio super Isaiam ad litteram* Leonine, 1974, *The Thomist* 43 (1979): 331–337.
Welter, J.-Th. *L'Exemplum dans la littérature religieuse et didactique du moyen age*. Paris: Occitania, 1927.
William of Auxerre. *Summa Aurea* IV, ed. J. Ribaillier. Paris: Éditions du Centre national de la recherche scientifique, 1980–1986.
William of Saint-Amour. *De periculis novissimorum temporum*, trans. G. Geltner, Dallas Medieval Texts and Translations 8. Paris: Peeters, 2008.
William of Tocco. "From the First Canonisation Enquiry." In Kenelm Foster, O.P., ed. and trans., *The Life of St. Thomas Aquinas: Biographical Documents*, 82–97. London: Longmans, Green, 1959.
Wippel, John F. *The Metaphysical Thought of Thomas Aquinas: From Finite Being to Uncreated Being*. Washington, DC: The Catholic University of America Press, 2000.
Zier, Mark A. "Sermons of the twelfth century schoolmasters and canons." In Beverly Kienzle, ed. *The Sermon*, 325–351. Turnhout: Brepols, 2000.

Index

Abelard, 91
   and Paris, 37, 422
   as scholastic, 424
   and Scripture commentary, 195
Adler, Mortimer, 15, 287
Alan of Lille
   De arte praedicatoria, 26
   Liber in distinctionibus dictionum theologicalium, 333
Albert the Great, 69, 103, 109
   Commentary on the "'Sentences,'" 140
   divisio textus, 75–76, 100
   resumptio address, 74–76, 99–100
Albigensians, 32
Alexander IV, Pope, 2, 81, 152, 364
Alexander of Hales, 2
   Summa fratris Alexandri (or *Summa Halensis*), 240, 344
allegory, 147, 170, 400, See also metaphor; Scripture, senses of
   Bonaventure's use of, 63, 133, 310, 332, 394
   and *dilatatio*, 133, 202
   Thomas's use of, 133, 202
analogy, 85, 254
   changes in, 336
   imperfect, 256
Anselm, 273, 424
   Cur Deus homo, 58
Anselm of Laôn, 195, 351
argumentation, 156, 162, 423, See also disputation
   in *dilatatio*, 57–58, 183
   as skill, 342
   in treatises, 355
Arians, 143, 389
Aristotle, 177–178, 180
   Ethics, 107
   Metaphysics, 286
   Protrepticus, 11
   radical Aristotelians, 365, 382
   and scholasticism, 422
   and *sermo modernus*, 423
Ars concionandi, 34, 52–54, 57, 59
associations, verbal, 54, 176
   and chaining, 209, 297, 330, 332
   in *dilatatio*, 47, 61, 65, 72, 106, 117, 128, 329
   in *distinctiones*, 221, 334
   as memory aid, 66, 175, 295, 388, 395–397, 408
   and *sermo modernus*, 70, 264
   as skill, 107–108, 135, 146, 183, 347, 416
   Thomas's use of, 223
   and word choice, 156, 181, 296, 324, 349
associations, visual, 61, 82, 117
Augustine, 104, 114, 153, 196, 236
   City of God, 181, 243
   De doctrina christiana, 26, 122, 278, 324, 336
   De magistro, 87
   De spiritu et littera, 112
   De trinitate, 85, 403
   on education, 259
   Literal Commentary on Genesis, 268
   preaching of, 200
   Quaestiones in Heptateuchum, 112
   on salvation history, 351–353
   on Scripture, 246
   and signification, 86, 112, 240, 245, 360
   on sin, 340
   Soliloquies, 254
   on the Ten Commandments, 374
authority. See also chaining
   argument from, 156, 175, 370
   of the author, 192
   divine, 175–176, 182, 371
   reference to, 342, 418
   and Scripture, 104, 108, 315, 359
Averroism, 195
Avicenna, 87, 179–180

bachelor, 99, 140
   Bonaventure as, 2, 306
   requirements of, 38, 42–43
   Thomas as, 140, 198
Bataillon, Louis, 165
beatitude. See also happiness
   and ecstasy, 404, 409
   final, 395
   as goal of learning, 187, 196
beauty
   Christ's, 215
   and memory, 66
   as motivation, 11

beauty (cont.)
    as motive, 279, 401
    in preaching, 211
    in Scripture, 136
    and wisdom, 400
Benson, Joshua C., 5, 8, 80, 252, 347
Bernard of Clairvaux, 149, 196, 416
Bernardo Gui, 148, 425
Boethius
    De trinitate, 155, 259
Boethius of Dacia, 195
Bologna, University of, 29
Bonaventure
    biography, 1–2, 233–234, 364–365
    Breviloquium, 40, 240, 344–347, 361–362
    coinages, 242, 354
    collations, 364–367
    Collations on the Seven Gifts of the Holy Spirit, 62–63, 376
    Collations on the Six Days of Creation, 383–385
    Commentary on the Gospel of John, 339
    Commentary on the Gospel of Luke, 319–321
    Commentary on the "Sentences," 61–62, 140, 290–292
    De reductione artium ad theologiam, 63, 80, 186, 252, 256, 261, 387
    distinctiones of, 333–337
    divisio textus, 253, 337, 349–351
    Legenda maior, 364
    philosophy of, 273
    as poet, 262, 297–298, 307–308, 337, 401
    preaching style, 33, 51, 140, 235, 333
    as preacher, 283, 353
    principium, 8, 79, 235, 247, 252–253
    resumptio, 240, 251, 288, 383
    rhetorical strengths, 327
    and *sermo modernus*, 235, 242, 289, 367, 411
    Sermon 1, *Veniet desideratus*, 64
    Sermon 29, 51
    Sunday Sermons, 48, 66
    as teacher, 335
    and Thomas Aquinas, 43–44, 162, 234–236, 342, 416–417
    use of allegory, 63, 133, 310, 332, 394
    use of chaining, 58, 235, 371, 391
    use of imagery, 268, 290, 307, 311–312, 350, 415
    use of metaphor, 61–62
    use of parallelism, 242, 262, 279, 386, 397
    writing style, 328, 363, 365, 379, 407, 416
Bordoy-Torrents, Pedro, 346
Bougerol, Jacques Guy, 347, 363, 367
Boyle, John, 109, 223
Brady, Ignatius, 8
brevity, 32, 42, 98, 236, 249
Brother Pacifico, 33

Carruthers, Mary, 116, 416
catena. See chaining
cathedral schools. *See studia generalia*
cause(s), 87–89
    cooperation among, 91, 325
    and effect, 53, 63–65, 179
    God as, 385
    knowledge of, 286
    persons as, 89
    of sin, 207
causes, Aristotelian, 106–108, 123, 166, 188–189
    efficient, 107–108, 167
    final, 107–108, 167, 248, 300
    formal, 107–108, 167, 242, 295, 298–299
    material, 106, 108, 167, 292
    use in disputed questions, 301
    use in *divisio*, 162–163, 236, 325–326
    use in prologues, 15, 167–168, 290
chaining, 202–203, 420
    in biblical commentary, 424
    Bonaventure's use of, 235, 371–372, 391–392
    of cause and effect, 63
    in *dilatatio*, 52, 58–59, 65
    as resource for preaching, 205, 208–209
    and *sermo modernus*, 213, 415
    Thomas's use of, 65
    and word association, 297, 330, 332
Christ. *See also* Word, of God; Incarnation, the
    Book of, 274
    as center, 387–388
    divinity of, 224–226
    and the Church, 119, 144–145, 163, 202, 391
    as fulfillment of prophecy, 170, 244, 254
    and grace, 377, 380
    as mediator, 326, 387
    name of, 160–161
    passion of, 296, 327
    and the sacraments, 184, 294
    as Son of the Father, 272, 388–389
    as source of Scripture, 311, 357–358
    as teacher, 87, 197, 280, 326, 357
    and virtue, 393–394
    as Wisdom, 86, 134, 141
Church, 386
    catholicity of, 349
    and Christ, 119, 144–145, 202, 391
    and grace, 120, 163
    orders of, 395
    and preaching, 27–31, 38
    and scholasticism, 40, 93
    as teacher, 362, 405
Cicero, 83
    De inventione, 121
    De officiis, 119
    Hortensius, 11

and oration, 106, 109, 128, 200, 423
Tusculan Disputations, 11
Clement of Alexandria, 258
collatio (evening sermon), 101–102, 215, 365, 414
   at the university, 42, 198, 414
collationes (distinction), 215, 365
collations (public lectures)
   Bonaventure's, 364–366
   protreptic in, 369, 376–377
   and *sermo modernus*, 369, 375, 378
   and sermons, 367–368, 376, 378, 386
   structure of, 368, 383–385
   thema shifts, 385
   Thomas's, 365
Cologne, 129
Commandments, Ten, 370–375, 399,
   See also law
commentaries, 43, 66
   preface to, 130
   prologues to, 140
   on the *Sentences*, 129, 147, 414
commentaries, biblical, 132
   and *dilatatio*, 202
   and disputation, 203, 212
   and *distinctiones*, 217
   and *divisio*, 227
   and preaching, 226, 423
   as preaching aid, 205, 211, 328, 333–337, 342, 414
   as product of *lectio*, 56, 207
   and *sermo modernus*, 17, 211, 328, 332, 342
   use of disputed questions. *See quaestiones disputatae*
Constantinople, Second Council of, 168
contemplation, 174, 185, 404
   and action, 117
   and anagogy, 72
   as end, 304
   exhortation to, 148
   and knowledge of God, 182
   and the sciences, 184
   and wisdom, 409
contraries, 53, 57, 386
creation, 292
   and humanity, 403
   and the Incarnation, 88, 146, 187
   as returning to God, 261, 268
   as vestige of the Creator, 238, 275–276, 283, 285, 401
Cruel, Rudolf, 422
culture
   as formative, 129, 200, 250, 343
   and memory, 116–117, 416
   and oral tradition, 16, 30–31
   of preaching, 101, 129, 222, 414, 421

d'Avray, David, 28, 36, 56, 422
definition of terms, 53–54, 110, 202,
   See also words
dialectic, 63, 195, 230, *See also* logic
dilatatio, 47
   argumentation, 52, 57–58, 423
   cause and effect, 53, 63–64, 236, 371
   chaining, 52, 58–59, 330
   comparatives, 52, 59–60, 211, 220, 354
   contraries, 53, 57, 386
   definition or classification, 47, 52–54, 227, 279, 284, 292
   distinctions, 420
   metaphor, 53, 60–62
   methods of, 52–65, 201–202, 328–329, 413
   and senses of Scripture, 53, 62–63, 133, 202, 219–220, 395
   as skill, 162, 342
   subdivision, 52, 54–56, 237, 257, 279
   as teaching device, 183
   in treatises, 263
dispositio, 82, 128
disputation, 17, *See also quaestiones disputatae*; argumentation
   and biblical commentaries, 203–204, 212
   distinguished from preaching, 17, 57, 301
   and preaching, 129, 418–419, 423
   as required practice, 96, 148, 342
   in support of preaching, 39, 199, 207, 278, 343, 424
   at the universities, 230, 250
distinctiones, 35–36, 72, 216–223, *See also* imagery
   Bonaventure's, 36, 333–337
   Thomas's, 208, 217–222
distinctions, 35, 205
   in biblical commentary, 205–206, 226
   in disputed questions, 341, 415
   in sermons, 64
divisio, 46–47, 49–52, 104, 128
   associations among, 237, 352
   and categories, 370
   comparatives in, 408
   definition or classification, 341
   as memory aid, 295
   modern use of, 349
   possible variations in, 52, 373–375
   and *sermo modernus*, 415
   as skill, 223–224, 227, 340, 342, 413, 415
   as structure, 73–74, 225–226, 349
   subdivision in, 47, 99, 306, 331, 379, 382, 407
divisio textus, 9, 14–16, 99–100, 110, 223
   in Aquinas's *Summa theologiae*, 132, 227–229
   in biblical commentary, 337, 424
   Bonaventure's, 349–351
   distinguished from *divisio*, 117, 370

divisio textus (cont.)
   importance of, 109, 121, 328
   of individual texts, 120, 131, 163–164, 225, 407
   as memory aid, 116–117, 348
   of the Psalms, 171
   purpose of, 164
   as skill, 111, 342
   as teaching device, 110–111, 123, 414
   as theological endeavor, 111, 125
   Thomas's, 118
docility, 122–123, *See also* student
   exhortation to, 148, 165
   necessity of, 14, 324
   to the Scriptures, 124, 131
doctrine, sacred, 95–96, 228
   communication of, 97–98
   as ordering principle, 197
Dominic de Guzman, 31
Dominicans, 304, *See also* mendicant orders
   formation of, 346
   as preachers, 31, 33, 115, 417
   at the university, 80
dualism, 89
Dulles, Avery, 187, 349, 353

education of preachers, 8, 28, 44, 117–118, 417–418
   and biblical commentary, 207, 424
   challenges of, 31
   and disputation, 229
   formation of habits, 148
   goal of, 41, 116, 126, 199, 422
   learning simplicity, 97, 418
   in *lectio, disputatio*, and *praedicatio*, 199, 363
   in the mendicant orders, 32, 34–35, 239, 414
   and prologues, 41–43, 127, 414
   and *sermo modernus*, 128, 413
   and *summae*, 345–346, 362
   and the universities, 35–41, 230, 329, 344
Eliot, T. S., 297
Étienne Tempier, 364–365
exempla
   nonscriptural, 419–421
   scriptural, 111, 113–115
exordium, 121–122, *See also* protreptic
   and *principium*, 131
   prologue as, 165

faith, 305, 331, 409
   and reason, 40, 179, 277, 304, 315–317, 393
   and Scripture, 351
Francis of Assisi, 32–33, 364
Franciscans, 261, 272, 304, 344, *See also* mendicant orders
   factions within, 364
   formation of, 346

   at Paris, 2, 367, 382
   preaching of, 32–34, 115, 417
Frederick II, Emperor, 148
friars. *See* mendicant orders
Friars Minor. *See* Franciscans

Galdericus, 14, 257
Gerard of Abbeville, 364
Giacomo da Fusignano, 46
Gilson, Étienne, 57, 423, 426
Giovanni di Fidanza. *See* Bonaventure
Gnostics, 357
grace, 163–164, 204
   Bonaventure on, 376–379
   and knowledge, 186
   and law, 76, 111, 351
   and order, 403
   in the sacraments, 184
   and sin, 207
   Thomas on, 119–120
   and wisdom, 191
grammar, 50–52, 277, 302
Gregory IX, Pope, 37–38
   Parens scientiarum, 37, 422
Gregory the Great, Pope, 38, 317
   Cura pastoralis, 26
Gregory X, Pope, 365, 383
Guibert de Nogent, 26
Guy of Aumône, 257

habits. *See also* practices
   development of, 150, 342, 415–416
   of masters, 129, 200–201, 382
   of preachers, 200, 328, 413, 424
   of students, 148
   in Thomas's *Summa*, 346
happiness, 248–249, *See also* beatitude
Henry of Ghent, 103, 105, 108, 121
heresy, 316
   avoiding, 143, 277
   in preaching, 32, 317, 417
   preaching against, 32
   at the universities, 195
hierarchy, 353–355
   in creation, 85
   of grace, 381
   of sciences, 258–262, 265–266, 269, 383
Holy Spirit, 60–61, 64, 95
   as author, 172, 244
   Gifts of, 381, *See also* grace
   and grace, 377
   inspiration of, 83, 136, 167, 170
   and Scripture, 126, 133, 315, 323
   and teachers, 323
homiletic revolution, 26, 29, 44, 413, 417–419

homily. *See* sermons
Hoogland, Mark Robin, C. P., 54, 101
Hugh of St. Cher, 36
   Commentary on Luke, 217
   distinctiones, 334
Hugh of St. Victor, 37, 277
   De sacramentis, 243, 246, 254, 351
   Didascalion, 258, 260, 383
Hughes, Kevin, 366–367
Humbert of Romans, 41
humility
   Christ as model of, 86, 357, 391
   and Scripture, 359, 400
   of students, 14, 96–97, 148, 324
   of teachers, 91, 93–94, 97, 124, 323–324
   and wisdom, 409

imagery. *See also* metaphor; allegory
   Bonaventure's use of, 268, 290, 307, 311–312, 350, 401, 415
   in *distinctiones*, 221
   and memory, 176, 295, 349
   modern use of, 146
   in Scripture, 69–70
   in sermons and commentary, 36, 72, 208, 268, 283, 415
   Thomas's use of, 94, 184, 219, 415
   and word association, 184, 413
Incarnation, the, 86, 88, 138, 143–144, 187–188, 341–342, *See also* Christ
   and creation, 282, 284
   divinity of, 189–190, 311, 357–358
   humility of, 400
   as intermediary, 85–87, 272, 275
   as medicine, 293
   and rational philosophy, 279
inception, 2–3, 38, 99–101, 328, 413, *See also* master
   addresses, 67, 79, 129, 251–252, *See also principium*
Innocent III, Pope, 32
interpretation, 323, 408, *See also* Scripture, senses of
   and education, 86
   and the Holy Spirit, 133
   and the literal sense, 168, 357
   modes of, 164, 187, 320, 360–361
   and proof, 282, 335, 351, 372
   symmetry in, 374
   of visions, 407
introductio, 153, 155, *See prothema*
inventio, 82, 128

Jacques de Vitry, 30
Jerome, 130, 168, 191

Joachimites, 32
John of La Rochelle, 103, 105
   divisio textus, 113
   resumptio, 106
   Summa fratris Alexandri (or *Summa Halensis*), 240, 344
John of Parma, 2, 93, 233
John Paul II, Pope
   Dominum et vivificantem, 187
John the Baptist, 341–342
John, the evangelist, 308–310, 339
justice, 53, 394
   definition of, 74

knowledge. *See also* learning; sciences
   acquisition of, 89–90, 354
   goal of, 267, 276
   of God, 64, 176–178, 182, 385, 404
   and the sciences, 186
   sense-, 270
   source of, 387
   and wisdom, 91, 407, 409

laity
   desire for preaching, 29–31, 44, 128, 188
   as educated, 29–31, 39, 44, 50, 414, 417, 425
   expectations of, 30
   preaching to, 28, 45, 413
Lateran Council, Fourth, 31, 39, 128, 277, 344
   and the homiletic revolution, 27, 29, 44
law, 74–76, 137, *See also* Commandments, Ten
   ages of, 204, 351–353
   divine, 107
   and grace, 76, 111, 377
   natural, 119, 352, 399
   and Scripture, 100, 103–105, 113–114, 137, 206, 351
   and wisdom, 399–400
learning, 89–90, *See also* study
   goal of, 196, 267, 288
   modes and methods of, 86, 147, 354
   through the senses, 274
   and wisdom, 148
lectio, 9, 199–200, 207, *See also* master, duties of; Scripture
lectiones. See commentaries, biblical
lecture, 3, 102, 140, *See also collationes*
Lewis, C. S., 10
logic, 259, 262, 266, 277, *See also* dialectic
   Christ's, 392–393
   and preaching, 342
   and scholasticism, 422
   and Scripture, 315, 340
   and the universities, 37, 39, 57, 229–230
Lottin, Dom Odo, 351

Louis IX, King, 37
Lyons, Second Council of, 81, 383, 408

MacIntyre, Alasdair, 10, 126, 147, 199
Mary Magdalene, 210–211
Mary, Blessed Virgin, 65–66, 102
    and John, 192
    and the Magdalene, 210
    as mother of Christ, 293–294
master, duties of, 8, 28, 39, 96, 250, 363
    as cultural practice, 200–201
    and *divisio textus*, 121
    and habits of mind, 129, 382, 415, 424
    interrelation of, 16–17, 199, 328, 342, 413, 418
    and prologues, 147
masters. *See also* teacher
    friars and seculars, 115, 151
    as intermediaries, 85–86, 93, 238
    requirements of, 100–101, 199, 414
    responsibilities of, 41, 152
    role of, 147
    seculars and friars, 2
Matthew of Aquasparta, 103, 109
    divisio textus, 113
Maurice de Sully, 35
memory. *See also* mnemonics; recollection
    arts of, 15, 30, 67, 164, 329, 413, 416
    of audience, 71, 128, 410
    and *divisio textus*, 116–117
    and imagery, 70
    in oral tradition, 30
    of preachers, 56, 58, 128
    and recollection, 15, 47, 388, 408
    of sermons, 66, 83
mendicant orders
    controversy with secular masters, 2, 81, 92–93, 151–152, 233, 364–365
    preaching of, 31, 34, 128, 336
    teaching at the universities, 37, 39, 44, 418
    training preachers, 31, 41–43, 239, 344
metaphor, 52, 60–62, 65, *See also* imagery; allegory
    Bonaventure's use of, 61–62
    in *dilatatio*, 53, 65, 133
    and figurative language, 61
    and rhetoric, 66
    in Scripture, 134, 136–137, *See also* Scripture, senses of
    Thomas's use of, 159–161
metaphysics, 185, 280, 389–390
Minnis, A. J., 166, 290
mnemonics, 48, 66, 82, 116, 307, *See also* memory; recollection
    divisio as, 295
    divisio textus as, 116–117, 164

and *sermo modernus*, 98, 182, 388, 413
thema as, 128, 156
and word association, 175–176, 395
monasteries, 27, 196, 417, *See also* mendicant orders
    schools at, 35
Monte Cassino, 1
Monti, Dominic V., 239
Moses, 74, 100
    as prefiguring Christ, 298
    as teacher, 323
Mulcahey, Michèle, 45, 421

Naples, University of, 148
negation, 404
nominalism, 419

Odo of Châtearoux, 69
    principium, 71–74
orators, ancient, 82, 116, 200
order
    created, 403
    and *reductio*, 268
    in *sermo modernus*, 382
    in sermons and prologues, 49, 342
    and wisdom, 223, 401
Order of Preachers. *See* Dominicans
orthodoxy, 31, 33, 44, 128, 277, 329, *See also* education of preachers

parallelism, 214
    Bonaventure's use of, 242, 262, 279, 386, 397, 416
    complexity of, 235
    in *dilatatio*, 340
    in *divisio*, 380
    imperfect, 214, 235, 265
    lost in translation, 218
    of phrases, 329, 340
    in *sermo modernus*, 50–51, 213, 307, 371
    Thomas's use of, 218
Paris, University of, 37, 421, 425
    courses of study, 128, 194, 260, 344
    culture of preaching, 17, 39, 101, 129, 250, 337, 414
    formation of preachers, 344, 382, 413, 422
    and the mendicant orders, 37, 39
    mission of, 29, 38, 269
    and preaching, 35–41, 230, 413, 417
    and scholasticism, 229, 422
    seculars vs. friars, 2, 92–93, 151–152, 154, 233, 289–290, 364
    writing requirements, 3, 42, 101, 111, 198–199, 289
partitio. See divisio textus

Peter Cantor, 8, 28, 39, 199, 203, 424
  Summa Abel, 35, 72, 216, 333
Peter Lombard, 290, 300
  Sentences, 245, 346
Peter of Poitiers
  Distinctiones super Psalterium, 216
Peter the Chanter. *See* Peter Cantor
Philo of Larissa, 12
philosophy, 265–266
  and investigation, 316
  moral, 265–266, 284
  natural, 260, 265, 280–281
  rational, 265, 277–278
Pieper, Josef, 393
Plato, 12, 88, 178–179
practices, 149, 199–201, 230, *See also* habits
  prologues as, 147–148
  sermo modernus as, 129, 328
praedicatio, 200
  as product of *lectio* and *disputatio*, 39, 199, 207, 278, 328, 418, 424
prayer, 131, 167
  metaphors for, 63, 72
  requirement of, 91, 148
  and *sermo modernus*, 376
preachers. *See also* education of preachers
  and *sermo modernus*, 66
  friars as, 42
  itinerant, 27, 32, 34, 417
  motives of, 317
  need for, 27
  office of, 39, 104
preaching aids, 42, 147, 413, 418
  biblical commentaries, 205, 208, 328, 333, 342, 414
  distinctiones, 35–36, 216–223, 333–335, 413
  exempla, 117, 419
  manuals, 34, 47–48, 53, 127, 328
  production of, 35–37
  sermon collections, 5, 34, 43, 235
  summae, 345–346
pride, 91, 409
  avoidance of, 148
  in students, 197
  and the universities, 230
principium, 3–6, 38, 140, 413, *See also* prologues; inception; *exordium*
  comparisons of, 234
  goals of, 124
  for an individual course, 42, 120, 414
  in aula, 2, 4, 99, 129, 199
  as prologue, 4, 43, 369
  regulations for, 79
  and *sermo modernus*, 4, 67–69, 414

  as teaching device, 123, 414
  types of, 3, 67, 102–103, 129, 199
prologues, 9–11, 42–43, 140, *See also principium*
  and biblical commentary, 227
  Bonaventure's, 347, 411
  and collations, 368, 386
  as cultural practice, 66, 147–148, 152
  and disputation, 301, 314
  as exhortation, 193–194, 317–318, 324–325, 414
  modern vs. medieval, 10, 125–126, 168, 188
  as preaching exercise, 43, 148, 198, 414
  and *principia*, 413
  purpose of, 172, 301
  and *sermo modernus*, 44, 56, 67, 129
  style of, 58, 346
  Thomas's, 157
  and treatises, 227–229
prothema, 47, 74, 141, 243, 375–377
protreptic, 11–14, 126, 148, 167, 287, 368
  and collations, 367–370, 376–377, 382
  and imagery, 401
  principium as, 414
  and prologues, 193–194, 317–318, 361
  prologues as, 11, 324–325
  purpose of, 194, 197
Pseudo-Dionysius, 353
  Celestial Hierarchy, 85
  Divine Names, 182
  Mystical Theology, 405

quaestiones disputatae, 363, 422, *See also* disputation
  and biblical commentaries, 203, 212, 337, 339, 341
  at inception, 99–100, 199
  in prologues, 301, 314
  and sermons, 58
  and subdivision, 56
  Summa theologiae as, 40, 346
  at the universities, 411, 425
Quintillian, 83
  Institutio Oratoria, 122
Quoniam in promotione, 2

recollection, 30, *See also* memory
  and association, 116, 175–176, 397
  and imagery, 176, 349
  and memorization, 408
  and memory, 15, 388
  and *sermo modernus*, 413, 416
  and structure, 124, 128
  and *thema*, 47, 98, 156, 182, 250, 307, 388
reductio, 276, 282
  as habit, 283
  metaphysics as, 390

reductio (cont.)
   as resource for preaching, 283
   and sciences, 302, 387
resumptio, 2, 5, 99–103, 370
   as continuation of the morning sermon, 252, 274
   and *sermo modernus*, 129
rhetoric, 121–123, 200, 277, 327
   and philosophy, 277
   and preaching, 342
   purpose of, 279, 316–317
   rhetorical questions, 57, 72
   in sermons, 48, 61, 66
   as teaching device, 137
   and use of grammar, 50–52
Rhetorica ad Herennium, 83, 121
Richard of St. Victor, 416
Robert of Basevorn, 51
   Forma praedicandi, 48–49, 52–53
Rouse, Richard and Mary, 27, 36, 420

sacraments, 144, 245, *See also* signification
   and grace, 380
   efficacy of, 297–298
   in the Pauline epistles, 164
   rooted in Christ, 184, 294
   as signs, 303
Schillebeeckx, Edward, 294
scholasticism, 17, 126, 250, 422–426
   and the Church, 40, 93
   and preaching, 423
   and Scripture interpretation, 356
   use of distinctions, 56
sciences
   division of, 184–185, 260–261, 265–266
   goal of, 268
   hierarchy of, 186–187, 255, 258–261, 269, 354, 383, *See also reductio*
   mathematics, 280, 391
   metaphysics, 185, 280, 389–390
   natural (physics), 185, 280, 390–391
   and Scripture, 196, 240–241, 254–256, 267, 288, 317
Scripture, 124, 238–239, 358–360, *See also* Testaments; *lectio*
   approaches to, 110–111, 125, 187, 193–194, 361
   as Christocentric, 167–171, 174, 187, 213–215, 356
   Gospels, 315–316, 327
   Hebrew, 110
   humility of, 14, 359, 400
   informed by the sciences, 283
   as intellectual, 14, 183, 187, 195–196, 255, 312, 317
   lay knowledge of, 30
   memorization of, 30, 388
   modes of, 108, 167, 313, 348, 359–360
   as perfection of sciences, 196, 267, 270, 286, *See also reductio*
   and salvation history, 125–126, 247, 352–353
   as science, 240–242, 254–255, 360
   in *sermo modernus*, 99–100, 103–105
   in sermons. *See* chaining
   as transformative, 126, 347, 353
   as wisdom, 242–243
   and theology, 162, 239–240, 345
Scripture, senses of, 246–247, 250, 355–358, 413, *See also* signification; interpretation
   allegorical, 63, 202, 270, 331, 336
   anagogical, 63, 72, 267, 270
   in *dilatatio*, 53
   in *distinctiones*, 216
   figurative, 245, 332, 360
   in interpretation, 72
   literal, 166, 356, 358–360
   literal and figurative, 107–108, 134–135, 170, 213–215, 245
   mystical, 330, 395
   and signification, 243–244
   spiritual, 62–63
   tropological (moral), 63, 270, 323, 332
   and wisdom, 400
semiotics. *See* words
sermo modernus, 6, 44, 128, 198–199
   as cultural practice, 17, 200, 234, 328
   departure from, 157, 323, 368, 414
   development of, 26, 45–46, 67–69, 128, 140, 413
   education to, 33, 41, 233
   elements of, 47, 58, 64, 257, 301, 342
   influence of, 151, 363, 382
   and *principia*, 42, 262–263
   and recollection, 102, 182
   and scholasticism, 422–426
sermons, 278
   ancient, 45
   and biblical commentaries, 202, 205, 208
   characteristics of, 279, 328
   and collations, 365, 367
   collections of, 5, 34, 43, 147, 235, 412
   crafting of, 61, 66, 82
   desire for, 30, 33, 425
   and disputation, 57–58, 301
   divisio of, 93, 99
   and *divisio textus*, 223
   and memory, 47, 116, 128
   principia as, 68, 129
   and prologues, 42, 67, 148, 188
   purpose of, 279–280
   and Scripture quotation. *See* chaining
   structure of, 48, 74–75
   at the university, 41, 101, 129, 198, 414

Siger of Brabant, 195, 364
signification, 86, 108, 278
   modes of, 176
   of numbers, 171
   reality as, 86, 240, 245, 275, 357
   in Scripture, 112, 133, 243–245
   and truth, 110
similitude, 272–273, *See also* metaphor
sin, 206–207, 340
St. Victor, School of, 35, 37, 422
Stephen Langton, 69
   principium, 69–71
Stephen of Besançon
   resumptio, 121, 123, 251
Stoics, Greek, 185
structure, 73–74
   of classes, 101
   divisio as, 225–226, 306, 349, 406
   and form, 298–299
   parallelism in, 224, 354
   of prologues, 140
   and *sermo modernus*, 368, 383, 416
   thema as, 105, 107, 320
student, 86, 172, 316, 322, 324, 368
   development of, 345–346, 413, 415, 417, 422
   duties of, 91, 96–97, 126, 148, *See also* docility
   and pride, 195
   and protreptic, 13
   and teacher, 86, 89–91, 325
studia generalia, 35, 344
study, 70, 91, 148, *See also* learning
   commitment to, 9–10, 126, 147, 288, 367
   exhortation to, 13, 126
   goal of, 110, 185, 269, 276, 287, 305
   order of, 258, 260, 383
   preparation for, 123, 165, 197, 414
   of Scripture, 312, 317, 345, 362

teacher, 52, 70, 86–88, 316, 322, *See also* masters
   clarity of, 392
   dignity of, 94, 96, 309
   goal of, 95, 126
   and humility, 124
   orthodoxy of, 34, 44, 90–91, 96
   proof of ability, 164
   responsibilities of, 86, 90–91, 95–96
   Scripture as, 165, 248–249, 400
   and student, 85–86, 89–91, 322, 325
   Thomas as, 86, 120, 417
Testament, New
   division of, 119
   and grace, 111, 119–120
   and law, 75, 100, 107
Testament, Old
   approaches to, 125
   and law, 75, 100, 103, 111, 118
   as prefiguring Christ, 167–171, 174, 187, 213–215, 244–245
Testaments. *See also* Scripture
   and *divisio textus*, 112–116, 253
   interrelation of, 16, 76, 111–112, 211, 350–351
thema, 45, 47–49
   as mnemonic device, 47, 82, 128, 156, 388, 413
   selection of, 48–49, 52, 263–264, 340, 347, 349
   and *sermo modernus*, 415, 423
   as structure, 105, 107, 384–385
   and word association, 83–84
Theodore of Mopsuestia, 168
theology, 162, 268
   arguments in, 176–178
   modes of, 304
   and natural philosophy, 281
   negative, 405
   and preaching, 28, 41, 59
   purpose of, 305, 354
   and sacred doctrine, 260
   as a science, 239–240, 286, 302–303, 317
   and the sciences, 288
   and Scripture, 125
   in sermons, 65–66
   Trinitarian, 62, 142–143, 155–156
Thomas Aquinas
   biblical commentaries of, 201
   biography, 1, 80–82, 98, 148–149, 152
   and Bonaventure, 43–44, 162, 234–236, 342, 416–417
   Catena aurea, 191
   Commentary on Boethius's "De trinitate," 155–156, 185, 258
   Commentary on Isaiah, 212
   Commentary on John, 208
   Commentary on the "Sentences," 141, 146
   Commentary on the Epistles of St. Paul, 114, 157
   Contra impugnantes Dei cultum et religionem, 152–155
   De veritate, 87, 90
   development of, 42, 140, 153, 172, 212
   distinctiones of, 217–222
   divisio textus, 80, 342
   and grace, 120
   Hic est liber, 99
   marginalia, 215
   On Being and Essence, 87
   On the Power of God, 179
   philosophy of, 177–178

Thomas Aquinas (cont.)
  as preacher, 201, 207, 222, 425
  preaching style, 235
  principium, 1, 7, 76, 79, 94, 158, 235
  prologues of, 149, 157
  on the Psalms, 168–171
  Quodlibet 3, 90
  rhetorical strengths, 327
  and senses of Scripture, 62
  and *sermo modernus*, 148, 154, 172, 198, 235, 365
  Sermon 1, *Veniet desideratus*, 54–56, 58–60
  Sermon 2, *Lauda et laetare*, 62
  Sermon 4, *Osanna filio Dauid*, 60–61
  Sermon 5, *Ecce rex tuus*, 46–48, 101–102
  Sermon 6, *Caelum et terra transibunt*, 60–61
  Sermon 9, *Exiit que seminat*, 154
  Sermon 11, *Emitte Spiritum*, 57, 60, 63–64
  Sermon 13, *Homo quidam*, 60
  Sermon 16 *Inveni David*, 166
  Sermon 18, *Germinet terra*, 65–66
  sermons of, 43, 48, 149
  Summa contra Gentiles, 110, 124, 223, 346
  Summa theologiae, 40, 64, 119–120, 227–229, 344–347, 373
  as teacher, 148–149, 181, 183, 197, 417
  use of allegory, 133, 170, 202
  use of chaining, 58, 65
  use of imagery, 94, 184, 208, 219, 416
  use of metaphor, 60–61, 159
  use of parallelism, 218
  writing style, 250, 328, 416, 426
Thomas, the apostle, 211
Torrell, Jean-Pierre, 82, 152, 165, 215, 420
translation, 145, 168, 293, 330
treatises
  prologues to, 345–347
  and *sermo modernus*, 263
  structure of, 262, 346
Trier, Council of, 34
Trinity, 51, 125, 155–156
  as community, 240
  eternity of, 292
  and the law, 373, 399
  Persons of, 62, 142–143, 388–389
  and Scripture, 239, 355
  vestiges of, 142, 401–402
truth
  Christ as, 254, 390
  and the intellect, 324
  and philosophy, 265
  and rhetoric, 122
  and Scripture, 110, 242, 249, 420

understanding, 80, 266, 308, 406–408, See also wisdom
universities. *Listed by city names.* See also scholasticism
  and the mendicant orders, 31, 40, 44, 81
  and preaching, 35, 57, 101, 148, 196
  and *sermo modernus*, 157, 198, 421
  training of preachers, 239, 344

Varro, Terence, 258
Vatican Council, Second, 118
virtue, 119, 159
  Aristotelian, 382, 393
  and faith, 393–394
  and grace, 380–382
  and prayer, 167

Waleys, Thomas
  De modo componendi sermones, 45
Weisheipl, James, 81, 148, 177, 194, 258
William of Auvergne, bishop of Paris, 37
William of Middleton, 2, 233
William of Saint-Amour, 152, 364
wisdom, 110, 398–401
  divine, 132, 144, 193, 300
  exhortation to, 382
  as habit, 305
  and knowledge, 409
  and love, 193, 404
  mediation of, 85
  vs. modern ethics, 186
  and order, 223
  and philosophy, 277, 280
  prerequisites of, 197
  and science, 91, 286
  and Scripture, 125, 134, 242
  source of, 13, 86, 387
  of teacher, 96–97, 124
  and understanding, 406–407
Word, of God, 182, 339–341, 390, See also Christ
  Incarnation of, 278
  as means of creation, 88, 275
  and Wisdom, 86, 406–407
words
  choice of, 52, 156, 274
  context and connotation, 296, 336, 343, 415
  senses of, 52, 202, 205–206, 208, 284, 290
  as signs, 245, 278, 360

For EU product safety concerns, contact us at Calle de José Abascal, 56–1°,
28003 Madrid, Spain or eugpsr@cambridge.org.

www.ingramcontent.com/pod-product-compliance
Lightning Source LLC
LaVergne TN
LVHW081527060526
838200LV00045B/2023